IN
COMMAND
OF
TOMORROW

Sterling Brubaker

IN COMMAND OF TOMORROW

RESOURCE AND ENVIRONMENTAL STRATEGIES FOR AMERICANS

A Resources for the Future Study

Published for
RESOURCES FOR THE FUTURE, INC.
by THE JOHNS HOPKINS UNIVERSITY PRESS
Baltimore and London

Resources for the Future is a nonprofit corporation for research and
education in the development, conservation, and use of natural resources
and the improvement of the quality of the environment. It was established
in 1952 with the cooperation of the Ford Foundation. Part of the work of
Resources for the Future is carried out by its resident staff; part is
supported by grants to universities and other nonprofit organizations.
Unless otherwise stated, interpretations and conclusions in RFF
publications are those of the authors; the organization takes responsibility
for the selection of significant subjects for study, the competence of the
researchers, and their freedom of inquiry.

The book was edited by Brigitte Weeks and Jo Hinkel.

RFF editors: Mark Reinsberg, Joan R. Tron, Ruth B. Haas, Jo Hinkel

Library of Congress Catalog Card Number 74-24401

ISBN 0-8018-1700-5

Library of Congress Cataloging in Publication Data will be found on the
last printed page of this book.

CONTENTS

PREFACE

This is a book about resources and environment—about the link between their very long-run requirements and current policies. It starts from the assumption that the availability of ample supplies of moderate-cost energy and materials and the preservation of a healthy and spiritually rewarding environment are basic to the continuation of a high-level industrial society. And it is written in the belief that the maintenance of such an industrial society, organized so as to spare natural systems from destruction, offers the best hope for the realization of human capabilities in all their individual forms.

Of course, there are many other equally pressing human problems that demand attention if man's future is to endure as long as his past. Even with the most myopic vision it is evident that among the problems man must deal with are war, racial conflict, income distribution, population control, providing for social and political participation, and such timeless and universal problems as the search for meaning in human life. But it is not possible to treat all of them here, so I have considered only resources and environment, the constraints they imply, possible avenues for release from constraint, the social attitudes and values of most use for dealing with resource problems, and the broad policy directions that would at least take mankind in the right direction. This already seems more than enough for one short volume, and so I ask forgiveness if I have omitted attention to some of the reader's favorite causes. But attention to resource and environmental problems will not prejudice desirable action on other fronts. On the contrary, appropriate resource policies, by helping to ensure the material base for society, will ease the other adjustments required.

The title is intended to convey the activist and optimistic thrust of this volume. It implies that we can take charge and mold our destiny rather than wait for it to happen to us. This is in the tradition of western man. But the subtitle reflects a change of emphasis that I feel is important. In the past, in a world of resource abundance, individuals in quest of their own advantage produced a result that was in the main socially satisfactory. In the future that result seems less apt to occur automatically; conscious and long-range social planning will be required to ensure an acceptable outcome.

This book deals with strategy rather than policy. Policy implies the choice among alternative short-term measures that might be used to achieve objectives on which there is a social consensus. By starting further back, I attempt first to discern what may be required by the resource and environmental imperatives for maintaining a high-income society. I also examine some elements of the existing social concensus on objectives. The juxtaposition of resource imperatives and social goals indicates the possible general direction of society. It seems necessary to start at this level lest policy prescriptions be oriented to very short-term problems and to decision criteria that have worked well in the past but may be inappropriate for the future.

Of course I cannot resist the temptation to say something about policy, but I have tried to do so in the context of a longer-term strategy. Thus the comments on policy are not as comprehensive or topical as they might be if this were exclusively a policy study. I believe that it is important to see policy issues in a longer-range context; consequently, I have foregone much policy detail in favor of developing a framework for the discussion.

This is primarily a book for Americans. Others can read it too, and indeed the long-range imperatives and means of coping are common to all mankind. But much of mankind is not presently in position to act on very many of these problems, while the United States is. It is in the United States that the problems of growing resource stringency and environmental degradation accompanying an advanced industrial society coincide with a national state of sufficient size, wealth, and organization to make a fundamental attack on the problems. The Europeans who face the problems in equal or greater measure are currently too disorganized to mount the attack, although both they and the Japanese can make a substantial contribution if they choose.

A second reason why the United States may take the lead derives from its great power status. However much others in the world may grumble about the exercise of American power, a great many of them would sorely miss us if we departed from the world stage. If the United States is to maintain itself as a world power, it has national reasons for seeking internal solutions to its resource problems. While Americans may proceed on the basis of self-interest, we can be pleased that any success we have will be broadly disseminated in the course of time. There is need for sensitivity to the effect of our actions on others over the shorter term, but we need not be paralyzed by the fear that we in the United States have behaved selfishly if we succeed in solving our own problems.

The plan of the book is simple. It commences with a most general and rather abstract look at the longer-range prospects for man insofar as they are affected by resources and the environment. The most fundamental problem to be dealt with is the problem of resource exhaustion. While this problem can be deferred through measures to restrict income growth and materials throughput, longer-term human occupancy of the earth must escape resource exhaustion either through reversion to the very modest scale that could be accommodated by renewable resources, or through technical advance that permits continuation of high income based on the exploitation of inexhaustible energy and common materials. This author frankly prefers the second path, which seems more consistent with the social goals presently accepted by society. But society at large does not recognize the need for this choice or the measures required to make a transition. An interim strategy is suggested that extends the time during which mankind can appreciate the nature of his choice and secure the transition. Since the time required for transition is long and the pressure of growth on resources is increasing, it is necessary to begin now to develop the new habits of thought and to start the measures necessary for this transition. This means above all diverting a sufficient share of our natural resources from current consumption toward investment in the technology of the future.

Chapters 2–6 are an attempt to work out some of these ideas in more detail, indicating the nature of long-term directions and the interim strategy this suggests. Only if the nation has some vision of what it is trying to accomplish and how policies are likely to affect it can short-term policies be made consistent with longer-term requirements. Special emphasis is given to land use decisions in Chapters 2 and 3, and to the crucial energy and minerals strategy in Chapters 4 and 6. Many aspects of environmental quality are dealt with in those categories, but the somewhat narrower question of pollution abatement recurs in Chapter 6.

The focus is on what Americans can do about the resource and environmental problems affecting them. Some of the suggestions made have the potential to disrupt prevailing international patterns of trade and investment, and the hopes that other countries have built on them. As a nation we do not wish to be insensitive to these concerns and I therefore discuss in Chapter 7 how they may be taken into account.

The final chapter reviews the basic thesis of the book, engages in a brief discussion of social choice, reviews the policy instruments available to us, and concludes with a summary on policy directions.

This volume is very much the outgrowth of the Resources for the Future environment. It had its origin in a suggestion by Joseph Fisher, former president of RFF, and has benefited greatly from his advice and encouragement. It also has drawn freely on the work of colleagues: I gratefully acknowledge the influence of Marion Clawson, John V. Krutilla, and Irving Hoch on Chapters 2 and 3; of Sam H. Schurr, Milton F. Searl, Harry Perry, and Joel Darmstadter on Chapter 4; of the late Orris Herfindahl on Chapter 5; of Allen V. Kneese on Chapter 6; of Hans H. Landsberg and Kneese on Chapter 7; and of Kneese and Edwin T. Haefele on Chapter 8. In many instances these colleagues supplied me directly with background material in all cases I drew on their written work.

My work was also the subject of a lively discussion within RFF. Valuable contributions to that discussion were made by all of those previously mentioned and by Ronald G. Ridker, Pierre R. Crosson, Leonard Fischman, R. Talbot Page, Henry Jarrett, Robert G. Healy, and Kenneth Frederick. Despite this institutional input, the book remains a personal document. There was no hope of reconciling all of the conflicting views and differences of emphasis among my colleagues. I can only thank them for giving the manuscript their attention.

I am also grateful to Brigitte Weeks and Jo Hinkel for their editorial assistance and to Gayle Underwood for secretarial help in preparing the book.

Sterling Brubaker

IN
COMMAND
OF
TOMORROW

1
RESOURCE IMPERATIVES AND SOCIAL GOALS

MODES OF PERMANENT HUMAN OCCUPANCY OF THE EARTH

Until recently there has not been general concern about the long-term capacity of the physical world to meet our expanding wants. Now that such concern is both necessary and widespread, we are subjected to conflicting and often inconsistent advice on the direction to take. The nation has no long-term strategy to guide short-term policy. It is easy to accept the idea that current policy should be consistent with a longer-term view, but this is difficult to achieve in the absence of agreement on what the longer-term options look like or which of them we choose. In modern societies with representative governments, consistency between long-term objectives and short-term actions is hard to attain in any case, for governments must be responsive to short-term demands that often are in conflict with longer-term goals. Nonetheless, clearer public understanding of long-term options favors a climate in which greater reconciliation between current policy and long-term goals is possible. With that in mind let us examine future modes of occupancy.

All civilized men are miners. Primitive hunters and gatherers were not; they depended upon and were limited by the current output of natural systems. But from the time when man first domesticated goats and made bronze, he has been mining the earth's soil and rock and debauching the environment. So long as the mine lasts, man gains partial release from the constraints of the natural ecological system. The faster the mine is depleted, the more he can increase in numbers and wealth.

Thanks to the original riches of the earth and to human technological ingenuity, he has extended the life of the mine. Yet we are all dependent upon exhaustible resources, and any mine, if worked long enough, runs out.

Men are not exclusively miners. We still make use of current biological output. In the case of agriculture, we have modified natural systems so as to increase greatly the earth's current yield of value to man, apparently on a sustainable basis. While sustainable, this use is not infinitely expandable; the supply of agricultural land is limited, and limits to the efficiency of photosynthesis may be expected. Moreover, our agricultural technology carries us down paths that may even challenge our capacity to sustain it. Sustaining or augmenting agricultural production under modern conditions also makes demands on exhaustible resources, thereby exposing us again to depletion. In addition, it places burdens on the capacity of the environment to absorb waste, threatening overload. Thus, while agriculture offers partial escape from the exhaustion of the mine, it still uses exhaustible resources, meets only a limited range of needs, creates environmental congestion and is itself subject to capacity limitations.

The environment also is a complex resource which renders direct amenity services to man and serves to assimilate his wastes. In some respects it is an exhaustible resource, for it can be permanently damaged. However, the mining analogy is not precise to the extent that regenerative capacity is involved. In most respects the environment is a renewable resource. It is subject to congestion if overloaded, and just as with land, there are capacity limits that may not safely be exceeded on a continuing basis.

All of these limits are aggravated by increased scale of human activity. Because of growth in both numbers and per capita consumption, the draft on resources and burden on the environment is increasing at a startling rate. A spate of recent writing has called attention to these problems. The emphasis has varied. In *Resources and Man*, the focus was on estimating the availability of traditional resources and probing the potential for certain innovations now on the horizon. Its overall tone was rather glum. Kenneth Boulding's celebrated article, "The Economics of the Coming Spaceship Earth," put forward the idea of the earth as a closed system where the objective must be maintenance of the stock rather than maximization of throughput. Many authors have focused on environmental and population problems. Several of these strands were brought together in *The Limits to Growth* where the stress was on the tendency of the system to overshoot, the imminence of this event if exponential growth continues, and the conditions under which equilibrium could be attained.[1]

The hysterical tone of some of the recent environmental concern does not appear to have been warranted, and it is tempting to discount also much of the concern about resource exhaustion as simply a new ripple in the long wave of worry about that subject. As we know, territorial expansion and technological ingenuity have brought us new supplies at constant or declining cost. The relentless logic of Malthus that, given fixed supplies of land, we could not expand food production fast enough to keep pace with population growth has not yet been verified. Still, it is impressive to observe how rapidly exponential growth threatens to exhaust finite stocks of conventional nonrenewable resources or available land, and most of us have become aware of the onerous burden of pollution that endless growth implies. These consequences loom even if active technological policy extends the availability of conventional resources and the capacity to abate pollution.

However, the focus on growth distracts attention from a still more fundamental fact. The problem is not just growth. While growth abbreviates the time when finite resource stocks are exhausted, permanent human occupancy of the earth cannot in any case be based on the use of conventional exhaustible resources. However successful we are in finding deposits or in recovering materials from lower-grade sources, eventually we disperse our supplies. Those who postulate a continuing stationary state somewhere near the present level based on recycling of exhaustible materials through the use of current energy flows underestimate the inexorable spread of entropy.[2] A prescription that reduces the rate of use defers, but does not avoid, the day of reckoning. Where the sustainable level of activity depends upon a level of land use and use of environmental assimilative capacity that may not be exceeded without permanent damage and reduction in their output a different constraint applies. Such renewable resources, if essential, indeed may limit growth and define a maximum level of per-

---

[1] National Academy of Sciences National Research Council Committee on Resources and Man, *Resources and Man* (San Francisco: W. H. Freeman and Company, 1969); Kenneth Boulding, "The Economics of the Coming Spaceship Earth," in Henry Jarrett, ed., *Environmental Quality in a Growing Economy: Essays from the Sixth RFF Forum* (Baltimore: Johns Hopkins Press, 1966), pp. 3–14; Donnella H. Meadows, Dennis L. Meadows, Jorgen Randers, and William H. Behrens III, *The Limits to Growth* (New York: Universe Books, 1972).

[2] Entropy here refers to the degradation of matter and energy toward an ultimate state of uniformity.

manent occupancy. By contrast, for nonrenewable resources, any level of use, however small or slow growing, ultimately exhausts the supply and implies not merely an end to growth but of the prevailing level of occupancy as well, provided these resources are essential. Reliance upon renewable resources implies a scale limit to occupancy, while reliance upon exhaustibles implies a temporal limit. Man can accommodate the scale limit but not the temporal one. Our present mode, dependent as it is on exhaustible resources, is not viable over the longest term.

Can the dilemma posed by depletion be avoided? Essentially two paths are open to man in order to secure permanent occupancy. One is to aspire to a modest but sustainable place in the natural system by changing to a technology that is nondepleting in character. This would mean reliance upon a current energy flow from the sun and on the biological cycling of materials. It would not rely on the continuing net acquisition of exhaustible materials. Man once held such a sustainable place when numbers were few, wants purely biological, and technology nil. In modern dress we might hope to manipulate the natural system through sophisticated biological methods and more efficient capture of the energy flow from, for example, sun, wind, and tides, so as to maintain numbers and a high standard of living. The more restrained our expectations with respect to population size and living standards, the more promising the outlook for this mode. Even so, it is difficult to see how this system could avoid degradation over time. The reason is that many uses of materials are inherently dissipative, and it is hard to imagine that we could divert a current energy flow large enough to permit us to recapture that which is dispersed. As dispersion proceeded we would lose access to our initial stock of exhaustible materials, including metals. If deprived of metals, hence of machinery and transport, this in turn would limit our capacity to capture and utilize current energy flow. Regression in population and income would appear inevitable. Advocates of this mode might view that result with equanimity, contending that it is still consistent with human happiness and the health of the planet. Indeed, on a sufficiently reduced scale, this mode is viable.

Part way down the path to such a system we encounter those who would substitute more "natural" technologies—a method that allows extension of exhaustible resources.[3] While they would seek to make more use of renewable resources and biological recycling, they have

---

[3] See, for example, Barry Connover, *The Closing Circle: Nature, Man, and Technology* (New York: Alfred A. Knopf, 1971).

not faced up to the full implications of the exhaustion of depletable resources.

It is convenient to call the first path a "low technology" course, although it must be recognized that this is a value-laden term. Some would argue that by achieving permanent balance with nature it represents the most sophisticated technology.

The other path would be a calculated effort to escape the constraints of resource exhaustion through new technologies. This differs from previous constraint-releasing advances in that it would not simply rely on enlarging the conventional supply of exhaustibles but rather would seek to replace them with inexhaustible resources. The difference is between a temporary reprieve and a permanent solution. The second path means finding an inexhaustible source of energy as a prerequisite to other technology that would make use of more common materials. Given ample energy, we might make a direct attack on entropy, using common rock and sea water as resources, or perhaps we could reach for the alchemists' dream of elemental transmutation.

Even this approach would not be without scale limits to growth—dissipation of heat and physical space still pose limits. (Presumably we could learn to synthesize nutrients chemically, so photosynthesis and the supply of agricultural land might not limit us.) Of course, an encounter with the heat limit also could be greatly postponed by more attention to efficiency and to less use of heat technologies. The important point is that, while we might face limits to the magnitude of activity at any time, we could hope to escape the time limit implied by exhaustion.[4] And, if this mode is combined with population restraint, it carries the potential for a higher standard of living for both developed and less-developed countries (LDCs). By contrast, when measured by current values, the first path implies a lower standard of living.

I have outlined these two modes as polar cases so as to dramatize the nature of the choice. They are not merely straw men, however; they are true ultimate choices. If we lean toward one or the other and progress in adjustment toward it, an encounter with the pure case may be long deferred, for consumption of depletable resources will be retarded as we move toward path one, and as we move toward path two supplies will increase. Although each path admits of many variants, the strategies suited for each path are antithetical in important respects. An interim strategy is proposed below (pages 14–22) that preserves the option to choose between the two modes, but neverthe-

---

[4] In cosmic terms there is still a time limit. But fusionable materials sufficient to supply current energy needs for 10^9 years will far outlast the human species.

less that decision cannot be indefinitely deferred. In practice, it seems likely that society will prefer a variant of the second path, and much of the discussion in subsequent chapters is consistent with that view.

There is no assurance that the second mode can be achieved. Is it not more risky than the first? Not necessarily; if the second path proves impassable, this does not preclude reversion to the first, although depending on population size at the time of transition, great suffering and a dramatic reduction in numbers would be likely. Indeed, return from one path to the other becomes harder the longer we pursue its opposite.

Postponement of decision is not a solution; there is risk in hesitation. The constraint-releasing option is perishable—we must seize it soon (given the prospective rate of resource exhaustion) or forever lose it. This matter of timing is very important. Since time is required to perfect constraint-releasing technology (if indeed it is successful), exhaustible resources should be viewed as buffer stocks to be drawn on while the desired technology is perfected. If we continue to consume exhaustible materials without advancing to a technology able to transform or transmute plentiful materials, then we may no longer have in stock the brute force of energy or the quantities of concentrated elements needed to secure the transition. If we tarry too long at the fork or move too far down the first path, abandoning much of our technology as we go, then we forfeit the option of the second path— in effect we choose path one for our heirs, if not for ourselves.

Mankind is largely unaware of the need for choice. Instead we mill about, increasing our appropriation of the stock for current consumption but not turning in a definitive way toward constraint-releasing technology of a sort that allows permanent occupancy. Is there still time to effect the transition before encountering resource constraints? Many doomsayers who say no are in fact expressing a preference for a romanticized version of path one. To the extent that they are also technological Luddites, there is a self-fulfilling element to their prophecy.

But if path two is selected, a prudent first step would be to seek a more efficient transformation of the natural capital represented by resource stocks into the constraint-releasing technology of the future. A consumer society that uses stocks only to increase current gratification is inimical to the second strategy. An antitechnological bias that denies resources for the development of new technology also frustrates the second path. On the other hand, measures to conserve exhaustible resources through more efficient use, recycling, or substitution of renewables are consistent with the second strategy. Policies that restrain our rate of use of exhaustible resources, extending the time period over which the stock is used, allow a longer time for transition to occur. However, such conservationist measures need to be combined with a technical strategy if they are to contribute to the success of the second path. Thus, the conservationist, preservationist, and environmentalist biases present in much of the current discussion can be reconciled with the second strategy, but the antitechnological biases cannot.

While conservation policies permit deferral of the choice between the two paths, ultimately a choice must be made. Our society already is a heavy user of exhaustible resources and there is danger of overstaying that mode. If we opt for the second path, we must do so on a timely basis while resource stocks allow time, energy, and materials for possible success. Also, we must have continuity with past technical achievements. We may be able to get there from here, but not if we wander too far away from the technological sophistication already attained. We must remember that we can always fall back on the first course, provided no cataclysmic damage has been done to the ecosystem in the process. Hence the manner in which we proceed is also of great importance to man.

The quest for constraint-releasing technology would have to be a conscious social choice with the decision made long in advance. There are several basic reasons for this, including the scale of the effort implied, the consequent need to divert resources, and the time required to effect change. The search is apt to be extended, expensive, and risky. In such a context, conventional market signals cannot be relied upon to effect fundamental change.

These points deserve emphasis. Based on present knowledge of conventional resources and with anticipated growth in consumption, many resource stringencies will be encountered by the end of the century (see Chapters 4 and 5). Even with the assumption of normal technical progress in finding and producing resources believed to exist, resource problems will multiply rapidly 50–100 years hence if exponential growth continues.[5] Fundamental changes in technology, if

---

[5] Note that at 4 percent annual growth rate, *annual* consumption 100 years from now would be nearly 50 times the current figure. Of course, we may not accommodate growth of that magnitude, but even lesser growth will suffice to shrivel supplies of many conventional resources. One hundred years is not a long time in human society.

pursued in an orderly way, may require fifty years or more from basic research through full deployment. For example, nuclear energy is expected to furnish 25 percent of the U.S. energy supply by the year 2000, a full fifty years after the Atomic Energy Commission began work on it. Complex technologies of this sort that are so expensive and require so long to bring to fruition will not be initiated by a private firm under day-to-day competitive pressure. Moreover, the social and environmental implications of new technologies may be such that they cannot be left to private firms. Yet society has a major stake in the new technology. Hence public decisions will be required to guide and fund the research and development effort necessary for the constraint-releasing strategy as a whole. A major role will remain for private firms in researching and deploying new technology.

Faced with two possible modes of permanent human occupancy, some might argue that only the first path is consistent with the fundamental nature of man because it stresses man in harmony with nature. They see the path as both ecologically and psychologically healthy. The extent to which contact with nature is important to man remains an unanswered question, although it is a matter that cannot be safely cast aside. At present, most of us are urban dwellers in infrequent contact with nature, and many rural people have a far from harmonious relationship to the soil from which they live. At some modest level of population, the vision of technological plenty is not inconsistent with the aspiration to preserve and relate to nature. A nonpolluting and sophisticated technology and a people deliberately restricting the territorial range of their activities might place less strain on the natural system than does our present intermediate technology which is extensive in land use. Escape from the resource constraint does not imply the destruction of nature, provided that man exercises self-restraint in his numbers and style of land use.

In sum, long-term human occupancy of the earth on the present basis is not viable. The alternatives are either path two, to escape resource exhaustion while retaining income aspirations, or path one, based on current flows, with population and income being trimmed as necessary. In either case there are limits (though quite different ones) to the scale of human activity at any time, but no necessary limits to its endurance. Those who have publicized the speed with which exponential growth threatens resource exhaustion deserve credit, as do those whose prescriptions would extend the time over which the present mode can endure. They help the rest of us appreciate the time dimension of our choice even if they do not pose its nature as clearly as they might.

RESOURCES AND GOALS FOR AMERICANS

Most of us manage to live from day to day without dwelling on the ultimate fate of man. However, we are quite likely to be part of a broad consensus on what we want our system to yield. Some of these goals have significance for resources and environment. Goals that are simultaneously considered desirable may be in conflict with one another as well as being inconsistent with the needs of long-term occupancy. It is worthwhile to identify goals widely accepted by Americans and to examine the extent of their compatibility and their significance for long-term occupancy.

Income Growth

Despite the existence of a vocal antimaterialist segment of the population, most Americans seem unprepared to halt or slow economic growth, at least for the intermediate term. The inertia of our expectations favors growth, and it appears one of the most promising ways of dealing with our social ills. Environmentalists take a more ambivalent view; some welcome the role of growth in paying for pollution abatement costs, while others decry it as a major cause of environmental problems. Possibly a more affluent future generation will be less enamored of income growth. Also, if income distribution becomes increasingly divorced from production, so that incentives are weakened and the lash of insecurity loses its sting, then we may be willing to forego some income growth. For the present, however, Americans place a high value on per capita income growth and especially on income security. Measures taken in the name of resource or environmental policy that threaten income growth, and especially those that threaten income security, bring quick reaction.

The significance of this aspiration for resource policy is clear. High and rising income implies adequate resource availability at moderate cost, for materials and energy provide the basis for other economic activity. If we are to have the wealth of goods and the diet that high income implies, we cannot spend a disproportionately large share of our effort in winning the basic material inputs. In fact, the long record of industrialization has been one of reduced real costs for raw materials and food, allowing an expanded materials supply to be provided by a shrinking percentage of the labor force.

As was observed earlier, a high-income society tends to speed the rate of exhaustion of nonrenewable resources and increase the burden on the environment. Therefore, it shortens the time during which the path two option is retained and may increase the risk that we lose it. On the other hand, high income devoted in substantial degree to constraint-releasing technological research offers the best prospect of gaining path two.

Environmental Quality

Americans also are widely committed to the preservation of environmental quality. This has many facets, but the heart of the public concern centers on pollution abatement. At first glance, this goal appears to be in conflict with the income objective, for high income tends to generate a greater environmental burden and pollution abatement can be expensive. If the concept of income is extended to a broader welfare standard, and if pollution abatement measures are well conceived, then there is no necessary conflict with welfare growth. Expenditures to control pollution will result in net improvements in welfare, that is, their value will exceed their cost. In practice only very deficient means of judging the damage caused by pollution exist, and control measures are not based on a careful weighing of costs and benefits, so the cost effectiveness of some measures becomes doubtful. Ill-conceived measures, if carried to extremes, will conflict with the goal of income growth, and backlash can be expected. When pollution control measures are properly assessed on a welfare basis, however, such conflict can be minimized. In any case, the public will probably demand visible progress in curbing air and water pollution in the years ahead; in fact, a legal basis for accomplishing this already exists.

There is also a long-term interest in pollution abatement related to those damages that are intergenerational in nature. Thus, irreversible damage to the earth's life-support system or to substantial parts of it would be harmful to long-term occupancy, whatever our mode. Likewise, damage to the human gene pool from environmental sources would be a very heavy burden to leave to future generations. Concern about these matters is not part of the popular consensus, but is widespread among influential segments of the population.

Supply Security

Another goal on which there is wide agreement is the need to ensure the security of supply of raw materials and food. Primarily, this is a matter of national security—the physical availability of supplies in time of crisis. In addition, there is an interest in avoiding the economic blackmail that may occur as a result of other foreign policy interests or of falling victim to severe disruption growing out of third-party disputes. The security argument is often a mask for domestic interests and must be appraised critically. Security may be in conflict with the income objective if, in deference to it, we must rely upon costly defensive measures or on more expensive domestic production. Moreover, to the extent that we use domestic nonrenewables in lieu of foreign resources, we accelerate depletion of domestic resources and accentuate our environmental problems.

From a security standpoint, the ideal arrangement would be to have domestic resources developed for possible quick access while refraining from use lest they be depleted. However, this usually is unrealistic. Often it is impractical to increase production much over a few months' time, even if mines, mills, and transportation facilities exist, because of the time needed to recruit and train a labor force. Furthermore, it is extremely costly to invest in production facilities and then allow them to lie idle. Therefore, a going but expandable industry is apt to provide the only true recourse for an intermediate-term supply interruption. Maintenance of stocks allows time for some of this adjustment and permits us to ride out short supply interruptions.

Reliance on domestic supply as a form of security carries inherent conflicts. The imperatives of growth and competitiveness and the consumer demand for low prices may favor imports. Broader foreign policy considerations of maintaining an open trading system available to us and our allies are also in conflict with domestic protection. At the same time, in a world of diminishing U.S. and Western influence and of growing economic nationalism, it may appear dubious practice to increase dependence on foreign supplies, especially the more critical ones, if there are reasonable alternatives.

Secondary Goals

Conservation. The foregoing seem primary goals. Several secondary and instrumental goals also may be mentioned. For example, conservation is viewed with favor by most who see it in terms of eliminating blatant waste of resources. Of course, resources usually are "wasted" when they are cheap and they may be cheap for a number of reasons traceable to government policy—farm subsidies, water control subsidies, depletion allowances, policies governing access to federal lands, tolerance of environmental damage, and governmentally tolerated freight rates and industrial structures. Fostering prices that reflect true social cost of production would be a minimum step toward restraining waste. This does not conflict with other social objectives.

In addition to restricting waste, a conservationist policy also would protect the sustainable productivity of the land and would extend the life of nonrenewable resources. The latter could be accomplished by more complete recycling of materials, substitution of renewables for nonrenewables, and sheer reduction of consumption. These measures, particularly if they are more costly in terms of economic resources, may conflict with the income objective; if consumption is repressed, the conflict is direct. Conservationist measures are generally consistent with the security and quality objectives since, by restricting new materials throughput, they reduce foreign dependence and the burden of materials cast out upon the environment. (It is not certain that substitution of renewables for nonrenewables has favorable environmental effects.)

Preservation. Preservation of wilderness, unique natural features and ecosystems, and genetic material is an objective often linked with conservation. Preservation is an alternative to development, and the fruits of development are what is sacrificed to achieve the preservation goal. In general, preservation withholds some of our natural capital from industrial use. Thus, there may be conflict with the income and security goals. However, preservation also insures the availablity of scenic and genetic resources and therefore has a value that should be measured as part of society's income; we cannot conclude that this value is less than the development alternative without examining each case in detail.

While discussed here as elements of the social consensus, preservation and conservation are of special significance in the choice of occupancy mode. Conservation measures are of importance in extending the duration of exhaustible stocks, thereby extending the length of the choice option. They also are serviceable in expanding or preserving the sustainable yield of renewable resources, whichever path is finally taken. Preservation measures assure whatever spiritual values man derives from exceptional natural beauty and contact with nature. In addition, the preservation of genetic material is likely to be of value to man along path two and would be absolutely essential to path one.

Efficiency. As an instrumental goal efficiency is serviceable to income growth, quality, and conservation. We usually think of efficiency in economic terms as minimizing total costs and thereby maximizing income. However, we may have conservation and environmental goals in conflict with the income goal and still seek the most efficient means of accomplishing them. Thus reduction of material requirements, resource exhaustion, and residuals generation per unit of output may be sought, even if they do not follow the lowest-cost path.

Equity. Policy also must be responsive to several dimensions of equity. Resource exploitation often generates large economic rents, and these may increase with scarcity. If land use regulations, environmental controls, and government incentives act to increase rents still further, many will question leaving the return in private hands. Measures to improve environmental quality may especially affect the poor through higher prices and loss of established jobs. Such inequity may be compounded by the inability of the poor (and perhaps other social groups as well) to influence collective decisions so as to reflect their values. Measures aimed at reducing private rents or limiting enjoyment of common property resources modify established rights and pose difficult problems of equity. Equity also implies attention to the interests of foreign countries in the U.S. markets and supplies, with consequences for all of other American goals. Indeed, the resolution of equity considerations may bring conflict with all of the other goals, though for a working society some overall sense of equity is a prerequisite if other objectives are to be attained.

Institutions. Some institutional features of American society are widely enough accepted that, in addition to being instruments through which we seek other goals, they have taken on a value of their own. Thus, whatever other goals are pursued, they must be sought in a fashion which allows widespread public participation in decisions and maximum latitude for individual tastes. This means a bias in favor of leaving to the private sector as many things as possible, relying upon it to provide full play for initiative and to generate alternatives. There is still a major role for policy in setting the context within which the market operates. Where collective choices are required, the bias favors making decisions at the local or regional level when possible and administering the rules at the lowest level consistent with the scope of the problem. Obviously, many decisions affecting security, resource availability, and environmental quality are national or even international in scope. However, many aspects of land planning and environmental quality management are amenable to lower levels of planning and perhaps to still more local administration. It greatly adds to the vitality of the society if responsibility for such matters goes to the local level, and it also is apt to result in more effective administration.

The foregoing goals for Americans pertaining to resources exist somewhat apart from the question of which path man shall take. In part this is because the goals reflect experience in our particular setting while the paths for man relate to a future as yet dimly perceived and poorly articulated. Moreover, our national goals reflect the fact that we live in a world of sovereign states and the United States enjoys a highly favored position in that world. Are the goals compatible with either or both modes of occupancy? They appear to be more consistent with path two than path one. This is almost entirely due to the high value that Americans still place on income growth and, for the present, on security. Because we sense that the only real hope for income growth and for security is continued technical progress, most Americans, if forced to choose, would prefer path two. However, values change and a future generation may lack the drive and confidence required to sustain the trek along that path. Meanwhile, it seems wise to behave in a way that prolongs the option. Most of the other goals widely subscribed to by Americans—especially those relating to environmental protection, conservation, preservation, and efficiency— all serve to prolong the option, with institutional and equity objectives in a somewhat anomalous position. On this basis an interim strategy can be discussed, which is consistent with widely accepted American goals and which attends to our particular present needs without foreclosing future options for mankind as a whole.

ELEMENTS OF AN INTERIM STRATEGY

An interim strategy for the next 50–100 years that is consistent with long-term occupancy must first preserve our option regarding choice of future mode. This means it must attempt to conserve the resource stock, restraining purely consumptive uses, and must seek to avoid irreversible damage to the earth's life-support system or genetic stock. Such performance is facilitated by population restraint, which has the added benefit of easing the transition to a lower level of resource use, should that ever be required. Technological innovation is essential to prolong the present basis of occupancy and is even more important if release from resource constraints is sought. All of this applies to a world system. Since man will continue to live in a system of national states for an extended period, interim strategy for the United States must also attend to national materials supply. Within the above context, Americans must seek means of relieving current environmental congestion and resource shortages. The watchwords of an interim strategy, then, are conservation, preservation, independence, innovation, and population restraint. Each requires fuller explanation, and their applications will be further illustrated in Chapters 2 through 7.

Supply Independence

Supply independence tending toward autarchy in basic materials is a malodorous concept in economics. It is associated with the protection of vested domestic production interests at the expense of consumer interests. It also is associated with unconcern for the interests of foreign sellers, which often are LDCs, and it may lead to aggressive nationalism among land powers in an attempt to secure supplies. Of course, trade in resource commodities also has been associated with aggressiveness for sea powers and with the colonialism and neocolonialism that are said to exploit the weaker traders from the LDCs.

The fact is that the complex economies of major industrial countries, whether alone or in trade groups, are becoming inordinately sensitive to supply interruptions. This applies to energy above all. The European Economic Community (EEC) and Japan already are very exposed, and the United States is becoming so. Such exposure is a comparatively novel situation for industrial countries. Where foreign suppliers are few and act in concert, insecurity of supply sorely restricts national sovereignty. To some, this might appear a compelling argument for the submergence of sovereignty into a larger world system, but the gap in outlook between industrial countries and LDCs is so profound and the prospect of bridging it sufficiently remote that industrial countries, having lost the determination to impose their will on others, cannot look to the world system to ensure greater security for such fundamentals as their energy supply.

Could industrial countries rely on mutual interest to ensure trade in resource commodities? In a world of growing nationalism and shifting alliances, mutual interest cannot be depended upon. While governments in LDCs often are most anxious to export resource commodities, some are learning to act in concert to restrict supply. Also, there are other spokesmen who increasingly complain that trade in raw commodities warps their domestic economies, promotes enclaves and corruption, and leaves them holes in the ground instead of the resources needed for their own future development. While this argument can be countered, it would take us far afield to pursue it. Yet another theme advanced both in the LDCs and among guilt-laden citizens of industrial countries is the charge that developed countries consume a disproportionate share of the world's resources, drawing much of them from LDCs. All of this contributes to a climate in which supply interruption becomes acceptable practice. We cannot count on simply going into the market to secure future resource supplies.

Increased self-reliance probably would not reduce consumption greatly in developed countries and therefore would not reserve more of the "world's" resources for future development of the LDCs. Since it would deprive the latter of markets they currently value, it would be viewed by many as illiberal. However, it would put an end to the charge of exploitation that presently bedevils relations between the two worlds. Since it would require development of substitutes for traditional energy and materials commodities, it would also be a step toward freeing other countries from the threat of early resource exhaustion.

From the standpoint of the developed countries, concern about supply interruption has less force for minerals than for energy. The potential for substitution among mineral commodities is great, long-term stockpiling often is feasible, and the consequences of interruption less severe. Of course, the LDC's own reservations about trade in mineral commodities will stand.

Where trade involves tropical agricultural products, dependence in most cases poses no threat to the security of the United States or other developed countries because the demand is highly discretionary. Overall dependence on outside sources for basic calories or protein in a world where surpluses are very thin would be an uncomfortable position for industrial countries to assume, but the United States does not face that problem.

Independence is not an absolute to be sought regardless of cost. It is a bias to be given more weight in crucial cases, such as energy, or where the instability of potential suppliers is troublesome. Moreover, it is an objective that can be compromised at times to meet other pressures, provided that a suitable strategy exists to make a turnabout. For example, we might condone the growth of energy imports during a transition period to a new energy system that makes us less dependent.

Conservation, Preservation, and Environment

Conservation incorporates the idea of extending the life of a fixed stock of exhaustible resources. For renewable resources, it implies maximizing the sustainable yield of the resource. Obviously, the substitution of renewables for nonrenewables extends the life of the stock of the latter and therefore is a conservation measure, provided we do not exceed the capacity of the renewable resource and do it permanent damage. Other means of extending the life of the stock include more complete extraction, more efficient refinement, reduced resource use per unit of output (that is, improved efficiency), restraint on certain types of output or on the specific resource inputs to them, and increased recycling of materials. Restrictions on consumption of output incorporating large components of materials or energy generally would also extend the life of the stock.

The operation of private markets that was seen as wasting materials in a time of plenty acts to conserve resources as they become scarce. At the same time, scarcity has sometimes been countered by technological measures that increase access to the resource base, thereby speeding depletion. Moreover, policy has favored development and use of virgin resources rather than measures to restrict use; this is evident in tax policy, land use policies, freight discrimination, and policy regarding disposal of residuals. Such policies are presumed to increase current income. Since we may anticipate a time when we need not rely on the conventional resources of today, why should we alter the current policy bias? Again, the rationale for conservation is that it extends the time during which the difficult transition can be made and it is conducive to the future-oriented cast of mind required to convert natural capital into the technical and scientific capital needed for the future. Moreover, as we attain greater affluence, deceleration of growth is not especially painful.

If higher raw materials prices result from a conservationist policy, this does not imply equivalent damage to the income objective. Resulting changes in industrial processes will bring at least partially offsetting higher efficiency in material use. Also, if income is interpreted as welfare, higher materials costs will restrain consumption and thereby have salutary effects through reduced environmental burden and improvement in the services the environment yields to man.

Environment is but another face of resources and pollution abatement another aspect of conservation. If we do permanent damage to the environment through human activity, we are consuming a stock.

In most respects the environment is a renewable resource that yields direct amenity services and assimilates wastes. Where chronic congestion (even if reversible) impairs the environmental quality standard we expect, then we have exceeded the sustainable yield of the environmental resource and reduced its current service flows to man. Conservation measures that restrict mining activity and materials throughput and promote recycling also conserve the environmental resource. Conceivably, incentives could be designed to increase both the cost of the materials and the cost of effluents, thereby conserving both materials and environmental resources. This would enhance the direct income yield of the latter and diminish the income penalty that conservation measures otherwise may entail. From an income standpoint, however, the potential tradeoffs are infinitely complex and can only be discussed in detail.

The preservation option is a special case of conservation. Here we choose between two types of consumption; preservation permits sustained yield of a particular kind of psychic income, while development generally means destruction of these values in favor of greater immediate yield of a different kind. Economic criteria tend to bias the case in favor of development, since the advantages of preservation are very long term, and hence subject to heavy discounting, while development is a near-at-hand option to be realized without heavy discount. More refined analysis permits rectifying some of this imbalance, but in the final analysis the preservation choice is likely to be influenced by ethical or prudential concern rather than by pure economic calculation. Development is essentially irreversible and its gains can always be claimed in the future if desired. Because preservation is of ascending value, a heavy interim bias in favor of preservation is defensible (see Chapter 2, pages 36–39).

Innovation

Technological innovation for the interim period will include both extensions of technology aimed at increasing the availability of conventional resources and improved efficiency in use to permit their conservation with least damage to income. It will also include basic research and pilot applications looking toward the technology required for transition to a period of plentiful energy and materials. In both cases the innovations must be brought forward with caution to ensure that they do not degrade the environment. We should strive hard to stay far enough ahead of resource and environmental constraints so as to avoid risky crash programs.

The first line of innovation will require improved means of locating and extracting minerals and fuels. Data acquisition via geochemical and geophysical techniques and the use of airborne or satellite sensors promise rapid advance in defining and locating the earth's stock.

Attention to recycling in all phases of production and use must be emphasized. Both processes and products will need to be designed with this in mind. This, in turn, will help reduce the burden on the environment, a matter that must receive current attention irrespective of recycling possibilities.

For basic research, attention inevitably will center about new energy systems, including those configurations affecting demand as well as supply. As is well known, the United States has ample resources of combustible fuels which could meet our needs for many decades or perhaps for hundreds of years. However, two considerations strip some of the comfort from this fact.

Whatever the amplitude of our own resources of fossil fuels, many other parts of the world are not so generously supplied. It is impossible to make an accurate projection of world demand and supply over the next hundred years or so, but if shortage arises during that time, it is not imaginable that we could comfortably continue energy use at several multiples of our present level while the rest of the world comes to a halt. The urgency of the need for transition to inexhaustible energy sources cannot be related solely to our own supplies.

The other question pertains to the environmental consequences of continuing combustion. One consequence is the unavoidable addition of CO_2 to the atmosphere on a much larger scale and with uncertain results. For another, combustion is often a thermally inefficient conversion technique that adds to the heat burden wherever it occurs. Finally, we have not so far been successful in fully containing or neutralizing other combustion products, whether in internal combustion engines or thermoelectric plants and metallurgical industries. Thus, we may encounter an environmental limit to the use of fossil fuels, even if we do not encounter a resource limit. For coming decades, combustion technology can be improved to stave off this limit, but our eye must fall on the environmental consequences as well as on supply.

An effectively inexhaustible and ample potential energy source is fusion materials. Solar energy (however collected) is a nondepleting (though not infinitely expandable) source, and valuable supplements may be found in wind, tides, and earth heat. All represent a major departure from the present energy system. Success in tapping these sources may eliminate supply concern, but energy-related environmental problems will remain. All energy sources other than naturally incident solar energy add to the earth's heat burden. This implies an ultimate environmental limit to the scale of human activity.

Measures to improve the efficiency of the end uses of energy not only extend the availability of fuels but also defer the approach of heat limits and therefore have an additional value that improved conversion techniques do not, since efficiency in use will be essential for a post-combustion age. The simplest and most obvious measures are space heating advances—insulation, utilization of waste heat, use of solar heat, etc. Much energy presently is used to overcome friction in transportation and industrial machinery; ingenious uses of vacuum tubes and magnetics in transport could reduce these requirements. Better organization of flows, whether in the machine, plant, urban area, or larger geographical regions also could minimize energy requirements. Metallurgical and chemical industries commonly are based on heat processes, but we probably could diminish this in a way that would have long-term value.

We have dwelt on energy as an example of longer-term research focus. Another area of research might be the problem of enlarging current organic production and making better use of it than we do. Some plant species are more efficient synthesizers of sunlight and nutrients than others, and if we could combine this characteristic with improved industrial capacity to convert biomass into nutrients, fiber, or fuel, we might greatly expand our renewable resource base. This would extend the life of exhaustible stocks and might be a low-cost resource even for a period of resource plenty. In any case, by making better use of current organic production, and perhaps by confining it to a minimum acreage, we reduce the pressure of man on the land, favoring preservation.

Population Restraint

Population restraint is part of an interim strategy. We cannot know what constitutes an optimum level of population even at present; any long-term optimum is apt to be at a shifting level, reflecting altered tradeoffs between population and income and shifting values with respect to income and to the preservation of nature. In the absence of a clear concept of an optimum, we can be reasonably sure that "less is more." Population restraint preserves our options in every regard, reducing the rate of use of resources, and having a similar effect on environmental quality and preservationist objectives. Should we take path one, the transition would be greatly eased, while restraint imposes no obstacles to, and probably facilitates, path two. Few Americans would disagree with the idea of population restraint, although it is not universally accepted in other parts of the world.

About the only positive case to be made in defense of population growth is the pleasure many people derive from children. If this brings a net reproduction rate exceeding one for society as a whole, all would agree that the result is insupportable in the long run. One may then ask why it should be indulged for one generation if forbidden to the next. Others might argue that human creativity is a rare quality and randomly distributed so that the largest supportable population means more such individuals. However, it seems likely that the conditions in which creativity can blossom are at least as important as its occurrence, and we may profit from it as much if a sparser population provides better conditions. As for other arguments, the United States has no vast empty lands beckoning the settler, or border areas to be occupied, or racial integrity to preserve, or armies in need of cannon fodder.

The main problems concerning population restraint are related not to its wisdom but rather to the human and social difficulties in achieving it. These involve both individuals and nations, ethnic and religious groups, and social classes. If education and inducement can achieve stabilization, the problem can be managed at the national level. If they cannot, the implied sanctions would be very divisive.

For the larger world community the problem is aggravated by worldwide sentiment for greater income equalization and by recognition that some of the environmental effects of population growth may be international in scale, giving each of us an economic and ecological stake in the size of other people's families. Present rates of population growth in many parts of the world are frightening in their possible import, not only for other countries but for the United States as well. The United States can offer a responsible example and technical advice where accepted, but we have no confident solution for this problem.

We are fortunate in the United States at present because declining fertility appears to have brought us within range of a net reproduction rate of one. So long as we are near that point, we can avoid compulsory measures to restrict fertility. It would be pointless to incur the large social costs involved for very minor gains. At the same time we must deepen our understanding of the social, psychological, and economic determinants of fertility, as well as of methods of contraception, so that should present voluntary trends reverse, we would have a better basis for policies to induce continued restraint. Such steps will also help parents to reduce the gap between intended and actual family size, ensuring that only desired children are born.

The U.S. population grows not only through natural increase but also through immigration. At one time we encouraged immigration for good national reasons. That time is past. And in a world where others decline responsibility for controlling their own numbers, we are perfectly entitled to restrict entry to the United States. Hereafter, immigration may be thought of in humanitarian terms of uniting families, asylum, or relieving vicims of temporary disturbances abroad than as a general demographic obligation.

What has been described as an interim strategy is by most standards a long-term view. It is intended to cover the time during which men must decide what type of long-term occupancy of this planet they will seek and must begin the transition to that system. As I argue, this interim strategy is one of retaining our option and extending the time during which it remains open. It is advisable because our vision is too imperfect and our habits of thought too frozen in a past mode to permit a clear decision now on the feasibility and desirability of other modes. It is noteworthy, however, that this interim strategy can be reconciled with goals widely held by Americans, including many environmentalists. It calls for modifications of a sort that environmental needs and resource scarcity will favor in any case, but asks us to be somewhat more self-conscious and reflective about what we are doing. It is a strategy for transition.

While government policy decisions should aspire to consistency with such a strategy, by their nature most of them will be responsive to more immediate demands. Some of these policy problems are examined further in the chapters that follow.

2
ISSUES
IN
LAND USE POLICY

Land use is basic to a future-oriented resource and environmental strategy. In the terms outlined in Chapter 1, land is the principal arena for the current flows of energy and the recycling of minerals required by path one. Hence, maintenance of the ecological health and productive capacity of the land would be prerequisite to that mode. Path two might be less dependent on the output of land, but land would still be a source of the materials and energy resources required for path two. For both modes, land would retain its role as a supplier of outdoor amenities and as a nurturer of genetic resources and as the site for all of the human infrastructure, however sizeable that may be. The focus in this chapter will be on the extensive or nonurban uses of land, recognizing that the economic needs of urban dwellers who occupy only a tiny share of the total surface nonetheless largely determine the general configuration of land use.

Land clearly is a finite or limited resource. However, that statement must be qualified. The productivity of land in most uses can be increased, so land is not quite the rigid limit to human occupancy that we might suppose. By adding other inputs—labor, natural and synthetic fertilizers, mechanical power, pesticides, and scientific selection and breeding—farmers have increased agricultural yields per acre manyfold. There are limits to the amount of photosynthetic activity possible over a given surface area, but they have not yet been reached. We also have increased the productivity of land for site use by improved planning and building techniques and the associated transportation developments that permit servicing larger centers at greater density. Even the amenity services yielded by land used for outdoor recreation can be enhanced by investments affecting access and by management techniques to avoid congestion. Despite these possibilities for increasing the services of land, scarcity can still cramp us; the total land surface and the area of good cropland are limited, and we can make only marginal changes in them.

While land is a finite resource, in normal use it is not a depletable one. Land continues to yield its services year after year if properly cared for. This is true irrespective of whether the land is in pastoral uses or is employed for sites. If land is to support photosynthetic production, then protection of the soil is essential. This means control of erosion above all. Preservation of genetic materials also is important to agriculture and medicine and will require that some land continue in wild state so as to nurture the species that may prove of future value. Land can yield most of its amenity services without destruction of its permanent qualities. Thus, a distinguishing feature of land is its eternal and renewable nature when not abused.

However, some shifts of land use tend to be irreversible in character, at least for very long periods. Fear of exhausting the land resource generally refers to the shift from more extensive to more intensive uses of land and concern that demands of the former type, especially for recreational use, will go unmet. Obviously, use of land for building sites is incompatible with pastoral uses of the same land, and there may also be conflict between uses of land in agriculture or forestry and its use for recreation, though in many cases these activities are compatible.

If the goals of high income, improved environmental quality, and security of supply are to be well served by land, then we must learn to improve the yield of land in each use and must devise methods for directing land to its best uses. If yields can be improved from this domestic renewable resource in an economical fashion without raising environmental burdens, this helps attain the income objective. At the same time, there are environmental and preservationist reasons for restricting agricultural and forest commodity production to the smallest acreage of land and to those lands best suited for such purposes, leaving the rest of the land in its "natural" state. This would be consistent with a strategy of retaining options and leaving the natural systems intact for future amenity use or as a fallback production base for path one.

Could society intervene to accomplish such objectives? In traditional agrarian societies the individual's relationship to the land was the very nexus of the social system. That bond was ruptured in the industrialized West, and land ceased to play the central role it once held; it became a commodity like any other. As land became more plentiful through territorial expansion and as employment opportunities expanded apart from the land, society abandoned much interest in land use control, especially in the United States. Now that we are more aware of the environmental and resource implications of land use and face rising competition for the limited supply of land, there has been a reassertion of social control over land use. That trend is sure to continue, despite rearguard resistance. Therefore, Americans need to reconsider their attitudes toward land use in order to understand more clearly what should be accomplished through social control. Land use planning is a means of structuring the various controls over land use; at the same time it promises to provide a forum in which new attitudes toward land can be formulated.

LAND USE PATTERNS

The United States has always been a land-rich country. When the early settlers brought European agricultural technology to a land more lightly occupied by hunters and gatherers, they were able to not merely displace the indigenous population but to increase manyfold the numbers that the land would support. Early land use policy centered about how to occupy the vast land for agriculture—the rate of opening, means of acquiring tenure, credit, transport, and the issue of slavery dominated land policy. Efforts to restrict supply were defeated by a land-hungry people drawn to the empty territory. American attitudes toward land were shaped in that climate of abundance. Government control over land was viewed as a denial of opportunity, and the challenge of the wilderness favored exploitation over conservation.

The retreat from these attitudes has been gradual. The closing of the frontier ended the sense of land abundance. Able propagandists soon made us aware of the need for conservation of our forests. A more affluent and urban society, now subjected to some pressures from congestion, turned to zoning as a device to protect neighborhood quality. The dust storms of the 1930s dramatized the neglect of our agricultural land and led to conservation programs directed toward farmland. Finally, the intense urbanization and spectacular prosperity of recent decades, together with the associated environmental problems, have brought problems of land use control into much sharper focus. All of these changes have been in the direction of restricting the unfettered property rights in land in favor of social controls and public programs.

Are we in danger of soon running out of land? Will we no longer have enough for agriculture, forestry, and the infrastructure of civilization? It is possible to conceive of circumstances where the fixed supply of land would be "inadequate" to meet needs of these sorts. Endless population growth would generate such a situation. Nevertheless, during the next 50–100 years we should have enough land to meet our needs. We do not expect the population to grow so dramatically or the domestic consumption of the products of the soil to increase so much that we will run short. For example, population projections for the year 2000 are on the order of 251–300 million, and continuation of current trends would yield about 300 million by 2020. Even in the face of growing population and improved dietary standards, total land in cultivation had declined for decades until the very recent surge of foreign demand occasioned some reversal. Very modest improvements in per acre productivity will allow us to feed our added population, even if more of our diet is consumed as animal protein. Since cities and other man-made structures presently require only about 3 percent of the total surface, there is certain to be ample space to meet these two uses over the interim period. (The only major uncertainty in this picture concerns the extent of foreign demand for farm and forest products.) Sheer space is not our problem, but rising competition for land in various uses does bring conflict.

The extensive uses of land in the United States are for agriculture (pasture, range, and cropland), forests, and those residual lands in mountains, tundra, swamps, etc. All of these categories serve multiple uses; they may provide recreational services (hunting and hiking at least), some offer wilderness experience, and all serve as ecological preserves to some degree. In 1970 nearly 28 percent of our land was in pasture and range, over 23 percent in forest and woodland, and 21–22 percent in the residual category, most of this in Alaska. An additional 3–4 percent was in parks, wilderness, and the like, excluded from development. Thus, well over three-fourths of our land surface is not intensively used for cultivation or sites. Land used for crops amounted to about 15 percent of the total, while in excess of 4 percent was cropland not harvested. Acreage harvested actually declined about 15 percent in two postwar decades, despite the rapid population growth of the period.

A mere 4.4 percent of the total was in use for infrastructure, divided about equally between habitation, transport and industrial uses, and public institutions. Included in these categories are urban recreational lands and extensive military installations, so less than 2 percent of the surface is devoted to intensive use as sites for man-made structures.[1] Of course, the value of such intensively used lands far exceeds the value of all rural land.

These classifications are in terms of primary use. Much of the countryside, whether farmland, swamp, or wilderness, produces game and recreation even if classified in other uses, and forest land and some cropland may be grazed part of the time. Primary use statistics can be deceptive in other ways—the mining scar on a distant hillside may occupy only a small area but can degrade the view for miles around. Likewise, land is one of the principal receiving media for residuals and, while its capacity is great, some uses on small acreages destroy the amenity value of much nearby land—no one wants to live or play next to the dump.

Our supply of land is relatively generous. We have about 11 acres per capita (9 excluding Alaska and Hawaii). Even under assumptions of high population growth, by the year 2000 we will have more land per head than most European countries have today. Because so much of our land is in extensive uses, our needs for urban and recreational land can be met by encroaching on these categories. Indeed, for a generation or so it is unlikely that the distribution of land by category of use will change much at all. Of course, there will be great regional variation in this pattern of change, and prime sites for urban and recreational use will be in much shorter supply in some areas than the aggregate picture suggests.

Our present supply of land and the flexibility implied by the pattern of land use are reassuring for some decades—even longer if population growth is moderate. Yet in the long term there are considerations that modify this assurance. First, while land is renewable in agriculture or forestry, it may be irrevocably committed to other uses. This is the case when land is converted to sites for the works of man. Because these site uses are enduring, and in a growing economy commonly lead on to still more intensive site use, the land is effectively excluded from further pastoral use. Conversion to sites has been governed mostly by convenience, with very little attention given to the inherent qualities of the land. Since powerful elements of inertia influence this decision when left to the market, land planning could play an

---

[1] Data on land use were taken from Ronald G. Ridker, ed., *Population, Resources, and the Environment*, volume III of Commission Research Reports, U.S. Commission on Population Growth and the American Future (Washington, D.C.: Government Printing Office, 1972), pp. 226–227.

important role in diverting to site use lands suited to that purpose that might lack qualities needed in other uses. Another nearly irreversible change occurs when wilderness lands are invaded for development. Theoretically, it should be possible to restore the land to wilderness by desisting from more intensive use, but once developmental investments have been made and the area opened to traffic, it is virtually impossible to return it to original condition.

Aside from its value in direct production of food and fiber and as sites, land as a resource holds the key to a wide range of other valued services. Land use greatly affects the severity of flooding and the recharge of runoff into underground basins. The esthetic pleasure that we take from the countryside also is an aspect of land use to which we have given almost no conscious attention. Land is a setting for outdoor recreation, for wildlife, and for wilderness. In all of these respects it is a renewable resource if not abused. Finally, as the site of terrestrial ecosystems, the land serves as our primary genetic preserve, nurturing species whose value to man may as yet be unrecognized. Again, this aspect of the land resource is poorly appreciated and not deliberately guarded. All this serves as a reminder that land is a trust held by each generation for use by the next, so preservation of its permanent qualities must be considered a duty.

An ample supply of land is a luxury that can be squandered on rising demands for land use or it can serve as a cushion for adjustment toward a rational long-term pattern. The opportunity presented here for positive action should not be missed. Long-term guidelines that I feel should apply to land use include:

1. Minimizing permanent damage
2. Maximizing sustainable yield on all land in each use for which demand exists
3. A bias toward preservation and toward a return to "the ecology" of lands not needed for crops
4. Development of agricultural technology so as to avoid current environmental damage
5. Exploration of alternatives to open-field agriculture.

MINIMIZING PERMANENT DAMAGE

In agricultural use land is a renewable resource. Even land that is comparatively exhausted by cropping can be restored to fertility by the application of artificial fertilizers. Soil structures may be damaged through the loss of humus that occurs with cropping, but in most cases cultivation practices can compensate for this. Even this loss is reversible, for it would be possible to restore humus content if economic and demographic pressures on the land were relieved. The most extensive permanent damage done to land is by exposing soils to erosion and through ill-considered and irrevocable decisions about land use.

In many cases erosion is a major threat because cultivation is attempted on poorly adapted lands—those too steep or located in areas where harsh climate or thin cover leave them vulnerable. Since the 1930s we have made considerable progress in controlling erosion through the creation of soil conservation districts. By a combination of physical works and cultivation practices it is possible to control erosion on much of our cropland. This involves withdrawal of steep slopes from cropping, retention of cover, contour plowing, and other means to prevent gullying and to slow runoff. The maximum possibilities here have not yet been realized, in part because few social responsibilities are currently imposed by land ownership. Given the fortunate supply of good cropland and the propensity to agricultural surplus in the United States, our society has been under little economic pressure to employ lands highly vulnerable to erosion. Why then, should the chance owner of the moment be allowed to preside over the destruction of the timeless quality of the soil? This has occurred in part because the cost to the farmer of corrective measures often exceeds the private income benefits to him. But if society perceives a sound reason for arresting erosion, surely this result can be secured through education, regulation, and subsidy affecting the private owner. Some of the social benefits such as watershed protection and reduction of siltation are easily perceived and are measurable in principle. We should proceed as promptly as benefit–cost standards dictate to ensure these benefits. In the longer run serious permanent damage to the earth's life-support system, of which the soil is an integral part, cannot be tolerated. Therefore, where private owners seek to realize a short-term gain at the expense of the ecosystem by more intensive use than the land can sustain, they must be restricted from doing so. In most cases, long-term retirement from cropping suffices to stem erosion; this could be secured by easement where necessary.

The government shares the blame for some of the erosion that occurs. Substantial acreages in the United States have been withdrawn from cropping under various crop support programs. All too often this is done on a year-to-year basis, with the land left uncovered. Particularly in the Midwest this practice exposes land to wind and water erosion. If support payments were made only on evidence that appropriate cover has been provided on withdrawn land, this would ease the problem. Moreover, the encouragement of longer-term commitments of land to acreage reserves would facilitate the provision of cover and permit more effective alternative uses (see pages 32–33).

Erosion is a function of many different elements, including soil structure, climate, and topography. There is little need to crop or log those lands most subject to erosion. Increases in per acre yields on the best lands in the United States permits us to spare the marginal lands from tillage. Of course, there is another sort of environmental tradeoff involved, since increased yield of good land is based on the use of more agricultural chemicals. Fortunately the problem here is not acute. We have ample agricultural land to meet domestic needs well into the future. Over a third of our cropland is considered to be adequately protected against erosion at present, and time still remains to progress toward more complete control.

Despite the urban dweller's perception of the matter, very little land is devoted to man-made structures. As we saw, less than 2 percent of our total surface goes to these uses, and population growth and increased urbanization may raise this figure to about 3–4 percent by the year 2000. From a short-term standpoint this is not an alarming shift. Nonetheless, if such trends should continue long thereafter, a significant amount of land would be diverted from pastoral uses. We could economize on site use by concentrating industry, residences, and transport rights-of-way on minimal amounts of land. For residences, this would mean smaller lot size zoning or more use of townhouses and apartments, while for transportation it implies use of mass transit and perhaps less commotion through better urban organization. Discussion of these possibilities is reserved for Chapter 3.

Irrespective of the amount of land used for man-made structures, there is a question of the type or quality of land diverted to such purposes. Too often we do not show proper respect for the physical features of the land. Building in the flood plain is the most obvious example of this. Flood plains are part of the natural river system and should not be incorporated into built-up areas. Thus, the policy of subsidizing flood plain protection is positively nefarious; even flood insurance programs take account only of private damages rather than broader social interests in maintaining the river system and its associated recharge basin. Of course, protection cannot be abandoned for areas already built up, but a resolute policy of land planning must be evolved to prevent such exposure in the future. Short-term, low-investment uses of the flood plain would still be viable.

INCREASING SUSTAINABLE YIELDS

A second guide is that of maximizing sustainable economic yields in each use for which demand exists with the aim of sparing depletable materials. At present we do not make intensive use of the land except for some cultivated areas. Rather we use the natural capital found in mineral deposits for current consumption while failing to harvest the sustainable current potential of the land. The principal reason is existing relative price relationships, which in turn owe much to the incentives provided to new mineral production. The most effective way to increase the current yield from the land so as to substitute for exhaustible raw materials would be to increase the price of the latter—a step that could be justified on environmental and security grounds in many cases.

Failure to maximize the yield of many outputs of the land also comes about because the social benefits of doing so cannot be captured by private owners. Small privately held woodlands are a case in point. In addition to providing a commercial product of interest to the owner, they also provide watershed protection and habitat for game, as well as esthetic and perhaps recreational values. The small owner is poorly equipped to realize any of these yields, some of whose benefits are not even in principle within his control. Thus he does not manage effectively, and some of the social benefits are lost. It should be possible to organize a set of institutions to deal with this problem—cooperative organizations to market hunting rights and subsidies or easements to encourage development of pure public benefits such as watershed and landscape protection.

Land use for crop production tends to be better managed. There is considerable incentive for the private owner both to protect the soil of good land and to use it intensively. For decades the problem has been one of surplus rather than insufficiency of output. In the face of food surplus, some contend that federal programs that increase productivity like research, reclamation and flood control are ill-advised. More recently there has been a growing longer-term concern that we may need the added productivity to restrain food costs, increase our supply of animal protein, meet the needs of a growing population, and provide assistance to a hungry world.

POLICY FOR UNCROPPED LANDS

The contradictory nature of U.S. farm programs is well known. We have restricted output as a device for raising farm income at the same time that other programs tend to increase output. Coherent policy requires an assessment of whether the long era of farm surplus is behind us. If surplus again becomes a problem, attempts to limit production will probably be resumed. Since acreage restrictions rather than marketing quotas have been the principal means of controlling farm output, some public attention should, as a minimum, be turned to the use of private lands withdrawn from crops under these public programs, and we should strongly question the rationale of new land development at public expense so long as the surplus remains. The first concern for withdrawn lands is that they be protected from erosion. If the farmer views these lands as more or less permanently withdrawn, he may have little interest in their protection. Therefore protection must be made a condition of payment. Beyond this, if some product is to be realized from withdrawn lands, then their management as pasture or for wildlife should be encouraged. This could be achieved if longer-term arrangements for withdrawal were to become the rule. Some movement of land into and out of cultivation is essential to meet fluctuations in output and demands, but a larger acreage could be consigned over varying periods of time to the reserve and managed for other socially useful products.

Acreage restrictions have the effect of concentrating crops on the best lands—those with highest productivity and least exposure to erosion. From a strict efficiency standpoint it would be preferable in many cases for withdrawn acreage to be concentrated in larger blocks of land—perhaps entire farms and wider regions. Local communities commonly object to this procedure because the loss of farmsteads destroys the local business community as well. It is worth noting that the concentration of cropped land into larger units is already having this effect, and the difficulties of providing a satisfactory level of public services and urban amenities in tiny farm communities suggest that these towns may be lost in any case. Politically, the decision remains very difficult.

Whether cropland is withdrawn in checkered fashion or in larger blocs, the idea of concentrating production on smaller acreages has much merit. It permits us to forego expensive reclamation and drainage projects and allows more of the land to be returned "to the ecology." Indeed, a preference for protecting and returning wetlands, streams, channels, and the like to wild use would be most productive of wildlife and would spare the public expense of developing or maintaining private crop production on marginal lands.

If surplus persists, this implies antidevelopmental policies with respect to new farmland and policies in favor of developing other land use values. Rural stream channelization projects are a case in point. If carried through, such projects commonly open new land to cultivation, or at least to more reliable and intensive use, thereby adding to the burden of surplus. The public must finance both the investment and the continuing cost of surplus production. At the same time the environmental effects are nearly all negative. Loss of habitat for wildlife, faster runoff that increases downstream flood danger, and loss of ground water recharge all occur. Far from generating the social benefits that would justify subsidies for such projects, they more often generate social losses.

If surplus is not a problem for the future, we can pursue more neutral policies. A simple requirement that private beneficiaries be forced to pay the cost of such projects after social benefits or losses have been computed would restrain much of this activity. In other cases, more use of easements or even acquisition of privately held wetlands, abandoned farmlands, and the like would permit their longer-term management for wildlife and, in some cases, for recreation or forest production.

TOWARD MORE SPARING USE OF CHEMICALS

Since prime agricultural land is less subject to erosion and permits greater per acre yields, the concentration of crop production on such lands seems desirable on environmental grounds, thereby sparing less suitable lands and leaving a larger total to nature. Intensive cultivation carries hazards of its own, however. The output necessary to meet our dietary standards on restricted acreage can currently only be gained by the application of agricultural chemicals. If the practice of open-field agriculture is to be continued, we must master less destructive techniques of pest control and learn to meter fertilizer application in line with plant uptake. Present policy approaches for pesticides include regulating the application of those potentially most harmful to man and to the environment and withdrawing from use some, such as DDT, which have gained the worst reputation. As initial steps these are hard to fault, but more remains to be done.

A broad approach to pest control would include far more sophisticated understanding of natural controls and how they can be fostered, whether through farm practices, release of predators, or by providing more habitat for predator production. More specific or confined use of chemicals is another possibility. The use of sex attractants and methods to interrupt the reproductive success of pests also hold promise. In a system with more balance, judicious use of chemicals could still provide insurance when needed, while some crop losses could be tolerated in view of the savings on routine pesticide use. Obviously, a lengthy process of learning and adaptation is implied, but an integrated pest control system should permit satisfactory per acre yields, holding total crop acreage down.

Likewise, in the case of fertilizer use, a detailed study of the manner in which fertilizer moves in the soil and the pace of plant uptake should be made in order to permit more exact application. Both for fertilizers and pesticides this kind of individualized treatment tailored to specific situations entails much diversity and may not be best suited to techniques of large-scale agriculture. Some substitution of labor for other inputs is implied. In general the substitution between land, labor, and chemicals is such that future production needs cannot be met while restricting all three. The use of increased labor has a quick impact on agricultural prices. As a short-term measure it is probably preferable to allow increased use of land to meet rising needs, while trying to perfect nonpolluting technologies that can be operated at high yield and low-labor input.

In a more remote future, population pressure on the supply of land and environmental damage from agricultural chemicals may compel much closer management of photosynthetic production. For the United States, there is no immediate need to contemplate abandonment of field agriculture. Nonetheless, Americans have a continuing interest in reducing agricultural costs, both for our own benefit and to help feed other parts of the world. There are limits on the capacity of most of our plants to synthesize nutrients. It is generally agreed that the next major advance in agriculture will involve selecting, breeding, and producing more efficient plants. This still implies an intermediate type of field agriculture and does not reach all the way to a fully controlled photosynthetic factory. Such plants, however, might speed the day when the latter would be possible, since they increase the potential yield under controlled conditions. Because this has the possibility both of controlling agriculture-related pollution and concentrating production on the smallest area, it is worth a small continuing research program.

CONFLICTS OVER FOREST USE

Forest policy in the United States is caught in the middle between those who wish to increase wood production and those who emphasize the use of forest lands for such nonharvest values as recreation, wilderness, or watershed. Both sides represent legitimate values. Conservationists seeking to subordinate timber harvest to other uses have enjoyed increasing success as they have opposed roads into forest lands, timber clear-cutting, harvesting of virgin stands, and the like. Meanwhile, the nation's housing goals, with special reference to low-income people and minorities, will require more lumber than ever. New methods of construction may in time relieve some of this pressure, but meanwhile wood remains a versatile building material with few adverse environmental effects.

Conflicts between wood production and the various conservation and recreational uses of the forest need not be as severe as sometimes appears. It is true that some uses are partially or wholly incompatible at the same site and the same time. But the conflict could be greatly reduced by allowing for the rotation of uses and employing practices already available. Even lands managed for maximum wood output could still yield important recreational and other benefits. A further escape from this conflict may lie in the intensive management of our most productive forest lands for wood production, leaving less productive lands unharvested. Often the less productive lands are among those most suitable for wilderness or recreation. Marion Clawson has argued convincingly that such a pattern of high-intensity forestry concentrated on the most productive sites would allow us to meet prospective demands for wood while sparing over three-fifths of the forest land from harvest.[2]

Our failure to maximize the sustainable yield from forest lands has made forest products a conspicuous exception to the general trend of falling raw material prices in the United States, and it has unnecessarily aggravated the conflict between wood production and other forest uses. It is estimated that the net growth of wood on forest lands is less than one-half of the potential. While sheer resistance to harvest on the part of conservationists explains part of this record (failure to cut mature stands impairs net new growth), many other causes are involved; among them are the ownership pattern, administrative failures,

[2] Marion Clawson, "Conflicts, Strategies, and Possibilities for Consensus in Forest Land Use and Management," in *Forest Policy for the Future* (Washington, D.C.: Resources for the Future, Inc., 1974).

economic considerations, policy deficiencies, and the dubious concept of good silvicultural practice followed in some cases.

Only in the larger private forests do economic criteria guide output, and even for them it is believed that economic yields could be greatly increased by added investments and more intensified management practices. For other forests, other criteria are still more important.

The many small private forests and farm woodlots (nearly 60 percent of the total area) are not predominantly managed for economic production of wood products, although they are the source of much output.[3] The small owner may not find it worthwhile to equip himself to manage his forest lands, may lack the capital to do so, or may have noneconomic reasons for holding the forest. Attempts to provide technical support to small owners have not been notably successful heretofore. An approach involving cooperative professional management or leasing arrangements might help. The latter would also provide necessary capital and would permit a continuing flow of income to the owner. Government payments for the social benefits of maintaining forests would also encourage better use of this asset. The diverse personal situations and objectives of the owners constitute a major obstacle to any cooperative approach.

Public forests, which contain half the nation's sawtimber, do not approach their sustainable yield. Part of the reason for this is conflicting recreational use and part is due to simple underfunding of management agencies, but beyond this, the concept of good forestry being followed has retarded the harvesting of mature timber, meaning that some of the old-growth stands on prime forest lands are making no net growth of wood. The necessary changes fall directly within the realm of public policy. If a policy of concentrating production on the best lands is followed, then it should be possible to designate substantial areas of public forest (over half according to Clawson) as not subject to harvest; output on remaining lands could be raised just as on private forest industry lands.

THE PRESERVATION OPTION

Our bias for preservation needs to be carefully examined at this point. How do we determine what to preserve? When the land was wilder-

[3] This discussion of forest problems has drawn on the Report of the President's Advisory Panel on Timber and the Environment (Washington, D.C.: Government Printing Office, 1973).

ness this was not a pressing question, and it was understandable that policy favored development. Now the balance has tilted very far toward development, with only about 50 million acres of *de facto* wilderness remaining in the United States. Some would argue that remaining wilderness and unique natural features should be preserved as a matter of course. This is an expression of strongly held values, and if these values are widely enough held, they can compel this result politically. However, the benefits of development cannot be ignored—the dam, mine, or timber cut which also serve social purposes. A current generation cannot arbitrate between these two positions with assurance because the development decision makes irretrievable commitments affecting future generations. Nonetheless, it is reasonably certain that present methods of evaluating the alternatives fail to consider all of the benefits of preservation and exaggerate development benefits.[4]

Wilderness and unique natural features cannot generally be produced by man. If submitted to development, their value as amenity resources is decreased. The attempt to compare this preservation value with the value of a development alternative commonly neglects to estimate the worth of retaining our option in a changing situation where development becomes irreversible. We could condone the destruction of wilderness in favor of development when the country was poor, our technological alternatives few, and the supply of wild lands generous. This situation is now reversed. Now demand for wild land will certainly grow faster than demand for the resource commodities it might yield if developed. Meanwhile the supply is not expandable. The appropriate response to this situation would appear to be a presumption in favor of preservation. Developmental proposals should bear the burden of demonstrating that they will yield a premium well above the values yielded by preservation in order to compensate for the option value sacrificed by development. Development also should be able to stand without any element of subsidy so that, apart from environmental costs, its value is not overstated in the usual efficiency sense. A smaller discount rate applied to the stream of benefits to be expected from the preservation option, to allow for future appreciation of this value as compared to development, would help to compensate for some of the present bias favoring development. As a pragmatic

---

[4] A thorough treatment of these topics is found in the writings of John V. Krutilla. See his "Conservation Reconsidered," *American Economic Review*, September 1967 (Resources for the Future Reprint 67); and "Evaluation of an Aspect of Environmental Quality: Hells Canyon Revisited," *Proceedings of the Social Statistics Section, American Statistical Association*, 1970 (Resources for the Future Reprint 93).

step we could think in terms of a moratorium on development in wilderness or *de facto* wilderness, with changes in status subjected to rigorous tests to include the loss of option value and the requirement that development be able to compensate those who lose their previous right to use of the wilderness. This same line of thinking can apply to private lands, which provide habitat for rare or migratory species. In this case, however, the social purpose might require subsidy to the private owner via easements or outright acquisition that would cause him to desist from certain uses of his property.

In the face of the limited wild land and the unique natural features that we can preserve, we will soon need to consider means of limiting access to these resources. Wilderness yields many different kinds of experience, and we need to limit access only to those uses that are threatened by congestion; for example, one type of hunting may need to be limited if a particular species is threatened, while other game could still be taken. Solitude, however, is a nearly universal feature sought in the wilderness, and its preservation will impose a general restriction on use. Restriction can be achieved by such as devices as price rationing, lottery, or first-come–first-served. Each has its drawbacks.

The use of price to restrict access to a desired level appeals to some. It means that only those who value the experience most will come, and therefore at any given level of use the highest value of the resource is realized. Such a high yield on wilderness use in turn helps it to compete against the development alternative. Moreover, it is sometimes argued that the clientele for wilderness recreation is predominantly a middle-class one for which price rationing is appropriate. The disadvantage, of course, is that with the existing income distribution many of the most avid outdoorsmen would be excluded from what they view as enjoyment of their common property rights—an exclusion for which they are offered no compensation. Among them is a class that is physically most able to use the wilderness and for whom a wilderness experience could be most enriching, namely, the young.

A lottery is a more egalitarian device, but it gives no preference to those who most value the experience. Thus the total economic value yielded by the resource is diminished, and there would be a lesser economic rationale for preservation. First-come–first-served gives preference to those with time to stand in line over those with money to bid for access. It still allows the most determined a chance to satisfy their desires but is wasteful of everyone's time. A reservation system is a variant of first-come–first-served. It is complex and destroys the element of spontaneity.

These and other problems pose severe challenges to wilderness and park managers. But management can also help to allay and defer the problem of congestion. Especially in national parks, greater dispersion of visitors and limitations on auto traffic would permit fuller utilization of carrying capacity, and even the solitude of the wilderness could be preserved under more intensive use through dispersion and scheduling. These areas should be reserved for persons who want the unique experience, while persons merely interested in outdoor camping are diverted to less exclusive sites. Criteria for determining what to preserve, how to ration access when necessary, and how to manage so as to maximize the kind of carrying capacity sought all are management decisions crying for answers at present. A collaborative effort of academic persons, public interest groups, and agency personnel will be required to define the option more precisely and to help arrive at answers.

LAND USE PLANNING

The basic policy guides (page 28) state the social interest in land use, and I have mentioned some of the steps that may take us in the desired direction. It is apparent that the social interest cannot be attained through simple operation of the market, for short-term gains from exploitation may lead to unwise but irreversible land use decisions, to permanent damage to soil, or to ecologically unsound agricultural practices. Dispersed private management may fail to realize potential yield in, for example, forestry, and will not act to preserve wilderness. It is incapable of organizing to develop an alternative to present agricultural technology.

Government intervention affecting raw material prices could throw the balance more toward maximizing production of renewables, and government is best suited to attaining the preservation objective. It also must play a leading role in guiding soil conservation and in promoting new technology. Implicit in all of this necessary government intervention is a greater direct responsibility for the outcome of the system. Even now the government helps to create land values, subsidizes desired objectives, and in turn abridges some of the rights of property in land. While this process already is embedded in our system, it has never been very explicit nor have the possibilities been boldly viewed. Further extension of social control over land is a recognition of the fact that land uses are organically related: my neighbor's use of his land affects my own possibilities, and I have a stake in what he does with his land, even though I have no ownership interest whatever.

Awareness of the irrationality of much present land use and of the conflicting pressures affecting land use underlies the attempt to pass national land use planning legislation. Legislative proposals so far considered provide for a planning apparatus and offer very little guidance on the objectives of land planning. It is unlikely that a comprehensive land use policy could be agreed upon at present. If we are ever to arrive at that stage, it will require a lengthy period of evolution and discussion for which the planning apparatus should provide both a stimulus and a forum.

At present, land use decisions are highly dispersed. About one-third of the nation's lands (762 million acres) are in the hands of the federal government. The Bureau of Land Management (BLM), the principal agency involved, holds about 450 million acres of the total, with the Forest Service (187 million acres), the Department of Defense (DOD), the National Park Service, and the Fish and Wildlife Service holding most of the remainder. Various federal laws govern the use of federal lands (especially mining and grazing laws), although it is a frequent lament that the BLM has no real institutional basis or clear guidelines for the lands in its jurisdiction. The federal government has no direct control over private land use. States have the power to regulate such use, but only a handful have comprehensive laws. Others attempt to regulate certain critical areas such as shorelines or flood plains, but most delegate land planning to local government, where often the jurisdiction is inappropriate for the scale of the problem and parochial and special interests may be decisive.

Legislation to revise the laws affecting federal lands may still be some time away. The issues are enormously complex and the outcome quite unpredictable. Since so much of our mineral and energy resources and usable timber are found on federal lands and since these include at the same time most of the remaining wilderness areas, the conflict between preservation and development is one of the major issues to be faced. However, only a small portion of the federal lands are candidates for wilderness preservation. For the rest, the issue is how to maximize sustainable yield of renewables (grazing, forests, and wildlife), and to enlarge domestic energy and mineral production on public lands while preventing environmental damage and meeting public standards of equity. In the management of all federal lands, protection of water quality and the visual aspects of the landscape are important considerations.

At one time public land policy was mostly a question of the terms of disposal. Now it is a question of the terms of use, with a growing consensus that disposal should be very limited and restricted mostly to administrative convenience. Even for mining properties there seems little rationale for the current practice of granting surface rights to claimants. For those lands where economic production rather than ecological preservation is the first objective, whether for mining, forestry, or grazing, there is need for modern management techniques. For grazing, this means arrangements that ensure incentives for range maintenance; for forestry, the harvesting of old growth and the reseeding of new; and for mining, new arrangements to foster the expensive and large-scale exploration which technology now makes possible (see Chapter 5).

Public land use must harmonize with planning for private land use. Formal liaison between the federal agencies and a separate apparatus at the state level for planning private land use is required. At present we have very little comprehensive state land use planning law affecting private lands. Proposed national land use policy legislation for private lands has found favor in the Senate but has never been passed in the House. The private land planning bill acted on by the Senate, although moribund at the time of writing, deserves discussion because it embodies an approach likely to be revived in future legislation. The bill lacks any statement of the objectives of land use planning. As drafted, it makes a general statement in favor of formulating a land use policy; offers encouragement to states to undertake such planning and offers financial help in staffing for it; encourages the states to focus on areas of critical environmental concern, key facilities, land uses with regional benefits, and large-scale developments; and provides for federal supervision over the states to ensure that they qualify for planning grants. It also sets up a mechanism for coordination among governmental units. The question of penalties for failure to establish the planning apparatus was a point of contention, but in the end the sanctions were weak.

The proposed legislation is procedural rather than substantive; it deals with how the planning is to be organized rather than with its content. Individual states are to be left with the responsibility for determining the objectives of land planning. The existence of a state agency will be an important change, however, for it will mean that local planning efforts will be under state supervision and will need to conform to state standards.

The implicit assumption of the bill is that, once a planning mechanism is established, men of goodwill working with proper information will be able to resolve conflicts on land use. It is uncertain that in the absence of federal guidelines this result will occur. Since the bill is not comprehensive, many land use decisions will continue to be made without a plan. (Three-quarters of all zoning is done without a plan at present.) Moreover, many land use actions occur in contradiction to existing plans or the plans themselves are in conflict. Enforcement will remain a problem, even if coordination improves between governmental agencies. The bill offers nothing to resolve conflicts between output-increasing and output-restraining programs in agriculture or to promote best use of rural land. There is no control on speculative profit arising from land use planning decisions. The bill will not prevent suburban discrimination against blacks and the poor. Thus, it falls far short of providing for comprehensive and internally consistent land use practices.

Still, one should not conclude that such legislation will be useless. Procedures do matter. If the bill ever passes, local governments will continue to generate plans, but there will be state supervision and a channel of appeal and some degree of federal involvement. Local vested interests may find it harder to influence land use decisions at higher levels of government where they will encounter better organized opponents, and there will at least be an apparatus for plan coordination. The proposal seems in tune with the national mood which may allow more land use planning but is unwilling to give such powers directly to the federal government. A number of states already are proceeding on their own to set up land planning agencies, some in anticipation of the federal law and in other cases for special purposes.

More ambitious planning efforts appear to be unrealistic at this point; we do not have enough planners or the necessary organization, and we have too little understanding of what we want. Yet if we ever should implement the present bill, we will establish a bureaucracy at both federal and state level that will be taking a broader view of the possibilities. These agencies will experience the need for broader policy guides and could prove receptive to strategies for more comprehensive and integrated land use planning.

Public policy affects land use in many ways other than through land use planning. The rationalization of farm production and conservation programs are pursued through incentives. Forestry practices on public lands can be altered through direct government intervention. Environmental regulations also have important impact on land use. Meanwhile, land use planning will focus on proposed changes in land use. The current possibilities for planning concern the siting of major industrial establishments (such as power plants), transportation (airports, interchanges), protection of coastal zones, flood plains, and wet-lands, and large-scale conversions of land from rural to urban use or major intensification of urban use (regional centers). In all of these cases a major change may be contemplated whose effects extend be-yond the boundaries of local jurisdictional units. Broader land use planning will permit these decisions to be made at a level more nearly appropriate to their scale. Strictly local decisions can continue to re-side at the lowest level of government. However, if the spirit of the proposed legislation is followed, states cannot continue to delegate unrestrained power to local zoning authorities simply because a pro-posed use falls within their physical boundaries.

As land use planning agencies staff and build their expertise, it is certain that they will soon have to confront some of the inconsisten-cies in public policy affecting land. The conflict between exclusionary zoning and the announced policies to encourage desegregation and housing for the poor will surely come into focus early. Likewise, the conflict between conservationists and the demand for timber to meet the same socially desirable purposes will be apparent. Planning that would deny building on flood plains may question developing them for agriculture as well. Finally, with planning decisions reviewed at higher levels of government and often pertaining to very major changes in land use, the spotlight will glaringly illuminate how much speculative profits in land depend upon a social process and on gov-ernmental decision. It will be much harder to defend such gains as the necessary motive force to convert land to higher use in a free land market when the decision is controlled by a public agency of high visibility. Where the public creates values, who could contest its right to tax them? Land use planning combined with a stringent tax on speculative gains through land use change could serve the cause of equity.

3
SETTLEMENT PATTERNS AND THE IMPLICATIONS FOR RESOURCES

The extensive uses of land (especially for agriculture) and the geographic distribution of natural resources once largely determined the regional distribution of the population. When most of the work force was engaged in agriculture, farm products comprised the bulkiest and heaviest output of human labor, and transportation was difficult and expensive, other types of endeavor tended to relate to the distribution of good farmland. The industrial revolution changed that, enlarging the bulk of materials required by industry, cheapening transport so farm products could move, and reducing the number of people required in the countryside. In the postindustrial age, much of industry is no longer bound to material sources and a more affluent population is able to locate in response to the attraction of amenities. Although the influence of inertia on the regional distribution of population is strong, a new fluidity has been introduced into that pattern.

However we are distributed regionally, the tendency toward urbanization is strong. It is reflected, not in the growth of central cities, but rather in increments to metropolitan areas outside the central city. Because we simultaneously concentrate in metropolitan areas and spread out in suburbs, the impression is one of endless urban growth, leading many to lament the inevitable loss of the countryside and "paving over" of the land. Perhaps this view is excessively myopic. If indeed there is hope for population stability within a generation or two, one major source of city growth will be withdrawn. Urban growth then would depend on internal migration from farms and small towns. This is not an endless reservoir. The nonmetropolitan population has dwindled to about 30 percent of the total, and the farm population is under 10 percent. For another generation or so population growth should continue and most of it will go into urban areas. During this period we will be coming to terms with our environmental constraints and with new transportation possibilities. We will have the opportunity to shape the cities that Americans will live in long thereafter.

Urban size and form make a difference. City size is related to a wide range of opportunities and services as well as to congestion and inconvenience. There is a tight bond between density and the type of urban transportation system used, and density also has implications for energy use and for all types of waste disposal. Thus city size and density are variables that we may seek to influence for resource and environmental reasons, as well as for other economic and quality-of-life considerations.

Built-up urban centers not only occupy their own land but powerfully affect surrounding land uses. Most obvious is the effect on the specific character of production on nearby agricultural lands. The transportation needs of cities spike the countryside with highways and dot it with airports, and their energy needs likewise impose power plants, transmission lines, and possibly refineries on outlying areas. Concentrated generation of solid and liquid wastes, if not recycled, means that land and water will be degraded as disposal sites. In the denser industrial areas of the country air pollution may pervade whole regions in addition to the concentration that occurs within urban centers. Plainly some of the consequences of urbanization are inflicted outside the urbanized area, and broader planning instruments are required to cope with them.

THE REGIONAL DISTRIBUTION OF ACTIVITY

Empty spaces on the map seem a challenge to some planners, especially if they are much aware of congestion in other parts of the country. They view the population distribution as unbalanced and feel that regional redistribution is required. This view, which may be combined with the advocacy of rural living, has been thrust forward by many who have a rural bias, including the U.S. Department of Agriculture. Not all of the intended host areas welcome more intensive development, and some have been outspokenly against it. Declining rural areas still charged with providing services for a dependent population generally are more receptive. In stable or growing areas, local support for development comes from those with vested interests in land or business.

From a national efficiency standpoint, the issue is whether there are compelling resource or environmental reasons for regional redistribution. It is hard to discern such reasons on the resource side. The proportion of our work force involved in the extractive industries falls steadily toward the vanishing point. There would be some transport advantage in consuming these products nearer to their source, but the mix of farm products, energy commodities, and forest products needed to sustain modern life does not occur on the necessary scale at one site. Some must be shipped and, given the existence of our transport net and the combination of sources, it is comparatively easy to assemble resource commodities in most parts of the country. One conspicuous exception to this line of reasoning is water needed for industrial and municipal uses and for cooling, as well as for local agriculture. It does not travel easily in the quantities required, and this helps to account for some of those empty spaces on the map.

There are some environmental advantages to regional dispersal, but, again, they are not compelling. Most environmental damage is highly local—an airshed over the city, a few miles of river. There are some regionwide problems, however. Streams heavily used by industry may not fully recover between metropolitan areas and some of them, repeatedly battered without surcease, finally succumb. Parts of the eastern United States are arriving at a stage where regionwide air pollution can be expected under meteorological conditions of some frequency.

Existing regional patterns have considerable inertia. The concentration in the East reflects an historical settlement pattern and a favorable logistical position. The latter is retained with the growth of the Atlantic trade with increased energy imports to coastal sites. Meanwhile substantial shifts have occurred in response to real economic forces. These include the depopulation of rural areas and the attraction of amenities, favoring growth in the South and West. It would be hard to reverse these trends. The only element of the regional pattern that causes disquiet on resource and environmental grounds is the heavy concentration in the Northeast and the consequent environmental burden.

Since we are committed to programs aimed at alleviating air and water pollution, they should be given an opportunity to work before we elaborate a national policy of population redistribution. Meanwhile, environmental controls may themselves have an effect on the regional settlement pattern. Some pollution abatement measures will favor dispersion of economic activity, but recent court decisions forbidding degradation of air quality in regions with pure air can foreclose development in unpopulated areas and force growth into areas where the environment already is heavily burdened.

THE ISSUE OF URBAN SCALE

In view of the fact that we will continue to concentrate in metropolitan areas, the issues of desired urban scale and form are far more pressing than that of regional distribution. Moreover, scale and form are interrelated, since large scale raises issues about form that otherwise might be avoided. There is an extensive literature concerning optimum size of cities. Much of it is rather utopian in nature, ignoring the interrelations between cities and the particular specialization and hinterland that individual cities have. Still, we face a real issue of whether we should encourage future metropolitan growth in new centers—and if so, of what size—or try to limit larger cities by directing growth to smaller metropolitan areas. It is all too easy to try to answer this question with reference to a limited range of economic or social factors, and that temptation is present when viewing cities from the standpoint of resource and environmental policies.

Large cities have become large because they have some special feature that makes them more productive. Once they attain large size, it is reinforced by the advantages of agglomeration. From a purely economic point of view, despite the problems of congestion, larger cities remain productive. Irving Hoch has assembled information showing that wages for a given job rise with increased city size after adjusting for North–South differences and for differences in living costs.[1] Employers are presumed able and willing to pay substantially higher money and real wages because they gain other efficiencies from their location in the city. The ready availability of financing, advertising, access to headquarters of other firms, and other specialized services explain part of the attraction the city has for firms. Employees, depending on their personal tastes, also may be attracted to the cultural, entertainment, public services, and other specialized services and the

[1] Irving Hoch, "Interurban Differences in the Quality of Life," International Economic Association Conference on Urbanization and Environment (Copenhagen, Denmark, 19–24 June 1972).

range of goods available in the city. For the individual, opportunities undeniably are greater in the city, and to some extent this advantage varies with size.

It has become more fashionable to decry the disadvantages of the city both for firms and individuals. These include the degradation of the physical and social environments and the psychic and monetary costs of coping with this degradation. At enlarged scale the waste-assimilative capacity of the urban environment is exceeded, and costly countermeasures must be undertaken both by firms and individuals. Congestion is commonly related to size, as is distance to work. Hoch was able to show that by most measures of environmental quality, including some social indicators such as crime rates, the larger city offers an inferior environment. He infers that higher wage rates in larger cities compensate the net psychic disadvantage of submitting to these environmental insults.

THE ROLE OF URBAN FORM

Plainly there are economic advantages to scale and these are accompanied by deterioration in the amenity aspects of city living. It is tempting to ask whether we may not preserve the advantages of scale and avoid environmental deterioration by alteration of urban form. Historically, cities grew in compact form, reflecting the prevailing transport technology (foot and horse carriage). Early mass transit technology reinforced this pattern and, though cities grew much larger, they were based on a high-density core. What has undone this pattern is that twentieth-century favorite, the automobile. Reliance on automotive transportation is incompatible with compact cities. Autos require too much space on the roads and at rest, create too much localized pollution, and encourage dispersal by allowing more remote residence and contacts not limited by transit routes.

This is reflected in trends in the city density patterns. Cities still demonstrate centrality—that is, the population per unit of residential land is highest at the center and decreases in negative exponential fashion as one moves away from the center. Moreover, the density at the center is greater for larger cities and is correspondingly higher in outlying areas. More sophisticated measures of person-hours spent in place (thereby capturing commuters) would accentuate this tendency for concentration in the center by populating the business district where few actually live. As cities grow larger, there is greater density at the center but more than proportionate increases outside the center. Thus, while density grows throughout the metropolitan region, it grows faster in the outlying areas and the peak at the center fades into a pattern of generally greater density.

The strength of the center has been based on its advantage as the market where people assemble to perform their economic functions. A location away from the center requires travel, so the price of land in the center is bid up and it is used more intensively. The individual has a choice between space and access—between a private yard and a longer trip to work. Of course, "distance" is modified by transportation routes, and there may be higher density and rents connected with transport nodes or near attractive amenities.

The effect of the automobile has been to reduce travel time from more distant points to the center. The more completely a community cooperates with the automobile through provision of parking and urban freeways, the greater this effect becomes and the lower the average density. This can be seen in the difference between northeastern cities that were built before the automobile and western cities that grew very largely in the automobile age. Density is much higher and centrality far more pronounced in the Northeast.

As was noted earlier, population growth within a metropolitan area tends to bring greater average density at all points but more than proportional increases in outlying areas. There are several reasons for this outward shift, but their relative strength is uncertain. Some have argued that the shift reflects a preference for the new housing found in outlying areas, and others have contended that the enlarged area can support subcenters so as to be less dependent on the downtown. Another argument is that increased density brings greater disamenities and encourages spread—a trend reinforced by highway building and higher incomes, permitting automobile ownership and suburban location. Yet another factor has been white flight from inner-city blacks and from the social deterioration of the center as reflected in crime and poor schools.

Granting that we cannot make an abrupt break with what we have, but recognizing that most of our prospective growth over the next two generations will be in metropolitan areas, what pattern do we want, whether in new towns or as modifications of old ones?

Should we follow the logic of the automobile and build at lower density? This is best imagined if we propose to abandon our focus on a central node, for it is difficult to see how auto transportation can ever be made compatible with a strong center. Some see little reason for a center based on cultural or political requirements. The substitution of communication for transport would enhance this possibility. Such a dispersed pattern based on a grid of roads would allow us to retain our personal transportation and personal living space. It would do so at a cost in transport efficiency, more extended urban space, poorer access to the country, and high energy and waste disposal costs. Some also insist that the city would lose vitality and be unable to provide the contacts, institutions, and conveniences of urban living. Still, a dispersed pattern seems to respond to preferences as expressed by the extensive suburban growth in recent decades. As was noted, part of this preference is based on the exclusionary character (race, income) of much of the suburban part of the metropolis and might vanish if exclusion were disallowed.

A return to greater compactness means sacrifice of personal space and transport. Properly designed, however, a compact city could still offer open space in the form of communal parks and playgrounds and it would greatly enhance convenience and access to work and leisure. There is dispute about the social and psychic effects of density—whether stable and active communities could avoid the blight of crime and anomie.

RESOURCE AND ENVIRONMENTAL IMPLICATIONS OF URBAN FORM

Since the pattern is away from density toward a dispersed metropolis, it may be argued that this is the preferred and efficient pattern. The fact of this evolution does not prove its economic superiority, however, for two principal reasons. The first is the importance of the social factor in motivating flight from the center. Second is the fact that dispersal has been favored by market imperfections and on balance by policy. With the overall record clouded by these factors, it is legitimate to review the resource and environmental implications of the two patterns.

A compact city is unequivocally land-sparing for populations of equal size. If population growth is in fact grinding to a halt, this will not prove terribly important, but even a slow rate of growth, if sustained, could make greater density necessary as a means of saving land. The compact form clearly requires less movement and hence less energy and material devoted to transportation. Moreover, it invites the mass transit that the dispersed form defeats, thereby multiplying the energy saving. As energy costs rise and environmental controls are reflected in transport costs, the compact form would enjoy an advantage. On the other hand, flexible computer-dispatched transit systems (taxi-buses) could increase the efficiency of the dispersed city, and more substitution of communication for transportation could reduce total transport needs and thereby dilute the advantage of the compact city.

Other energy savings are feasible with compactness. High-rise buildings or even townhouses present less outside surface for temperature control. By contrast, the suburban house may have greater potential for use of solar heat—a nonpolluting and renewable form of energy. The compact city offers the possibility for economical use of otherwise wasted heat and of unused heat sinks because of the scale that could be achieved using a dense common delivery grid.

In general, utility delivery and collection systems are more efficient with density—electricity, gas, sewage, and garbage. The advantage is not decisive, however, for the denser pattern requires higher engineering standards for some of these services, as well as for house construction. Disposal of collected wastes presents a mixed picture. Disposal to landfill, to streams, or through burning is more tolerable if the scale is small and dispersed. However, it can be taken for granted that environmental standards of the future will severely limit disposal to these media, so extensive processing and recycling of waste will be required. Usually this is best done on a large scale. Certainly the same is true of solid waste recovery. Scale, of course, is a function of the size of the metropolitan area, but cost of assembly at one or a few processing points is smaller for the compact city. So long as we rely upon fuel combustion for motor transport, the dispersed city is at a disadvantage with regard to air pollution since it offers no mass transit alternative. Compact cities have an unavoidable disadvantage with respect to noise.

Some believe that we will devise a technology for energy conversion and waste disposal suited to a household scale. Such changes would favor dispersal. Until this possibility is proved, it seems fair enough to argue that dispersal made sense when environmental insults were moderate and standards less stringent, but the balance swings to compactness if we raise standards and require strict control. On balance, given our attitudes toward air and water pollution already expressed in law and our concern for energy conservation likely to be expressed in price, the compact pattern appears more workable.

SOME SUGGESTED POLICY GUIDES

There are enough questions about this matter to warrant a cautious approach. The least that we should do is to unstack the deck. We should see that the costs of dispersal are more nearly met by those who choose that style and that tolerable alternatives in terms of social climate and urban design are offered for those who opt for the denser patterns. Within the city this means adequate common open space, a truly convenient transportation system, assurance of good schools (a voucher system?), and some imagination in design. The exclusionary characteristics of outlying areas need to be broken up if the social issue is not to dominate other considerations in determining urban form. The cost of utility services both in the center and in outlying areas should be reflected in utility and tax bills. Credit and tax incentives favoring private home ownership could be equalized between the two areas, whether through greater encouragement to ownership devices adapted to urban conditions (for example, condominiums), or through renter's tax breaks. Serious enforcement of air quality standards that force suburbanites out of their automobiles would do more than anything else to halt sprawl, while improvements in schooling and public safety in the city would be most effective in enhancing its attractiveness. If some of these changes are made, the allure of suburbs may fade and a better measure of unfettered consumer preferences regarding urban form will be revealed.

No matter what style of urban form is favored, more effective planning instruments are needed in order to realize the desired system. Proposed national land use planning legislation will help in this regard by forcing consideration of the issues and by ensuring some state and federal surveillance and coordination in matters affecting the metropolis. By influencing land use about the urban fringe and by playing a similar role with regard to airport and highway construction, utility plant siting, waste disposal siting and technology, and flood control measures, the higher units of government can very significantly affect resulting urban form. And indeed they should affect it, for the resource and environmental consequences are a matter of more than local concern.

Within the metropolitan area, however, most detailed decisions on land use will be taken by local authorities. With land use planning expected to be a very prominent subject of discussion nationally, it will also assume a greater importance locally. Perhaps this will give renewed force to zoning as an instrument for controlling changes in land use and shaping the metropolis. Nonetheless, complete reliance on this apparatus subjects the process to the constant attempts of would-be developers to manipulate the system. Some of the gains from governmentally controlled changes in land use should definitely be recaptured for the public. One device to gain such a result would be to auction zoning rights that would be compatible with the plan. In other cases, projects of ambitious scale, particularly within the city, can be accomplished only through public acquisition of land and control of its subsequent use. So-called land banking, or public acquisition of land, to which future development is channeled is another promising device for recapturing development gains for the public. If our social requirements in the future demand that we pursue a defined concept of urban form in order to spare resources or environment (or indeed for social reasons), then the abridgements of private property rights may become so great that public acquisition is the only reasonable alternative for key parcels of land.

4
ENERGY ALTERNATIVES FOR THE UNITED STATES

THE ENERGY CRISIS

All Americans by now have become acutely aware of the energy crisis. Prior to the October 1973 outbreak of fighting in the Middle East, our awareness of it came mostly through the media. Since then we have all been inconvenienced to varying degrees. While the aftermath of the October War has sharply aggravated previous supply difficulties, many of those difficulties would have been encountered in any case. By dramatizing the problem, forcing public discussion of it, and throwing in doubt an easy reliance on imports, the present crisis may help us to deal more effectively with long-term energy strategy. We cannot escape considerable short-term inconvenience. Even apart from the war, a short-term problem existed of the supply of desired types of fuels. This problem was in part created and much compounded by new environmental requirements. The energy crisis also carries implications for the value of our currency. Already it has meant great change in the structure and level of energy prices. Longer term, the energy crisis is the specter of the exhaustion of finite supplies of traditional fuels. It raises the issue of the research strategy required to produce substitutes on a timely basis.

Industrial society is built upon the expanding use of energy. Throughout our history Americans have enjoyed access to cheap and abundant energy sources—so much so that we have given little thought to the consequences of a change in that situation. Yet the importance of energy is so pervasive that even a temporary shortage can create great disruption, while more prolonged shortage and higher costs imply a still more severe impact. The future availability of energy and its compatibility with the environment is the most critical factor in determining whether man can extend the industrial system and live with it long term.

What has changed? Long before the October War the United States had begun to encounter increasing signs of energy shortage. Industries using interruptible supplies of natural gas were finding (often for the first time) that such supplies are indeed interruptible. Utility firms were refusing to sell natural gas to new customers because they could not be assured of supplies. It was clear that far more natural gas could be sold at current prices, but much of the demand was not being filled. The shortage applied to petroleum products as well—unheated schools, idle grain dryers, and rationing of sales by some suppliers during the winter of 1972–1973 provided the evidence. We had a whiff of gasoline shortages in early 1973. Where once we imposed import quotas on oil to protect our unused domestic production capacity, we now had brought nearly all that capacity into production and were seeking imports to meet demand.

Prior to the Middle East war, 30 percent of our petroleum was imported, and the East Coast was getting 90 percent of its fuel oil from abroad. Even coal supplies—where air quality standards had not constrained their use altogether—were somewhat tight on occasion. The failure of nuclear plants to come into operation on schedule threw more of the burden on coal. Meanwhile new safety laws slowed operations in some coal mines. Many coals are too high in sulfur content to meet new air pollution standards, forcing a resort to remote deposits. Investment in new coal mines lags, in part because we have not defined the place of coal in the future energy system. Electricity brownouts also have become a feature of recent years. For the most part, this has not been caused by a fuel shortage but rather by inadequate generating capacity. Demand has exceeded expectations and the increased lead times for building new plants, especially nuclear plants, have embarrassed utility executives.

While some of these problems appear transitory in nature, they are symptomatic of more fundamental difficulties. Although energy producers have profited from the shortage, it is not merely something contrived by them for short-term gain. The manner in which we respond to current shortages will condition the kind of energy system that we are to have over the next fifty years. A very basic decision concerns the extent to which we wish to rely upon imports. When foreign supplies are available, the temptation is always to increase imports to alleviate current domestic shortage. It is the quickest way to increase supplies to an uncomprehending public and it can bring fuel of the desired sort. Yet allowing ourselves to drift into a policy of expanded imports has serious implications that cannot be ignored. We will return to this issue below (pages 57–61).

ENERGY POLICY OBJECTIVES

For the longer term the United States must face up to the fact that nearly all of the energy sources currently in use are exhaustible, and their use also carries environmental penalties. An interim strategy requires an energy system that is compatible with the goals outlined in Chapter 1—one which both meets current needs and helps preserve our long-term options. As a means of preserving options, it is appropriate to pursue measures that will extend the time over which present forms of energy are available. This means incentives and research to improve our capacity to find and recover fuels, to substitute more plentiful and inexhaustible sources, and to increase the efficiency of conversion and use, including measures to discourage the profligate use of energy.

A policy of preserving options also requires that we restrict permanent damage to the earth's life-support system. One potential danger of this sort is the creation and release of large amounts of long-lived radioactivity. A danger with a shorter duration but uncertain consequence is the increase of CO_2 in the atmosphere and its effect on the global climate. Landscape deterioration from mining activities is another permanent effect, albeit not on a scale that seriously impairs life support.

Finally, the policy of preserving options means that we must be alert to the threat of exhaustion and to the time span required to introduce and perfect a new energy system. Since the time required is long and success uncertain, and since the survival of technological society depends upon a solution, prudence requires that we act long in advance to secure new sources.

Attention to social goals will include continued advance in personal income. Energy use is essential to every facet of modern life, including pollution control. Up until the recent price surge, raw energy comprised about 3 percent of the total GNP. By any standard it has been abundant and cheap. Unless there are compelling resource or environmental reasons to restrict the use of energy, we should allow it to continue fueling a high-income society. Even if we discern reasons to restrict use, it is still desirable to produce energy at the lowest social cost, however it may be priced. Over the short term there is conflict between the goal of energy abundance and the strategy of extending the period of use, but to the extent that conservation measures serve to improve efficiency and avoid waste, as distinct from impinging on the useful services derived from energy, then the conflict is mitigated.

Another goal with special significance for energy is to attain environmental acceptability. While the avoidance of permanent damage is necessary to the retention of our long-range options, current environmental acceptability is largely a matter of the current health and amenity consequences of energy use. The principal damage to health comes from air pollution incurred during energy conversion. This is largely the consequence of combustion, and since combustion will be a major form of energy conversion for decades, the requirements for environmental acceptability will focus on improvements in combustion technology and on means of producing fuel that burns clean. Another threat to health comes from the possibility of the release of radioactive materials, either routinely, deliberately, or accidentally. Throughout the spectrum of energy production and conversion there are other environmental threats of varying gravity—oil pollution of sea and shore, thermal pollution of inland water, acid drainage from mines, brines from oil wells, esthetic objections to plants and power lines, landscape damage from mining—all of which affect current environmental quality.

The extraction and use of energy creates many kinds of equity conflicts. The industry draws on natural capital and seeks a profit in a climate of incentives and regulations that departs far from the competitive ideal. In the process, economic rents may be collected that are difficult to defend on equity grounds and that often are very remotely related to any necessary inducement to invest. Incentives necessary to a proper level of investment are part of the cost, but if the cost of finding and developing some forms of energy is far below price, then there is little reason why the resulting rents should go to private operators. It is a difficult challenge to the ingenuity of government to so arrange the incentive structure that private operators will undertake to produce a social resource under risky conditions while still minimizing private rents. Should it be necessary to restrict energy consumption (for example, to meet air pollution regulations), then the way in which supplies are allocated also will have profound equity implications.

The consumer interest in low cost meant some conflict with the security objective so long as we could assume that secure supplies would be more expensive. Current price relationships that make imports more expensive than the long-term cost of domestic fuels dissolve this conflict for the time being. In any case, there are various means of achieving security of supply and various levels of security to be had. Some cost penalty may be incurred in the future if we seek greater security, but it may be justified by the potentially greater risk if we forego such measures.

Bearing in mind the desirability of not foreclosing our option and also the goals that have been mentioned, what would be an ideal energy system? It would need to have an ample and inexhaustible resource base; the supply should come principally from domestic sources; the real cost of energy should be low; it must be available in forms to serve mobile as well as fixed site uses; it must be environmentally acceptable in all phases; and if consumption restraint is required by such environmental constraints as esthetic considerations or approaching global heat limitations, we should strive to achieve it by improving efficiency in use in preference to foregoing the services that energy provides. We do not arrive at such a system in a single bound, so we will wish to have our intermediate system approximate the ideal as far as possible. We should be suspicious of energy policy steps that take us away from rather than toward the desired system.

SECURITY AND IMPORTS—A BASIC DECISION

The most basic element of an energy strategy is the extent to which we will rely on domestic resources as opposed to imports. Reliance on domestic sources means that over the next ten to fifty years—what is called an intermediate period in this chapter—this country will need to turn away from oil and gas toward other energy sources because domestic petroleum and gas resources will not support the cumulative demand. President Nixon committed the nation to a policy of self-sufficiency, but if we are to persevere in that policy, the arguments must be clearly understood. The case for use of domestic supplies is grounded in the crucial importance of energy and the severe consequences of even short interruption. The consequences of even a partial interruption have been impressed upon us recently. Because foreign suppliers recognize the importance of energy to us, they may gain unacceptable leverage over us—whether financial, military, diplomatic, or other. The contrary case is based on the argument that foreign supplies are ample and are produced at lower cost, that their use permits conservation of domestic reserves and protection of the domestic environment, and that we can shelter ourselves from the threat or actuality of interruption by appropriate measures.

It is unclear what the long-term foreign price will be. Following World War II, foreign oil supplies were priced far below U.S. oil, and import quotas were designed to protect the domestic industry from its low-cost competitor. Recently, foreign supplying countries have dramatically raised their prices, and the price of foreign oil presently is above the price of most domestic oil. It can be argued that imports must be priced well below domestic production if we are to realize real savings from imported oil because domestic production costs include transfers within the domestic economy that are lost when we import, and because domestic oil production also entails low-cost gas not available with imports.

Domestic production capability may prove the most effective restraint on foreign price. The foreign price has moved up despite the existence of reserves abroad that under market conditions should call for a very low price. In fact, it is estimated that the actual cost of production from those reserves in the Middle East is between ten and twenty cents per barrel. At this writing such oil sells somewhere between ten and eleven dollars per barrel. The price has been supported through a producing country cartel that has set terms for the international oil companies that produce and market the oil. The history of cartel arrangements is that they tend to fall apart, and many await that result in this case. Moreover, it has been argued that if the international companies ceased their marketing of crude oil for the producing countries and if governments of consuming countries acted in concert, then the cartel could be broken. This would imply a return to very cheap oil and an impressive cost advantage for foreign supplies.[1] There would remain some doubt about the longer-term adequacy of supplies to meet what would then become an explosive worldwide demand for oil, but for a decade or two, and perhaps longer, that would not be the problem.

The producing countries appreciate the discrepancy between their production cost and sales price. Their incentive to maintain the cartel is very great, despite the squabbling that may occur among them. Moreover, as their financial reserves grow, they gain a degree of immunity from pressures that could be brought against them, and as their technical competence grows, they become still more independent. In fact, some of the countries may build such a large reserve of

[1] For an excellent exposition of this possibility, see M. A. Adelman, *The World Petroleum Market* (Baltimore: Johns Hopkins Press for Resources for the Future, 1972).

foreign currency that, far from cutting price to increase sales, they may be restraining output to prevent growth in their holdings of foreign currency. (At current prices total annual oil revenues of Middle Eastern and North African producing countries will be tens of billions of dollars and with increases in production their balances could attain hundreds of billions.) Plainly neither the United States nor other developed countries can rely on foreign sources to supply the amounts of energy needed for continued growth. It is highly questionable whether the U.S. balance of payments or the international financial system could support transfers of such magnitude. In the face of the strong position of producing countries, consuming countries might be tempted to use their greater industrial and military power to impose terms on producer countries, but this seems a hazardous basis for policy.

Other defensive measures could be taken to lessen vulnerability to foreign dependence. The development of multiple supply sources is an example. However, at present only the Middle East and North Africa have oil on the scale required to meet world demands for an extended period. Some proposals have amounted to an exchange of hostages. For example, in return for a favored position in the U.S. market, a Saudi Arabian spokesman once proposed to invest earnings in the American distribution system, leaving the Saudis subject to loss or vulnerable to countermeasures should they interrupt supplies or expropriate American investments. Use of oil revenues for large-scale development projects in producing countries also creates a reason for producing countries to keep supplies flowing. The suggested long-term purchase of natural gas from the Soviet Union is being discussed in the context of equally vital American sales of grain to them—an indirect but still apparent coupling. Finally, any measures to store energy in the United States or to develop standby capacity at home reduces vulnerability to foreign pressures or stoppage. We can buy varying degrees of security at some cost, even if we are dependent on foreign supplies.

If the foreign cartel endures over coming decades, the limit on the price of imported supply will be set by domestic alternatives. Already the cartel appears to price oil with such alternatives in view. Likewise, vulnerability to supply interruption that may occur for whatever reason can only finally be prevented by developing domestic supplies. To rely on foreign supply is to gamble control over energy cost and availability and hence over much of our economic, diplomatic, and military future in hopes of low cost. A decision to rely largely on domestic sources means that we must ensure protection in domestic markets if we are to encourage required investment, and, based on present resources and technologies, it implies moderately high cost energy in comparison to what we have known.

DOMESTIC ENERGY RESOURCES

What about the resource base for domestic production? Plainly, domestic resources do exist that should be adequate during the intermediate period. At the same time, it appears that oil and gas will not serve their present share of the market throughout the period. Lags in developing alternatives are such that concerted effort will be required to avoid increased reliance on foreign oil over the short term.

Estimates of resources often are confusing, both because of lack of knowledge of their physical extent and uncertainty about ultimate recoverability. Also, the units used for reporting frequently are variable and add to the confusion. Hydrocarbon fuels exist in defined deposits in sedimentary rocks; they are not dispersed in low concentration throughout common rocks. From knowledge of the distribution of favorable formations and the experience of intensive exploration of some of them, we can extrapolate to an estimate of oil or gas in place. This estimate, however inexact, is an attempt to set the absolute physical amount of the resource. The resource is not called a reserve until it has been discovered and determined to be recoverable at a cost that is economically viable. Because exploration is expensive, there is a tendency to limit the inventory of proved reserves to a comfortable amount. Hence, proved reserves are by no means the total physical resource that we expect to be able to recover at present cost. Estimates of these added amounts, though not very good ones, can be made. Over time, cost relations change, and resources that are not economical at present may become so, either because of reduced production costs or rising prices. Even so, not all the physical resource will be recoverable because the techniques of recovery do not allow it. Recovery techniques too are subject to improvement, but they can never approach perfection.

About three-fourths of the energy we consume at present comes from oil and gas. This represents a long-term shift from coal as our major energy resource. The shift reflects the convenience of oil and gas, especially for use in transportation and space heating, the very low price at which gas has been sold, and the environmental superiority of gas in several uses. At the same time, resources of oil and gas are far less substantial than those of other fuels.

Conventional Resources

Oil. Looking first at petroleum, the largest estimate for the United States of oil originally in place is around 3,000 billion bbl. with other estimates going as low as 660 billion bbl.[2] About 450 billion bbl. have been discovered and over 100 billion bbl. produced. Estimates of the amount of oil ultimately recoverable under current conditions range from 300–600 billion bbl. Recoverability from known deposits depends on technical and economic factors and presently is about 30–35 percent of the oil in place. Obviously, if the recovery ratio could be raised significantly, it would greatly expand recoverable reserves. Of the high estimate of oil in place, some estimate that about one-half is offshore and about two-fifths of the recoverable amount likewise is offshore. Other estimates are more conservative in attributing either total or recoverable oil to offshore sites. Since over 100 billion bbl. of the original oil already have been produced, remaining recoverable oil is still less impressive. Moreover, not all of the theoretically recoverable oil will be found; some suggest that about 80 percent of it is all that we may ever discover, and the figure surely is lower if we are relying heavily on Outer Continental Shelf deposits. Meanwhile we have available only about 52 billion bbl. of discovered and recoverable reserves.

Since a range of 200–500 billion bbl. is the most generous estimate of the amount that (based on current recovery capability) we might still recover if we can find it, how long would it last? This depends on our assumptions about the rate of growth of demand for energy and the portion of this met by oil. At present, oil provides about 44 percent of the energy used by the United States and total U.S. energy consumption grows at about 4 percent per year. If such a growth rate were sustained, present annual consumption of 6 billion bbl. per year would triple by the end of the century. At this growth rate, reliance on domestic resources would result in their depletion late in this century or early in the next, depending on the estimates of recoverable oil

[2] Resource estimates used in this section are derived principally from P. K. Theobald, S. P. Schweinfurth, D. C. Duncan, *Energy Resources of the United States*, U.S. Geological Survey Circular 650 (Washington, D.C.: Government Printing Office, 1972).

used. Of course the estimates of recoverable oil could err on the high side or we may not find much of it, so that depletion could occur earlier; on the other hand, recovery techniques might be improved to allow up to 60 percent recovery, in which case the life of the resource is extended a couple of decades.

Gas. For natural gas the picture is no better. Estimates of gas originally in place range from about 2,000 to over 7,000 trillion ft.[3], of which about 750 trillion ft.[3] have been discovered and of this, about 450 trillion already were used by the end of 1972. The distribution between onshore and offshore deposits is similar to oil. Estimates of gas ultimately recoverable under current conditions, provided it can be found, range between 1,000 and 2,700 trillion ft.[3]. The most frequently cited figure for recoverable gas still in place (including Alaska) is about 1,450 trillion ft.[3]—an amount equal to fifty times the current production.[3] The recovery factor for gas is very high—about 80 percent—so we cannot hope for great increases in supply through improved recovery techniques. However, in the case of gas, an artificially low price diminishes the amount of gas judged recoverable at present, so the figure for recoverable gas could be still higher if prices were to rise significantly. About 290 trillion ft.[3] of recoverable reserves and another 170 trillion ft.[3] that are submarginal at current prices have been identified.

Gas has claimed a rising share of the energy market, growing at over 6 percent per year. If this rate continues, we shall deplete our ultimately recoverable gas supplies (using the 1,450 trillion ft.[3] figure) somewhere around the end of this century. A slower rate of growth in consumption of 3 percent would extend this period only a few years and a larger supply would have a similar effect.

Coal. Although there has been a shift from coal to oil and gas, coal remains the domestic energy resource in most ample supply. If we continue to burn domestic hydrocarbon fuels well into the next century, almost inevitably they must be derived from coal or perhaps from oil shale. Our coal resources are so great that they often are viewed as almost inexhaustible. Indeed, at recent rates of coal production they will last a very long while, but if they must sustain more of the burden of the total energy supply, then even coal deposits do not appear as plentiful as we might suppose.

Our knowledge of domestic coal resources is more extensive than

[3] *Oil and Gas Journal*, vol. 71, no. 53 (December 31, 1973), p. 72.

that for oil and gas. Total coal resources are estimated at around 3,200 billion tons, about half of which is in deposits already identified. Somewhere between 200 and 400 billion tons are thought recoverable, based on seams of a thickness and depth now minable. Obviously, far more could be had at a higher price or with improved technology. Under present circumstances, the attractiveness of coal is related to its sulfur content. Of the identified deposits, about 65 percent are low-sulfur coals found in the Great Plains and Rocky Mountain areas, while the developed coal resources of the Appalachian area are predominantly medium and high in sulfur content.

Coal presently supplies less than one-fifth of our total energy. If we make greater reliance upon it as a source of synthetic fuels to substitute for oil and gas, this proportion could soar. At the current rate of use, identified and recoverable coal resources could last for hundreds of years. At a growing rate and on certain assumptions that it would substitute for other fuels, the presently recoverable supplies could be exhausted by the middle of the twenty-first century and we would have to resort to less accessible supplies.[4]

Oil shale. Our remaining hydrocarbon resource is oil shale, a large potential source of energy but one heretofore not economical to develop. There also are many uncertainties about the environmental consequences of producing shale oil. The mere size of the source is impressive. Total resources in place dwarf those for petroleum. Identified resources are around 2,000 billion bbl. The identified and undiscovered resources that might be recovered at an oil price of four to five dollars per barrel were estimated in early 1972 to be 1,500–2,000 billion bbl. Current and prospective oil prices now exceed that level, but meanwhile rampant inflation has made previous cost estimates obsolete. Even so, shale now is a resource to be considered. We do not know how the technology for mining and processing shale may develop nor the gravity of the environmental problems it would pose, but the government has recently accepted bids for initial leases on shale lands. If the environmental consequences are tolerable, shale provides one means of extending our hydrocarbon resources in case we fail to develop other sources of energy on a timely basis.

Canadian tar sands. Although we have only considered U.S. resources in this discussion, mention should be made of the Canadian tar sands, a

---

[4] *Summary Report of the Cornell Workshop on Energy and the Environment,* Committee Print, Senate Committee on Interior and Insular Affairs, 92 Cong. 2 sess. (1972), p. 163.

potentially large source of oil that could be developed commercially with very little further research. We cannot project the terms under which this might be available to us, but the Canadians are likely to price it at the world market price.

Nonconventional Resources

After shale oil we cross the boundary into the range of resources that become available to us with further research and development. Of course not all of our undiscovered conventional resources are likely to be found or developed without further technical advances, but for the range of noncombustion energy sources, research is one way of changing cost relationships so as to permit development. Since we cannot predict the outcome of research, it is impossible to state with assurance what our domestic energy resources from nonconventional sources will be. Nonetheless, some orders of magnitude for the possibilities may be useful.

Nuclear reactors. The light water nuclear reactors already being built provide one alternative. Although there is dispute about the size of the uranium reserves, if figured at present cost plainly they are not large by comparison with conventional fuels. Total domestic resources of uranium ore recoverable at less than $15.00 per ton of U_3O_8 have been estimated at about 1.6 million tons, about half of it recoverable at $8.00 per ton. To give some sense of proportion, these identified and recoverable resources of uranium are sufficient to supply total current U.S. energy demand for two to three years. The foregoing figures for reserves are often contested as too low because they exclude more costly ore. The cost of nuclear energy is relatively insensitive to the cost of uranium. For example, a $10.00 increase per ton of U_3O_8—that is, a more than doubling in price—would increase generating cost only about 0.6 mills per kilowatt-hour, less than 10 percent. As cost restraints are relaxed, the amount of ore balloons rapidly, and uranium contained in phosphate rock, shale, granite, and seawater must be considered as possible resources. Supplies of thorium which can be used in high-temperature gas reactors also greatly extend our resources of fissionable materials.

Breeder reactors, if they are developed and work as planned, will extend the uranium resource about fifty times. Breeders will generate fissionable materials from presently unfissionable materials that are in more ample supply. Since the breeder is much less sensitive to uranium costs than light water reactors, the total amount of uranium that could be made available for the breeder becomes astronomical. In this case environmental limits may well be encountered before resource exhaustion.

Fusion reactors. It is not profitable to discuss reserves of our remaining unconventional resources since we have only the poorest idea of what use could be made of them. Clearly, fusionable materials are in the most ample supply—virtually infinite by the human reckoning. Geothermal resources also are large if we can tap the contained heat of rocks deep in the earth. So far, little can be said of this possibility or of the resource limits applying to it, although some scientists are becoming more optimistic about it. Of all the exhaustible resources, based on present knowledge, the possibility of fusion reactors gives the best hope of energy in environmentally acceptable form on such a scale as to solve man's long-term problem. All others, assuming plausible rates of growth in energy demand, could be exhausted in a matter of decades to centuries, or they raise serious environmental questions.

Solar radiation. The chief renewable energy resource is solar radiation. It is the engine that drives such derivative renewable resources as hydropower, wind, and thermal sea gradients. Direct solar radiation is nondepletable and the continuous supply is generous enough, if it can be captured, to sustain any future level of consumption that we might attain for a very long time. Moreover, for space heating, and perhaps for other uses, solar energy has immediate potential. The economics of collecting it for generating electricity are still dimly seen. Conceivably, the natural supply of solar energy could be augmented by collection in space and transmission via microwave to the earth. Natural solar energy is singularly free of environmental objections (except the space required for collectors and the attendant asthetic objections) and its use does not exert pressure against any conceivable ultimate heat barrier.

ENERGY STRATEGY—A TIME-PHASED APPROACH

This recital of the perils of foreign dependence and of the extent and limits of domestic energy resources supports a basic strategy. We can remain in control of our energy sources and costs by developing domestic supplies. Since the preferred fuels (oil and gas) are subject to earliest depletion, we will have to adapt our more plentiful coal or shale resources to serve the markets now held by oil and gas and convert the coal to environmentally acceptable form. Since these resources in turn face possible depletion within the next century and since their use on the prospective scale may pose intractable environmental problems, we must begin the orderly search for alternative energy systems. Abrupt changes are very costly. Over a short-term period until about 1980–85 we can alter our reliance on oil and gas only marginally. It will require much effort to restrain our growing dependence on foreign sources of those fuels. During the period from then until the end of the century we can make use of other domestic fuels (coal and shale) if we organize ourselves properly to do so, and we can make increased use of nuclear energy. We also may find geothermal energy to be of significant help. By the end of the century we should strive for proved technology that will allow us to go on to the use of inexhaustible energy sources (fusion and solar energy) as advances in those technologies invite it or as fuel shortages compel it. Time lags are such that all aspects of this strategy must proceed simultaneously.

BAND-AIDS FOR THE SHORT TERM

For the short period, the suggested aim is to try to avert serious energy shortages while minimizing foreign dependence. At the same time we should act in such a way as not to preclude achievement of our objectives for the next period. Some increase in imports is likely to be required if we are to avoid shortages, but our exposure can be reduced, despite increased imports, if we act promptly.

There are limits to what we can do to affect either domestic supply or demand in the short-term period. Self-sufficiency by 1980 as called for by President Nixon does not seem attainable unless consumption is severely curtailed. Even conventional measures for increasing supply take time. An oil field, once discovered, may require three to five years for development to full production. A refinery is often three years or so abuilding. Coal mines may require a similar lead time for development. Major electric plants are running six to ten years from decision to operation. In view of these lags, we cannot affect the energy supply system very drastically before 1980, even if we know clearly what we want to do.

On the demand side, much energy is consumed in installations or equipment that represent substantial investments whose energy use characteristics are not easily changed. Most of them will remain in operation, even in the face of sharp changes in energy price, because energy cost will remain small relative to total operation and depreciation costs or to replacement alternatives. This applies both to energy conversion plants and to final energy consumption. Energy-conserving generating plants, smaller autos, and better insulated houses all take time to work their way through design and production and into the stock in use—often more time than we consider in the short period. They can make only a small contribution over the next few years. Of course we can suppress demand by energy rationing or allocation schemes that can be set in motion with short lead times, and price increases will have some further effect in reducing demand. In an atmosphere of crisis, energy-saving measures become socially responsible behavior and will be fashionable for a while. In some cases, such as with reduced interior temperatures or increased car-pooling, they involve little real sacrifice.

If demand is not suppressed, then we have in prospect an increase in energy consumption between 1970 and 1985 of about 84 percent. The National Petroleum Council (NPC) prepared four sets of figures indicating how this might be supplied.[5] The estimates were arranged by degrees of optimism for domestic supply. Thus, the most optimistic case (case I) projected maximum effort to develop domestic supply, with 5.5 percent annual increases in drilling for oil and gas and a high rate of discovery, 5 percent annual increases in domestic coal consumption, maximum effort to produce synthetic fuels, all new base load generating plants being nuclear fueled, and easing of environmental constraints. The most pessimistic case (case IV) assumed recent trends in drilling activity and drilling success, continued problems with nuclear siting and licensing, no new incentives for coal, and continued environmental constraints. In between were two intermediate cases. Case III seems particularly interesting; it assumed a 3.5 percent annual increase in drilling, continuation of recent experience in its success, nuclear development according to the Atomic Energy Commission's (AEC's) most favorable forecast, and coal production up 3.5 percent per year.

If we follow the case III projection, oil and coal almost hold their shares of the total energy market, sagging only slightly to 43 percent and 17 percent of the total, respectively, while the shortage of gas causes its share to decline from 34 percent to 24 percent. Nuclear power is expected to fill most of this gap, increasing from less than 1

[5] National Petroleum Council, *United States Energy Outlook: A Summary Report of the National Petroleum Council* (1972).

percent to over 16 percent by 1985. The striking change is the degree of foreign dependence for oil and gas. By this projection the share of imported oil would rise from 26 percent in 1970 to 53 percent in 1985, while imported gas would go from 4 percent to over 21 percent. Moreover the source of the foreign oil would shift from the Western Hemisphere to the Middle East and North Africa. By 1985 anticipated oil imports would match the total consumption of 1970.

While these estimates have since been overtaken by events, they do illustrate the nature of the problem faced if we wish to avoid the heavy dependence on imported oil that they imply. One possibility for current policy to consider is acceleration of the use of coal. Our coal resources are large and their location is established. There would be difficulties in increasing production rapidly. For one thing, the industry is not well capitalized. Presumably this could be overcome by use of outside funds. But equipment, transportation capacity, and new mine shafts all have considerable lead times. Labor will be a problem in any effort to expand underground mining rapidly. Moreover, the desirable low-sulfur coals are located in the West, far from the chief pools of mine labor, and coal miners are notoriously reluctant to leave their familiar homes. Strip mining requires less labor and less lead time. On the steep Appalachian slopes it is highly destructive of the terrain and leaves the hillsides virtually unrestorable. While there are environmental problems of restoring cover to stripped land in the arid West, these seem less intractable for semiarid terrain than reclaiming land on the steeper Appalachian slopes.

Even if substantially more coal can be produced, the environmental problems of its use may foreclose this option. It is questionable whether the technology of coal liquefaction or gasification could be far enough developed in the short run to make this a promising alternative. Techniques of sulfur removal, whether through stack scrubbing, precombustion, or via improved combustion, have so far been disappointing. We can hope for some progress on this front by 1980. Thereafter, coal could begin to play a more important role, if problems of production, transportation, and conversion can be managed. For the short period, however, coal will be fortunate if it can retain its share in the total energy picture.

Nuclear power offers even less promise over the short-term period. In view of the lead times involved, plants put under construction now would begin to feed into the power grid by the end of the period. They would have to be conventional reactors rather than breeders. However, all such projects have been beset by environmental objections and there are still unresolved problems of reactor safety. It is doubtful that we should crash ahead until these matters are settled, and equally doubtful that we could sharply accelerate the pace for a few years even if we chose. Again the NPC estimates may overrate the short-term help from nuclear power.

There remains the possibility of speeding the production of domestic oil and gas. The proved reserves to support this expansion are thin and the overall resource picture is not optimistic in the intermediate period, but over the short term we probably could find and produce more oil and gas. This would involve more intensive search of offshore areas in particular, since they are believed to be richest in undiscovered oil. Some knowledgeable analysts suggest that oil production could be increased as much as 40–50 percent over the NPC case III estimate by 1985. The recent increase in real crude oil prices makes this a more realistic possibility. Such production increases assume that objections to production of known deposits such as those of the Santa Barbara Channel, the Naval Petroleum Reserves, and the Alaskan North Slope are withdrawn. Under this assumption it is argued that the 1985 import share could be held to about 30 percent—not far from the current level. Optimism about gas production potential also has risen considerably because of higher prices and a generally more favorable regulatory climate. A quick increase in oil and gas production would be possible only if we acted promptly, since the lead time for discovering and developing new production may be three to seven years.

To achieve this result, the petroleum market must be structured so as to provide adequate incentive for domestic exploration and production. Current domestic prices surely are adequate to stimulate new output, provided the industry views them as a long-term expectation. The chief uncertainty is the possibility of the breakup of the cartel and a sharp fall in imported oil prices. Thus, for a policy of domestic production, some means of import restriction must still be available.[6] A policy of domestic production with prices at or near the current level leaves domestic oil competitive with foreign supplies but far above the historical level in this country. Such prices increase the rents on known reserves. The public will perceive the industry's increased earnings on known deposits resulting from a national policy of

[6] Until recently the import quota system simply allowed imports to fill the gap at an acceptable domestic price. President Nixon's energy program of April 1973 revised this system, substituting a license fee for imports above the old quotas. Future increases in the fee could provide protection for domestic production, but the degree of assurance might not be sufficient to speed domestic output were it not for the subsequent increase in the price of foreign oil.

self-sufficiency as inequitable, and the industry is sufficiently unpopular to make this politically very unpalatable.

It is hard to escape this problem. We want to stimulate new production but not to reward present operators unduly. The current approach is through the price control apparatus, with the government imposing controls on the price of oil produced from known reserves while encouraging exploration through a higher price for new oil. This two-tier price system will be difficult to police and will result in severe market distortions as time passes. A more rational approach would be to allow all oil to be sold on the same basis while taxing production from known deposits. The tax could be forgiven for stripper wells and need not apply to the new discoveries that we want to stimulate.

Other steps can be taken to raise domestic production. Since many of the sites most promising for exploration lie offshore, it is within the power of the government to make more of them available for leasing. The government has moved slowly on this because of environmental reservations about offshore production. It is now believed that most of the oil contaminating the ocean comes from ships rather than wells. Greatly expanded offshore production might pose a new problem, but this possibility may be disregarded when we are faced with the reality of an energy shortage.

At present incentives for production abroad are equal or better than those at home. American firms can take depletion allowances and charge off their drilling costs abroad as current expenses just as they do in the United States and, in addition, may defer tax on earnings until they are repatriated. This policy seems inappropriate at a time when we wish to stimulate production at home. Moreover, since depletion allowances often go to compensate the landowner rather than to stimulate new investment, new legislation could require that such allowances be reinvested in the domestic industry.

An assured domestic market at current prices also should stimulate a higher rate of recovery from known deposits. This effect also could be supplemented by tax incentives. As the cost of finding oil rises and foreign supplies are restricted, it will become profitable to improve recovery rates above their present level. Each 1 percent increase in the rate of recovery from known deposits has a substantial impact on available proved reserves and, hence, on total output.

While the foregoing discussion has been focused on oil, much the same story applies to gas. The two fuels normally are found in association and the incentives applying to one also affect the other. To date the United States has imported little gas (except from Canada) because the technology for shipment by boat is new and domestic prices have been low.

Gas differs from oil in that the price of domestic gas sold interstate has been controlled at a low level and it is sold on long-term contracts. This has depressed the search for gas and stimulated its consumption (often in low-priority uses), finally resulting in our present shortage. This artificial situation leaves us now faced with the prospect of producing expensive synthetic gas or buying equally expensive imports. It is difficult to support controls that force us to resort to more expensive sources when a higher domestic gas price would call forth more domestic production. At present, the policy is to increase the allowable price on new discoveries so as to provide some incentive. However, this regulatory initiative is very hesitant and fails to keep up with demand, forcing more resort to high-cost alternatives.

Gas is an environmentally attractive fuel well suited to use in dispersed (or even mobile) uses where emission control devices are difficult to design and control. Gas could be reserved for these more sensitive uses by adopting end use controls in conjunction with price changes to favor its diversion from use as boiler fuel, where other fuels would serve. Because of its environmental attractiveness, there will be a strong temptation to increase the supply of gas through imports. Prospective foreign sources include North Africa as well as the USSR and the Middle East, so we face a somewhat less concentrated exposure on imports. Moreover, there are some foreign policy reasons for increasing gas imports from the USSR. The specialized ships and handling facilities for gas imports will take some years to construct and they imply a longer-term commitment to imports. Very probably we could produce an equal or greater amount domestically over the short period by concentrating the same investment on increased domestic output. Meanwhile, imported gas will not be cheap. Apparently, synthetic gas can be produced from domestic coal at the same price or less. Since this is a direction that we are likely to want to take for the intermediate period anyway, it seems preferable to concentrate on raising the output of domestic gas while pursuing the technology of coal gasification rather than greatly to expand imports.

The most troublesome issues to be faced when protecting domestic production relate to the consumer interest in low price, the producer need for a long-term expected price high enough to meet costs, and the equity problem of allowing large rents through public policy to owners of oil and gas properties and leases. Although the price of imported oil could fall sharply in some circumstances, the cost of the domestic alternative seems the most effective limit on the pricing policy of the foreign cartel; thus, so long as the cartel holds, higher energy costs cannot be avoided. The equity question is most difficult for existing properties. I have already indicated my own preference for a tax on production instead of the present two-tier price control plan. Since the government owns the sites for much future production, it can set the leasing terms so as to recover much of the rent accruing on new leases. At the same time, in so uncertain a business as oil exploration, some firms will make spectacular killings, and this possibility is part of the attraction for private firms. If this is too unpalatable, a public corporation could be established to explore new terrain. This seems an unlikely possibility for the short term, but if private firms become too opulent, pressure will grow for a national oil corporation to serve as a yardstick.

Whatever our success in increasing domestic energy production in the short-term period, it is unlikely to match the growth of demand for oil. The share of imports may be held near the present level if we are lucky, but even then the total volume of imports will grow apace. This leaves us still quite vulnerable to supply interruption; for the U.S. East Coast, the dependence on foreign oil is almost complete, and it would be very difficult to shift the source abruptly. Therefore, we must consider means of ensuring against interruption during the period of heavy and perhaps growing dependence. Conceivably, some alteration in diplomatic posture would lessen the likelihood of interruption, but energy supply is not the only issue at stake here. A long-term arrangement of the sort once proposed by Saudi Arabia also offers a means of diminishing the chance of interruption. This has the attraction of offering balancing trade and investment flows that would ease our short-term payments position. Its disadvantage lies in sacrificing control over some aspects of the domestic economy and in freezing the United States into a longer-term position of dependence that may not be acceptable. It also breaks the unity of the international petroleum market and would foster an every-nation-for-itself attitude from which some would suffer.

Another alternative is storage. When this has been discussed in the past it has been in terms of the relative ability of the two sides to hold out in a bargaining situation. That balance has shifted greatly in favor of suppliers as their monetary reserves have grown, and the new balance may need to be thought of as the time required to shift to other fuels and to arrange production, transportation, and processing facilities. Even if such programs were launched on a crash basis, this implies a storage capacity equal to perhaps two years of imports. Should we build storage to hold a reserve of this size? It would be expensive, and stocking the reserve would bid up the price of oil at the same time. Given the time required to put it up and the money to stock it, we might with the same time and money move at least part way toward the alternative system on which we will rely later. No doubt our storage should be enlarged and better standby end use controls should be devised, but for the next decade there cannot be full escape from foreign dependence without severe restraint on consumption.

The outlook for the short period, then, is one in which only a limited range of measures is available. If demand for energy services is to be met, then consumption cannot be curtailed much by technical changes that economize on use. Moderate price changes will not slow consumption much initially. Demand can be left unfilled (severe price increases or rationing), but that means a reduction in real energy services in many cases. Conventional supply alternatives cannot make much impact until the end of the period. A possible exception is domestic oil and gas, whose output probably could be increased significantly in five to ten years with the necessary commitments. Even if we are successful in that, the share of imports will rise somewhat. If we are not successful, imports will become a critical part of our total energy picture, and strong insurance will be needed against supply interruption through increased storage. All of this assumes that the United States does not waver in its policy of self-sufficiency.

AN INTERMEDIATE PERIOD—WIDENING POSSIBILITIES

Beyond the next ten years, the energy options open to our society begin to widen, provided the necessary research and investment program to bring them within range is undertaken. Some of the things we do now to improve the short-range energy outlook, such as accelerating domestic production of oil and gas and increasing output of low-sulfur coal, will continue to have effect to the end of the century. Moreover, while energy demand can be altered only minimally over the next decade without foregoing energy services, over a longer period we can hope to conserve energy without such penalty. Both on the supply side and the demand side, the realization of longer-term possibilities will depend upon the kind of research and development policy pursued by this country. If the objective of minimizing foreign dependence while still meeting a high level of energy service at moderate cost is maintained, then this will be the period of greatest draft on our hydrocarbon resources, especially coal and shale.

The present system is based largely on oil and gas and, as already mentioned, the best short-term prospect for expanding energy output is for increased output of these fuels. The resource position is such that we cannot depend on them to sustain the load by the end of the century. Nonetheless, they can supply much of our needs during the intervening years and perhaps beyond, provided that two developments occur—techniques both for finding and recovering oil and gas must be improved.

As observed above, much of the remaining undiscovered oil is believed to be offshore on the Outer Continental Shelf. Operational problems make it expensive to work in this environment and favor improved means of selecting promising sites to explore. Other areas such as Alaska have not been thoroughly explored, largely because of the lack of clear prospects for getting the oil out. Both offshore and in areas already explored on the continent, substantial amounts of oil are believed to lie in stratigraphic traps, which up to this point have been difficult to identify. The normal evolution of geophysical techniques can be expected to improve the capacity to find oil. Also, a decade from now production and transport of Alaskan oil should be on stream.

One of our major petroleum resources is discovered oil that presently is uneconomical to recover. Rising oil prices and improved techniques gradually bring more of this into use. Of over 400 billion bbl. of oil discovered, only a little over 100 billion bbl. have been produced. Plainly, improvement of the present recovery ratio by even a few percentage points would open sizeable resources. For gas, the situation is not comparable, recovery rates already being high, but again there are sizeable deposits not presently minable that could be made so by underground fracturing.

While nearly all transportation systems and many stationary burners are set up to use petroleum products, as supplies of these fuels dwindle equivalent amounts of other fuels need not be converted to liquid form. In electricity generation, process steam, or space heating, other fuels will serve as well, and in most mobile uses gaseous fuels or electric propulsion can be used in lieu of liquids.

But what governs the use of remaining domestic hydrocarbon resources? Three considerations will influence the decision—resource availability and conservation, environmental effects of the system in all phases, and cost as affected by the first two considerations.

Resource availability already has been discussed. Plentiful resources are coal and shale. We know where they are located and we have assurance concerning their extent. Technologies exist that permit their use as sources of gaseous or liquid fuels, albeit with environmental consequences that are less than ideal at present. It is reasonable to expect that these could be improved to acceptable standards. The other certain resource is at present conventional nuclear energy. However, if fission reactors are to provide a quarter of the energy supply by the end of the century and sustain it far beyond that date, this implies development of a workable breeder reactor. Other energy sources such as geothermal or solar energy may become important by the end of the period if we press ahead with their development. Solar energy has most immediate promise for water and space heating and will be incorporated only slowly in new construction. Geothermal, if it proves workable, could be brought rapidly into use for electricity generation once the technology is established. Fusion is unlikely to play a significant role in this period. Given the limited potential for oil and gas and the uncertain prospects for unconventional energy sources, it appears that the best strategy is to develop technologies for use of coal and shale while continuing to explore the unconventional sources.

If we are able to foresee demand correctly and phase in new energy production on a timely basis, we should not encounter an energy shortage during this period. The conservation of energy will be less urgent from a resource standpoint than it will be for environmental reasons. Perversely enough, we may require a larger input of energy in order to accomplish the conversion to environmentally acceptable form. If we are to use coal as the principal energy source, then we will have to convert it to gas for many purposes. While improvements in coal combustion techniques may allow its use to continue under boilers, if coal is used on a massive scale, such combustion products as fine particulates and sulfur would threaten environmental values. Recourse to low-sulfur coal helps, but most of this is located far from the market, and it may be simpler to convert it to gas for shipment in any case. For uses in transportation and space heating, the gaseous form would always be preferable. The conversion process inevitably entails loss of some of the calorific value of the coal and results in fuel that will have higher Btu costs. Since it will require fewer controls in combustion, the net increase in cost as burned will not increase proportionately.

Energy in the form of coal gas promises to be fairly expensive in comparison to what we have known in recent decades. Comparison with artifically low natural gas prices would be unfair, but even when compared to recent oil or coal prices, the cost will be higher. As of early 1972, prospects were for high Btu coal gas in excess of $1.00 per million Btu, depending on assumptions about the price of coal. Of course, two or three decades hence the technology for conversion may be much improved, and the cost of producing western coals could be very low. At the same time alternative fuel costs will rise. Oil at a price of over five dollars per barrel implies Btu costs per million in the neighborhood of eighty-five cents; of course much domestic and imported oil already is far above that price. And oil does not enjoy the environmental acceptability of gas. The principal environmental reservation about this energy system is the landscape damage and water requirements implied in processing such large volumes of coal. Western terrain is more hospitable to replacement of disturbed materials, but restoring cover will be more difficult than in the East.

Coal can be used to produce oil (the Germans did it on a large scale in World War II) but it is an expensive process, in part because the hydrogen content of coal is low. If we continue to need oil or wish to diversify our resource base, shale is available as a source of some of our liquid fuel. A frequently cited obstacle is the shortage of water for shale processing in the Green River area. However, interbasin transfers would be possible if the need for shale oil becomes strong enough. The relative costs of shale oil and coal tars are in flux at the moment. In early 1972 estimates of the cost of producing oil from high-grade shale were about $5.00 per barrel based on current technology and perhaps under $4.00 in the future—a figure that compared well with current oil costs. Even at $6.00 per barrel, shale would provide fuel at $1.00 per million Btu, or about what was expected from coal gas. As a source of liquid fuel, however, shale seemed preferable to coal on economic grounds since it was expected that oil from coal would cost $6.50–$7.50 per barrel. All of these relationships have been disturbed by rapid inflation, apparently to the disadvantages of shale. The mining of shale involves extensive landscape damage just as with coal—probably more damage. It also will probably involve water pollution in an area little able to sustain it. The landscape damage in both instances occurs in remote areas. It should be more feasible to repair it in coal operations than in shale. In any case, some damage will be a necessary price to pay for energy from these sources.

Apart from damage at the site of production, it should be possible to hold current environmental damage within acceptable limits in other phases of energy use from these sources. Both would be transportable by pipeline from inland source. Both burn efficiently in most uses. Gas is relatively clean in combustion. Both are as amenable to more efficient electric generating cycles as any other fuel.

What steps are necessary to ensure the availability of these fuels in acceptable form? Reasonable assurance on price is the first requirement. The second is organization of necessary research and development efforts. Finally, since most of the shale is on public land, a system of leasing compatible with the needs of the industry must be established. Over the intermediate period, given the level of world demand, the threat of cheap fuel imports may no longer impair the development of these domestic resources. Still, we should be willing to impose import controls if needed to permit development to continue. More stringent environmental controls will favor the use of gaseous fuels and inland sources. Already the industry is showing an interest in high-priced gas for this reason. Joint government–industry pilot plants for production of coal gas will speed the gas conversion technology. The bright prospects for shale oil production of two or three years ago have clouded, and the government may need to reevaluate the advisability of a joint research program in that field. While the government should not be hasty about disposing of its shale resources before their economic value is ascertained, leasing policies adapted to other minerals should not be allowed to constrain shale production.

The principal controversy concerning nuclear energy is the role that the breeder reactor will play during the intermediate period. By that time current disputes about licensing and light water reactor safety are likely to be resolved, and we will have a breeder technology available.

As noted, nuclear energy is expected to supply up to 25 percent of all energy by the end of the century. Only fission reactors can presently be counted on to meet this demand, since the scientific feasibility of no other nuclear technology is established. Must we be heavily dependent on the breeder if nuclear energy is to play a growing role in our energy economy? Some argue that electricity demand estimates are too high or that resources of uranium and thorium will prove sufficient, so that we will not need the breeder, or they may point to our still generous hydrocarbon supplies as grounds for deferral. They would have us explore solar and geothermal sources first and hope that fusion will come along in time. Others would even prefer to see restricted energy use rather than production of energy from this source. The basic reservations concern safety and the uncertainties of long-term disposal and control of nuclear wastes.

Like any fission reactor, the breeder carries the possibility of catastrophic accident. Although it is a more difficult technology than present light water reactors, it is uncertain that it need be more dangerous in operation. It may be possible to design in sufficient redundant safety features to hold accidents within the same limits, and more thorough attention to siting can be expected for future plants. A more serious dilemma is the longer-term one. Highly toxic materials, especially plutonium, will be generated, which will endure far beyond our present range of vision. There is the real possibility that these may escape tight social control, whether in periods of upheaval or through the action of social aberrants. Both the operating safety and long-term control of breeders present more unknowns than do conventional fission reactors, but the problems are qualitatively similar for any fission technology. Even if the heyday of the breeder lasts only for a matter of a few decades, this legacy of radioactive wastes will remain, but again much the same can be said for the light water reactors to which we already are committed and which some see as an alternative to the breeder.

Against the disadvantages of the breeder must be set the possibility that it will provide moderate cost and otherwise comparatively clean energy. With conventional fuel costs rising, abundant resources usable only after transformation, and unconventional sources unproved, the breeder could become an attractive source of power. Moreover, if combustible hydrocarbons, even if transformed to desirable forms, must bear the full energy load, they will place a growing burden on the capacity of the atmosphere to absorb wastes. The CO_2 burden, for example, could then begin to have bite. The breeder could reduce that load while greatly extending the resource horizon. Furthermore, in an uncertain world it is always useful to have alternatives available, although in this connection an argument could be made for deferral of full deployment until the course of proposed alternatives becomes clearer.

We are in fact proceeding with the breeder. Whatever the wisdom of selecting this strategy, we now have a considerable investment in it. The breeder could be halted, but in an atmosphere of energy crisis probably will not be. There is no way of providing absolute assurance of long-term security for the nuclear materials to be generated by fission technology. Greater short-term security against accident or terrorists could be gained by putting plants and materials storage underground from the beginning, and recourse to such nonbreeder reactors as high-temperature gas reactors would lessen the proliferation of plutonium. In any case, the whole question of breeder strategy and degrees of safety should be brought out from behind the technocrats for public discussion.

The intermediate period is one during which active research must be undertaken for a permanent solution to the energy supply problem. However, the intermediate period could be extended by exploring the use of geothermal and solar energy. Because of promising cost and environmental characteristics during a time when both of these features will be under pressure from the use of conventional sources, the payoff, if new resources can be brought in, will be great.

A major tenent of my argument here is that we should seek to supply energy to the economy at lowest possible social cost so as not to restrict the flow of services it can yield. This is at the same time consistent with nonprice energy-conserving measures, and the intermediate period is long enough to give these some play. Measures to restrain energy use without depriving the economy include more efficient energy extraction and conversion techniques, fuller utilization of energy produced, and improved management throughout the system prior to delivery to end users. Energy saving also can be achieved in numerous end uses without sacrifice of function, and less energy-intensive processes could also be employed in industry. Many of these economies in energy use will cost other resources, but in some cases the cost is small, so that real economic savings can be achieved. There is also a gray area where, at some cost in convenience or service, energy saving can be attained. This violates the principle of avoiding any restriction on the services energy can yield, but where the inconvenience is minor in relation to the saving, it is worth looking at. Finally, some uses of energy are truly frivolous and could be halted without any offsetting loss.

The intermediate period allows for conservation measures in nearly all phases. Most attention has focused on household uses where about 20 percent of all energy is consumed at present, over half of this in temperature control. Since we will be adding to or replacing a sizable share of our housing stock over this period, the opportunity for savings on this use through improved insulation and more efficient heating and cooling equipment is very great. The possibility of using heat pumps is especially promising in this regard. These measures generally require other resources and mean greater initial costs. The organization of housing markets discourages resort to energy-saving measures that raise initial house costs, even if, when computed over the period of use, they are less costly. Serious concern about energy conservation would justify more stringent building codes and standards for heating and cooling equipment. If housing costs are computed to include temperature control, such measures should not deny anyone access to the new housing market who otherwise would qualify. Other possibilities for households involve the substitution of gas for electricity in space conditioning, water heating, and cooking. Economies in gaining interior temperature control also can be realized in commercial and industrial building, primarily through reduced use of glass.

Transportation currently accounts for about one-fourth of all our energy consumption, with automobiles responsible for over half of this. Auto transport is notoriously inefficient in terms of energy cost per passenger mile in comparison to nearly all other modes. The present American urban configuration reflects the dominance of the auto and will continue to do so for decades. We cannot dispense with cars. The most immediate energy-saving step would undoubtedly be to shift to smaller cars—a transition that could be accomplished in a few years, given the life-expectancy of a car. A stiff horsepower or gross weight tax together with rising fuel costs should be effective in this regard. At the same time we have an extensive and flexible road net that invites imaginative use for various types of road-based public transit, whether taxi–buses, or conventional fixed line buses. A shift of much traffic to buses is attainable if we improve service through more frequent scheduling and reserved traffic lanes and if we discourage private cars by high parking charges. Note that these changes are not without costs in terms of comfort, convenience, and safety, but the energy savings and environmental benefits should be substantial. Freight movement has shifted in recent years away from rails toward highway transport at considerable cost in energy efficiency. If rail regulations, management, and labor practices could be reformed to take advantage of the inherent economies of railroads for hauls of intermediate distance, then this shift could be reversed.

Our total need for movement, both of people and goods, could be reduced by changes in urban form toward greater compactness and rationality in transport modes. This is a matter on which significant progress could be made over the intermediate period. Changes that make auto transport more inconvenient and expensive in town will tend to accelerate this process.

Another area for significant savings in energy use is in electricity generation and transmission. The present steam cycle is wasteful of energy, since at most only 40 percent of the calorific value of fuel burned ends up as electricity. Two approaches are possible. One is to make some use of the reject heat that presently is wasted. This involves identifying and locating industries for which this low-grade heat could be valuable. Some waste treatment processes, agricultural and aquicultural activities, and perhaps others are good candidates. Other schemes would build elaborate energy complexes combining power generation with desalinization plants and various uses for low-grade heat. The other approach is to convert more of the calorific value of the fuel into electricity. So-called topping cycles are one example, building on existing technology. Another would be to perfect fuel cells, which allow recovery of a much higher share of the energy content. So far none of these approaches has been proved out, but as fuel costs rise the incentive to perfect them will also increase.

Industry, apart from utilities and transportation, uses a whopping two-fifths of all energy consumed. The applications, whether for process steam, direct heat, electric drive, internal transport, or whatever, are very diverse, and one cannot readily generalize about where savings might occur. It is worth noting, however, that energy heretofore has been a small part of total costs in most branches of industry; therefore the incentive to conserve on use has likewise been small. As energy costs rise, customary processes will be reexamined. An example is the primary aluminum industry where energy costs always have been a significant factor in total costs. It is noteworthy that in the face of rising energy costs one firm recently announced plans to try a basic change in the technology of this industry that it hopes will save one-third or more of the energy required in the traditional process. Other metallurgical industries will face analogous challenges. In general, heat and brute force have been used in industry because they have been cheap. As computer-controlled automatic processes give better control over materials, we should be able to master more subtle means of transforming and fabricating them.

THE LONG TERM—RESEARCH DIRECTIONS

Prospective energy systems for the short and intermediate terms rely principally on exhaustible energy sources—hydrocarbons and uranium. Properly developed and managed (including attention to the environmental effects of their use), these can most likely carry us for fifty years or more—surely more with zero population growth and energy conservation. Still, if we do not stint on the services energy can provide, these should be years of continued economic growth that will increase dependence on a high level of energy availability. That availability cannot be assured throughout the lifetime of those born today unless we develop new energy sources, and because of the lead times involved, now is the time to explore those possibilities. For the present, a long-range energy strategy is a strategy of research and development.

Current energy flow from the sun is the resource mankind is most certain of over the long term. The amount we receive is stupendous. How much can be captured and used remains uncertain. That which is converted to organic matter through photosynthesis lends itself to use as energy, whether through direct combustion or through more intricate cycles. This, however, is a comparatively modest source of energy and offers little promise to meet a high-level of expanding energy demand. A great deal more could be done with wind power than at present, but again the limits would soon be encountered and the environmental consequences (the plains forested with steel towers) would be considerable. Direct solar radiation holds real promise as a major and continuing source of energy. It is nondepletable and available in generous supply. As mentioned, it already could have application to temperature control. It is still not economical in electricity generation, but with advances in technology and changes in cost structure it might become so. Collectors of solar energy on the earth's surface will occupy a great deal of land—50–200 km.^{2} for a 1,000 MW capacity. Moreover, prospective efficiencies in electricity generation are such that the insolation we receive would not support unlimited growth. At present better prospects exist for using solar energy as direct heat. This deserves attention now because it will have application for the intermediate as well as the long term.

Given the prospects for solar energy and the limitations that environmental concerns impose on it (that is, space required by collectors), neither it nor any of its derivative forms promises a long-range solution to the energy supply problem in a growing economy. It does promise to be a useful supplement. Of course, if rather than a growing economy only a stabilized one is envisaged, then solar energy could provide for some level of activity.

For a growth economy that is not restrained by energy availability, Americans must turn to other sources. Too little is known about geothermal potential to be able to comment on its prospects. The volume of hot rock close enough to the surface to be drilled and our success in fracturing it will be the important considerations. Although potentially a large source of energy and hopefully an environmentally acceptable one, this is nonetheless a depletable resource. We may use it in accordance with its cost and environmental characteristics just as we do any other exhaustible resource, but so far it does not appear to be an ideal long-run solution. Nonetheless, the potential is great enough to merit investment now to explore its feasibility.

The most promising avenue open to us is to pursue research on the fusion reactor. The resource base is effectively infinite and the environmental characteristics, as far as they can be discerned, are promising. The feasibility of this concept has not yet been established. We should proceed in an orderly way to establish scientific feasibility. This will be a large but not a massive program extending over perhaps a decade. If that is successful, a larger investment in engineering it to a pilot stage would be indicated. By the end of the century, if all goes well, we should aim at having an estimate of the economic cost of fusion power. At that time, since other fuels and breeder reactors will still be available, a decision can be made, based on cost and environmental considerations, whether we wish to proceed further. An investment of a few billion dollars to the end of the century to develop what may be a permanent solution to the energy problem does not appear excessive. If prospects for economic feasibility look good in the face of rising costs for alternative energy sources, then the process can be accelerated.

Some would argue for the pursuit of fusion research on a more active basis, hoping to avoid reliance on breeders. According to this scenario we would burn our fossil fuels over the next half century, perhaps supplemented by some solar or geothermal energy, while counting upon the fusion reactor to come in on time. Essentially, this trades away the longer time margin of security that the breeder's more certain technology offers against the environmental and social reservations about breeders. It is difficult to accelerate the basic research needed to develop fusion reactors, although different approaches could be tried simultaneously to improve the chances of early success. If we proceed methodically and appear to be getting good results by the end of the century, then our investment in breeders can still be written off, but meanwhile a case can be made for proceeding with their development.

Whatever long-term energy system man finally arrives at, the means of storing energy and adapting it to its diverse uses will still be needed. Solar energy used in temperature control can be managed well enough by transferring the heat to water or other fluids. Geothermal energy can be regulated to the rate desired. Most future energy probably will be based on electricity generation, and electricity is a notably perishable commodity. The use of electricity to generate hydrogen via electrolysis of water provides at once a means of energy storage and a versatile fuel for many uses. Hydrogen can be transported by pipeline, stored in liquid form in tanks, and burned cleanly in vehicles, fuel cells, or at dispersed sites. It promises the flexibility of a fuel for use in metallurgy and transportation while avoiding the environmental penalty of other fuels.

The rationale for restricting energy use is generally based either on the exhaustible nature of energy resources or on the environmental consequences of production and use. Success in perfecting an ample and inexhaustible source would of course eliminate the first reason.

Moreover, reliance upon solar energy and fusion-based electricity with a hydrogen cycle also dissolves most environmental objections. The ones that remain are the esthetic objections to the presence of energy production and transport equipment, the danger of accident (mostly in handling hydrogen), and the problems of managing heat. The first two are health and amenity considerations for which cost–benefit decisions can be made. While we are very far from encountering global heat limits, in local situations heat dissipation is becoming a real problem. Restraining use will, therefore, remain a consideration, but for a long while it will not govern our actions. The conservationist steps to restrain consumption that were suggested for the intermediate period deserve continued development for the longer period. In a world of plentiful energy, measures to improve efficiency in use may be a sufficient response to environmental requirements, and there is hope of avoiding restriction on energy services.

ELEMENTS OF A COORDINATED ENERGY POLICY

The lament that the United States has no national energy policy has become one of the clichés of the day. Oil executives, consumer representatives, government officials, politicians, and environmentalists all cite the need for a policy. This in itself is a reflection of the change in contemporary attitudes. It is widely recognized that our energy policies are in conflict and ill coordinated. When the supply of domestic fuels was abundant and the environmental consequences of their use a fraction of the present ones, the absence of a coordinated policy was tolerable. Instead, we managed with a mélange of policies, each applying to a particular fuel or range of problems. Competition, however unequal, was allowed between energy forms.

Little regulation has been imposed on coal. It is a dispersed resource, found widely on private lands and exploited by many producers. National policy related mostly to regulating mine safety and coal freight rates. Lately, some modest regulation of strip mining has been imposed, and of course other environmental regulations have impacted strongly on the uses of coal. Only with the current research program on coal gasification does the place of coal in our energy system begin to be defined. At the same time, otherwise desirable safety and environmental measures pertaining to coal are being taken without much regard to energy needs.

Government policies with respect to oil and gas have been more numerous and still more in conflict. In part, they have sought to stimulate domestic production through tax incentives and import controls. An elaborate system to sustain domestic oil price (prorationing) also had this justification. However, these measures can be explained as much as a response to producer interests and their effectiveness in influencing policy as by any national purpose. For example, while the government provides domestic tax incentives for production, it also offers the same incentives to the foreign production of American firms. The incentives provided to the industry through the tax structure have not zeroed in on either domestic exploration and production or on equitable treatment of earnings. Government leasing policy, dominated by an interest in maximizing government revenue from a public resource, prevented domestic production of oil and gas from advancing as fast as it might. Meanwhile, the consumer interest in low price weighed in favor of greater oil imports, to the detriment of long-term domestic price expectations and hence domestic production. The consumer interest in low price also brought regulation of the field price of gas to the detriment of production and warped its consumption pattern. New environmental regulations placed an added demand on gas and oil as well. In the face of this, government was slow to lay out a credible emergency strategy as imports grew, or an effective long-term policy for limiting imports.

Utilities are highly regulated but do not enjoy a clear policy climate. In the absence of a basic energy strategy, they cannot know the source and nature of their fuels. They are expected to provide economical and reliable service, but are beset by environmental and regulatory uncertainties that delay expansion.

Nuclear energy has developed an inertia of its own. Blessed by relatively generous funding, it has proceeded without much consideration of what a similar research effort would yield in other energy industries.

Energy policy apparatus in the United States has been very fractionated and was designed in response to the specific problems of the various energy industries and the conflicting aims of different groups. It has been ill adapted to the changed circumstances of energy shortage and environmental concern in which we now find ourselves. The burden of the argument in this study has been that income and environmental goals are broadly reconcilable in the energy field. It must be the responsibility of energy policy to orchestrate the changing sources and supplies so as to permit this to occur. The paralysis of decision probably can do more damage to particular interests than would result from any of the likely range of policy decisions.

The most urgent need is to elaborate the main assumptions and directions of energy policy so they will be entirely clear to the industry and to the public. These directions should have some degree of stability, and it would be wise to seek legislative approval for the basic propositions, with provision for thorough review at intervals. Among the basic premises that the policy needs to contain are the extent of intended reliance on foreign sources, and the research and development directions to be pursued in the future for domestic sources. Another general policy might state the principle that energy should be priced to reflect the full environmental consequences of production and use, so that producers and consumers would both have incentives to minimize these costs. Of course, some possible hazards—such as those encountered in nuclear energy production—do not fit within a cost framework and will require specific legislative guidance. There should still be room, however, for considerable competition among the various forms of energy.

A single coordinating unit is required to ensure that all forms of energy production adhere to the rules and to ascertain whether their individual plans will meet both supply and environmental needs. The Federal Energy Administration created by President Nixon can evolve in this direction provided it does not give exclusive attention to short-range problems. The newly created Energy Research and Development Administration gives hope that longer-term research directions will take a more rational form. A rational energy policy cannot be evolved piecemeal. Explicit decisions must be made on its main lines. Thereafter, the elaboration of specific policies will at least carry the hope of consistency.

5
DILEMMAS
FOR
MINERAL POLICY

Heretofore, minerals have been an unexciting subject. Unlike energy they have not yet become the focus of a crisis, but problems of supply and dependence, in some ways analogous to the energy crisis, lie over the horizon. Along with energy, minerals are the resources par excellence of the industrial system.

While we have some idea of the steps and timing of measures required to secure energy supplies over the long term, the strategy for minerals is considerably murkier. Minerals also differ from energy in a fundamental way because they can be recycled. Over time increased reliance on recycling and on low-grade virgin resources will develop, but the pace of transition is much harder to discern and the sense of urgency is not the same. Meanwhile, an expanding supply of minerals must be found and recovered with reasonable attention being given to such matters as cost, security, and environmental quality.

SOME CHARACTERISTICS OF NONFUEL MINERALS

Mineral deposits are a depletable resource and, just as with energy, there is great interest in how long they will last. The resource base for minerals is much harder to define than for fossil fuels. Fuels have been laid down in defined deposits over geological time. Minerals also occur in concentrations in the rocks that we classify as ores, but often the basic mineral elements are found in other rocks (or in the sea) at lesser concentrations but in larger amounts. Widely different grades of shales and considerable differences in the quality of coals exist, so there is some parallel to fuels, but the fact that fossil fuels exist only in defined deposits still sets them apart from many other minerals. While it is reasonable to speak of supplies of fuel originally in place as an ultimate limit on their availability, the concept of ultimate supply seems to vanish in the mist if applied to diffused mineral elements at low concentration. Moreover, unlike energy, which generally is irretrievably lost when used, all minerals carry the possibility of recycling, with relative cost playing the crucial role in determining whether they will be recovered. Mineral supply is very much an economic question, and a figure for the ultimate availability of mineral resources is not very illuminating.

Yet geologists insist on the finiteness of the earth. In the very longest terms and projecting a high technology mode with full recycling, crustal abundance of each mineral becomes the ultimate supply limit.[1] Some metals that have played an important role in technology to date are not abundant materials—for example, copper, zinc, lead, nickel, molybdenum, tin, and tungsten. Others—notably, aluminum, iron, and titanium—are very abundant.[2] Even good success in finding, recovering, and maintaining the stock of less abundant materials may not suffice to allow them to continue their relative places in material use at the much higher rates that could be projected for a remote future. In many instances abundant minerals or other materials could substitute for the less abundant without serious difficulty. But the cost of maintaining the stock (measures to avert dispersal) and of forced reliance on less suitable materials could become burdensome to growth.

Since an industrial system cannot run without minerals, it is tempting to demand the same kind of national supply security for them as for energy. The problem is really quite different, however. Minerals span a wide range of characteristics and uses. Substitution between metals is possible for many uses, and even in the case of industrial chemicals there is some range of possible substitution. Nonmineral materials also can be used in place of minerals in some applications. Substitution does not represent an ideal solution when faced with short-term adjustments, but given sufficient lead time, it often is feasible. Substitution in response to commercial pressures is common. Since metals and many other minerals are easily stored, it is much easier to

---

[1] This ignores the possibility of elemental transmutation—a possibility that cannot be ruled out if the high technology mode is preserved.

[2] Donald A. Brobst and Walden Pratt, eds., *United States Mineral Resources*, U.S. Geological Survey Professional Paper 820 (Washington, D.C.: Government Printing Office, 1973), pp. 22–23.

maintain stockpiles as security against abrupt interruption of supplies than is the case for liquid or gaseous fuels. In fact, this has been done as part of our emergency planning in postwar years. And since minerals go mostly into industrial products and demand for them often is postponable, a short-term interruption in supply is much less critical than for energy, which is essential to the day-to-day operation of the entire economy and to public health and safety in many circumstances. American society could survive a long while if supplies of some minerals were interrupted, though if many were affected and the period overlong, it would become increasingly difficult. Again, unlike fuels, imports of minerals come from many parts of the globe; as a class they are not concentrated in a particular geographic region that may be especially hostile or subject to turmoil. For specific mineral products, however, the sources of supply may be few, and in general U.S. imports tend to come from the less-developed countries (LDCs) where economic nationalism is working to make supplies less dependable and terms more onerous.

Since minerals are traded widely on world markets, there has been a tendency for prices to equalize between countries. A nation that sought an autarchical position would be at a considerable competitive disadvantage in industrial markets if (as could be expected) its materials costs were substantially higher than those for other countries. To the extent that a country relies upon high-technology industries for its export trade, it might avoid some of the disadvantage (such industries use comparatively little material in relation to value of product), but it would remain vulnerable on the import side where goods produced with cheaper foreign materials could flood domestic markets.

There is a less compelling case to be made for supply independence than in the case of energy, and since domestic alternatives often may be high cost, the policy toward minerals can be more flexible than that for energy. Still, balance-of-payments considerations, the international tensions accompanying foreign investment in resource commodities, and the myriad possibilities for supply interruption or monopoly pricing all favor a degree of independence if the cost difference is modest.

U.S. MINERAL RESOURCES AND THEIR USE

One reason why minerals have been an unexciting topic to Americans is that we have never really been exposed to serious shortage. This is not owed entirely to our own basic endowment; increasingly, we have had recourse to foreign sources of supply. So far foreign supplies have generally been forthcoming on a reliable and competitive basis. Since shipping costs on bulk commodities permit them to move readily in trade, greater reliance on foreign sources often reflects cost relationships and accessibility rather than the exhaustion of domestic supplies. Let us first examine the U. S. resource in minerals.

Published figures on mineral reserves generally refer to the amount of known deposits that could be recovered with known technology at current prices. They include amounts that are estimated or "inferred," based on geological evidence, in addition to those that are proved or measured. These figures are not comparable to the estimates of oil and gas in place, which were discussed earlier, because they do not attempt to include minerals in unexplored structures or unknown districts. Further discoveries of minerals can be expected, some of them minable at current costs, as exploration proceeds. The pattern in the mineral industries is to maintain a satisfactory inventory of reserves relative to production and to push hard on the search for new reserves when the inventory ratio begins to shrink. The amount of undiscovered and unestimated reserves of the quality presently used is unknown. However, the fact that production moves abroad suggests that it has become easier to find minerals of good quality elsewhere. This would be consistent with the fact that the United States is more thoroughly explored than many parts of the world and has had a longer history of intensive exploitation. Newer geological techniques, however, should permit discovery of an increasing share of those presently undiscovered reserves both here and abroad that do not enter the figures.

Reserves are a function of price and technology as well as of the physical grade of the ores. Improved technology permits the mining of inferior ores at constant cost, copper being the usual example. Whether technology improves or not, the physical volume of resources widens out markedly if the cost constraint is released. Thus, if the price of minerals rises to one and one-half to three times the current level, for many minerals, reserves increase by multiples of the present figure. Furthermore, by moving from concentrations of the mineral in question toward the more diffused sources that could be used at yet higher cost, the quantity of the mineral that could be produced expands still further. Obviously, for a long time, cost—rather than physical limits on the supply—becomes the crucial concern, and cost will be determined by future technology. Nonfuel mineral production presently accounts for about 1 percent of the

GNP. Even if technology and cost do not develop favorably, still only a few percent of the GNP will need to be devoted to the acquisition of these materials, always assuming that the supply of energy is abundant and of moderate cost.

Returning to the figures for reserves identified and inferred at current costs, what do we find? Data on reserves were matched against estimates of cumulative demand out to the year 2020 in work done by Resources for the Future for the Commission on Population Growth and the American Future.[3] Out of eighteen minerals, including the principal metals and the key inorganics needed for fertilizers and chemicals, only for three (four, if atmospheric nitrogen is added to the list) are domestic reserves in excess of projected cumulative demand. These are the fertilizer minerals (phosphorus and potassium) and magnesium which is available from the sea. For both magnesium and nitrogen, the key to future supply is the availability of energy to extract them from sea and air. As the report notes, iron and nickel present little problem because Canadian supplies are adequate to meet demand in the United States and are assumed to be available.

On a world basis, in addition to the ample supplies of magnesium and fertilizer minerals, there apparently are sufficient reserves to meet expected demand for iron, nickel, vanadium, chromium, and cobalt, but the United States will have to rely on foreign sources for part of its supply. The United States has hardly any minable chrome ore and has always depended on South Africa, Rhodesia, and the USSR for its supply. Under present conditions our best recourse is to maintain a sizeable stockpile. At first glance, vanadium appears to be a case of dangerous dependence, since domestic ores are modest in relation to demand, and the principal world source is the USSR. However, vanadium is a common element found in other metal ores, especially uranium ores, from which it is recovered as a by-product. If by-product sources become inadequate, the United States has extensive low-grade resources from which the metal could be recovered at higher cost. No crisis is in store with regard to this metal. Cobalt is a metal that must be imported under existing conditions. World reserves are well dispersed in Zaire, Canada, Morocco, New Caledonia, Zambia, and Cuba. In addition, we have low-grade domestic resources that could be exploited at higher price and other ferroalloys can be substi-

[3] Ronald G. Ridker, ed., *Population, Resources, and the Environment*, U.S. Commission on Population Growth and the American Future, vol. 3 of Commission Research Reports (Washington, D.C.: Government Printing Office, 1972), pp. 87–88.

tuted in many instances if need be. The stockpile seems the appropriate security response at present.

Where world resources are inadequate to meet prospective demand, the problem is different. In some cases new reserves can be found, but in others this country must rely either upon outtrading others for needed supplies or on finding substitutes for them. A number of important materials fall in this category—among them copper, lead, zinc, aluminum, manganese, molybdenum, tungsten, and sulfur. For example, sulfur reserves appear limited, but increased by-product recovery from oil and gas and perhaps eventually from coal would greatly expand the supply. Sulfur also could be recovered from gypsum should the need be urgent enough. Likewise, aluminum is a very common material in the earth's crust and the exhaustion of bauxite reserves would mean a shift to other sources at a fairly modest cost penalty. Possible shortages of tin may be delayed by bringing in lower-quality ores, but even if this does not occur, we would not suffer greatly by using other materials for most uses of tin. Aluminum (given the electricity to produce it) promises to be a plentiful substitute for a number of other metals, including many uses of tin, copper, and zinc.

Some of the steel alloys remain troublesome, however. Tungsten is scarce and found mostly in China. Substitutes are less satisfactory and some of them are also on the short list. While secondary recovery may be improved, adjustment of industrial operations may also be necessary so as to make less use of tungsten alloy cutting tools. Manganese is an important steel alloy for which we must rely on foreign sources. While shortage is indicated, lower-grade resources are known to exist that could be exploited at higher price, and manganese nodules from the sea floor are likely to become an economical source as price rises.

The list of materials could be extended, but the kinds of problems encountered would fall within the range illustrated by the foregoing examples. Our nonfuel mineral supply prospect is one of increasing dependence on foreign sources and quite possibly of rising costs. The supply does not face an abrupt end because there are opportunities for substitution, for recycling stocks in use, and for extending mining to lower-quality ores. Likewise, while there is exposure to interruption of foreign supplies in an uncertain world, the greater diversity of sources, the fact of competition among materials, and the practicability of stockpiling all ease this hazard. No clear-cut strategy can be proposed to ensure the permanent availability of minerals. The problems are too specific for each material and the unknowns too great to allow this, and there is no sense of imminent crisis. Avoidance of needless dissipation of stocks seems reasonable, but no crash program to reduce demand or ensure an infinite supply is called for. Ever lower quality ores can be mined, which still are preferable to common rock. As the approach to common rock draws nearer, cost factors will indicate whether we should place more effort on recycling or should restrict use. That day can be long deferred by investing at a reasonable pace in sophisticated geological exploration. However, it may be brought closer if world conditions become inhospitable to production and trade in minerals, and compel earlier reliance on domestic supplies.

THE UNITED STATES AND FOREIGN SUPPLIES

Growing U.S. dependence on foreign mineral supplies occurs at a time of important changes in the condition of world supply and demand and in the relative position of the United States. The net result of these changes is to make prospective supplies both more uncertain and potentially more costly. In combination, and when joined with the implications for the balance of payments of imported energy and minerals, these factors may hasten the search for domestic substitutes, including greater secondary recovery.

The dependence of the United States on foreign sources of metals increased over the past two decades for nearly all metals. The major exceptions were copper and mercury, where the share of primary supply derived from imports declined, and molybdenum, where we remained self-sufficient. About a third of our iron is now derived from foreign sources, more than twice the share of 1950. Our dependence exceeds 90 percent for aluminum ore, a sharp climb from early postwar years, and dependence on foreign zinc also is up sharply. For such metals as chromium, cobalt, manganese, tin, and tungsten, dependence is high and rising. Projections to the year 2000 prepared by the National Commission on Materials Policy offer no cases where U.S. mine production will keep pace with rising consumption.[4]

This change has not come about suddenly, but much of it occurred during a period of restrained foreign demand, allowing the United States easy access to foreign supplies. Rapid growth in other de-

[4] The National Commission on Materials Policy, *Towards a National Materials Policy: Basic Data and Issues, An Interim Report* (Washington, D.C.: Government Printing Office, 1972).

veloped countries and no longer negligible demands of the LDCs are changing this situation. Exponential growth in demand from so many sources could dissolve the world's long-standing glut of mineral resources. Meanwhile exporting countries are beginning to take joint action to raise the price of their commodities. Such countries long have chafed under the price at which their raw materials enter trade, viewing it as the result of dark machinations by international monopolies rather than a consequence of supply-and-demand relationships. In a changed supply situation their capacity to hold cartels together to exact a greater return will be much enhanced. In zealous exercise of their newly won sovereignty such countries often make it difficult for foreign enterprises to operate and thereby perhaps unwittingly depress supply and strengthen the bargaining position of producing countries. This has the effect of negating some of the potential of new geological techniques that otherwise would act to expand supply.

In early postwar years the United States enjoyed a preeminent position in the world minerals economy. We had a monopoly on the best technology, were the principal source of investable funds, and possessed unchallenged power and prestige. In such circumstances our commercial firms could deal with the governments of producer countries with assurance. Of course, our situation no longer can be described in those terms. Others have caught up in many aspects of technology and general economic strength and surpass us in their ability to control commercial arrangements in accord with national purposes. Our favored position is gone, and both the security and cost of supplies will suffer.

It might be possible to make bilateral arrangements with suppliers that would mitigate these consequences. Canada is one of our most important suppliers and has a far-ranging stake in its relations with the United States. In all cases, however, foreign governments will understandably be tempted to exact the full rent on their resource and to shift among buyers as needed in order to accomplish this. Moreover, in many of the less stable countries domestic political groups will capitalize on the theme that sale of minerals yields no real benefit to the general public. They will find a sympathetic audience elsewhere among conscience-stricken citizens of advanced countries who argue that the United States and other developed countries preempt too large a share of the world's resources and deplete them before others have had a chance to use them for their own industrialization. So long as there seems to be no escape from this logic, its moral force will weaken all U.S. efforts to secure supplies abroad.

MINERAL POLICY GUIDES FOR THE UNITED STATES

The perverse fact that many minerals essential to a growing industrial economy are not to be found at moderate cost in the United States forces compromise on some of our goals. In particular there is conflict between income growth, which requires abundant and low-cost resources, and security, which would favor resort to the scarcer and more expensive domestic sources. Likewise, there may be conflict between environmental protection and other objectives. There is no reasonably simple or final solution.

The discussion here can only indicate a possible direction.

One aim would be to minimize dependence on foreign sources, but to require that this be pursued only if the cost differential is moderate. Obviously, a case-by-case approach is required. Some minerals are more important than others. For example, steel is so important that complete dependence on foreign sources would be intolerable, even if domestic costs were far higher. At the same time, the price of steel is basic to competitiveness in many other lines of trade so the other extreme of complete independence at very high cost would not be feasible. Within a considerable range we can take advantage of the cost and logistical advantages of imports while retaining a major capability of our own. A mix of policy and economic factors already produces this result in steel and copper. Our dependence on foreign bauxite is nearly total, but many of the sources are reasonably secure. Given a little lead time, production could continue with domestic alternatives, so the decision to import does not expose us badly. Of course if foreign cartels succeed in sharply raising prices, then domestic production looks still more favorable.

For minor metals and steel alloys, this country is often heavily import-dependent. In some instances, Canada is able and willing to meet our needs. In other cases, the only real option is stockpiling to guard against interruptions over a time span that would allow other adjustments. Our present stockpiles were established with reference to military emergencies of defined duration. As those assumptions were changed, the government determined some stocks to be excessive. Nonwar interruptions or shortages were not considered. Because stockpiles are readily marketable assets, the temptation to sell in periods of budget stress is strong and is supported by purely economic analysis of the cost of holding such an asset. However, from the standpoint of a comfortable materials policy for the longer term, the maintenance of sizeable stocks may prove more rational than disposal.

An attempt to maintain a degree of self-sufficiency comes at the cost of added domestic environmental burden. An exception may occur to the extent that self-sufficiency is sought via more complete recycling, though even in that case there are added energy costs, and some recycling processes also entail direct environmental damage. Such environmental costs may be avoided if mineral supplies are conserved by diminishing use, and they may be mitigated by the pursuit of an active abatement policy.

Environmental damages from minerals production occur at the mining stage and during refining or smelting. Underground mining operations require comparatively small land areas but do result in unsightly tailings and often dust and noise. In some cases, underground and surface waters are degraded through exposure to minerals in mining or in concentrating. Beyond this, underground mining requires access roads which often penetrate remote areas, opening them up for other traffic and development. For this reason, mining is not consistent with pure wilderness preservation, though it is possible to conceive of controls that would tightly limit the environmental insult.

Surface mining disturbs a much larger area and carries the other detrimental effects of mining. Its advantage is that it frequently is cheaper and permits the exploitation of low-quality ores. This presents a fundamental kind of tradeoff. In many mineralized parts of the country population density is low and the landscape undistinguished (though some will always love it). In such cases the inevitable landscape damage could be sustained. Where these conditions are reversed, or where designated wilderness is involved, more exacting standards of need can be required before mining is allowed. Likewise, for wilderness the presumption is against development unless an overriding need for the mineral is demonstrated. If the deposit is near the surface, restoration is sometimes possible, and in other cases the excavation can be turned to an asset as a lake or landfill.

Frequently, minerals processing is a highly polluting activity that affects both air and water. Ores often must be ground and concentrated near the site if the mineral content is low, while such materials as iron ore and bauxite are rich in metals and can travel with little preliminary processing.

Where concentration is feasible or the ore is high in mineral content there may be some flexibility in the location of smelters, but in other cases economics may dictate a site near the mine. Tightened air and water standards threaten the economic viability of many smelters and can inhibit the development of new ones. An escape is possible if new processes can be devised for treating ores in conformance with environmental standards. New promise has been offered by proposed processes in copper and aluminum smelting. Otherwise we face the prospect of increased foreign dependence as the cost of environmental purity at the same level of materials use.

To the extent that we can increase recycling of minerals, part of our dilemma can be avoided. Metals in particular lend themselves to re-melting, often at resource costs that are a small fraction of the cost of virgin materials. Once materials become embodied in final goods, the problem is the collection and separation of metals to get a uniform-quality scrap. Final products could be designed to permit easier separa-tion, at least in consumer durables. Containers and packaging remain an unpromising field for recovery if anything is allowed for the cost of collection. Materials used in construction remain locked up for long periods and often are lost or relegated to low-value uses when demol-ished according to present techniques. Recycling is not likely to be a panacea for materials supply or environmental protection, though it can assist in both cases.

It is frequently lamented that the U.S. incentive structure favors virgin materials over recycled products, making the latter too expen-sive for economic viability. Virgin materials of all sorts benefit from the depletion allowance and expensing provisions of tax law and, for overseas investments, from the provision for deferral of tax until prof-its are repatriated. In addition, governmentally regulated freight rates are alleged to favor virgin materials, although the structure of rates is too complicated to permit easy generalization and there may be oper-ating efficiencies that justify the lower rates on raw products. As with oil and gas, the tax incentives that favor foreign production could be eliminated (including investment guarantees for mining properties) and those that relate to domestic production could be more closely tied to exploration and investment. Since it will probably be desirable to encourage domestic production of minerals, we cannot lightly pro-pose dismantling the domestic incentives entirely. At the same time, special incentives to encourage recycling are consistent with security and environmental considerations.

In all phases of the minerals industries from exploration through mining, concentration, refining and smelting, and recycling only inno-vation offers real hope of extending our resources and ensuring com-patibility between exploitation and environment. We have not pursued this as actively as we might because we have grown content with our access to cheaper foreign supplies and have not pushed hard enough on domestic alternatives.

Conventional exploration techniques have relied largely upon sur-face manifestations to reveal underlying mineral deposits. Clearly, a developed country such as the United States is more thoroughly explored than many other parts of the world, and it has proved easier to find rich deposits elsewhere. So long as conditions favored development of foreign deposits by U.S. firms, foreign production enjoyed competitive advantage and provided a satisfactory degree of supply security. As those conditions change, inferior domestic deposits look more attractive. The advance in geological techniques to make use of highly sophisticated sensors to provide indications of possible deposits should allow discovery of many presently concealed resources. Satellites are already deploying such sensors, and the art of design and interpretation of these techniques can be advanced if we wish to devote more resources to it.

Advances in mining technology have permitted the use of lower-quality ores without increase in cost. Mining is essentially a matter of loosening and moving materials. It has benefited greatly from the increase in scale of earth-moving machinery, especially for surface mining. For underground mining, an added consideration is the need to maintain a safe working environment (ventilation, dust control, and shoring) for miners. At some stage, advances in automatic control techniques and rising standards of industrial safety may favor an attempt to go to more automatic systems. Meanwhile the development of more efficient equipment for underground use continues.

As noted earlier, many minerals must be concentrated or refined near the mine. More stringent environmental standards are driving up the cost of processing in the United States, thereby favoring foreign mines. In some cases new processes can be adopted to meet U.S. standards. Where an operation already is marginal, the added investment may prove too much and force closure. Environmental standards for air and water may be excessively rigid and lack provision for less demanding adjustments to local ambient conditions. However, it is a lamentable fact that mineral policy needs are not considered jointly with environmental standards. Since minerals must be mined where they are found, and the areas often are remote from human population, the opportunity for adjustment in local situations will often be present if we are not too dogmatic about uniform environmental standards.

The tension between incentives for mineral production and the equity claims and consumer interest of the public pose difficulties just as in the case of oil and gas. The public interest is in obtaining an ample and low-cost supply of materials, yet incentives to secure them may unduly enrich some. The fact that much of the U.S. mineral supply has been found on public lands gives the government a special responsibility for protecting the public's assets at the same time that it seeks to expand output. These complex issues are the subject of the section which follows.

THE PUBLIC LANDS AND MINING LAW

About one-third of the nation's lands (one-fifth if Alaska is excluded) is held by the federal government. Most of this is in the West and most of it is administered by the Bureau of Land Management. The government also has jurisdiction over the Outer Continental Shelf and retains mineral rights on some 62 million acres of once-public lands now in private hands. Much other mineral production occurs on purely private land, some of it once public, that was acquired under mineral law. However, a very large portion of our hard rock minerals (except for iron ore) comes from western states, and the public lands of the West are a potential source of much of our future production.

Mineral production, which is generally recognized as essential to the economy, often becomes a bone of contention when any specific site is under consideration. The difficulty is that mining often conflicts with other uses of the site or of nearby land, and policy must have some means of resolving these disputes. If mining is permitted, the arrangements become very important insofar as they affect the incentive to explore, in limiting the damage that occurs, and the sharing of rents from the operation. In practice all of these issues have been entangled in the body of mineral law that has grown up.

The present system generally gives priority to mining on public lands over other uses. There are important exceptions to this, but the original mining law—known as the location system—allowed private persons to stake a claim and proceed through stages to production without any payment to the public.[5] Originally, the location system applied to all minerals, but subsequent acts have removed some minerals from the system in favor of leasing arrangements, and other "common varieties" such as sand and gravel are sold or may be given away. Some lands (for example, national parks) are excluded from the location system.

If the land is open to location, the prospector may enter and explore without restriction. He can stake a claim and register it under state

[5] For a brief discussion of mining law, see The National Commission on Materials Policy, *Final Report* (Washington, D.C.: Government Printing Office, 1973), chapter 7.

law. To remain valid, specified assessment work must be performed, but only a rival claimant can take it away from a negligent holder. The criterion of a valid claim is whether a valuable mineral deposit has been discovered—not a very clear standard. Anyone with a valid discovery can mine without payment to the government.

The surface rights of a claim holder presumably are limited to his needs for mining. If he "patents" his claim by establishing that he has discovered a valuable (marketable) mineral, he gains full control over surface rights. Many claim holders have behaved as though they owned the surface, and the failure of the federal authorities effectively to contest this behavior led many to file ostensible mining claims (often based on discovery of common variety minerals) in order to gain valuable surface rights, such as timber or vacation homesites. Such behavior is more difficult under current law, which excludes common varieties from the location system.

As noted, certain minerals are not subject to the location system. Some were removed under the provisions of the Mineral Leasing Act of 1920 (and subsequent amendments); among them are coal, oil, gas, shale, phosphate, tar sands, potassium, sodium, and others of less importance. If the Interior Department believes that workable deposits exist in an area, it may put the land up for lease on competitive bid. One may also explore for leased minerals on other land by obtaining a permit. If this results in a discovery, exploitation can be arranged on the basis of a royalty payment.

Yet another modification of the location system occurs in wilderness areas. Under the terms of the Wilderness Act of 1964, private mineral rights remain in force but no new ones may be created after 1983. Claims made before 1984 can still be operated but this must be done in a manner compatible with wilderness preservation, and those claims dating after 1964 carry only limited surface rights. The requirement pertaining to compatibility with wilderness preservation could be a very onerous condition for a mining operation.

This structure of law gives mining priority over other uses of land in allowing exploration and production of federal lands. However, withdrawals of land from mineral entry for various reasons and the restrictions imposed on operations in wilderness areas modify this priority, while the minerals subject to lease do not enjoy it in the same degree. Still, for most of the land no consideration need be given by mine operators to the recreational or scenic uses of the areas.

If it is determined that the land is open for mining, there are still important issues of efficiency and equity. For example, the system provides little security of tenure during the exploration phase. With modern techniques, exploration via remote sensors may occur far from the actual site of the deposit. Also, under present law when a deposit is located it may be difficult to claim sufficient surface acreage for an efficient operation. These features raise the cost of exploration and may result in premature exploration in order to establish valid claims not yet suitable for mining. The lack of a central registry of claims adds to the cost and risk of producing on public lands, since it is difficult to establish that there are no prior claims. On the equity side, the location system yields the public nothing for the minerals recovered from public land, while private operators are able to claim the entire rent.

Past changes in the law have acted to reduce such abuses as the acquisition of mining claims for homesites or for removal of timber. However, aside from the limited provisions of the Wilderness Act, little has been done to resolve the issue of competing claims for the services of federal lands, especially the question of recreation and wilderness versus mining.

The present law could be tidied up to eliminate some clearly undesirable features while leaving the essentials intact. One useful change would be to require that claims be filed with the federal government and be subject to refiling periodically or else be considered abandoned. Required assessment work on claims could be rationalized so as to yield more information—for example, test borings could substitute for trenches. There seems little reason to allow surface rights to go to new patent holders, and the provisions of the Wilderness Act could be extended in this respect. More efficient exploration could be promoted by granting exclusive, though temporary, exploration permits over a larger area. The foregoing suggestions would not deal with a situation where locatable and leasable minerals occur on the same land. Moreover, if the suggested changes were made, they would still allow mining to occur in many areas without much concern for other uses, would allow claimants to enter on their own initiative, and would grant claims without consideration of the value of the deposit—all questionable features.

More fundamental changes of the location system also could be considered. For example, a limitation on the surface rights acquired by patenting a claim and a requirement for "restoration" of mined areas would circumscribe some of the priority that mining now enjoys. A still further limitation might require that exploration permits be granted according to rules to be laid down instead of simply allowing anyone to stake a claim on his own initiative. If such permits were not issued automatically, public control over mining on the public lands could be reasserted.

Among the suggestions considered in public discussion of mining law is a proposal to go to a system of leasing for all minerals. The administering agency could select areas for lease, perhaps with advice from mining companies, and offer them for auction. Operations would be subject to environmental regulations. Failure to engage in actual mining after an appropriate period would result in termination of the lease. Such a system would provide the public some means of determining whether mining was to occur and some control over the nature of the operation. It would resolve the problem of leasable and locatable minerals on the same site. The lease auction would provide a return on the resource to the public. A comparatively low royalty might be combined with this, but an excessive royalty would result in failure to recover minerals that otherwise should be mined. The termination provision provides incentive to produce on a timely basis.

While a leasing system would allow public control over the issues of whether mining is to occur and how it is to occur, criteria are still needed for resolving these questions where mining conflicts with other uses of the site. At this point land planning legislation applying to the public lands (see Chapter 2) could assume great importance. So far our criteria for land planning are very underdeveloped, but it is clear that planning must be flexible to adapt to changing circumstances, must be long term in nature, of broad focus, and must avoid undue permanent damage to land or environment, even at some cost in current economic return.

Our basic mining law reflects a developmental bias and lack of concern with environmental damage. The present tendency is to swing in the other direction. This occurs at the very time that rising domestic costs and increasing foreign dependence would logically call for measures to increase output. The technical and administrative challenge ahead will be how to devise more acceptable methods of mining under public control without impairing an industry that we all depend upon.

6
ABATING POLLUTION IN A GROWING ECONOMY

POLLUTION ABATEMENT AND OTHER GOALS

Pessimistic scenarios for man's fate hold that either resource scarcity or environmental damage will bring about collapse of the industrial system. If one does not get us the other will. The prescription following from this diagnosis becomes to retard or arrest economic and demographic growth; the longer-term future is left somewhat vague.

In this book the prognosis has been rather more hopeful on the resource side; the author looks to a technological strategy to develop long-term energy alternatives and to help us solve other resource problems as well. Such optimism is qualified by awareness of the congestion that ill-planned growth implies for land resources, especially for pastoral and wilderness lands. Yet if the demographic component of growth is eliminated, if our occupancy of space is land sparing, and if the permanent qualities of the land are protected, then we should be able to cope with the pressures of long-term economic growth on the land as discussed in Chapter 2. Under those conditions we could continue to enjoy the direct productive services of the land, as well as to experience the awe inspired by the natural order of wilderness and the esthetic and spiritual values derived from an orderly cityscape and landscape. There are a great many ifs in the foregoing, but success in this regard would protect many of the attributes that should be included in the term *environmental quality*.

But how about the burden of pollution that a growing industrial economy entails? Whether this burden is visited upon land, water, or air, it offends the senses and may have profound effects on health, genetics, and the earth's life-support system. At some level protection of environmental quality becomes a necessity. Clearly, the burden must be managed in order to maintain a high-level industrial society.

Public awareness of environmental ills has grown to the point that pollution abatement has become almost a moral crusade. Even though the energy crisis has blunted the force of the environmental movement, it remains powerful. The energy crisis also has pointed up the potential conflict between some pollution abatement measures and the still widely held objective of secure and growing incomes. As more Americans are jarred into awareness of these conflicts, the need increases for more effective means of reconciling goals.

Longer term, does the growth of per capita economic activity (assuming control of population growth) imply an unmanageable environmental burden? The threat cannot be dismissed, but it does not seem so imminent as to require the sacrifice of income aspirations.[1] It is important to distinguish between different kinds of threat. A first distinction is between current and long-term damage. Our obligation to future generations is to avoid irreversible damage to the large global systems, to the human gene pool or other genetic stocks, and to ecosystems. It is difficult to identify possible catastrophic damage of this kind arising from prospective activities over the next generation or so. Conceivably, unrestrained combustion of fossil fuels could alter climate, and the massive release of radioactivity could do severe genetic damage in addition to its effects on the health of current generations. Uncontrolled use of pesticides or other toxic materials and dispersed human land occupancy could result in major ecological damage. But we are moving to guard against such events, and the sheer scale of human activity will not make them inevitable over the next generation or so, provided that current means of coping are employed. A subsequent generation will have to reevaluate these matters. The greatest danger is the possibility of unforseen damage, perhaps from new technologies whose effects remain latent or unnoticed until a critical threshold has passed. The danger of this happening is multiplied by the pace of technological change, although a system of technology assess-

---

[1] Work done at RFF indicates that dramatic reduction in emissions of common pollutants from current levels could be achieved by the year 2000 through application of an active abatement policy using technologies already known. This would be possible, even allowing for the highest reasonable levels of population and economic growth. See Ronald G. Ridker, ed., *Population, Resources, and the Environment*, volume 3 of Commission Research Reports, U.S. Commission on Population Growth and the American Future, (Washington, D.C.: Government Printing Office, 1972), p. 48.

ment is being slowly evolved that should help to reduce the number of surprises. However, no protection is absolute.

Developments a generation or more hence cannot be forseen well enough to say that we will be able to cope with damage to global systems at an expanded level of activity. Yet there is no reason for pessimism a priori. Pollution abatement technology is still in its infancy, and the emphasis is on patching up processes not designed with pollution control in mind. As a newer technology emerges for some of our major economic clusters, such as energy, transportation, and the production of food and fiber, more systematic approaches to pollution abatement can be built in, which should greatly extend the ability of the environment to accommodate growth.

Irreversible damage, whether to global systems or through cumulative action, is difficult to defend. Application of conventional discounting to the future benefits of averting such damage through actions taken now would offer little current incentive to protect the environment. Instinctively, everyone feels a duty to pass the earth on intact to his heirs, and damage of this sort is indefensible if it can be identified. Obviously, there is conflict between current income and longer-term environmental quality in cases of irreversible damage.

Most environmental damage, however, is neither of the permanent or irreversible kind nor does it affect global systems. Rather it is localized congestion of environmental media that may be either sporadic or chronic. The damage most commonly is to human health and amenities, although localized ecological damage affecting other species also is common. The effects of these sorts of damage are felt by the current generation and most often by people near the source of the insult. Although current damage may be reversible and limited in reach, it can still be intolerable to the affected population, especially if damage to health is involved.[2]

Pollution damage represents a loss of current income and its abatement entails a current cost. In principle most pollution damages are measurable, and theoretically our income would be improved by spending for abatement as long as the damage averted exceeds abatement cost. If this standard could be applied, there would be no necessary conflict between the income and environmental objectives when dealing with reversible damage. Income as measured by the conventional GNP accounts would be somewhat deceptive, however. Since a

---

[2] A more complete discussion of the various kinds of environmental threats and of possible reactions to them is found in the author's *To Live on Earth: Man and His Environment in Perspective* (Baltimore: The Johns Hopkins University Press, 1972).

pollution-free environment represents part of our income, and since increasing expenditures are required to maintain it in the face of economic growth, part of our apparent income growth is spurious—it simply goes to maintain what we have.

Pollution abatement policies also conflict with other social goals. For example, they may raise domestic costs and induce greater foreign dependency; they need not always promote conservation; and they can pose difficult equity and institutional problems. Some of these conflicts are diminished to the extent that growth is retarded. Almost all aspects of energy and mineral refinement are polluting in nature and the burden could be reduced by lowering the level of activity. It would also be possible to reduce the domestic environmental burden by relying upon foreign production, but for security reasons the United States chooses to maintain domestic capability. As a consequence of environmental requirements here there is a tendency for metal smelters and refineries and for oil refineries to locate abroad, while mining operations are frustrated in myriad ways. For conservation the result is a mixed bag. Reliance on foreign supplies, forced by domestic environmental rules, conserves our own resources, even if they are not accessible short term, and the higher costs occasioned by pollution control retard demand. However, some environmental measures, such as coal gasification or auto pollution controls that decrease gas mileage, may result in faster depletion. The fact that the cost of pollution control measures, whether reflected in private costs or in public budgets, falls on individuals according to a different pattern than pollution damages means that control generates important questions of equity.

While the increase in economic activity enlarges the potential environmental burden and exacerbates the conflict among goals, not all of this result is necessary. The problem has been aggravated by institutional failures that have inhibited us from coping with environmental damage by using the range of methods available. One failure concerns the free use of common property resources to receive discharges. Individuals, firms, and governmental agencies have been allowed to discharge residuals into the environmental media—principally air and water—without payment. As a result there has been little incentive to restrict discharges and the media have become overloaded. When they are overloaded beyond their capacity to receive and neutralize discharges via natural processes, the resulting damages may increase at a faster rate than the increased load. The heart of the pollution abatement problem is how to restrict access to the environmental media.

Assuming that a high-level industrial system is desirable, then the environmental burden that the system tends to generate must be controlled if we are to enjoy the income represented by a reasonably clean and agreeable environment. Control can be achieved through technical measures that restrict the production and release of pollutants, through management systems that relate releases to the capacity of receiving media, and through adoption of consumption patterns that may be less demanding in their impact on the environment. Such changes do not occur automatically. They can be sought by social control, and through market-type incentives.

The first control problem is to set the environmental standards that we wish to maintain—so-called ambient standards. Complete purity—that is, allowing no discharge to the environment—is incompatible with the maintenance of an industrial system (or almost any form of activity!). If ambient standards are set at very high levels of purity, the cost of achieving them rises abruptly. Obviously, a balance is needed, allowing some use of the common property resources to receive wastes but not permitting use to the point of serious damage. The idea of proceeding to the point where the value of added abatement is equal to its cost has appeal. In practice this point is difficult to ascertain. It also creates equity problems. Individuals differ in their willingness to tolerate pollution. Some might set an infinite value on the pristine condition of a stream, and their right to have it maintained in natural condition is not inferior to that of a would-be discharger to use it for waste disposal. There generally is no way that all of the damaged parties can be compensated. Moreover, the techniques for estimating damages and benefits are very imperfect. While it is useful to make the best estimates possible of the benefits and costs of various levels of abatement, in the end the setting of ambient standards is a matter for social choice through the political process. Not everyone can meet all of his objectives in this way, but with improved methods of social choice ambient standards could be established in a manner that articulates the various interests at stake and permits each social group to defend its interest. Further discussion of this problem is reserved for Chapter 8.

The design of ambient environmental standards is made even more complex by the fact that pollution arises from multiple sources and normally can be deposited in more than one medium. Attempts to correct insult to one of the receiving media may aggravate the problem of another. Our aim must be to achieve an acceptable quality for the entire ambient environment. Basic control legislation is organized about the principal receiving media—air and water—while other special types of emissions (for example, noise) or pollutants that affect more than one medium (for example, pesticides) are treated separately. This approach is convenient for many purposes, but it tends to deemphasize the interrelatedness among media and types of residuals. It is still true that (except for heat lost to space) materials are not consumed but only displaced. Everything must go somewhere, as we are told. The new interest in land use planning is in part a reflection of dissatisfaction with narrower technological approaches that try to deal with residuals after they are generated without consideration of how siting and concentration complicate the problem. In order to continue economic growth, we must learn to make more effective use of the assimilative capacity of the environment, so that it can receive residuals without damage or offense to man.

Assuming that an acceptable set of ambient standards has been defined, the next question concerns the most efficient way of achieving them. The prevalent tendency in government is to seek objectives by means of appropriate regulations. If an ambient standard is set, then the next step ordinarily is to set emissions standards or to ban the release of certain effluents as a means of achieving the ambient standard. Often these steps may be supplemented by a subsidy, especially if local governments are involved. Direct regulation may be required when dealing with toxic materials or those that imply long-lived damage. The receiving media cannot be viewed as a continuing and renewable sink for long-lived materials, because discharges simply deplete the more or less fixed capacity of the media to absorb them.

In the case of common air and water pollutants, the receiving media can absorb, disperse, and neutralize the burden on a renewable basis through biological and meteorological processes. This assimilative capacity must be efficiently used on a continuous basis consistent with the ambient standard defined for the media without doing permanent damage to the media or to their capacity for continued absorption. The capacity of the media to render this flow of services can be increased by various systems management measures. The burden upon the receiving media can also be reduced by changes in processes, end products, or through recovery and recycling measures, and damage can be limited by measures to neutralize necessary discharge. Such measures are extremely complex in practice. An attempt to accomplish them exclusively by regulation implies that government officials can make detailed choices about costs and processes available to industry. In fact this is implausible, for government lacks the detailed information required, and industry is adept at frustrating this type of detailed government regulation. Even if government successfully imposes its will, the result is not likely to be efficient in use of resources.

This difficulty in making regulation truly operative and doubts about its implications for economic efficiency have led many economists to argue for effluent charges as a means of allocating the assimilative capacity of common property resources that would be consistent with the socially established standards for them. It is true that in the United States we have had comparatively little experience with this approach (there is more abroad), and it is also true that the approach would not be effective in all circumstances. Yet ingenious application of this concept could be made in a great many situations. Its great advantage would lie in providing business with incentive to find the cheapest way of abating pollution, while sparing the costs and frustrations of an elaborate regulatory apparatus. If the twin goals of income growth and improved quality are to be reconciled, we cannot afford to ignore these questions of efficiency.

The rather general observations of this section are worked out in more detail in the remainder of this chapter. For expositional convenience I have followed the traditional air, water, solid waste breakdown but I will try to give some indications of the interrelationships along the way.

IMPROVING AIR QUALITY[3]

Air pollution is largely the result of combustion or of the volatilization of combustible fuels. It also originates in the processes of a few industries—especially chemicals, metal smelting and refining, and pulp and paper. In addition, air may serve to transport residuals not ordinarily thought of as air pollutants, such as pesticides, radioactive materials, and lead and mercury. The common air pollutants arising from combustion include carbon monoxide, carbon dioxide, nitrogen oxides, hydrocarbons, sulfur, and particulates. Their proportions vary, depending upon the fuel and the conditions of combustion. Two unavoidable consequences of combustion are carbon dioxide and heat. (Water ordinarily results as well, but it may be considered innocuous.) The amount of other pollutants may be reduced by varying fuel inputs or by varying fuel handling and combustion conditions, and

[3] Both this section and the one to follow have relied heavily on information supplied to the author by Allen V. Kneese, a former member of the RFF staff.

they may be controlled by devices to capture or alter the wastes generated.

The atmosphere is not a permanent sink for these emissions, though their residence time in that medium may be long (perhaps very long for CO_2). Natural processes of breakdown, washout, or incorporation into the life cycle ultimately remove them from the atmosphere. These processes may take days, weeks, or years; meanwhile we rely on dispersion via meterological activity to dilute emissions until they are removed from the atmosphere.

While man is subject to chronic exposure from common air pollutants, they pose few serious threats to global systems at present. Increased CO_2 in the atmosphere from combustion may significantly affect the global climate. This and potential loss of the ozone shield from the operation of SSTs are the most plausible threats so far identified. They deserve careful study and monitoring but call for no immediate action.[4]

Since air pollutants are so largely the result of industrial processes, space heating, operation of automobiles, and the combustion associated with electricity generation, they tend to be concentrated in urban centers and specialized industrial areas. The capacity of the air to assimilate and disperse pollutants depends on many factors, including the amount, type, timing, and spatial distribution of discharges, the physical pattern of airflows, and specific weather conditions. Cities, for example, not only generate large amounts of gaseous residuals but also inhibit their dispersion by impairing wind velocity and by creating inversion layers that block upward diffusion. Assimilative capacity is varying and random in nature, changing over the time of day, season, and from year to year. Although we occasionally have regional concentrations, air pollution usually is a highly local phenomenon with peak concentrations also quite limited in time. It is much easier to control the peaks (through temporary cessation of polluting activities) than to control the average level of pollution.

Most of the damage from air pollution that concerns us is the effect on health, though esthetic or amenity considerations and damage to plants, animals, and property also are important. Because of the subtle nature of the effect of air pollution on health, it is very difficult to establish the seriousness of the problem or to relate it to different

[4] Recently, concern has been voiced that freon gas used as an aerosol propellant also may significantly reduce the ozone shield. Although not yet thoroughly evaluated, the danger seems plausible enough that it may require early action to halt this use.

states of the atmosphere. For example, acute air pollution episodes are known to be fatal to many of the more susceptible individuals in the area, but we are unsure about the effects of low-level chronic exposure. Available evidence suggests that air pollution is intimately associated with a range of respiratory diseases, that it works as an additional stress and is far more harmful to susceptible individuals than to others, and that its pure economic costs would warrant a large-scale effort to correct a major share of the problem. Of course, the public does not view health exclusively in economic terms, and we may wish to control air pollution beyond the point at which net economic benefits can be established.

Our approach to air pollution control is embodied in the Clean Air Act Amendments of 1970. Prior to 1970, federal law sought to establish regional airsheds, which were to set their own ambient standards and control programs. The 1970 legislation provided for national air quality standards, distinguishing primary standards based on health needs from secondary standards to protect the public welfare (esthetics, vegetation, and property). Ambient standards were set pursuant to the act for six common pollutants—particulates, sulfur oxides, carbon monoxide, hydrocarbons, nitrogen oxides, and photochemical oxidants. To help achieve these ambient standards, emission standards were established for a number of sources, notably automobiles and aircraft. The act also allowed for emissions standards for new stationary sources or for those undergoing modification. Emissions standards also apply to hazardous substances (for example, mercury, asbestos).

The law intended an important role for the states in devising and implementing plans to meet the ambient standards for the common pollutants in their various air pollution control regions. Usually states plan to rely upon some form of permit system affecting new construction as a means of enforcing compliance with pollution control standards. It is unclear how these permits will be related to the ambient standards they seek to achieve. Moreover, a permit system is not an economically efficient way of achieving the standards. States were slow in bringing forward plans to meet ambient standards and many sought extensions of the time limit as is permissible under the law. In other cases states have in effect thrown the problem of devising a plan back on the Environmental Protection Agency (EPA). The problem is complicated by the shortage of low-sulfur fuels, the unavailability of reliable sulfur-removing technology and equipment, and by delays in achieving the mandated auto emissions standards.

One major thrust of plans put forward has been for emission controls and better maintenance on older cars and for restrictions on auto traffic in cities. Corrective measures on autos can be provided readily enough for unburned hydrocarbons and carbon monoxide, but not for nitrogen oxides. Measures to restrict traffic vary from parking charges and restrictions all the way to the celebrated proposal to limit drastically fuel availability in Los Angeles. If such an approach is not to destroy the economic viability of communities grown dependent on auto transportation, it must include provision for alternative transport, but air pollution control authorities are poorly positioned to effect this. For cities, given the short time frame, changes in the transportation system can only mean buses, taxi-buses, or inducements to car pooling. So far there have been only hesitant movements in this direction other than those compelled by gasoline shortages. Apparently we don't really believe that what the law mandates will be done.

The 1970 law, while allowing for a degree of state and local administration, is based on uniform national ambient standards and in many cases on uniform emissions standards. Uniform ambient standards can be defended where public health is at stake (primary standards) but are more dubious in the case of secondary standards. The presence of some classes of pollutants might greatly reduce visibility, for example, in the arid West, while they would have less noticeable effect in more humid climates. Also, the economic burden of a given secondary standard falls differently on different regions. A case could be made for allowing some latitude on amenity considerations so long as health is protected. A range could be established, within which variation is allowed, that would moderate interregional competition based on degradation of the ambient air while still allowing the neediest areas an opportunity to preserve or extend their industry.

The case for uniform emissions standards to facilitate the attainment of ambient standards is even harder to make. For automobiles, scale economies in manufacture and their inherent mobility may make this a useful device. Uniform emissions standards for industrial plants might be justified out of desire to discourage control laxity as a form of interregional competition. However, some of the plants to which emissions standards apply are not in the national market, so unfair competitive advantage is not of concern. Moreover, in lightly populated regions where ambient standards are under little pressure, it would again make sense to allow some latitude in emissions standards as an aid in attracting industry if the area so chooses. It would be preferable to place industry where costs of control could be lower. Basically, the use of uniform emission standards appears to betray a lack of faith in the principle of local initiative in attaining the ambient standards.

Finally, whether the responsibility for achieving ambient standards is left to local devices or not, in many cases emissions standards may not be the best way of achieving the ambient standard. As was argued earlier, an emission charge scaled to force reduction to the desired total level often would be more efficient in that it would give incentive to seek out least-cost methods of reducing emissions, while allowing those for whom the privilege of using the atmosphere's capacity is most valuable (that is, for whom alternatives would be most costly) to continue to do so within the ambient limits. By contrast, a system of regulation, whether employing permits or emissions standards, cannot take efficiency into account in a satisfactory manner because regulators simply lack the detailed information required. In consequence, their prescriptions often are unduly burdensome.

Emissions charges are not a panacea. Their use implies an effective system for measuring actual discharges, and they are ill suited to situations where essentially no escape of the pollutant is the objective. For some toxic substances, the environment does not provide a continuous and renewable assimilative capacity—the objective here is not allocation of capacity but exclusion of the pollutant. In that case the most stringent emission standard enforced by regulation is called for. Also, for common pollutants from many dispersed sources, the difficulty in measuring effluents presents a real problem. Where the pollutants are generated by standard industrial products (for example, home furnaces, autos) there are many options involving design and operation of equipment. Equipment design could be required to meet certain emissions standards—a regulatory device; or use of the equipment could be licensed according to a fee system based on its average performance—essentially an emission tax approach. It is worth examining two opportunities for use of emissions charges.

Sulfur oxides are an important airborne residual apparently damaging to health. (There is dispute about whether at relatively low levels they act only in combination with other pollutants or are dangerous in their own right.) Moreover, they increased steadily over three postwar decades before apparently leveling off. Some of our most ambitious and expensive control programs have been directed at sulfur emissions. Since it is difficult to remove sulfur from fuels (except natural gas) prior to combustion, and since the technology for removal after combustion is unperfected, the principal defense has been to require use of low-sulfur fuels. This in turn has been costly and has aggravated the energy crisis, such fuel being in short supply.

Sulfur seems well suited to the use of an emission charge. The Nixon Administration proposed such a tax in 1972 as a means of internalizing pollution costs and testing the efficacy of incentives. The tax was to be imposed on sulfurous emissions from sources where this could be measured and on the sulfur content of fuels in other cases. It was to be scaled higher where ambient standards were not being met and would revert to nil if all ambient standards were met. Such a tax would place a premium on low-sulfur fuels and stimulate their production and transport. It would also speed the development of techniques for cleaning fuels or scrubbing emissions. Congress has not approved this innovation, and regulatory devices remain the only recourse. There is a growing sense that enforcement cannot be sustained in view of the shortage of low-sulfur fuels and the hardship that would be created by strict adherence to the law. Pressure to relax or defer application of the secondary standards was mounting, even before the energy crisis became acute. The story is a familiar one.

Over a long-term period as energy use grows, it is questionable whether a regulatory approach can hold sulfur or the other consequences of combustion within acceptable limits. Even use of more low-sulfur fuel may not suffice if total fuel consumption expands far enough. An energy strategy that seeks to transform coal into clean-burning gas comprehends this need. Since this technology cannot be perfected and brought into general use for well over a decade, even with a major research effort, there is all the more reason to try in the meantime to stimulate abatement techniques of the sort that would result from a sulfur tax.

American experience with auto pollution controls provides another example of the difficulty of a simple regulatory approach. In this case the law originally mandated a 90 percent reduction between 1970 and 1975–1976 for three common pollutants in all new cars. The force behind this act was understandable. Automobiles were the largest source of air pollution. Enforcement against individual owners would present enormous difficulties, while changes at the design stage are an efficient way of attacking the problem. Yet as the deadline for control targets approached, manufacturers pleaded that technology was not available, was untested, would be costly, and would aggravate the energy crisis by reducing gas mileage. An attempt to enforce the deadlines in the face of this posture becomes increasingly unlikely. Could we seriously entertain the thought of closing down Detroit, with the subsequent economic disruption in supplying industries, dealerships, finance, etc., not to mention the balance-of-payments effects of buyers scrambling to purchase foreign cars that may meet the standards? In this situation a strong law becomes a weak reed.

Since auto manufacturers recognized that the law would be difficult to enforce, they did not strain overmuch to comply with it. Faced with deadlines and the need to make some show of compliance, they have abjured fundamental new approaches in favor of catalytic converters attached to present engines. There is a strong possibility that the stern enforcement strategy will saddle us with a nonoptimal solution for years to come. Had we chosen another path of giving manufacturers a financial incentive to produce a clean running car we might be much further ahead. For example, a graduated tax could be imposed on the maker, based on how a sample of his products perform in actual use. The tax would be nil if the mean performance meets the standards but progressively higher the more it departs from them. Manufacturers would then be competing across the range of technological possibilities for the lowest-cost way of meeting standards—probably through new types of engines. Buyers would be mindful of how other aspects of performance were affected by pollution control measures.

The EPA Administrator in a solomonic decision has allowed a one-year extension of the 1975 deadline for meeting hydrocarbon and carbon monoxide standards. At the same time he has established interim standards for that year and more stringent ones for California where auto-related pollution is more acute. By itself this decision simply demonstrates the weakness of the law. Neither industry nor environmentalists are very happy with it. Perhaps a new examination would favor granting delay in application of the standards if the industry committed itself to vigorous pursuit of alternatives to the add-on devices.

Whether we rely upon an enforcement strategy or an effluent charge system, it is clear that a major defect of our present system is the failure to think in large enough terms. With automobiles we look at what comes out the exhaust pipe and become lost in the search for means of reducing this. The emissions are the product of fuel consumption. EPA data show that fuel comsumption per mile is directly related to vehicle weight. Why isn't there a stiff tax on weight or horsepower? It would save fuel and all of the materials that go into a car without necessarily reducing the service it renders—some luxury cars built abroad are much lighter than standard U.S. models. Higher fuel costs are beginning to move us in this direction. But go the next step. Can we reduce total vehicle miles traveled? Clearly this is possible, at least in getting to work, if more people travel in each vehicle. Our road system and computer capacity can be used to design service that would not inconvenience the public. Public stimulus through providing bus service alternatives and higher parking charges or tolls on single-passenger vehicles would help. In fairness, the existence of the alternative must accompany the incentive to use it. While proceeding along this path we may finally arrive at the conclusion that land use controls to restrain dispersion will aid still more in containing pollution problems and conserving resources of land and energy.

The same kind of thinking based on environmental concern could be applied to other energy use wherever combustion serves as a source of energy. We can have temperature control in our houses, but why not do it efficiently? Evidence that the cooling output of home air-conditioners varies over a wide range for a given power input argues either for regulation of the efficiency of such products or a tax based on their failure to meet a standard of reasonable efficiency. Building codes and financial regulations could compel use of energy-conserving materials and equipment in new construction. Present incentives favor marketing a low-priced product; standards, whether enforced by regulation or tax, could again conserve on resources and environment. If lenders can be compelled to take operating costs into account, energy-conserving requirements need not deny access to the product to anyone who otherwise would qualify. If industry proves slow in adjusting to the new market potential, then government can mount demonstration research efforts of its own, whether in perfecting a clean engine or a better insulated house. Such efforts, backed by government power to require adoption of superior technology, once demonstrated, could help to shake the kind of lethargy witnessed in the case of the auto industry.

A special dilemma for policy is the predicament of metal smelters. The United States has an interest in the health of this industry on security grounds. It is disquieting that the nation already is so dependent on foreign sources. The imposition of air pollution controls on smelters undoubtedly will accelerate this trend toward foreign supplies. This could be counteracted by providing protection for the domestic industry to allow it to compete, but this provides little incentive for improved pollution abatement technology. If emission controls were not uniform, then smelters in many locations might be able to adjust to local secondary ambient air quality standards at reasonable cost. Some regional latitude in the level of secondary standards also would allow consideration for the local importance of the industry, very likely with favorable effects on national metals supply. After a period of panic the industry has settled down to search for ways of complying with national standards; there have been some encouraging developments, but the overall effect is hard to appraise. An overly rigid air quality program, especially when applied to plants in remote and desolate locations, can defeat other national purposes.

WATER QUALITY MANAGEMENT STRATEGY

Water quality problems have less urgency than air pollution—after all, we can avoid water, except for household service, while we have no such option with air. Water treatment technology shelters us from most of the health hazards of pollution. Nonetheless, men always have had a special affinity for water as a source of esthetic delight, for recreation—and of course it is also vital for use in industry. Employing water to receive wastes often is in conflict with these other uses. We have had considerable experience in trying to regulate water quality, and it is instructive to see how it has turned out.

Even the cleanest natural waters normally carry some burden of pollutants—for example, microorganisms, organic matter, and mineral salts and acids. If the burden of these materials is not excessive, then they may be eliminated or neutralized by natural processes occurring in water, or they may be tolerated. For example, stream biota can decompose the organic matter, incorporating it into the life cycle in the water. Heat and pathogens are also degradable pollutants subject to elimination by natural processes. Salt content makes the water harder, but in dilute form salts and acids are not harmful to most aquatic life or to water quality for most uses. Usually dilution and flushing control damage from these materials if they are allowed to enter water. However, for some industrial and municipal uses the presence of such chemicals may cause corrosion or other damage, and the water must be treated to remove them prior to use. Heavy metals, synthetic organic chemicals such as pesticides, and radioactive materials can be very damaging to aquatic life, even in tiny amounts, and if they find their way up the food chain they can damage other species and man as well. There is no effective way of dealing with these except to prevent their entry into watercourses.

One of the commonest forms of water pollution is the presence of excessive organic matter. It may derive from direct discharges in the form of sewage, animal wastes, food processing residuals, papermaking, or the chemical industries. Another source is aquatic plants whose growth is stimulated by the presence of nutrients from the foregoing sources and from agricultural activity. As aquatic biota feed on these

organic materials and break them down into their inorganic components, they consume some of the oxygen normally dissolved in clean
water. If the oxygen supply is exhausted, most forms of aquatic life
cannot survive and the water becomes dark and smelly—unsuited for
most use.

The amount of organic material is conventionally measured by the
biochemical oxygen demand (BOD) that it imposes on the water. It is
estimated that industry is the source of about half of the potential
BOD, predominantly from the industries mentioned above, with livestock and urban areas dividing the remainder. Will the growth of
industry mean ever-increasing amounts of BOD in the water? Assuming no treatment, the potential load could increase about 150 percent
by the year 2000, with the chemical industry then being the source of
about one-half of the total. This is not expected to occur, for secondary treatment could reduce actual discharges to only about one-tenth
of the untreated amount and advanced treatment could do still better.
Thus, expanded economic activity does not entail pollution on this
scale, provided action is taken to counter it.[4]

Dissolved and suspended solids also provide gross measures of water
pollution. Again, industry is the source of over twice as much of these
pollutants as is the urban population. The primary metal industry is a
major source, with the chemical, petroleum, and food industries also
contributing heavily. The livestock industry is by far the largest
source of suspended solids.

Livestock operations also are a major source of nutrients, a large
quantity of which enter streams. Presumably, industry also is a major
source of nutrients, since the latter result from decomposition of organic matter and industries that are large contributors of BOD must
therefore also be responsible for nutrients in the water. Nutrients in
turn stimulate plant growth and BOD. One of the nutrients, available
nitrogen, can be harmful to man at sufficient concentration and in
some of its forms. Again, from a technical standpoint it should be
possible to prevent much of this burden from entering water.

So far we have not done too well. Federal legislation to protect
water quality has developed through a series of acts since 1948. The

---

[4] These data and those in the following two paragraphs were taken from Ivars
Gutmanis, "Waterborne Residual Generation and Emissions in the United States
and Selected River Basins, 1970," (Washington, D.C.: National Planning Associa-
tion, 1972), and from Leslie Ayres and Ivars Gutmanis, *A Model for Strategic
Allocation of Water Pollution Abatement Funds* (Washington, D.C.: International
Research and Technology Corporation for the Brookings Institution, 1970).

amendments of 1956 provided authority to regulate discharges to interstate waterways. This role was expanded in 1965 with the provision for setting up water quality standards enforceable by state and federal governments, while subsequent legislation provided for a state certification procedure to maintain standards. From the beginning there were elaborate procedural safeguards that required study, hearings, findings, and conferences before suit in a court to enforce compliance. Together with appeals and rather feeble penalties upon conviction, the net result has been that the enforcement process has held few terrors for polluters. Various amendments prior to 1972 addressed this frustration, seeking to broaden federal authority, shorten delays, and accelerate the appeals process. Meanwhile incentives were provided via a program of matching grants for municipal sewage systems, federal research and development programs, assistance to states in setting standards, and surveillance over states, with federal authority to supplant unacceptable state standards.

There is widespread feeling that the strategy embodied in the law prior to 1972 was a failure. This cannot be established in a definitive way. No single measure reflects water quality, and the amount of pollutants going into streams is not accurately measured, but the belief that water quality has continued to deteriorate in the face of past control efforts underlies the far-reaching efforts of the 1972 law. There has been some success in removing suspended solids, with favorable esthetic effects. The trend of BOD moved up over most of the period since 1956, although recently it apparently has declined a bit. Eutrophication has continued, and the discharge of toxic materials has increased. The EPA estimates that one-third of our stream miles are generally polluted (that is, violate water quality criteria), and only 10 percent of watersheds are characterized as unpolluted. Apparently the problem of nutrients is worsening, partly from nonpoint sources such as fertilizer use.

As noted, the federal strategy has been based on two main elements. One has been financial support to municipalities for waste treatment plant construction of up to 55 percent of cost. Authorized grants to municipalities under the 1966 act were not achieved in practice. Industry benefits from these grants to municipalities if their plants are connected to sewers. Industry also has been permitted rapid tax write-offs for industrial waste treatment facilities.

The second element is direct enforcement against individual dischargers. This power was steadily strengthened so that in theory it applied to nearly all sources. The 1965 act required states to set water quality standards for interstate waters and to propose a program for achieving them, but not all states complied. In addition, the federal government retained considerable enforcement powers.

This strategy has not been a notable success. Much of its failure was attributed to underfinancing of both the grant program and the enforcement apparatus, but it also appears that the basic concept may have been at fault. A subsidy for waste treatment plant construction is not by itself an inducement to build. If only a part of the cost is subsidized, it is still cheaper to forego the plant and discharge the sewage. Subsidy must be linked with enforcement if it is to have effect, but this did not occur. Also, there was no sense of priorities in allocating grants. In practice, funds have gone to those most ready to use them. Allocations by state are according to a formula that takes little account of the seriousness of local problems. Moreover, in many instances where subsidy made funds abundant, works have been over-designed and underutilized, while in other less favored jurisdictions systems are overloaded. Finally, the construction grants do not affect the efficiency with which a plant is operated. Often more attention to this matter would permit a smaller capacity to do the job. The net result of the subsidy program could well be negative, since the sums provided have been modest and, in anticipation of a grant, local authorities may have delayed works they otherwise would have undertaken on their own.

The enforcement program likewise was no flaming success. It relied largely on the enforcement conference that could be called by the EPA or at the request of a state when the pollution was intrastate. The conference advised the EPA Administrator who then could issue recommendations. Subsequently, he could convene a hearing board to produce formal recommendations and eventually seek an injunction. This procedure at the minimum required in excess of a year to complete. Presumably, states could act within the terms of their implementation plans for meeting state water quality standards, but in practice their position was weak. Prior to the 1972 act some fifty-odd conferences were convened. In only a handful of cases did the government go to the hearing stage and in one case to a legal proceeding. Of course, the process may have been more effective than this implies, for firms fearing adverse publicity may have taken actions to avoid it. However, when enforcement is rarely invoked the whole process loses force. With so little chance of penalty, foot-dragging is a rational response for polluters. Enforcement is difficult in any case. The government does not have complete and accurate information on what is discharged and hence does not know where to bring action against polluters. To deal with each source of pollution would require an army of bureaucrats.

In 1970 the government exhumed a provision of the 1899 Refuse Act that prohibits discharge of wastes into navigable waterways without a permit from the Army Corps of Engineers. It started to issue permits, although it was unclear how these related to state water quality standards or state implementation plans. Court tests soon threw this effort into confusion and were one factor that brought about the 1972 amendments.

The 1972 act is a determined and comprehensive effort to improve water quality. It sets up two general goals and offers deadlines for their attainment—first, to achieve water clean enough for swimming or other recreation and safe for fish, shellfish, and other wildlife by mid-1983; second, to end discharge of pollutants into waterways by 1985. It provides for much stronger and quicker-acting enforcement, and the enforcement emphasis is shifted from a general effort to maintain a standard to detailed regulation of discharges from point sources.

The new law extends federal control to all navigable waters. Strict deadlines are laid down. Industry must convert to the best practicable technology (economic factors considered) for controlling discharges by July 1977, and to the best available by July 1983. Comparable deadlines apply to municipalities. New industrial sources must use best available technology as of May 1974. States are still required to submit water quality standards and implementation plans for their streams (now including intrastate waters) subject to EPA approval. If use of best available technology by 1983 does not suffice to achieve standards, the EPA may require states to limit discharges to certain maximum amounts. Toxic pollutants (those harmful to life) are subject to strict effluent limitation or outright prohibition. The new law has incorporated the 1899 permit system, applying it to all point sources. EPA provides guidance and review for the permit system but administration and enforcement is shifted to the states. The permits are to be consistent with effluent limitations and are of limited duration. For the first time, polluters are required to keep records of discharges. The old conference enforcement procedure has been abandoned in favor of streamlined enforcement via administrative order or court injunction. States which are lax in their enforcement endeavors can be superseded by the EPA. Penalties for violations of the law can be severe for repeated violations. Citizens are given the right to take court action against anyone violating standards and can also take EPA to court for failure to carry out its mandate.

The subsidy feature of the 1972 law was a greatly expanded grant program, providing authorizations of $18 billion during the 1973–1975 fiscal year period for construction of treatment plants, with the federal government prepared to pay 75 percent of the cost of new facilities. This aspect of the bill was greeted as a budget buster by the Nixon Administration and was the occasion for a presidential veto that subsequently was overridden. The EPA, convinced that the money cannot be spent efficiently at the indicated pace, attempted to impound some of the funds. Since both Congress and the courts are challenging impoundment, it is difficult to know how much money will in fact be spent. In any case, the cost of treatment plants is only a small part of the total public and private costs that would be required by a serious effort to reach the no-discharge goal.

It remains to be seen whether the new law will prove more effective than its predecessors. The ingredients—enforcement and subsidy—are much the same, although both are to be attempted on a grander scale and with more intensive federal involvement. Even if the act is successful in forcing back the tide of pollution, it may prove a needlessly costly way of doing so. While some features of the law encourage citizen participation and leave a role for states, the overall thrust is toward centralization of control in the federal bureaucracy and toward uniformity between regions. It reflects a desire for a final solution (no discharge) which is unrealistic. What is needed is rather the recognition that water quality is a continuing problem requiring regional responsibility and allowing room for local diversity.

Certainly the more direct enforcement procedures and stiffer penalties give the government a stronger hand, and its right to intervene where states have failed to act avoids any blank spaces on the enforcement map. Retention of the permit system betrays some lack of faith in the stated goal of zero discharge. The intermediate steps of best practicable and best available technology also fall short of zero discharge and are subject to considerable interpretation. An attempt at strong enforcement exercised on behalf of unrealistic goals soon leads to pressures that force either revision of the law or breakdown of enforcement.

The zero-discharge goal ignores the effect on other media if the residuals usually discharged to water are put elsewhere. We cannot end their generation and disposal completely, for some of these are inherent in the industrial process. The solids and dissolved matter removed from waste water accumulate as sludges and brines. They must then be disposed of on land if we are to have no discharge to water, or, in the case of organic sludge, incineration is possible at cost to air quality. Financial cost of sludge and brine disposition also is high and will rise in the process of recapturing more of that formerly committed to streams. Perhaps land disposition is preferable, but this surely will not be so in every case, and the option of using water as a disposal medium should be retained where it has greater capacity than other media.

In addition to its onerous demands for information and personnel, the enforcement strategy also fails to meet the test of economic efficiency. The imposition of uniform effluent standards takes no account of differences between regions or between industries. If control were focused where costs of reducing effluents is least, the attainment of ambient standards should be possible at greatly reduced cost. An effluent tax would greatly facilitate this goal. It affects decisions to produce and generate residuals at every level. The kind of inputs, processes employed, and final products all are affected. To the extent that costs are passed along to consumers, demand for environmentally damaging products also will be limited. Moreover, payment of the tax means that those who can take inexpensive measures to reduce discharges will be motivated to do so to escape the tax, thereby reserving whatever capacity of the stream we want to devote to waste absorption for those for whom control measures would be more costly. From a social standpoint this is a sensible approach and one that would accrue automatically from a tax at the appropriate level, without requiring a great deal of technical information to enforce. Of course this approach is keyed to the maintenance of acceptable ambient standards. It is not useful if we aim at zero discharge nor is it compatible with the imposition of effluent standards deemed "practicable" or "best available."

The subsidy–enforcement strategy biases control measures toward building treatment plants instead of requiring internal measures that may be cheaper or providing incentive to operate treatment plants more effectively. By contrast, the effluent charge influences both the design of processes and the operation of equipment.

Although the present law provides for setting ambient standards, it fails to realize the full opportunity for treating river basins according to systems management techniques. The main emphasis of the law is on regulating effluents and, as I have argued, it does this inefficiently. But the ambient quality of water can also be improved by measures that increase its capacity to absorb wastes. Essentially, these involve flow regulation to ensure sufficient water for dilution, mechanical aeration to increase oxygen content in some circumstances, and timing of discharges to conform with stream capacity. It has been argued that such basinwide schemes would reduce costs of attaining a given standard by as much as one-half. The present strategy pays scant attention to this approach. To be effective it would require a major effort in institution building to establish river basin authorities with sufficient scope, imagination, and resources to actually manage the stream continuously. They would need power to build and operate works as well as to regulate discharges. If effluent charge revenues were designated for use by such authorities, the latter would quickly become a force to be reckoned with. Instead the new law is moving in the direction of greater centralization and is limited pretty much to regulating effluents.

One of the most difficult quality management problems is the preservation of estuaries and coastal waters. Much of past strategy of managing inland water quality was designed to pass pollutants through the sea where they could be forgotten. The result is a concentration of residuals in estuaries and coastal waters, which are most intensively used by man for recreation and as a source of seafood and by the ocean ecosystem as the "nurseries of the sea."

To the extent that point sources are controlled upstream the burden on coastal waters can be reduced. However, management of estuarine waters and bays is a very complex problem. They may receive inflow from several watersheds, each managed for different purposes. Moreover, the strategy of controlling point sources of discharge still allows a great deal of material to enter water, whether from atmospheric washout or leaching through the soil. Agriculture is a major offender as a source of nutrients. Ultimately nutrients come to rest in the sea, which has been a sink for terrestrial residuals over the ages but is one now receiving an enlarged burden concentrated at the margins. Since tidewater is also a favored site for industry, the direct contribution from this source also may be great.

In view of the complexity of the ecosystem and the economic uses involved and the diverse sources of incoming residuals, coastal water quality cannot be managed as precisely as inland waters. Steps have been taken to control ocean dumping, restricting hazardous substances and placing dredged material and other wastes on a permit basis. At the same time the National Oceanic and Atmospheric Administration has been charged with research on the effects of dumping and other man-induced changes. But for the coastal zone the pervasive interrelatedness of environmental problems is apparent in the highest degree. Planning cannot focus on water management alone but must include attention to land use within the coastal zone, and ideally even beyond it, if water quality is to be maintained. The Coastal Zone Management Act makes a start in this direction, but so far it has not been very effective, in part due to lack of funding. Meanwhile, several states are taking the initiative, each reflecting its own situation. Any hope for success in controlling pollution in bays and estuaries must clearly reach for more comprehensive systems that include the interrelationships among receiving media and the kinds of governmental institutions required.

THE WASTELAND INHIBITED

If water discharge is to be forbidden and air emissions sorely restricted, there will be pressure for increasing disposal of residuals on land. This will add to the growing volume of solid wastes already accumulating. For most nutrients and many minerals and pathogens, land disposal is a harmless or even beneficial disposition provided the material is contained at the site. There is a danger that some of these materials may return to watercourses or, if distributed on agricultural land, that some of the heavy metals or toxic chemicals may be taken into the food chain. For the most part, however, the issue is one of space, cost, and public reaction to the esthetics of close-in disposal sites for solid wastes. Land disposal of most industrial and household trash does not pose a major threat to health or ecological integrity, although conservationists will be concerned that we fail to salvage what we might from our solid wastes.

Federal efforts in the solid waste management field have consisted mostly of research and demonstration projects on refuse handling and disposal or on the recovery of materials. Recently these programs have been severely curtailed on the grounds that solid waste management is a local responsibility, and for budgetary reasons. Solid waste management surely is not a federal responsibility, but it may require regional rather than purely local authorities. No one wants the dump, but some sites may have the potential to serve a wider jurisdiction, and this potential should not be lost because of purely local political boundaries. Moreover, economies related to scale in disposing of or salvaging some specialized materials can be expected. Federal policy could be used to stimulate regional approaches. It could also be used to ensure that appropriate liaison between air and water authorities and regional solid waste management groups is maintained. If one control authority proposes measures that throw a burden on the other, an explicit means of resolution must be found. This implies larger-area governmental units with authority that spans at least the environmental field.

While management should not be a federal responsibility, there is still a federal role for research and demonstration projects. The modest scale of many solid waste disposal operations precludes them from undertaking their own research, and of course they have no responsibility for the national interest in materials supply. There is need both for technical research on recycling possibilities and on incentives that reduce the burden or facilitate management. For example, penalties on disposable packaging should be studied and local innovations, such as those in Oregon, should be carefully monitored. The federal government should sponsor a study of those changes that would facilitate recycling, including material separation and collection.

Since land disposal entails environmental damage to the affected land, one could also justify incentives to increase materials recovery. This would reduce the area required and therefore the damage incurred. Yet another possibility is to diminish damage to the land by making more positive use of filled sites, converting the site to productive use (for example, recreation) upon completion of the fill.

Experts in the field of solid waste management have not been optimistic about reducing the cost of materials recovery from household refuse so as to allow recycled materials to compete with virgin supply. As prices for virgin materials rise to reflect their true costs, this equation may change. Also, if the householder could be induced to assist by separating metals, glass, and natural fibers, the cost of recycling could be reduced and some of the disposal costs would be saved. For some products, design changes would facilitate materials segregation. There is also the possibility of using organic refuse as a heat source to fire boilers, thereby gaining some value and reducing bulk for disposal. Incentives for recycling need not aim to restrict consumption or the output of virgin materials but should make processing and recycling of secondary materials more attractive, thereby reducing environmental damage from the excessive load that their disposal presently imposes.

Industrial wastes have more potential for recycling. Many forms of scrap already are used at the plant or have well-developed markets. In other cases where a homogeneous residual must be disposed of, industry has been able to find uses for it as a construction material and the like.

Industrial brines and sludges and sewage sludge from municipal treatment plants pose difficult problems. In the past these often were committed to watercourses and ended up in the sea. This no longer will be permissible. The nutrients in sludge can be accommodated on land if sufficient space is available. Since sludge often contains heavy metals and toxic chemicals as well as nutrients, it is still somewhat uncertain what the consequences of land disposal will be. Likewise, industrial chemical wastes and brines are dubious candidates for land disposal since it is difficult to keep the material out of surface waters or underground aquifers. Since the material is deposited in the first instance on private property rather than common property and may reach the latter only through indirect routes, a system of charges would be hard to implement. This appears to be a case where regulation affecting the conditions of disposal will be required. In the long run, more attention must be paid to means of rendering these materials innocuous before disposal. Even if they remain confined to the site on private land, the trusteeship principle (see Chapter 2) in regard to land precludes complete freedom if disposal results in irreparable damage.

The problems of land disposal of residuals illustrate the many trade-offs available to society. The burden on the land is increased by restrictions on the use of air and water. Incineration of sludge and paper or other organics could greatly reduce volume for land disposal. Also, mineral salts damaging to land traditionally have been flushed to the sea. Land may be the preferred disposal medium in many cases because of its generous availability and lesser sensitivity to damage and less intimate connection with human health. However, if we are to be sensitive to esthetics, the cost often is high. The burden on land can be reduced by going further back into the consumption and production process to restrain the generation of residuals or to put them to reuse, but it should be recognized that doing so often entails sacrifice of current income.

OTHER RISKS AND RESPONSES

The approach to other environmental burdens that do not fit neatly into the air–water–land classification is necessarily varied. In some cases a strict regulatory policy aimed at keeping toxic materials out of the environment is the only apparently feasible path. If the economic advantage of generating such materials seems to merit continuation, then a part of the cost is their containment. But what if they are eternal? An obvious case is radioactive materials. Because they give us an option on energy supply, American society has acquiesced in their continued production, but we demand essentially a no-discharge policy for their control. There is still dispute about whether the likelihood of accidental discharge is low enough to justify this risk and the issues involved in maintaining permanent social control over high-level radioactive wastes have not been seriously faced.

The laissez-faire policy with respect to pesticides has been abandoned, and we now require that they be registered, that applicators be certified, and that tolerances for pesticide residues on food be established. This has strengthened the government's hand in regulating the use as well as the manufacture and sale of pesticides. Many of the hazards from pesticides derive from misuse of materials that can be beneficial under proper handling. The regulation of application is a sensible response; it allows choice between the benefits and only the necessary consequences of pesticide use. A still broader approach would involve questioning the need for chemical pesticides and devising alternatives to them. In some cases the chemicals become counterproductive over time and their continued use makes no economic sense, or the losses they prevent would be a small price to pay for the environmental benefits of abstention. However, agricultural and forest production and prices are of universal concern, and no immediate and total substitutes for pesticides are available. The best course is to lay out a research program aimed at perfecting biological and cultural controls that will allow reduced use of chemicals while exercising more control in the licensing, testing, and application of those that are essential.

Sometimes simply greater awareness of problems is a great help. Take noise as an example. It is episodic and derives from diverse sources. An "effluent" charge would make little sense. Under the law, emissions standards are now applied to aircraft and to certain products sold in interstate commerce. Noise inflicted on others has simply not heretofore been a design consideration for most products and most environments. The present law increases awareness and stimulates new thinking. As it permeates into the design and positioning of buildings and transportation facilities and into product design, the results should begin to go beyond the fruits of regulation. Often this can be accomplished at only trivial cost. This is a case where attention to urban form and transportation needs could do a great deal to alleviate an environmental insult.

Much of this chapter has been devoted to discussion of comparatively short-term means of coping with the residuals of an industrial society. Many fear that continued economic growth will overwhelm possible defensive measures to protect the environment. This may prove to be the case at some point, but by taking the proper steps the capacity of the environment to accommodate human activity without degradation can be greatly extended. Efforts to internalize more of the costs of pollution by imposing appropriate charges and regulations and to increase environmental capacity via systems management techniques are steps in the right direction whatever the ultimate environmental limits may be.

7
RESOURCES
AND INTERNATIONAL
RESPONSIBILITY

In the long view it is possible to conceive of a "world without borders" in which the riches of the earth would be equally shared among peoples. That would require enormous institutional change. The decline of national sovereignty would carry a threat to diversity and would require still undefined forms of organization that might be of unmanageable scale. If the change were to be peaceful, it would require a huge and sustainable increase in output so the rich could acquiesce to the new arrangement without degradation of their standard. It also would demand equalization of birthrates among groups at a modest figure so that income aspirations could be met. The obstacles to attainment of such a world are immense. Moreover, the vision of a pool of resources to be shared is a constricting one. The pool appears too small to support the required growth. What happens when it runs out?

This view must be transcended. If technology is seen as the world's basic resource and its development and transfer as the basic problem, then the idea of world community is more easily restored. Much of this book has been concerned with the steps that Americans might take to assure an income base under which changes toward a world community would be feasible. The focus has been on developing and transferring sustainable income-generating capacity to future generations, but it can be extended to include transfer between nations. The transfer between generations is more acceptable to most of us than a transfer between nations because our sense of community with our progeny and identity with the nation is stronger than with our contemporaries elsewhere. It is technically harder to transfer income-generating capacity among nations. Transfers of wealth or of current income, while feasible, are apt to be dissipated if not accompanied by institutional development and population controls. Therefore, the establishment of a sustainable long-term basis for occupancy seems the most urgent task, even though this arouses skepticism among the currently disadvantaged. If the U.S. draft on world resources and environment is used to develop a pollution-free technology that expands the resource base, it can be justified both to future generations and to other nations.

Even if we seek to limit the U.S. call upon the world's natural resources and environmental capacity, many problems nonetheless extend beyond national boundaries. Policy must be mindful of the international dimension, trying not to exacerbate current difficulties while preparing for a different long-term relationship.

SECURING FOREIGN SUPPLIES

As a continental power well endowed with resources, the United States has not heretofore been greatly concerned with the international aspects of the resource problem. It produced a large share of its resource needs and was confident that it could trade for the rest.

Lately a string of accusations that the United States preempts world resources, depletes those needed for future development in the less-developed countries (LDCs), pays "unfair" prices for the raw products it imports, and "exports pollution" has become a familiar litany. In defense it could be argued that resource commodities have not been in short supply on a world basis, so as yet no one has been deprived, that further development of the LDCs may not require the same kind of resources that we use now, and that sellers are anxious to sell. In any case, sellers can adopt measures to raise prices and defend their own environment, subject always to the constraint of buyer substitution among sources and materials. Nonetheless, this country is part of an international system, and it is incumbent on us to avoid abrupt changes that force sudden adjustments upon others. As reliable trading partners we must take the interests of others into account.

From a purely national standpoint we have stressed the desirability of limiting dependence on foreign sources. This rests on the security argument, with security construed more broadly than in purely military terms. Vulnerability to supply interruption depends on the sources of the material in question (whether nearby, from a friendly country, and how stable politically), and on how vital the material is to the daily operation of the economy. Also, the United States may be dependent but not highly vulnerable if a long-term supply of a material can easily be stored and if we are willing to maintain stocks. Continuing review of the supply situation on a product-by-product basis is necessary to ensure that the question of the relative importance of the material, security of source, and level of stocks yield a satisfactory position.

The question of how much security is necessary must also be posed. Complete longer-term supply independence could be very expensive and is a doubtful goal. One strategy might be the maintenance of sufficient domestic production capacity whenever possible to ensure essential military needs, while taking advantage of lower-cost foreign sources for most commercial purposes. However, where the material is of such urgent and pervasive importance to the entire economy as energy or basic food supply, and demand is not easily postponed, the case is strong for a higher degree of self-sufficiency. This is the more compelling when a considerable degree of self-sufficiency can be had at very little extra cost, as is true for the United States in energy and food.

Apart from military security and essential social needs, commercial dependence carries such other hazards as unpredictable supply, consequent abrupt price movements, and balance-of-payments problems. The rationale for trade in resources is access to less expensive materials on average—otherwise we would rely on domestic supplies or substitutes. Supply unpredictability and price instability often can be countered unilaterally by adequate stockpiling and on a multilateral basis by commodity agreements or through bilateral understandings. Stockpiling is a rational response for many short-term hazards.

In a world of ample supply the United States heretofore has preferred minimal interference with international markets and has relied on its own commercial strength to ensure continued supply. A future world is likely to see foreign supply tied more closely to specific investment arrangements on a bilateral basis. However much violence this does to the open trading ideal, the United States will have to learn to play this game if, as seems likely, it becomes the prevailing pattern. It will likely mean more direct government participation in securing agreements and more support for private firms once the agreements are in force. Such arrangements depart from the normal operation of markets. The likelihood is that we will end up paying a higher average cost for materials in return for somewhat greater assurance of supply.

From the standpoint of our income objective we have an interest in securing materials at the lowest cost, and considerations of international competition require that U.S. costs not be out of line with what other countries pay. The low-cost objective conflicts with the aim of LDCs to maximize their return on resource commodities as an aid to development. In turn, the United States has sympathized with and supported their development and has financed their resource industries for mutual benefit. In a world of ample material supply, competition served to restrain the price of materials.

Many efforts have been made to "stabilize" commodity prices, generally with very modest success. Two fundamental changes give the LDCs more promise now. Rising world demand associated with the affluence of Europe and Japan may strengthen longer-term prices of many minerals (especially the less plentiful metals) and farm products. Also, the ripening sovereignty of once-dependent countries gives them enhanced bargaining power. This is expressed both in the concession arrangements they make with foreign operators for exploitation of their resources, and in the cohesion of producer countries in controlling supply to their benefit on price. The success of the oil cartel in the face of generous world reserves is evidence of the latter. Meanwhile all types of concession and contract arrangements shift in favor of the LDCs.

On the side of price restraint are the possibilities for substitution of domestic supplies and synthetics. In many instances domestic sources could be substituted with only moderate increases in cost (for example, aluminum and energy). These possibilities set limits to the prices LDCs may expect, whether through the operation of free markets or through bargaining. They also set limits to the premium that is necessary to ensure supply; anything beyond that should be viewed as aid.

Often it is suggested that sensitivity to the needs of LDC suppliers of resource commodities would require us to avoid measures that would inhibit their sales to us. Certainly an abrupt halt in purchases would have a devastating effect on the economies and development plans of many developing countries. Longer term, these same countries often harbor ambivalent views about accelerated exhaustion of their depletable resources via exports. A policy to limit the increase in foreign dependence could be mindful of both of these currents, not moving so quickly as to create disturbance and yet not insisting on continued supply in the face of obvious resentment. In any case, no abrupt shift is in prospect. In fact, the trend is all in the direction of growing dependence, and a gradual shift away from this, initiated now, would allow continued growth in LDC resource exports to us, even while building some hedges against extreme dependence.

For depletable resources there is an inherent conflict between present and future production. A nation that attempts to reduce dependence via increased domestic production diminishes its future resources. An eye to the future would suggest conservation, slowing the rate of use, and perhaps would welcome foreign supplies as conserving domestic resources. Owners of resources, whether individuals or nations, may feel that their best interests lie in realizing the potential gains from the resource as quickly as possible. Refusal to exploit a resource out of conservationist objectives risks the possibility that it will be made obsolete by subsequent technical developments. In the face of these uncertainties, a reasonable course is to develop and use the resource efficiently while at the same time perfecting the technology needed to produce substitute materials.

THE UNITED STATES AS AN EXPORTER

The United States is an exporter of resource commodities as well as an importer. It has recently been clearly demonstrated how, under certain conditions of world demand and with altered currency exchange rates, domestic production can be sucked into foreign markets, with severe consequences for domestic availability and price. The most spectacular examples were grains and timber, where foreign bidding produced a sharp impact on the domestic price structure. This unhappy result must be balanced against our own need to earn foreign exchange and the fact that the production of these commodities is one area where we hold a competitive advantage. Moreover, buyers often are other developed countries with whom good relations are extremely important and who are very anxious to buy. To them the problem of reliable supply is similar to that faced by the United States with regard to foreign energy and mineral supplies.

Export quotas are a device for insulating the domestic market from the world price level. If imposed abruptly so as to interrupt usual trade, they can cause great consternation among regular customers. However, domestic social goals in housing and nutrition can be threatened by large increases in the price of food and timber, and it becomes politically unacceptable to allow world demand full play in the domestic availability of home-produced goods of this sort.

Recent price relationships may prove transitory and a surplus could recur, but strong demand from other developed countries now in the process of upgrading their diets makes this questionable. Since this country cannot feed the world, a decision must be made as to whether we want to allow world prices to prevail in domestic markets or to retain domestic prices more closely related to domestic production costs. A purely economic answer would allow the domestic price increase, perhaps using subsidies or income supplements to meet other social goals. Such a broad segment of the population would be adversely affected by this approach that it does not appear politically feasible. The public will remember that in the past, when the problem was oversupply, domestic price was maintained above the world level to protect producers. If strong foreign demand continues, one possible means of restraining domestic price would be to offer a guaranteed level of exports to regular customers, with further supplies to be auctioned off when available.

In addition to the price and social consequences already mentioned, an open-ended commitment to supply farm and forest products to the world market might have major domestic environmental consequences over the longer term. Since world population and income growth is in an explosive phase, foreign demand for the products of our land could dictate land use in the United States. The pressure to harvest marginal lands and to employ added agricultural chemicals would have adverse effects on the quality of the rural environment. In a world where Americans have no control and very limited influence over developments elsewhere, we might properly be reluctant to surrender control over domestic land use policy in the name of free trade or some larger concept of world resource equity.

This discussion completely ignores the humanitarian aspect of possible food shortages on a world scale affecting the LDCs. In the past this country has been able to assist them through donations of surplus. If strong world demand eliminates surplus, then at any given level of production we shall face the dilemma of foregoing commercial sales to customers in developed countries who could outbid the LDCs or of reducing our own consumption if we wish to help. Quite possibly we may wish to share responsibility for dealing with this problem with the international community should matters come to such pass.

ENVIRONMENT IN THE INTERNATIONAL SETTING

If the environmental dimension is added to international materials supply problems, still more complications arise.[1] Mining and refining of

[1] This section has drawn heavily from two pieces done by RFF colleagues: Clifford S. Russell and Hans H. Landsberg, "International Environmental Prob-

minerals, wherever done, commonly results in environmental damage. If resources are plentiful and dispersed, there is the option either to exploit the deposit or leave it undeveloped; in the latter case, choice regions or fragile areas could be spared damage. More often there are strong pressures to develop, including, of course, the commercial interests of the deposit owner. There also are national and consumer interests in materials supply and cost as well that favor development. Mining can only be done at the site of the deposit. In practice some phases of refining often are restricted to the site also.

Imposition of environmental controls on domestic resource exploitation raises domestic costs and favors foreign sources, assuming they do not impose like controls. Increased foreign dependence and balance-of-payments costs are the consequence. Assuming the domestic industry was competitive, we may pay more for the foreign supply. There also will be adjustments in the domestic employment structure that may be painful because they are concentrated in small communities without a diversified employment base.

The shift to foreign sources is often criticized as "exporting pollution." From a global standpoint this may be desirable if the new producing country is not subject to the same degree of environmental pressure. Since such shifts most often are to the LDCs with less industrial development, ordinarily they could more easily accommodate the expanded industry. This is not always the case, for some urban centers in the LDCs are among the most polluted. Nevertheless, they do have the option of refusal if they find that the increased environmental burden outweighs the economic benefits of expansion.

If the host is truly sovereign, concern about exporting pollution may be unwarranted. The country affected can defend itself by internalizing pollution control costs or, if desired, by imposing terms that make production unattractive, assuming that it has the scientific and administrative capacity to do so. The real issue, then, is the domestic dislocations, balance-of-payments effects, and increased dependence that enviornmental controls in the United States may generate.

No generalized policy can respond to these concerns. So far there is little convincing evidence of extensive damage to domestic resource industries. The earlier suggestion that there should be greater latitude in local ambient conditions and that national emissions standards are unjustified in many cases is apropos here. It would allow more domes-

lems—A Taxonomy," *Science*, vol. 172 no. 3990 (June 1971), pp. 1307–1314; and Ralph C. d'Arge and Allen V. Kneese, "Environmental Quality and International Trade," *International Organization*, vol. 26, no. 2 (Spring 1972), pp. 419–465.

tic production while still minimizing environmental damage, particularly damage to health.

Balance-of-payments considerations and industrial adjustment problems arising from environmental controls are not wholly dissimilar to those created by other import-liberalizing measures; they can be countered by industrial shifts in line with the principle of comparative advantage and by adjustment assistance specific to the situation. However, unlike tariff reductions that stimulate trade, environmental controls favoring imports bring no compensating concessions from trading partners. Also, the issue of increased dependence must still be weighed in terms of its gravity and the measures taken to counteract vulnerability.

Leaving the issue of dependence to focus on the implications of environmental controls for trade, whether in resource commodities or other goods, some rather simple principles appear to govern. In some cases environmental damage occurs in the course of production, while other damage is associated with consumption. Each country is entitled to defend itself against such damage as affects it.

Let us look first at the consumption side. If the United States imposes requirements on automobile performance, they will apply both to foreign imports and domestic cars. By the same token, export models need only meet the standards of the country of destination. A tax imposed equally on domestic and imported consumption will discourage consumption of a product or force it to pay for damage caused. The temptation to use controls in an arbitrary or discriminatory manner to disqualify imports must be resisted.

Where the damage is associated with production, ordinarily it affects the producing country, and control measures should be taken in conformity with each country's own standards. If the United States imposes stringent controls that raise domestic costs and a competitor does not impose such controls, the cry of unfair competition will be raised. However, this situation does not differ greatly from many other competitive inequalities. Competition is always unequal to the extent that differential labor costs, subsidies, and the like give some the advantage. Unless there are security reasons for protecting domestic production, environmental standards can be set and the market will determine where production occurs. At the same time, some equalization of trading advantage could be encouraged, at least among developed countries. It would help if each country required internalization of costs and refrained from subsidy. There might still be differences arising from different national environmental standards, although in the Organization for Economic Co-operation and Development

(OECD) countries efforts at "harmonization" of standards also are being made.

In general, environmental controls in developed countries should be to the advantage of LDC producers so long as their unused assimilative capacity is greater or they do not match developed country standards. Contrary influences arise if environmental controls in developed countries force up the price of their exports to LDCs or restrain imports from them. It would be hard to justify any requirement that LDC goods be produced under equally stringent conditions so long as the product itself is not contaminated. If the product carries a hazard (for example, pesticide residues on food products), then consuming country standards should apply to imports. However, if the production process imposes a burden on global systems, then other countries have a stake in the conditions of production.

Adherence to the foregoing principles would permit maximum flow of trade and be entirely consistent with national sovereignty for most environmental matters. Under the doctrine of comparative advantage this also would be to the benefit of income in all countries.

Not all international environmental problems can be subsumed under trade realtions, however. Pollution originating in one country may cause environmental damage in another. Frequent examples are the pollution of the lower Rhine or the acid rain of Scandinavia, both originating in other countries. But for the existence of national borders, these problems are not different from those contained within a single country. The logical course would be to apply the polluter-pays principle and either compel him to invest in abatement or to compensate the damaged party. The 1972 UN conference in Stockholm adopted this principle and urged its extension to international law.

In practice it will be very difficult to apply the principle across borders. Decisions that could be made politically within a country are far harder to arrive at through international legal proceedings. The latter require the establishment of a cause-and-effect relationship, an assessment of damage, and a means of decision and enforcement. So far no effective institutions exist to accomplish this.

Moving from the upstream–downstream type of problem to truly global problems such as global climate modification, ocean pollution, and the spread of long-lived toxic substances, the problem is even less manageable. In these cases it is still harder to trace causes and effects so as to know where to assess charges or pay compensation. In many cases the damage is still hypothetical and there are national differences in willingness to incur risk. Some arrangement might be possible whereby the risk-averse compensate those who are less concerned to induce them to refrain from activities threatening global damage. Except for ocean pollution, there do not appear to be urgent questions of this sort requiring early attention. A world ocean regime dealing with resources as well as pollution would provide an excellent start toward institutions to manage other threats as they arise. International scientific agencies are moving to provide baseline data and monitoring to ensure early warning on other global threats.

Yet another class of international environmental problem involves actions by one country within its own territory that nonetheless deprive others of part of the world's geological, biological, or cultural heritage. Excess harvesting of migratory birds or animals, extinction of rare or exotic life forms, obliteration of scenic wonders, and so forth are often of interest to peoples outside the borders of the host country. The best posture for Americans in regard to this kind of problem should be, first, to act responsibly ourselves and, second, to encourage others to do so by means of education, technical help, and perhaps financial assistance.

At the Stockholm conference LDCs strongly argued for two principles termed *compensation* and *additionality*. Compensation was intended to reimburse the LDCs for declines in their export earnings as a consequence of environmental restrictions adopted by developed countries. It is virtually impossible to imagine how this principle could be applied. Amid all of the currents affecting international trade, it would be difficult indeed to say what portion of a given change in demand from a particular source was owed to the adoption of environmental restrictions elsewhere. Moreover, it is hard to understand the equity of the principle. Each country is entitled to defend its own environment, and if consumption of a given imported commodity is antienvironmental, why should it be exempted simply because it is produced in an LDC?

Environmental consciousness on the part of developed countries has been extended to foreign aid programs. International financial institutions and national aid organizations are properly requiring that the environmental consequences of aid projects be considered. However, it is quite another matter to impose the standards of developed countries on such projects where the consequences are limited to the recipient country. The additionality principle argued that if advanced countries required expensive environmental features on aid-financed investments, the donor should add the cost of these features to the amount of aid. Both additionality and compensation are attempts to ensure that the environmental concern of developed countries shall not retard LDC earnings or investments. While this attitude of the

LDCs is understandable, it is hard to see how either of these principles could be imposed on unwilling developed countries. The LDCs may justifiably oppose imposition of unwanted environmental restrictions, but their aid objectives would be better served directly rather than through complicated compensation or additionality schemes.

The United States has resisted these proposals, and meanwhile finds itself in the dubious position of applying the environmental impact statement requirement of the National Environmental Protection Act (NEPA) to foreign aid projects. If the statement is used as intended (to affect seriously the decision process), then on environmental grounds, we may be denying projects desired by the countries concerned. The impact statement would be useful in providing LDCs with additional information, in assisting design so as to minimize damage where this is possible at minor cost, and in protecting the U.S. interest in avoiding international or global damage. But where the damage is confined to the recipient country, substitution of an alien judgment for theirs would be an unfortunate result of the application of NEPA.

In view of the conflicts of sovereignty, diverse national circumstances and values, and lack of international institutions to manage transnational environmental problems, the United States can stress two approaches. The first is to do all in our power to avert and alleviate international environmental problems on a unilateral basis. This may entail use of our trading and financial strength to defend international standards while displaying a willingness to join in cooperative agreements. A second approach is through example, research, information, and persuasion. In a world where this country has some of the earliest and most extensive experience in managing environmental problems, we should not underestimate the value of this experience to others. We can take the lead in financing and supporting the UN environmental agency to ensure that global monitoring is pursued, that information is diffused, and that feasible agreements are reached. An elevated environmental consciousness on a world basis is essential to the solution of global problems so long as national sovereignty prevails.

8
POLICY CHOICES AND THEIR IMPLEMENTATION— A SUMMARY

Recurrent themes of this study have been (1) the need for a long view of the resource and environmental problem so the constraints and the fundamental choices are revealed well in advance, (2) the value of an interim strategy that meanwhile retains options, and (3) an awareness of diverse goals and of the potential of broader planning for minimizing goal conflict and increasing policy coherence. These themes, which comprise a framework for policy, are reviewed briefly in this section. Up to this point little attention has been given to the governmental policy decision process itself, to the appropriate level for decision, and to the place of various policy instruments—including the role of the market, in implementing policy. Those matters will be dealt with in subsequent sections. A final section serves as a general review and summarizes the main policy conclusions reached by the author.

BASIC THEMES

The discussion has been set in the context of a long view. A truly long view implies the recognition of imperatives that compel fundamental choices. The problem of depletion is the most fundamental imperative or limit; as we saw in Chapter 1, it compels a choice between paths one and two—between a smaller system based on current flows and a more ambitious one based on constraint-releasing technology. Mankind cannot have it both ways. It is necessary to find an escape from depletion or change utterly our economy, technology, and population.

But once this choice is made, there are other implementing imperatives that come into play. For example, opting for the high-technology path requires timely investment to perfect the technology implied by that mode. Otherwise the attempt to follow that path leads to disaster through premature resource exhaustion. Of course the rate of depletion can also be altered, thereby determining the point of decision between the two paths.

In other cases the choices are not so constrained; for example, even with path two, we can choose how much of the natural system we wish to preserve. There are reasons for preserving a major part of it, even if it is not essential for production. If it is to be preserved, then space must be allowed for natural processes. We then face the imperative of limiting population and areal spread, and since there are many ways to accomplish this, again the range of choice is wide. We can trade off between population and income, can opt for different levels of environmental quality, and by shifts in tastes, consumption patterns, technology, and land use could accommodate far more people while still preserving the natural system.

Mankind is not accustomed to thinking in truly long-range terms, and neither governments nor private institutions are organized to accomplish it. Indeed the individual psychology is not well adapted to it, since many plan hardly at all, and even the most future-oriented attempt little more than planning for a single life span. Market signals, subject as they are to discounting, do not have the required reach. Therefore, if men are to think and act collectively in a long-term fashion consistent with permanent occupancy, the basic incentive will not come from pursuit of any individual interest but rather from a sense of continuity in a larger scheme of things. Individual and social conduct will need to be governed by this sense of what is right and necessary—in brief, an ethic which reflects the long-term requirements of the race. This is something that primitive people living in stable harmony with the natural system were able to achieve, but in the present period of rapid transition it has been lost. Reconstruction of a set of values responsive to long-term social needs will be one of the imperatives of technological man in the future. Policy can only be a reflection of these values whose development and elucidation will occur largely outside of government.

Any view of the future will always be imperfect and tentative and the reconstruction of values is not quickly accomplished. How can Americans be sure that our actions over coming decades are reasonably consistent with long-term occupancy? The attempt to elaborate an interim strategy in Chapter 1 recognized the difficulty of establishing principles of conduct prior to fundamental choices about future mode. The intent was to preserve options while considering the choice. The set of policy biases outlined there stresses preservation of the natural system and restriction of population growth, both of which are consistent with either path. At the same time these policies would have us employ our depletable resources so as to advance us along path two rather than simply to use them for consumption. It could be argued that the bias toward preservation is pointless, since my inclination plainly is toward path two which is less dependent on the natural system. However, even in that mode it seems wise to retain the natural system, not as the basic source of human sustenance, but rather as a spiritual anchor.

The interim policy biases also are responsive to the principal social objectives at present recognized in the United States. These objectives are discussed in more detail in the section entitled "A Summary of Policy Directions."

While there is inherent conflict between some of the widely accepted social goals of our society, a satisfactory level of attainment of these goals should be possible for decades without serious clash; indeed, much of the seemingly inevitable clash may be averted if technical progress is sufficient.

Policy coherence can never be complete in the face of conflicting goals, but broader governmental planning to encompass a wider range of objectives could minimize the conflict. Principal clashes at present are between the income objective and environmental quality and between both of these and security. Lesser conflicts center on the clash between conservation and preservation objectives and those of income and security. Not all of these conflicts need be so acute. Indeed, now is the time to invest in restoring quality. Even though this will have a partially adverse effect on growth, if our technology is properly adapted, the adverse effect on growth will not be great on a continuing basis. If, however, our quality problems are attacked without concern for the effect on income—particularly, on a crash basis and in piecemeal fashion—the clash will be severe. Thus, the speed and manner of action is quite as important as the determination to act.

PUBLIC CHOICE—SCOPE, UNITS, AND PROCESSES

Scope of Governmental Activity

I have argued that some decisions will be forced upon man and that if the race is to survive man must make the choices that permit survival. One of the most difficult problems is to achieve sufficient consensus on long-term requirements and goals so as to permit short-term political decisions that do not, out of expediency, conflict with long-term requirements. My argument was that a cast of mind conducive to making the survival choice is best embedded in the basic values of the society; such matters need not be always open for fresh decision. But the implementing decisions are always open and comprise the substance of policy. Also, the weighting among goals is a matter on which tastes may vary and change. In brief, how can the political system be made to operate effectively to generate efficient alternatives and to accurately reflect public desires, and how can private individuals and enterprises be encouraged to play their appropriate role in promoting social objectives?

An effective political system must agree on the issues that are to fall within the range of governmental decision, the level at which the decision is to be made, and means of framing the decision so the public can express its preferences through the political process. At the substantive level, decisions are required on the pace and degree to which objectives are to be pursued, how the income distribution and other aspects of equity are to be affected by policy measures, and what means will be used to achieve objectives, recognizing that these affect both income distribution and efficiency.

Since governmental decisions on resource and environmental matters will reflect the prevailing social ethic, much private conduct will conform to this ethic as well, thereby reducing the necessary role of government. Plainly a decision so far-reaching as whether to proceed by path one or two will not be the result of a single decision taken at some point but rather of a social consensus reflected in numerous subsidiary government decisions.

Some policy directions, such as the intended level of income, the rate of resource consumption, and the degree of supply independence, are matters for governmental consideration at the national level, wherever and however they are implemented. When it comes to the actual provision of resource commodities, however, this historically has been left to private markets. The role of the government has consisted of the protection of the national market (agriculture, energy, some minerals), making the public domain available for exploitation (land sales, homesteading, mining law), and the provision of infrastructure and research (railroad land grants, other assistance to transportation, research on agriculture and minerals). In a world of plentiful resources subject to exploitation the private market was effective in making resources available, but it did not operate to protect the environment. Since common property resources clearly are public goods whose quality is of interest to all, the need for a public regime governing them is plain.

The market promises to be a less effective provisioner of resources in a more constrained world where longer-range and larger-scale decisions are required to ensure supply and environmental quality. Social choices about rates of use and about research directions and budgets will become more vital in the future for a range of supply matters heretofore left to private markets. Thus, both in setting environmental standards or in providing for the future level of supply, public decisions will play a more important role. It is a public responsibility to discern the future constraints affecting both resource supply and environmental management and to set policies that take account of these imperatives. This goes far beyond criteria for the shorter-term provision of public goods (a subject that occupies so much of social choice theory) to the question of social strategy.

Established theory has argued that with a given income distribution and with other assumptions about competition, individual choice working through markets gives the best expression of social welfare because it allows maximum diversity and encourages efficiency. The theory for providing public goods represents an effort to approximate a market result even in the absence of actual markets. But for the kind of long-term strategy considered here, private action (or its surrogates) with its shorter time horizon and objective of current maximization cannot be expected to act in a way consistent with either mode of occupancy. Private choices that may be feasible short term can be disastrous in their consequences for the long term. If long-term policies are clear, however, the market can be used as an instrument of policy, even though it does not substitute for long-term social choice.

The market is best at allocating limited resources and in encouraging efficiency and innovation within its terms of reference. For example, in the actual production of minerals there is no reason to suppose that a government enterprise would do better. The private firm is apt to be more nimble, and competing firms will undertake varying innovations. Private exploitation raises questions of equity, but proper leasing and tax policies can deal with many of these questions.

If I am right in thinking that resource supply in the future will be less closely attuned to unfettered demand and more affected by government policy with regard to the level of domestic supply, more dependent on government or government-industry cooperative research, more restricted with respect to environmental regulations, and demand itself subject to government growth and materials policies, with recycling promoted by subsidy or regulation, then the role of private markets will be considerably curtailed. Nevertheless, competition between firms will still be possible and competition between materials likewise. Profit-making firms will have the added burden of demonstrating that their operations are consistent with social standards for the environment and conservation but will have wide operating freedom to the extent that they control residuals and make use of common materials. In brief, a substantial role for the market in resource supply will remain, within the context of national growth and materials policies and environmental standards.

Since the receiving media for society's residuals have escaped private ownership, the market has played little role in abating pollution. Firms, individuals, and local governments alike have made use of these media without any payment. They have lacked incentive to minimize their discharges. In consequence, the task of controlling pollution has been almost exclusively the province of regulation, and, as we have seen, the results have been meager. Economists have argued cogently enough for the value of internalizing the environmental costs of production or use. Regulation can be used as a means of internalizing costs but it is clumsy, often of doubtful effectiveness, and does not make use of the potential efficiencies that a management with more latitude could devise.

A charge for the use of the environment permits such economies to be realized and will serve to allocate the use of environmental capacity to those to whom it is most valuable—that is, those to whom the cost of reducing residual discharge is greatest. A system of environmental charges provides incentive to economize on use. When used with government-established ambient standards, the charge can be scaled to preserve the socially desired standard. Emissions standards and regulations to enforce them are inconsistent with the effluent charge approach. So far not much use has been made of the effluent charge. But an instrument of such promise deserves a try in those situations where it is suitable. Ironically, at a time when the role of the market may be constricted in the field of material supply, it may be expanding into the hitherto unoccupied terrain of pollution abatement.

Appropriate Decision-Making Units

The foregoing discussion of the scope of governmental activity in the resource and environmental area anticipates some of the things to be said about where decisions are to be made. One aim of jurisdiction is to ensure that those who are affected by the decision make it. Grander questions of supply strategy and the division between public and private actions are matters to be decided nationally. It is the environmental quality issues, especially those involving land use, that present a more uncertain basis for locating decisions.

Many issues of land use are a fit subject for federal policy because they involve resource supply. In other cases the national government assumes the role of decision maker because of extensive federal land holdings. However, public land management practices also are matters of vital local interest in many communities, and there is no inherent reason why federal policies should override these local interests. With regard to wilderness preservation, a basic national system seems to be the only socially reliable means of assuring this nonlocal objective. Other aspects of land use traditionally have been local responsibilities.

The government now imposes national environmental standards that in turn constrain local land use practices. It has been argued here that it is a dubious matter for the national government to enforce national ambient standards. If the standard is based on protection of health, one could argue that a national minimum should be applicable everywhere. But even health standards involve arbitrary decisions on the amount of exposure permitted or risk to be sustained; in other areas of public health local discretion is allowed, and for many sorts of health exposures individual discretion. Of course if the hazard extends beyond the area of local jurisdiction, the case for national health standards is stronger. Where environmental measures relate to amenity considerations restricted in areal extent, there is less justification for mandatory national standards. Why shouldn't those immediately affected make the decision? Curiously, there is more justification for external intervention in land use planning, traditionally a local matter, because it involves permanent commitment of a limited resource and therefore is of concern to all citizens and to the national government as trustee for future generations.

When a problem, though local, is nonetheless general across the country, it may be more efficient to attack it through a national regulation. Auto emissions controls at the manufacturer level are a case in point. But management of a watershed or airshed is best handled at the basin or airshed level. Moreover, these physical units do not conform with existing political units nor do they coincide with each other. A management organization established to conform with the scope of the problem has no legislative body of equivalent jurisdiction to give it guidance. Intergovernmental bodies are usually very clumsy instruments in this regard.

We could devise governmental units that are more flexible and in better conformance with the scope of the problem they must deal with. An ingenious suggestion offered by Kneese and Haefele proposes a building block system of representation, with a general purpose representative from each district serving as its delegate to other special purpose authorities (for example, air, water, land management). Such authorities would have tax powers and be in a position to provide service to the district. With revenue authority and benefits both conforming to the scope of the problem, and with frequent elections to keep the representatives in close contact with the current wishes of their constituents, the legislative group would be competent to give policy direction to a regional management authority. Moreover, voting participation might improve if the districts were small enough and elections frequent, thereby drawing participatory democracy within the institutional system.[1]

The Decision-Making Process

If the questions of scope and jurisdiction are settled satisfactorily, then the problem becomes one of a choice of mechanism to arrive at decisions where (1) actions are often interrelated and come as a package with multiple purposes and joint costs, (2) some results unwanted by many must accompany any action, and (3) there are great variations in intensity of feeling about any given result. The presumption of a democratic system is that the best result is achieved in a rough way through representative government.

In actual fact, decisions often are not made by those affected, and the

[1] Edwin T. Haefele and Allen V. Kneese, "Residuals Management, Metropolitan Governance, and the Optimal Jurisdiction," in Haefele, *Representative Government and Environmental Management* (Baltimore: Johns Hopkins University Press, 1973), pp. 89–115.

system is not especially sensitive to citizen desires. Decisions are framed in expert commissions, planning boards, or congressional committees and ratified by legislative groups that do not conform to the scope of the problem. Commonly special interest groups are most effective in seeing that the proposals put forward conform to their views. A capsule critique of the present system has been offered by Haefele.

> We thus have the worst of both worlds—technical analysis debased by political judgments, and political deals in which only a small number and perhaps the wrong people play. . . . the technical analysis does not cover the full range of technical possibilities and . . . is tempered by what the technician judges to be political reality. Both are grievous faults. The political process is faulty because, first, it is conducted by the wrong people (say, for example, the Public Works Committee) and second, it is hidden behind technical surveys that purport to be objective.[2]

Haefele argues for revitalization of the institution of representative government to recapture policy decisions from the executive branch and its experts. In a legislature where many issues are to be voted on and diverse coalitions can be expected, a system of vote trading allows representation and influence for strongly held views, giving hope even to the minority on some issues and mitigating the tyranny of the majority. Moreover, the two-party system, with its inherent attempt to put together winning coalitions across many issues, offers the best chance for framing decisions so that the conflicting desires of real people can be most truly expressed. Parties become identified with programs over longer time horizons; they are the only groups in the society that have responsibility for program formation.

A legislative body is the appropriate institution for policy formation but is ineffective at administration. Administrative agencies in turn flounder when policy-making functions are thrust upon them. Proper policy guidance that sets goals or standards and broad institutional means of achieving them still allows flexibility to the administrative agency in detailed planning and enforcement.

This discussion of social choice is best terminated by returning to the starting point. However adept society becomes at defining the proper role of government, in assigning problems to the appropriate jurisdiction, or in devising more responsive institutions, it does not follow that we will make the survival choice. That depends on timely recognition of the imperatives of the situation and on a future-

---

[2] Ibid., p. 19.

oriented cast of mind that values succeeding generations equally with our own. It is asking much of man to accommodate these needs— perhaps more than we are capable of collectively.

POLICY INSTRUMENTS AND THEIR USES

Most of the policy instruments available to government have been illustrated by the discussion in preceding chapters. Government has the power to tax or to raise revenue and the power to spend its revenue where it chooses. The other chief government power is the power to regulate—the most obvious and direct form of action in the common view. In addition, government is a large landlord, so it can be a direct operator in land management and other fields. Finally, government can stimulate private action or the actions of subordinate governments through all of the foregoing instruments.

Direct Federal Operations—Taxes, Spending, Management

General taxes are intended to raise revenue. Changes in their level can be employed to regulate the economy. General taxes are not well suited for affecting the disposition of resources in particular lines of activity, but the system can be juggled. Investment can be made more attractive in some lines by tax concessions that directly improve after-tax yield in activities requiring stimulation. Writeoff provisions and depletion allowances have this character. To inhibit demand for a particular line, an excise tax can be employed. Such a tax has potential as a conservation measure; the proceeds also could be used for research on constraint-releasing technology. A serious desire to promote recycling of materials, almost surely must involve creating a tax differential favoring recycled materials through some combination of tax concession to recycling or an extraction tax on virgin materials. A tax on virgin materials, whether to inhibit demand for the material or to promote recycling, would need to be imposed on imports as well as domestic production if it is not to disadvantage the latter. The first candidates for such a tax would be some of the depletable resources; it should be reserved for situations where a tax seems likely to bring forth viable recycling industries or where the urgency of finding substitutes is greatest.

Since encouragement of domestic production in essential lines is one of the means of reducing vulnerability to foreign suppliers, the tariff has an important role to play. A tariff generally is less offensive to foreign sellers than are other means of exclusion and is a straightforward and visible statement of policy. At the same time, depending on its level and stability, it keeps a certain amount of competitive pressure on the domestic industry to perform if it is to hold its market share.

The difficulty with tariffs or other tax concessions is that they are susceptible to abuse. They may be sought as windfalls for the domestic interests that benefit, instead of being restricted to circumstances where they serve a clear national purpose. This concern leads some to argue against tariffs, special taxes, or tax breaks. They would use the tax side of the fiscal operation only to raise revenue and for no other purpose, or at most to serve as a regulator of general activity as distinct from particular activities. However, the potential for use of taxes to restrain or encourage particular lines is too strong to be foregone and is well embedded in our system. A clearer sense of direction in resource policy should help bring tax concessions into sharper focus and permit use of the tool when appropriate, while culling out those tax concessions which serve only a private interest rather than a public purpose.

Yet another use of the fiscal system is the tax or charge imposed for the use of publicly owned resources. Such charges could be based on any of a number of principles, whether to stimulate an industry, restrict some activity, pursue redistributive aims, or raise government revenue. Most attention of late has focused on the possibility of using emissions charges as a means of encouraging pollution abatement. Although revenue would be generated and could be applied to administering abatement programs, the principal objective is regulatory rather than fiscal.

Other government-owned resources are made available under various management principles. For example, grazing leases on the public lands are a means of restricting access; they are used in an increasingly rational way to maximize revenues while protecting the sustainable yield of government lands. Historically, arable land in the public domain was made available for farming in pursuit of broad social objectives. Access to wilderness areas has not been governed by fiscal objectives but rather by the presumed physical needs for protecting the integrity of the area. Mineral leases in recent years have had a strong element of revenue maximization, though currently more attention is given to stimulating production. A longer range resource and environmental policy which seeks to conserve resources and protect the environment is apt to make greater use of charges for regulating access to publicly owned resources, though the possibilities for flexibility remain great.

On the spending side of the fiscal ledger the flexibilities are still greater and the possibilities for abuse and waste likewise greater. Government can operate programs directly or induce others to operate them via financial incentive or provision of other stimulus.

Government generally has stayed away from the operation of resource industries that produce a salable product. The major exceptions have been hydroelectric power, enriched uranium, and some outdoor recreation. The production of hydropower relies on a public resource —falling water—and usually requires some regulation of the stream, which affects other public purposes. These public requirements can be met by licenses and regulations rather than by direct operation. Direct operation has been justified as providing the government with a yardstick on costs which can be used in regulating commercial operators. If operated on that basis, such enterprises, of course, should be a source of revenues rather than net expenses. In other cases government investment has been justified as an aid to regional development. The development objective may demand public investment, but it does not require public operation if responsible private operators can be found. On the other hand, the argument for a public corporation to develop offshore oil resources is based on concern about whether private operators will respond to the full range of public interests including competitiveness, environmental responsibility, and rate of investment. The long-standing bias of the country is to rely on private domestic oil production. If other measures of that sort are taken without expected results, then a second look could be taken at a government oil corporation.

The commonest sort of direct government operation is in major investment programs where the salable product is nil or at least insufficient to repay costs. Water development projects and many government land management programs fall in this class. In such cases an attempt is made to measure the net social benefit of undertaking an investment. The literature on that subject is immense and does not need review here. The great difficulties in estimating all benefits and the propensity to employ too low a discount rate are major drawbacks, but measurement difficulties should not foreclose government resource development that is consistent with broad social objectives. However, especially with water projects, we should not proceed before reviewing our needs for agricultural commodities, the potential of reclaimed land for other uses, alternative uses of the water, and the expected ecological effects.

Another sort of direct government operation would be in larger systems management of watersheds, airsheds, or solid waste disposal. The intricate pattern of private and government property involved and the dependence on government police power to enforce requirements on private operators make this a function for government. If combined with an emissions charge system, net government expenditures easily could be nil. Initial investment may be considerable, however. As discussed earlier, the proper agency would be a management authority responsive to an appropriate regional legislative policy-making body.

Subsidies and Grants

Subsidies and grants provide a means for inducing others, whether private operators or other governments, to conform with public policy. Subsidies may be offered to defray part of the cost of a desired course of action. Unless supported by regulations requiring the action or by a strong sense of responsibility, a subsidy is not likely to prove effective. It also is not efficient from an economic standpoint, since ordinarily the subsidy is paid for a very restricted form of action whereas other means might prove more effective. Subsidies to induce production of commodities incur objections from trading partners. Moreover, since private cost data are not available to the government, the appropriate level of subsidy is not known and the device is subject to abuse. Subsidies to the farm sector were rationalized on social grounds and have been extended to some minerals on a temporary basis, but an extensive system of subsidies is appropriately viewed with skepticism.

Grants to other levels of government have some of the same deficiencies as subsidies in that they tend to restrict the range of action, particularly on capital projects. Nonetheless, where the policy decision is made at one level of government and administration is more appropriately centered elsewhere, the grant is a useful device. In this case the effect is much like hiring the work done, but local authorities will have a voice in the manner in which it is done. Grants are favored devices for inducing local governments to initiate programs in which there is a national interest but whose detailed planning and administration must be local. An obvious case is land planning, where states have been slow to exercise their powers.

Governments can stimulate planning via grants to other governments and can engage in planning and in research and development on their own account. It has been my contention that, particularly in matters of materials supply and above all energy, the need for governmental initiative is great. However, much of the expertise in these areas is found in the private firms operating in the field. Where there is industry agreement on the necessity for major technological breakthroughs on a large scale, there is a role for government, especially when a successful breakthrough would threaten the competitive structure of the industry if achieved by only one firm. In such cases research and development programs or demonstration projects using joint government–industry funds serve a useful role.

Regulation and Charges

In the common view, regulation is the policy instrument par excellence that is available to government, especially in the field of environmental quality. Its limitations in that regard have already been covered at some length. The setting of ambient standards, a policy function expressed in regulation, is a clear government responsibility. Some would seek an economic criterion, arguing that the standards should be set at that level of quality where net additional social benefits just match added costs. But this presumes far too much about our ability to measure either social benefits or costs, and it disregards the distributional aspects of attaining that standard. A rough measure arrived at by our system of social choice is currently the best compromise.

While the setting of ambient standards is a proper regulatory function, detailed performance standards may be inadvisable. They often fail the efficiency criterion and therefore are damaging to income. Where discharge is to a common renewable environmental medium, a system of charges to hold total discharges to the acceptable level would be preferred. Surcharges could be used to cut emissions at peak periods, and, with experience, we should be able to anticipate required alterations in the charge structure so that industry could adjust smoothly. The charges would be adjusted so as to maintain the integrity of the environmental medium, with standards set by a policy-making body. Since they would not be set according to an economic criterion, the charges are not strictly a case of internalizing costs—they might exceed or fall short of that standard. Nonetheless, they act in that direction and generate revenues usable for environmental management and for extending its capacity through systems management techniques.

A charges system is a means of allocating a limited resource—for example, that part of the waste assimilative capacity of an airshed or watershed which is consistent with maintenance of standards. When dealing with a nonrenewable resource or an irreversible change, a different order of problem arises. Some toxic materials, such as heavy metals or exotic chemicals, are virtually indestructible. Once discharged to land or water, they reside there permanently and may be damaging to man or other life. Tolerances often are unknown and there may be no safe threshold of exposure. If some specific level of contamination was known to be harmless, we could auction off rights to that amount. More often nothing is certain, and the only recourse is to forbid discharge.

Some shifts in land use—namely, from wilderness to development or from rural to urban—are essentially irreversible. Moreover, such changes are fraught with enormous consequences for public budgets and for general welfare. The public has little control of these changes through market mechanisms. Only land planning provides a framework within which changes could be allowed. However, if the plan is followed, it allows intensified use for some land and denies it to other lands. It is grossly inequitable to leave these publicly created gains in the hands of the fortunate few. The value of development rights could be taxed away or permits for development could be auctioned off instead of being given away as windfalls. These devices, while they have a fiscal dimension, are essentially regulatory in nature, the aim being to take the profit out of speculation about the actions of public agencies and to allow planning criteria rather than manipulation to determine the direction of development.

Resource policy which has a substantial element of domestic supply as one of its foundations must have some means of restricting imports. Likewise in a world of violently fluctuating commodity markets, and especially in a situation of strong world demand for food, Americans may question whether they want to see domestic dietary standards supplanted or domestic production fully exposed to the draft of world demand. Export and import quotas are one means for pursuing a stable resource policy. If used, they should be part of a resource policy whose broad outlines are well understood by trading partners and not subject to abrupt change. In that context their use could be anticipated and should be no more objectionable than the policy itself.

A SUMMARY OF POLICY DIRECTIONS

Initially two possible modes of permanent occupancy were defined in this study. Because this is a matter that has not been the subject of much popular discussion, which direction an informed public would take is not clear. The immediate need is to define the nature of the choice and the necessity for it. Nonetheless, I conclude that an attempt to try for path two is the approach that would be most consistent with commonly held goals. It holds the most potential for both the United States and other nations. Above all, it holds options open that the other path would close; as noted, we could revert from path two to path one, but too long a delay would prevent us from making the reverse trek. We need time to appreciate the necessity for choice and still more time to accomplish the transition.

Most of this discussion has been based on the assumption that path two will be the preferred choice. It then follows that, as a broad proposition, we should aim at converting natural capital into constraint-releasing technology rather than squandering it on current consumption. Such transformation is consistent with varying rates of use of depletable resources so long as the proceeds are properly directed. Extraction taxes devoted to financing a research budget would be a direct expression of this principle. Meanwhile, measures aimed at ensuring that resource prices reflect the full social costs of their production and use will help to restrain demand and prolong the option. And since the key constraint that brings the necessity for choice to a head is the depletability of resources, measures to substitute renewable resources also serve to prolong the option.

Population Control

I have not dwelt much on the need for population restraint, not because it is unimportant, but rather because currently in the United States we appear to be behaving responsibly on an individual basis. Public policy need not intrude so long as that is the case; nonetheless, an attempt should be made to understand the forces at work and how they can be influenced should that become necessary. Such understanding is all the more advisable because the built-in wave of population growth ahead will be combined with the heavy draft on resources and environment that continued income growth entails. Although the

United States will be affected by population trends in other countries, particularly in the rapidly growing LDCs, we do not have very strong leverage for influencing those trends at present. This study cannot pretend to treat the many difficulties of coping with that important problem.

National Security

A decent concern for national security should not be dismissed as jingoistic nationalism that is unmindful of the rest of the world. On the contrary, if it leads to technical innovations that expand the resource supply and these innovations are available to all, as they would be, then it is broadly serviceable to mankind. The United States is well positioned to serve this function by reason of our state of consciousness, national capacities, and national needs.

Land Use

Current policy decisions must be made with these longer-term considerations before us, and land use provides an excellent starting point, since it is so fundamentally related to our longer-term options. Land use changes, especially the invasion of wilderness or the conversion of land to urban use, have a degree of irreversibility. Preservation of the health and productivity of the land and its genetic stock is essential to path one and important to path two.

Land often is a resilient resource and it can recover from considerable abuse, although this varies, depending on its location and other characteristics. Generally, the biotic community can recover from abuse more readily than the soil itself. The most serious kind of permanent damage is soil loss from erosion. There is a program to control this and it should be pursued methodically, so that necessary works are built and desirable cultivation practices followed. Erosion control can be assisted by concentrating production on the best lands. Acreage limitations have acted in this fashion on the individual farm. Proper cover of abandoned cropland should be required as a condition of payment. Cover would be fostered if withdrawals could be arranged on a longer-term basis, permitting development of alternative uses for the land. Regionally, withdrawal of unsuitable lands can be speeded by acquiring easements on those that have special ecological characteristics (especially wetlands and floodplains) and by assisting in the shift of farm people in less productive regions to alternative employment. However, if the United States is called upon to contribute to a fundamentally enlarged world demand for agricultural commodities, the emphasis will shift from management of withdrawn lands to measures to protect marginal lands brought into production.

Land use planning for the countryside should attempt to be more closely attuned to the physical capabilities of the land. Why not spare agricultural land from site use for building whenever alternative lands are available? Property tax breaks in return for long-term commitments to agricultural use and a determination to capture for the public any eventual development gains should be useful in sparing farmland site use for buildings. By preserving our best agricultural land and concentrating farm production there, we can avoid the financial costs and ecological damages now entailed in many reclamation and flood control works. Stream channelization and flood control destroy ecologically valuable wetlands and recharge areas. Subsidies for these projects should be ended and no protection should be provided for further encroachments on the floodplain. Where private capital threatens to develop wetlands, serious attention should be given to preservation through easements or acquisition.

If a policy of withdrawals, easements, and termination of reclamation subsidies helps concentrate cultivation on the best lands, then a policy to increase the yield of uncropped lands is needed. The prospect of longer-term dedication to noncrop uses will help to generate the kinds of investments and management expertise required. Apart from wetlands, where the government should take a direct role, and grazing lands, which responsible property owners can manage well enough, the yield of woodland and the production of game could be increased by providing technical assistance or devising cooperative management schemes carrying assurance that the owner would realize the gains. There is a public interest in promoting such institutions so as to maximize the yield of our renewable resources.

While it is our aim to increase output from appropriate land uses in settled areas—whether from crops, grazing, woodland, or recreation and wildlife—the preservation of wilderness and of genetic material is motivated by prudential concerns and is not determined by alternative current yield. Because preservation is an alternative to development, it has a cost, and what that cost is must be understood in detail. Our stance might then be to preserve as much wilderness as we can afford, recognizing that its value to us as wilderness will be increasing in ways that are both measurable and unmeasurable. This stance need not be dogmatic. Most highly productive timberlands are not candidates for inclusion in wilderness and, while wilderness should include some prime forest land, most prospective wilderness is too remote, steep, or high to be very productive. Where prospective wilderness holds deposits of scarce and essential minerals, the presumption should still be for nondevelopment. If the social need to exploit the deposit is overwhelming, it should be possible to do so in a manner that shows maximum respect for the character of the site. Indeed, the longer development is postponed, the greater the likelihood that the price of the commodity will sustain the cost of environmental protection or restoration at the site. Since wilderness area is limited and demand for its use as wilderness will grow, management techniques to increase its capacity without destruction of its quality as a recreational experience will need to be perfected. Joint government and academic research will be required to accomplish this. Some means of limiting access will be required; although an economic case can be made for use of market prices to limit demand, a more egalitarian system of rationing would be consistent with the joint heritage nature of this resource.

The management of forest lands outside of wilderness areas has become increasingly controversial. They must be managed so as to include attention to watershed, recreational, wildlife, and scenic values as well as wood production. However, wood production should not be neglected, and; except for wilderness lands, it need not preclude attention to the other goals. In fact, by rotating the use of timberland the yield of timber can be increased while providing improved range for game and sufficient recreational opportunities. The need is for nondestructive harvesting, using selective cutting whenever consistent with regeneration, but in recognition that harvesting is part of the cycle.

Man has been very successful at channeling photosynthetic activity so as to be of most use to him, but increasingly this occurs at the cost of current environmental damage. The use of agricultural chemicals, particularly pesticides, must be curtailed. Integrated pest control programs making use of natural controls or sex attractants as well as limited use of pesticides has much promise. The research required to perfect this should be pursued in many different parts of the country and for many crops. Bringing more land into cultivation is an alternative to pesticide use. In the current period of high demand this offers less latitude; it also foregoes the advantages of concentrating production on best land. Research on plants that have high capacity to synthesize would be appropriate at this stage in prolonging open field agriculture in the face of growing environmental pressure. Such plants would be highly valuable if it becomes necessary to move toward a more controlled agriculture.

For the present, there seems no imperative reason to pursue a policy of population redistribution among regions, so far as resource or environmental considerations are concerned; however, in the future we might choose such a policy for social reasons or on other grounds. Many types of governmental programs, including resource and environmental programs, may have an unintended redistributional effect —a matter that should be given more attention. But the regional distribution of population is the result of balancing many preferences and is not well enough understood to warrant confident intervention.

Within regions there is evidence that cities of large size have economic advantages that appear to compensate for their less desirable environmental quality. The evidence is not so conclusive as to rule out experiments in dispersing the population to new towns or smaller towns, but it does suggest the desirability of urban forms that preserve the efficiency of size without the penalty of degraded environment. Cities of a given population size can be organized at different average densities and with different degrees of centrality.

Urban form does have resource and environmental significance. A compact, centralized city is incompatible with reliance on private auto transport. Organized around mass transit facilities, a city can provide economies in energy and utilities and could avoid much auto-related pollution. If effluents are strictly controlled and less use is made of the environment to receive wastes, then the compact form is apt to be more efficient in waste management. In actual fact, the trend has been in the opposite direction, and despite the cost in energy, space, and pollution, this may prove a viable mode if we can clean up the private car, can reduce transportation requirements, and decentralize waste disposal and electricity generation. Assuming a stable population, the increased demand for space required by lower density is not serious. Any attempt to recentralize our cities must be accompanied by solutions to the problems of adequate schooling and personal safety.

The author personally cannot escape the sense that on balance further dispersion is wasteful of resources and environment. Attempts to enforce air quality standards in the face of reliance on auto transportation dramatize this problem. One solution might be the provision of alternatives to dispersion in well-designed urban environments that cluster housing and preserve common open space—compactness without crowding. If accompanied by subsidies for mass transportation and improved public safety and assurance of school quality, this would provide a good test of the public response. Meanwhile, we should take steps to end those exclusionary practices in the suburbs that are inconsistent with democratic ideals, and should adopt a hard-nosed policy of charging full cost for the provision of utilities and public services in suburbia.

Because the population continues to grow and move to cities, more land will be needed for future urban use. Land use planning can supplement other tools in shaping the emerging urban form. In particular, decisions about location of airports, highways, utilities, waste disposal facilities, and open space should be in conformance with a broad land use plan. If the plan is followed, it will determine which lands increase in value as a result of this public decision. There is no reason why some favored landowners should profit from this process. Public policy should move to capture development gains by way of taxation, land banking, auctioning zoning rights in conformance with the plan, or, where feasible, by public acquisition at undeveloped value.

Energy

Energy policy must aim at providing a dependable and moderate-cost supply without unacceptable environmental damage or affront to our sense of equity. At the same time it must look far enough into the future to mount the research necessary to guard against depletion.

Basic to energy policy is our attitude toward foreign supply. Known foreign oil supplies are large, the cost of exploitation is low, and oil is a preferred fuel for many uses. However, in my judgment the dependability of supply is too uncertain and the price not likely to be sufficiently advantageous to warrant the risk. In fact, the price of foreign oil may depend very much on our capacity to supply ourselves. Although growth in short-term reliance on foreign supply is inevitable, a domestic strategy that minimizes dependence is feasible even in the short run, and over a longer period it has still greater potential. Such a strategy is preferred. It implies extensive use of coal and shale oil over an intermediate period during the search for more enduring solutions.

Energy strategy requires a time-phased approach. For the next decade or so, embarrassing problems of supply are inevitable. While there are some methods of restraining demand, an attempt to solve our problems exclusively on the demand side would involve considerable cost to welfare. Accordingly, policy must provide incentives to domestic production so as to ensure supply and limit foreign dependence. The greatest possibilities appear to lie in increasing the domestic production of oil and gas. This is possible in the short period only in a climate that makes investment attractive—one that promises recovery of long-run costs. Some mechanism for restricting imports is essential. Provided the determination is clear to all, a variable import levy is the preferred means, since it captures for the public any difference between foreign and domestic price. At the same time it can be used flexibly to keep some competitive pressure on domestic producers. A protected domestic market carries the possibility of large rents on production, but at the same time, by providing stability, it reduces the prospective yields required to induce investment. Therefore, leasing and tax policies need not be directed toward encouraging high returns. Rather, they can place a premium on increasing output. If the depletion allowance is retained, it could be tied directly to reinvestment, and leasing terms should encourage early production and full recovery. Leasing should be accelerated as rapidly as environmental considerations permit.

Since the aim is to increase domestic production, the tax benefits presently favoring production abroad should be modified. In particular, deferral of tax on unrepatriated profits from new investments in foreign petroleum production should be ended, and depletion allowances on such investments should be permitted only if directed to domestic production. Also, the practice of allowing foreign tax payments to reduce U.S. income tax liability is an anachronism at a time when the aim is to direct resources toward domestic production.

If we do not pursue a longer-term strategy of domestic supply, then, as a minimum, a large-scale program of building storage should be undertaken along with a standby of allocation and rationing. If we do emphasize domestic supply, we may take our chances during the intervening period of exposure with a greatly reduced storage plan. Meanwhile, work must begin on measures that will ensure other sources of supply and dampen demand over the intermediate period.

The period of ten to fifty years hence will require massive draft on coal and shale oil resources. Domestic petroleum and natural gas resources are not adequate to maintain their share of the energy market by the end of the period. Assuming a strategy of domestic supply, we shall have to make use of the full range of domestic hydrocarbons. While protection should be offered for the domestic market so as to promote investment, there is a good chance that protection will not imply higher price—ample domestic resources may prove quite competitive with the cartel-controlled price of foreign supplies. Leasing policy for shale lands must reflect the needs of an effective private operation. Research should now be directed toward limiting the environmental damage from hydrocarbon extraction in such sensitive environments as offshore oil operations or surface mining in semiarid regions of the west. In view of the air pollution control measures being established on a national basis, research on coal combustion and gasification must be hastened. Joint government–industry programs appear to be the appropriate path. Combustion must be limited as much as possible. Research on geothermal and solar energy sources should be pursued actively, and government housing programs should seek to establish feasibility of solar temperature control and to have this feature recognized in financing.

The most disquieting feature of this emerging intermediate strategy is the role of the breeder reactor. In the end it must be decided whether the increased supply assurance and flexibility that the breeder represents is more esteemed than the undeniable uncertainties that accompany it. If the decision is made to go ahead, cooperation between government and industry regarding design and siting will be required to reduce the likelihood and consequences of accident.

The intermediate period allows time for measures to restrain energy consumption without loss of welfare. Upgrading of insulation requirements through housing agencies is one path. A second is to economize on energy use in transportation. Land planning that averts sprawl also will have an effect over this period. Finally, research efforts can be directed toward improving the efficiency of energy conversion and to utilizing waste heat in order to hold down the draft on energy resources.

Over the longer term, U. S. energy policy is mostly a research and development strategy designed to find inexhaustible and environmentally acceptable sources. If it is successful in both respects, so much emphasis on energy conservation will be unnecessary, but until the environmental compatibility of greatly enlarged energy consumption is established, research approaches that promise efficiency in conversion and use are preferable. Sources of most promise appear to be solar energy and fusion reactors, both of which score well on environmental grounds. Fusion is the more promising if combined with a hydrogen cycle that gives it many flexible uses.

A coordinated energy policy that has current internal consistency and long-term continuity must rest on a clear sense of direction. I have stressed the need to define policy toward foreign dependence. Thereafter it becomes a matter of designing domestic incentives and mounting necessary research and development to secure the domestic supply. If we are optimistic about potential supply and do not want to restrain demand artificially, we must favor prices that reflect full social cost and continued competition among fuels on that basis. This would be a departure from the current trend in policy toward excessive reliance on regulation.

Minerals

Problems with nonfuel minerals include their long-run depletability, increasing dependence on foreign sources, and the inherent conflict between mineral exploitation and the maintenance of environmental quality. Supply can be prolonged without serious damage to welfare by increased proficiency at recycling and by recovering lower-grade materials at moderate cost. Dependence can be reduced by developing more domestic supply, but in many cases this entails a cost penalty. However, vulnerability to supply interruption is less severe than in the case of fuels and can be reduced effectively by stockpiling. In the conflict with the environment, technical measures and careful management will help, but a balancing of the needs for minerals and environment requires their joint consideration in a fashion not hitherto attained.

To prolong and enlarge supply research is crucial. Techniques of finding deposits can be advanced by government-supported programs at universities and elsewhere and through direct operations of the U.S. Geological Survey. Large-scale deployment of sensors via satellites and aircraft is very promising in this regard, but no crisis of supply requires dramatic acceleration of these efforts at present. Private exploration could be encouraged by changes in mineral law to allow full use of modern techniques of exploration and mine operations. Mining and refining advances are mostly the province of private firms. Normal operation of markets has been effective in holding down costs despite the exploitation of lower-grade ores. Recent environmental measures will place new pressure on costs, but at the same time they may lead to different processes that will limit costs.

Recycling of mineral stocks also prolongs supply. As a first step, any positive discrimination against recycled materials should be ended, for example, freight rate differentials should be studied to determine if this occurs. Research on materials recovery from solid wastes should be pursued under governmental auspices, with attention extending into product design as well. Most opportunities existing in industry will respond to the relative costs of virgin and recycled materials.

Recycling could be favored by ending the incentives to produce virgin materials present in our tax and mining laws, and conceivably we could go further by imposing an extraction tax on newly mined minerals, although the aim of increased domestic mineral supply would not be promoted by the latter step. At this stage it seems best to proceed with research and to terminate discrimination against recycled materials rather than to shift the balance toward disincentives for new production.

This strategy is the more compelling because our principal hope of containing growing dependence on foreign supply is to encourage new domestic production. Those measures suggested to prolong and enlarge supply are applicable here, with focus on the United States and especially on mining law. As with oil and gas, the application of tax law which grants equal favor to mineral investments abroad and does not require domestic reinvestment of depletion allowances is questionable. However, the case is not so strong as for petroleum, since vulnerability is less. Provided that we do not dissipate our stockpiles, considerable reliance on foreign supply can be tolerated. Since considerable foreign dependence is inevitable, we should study whether the present path of encouraging private investment abroad via tax and insurance provisions will be viable in the future, or whether more direct government involvement in such arrangements is advisable.

The conflict between mining law, which gives high priority to mineral production, and environmental regulations, which give scant attention to the need for minerals, must be faced. While the environmental consequences of mining are felt mostly by local communities, the present trend is to subject them to national ambient and emissions standards. More local flexibility, particularly on secondary ambient air quality standards and on the emissions consistent with them, should be allowed. This would promote the national interest in mineral production. At the same time, the theoretically unrestrained right to locate and produce minerals should be subjected to control. Replacement of the location system with a leasing system on public lands would permit systematic evaluation of environmental values along with the need for production but still be consistent with some latitude in local ambient standards.

Reliance on a leasing system is attractive in that it would permit some form of tenure during exploration and allow the use of modern exploration techniques with hope of asserting a claim. It also would permit the public to recover some of the value of the resource, to designate the areas to be open for development, and to regulate the character of exploration. If this were done in the context of a land use plan, it would help to reduce site use conflict.

Pollution

Income growth can continue indefinitely only if means of pollution abatement are found that are economically efficient and physically effective at higher levels of output. Desirable ambient environmental standards are a matter for social choice along with the myriad other common decisions that must be made. The decision should be made with an awareness of what a given level of quality costs—that is, what we sacrifice to gain it. Because there are several receiving media to defend whose conditions are interrelated and there are many devices for improving quality that may be quite different in cost and effect, we need to think in terms of broader regional residuals management systems. There can be little confidence that the present system is either efficient or effective.

Decision making in air pollution programs has moved in the direction of centralization. The setting of national primary standards give little cause for objection, but nationwide secondary standards seem unnecessary and do not allow the desirable degree of local latitude. In any case, national ambient standards do not imply national emissions standards. For example, little justification can be found for most national fixed point emissions standards, except for control of toxic materials. Mobile sources, by reason of their movement across jurisdictions, the difficulty of control on an individual basis, and the logic of measures at the stage of design and manufacture, offer a better target for emissions standards. But other means of attaining the desired ambient level should be explored. An emissions charge is one such method, and a sulfur tax would be an excellent start.

For autos, a tax could be levied on manufacturers whose products fail to meet standards, the tax to increase in relation to the extent of the failure and to rise each year after the standards become effective. Meanwhile, measures such as a tax on weight and horsepower and diversion of gas tax funds into mass transit help to reduce emissions by permitting reduction in local traffic without serious economic loss. Like reasoning applies to use of financial and regulatory measures to upgrade insulation standards in housing, again reducing energy use and resulting pollution.

Because air pollution is largely a regional problem and has certain linkages with the use made of other receiving media and with land use planning, decisions on how to achieve mandated standards will have to be decentralized to governmental units that have sufficient scope to encompass the whole range of these problems.

The federal program of water quality management has not been very successful in stemming the deterioration of our streams. Recent amendments set an unrealistic goal of no discharge (thereby forcing residuals upon other media), rely upon the same basic strategy as past programs, and again are centralizing decisions that are regional in nature. As with air pollution, effluent charges could be tried as a means of implementing quality standards at less cost. The advantage of establishing appropriate management institutions is even greater in this case because the assimilative capacity of watercourses can be increased through systems techniques. However, the goals and standards mandated nationally under present law are a straitjacket that would frustrate more flexible techniques.

While Congress has asserted an exaggerated federal role in air and water quality programs, the Nixon Administration had withdrawn from the solid waste management field. Continuing research is needed on waste management and disposal, which industry is ill-equipped to do, and from both a resource and environmental standpoint continued work on resource recovery is needed. State and local attempts to penalize use of disposable packaging should be carefully evaluated and the possibilities examined for design changes and disposal taxes that make recovery easier or that pay for the costs of removal. The federal government also has a role in stimulating regional approaches to solid waste management, preferaby in conjunction with regional water and air quality authorities and land planners.

The International Dimension

U.S. policy with regard to imports and resource commodities must strike a balance between excessive dependence on foreign supply in critical commodities and high-cost domestic production. At least with respect to energy and food, substantial dependence is both ill-advised and unnecessary. For many minerals the balance tilts the other way, but often some domestic production capability can be maintained, and where this is impossible, stockpile levels should reflect commercial as well as military contingencies. Any shift in posture, whether toward restricting the growth of imports or increasing them, should be gradual and should give some weight to the attitudes of trading partners.

As an exporter of resource commodities the United States is torn between the desire to earn foreign exchange in lines where it may have an advantage and reluctance to see domestic supplies depleted and prices increased by foreign demand. Since the opportunities and the problem arise in the case of food and timber products, both of which have important domestic social implications, it may be desirable to ensure some stability in domestic markets through export quotas. This is compatible with stable relationships with regular trading partners. Decisions about diversion of scarce foodstocks to famine areas must be taken by the international community if the consequences are to be spread equitably.

We must also be concerned with the international environmental implications of our acts. This does not mean attempting to impose our environmental standards on others who sell in our market—they must defend their own environment. If their production adversely affects the global environment, then the United States does have a cause for action through international channels. So far there are not effective international institutions to implement this proposition, and we must work to establish them. Where the United States has an interest in matters that lie within the control of another country, we may use such persuasions and inducements as we can to affect their behavior.

Reorganization of Decision Units

Whether we deal with problems of resource supply and environment on the domestic or international level, one of our most pressing needs is to deal with the matter on a scale appropriate to the problem. Existing domestic and international institutions rarely are appropriate for this and lack flexibility for adapting to new requirements. Yet for most matters of resource supply, the United States is large enough and has sufficient technical resources to pursue its own strategy in an otherwise uncertain world.

Domestically we have far to go before decision making and administration are done at the appropriate level, especially in matters of land use and environmental management. Most often these are local or regional problems. Smaller units of government sorely need revitalizing to give them real authority in these fields within a broader national consensus on our longer-range direction. In the end, general purpose governments with jurisdiction over the full range of interlocking problems provide the only hope for the coordination required to minimize goal conflict.

A FINAL WORD

At this writing a profound sense of unease surrounds questions of materials supply and environmental management. It is a time of inflation, unemployment, international tension, and international financial stress, all closely tied to resource problems. For many this leads to a shortened time horizon, a refusal to look at long-term realities, and a propensity to defend personal and social consumption standards. In that attitude lies the greatest threat to industrial man. Others, who take a longer view, often despair as they look at the prospect of declining availability, rising cost, growing dependence, and environmental damage. This book has sounded a rather more hopeful note, suggesting a national path for coping that is not harmful to others and that seems within our reach.

The present mode of human occupancy of the earth cannot survive unchanged, principally because of the pressure of exponential growth on resources. The United States can pioneer a future mode over the next 50–100 years based on population restraint, a restricted style of land use, a shift to inexhaustible energy sources, and greater use of common materials and renewable resources. There is no inexorable requirement for return to a primitive state or even for a no-growth society. A shift of the sort described will require conscious social decisions so as to divert the necessary resources within the required time frame.

Why the United States? If the problem is common to all mankind, should not the solution be sought on a broader basis? Present international institutions, reflecting the urgent needs of most of the world's people, see the problem as one of the equitable sharing of the world's resources. I see it rather as one of the timely diversion of sufficient resources to perfect a technology for escape from resource exhaustion, without which there will be little to share. If the transition to a new mode must be accomplished over the next 50–100 years, and if that in turn requires that we start now, then the national state is what we have to work with. The United States has limited influence over actions elsewhere that contribute to man's common dilemma, but it does have the wealth and the technical resources needed for the transition, provided it can summon the will and tenacity to apply them. By pursuing such a course on an autonomous basis, if necessary, Americans will help to assure a tomorrow not only for themselves but for all mankind.

INDEX

THE JOHNS HOPKINS UNIVERSITY PRESS

This book was composed in Janson text and Airport display type
by the Maryland Linotype Composition Co., Inc., from a design
by Patrick Turner. It was printed on 60-lb. Warren 1854 paper
and bound in Holliston Roxite cloth by The Maple Press Company.

1—333—BRUBAKER JHP   8-9x26 Janson

LIBRARY OF CONGRESS CATALOGING IN PUBLICATION DATA

Brubaker, Sterling.
    In command of tomorrow.

    "A Resources for the Future study."
    Includes bibliographical references and index.
    1. Environmental policy—United States. 2. Con-
servation of natural resources—United States.
3. Energy policy—United States. 4. Pollution—United
States. I. Resources for the Future. II. Title.
HC110.E5B77   301.31'0973   74-24401
ISBN 0-8018-1700-5

INTERNATIONAL FINANCE

THE MARKETS AND FINANCIAL MANAGEMENT OF MULTINATIONAL BUSINESS

McGraw-Hill Series in Finance

CONSULTING EDITOR:
CHARLES A. D'AMBROSIO, *University of Washington*

INTERNATIONAL FINANCE

THE MARKETS AND FINANCIAL MANAGEMENT OF MULTINATIONAL BUSINESS

SECOND EDITION

Maurice D. Levi

Bank of Montreal Professor of
International Finance
The University of British Columbia

McGraw-Hill, Inc.
New York St. Louis San Francisco Auckland Bogotá
Caracas Lisbon London Madrid Mexico Milan
Montreal New Delhi Paris San Juan Singapore
Sydney Tokyo Toronto

This book was set in Times Roman by Science Typographers, Inc.
The editor was Suzanne BeDell;
the production supervisor was Friederich W. Schulte.
The cover was designed by Eric Baker.
Project supervision was done by Science Typographers, Inc.

INTERNATIONAL FINANCE

The Markets and Financial Management of Multinational Business

4 5 6 7 8 9 0 WHT WHT 9 0 9 8 7 6 5 4 3

ISBN   0-07-037483-X

Library of Congress Cataloging-in-Publication Data

Levi, Maurice D., (date).
    International finance: the markets and financial management of
multinational business / Maurice D. Levi.— 2nd ed.
        p.   cm.
    Includes bibliographical references.
    ISBN 0-07-037483-X
    1. International finance.   2. International business enterprises —
    Finance.   I. Title.
HG3881.L455   1990
332'.042 — dc20   89-13871

ABOUT THE AUTHOR

Since receiving his Ph.D. in economics from the University of Chicago in 1972, Maurice D. Levi has taught and done research in a variety of areas of finance and economics. His broad range of research and teaching interests form the foundation for this book in international finance, a subject that he believes to be best treated as an application of economics and financial principles, rather than as a separate and isolated subject area.

Professor Levi has published research papers on the effectiveness of monetary and fiscal policy, the relationship between inflation and interest rates, the effect of taxes on capital flows, and the link between inflationary expectations and unemployment, as well as in the numerous areas of international finance that are reflected in this book. He has also written in the areas of econometric methods, macroeconomics, labor economics, money and banking, and regional economics. His papers have appeared in just about every leading research journal in finance and economics including *The American Economic Review*, *Econometrica*, *Journal of Political Economy*, *The Journal of Finance*, *Journal of Monetary Economics*, *Journal of Money, Credit and Banking*, *Journal of International Money and Finance*, *Journal of International Economics*, and *Journal of Econometrics*. He is also the author of *Economics Deciphered: A Layman's Survival Guide* (Basic Books, New York, 1981) and *Thinking Economically* (Basic Books, New York, 1985) and the coauthor, with M. Kupferman, of *Slowth* (Wiley, New York, 1980).

Since joining the Faculty of Commerce and Business Administration of the University of British Columbia in 1972, Professor Levi has held visiting positions at the Hebrew University of Jerusalem, the University of California, Berkeley, MIT, the National Bureau of Economic Research, and the London Business School. He has received numerous academic prizes and awards including a Killam Postdoctoral Fellowship and a Bronfman Award.

Maurice Levi is currently the Bank of Montréal Professor of International Finance at the University of British Columbia. His interests include astronomy, fishing, and enjoying his family: wife Kate and children Adam, Naomi, and Jonathan.

v

To Kate

CONTENTS

PREFACE

This book is intended for use in MBA or upper-level undergraduate courses in international finance which cover both the management and markets of multinational business. The book is specifically designed for students who have taken introductory economics and corporate finance, and who wish to build upon the basic economic and financial principles they have acquired in these areas. By assuming these prerequisites, this book is able to go further than competing textbooks in international finance. It is able to introduce the student to the new and exciting discoveries in the dynamic and rapidly expanding field of international finance. These discoveries, many of which have occurred during the last decade, are extensions of the central paradigms of economics and corporate finance.

Of course, it is necessary to recognize that students of business, whether concentrating in finance or in international business, have a practical interest in the subjects they take. Consequently, any good textbook in international finance must cover managerial topics such as where to borrow and invest, what different types of bonds can be used to raise capital, how exchange rates affect cash flows, what can be done to avoid foreign exchange risk, and the general financial management problems of multinational enterprises. However, even these highly practical topics can be properly dealt with only by applying basic financial and economic principles that most other international finance textbooks seem reluctant to use. As a result, despite adequate levels of preparation, generally including an introduction to economics and finance, the student often receives a rather descriptive treatment of these topics which fails to build on the foundations of previous courses. For this reason, many second-year MBA students and undergraduate business majors with solid backgrounds in, for example, the principles of capital budgeting or the advantages of portfolio diversification feel they move sideways rather than forward into international finance.

The topics in this text are covered from the perspective of a person who wishes to learn about the financial management of an internationally oriented business. However, it is important that managers also understand international financial developments on an overall macroeconomic level. Such an understanding enables managers to predict economic changes and to adjust to what they expect to occur. Because of this double level of interest in the forces behind events and the consequences of these events for the firm, this book includes a backgrounder on the international finance of the economy. However, even at this macroeconomic level, a managerial perspective is taken, and for the benefit of instructors who emphasize international financial management, the backgrounder is placed as an addendum at the end of the book.

This book represents a very substantial revision to the first edition of *International Finance*. Several entirely new chapters have been included to broaden the managerial coverage, and topics previously covered have been considerably rearranged and reintegrated. In addition, a number of new topics have been included—currency options, the J curve, countertrade, forfeiting— and every chapter without exception has been reworked. The guiding principle throughout this revision has been to bring the book closer to the syllabus that seems to this author to be emerging in one-semester international finance courses in MBA and top-level undergraduate business programs. Of course, no book can escape the idiosyncrasies of its author, and so even this radically revised edition reflects what the author believes to be important. However, the author has taken more pains than in the first edition to suppress his own interests. Furthermore, the few such special topics that remain are included as appendices, or as asterisked sections which can be omitted without loss of continuity.

The grand scale of revision has become necessary because the international financial developments that have occurred since this book first appeared have been nothing short of spectacular. For example, since the first edition was published in 1983, the United States has gone from being the world's largest net creditor nation to being its largest net debtor. During this same period, exchange rates have been so volatile that they have on occasion grabbed the headlines, not of the business section of the newspaper, but of the front page. News reports have also been full of actual or imminent defaults of third-world debtors as well as economic summits of the world leaders dealing with periodic financial crises. At the same time, new international financial instruments such as currency options have appeared, and there has been an explosion of published research in international finance. The revisions to this book reflect these developments and the important research that has greatly sharpened the insights gained from studying this exciting subject.

This book has evolved over a number of years while I have been teaching at the University of British Columbia and also at the School of Business Administration of the Hebrew University, Jerusalem; the School of Business Administration of the University of California, Berkeley; the Department of Economics at the Massachusetts Institute of Technology; and the London Business School. I am indebted to all these institutions, especially the University of British Columbia, which has been my home base since receiving my Ph.D. at the University of Chicago.

An author's debts are a pleasure to acknowledge, and I have incurred many that I would find difficult to repay. The help offered by reviewers of the numerous drafts of this and the first edition has been immensely important in improving the final product. Charles D'Ambrosio and Laurence Booth examined several chapters and provided advice on the presentation of material. Richard Levich conscientiously and carefully checked portions of the manuscript and generously gave the benefit of his wise, professional judgment. Richard Brealey helped me avoid numerous errors and confusions and offered perceptive and valuable comments on virtually every aspect of the text. Carl Beidleman, Richard Bond, Kerry Cooper, Paul Fellows, Seymour Goodman, Roger Huang, James Hugon, Kenneth Kasa, David Leonard, John Murray, Bruce Resnick, and J. Fred Weston also provided detailed and valuable comments. Suzanne BeDell, Catherine Woods, and the expert staff at McGraw-Hill most professionally handled the coordination of reviews and numerous other editorial jobs involved in producing this second edition. I am especially grateful to Suzanne BeDell for her encouragement throughout the very long revision process.

I have had the good fortune of obtaining help from individuals at universities I visited while writing this book, especially from David Babbel, University of California at Berkeley; and Donald Lessard, MIT. In addition, Alan Shapiro, David Backus, Sarkis Khoury, and most especially Piet Serçu have provided generous help while they were visiting and teaching at the University of British Columbia.

I would like to thank my colleagues at the University of British Columbia who have provided input at various stages. In particular, I must single out Josef Zechner, who has patiently considered questions I have thrown at him about material in just about every chapter of the book. The quality of his answers is reflected throughout. Raman Uppall has also made a vital contribution by giving valuable advice on numerous topics. Last but not least, my good friend and former colleague Eduardo Schwartz has been a major help.

Barbara Weeks provided superbly professional and indispensable help in typing and preparing this manuscript. Too numerous to mention individually but of great importance were the students in my graduate and undergraduate courses in international finance at the University of British Columbia, whose reactions have been a crucial ingredient in various revisions of the text.

It is to my wife, Kate, that I owe my greatest and sincerest thanks. She provided the moral support and encouragement that have made this book a shared labor of love.

Maurice D. Levi

INTERNATIONAL FINANCE

THE MARKETS AND
FINANCIAL MANAGEMENT OF
MULTINATIONAL BUSINESS

CHAPTER 1

THE IMPORTANCE, REWARDS, AND RISKS OF INTERNATIONAL FINANCE

THE IMPORTANCE OF INTERNATIONAL FINANCE

The Scope of International Finance

International trade has a pervasive importance for our standard of living and our daily lives. In the department store we find cameras and electrical equipment from Japan and clothing from Hong Kong. On the street we find automobiles from Germany, Japan, Britain, Sweden, and France using gasoline from Venezuela, Saudi Arabia, Great Britain, Mexico, and Kuwait. At home we drink tea from India, coffee from Brazil, whiskey from Scotland, beer from Germany, and wine from France. Every one of these commodities which has reached us from some other land has involved international investments and the movement of money along the channels of the payments network that is the subject of this book on international finance.

The network of payments and the international investments have elevated the study of finance to a multinational scale. Events in distant lands, whether they involve changes in the prices of oil and gold, election results, the outbreak of war, or the establishment of peace, have effects which instantly reverberate around the globe. The consequences of events in the stock markets and interest rates of one country immediately show up around the world, which has become an increasingly integrated and interdependent financial environment. The links between money and capital markets have become so close as to make it futile to concentrate on any individual part. It is these developments which have made it imperative that every actual and aspiring manager take a good look into the exciting and dynamic field of international finance.

1

Benefits of Studying International Finance

A knowledge of international finance helps in two very important ways. First, it helps the financial manager decide how international events will affect a firm and which steps can be taken to exploit positive developments and insulate the firm from harmful ones. Second, it helps the manager to anticipate events and to make profitable decisions before the events occur. Among the events that affect the firm and that the manager must anticipate are changes in exchange rates, interest rates, inflation rates, and national incomes, as well as the prospects for change in political environments. These events are intricately linked, and it is crucial that the links be understood if profitable decisions are to be made and harmful effects avoided.

We are concerned with the problems faced by any firm whose performance is affected by the international environment. Our analysis is relevant to more than the giant multinational corporations (MNCs) that have received so much attention in the media. It is just as valid for a company with a domestic focus that happens to export a little of its output or to buy inputs from abroad. Indeed, even companies that operate only domestically but compete with firms producing abroad and selling in their local market are affected by international developments. For example, U.S. clothing or automobile manufacturers with limited or zero overseas sales will find U.S. sales and profit margins affected by exchange rates which influence the dollar prices of imported clothing and automobiles.

GROWING IMPORTANCE OF INTERNATIONAL FINANCE

While we shall concentrate in this book on the managerial issues of international finance, it is important to recognize that the international flows of goods and capital that are behind the subject of international finance are important for our well-being. Indeed, with rapid growth in the flows of goods and capital, international finance is a subject of growing importance. Let us therefore pause to consider the evidence of the growth of the international movement of goods and capital. We shall also take a look at the sources of gains from the flows of goods and capital. We shall see that international finance is a subject of immense and growing importance.

International Trade versus Domestic Trade

Peoples and nations have been trading from time immemorial. During the period since records have been kept the amount of this trade between nations has typically grown at a faster rate than has domestic commerce. Even in the period since 1960, a mere moment in the long history of international trade, the proportion of trade that is between nations relative to total trade has almost doubled. This is seen in Table 1.1, which shows that global exports have risen from 9 percent of the global gross domestic product in 1960 to approximately

TABLE 1.1
AGGREGATE INTERNATIONAL TRADE VERSUS GDP

Year	World exports (market economies), billion US$	Exports / GDP, %
1989	$2,668*	17.0*
1985	1,798	15.1
1980	1,892	17.7
1975	822.4	15.0
1970	290.6	10.2
1965	173.4	9.2
1960	120.1	9.0

*Estimate.
Source: International Financial Statistics: Supplement on Trade Statistics, International Monetary Fund, Washington, D.C.

17 percent by 1989. More and more of production is exported, which is the mirror image of the increasing proportion of consumption that is imported.

The growing importance of international trade is reflected in the importance of trade to most major industrialized nations. For example, Figure 1.1 shows that in the United States the proportion of consumption consisting of imported goods and services has more than doubled since 1962; it has increased from only 6.8 percent in 1962 to 15.3 percent by 1986. Figure 1.1, which shows the fraction

FIGURE 1.1
Percentage of consumption consisting of imports. *Source:* International Monetary Fund, *International Financial Statistics*, July 1989.

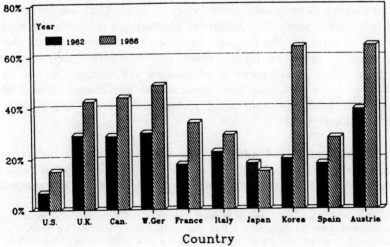

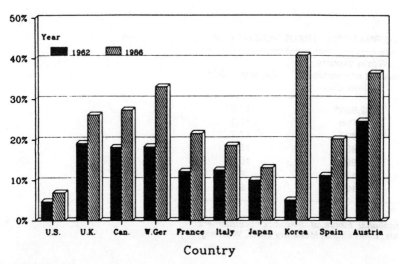

FIGURE 1.2
Percentage of GDP arising from exports. *Source:* International Monetary
Fund, *International Financial Statistics*, July 1989.

of consumption consisting of imports, and Figure 1.2, which shows the fraction
of GDP that is exported, reveal clearly that international trade is a matter of
growing importance in the U.S., Britain, Canada, West Germany, France, and
just about every leading country, whether we measure trade by imports or
exports. It is worth pausing to consider the rewards and risks that have
accompanied this expansion in importance of international trade.

The Rewards of International Trade   The principal reward of international
trade is that it has brought about increased prosperity by allowing nations to
specialize in producing those goods and services at which they are relatively
efficient. The relative efficiency of a country in producing a particular product
can be described in terms of the amounts of other alternative products that
could be produced by the same inputs. When considered this way, relative
efficiencies are described as **comparative advantages**. All nations can and do
simultaneously gain from exploiting their comparative advantages, as well as
from the larger-scale production and broader choice of products that is made
possible by international trade.[1]

The Risks of International Trade   The rewards of trade do not come
without added risks. The most obvious additional risk of international versus
domestic trade arises from uncertainty about future exchange rates. Unexpected

---

[1] For those readers who have not learned or have forgotten the principle of comparative
advantage, a summary is given in Appendix 1.1 at the end of this chapter. The gains from
exploitation of comparative advantages are no different from the gains from specialization within a
country.

changes in exchange rates can have important impacts on sales, prices and profits of both exporters and importers.[2] For example, if a U.S. whiskey exporter faces an unexpected increase in the value of the dollar from DM 1.6 (meaning Deutsche or German marks) to DM 2.0, a bottle of whiskey sold for $10 will increase in price in Germany from DM 16 to DM 20.[3] This will reduce sales, and since the U.S. exporter receives $10 before and after the change in the exchange rate, it reduces the exporter's profit. In a similar way prices, sales, and profits of importers are also affected by unexpected changes in exchange rates.

Whether unexpected changes in exchange rates affect prices, sales, and profits of exporters and importers depends on whether changes in exchange rates really make a firm's goods cheaper or more expensive to buyers. For example, if an increase in the value of the dollar from DM 1.6 to DM 2.0 occurs while the price of a bottle of whiskey for export from the United States goes from $10 to $8, a bottle of whiskey will continue to cost DM16 in Germany. This is because the dollar price multiplied by the exchange rate, which gives the mark price, is unchanged. Our example shows that in order to determine the effect of changes in exchange rates, we must examine inflation and how inflation and exchange rates are related. This requires that we study international finance at the level of the economy as well as at the level of the individual firm.

The risk faced by exporters and importers resulting from the impact of exchange rates on prices, sales, and profits is only one, albeit probably the most important, of the additional risks of international versus domestic trade. Another risk of international trade is **country risk**. This is the risk that, as a result of war, revolution, or other political or social events, a firm may not be paid for its exports. Country risk applies to foreign investment as well as to credit granted in trade, and exists because it is difficult to use legal channels or seize assets when the buyer is in another jurisdiction. Furthermore, foreign buyers may be willing but unable to pay because, for example, their government unexpectedly imposes currency restrictions. Other added risks of doing business abroad include uncertainty about the possible imposition or change of import tariffs or quotas, possible changes in subsidization of local producers, and possible imposition of nontariff barriers.

Practices have evolved and markets have developed which help firms cope with the added risks of doing business abroad. For example, special types of foreign-exchange contracts have been designed to enable importers and exporters to **hedge**, or **cover**, some of the risks from unexpected changes in exchange rates. Similarly, export insurance schemes have been established to help reduce country risk, and **letters of credit** have been developed to reduce other risks of trade. With international trade playing an increasingly important role in just about every industrial nation, it is increasingly important that we

---

[2]To the extent that changes in exchange rates are expected to occur, they do not contribute risk. Risk results from randomness and therefore is due to unexpected changes in exchange rates.

[3]This ignores taxes, shipping costs, and so on. It also assumes that the U.S. dollar price of whiskey remains unchanged as the exchange rate changes, an assumption we relax later.

learn about these risk-reducing practices. It is also increasingly important that we learn about the fundamental causes of the special risks of trade. These are two important topics of this book.

Increased Globalization of Financial and Real-Asset Markets

Alongside the growing importance of international versus domestic trade, there has been a parallel growth in the importance of foreign versus domestic investment in the money market, the bond market, the stock market, the real-estate market, and the market for operating businesses. At times, the importance of overseas investments and investors has swelled to overshadow that of domestic investment and investors. For example, there have been periods when purchases of U.S. government bills and bonds by Japanese, German, and other foreign investors have exceeded purchases of these instruments by Americans. Foreign buyers can be so crucial to the successful sale of securities that the U.S. Treasury and private brokerage firms must watch overseas calendars to ensure they do not launch a major sale when, for example, Japanese or European financial institutions are closed for an official holiday. The horizons of investors and borrowers have clearly become global.

In catering to the expanded horizons of investors, there has been an explosion of internationally oriented financial products such as internationally diversified, global, and single foreign country mutual funds. The popularity of these products is a sign of the internationalization of financial markets. For example, the large internationally diversified funds such as Fidelity Overseas, Paine-Webber Atlas, Putnam International Equities, T. Rowe Price International, Scudder International, and Shearson-Lehman International are all no more than a few years old. Similarly, virtually all the global funds which combine domestic and foreign opportunities are no more than a few years old. For example, from being the only fund of its kind 10 or so years ago, the Templeton World Fund has become but one of a long list of global investment funds with such new arrivals as the Prudential-Bache Global Fund, the Dean Witter Worldwide Fund, Templeton Global II, and the Merrill Lynch International Fund.[4] Single-country mutual funds have also become commonplace in very recent years, with the arrival of Korean, Australian, Italian, Taiwanese, Japanese, Mexican, Malaysian, and other country funds. The buying of foreign securities directly by individuals without the use of mutual funds has also enjoyed explosive growth in recent years and has helped transform the international departments of securities firms into major profit-growth centers. Real estate and other markets have also experienced transformations from the phenomenal pace of globalization. For example, foreign ownership of U.S. real estate expanded by an average rate of 39 percent per annum during the period 1976–1986.

---

[4]Even in the short period 1984–1989, the number of open-ended mutual funds investing globally grew from 36 to 171. See *Global Custody*, special supplement to *Euromoney*, March 1989, p. 4.

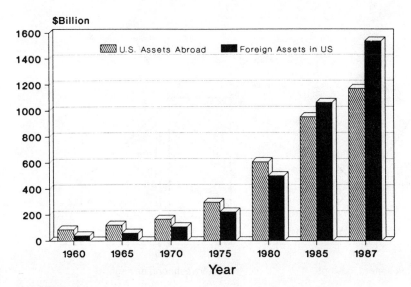

FIGURE 1.3
International investment position of the United States. *Source:* U.S.
Department of Commerce, Bureau of the Census, *Statistical Abstract of the
United States*, 1989.

The growth in globalization of investment viewed from a U.S. perspective can
be seen from Figure 1.3. In the decade 1976–1986 Americans increased their
investment abroad by over 300 percent. During that same period foreigners
increased their investment in the U.S. by 500 percent. A similar picture emerges
in other countries. However, as with the expansion of the relative importance of
international versus domestic trade, the increase in globalization of investment
has brought both rewards and risks.

Rewards of Globalization of Investment and International Flows of Capital
Among the rewards of the globalization of investment have been an improvement in the global allocation of capital formation and an enhanced ability to
diversify investment portfolios.[5] The gain from the better allocation of capital
arises from the fact that international investment reduces the extent to which
investments with high returns in some countries are forgone for want of
available capital, while low-return investments in other countries with abundant
capital go ahead. The flow of capital between countries moves rates of return in
different locations closer together, thereby offering investors overall better

---

[5]There is an additional gain from increased globalization of financial markets enjoyed via an
enhanced ability to smooth consumption over time by lending and borrowing. This gain is not as
straightforward as the gain from more efficient allocation of capital and is described in Appendix
1.2.

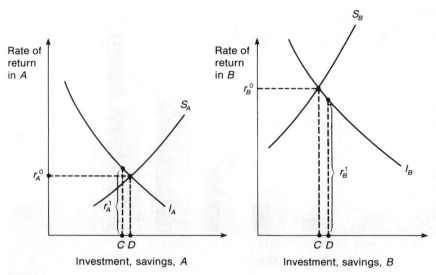

FIGURE 1.4
THE GAIN FROM THE BETTER ALLOCATION OF CAPITAL. The heights of the curves I_A and I_B give the rates of return on an extra dollar's worth of investment in countries A and B. These curves slope downward because as more is invested, incremental projects offer lower returns. The curves S_A and S_B give savings at different returns on savings in the two countries. With no flow of capital between countries, returns will be r_A^0 and r_B^0. Each dollar moving from A to B will result in a forgone return in A given by the height of I_A, and a return in B given by the height of I_B. For example, the first dollar to move from A to B raises the global returns on investment by $r_B^0 - r_A^0$. After CD dollars have left A for B, the added global return from another dollar is $r_B^1 - r_A^1$.

returns. This gain from the international flow of capital is illustrated in Figure 1.4.

The heights of the curves I_A and I_B in Figure 1.4 give the rates of return on investments in countries A and B at different rates of investment. The curves slope downward because countries run out of good investment projects as their rates of investment increase.[6] The curves labeled S_A and S_B give the amounts saved at different rates of return on savings. If there is no flow of capital between countries, the equilibrium returns in A and B are r_A^0 and r_B^0.

The first dollar to flow from A to B means a forgone investment return in A of r_A^0 for a return in B of r_B^0. This is a net gain of $r_B^0 - r_A^0$. After \$$CD$ of capital has moved from A to B, an extra dollar of capital flow produces a net gain of $r_B^1 - r_A^1$. It should be clear from the figure that there is a global gain in return from investment until enough capital has moved to equalize returns in the two countries. The figure demonstrates that there are gains from the flow of capital between countries, just as the principle of comparative advantage shows that there are gains from the movement of goods. Since international finance is

---

[6]The height of I_A or I_B is referred to as the **marginal efficiency of investment**.

concerned with the study of the international flows of goods and capital and all these flows entail, we can see that international finance is concerned with activities from which people benefit.[7]

A further gain from the international flow of capital has been an increased possibility of diversification of investment portfolios because the economic ups and downs in different countries are not perfectly synchronized. This has meant that investors have been able to achieve a higher expected return for a given degree of risk, or a lower risk for a given expected return.

Costs of Globalization of Investment The benefits of the globalization of investment have not come without a price. The price is the addition of exchange-rate risk and country risk.

Unanticipated changes in exchange rates cause uncertainty in investors' home-currency values of assets and liabilities. For example, if the exchange rate is $2 U.S. per British pound (£), a bank balance of £100 in London is worth $200 to a U.S. investor. If the British pound unexpectedly falls in value to $1.5, the U.S. investor's bank balance falls in value to $150. If instead of having an asset the U.S. investor has a debt or liability of £100, the unexpected change in exchange rate from $2 per pound to $1.5 per pound means a reduction in the dollar value of what the American owes. The dollar value of the liability will decline from $200 to $150.

In the case of a foreign-currency-denominated bank balance or debt, ex-change-rate risk is due to uncertainty in the future exchange rates at which the asset or liability will be translated into dollars. Any asset or liability for which the home-currency value is affected by unexpected changes in exchange rates is subject to exchange-rate risk. This means that foreign stocks, bonds, property, and accounts receivable and payable may be subject to exchange-rate risk if their value in home currency (the U.S. dollar for a U.S. investor) is affected by exchange rates. However, we should note that the mere fact that an asset or liability is in a foreign country does not mean that it is subject to exchange-rate risk, and the mere fact that an asset or liability is at home does not mean that it is *not* subject to exchange-rate risk. Let us consider why.

If a foreign asset can predictably be presumed to increase in value in terms of its home currency at the same time as the foreign currency falls in value, the foreign asset may not be subject to exchange-rate risk. For example, if real estate increases in value at the overall inflation rate in a country, say 6 percent, and if the foreign exchange value of a currency falls by the rate of inflation, that is, also by 6 percent, then the translated value of the real estate is not changed by future changes in exchange rates; we have an asset that is worth 6 percent more in its local currency, but that currency is worth 6 percent less, leaving the value of the foreign asset in the investor's home currency unchanged. As we

---

[7]This is not the place to describe the distribution of the benefits from the international flow of capital, any more than Appendix 1.1, which explains the principle of comparative advantage, can describe the distribution of the gains from international trade. In order to describe distributional effects we need far more elaborate frameworks than we use here.

shall see, there is reason to expect compensating movements in exchange rates and local currency values of some assets, at least over the long run.

While some foreign assets are not subject to exchange-rate risk, some domestic assets are. For example, suppose that when the exchange rate of a country's currency falls, the central bank in that country increases interest rates to arrest the decline in its exchange rate. In such a case, the value of the country's bonds will fall when the country's exchange rate worsens. Even though the asset is a domestic asset, it is subject to exchange-rate risk. This is because exchange-rate risk exists whenever unexpected changes in exchange rates affect the values of assets or liabilities expressed in the investor's currency.

Contributing to the increased importance of exchange-rate risk resulting from the globalization of investment is the interdependence it has created between financial markets in different countries. An interpretation of the circumstances surrounding the stock-market crash of October 1987 illustrates this interdependence.

The U.S. dollar had declined substantially in value in the two years preceding the crash, but the U.S. trade deficit had stubbornly refused to show any improvement. Indeed, the U.S. trade balance had worsened even while the dollar declined. It is believed by many economists that people were worried that, in anticipation of a further decline in the value of the dollar, foreign investors might sell the large volume of U.S. stocks and bonds they had accumulated; this large volume of U.S. stocks and bonds held abroad was itself a result of the globalization of investment. While other explanations of the crash are plausible, one view is that the release of the U.S. balance of trade statistics in the week before Monday, October 19, 1987, which were far worse than expected, turned market fear into panic. Even if this interpretation of the crash is not accepted, few could argue with the view that the globalization of investment contributed to the world-wide panic selling. Therefore, the crash of 1987 illustrates a cost of the globalization of investment. It also suggests that macroeconomic phenomena, such as the balance of trade, cannot be ignored, even if our interest is only in financial management at the level of the firm.

The globalization of investment has not only meant foreign exchange risk which has been exacerbated by the resulting increased interdependence. The increase in ownership of foreign assets has also meant that investors face increased country risk. As we have already mentioned, country risk involves the possibility of expropriation or confiscation of property, or its destruction by war or revolution. It also involves the possibility of changes in taxes on foreign income or the imposition of restrictions on repatriating income. As in the case of foreign exchange risk, this book is devoted to showing how practices and institutions have developed to help reduce country risk.

Increased Volatility of Exchange Rates

The more rapid growth of international trade versus domestic trade and the expanded international focus of investment that we have documented offer in themselves more than adequate reason why it is increasingly important for

TABLE 1.2
THE VOLATILITY OF EXCHANGE RATES

Period	Volatility, %			
	Can$	UK£	DM	¥
1950 – 1959	4	0*	0*	0*
1960 – 1969	4	6	2	0*
1970 – 1979	6	13	21	18
1980 – 1987	6	21	18	21

*Less than 0.5 percent.
Source: Standard deviation of month-end-to-month-end exchange rates as published in *The Wall Street Journal*, divided by the mean exchange rate over the period 1950 – 87.

students of business to study international finance. There is, however, an additional reason why knowledge of this exciting discipline has become imperative.

Exchange-rate risk has risen far more than the amount of foreign trade and overseas investment because exchange rates have become increasingly volatile. This volatility has been so substantial that at times the plight of the dollar or the soaring or sinking value of some other major currency have become headline material even outside of the business press. Prompted at times by tensions in the Middle East or some other politically sensitive part of the world, and at other times by news on the economic health or malaise of some major country, exchange rates have jumped and dropped by startling amounts. Billions of dollars—and yen, marks, pounds, and francs—are made and lost in a day as a result of these currency swings. Never before have exchange rates darted around as much as they have in recent years, and therefore never before has exchange-rate risk been so important.

Table 1.2, which is shown graphically in Figure 1.5, reveals the increased volatility in exchange rates that has occurred during the postwar period. The volatility is measured by computing the standard deviation of month-to-month exchange rates and dividing by the mean to allow comparison.[8] The table and figure show how dramatically exchange-rate volatility has risen and how much more risk is consequently faced even on a constant amount of international trade and investment. If we add to the higher volatility the fact that international trade and investment are both far more important than they used to be, we can see why it has become so essential to understand the nature of exchange-rate risk and how to manage it.

There is no consensus as to why exchange rates are more volatile than in the past. Some blame the switch to flexible exchange rates that occurred around 1973. However, others say the previous fixed-exchange-rate system could not have coped with the larger shocks that have occurred since that time—jumps and drops in oil prices, international conflicts, and so on. What is fairly certain

---

[8]This statistic is called the **coefficient of variation**.

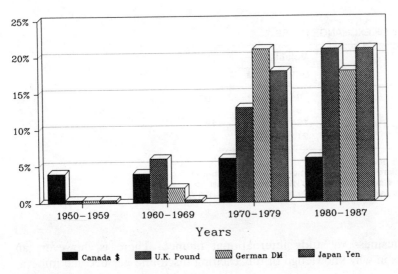

FIGURE 1.5
The volatility of exchange rates. *Source:* Standard deviation of
month-end-to-month-end exchange rates as published in *The Wall Street
Journal*, divided by the mean exchange rate over the period 1950–1987.

is that the increased globalization of investment played a role by being associated with more "hot money" skipping from financial center to financial center
in search of the highest return. Another factor may have been the technology
for moving money and transmitting information, which has allowed both to
move at the speed of light. Whatever the reason, a consequence of the greatly
increased exchange-rate volatility has been a parallel increase in the importance
of understanding the methods for managing foreign-exchange risk, and the
other topics covered in this book.

TOPICS COVERED IN THIS BOOK

Part 1, consisting of Chapters 2 and 3, explores the foreign exchange markets.
An introduction to the structure of the markets and the form in which currencies are exchanged is essential background to the study of international financial
management. Chapter 2 explains the nature of bank-note markets and bank-draft
markets—the former involving the paper currency in our wallets and the latter
involving checks. It is shown that the ability to choose direct or indirect
exchange between currencies allows us to compute all exchange rates from
exchange rates versus the dollar. Transaction costs are shown to cloud the link
between currencies.

Chapter 3 examines the forward and futures exchange markets and explains
how they work. These are markets in which it is possible to contract for future

sale or purchase of a foreign currency so as to avoid being affected by unanticipated changes in exchange rates. The similarities and differences between forward exchange and currency futures are described, along with definitions of some important terms. We consider the extent to which the forward and futures markets are linked. Chapter 3 also introduces currency options, explaining what they are and how they differ from forward and futures exchange contracts. The chapter concludes with a brief account of the situations in which forward, futures, and option contracts are useful, although the full account of these situations must await later chapters.

Part 2, consisting of Chapters 4 and 5, examines the determination of exchange rates. The purpose of these chapters is to give the reader a firm understanding of the factors which can make exchange rates move up and down. Such an understanding is essential for successful financial management in the international environment. Chapter 4 looks at the structure and meaning of the international balance-of-payments accounts, where the factors behind the supplies of and demands for currencies are recorded. Indeed, the balance-of-payments account is viewed as a record of the causes of supply and demand for a currency. Chapter 5 examines the supply and demand curves for currencies and the nature of the equilibrium they determine. It is shown that there is a real possibility that the exchange-rate equilibrium is unstable. This possibility is related to a phenomenon known as the J curve, whereby changes in exchange rates have unexpected effects. For example, it is shown that a depreciating currency—a currency with a falling foreign-exchange value—can actually make the balance of payments worse. This possibility has attracted considerable interest in recent years because the U.S. balance of payments since the mid-1980s appears to have been tracking the path of a J curve.

Part 3, consisting of Chapters 6, 7, and 8, introduces two central principles of international finance, the purchasing-power parity (PPP) principle and the interest parity principle. The PPP principle states that exchange rates will reflect the relative local currency prices of products in different countries, and that changes in exchange rates will reflect differences in countries' inflation rates; countries with relatively rapid inflation will have depreciating currencies, and vice versa. Chapter 6 examines both the theory behind the PPP condition and its empirical validity. The interest parity condition says that when exchange rate effects are incorporated in investment yields and borrowing costs by using forward exchange contracts, interest rates must be the same everywhere. Chapter 7 examines the theory behind interest parity as well as its validity, and in the course of doing so explains how to compute investment yields and borrowing costs that incorporate the effects of exchange rates.

If there were no differences in interest yields and borrowing costs between countries, it would not matter where investment or borrowing occurred. However, there are differences in yields and costs, and the reasons they exist are explained in Chapter 8. It is important that we understand why these yield and borrowing-cost differences exist, because they have implications for international cash management. Indeed, in the course of explaining why yield and borrowing-cost differences exist, we are able to show how to decide on where to invest and borrow in the international context.

Part 4, consisting of Chapters 9 and 10, considers the nature of foreign exchange risk and exposure, and how exposure may be hedged by the use of forward, futures, and option contracts, as well as by borrowing or investing in the money markets. Chapter 9 is concerned with the definition and measurement of foreign exchange exposure, which is what is at risk to changes in exchange rates. Different types of exposure and the factors determining the size of each type of exposure are described. In addition, exchange-rate exposure is carefully distinguished from exchange-rate risk. Because the accounting conventions that are used can affect exposure as it appears in financial statements, we examine accounting procedures for international transactions. We also explain the notion of real changes in exchange rates and their relation to exposure.

Chapter 10 begins by considering why it may or may not be a good idea to reduce the amount that is exposed to risk from unanticipated changes in exchange rates, that is, to hedge or speculate. The many techniques for hedging, and speculating are described and compared. These include forward, futures and options contracts, as well as swaps. A simple graphical technique is used to compare the consequences of using the different hedging and speculation techniques.

Part 5, consisting of Chapters 11 and 12, is concerned with short-term financial markets and management. Chapter 11 describes the nature of short-term international financial markets. The first part of the chapter focuses on the offshore currency market, of which the Eurodollar market is an example. Eurodollars are U.S.-dollar-denominated bank deposits held outside the United States. Other-currency-denominated bank deposits are also found in foreign countries, and along with Eurodollars constitute the offshore currency market. Chapter 11 explains why the offshore currency market has developed, and how it works. The chapter concludes with a description of the organization of international banking, because offshore currency deposits result from the structure of international banking.

Chapter 12 focuses on short-term cash management, and explains why a multinational corporation might want to centralize the management of its working capital. It is shown that the same factors causing differences in investment yields and borrowing costs between countries described in Chapter 8 are the factors affecting cash management. A central issue is whether foreign exchange and money markets are efficient, because if they are, there is no expected return from trying to "beat the market" with investment and borrowing decisions. The chapter therefore concludes with a discussion of the theory and testing of the efficiency of foreign exchange and money markets.

Part 6 is concerned with longer-term international financial markets and management. Chapter 13 considers portfolio investment, and how investors can choose between investments in different countries' stock and bond markets. Considerable attention is paid to the benefits of an internationally diversified portfolio of securities. It is shown that because economic conditions do not move in a perfectly parallel fashion in different countries, it pays to diversify internationally. The theory and evidence on whether securities are priced in an internationally integrated or a segmented market setting are examined within the context of the capital asset pricing model.

Chapter 14 is devoted to issues concerning medium- and longer-term financing, such as the choices between issuing bonds denominated and paying interest in different currencies, and/or sold in different countries. It is shown that certain types of bonds enable a firm to reduce foreign exchange exposure and/or country risk.

Part 7 turns to the question of foreign direct investment, which is what occurs when, for example, a company builds a manufacturing plant in another country. Chapter 15 shows how to evaluate foreign direct investments, including the discount rate and tax rate to employ, the way to handle concessionary financing, restrictions on repatriating income, and so on. Chapter 16 looks at the factors behind the growth of the giant multinational corporations which have been the result of foreign direct investment. It also considers problems caused by the growth of MNCs, and how corporate costs and earnings can be allocated among divisions of MNCs by internal transfer prices for items exchanged between corporate divisions. Since a primary concern of MNCs is country risk of foreign facilities being seized and of taxes being imposed on repatriated earnings, Chapter 16 looks at the measurement of and avoidance of country risk.

Part 8 considers the practices and risks associated with exporting and importing. Chapter 17 looks at the practical side of exporting and importing. It describes the documents that are involved in international trade, the methods of financing and insuring trade, and so on. Because a substantial part of international trade takes a special form known as countertrade, an account is given of the nature of and possible reasons from this practice. Chapter 18 uses the standard tools of microeconomics to discover the factors affecting how prices, sales, and profits of exporters and importers are affected by unexpected changes in exchange rates.

The book concludes with a backgrounder on the international financial and economic environment. This appears as an Addendum for inclusion in international finance and financial management courses that include an account of the broader environment in which exchange rates are determined and in which financial decisions are made.

The Addendum begins by looking at the international financial systems involving fixed exchange rates that have been practiced throughout history, and how these systems dealt with deficits and surpluses when they occurred. This involves a discussion of the gold standard, the Bretton Woods standard, and the European Monetary System. This leads us into a discussion of the automatic adjustment mechanisms involving prices, national income, and interest rates. While it is less important to study fixed exchange rates today than when exchange rates were formally fixed, we should pay some attention to issues concerning fixed exchange rates because the international financial system has moved away from complete flexibility in exchange rates since 1985, and because fixed rates still exist in a number of countries, including the majority of members of the European Economic Community. Furthermore, the international financial system could well return to fixed exchange rates.

The Addendum compares fixed and flexible exchange rates and looks at some of the compromise systems between these extremes. There is also a discussion of a number of new theories of exchange rates that have been used to make forecasts and explain the increase in exchange-rate volatility.

The economic and financial environment backgrounder in the Addendum is self-contained and can be used at any point in the book. However, the most appropriate place for inserting the Addendum is after Chapter 5, which discusses the determination of flexible exchange rates. This allows a natural transition into the fixed exchange rate systems that have been practiced or are still in use. The Addendum can be used in full or in part, depending on how much preparation the student has in international economics. All topics are treated at a basic level that assumes only a previous course in introductory economics.

SUMMARY

1 Every good or service reaching us from abroad has involved international finance. Knowledge of the subject can help managers avoid harmful effects of international events and profit from these events.

2 International trade has grown more quickly than trade in general. This has brought rewards and costs.

3 The principal reward for international trade is the gain in standard of living it has permitted. This gain comes from exploiting relative efficiencies of production in different countries, known as comparative advantages.

4 The costs of international trade are the introduction of exchange-rate risk and an increase in country risk. Methods and markets have evolved that allow firms to avoid or reduce these risks, and since international trade has become more important it has become more important to learn about these methods and markets.

5 International finance has also become a more important subject because of an increased globalization of financial markets. The benefits of the increased flow of capital between nations include a better international allocation of capital formation and greater opportunities to diversify risk. However, globalization of investment has meant new risks from exchange rates, political actions, and increased interdependence of financial conditions in different countries.

6 Adding to the increase in relevance of exchange-rate risk from the growth in international trade and the globalization of financial markets has been an increase in the volatility of exchange rates. All these factors combine to make it imperative that today's student of business study the factors behind the risks of international trade and investment, and the methods of reducing these risks.

BIBLIOGRAPHY

Aliber, Robert Z.: *Exchange Risk and Corporate International Finance*, Macmillan, New York, 1978.

Coombs, Charles: *The Arena of International Finance*, John Wiley, New York, 1976.

Dufey, Gunter, and Ian Giddy: *The International Money Market*, Prentice-Hall, Englewood Cliffs, N.J., 1978.

Grubel, Herbert, G.: *International Economics*, Richard D. Irwin, Homewood, Ill., 1977.

Henning, Charles N., William Piggot, and Robert H. Scott: *International Financial Management*, McGraw-Hill, New York, 1977.

Lessard, Donald R. (ed.): *International Financial Management: Theory and Applications*, 2d ed., Warren, Gorham and Lamont, Boston, 1985.

Mundell, Robert A.: *International Economics*, Macmillan, New York, 1968.

Pippenger, John E.: *Fundamentals of International Finance*, Prentice-Hall, Englewood Cliffs, N.J., 1984.

Robinson, Richard: *International Business Management*, 2d ed., Dryden, New York, 1978.

Stern, Robert: *The Balance of Payments: Theory and Economic Policy*, Aldine, Chicago, 1973.

Tarleton, Jesse: "Recommended Courses in International Business for Graduate Business Students," *Journal of Business*, October 1977, pp. 438–447.

Vernon, Raymond, and Louis Wells, Jr.: *Manager in the International Economy*, 5th ed., Prentice-Hall, Englewood Cliffs, N.J., 1986.

Weston, J. Fred, and Bart W. Sorge: *Guide to International Financial Management*, McGraw-Hill, New York, 1977.

Parallel Material for Case Courses

Carlson, Robert S., H. Lee Remmers, Christine R. Hekman, David K. Eiteman, and Arthur Stonehill: *International Finance: Cases and Simulation*, Addison-Wesley, Reading, Mass., 1980.

Dufey, Gunter, and Ian H. Giddy: *International Finance: 50 Cases and Problems*, Addison-Wesley, Reading, Mass., 1986.

Feiger, George, and Bertrand Jacquillat: *International Finance: Text and Cases*, Allyn and Bacon, Boston, 1982.

Zernoff, David B., and Jack Zwick: *International Financial Management*, Prentice-Hall, Englewood Cliffs, N.J., 1969.

APPENDIX 1.1: The Gains from Trade in Goods and Services

THE PRINCIPLE OF COMPARATIVE ADVANTAGE

Comparative advantage is not one of the most intuitive results in economics, and it can require a little thought to leave the reader convinced of the validity of the argument. Discovered by the English stockbroker-millionaire David Ricardo, the idea helps answer the following question:

> Suppose that Japan is much more efficient than the U.S. in producing steel and marginally more efficient than the U.S. in producing food, and that steel and food are the only items produced and required in both countries. Would both countries be better off by having free trade between them than by prohibiting trade?

TABLE 1A.1
THE SITUATION UNDER AUTARKY*

Output	U.S.	Japan
Number of people employed per ton of output		
Food	25	20
Steel	10	4
Opportunity cost per ton of output		
Food	2.5 tons steel	5.0 tons steel
Steel	0.4 tons food	0.2 tons food
Millions of people employed		
Food	75	40
Steel	75	40
Autarky output, millions of tons		
Food	3	2
Steel	7.5	10

Autarky means no trade across national borders.

When faced with this question, it is not uncommon to hear people say that while Japan would be better off from free trade because it is more efficient at producing both products, the U.S. would be worse off. The reasoning behind this view is the presumption that Japan would be able to undercut U.S. prices for both products and thereby put Americans out of work. What the principle of comparative advantage shows is that in fact *both* countries are better off from free trade than no trade, and that it is *relative* efficiencies rather than *absolute* efficiencies of production that determine the pattern and benefits of trade. These relative efficiencies of production are referred to as **comparative advantages**. Let us explain this important principle of comparative advantage by taking an example. This example will also clarify what we mean by this concept.

Suppose that the amounts of labor needed to produce a ton of steel and food in the U.S. and Japan with the given stock of land and capital with which the labor can work are as shown on the top of Table 1A.1. These numbers assume that Japan can produce both products with less labor than the U.S., which means that Japan has an **absolute advantage** in both products.

If the U.S. were to produce one more ton of food by moving labor from producing steel, the forgone output of steel—that is, the opportunity cost of food in terms of steel —would be 2.5 tons of steel.[9] On the other hand, if the U.S. were to produce one more ton of steel by moving labor from producing food, the opportunity cost would be 0.4 tons of food. Similarly, in Japan the opportunity cost of one more ton of food is 5.0 tons of

---

[9]Of course, it is individuals, not nations, that make production decisions. However, referring to countries as if they made production decisions is a convenient anthropomorphism.

TABLE 1A.2
INPUT / OUTPUT UNDER FREE TRADE

Output	United States	Japan
Millions of people employed		
Food	125	12
Steel	25	68
Total output, millions of tons		
Food	5	0.6
Steel	2.5	17
Consumption amounts under trading division		
Food	3.2	2.4
Steel	8	11.5

steel, and the opportunity cost of one more ton of steel is 0.2 tons of food. These numbers are shown in Table 1A.1. We see that the U.S. has a lower opportunity cost of producing food, while Japan has a lower opportunity cost of producing steel. These relative opportunity costs are the basis of the definition of comparative advantage.

A comparative advantage in a particular product is said to exist if, in producing more of that product, a country has a lower opportunity cost in terms of alternative products than the opportunity cost of that product in other countries. Table 1A.1 shows that the U.S. has a comparative advantage in food and Japan has a comparative advantage in steel. It should be clear that as long as relative efficiencies differ, every country has some comparative advantage. This is the case even if a country has an absolute disadvantage in everything. What we will demonstrate next is that by producing the good for which the country has a comparative advantage and trading it for the products for which other countries have a comparative advantage, everybody is better off.

Table 1A.1 shows the number of workers (available labor power) in the U.S. and Japan. The table also gives the outputs of food and steel in each country, assuming half of the working population in each country is employed in each industry. For example, 75 million Americans can produce 3 million tons of food when 25 million workers are required per ton, and the other 75 million who work can produce 7.5 million tons of steel. The total world output of food is 5 million tons, and the total world output of steel is 17.5 million tons.

Suppose now that 28 million Japanese workers are shifted from agriculture to steel, while at the same time 50 million American workers are shifted from steel to agriculture. The effect of this on the outputs of both countries is shown in Table 1A.2. We find that with Japan specializing in steel and with the U.S. specializing in food, the outputs for the two countries combined are 5.6 million tons of food and 19.5 million tons of steel. The combined outputs of both items have increased by 10 percent or more merely by having Japan concentrate on its comparative advantage, steel, and the U.S. concentrate on its comparative advantage, food.

The U.S. and Japan can both be richer if they trade certain amounts between themselves. One such trading division would be for the U.S. to sell to Japan 1.8 million tons of food and to buy from Japan 5.5 million tons of steel, giving a **terms of trade** of approximately 0.3 tons of food per ton of steel. The U.S. and Japan would then end up consuming the amounts in the bottom rows of Table 1A.2, all of which exceed what they could consume under autarky as shown in Table 1A.1.

The gains shown by comparing Table 1A.2 with Table 1A.1 are due to specializing production according to the countries' comparative advantages. The benefit of specializing production is only one of the gains from trade.

Given our assumption that Japan is relatively more efficient in producing steel than food, and the U.S. is relatively more efficient in producing food than steel, under autarky we can expect food to be cheap relative to steel in the U.S., and steel to be cheap relative to food in Japan. This suggests that by exporting food to Japan, where food is relatively expensive in the absence of trade, the U.S. can receive a relatively large amount of steel in return. Similarly, by exporting steel to the U.S., where steel is relatively expensive in the absence of trade, Japan can receive a relatively large amount of food. Therefore, via exchange of products through trade, both countries can be better off. The gain is a **pure exchange gain** and would be enjoyed even without any specialization of production. That is, there are two components to the gains from trade due to comparative advantage: the gain from adjusting the pattern of production (the gain from specialization) and the gain from adjusting the pattern of consumption (the pure exchange gain).[10]

FURTHER GAINS FROM INTERNATIONAL TRADE

The number of people required to produce the food and steel in our example is assumed to be the same whatever the output of these products. That is, we have implicitly assumed **constant returns to scale**. However, if there are **increasing returns to scale** it will take fewer people to produce a given quantity of the product for which the country has a comparative advantage as more of that product is produced. In this case of economies of scale there are yet further gains from international trade. Returns to scale can come in many forms, including pure technological gains, benefits of learning by doing, and so on. In addition, if there is monopoly power within a country that is removed by trade, consumers enjoy an additional benefit in terms of lower prices due to increased competition. Yet a further gain from trade comes in the form of an increase in product variety. Therefore, the gain from exploiting comparative advantages is only part of the total gain from free trade.[11] Furthermore, there are gains from the free international movement of capital that are in addition to the gains from free trade in goods and services. The gains from the movement of capital are described in Appendix 1.2.

[10] The pure exchange gain that comes from adjusting consumption cannot be shown in terms of our numerical example. This is because demonstration of this gain requires measurement of relative satisfaction from the two products. This in turn requires the use of utility theory. Formal separation of the specialization gain from the pure exchange gain is best left to courses in the pure theory of international trade.

[11] An account of the numerous sources of gains from trade can be found in Cletus C. Coughlin, K. Alec Chrystal, and Geoffrey E. Wood, "Protectionist Trade Policies: A Survey of Theory, Evidence and Rationale," *Review*, Federal Reserve Bank of St. Louis, January/February 1988, pp. 12–26.

APPENDIX 1.2: The Gains from the International Flow of Capital

In the previous appendix we showed that everybody can simultaneously benefit from international trade in goods and services. In this appendix we show that everybody can also simultaneously gain from the international flow of financial capital. Between them, the international flow of goods and services and the international flow of capital constitute the sum total of reasons for the supply of and demand for foreign exchange. Indeed, the two major subdivisions of the balance-of-payments accounts—the current account and the capital account—report respectively the demand for and supply of a country's currency due to trade in goods and services, and the supply of and demand for the currency due to the flow of capital. Therefore, what this and the previous appendix do is show that the very bases of the study of international finance—the flow of goods and services and the flow of capital—are both important contributors to our well-being. It is not, as is often thought, just the international flow of goods and services from which we benefit.

We have already noted in the text of this chapter that the international flow of capital means that a project with a very high yield in one country is not forgone for want of funds while a low-yield project in a country of abundant capital goes ahead. This benefits everybody because the investors in the country with the low-yield project can enjoy some of the high return offered in the other country, while the country with the high-yield project gets to fund what might otherwise be postponed or forgone.[12] This is potentially a very important gain from the international flow of capital, but it is not the only gain. There is a further benefit of the international flow of capital that comes from the smoothing of consumption that is permitted by lending and borrowing. This gain comes from the fact that if a nation were unable to borrow from abroad it would have limited scope to maintain consumption during temporary declines in national income.[13] Similarly, if the nation were unable to invest abroad, it would have limited scope for dampening temporary jumps in consumption during surges in national income.

It is frequently assumed that people are subject to diminishing marginal utility of income and consumption. Indeed, this is a basic rationale for the postulate of risk aversion which is essential to much of the theory in finance. Diminishing marginal utility of consumption means that a more even path of consumption over time is preferred to a more erratic path with the same average level of consumption. The reason for this preference for a smooth path of consumption over time is illustrated in Figure 1A.1.

The curve labeled TU shows the total utility derived from different amounts of consumption per period of time. Because the curve slopes upward throughout its range,

---

[12] The gain from funding high-yield projects rather than low-yield projects due to the flow of capital can be computed from the rate-of-return schedules of the two countries and the flow of capital between them. (The rate-of-return schedule is the downward-sloping curve that shows rates of return on extra investments on the vertical axis, and the amount invested on the horizontal axis.) The gain from capital flows is the area under the rate-of-return schedule in the high-yield country for projects funded from the capital inflow, minus the area under the rate-of-return schedule of the low-yield country for projects not funded due to the outflow of capital.

[13] National income, which is roughly equivalent to the gross national product and usually denoted by Y, can be classified into consumption C, investment I, government spending G, and exports minus imports (Ex − Im). This classification is met frequently in macroeconomics as the national income identity, $Y \equiv C + I + G + (Ex − Im)$. We see that for a decline in Y not to involve a decline in consumption it would be necessary to suffer a decline in investment, government spending, or exports minus imports. All these alternatives involve costs.

Total utility

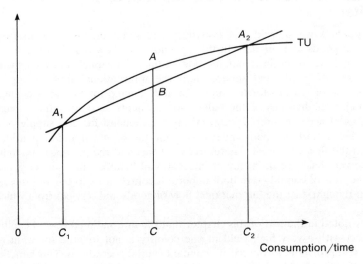

FIGURE 1A.1
UTILITY FROM DIFFERENT CONSUMPTION PATTERNS. If a country
faces variable consumption, being with equal frequency C_1 and C_2, the
average total utility level that it enjoys is distance BC. This is the average
of distances A_1C_1 and A_2C_2. If the country borrows from abroad during
bad times and lends abroad during good times, and thereby enjoys
consumption at C every period, it enjoys a utility level given by distance
AC. The gain from smoothing consumption via borrowing from abroad
and lending abroad is distance AB. This is a gain from the international
flow of capital.

it shows that higher levels of consumption are preferred to lower levels; that is, total
utility from consumption increases as consumption increases. However, the rate at which
total utility increases with consumption diminishes as consumption expands. This is
revealed by the lower slope of curve TU as consumption increases, that is, as we move to
the right along TU. The slope of TU gives the increase in total utility per unit of added
consumption and is called the **marginal utility**.[14]

If a nation is forced to vary consumption from year to year because it cannot borrow
and invest internationally and prefers not to vary other components of its GNP, it may
find itself consuming C_1 in one year when national income experiences a decline, and C_2
in the following year when national income experiences a favorable fluctuation. The total
utility from consumption of C_1 is given by the distance A_1C_1, while the total utility from
C_2 is given by A_2C_2. The average of A_1C_1 and A_2C_2, which is the average utility of
consumption, can be found by drawing a straight line between A_1 and A_2 and finding
the height of this line at its center. This follows because the height of the line halfway

---

[14]Most introductory finance textbooks deal with the notion of diminishing marginal utility of
consumption and its role in risk aversion. See, for example, Richard Brealey and Stewart Myers,
Principles of Corporate Finance, 3d ed., McGraw-Hill, New York, 1988.

between A_1 and A_2 is the average of A_1C_1 and A_2C_2. We find that the average utility from the two years of variable consumption is BC.

If the nation can borrow it might borrow the amount of C_1C during the economic downturn allowing it to consume OC. The nation might then lend amount CC_2 during the upturn and therefore also consume amount OC during this time.[15] With consumption of OC in both periods, and with total utility given by the distance AC in both periods, the average total utility is simply AC. It is immediately clear by inspecting Figure 1A.1 that the utility when consumption is smoothed by international borrowing and lending is higher than when borrowing and lending does not occur. Intuitively, this outcome is because the added or marginal utility of income during the period of higher consumption is smaller than the marginal utility lost during the period of lower consumption.

The empirical relevance of the preceding argument has been examined in a paper by Michael Brennan and Bruno Solnick.[16] They start by calculating what consumption would have been without international capital flows. This is determined by subtracting private capital flows from actual consumption during years when there was a net capital inflow to the country, and adding private capital flows to actual consumption during years of net capital outflow. This tells us what would have had to happen to consumption if borrowing and lending had not occurred.[17] All consumption data are put in per capita terms and adjusted for inflation.

Brennan and Solnik compute the standard deviations of the growth rates of consumption adjusted for capital flows and compare these with the standard deviations of the growth rates of actual consumption. This comparison is made for eight countries. They find that on average the standard deviations of actual consumption growth rates are less than half the standard deviations of adjusted consumption growth rates. The reduction in standard deviation is apparent in every country they examined, and for all measures of capital flows they considered. It would appear that there has been a distinct smoothing of consumption as a result of the flow of capital between nations. This gives us more than adequate reason to study these flows and the factors which affect them.

---

[15]Borrowing and lending involves paying and receiving interest. However, if the amount borrowed equals the amount subsequently lent, and if the periods are close together so that time value of money is unimportant, payments and receipts of interest cancel and can be ignored.

[16]See Michael J. Brennan and Bruno Solnik, "International Risk Sharing and Capital Mobility," Working Paper 8-88, University of California, Los Angeles, January 1988.

[17]This assumes all borrowing and lending affects consumption and not the other components of national income. Of course, borrowing and lending do in reality affect government spending and net investment. However, a smoother pattern of government spending and investment should contribute to smoother consumption. Furthermore, consumption is often considered as the end purpose of economic activity. This supports the case for concentrating on consumption.

INTRODUCING THE FOREIGN EXCHANGE MARKETS

Part 1 introduces the reader to the numerous ways that exist for exchanging currencies. Chapter 2 begins by considering the exchange of bank notes, such as the exchange of U.S. Federal Reserve Notes ("greenbacks") for British pounds. Chapter 2 also explains how money in the form of bank accounts is exchanged via the interbank spot foreign exchange market. An understanding of what actually happens when a person calls a bank to buy a foreign currency requires that we know how customers are credited, how the banks trade with each other, and how the banks settle transactions between themselves. This is all explained in Chapter 2. The chapter ends by showing why knowledge of exchange rates of each currency against the U.S. dollar allows us to calculate all possible exchange rates. For example, it is shown why we can calculate the exchange rate between German marks and British pounds from the German-mark–U.S.-dollar exchange rate and the British-pound–U.S.-dollar exchange rate. It is also shown why this ability to compute so-called "cross exchange rates" is nevertheless limited in reality by the presence of foreign exchange transaction costs.

Chapter 3 describes several other types of foreign exchange markets which play a very important role throughout the remainder of the book. The first of these markets is the interbank forward exchange market. Forward exchange involves a contractual arrangement to exchange currencies at an agreed exchange rate on some date in the future. The forward market plays an important role in avoiding foreign exchange risk (hedging) and in purposely taking risk (speculating). Chapter 3 provides the necessary background so that we can show in later chapters how forward exchange can be used for hedging and speculating.

After explaining the forward market, Chapter 3 turns to currency futures. These are similar to forward exchange contracts in that they help fix exchange rates for future transactions. However, currency futures trade on formal exchanges such as the Chicago International Money Market, have only a limited number of value dates, come in particular contract sizes, and can be sold back to the exchange. There are also a few other institutional differences that we will describe. These differences make forward contracts and currency futures of slightly different value as methods of hedging and speculation, and this is why Chapter 3 explains the specifics of each.

Chapter 3 also describes currency options. Unlike forward contracts and currency futures, currency options allow the buyer discretion over whether to exercise (complete) the contract. The different types of options are described, as well as the factors which affect the market prices, or premiums, on options. The advantages of using options to hedge and speculate are only briefly covered in Chapter 3. The details of the use of forwards, futures, and options are left for the chapters in which hedging and speculation are covered in greater depth. In Chapter 3 the purpose is primarily to introduce the reader to the institutional details of these important instruments.

CHAPTER 2

CASH AND SPOT EXCHANGE MARKETS

To the ordinary person, international finance is synonymous with exchange rates, and indeed, a large part of the study of international finance involves the study of exchange rates. What is not always known to those with a limited knowledge of international finance is the variety of exchange rates that exist at the same moment between the same two currencies. There are exchange rates for **bank notes**, which are, for example, the Federal Reserve notes with pictures of former U.S. presidents, and the equivalent Bank of England notes containing pictures of the Queen. There are also exchange rates between checks stating dollar amounts and those stating amounts in pounds or other currency units. Furthermore, the rates on these checks depend on whether they are issued by banks—**bank drafts**—or by corporations, on the amounts they involve, and on the dates on the checks. Exchange rates also differ according to whether they are for the purchase or sale of a foreign currency. That is, there is a difference, for example, between the number of U.S. dollars required in order to purchase a British pound, and the number of U.S. dollars received when selling a pound.

We will begin by looking at exchange rates between bank notes. While the market for bank notes is only a small proportion of the overall foreign exchange market, it is a good place to begin because bank notes are the form of money with which people are most familiar.

THE FOREIGN BANK NOTE MARKET

The earliest experience that many of us have of dealing with foreign currency is on our first overseas vacation. When not traveling abroad, most of us have very little to do with foreign exchange, which is not used in the course of ordinary

TABLE 2.1
EXCHANGE RATES ON FOREIGN BANK NOTES
Traveler's Dollar — May 18, 1989

	Foreign currency per U.S. Dollar	
	Bank Buys	Bank Sells
Australia (dollar)	1.34	1.30
Austria (schilling)	14.12	13.60
Belgium (franc)	42.00	40.50
Canada (dollar)	1.21	1.17
Denmark (kroner)	7.82	7.52
Finland (markkaa)	4.50	4.25
France (franc)	6.82	6.55
Germany (Deutsche mark)	2.01	1.93
Greece (drachma)	170.00	163.00
Hong Kong (dollar)	7.92	7.60
Ireland (pound)	0.74	0.71
Israel (shekel)	1.85	1.78
Italy (lira)	1470.00	1400.00
Japan (yen)	141.00	136.00
Mexico (peso)	2475.00	2385.00
Netherlands (guilder)	2.25	2.17
Norway (kroner)	7.22	6.95
South Africa (rand)	2.76	2.64
Spain (peseta)	125.00	120.00
Sweden (krona)	6.80	6.52
Switzerland (franc)	1.80	1.73
United Kingdom (pound)	0.63	0.61

commerce, especially in the United States. The foreign exchange with which we deal when on vacation involves bank notes, and, quite frequently, foreign-currency-denominated traveler's checks. Table 2.1 gives the exchange rates on bank notes facing a traveler on May 18, 1989. Let us take a look at how these retail bank note rates are quoted.

The first column of Table 2.1 gives the exchange rates in terms of the number of units of each foreign currency that must be *paid to the bank* to buy a U.S. dollar. For example, it takes 1.21 Canadian dollars (Can$1.21) or 0.63 United Kingdom pounds (£0.63) to buy a U.S. dollar. The second column gives the number of units of each foreign currency that will be *received from the bank* when buying the foreign currency with U.S. dollars. For example, the traveler will receive Can$1.17 or £0.61 for each dollar.

The rates of exchange posted for travelers in bank and currency exchange windows or international tourist centers are the most expensive or unfavorable that exist. They are expensive in the sense that the buying and selling prices on individual currencies can differ by a large percentage—frequently as much as 4 or 5 percent. The difference between buying and selling prices is called the **spread**. Table 2.1 shows that, for example, the 8-cent difference between the buying price and the selling price on the German mark is a spread of approximately 4 percent.

Our experience changing currencies on vacation should not lead us to believe that large-scale international finance faces similar costs. The bank note market used by travelers involves large spreads because generally only small amounts are traded, which nevertheless require as much paperwork as bigger commercial trades. Another reason why the spreads are large is that each bank and currency exchange must hold many different currencies to be able to provide customers with what they want, and these notes do not earn interest. This involves an opportunity or inventory cost, as well as some risk from changes in exchange rates. Furthermore, bank robbers, in which the United States does not have a monopoly, specialize in bank notes; therefore, those who hold large amounts of them are forced to take security precautions—especially when moving bank notes from branch to branch.[1] A further risk faced in the exchange of bank notes is the acceptance of counterfeit bills which frequently show up in foreign financial centers.

While the exchange of bank notes between the ordinary private customer and the bank or currency exchange takes place in the retail market, the banks trade their surpluses of notes between themselves in the wholesale market. The wholesale market involves firms which specialize in buying and selling foreign bank notes with commercial banks and currency exchanges. These are **bank-note wholesalers**. They exist only in leading banking centers and do not have names that are readily recognized by the general public.

As an example of the workings of the wholesale market, during the summer a British bank might receive large numbers of German marks from Germans traveling in Britain. The same British bank may also be selling large numbers of Italian lire to the British leaving for vacations in Italy. The British bank will sell its surplus German marks to a bank note wholesaler in London, who might then transport the mark notes back to Germany or to a non-German bank in need of mark notes. The British bank will buy lire from a wholesaler who may well have transported the lire from Italy (or brought them from banks in Europe which in turn bought them from Italians engaged in the popular sport of smuggling lire out of the country to avoid exchange controls). The spreads on the wholesale level are less than the retail bank note spreads, generally well below 2 percent, because larger amounts are generally traded.

THE SPOT FOREIGN EXCHANGE MARKET

Far larger than the bank note market is the **spot foreign exchange market**. This is involved with the exchange of currencies in the form of checks drawn on different currency-denominated bank accounts. In the spot market, instructions

---

[1]Because banks face a lower risk of theft of traveler's checks and because the companies that issue them, which are often themselves banks, will quickly credit the banks that accept them, many banks give a more favorable exchange rate on checks than on bank notes. The spread might be as much as 2 percent lower than for bank notes.

to exchange currencies take the form of **bank drafts**, which are checks issued by banks. Delivery, or **value**, from the bank drafts is "immediate"—usually in 1 or 2 days. This distinguishes the spot market from the forward and futures exchange markets which are discussed in the next chapter, and which involve the planned exchange of currencies for value at some date in the future—after a number of days or even years.

Spot exchange rates are determined by the supplies and demands for currencies being exchanged in the gigantic interbank foreign exchange market.[2] This market is legendary for the frenetic pace at which it operates, and for the vast amount of money which is moved at lightning speed in response to the tiniest differences in price quotations.

Organization of the Interbank Market

The interbank foreign exchange market is the largest financial market on earth, with a daily volume in excess of $100 billion. It is an informal arrangement of the larger commercial banks and a number of foreign exchange brokers for buying and selling foreign currencies. The banks and brokers are linked together by telephone, Telex, and a satellite communications network called the Society for Worldwide International Financial Telecommunications, SWIFT. This computer-based communications system, based in Brussels, links banks and brokers in just about every financial center. The banks and brokers are in almost constant contact, with activity in some financial center or other 24 hours a day.[3] Because of the speed of communications, significant events have virtually instantaneous impacts everywhere in the world despite the huge distances separating market participants. This is what makes the foreign exchange market just as efficient as a conventional stock or commodity market housed under a common roof.

The efficiency of the foreign exchange market is revealed in the extremely narrow spreads between buying and selling prices. These spreads can be smaller than a tenth of a percent of the value of a contract, and are therefore about one-fortieth or less of the spread faced on bank notes by international travelers. The efficiency of the market is also manifest in the electrifying speed with which exchange rates respond to the continuous flow of information that bombards the market. Participants cannot afford to miss a beat in the frantic pulse of this dynamic, global market. Indeed, the bankers and brokers that constitute the foreign exchange market can scarcely detach themselves from the video screens

---

[2]The supply and demand curves for currencies are derived and used to explain the economic factors behind exchange rates in Part 2.

[3]Indeed, in the principal centers like New York, London, Tokyo and Toronto, some banks maintain 24-hour operations to keep up with developments elsewhere during other centers' normal working hours.

that provide the latest news and prices as fast as the information can travel via the telephone lines and satellites of the business news wire services.

The banks and foreign exchange brokers, in all countries, collectively determine exchange rates. Each dealer gets "a feel for where the market is going" and takes positions to buy or sell on the basis of this feeling and according to orders received from clients. The feel for the market in each currency, as well as a desire to balance the books, is what determines the position the banker is prepared to take. If it is decided that the bank's pound position should be balanced and, further, customers wish to sell pounds, the bank will enter the market to sell these pounds.

Once the desired amount of buying or selling of a currency has been determined, the banker will call foreign exchange dealers at other banks and "ask for the market." The caller does not say whether he or she wants to buy or sell or state the amount to be traded. The caller might say, "What's your market in sterling?" This means, "At what price are you willing to buy and at what price are you willing to sell British pounds for U.S. dollars?" In replying, a foreign exchange dealer must attempt to determine whether the caller really wants to buy or to sell and what his or her own position is. This is a subtle and tricky game involving human judgment. Bluff and counterbluff are used. A good trader, with a substantial order in pounds, may ask for the market in Canadian dollars. After placing a small order he or she might say, "And by the way, what's the market in British sterling?" Dealers are not averse to having their assistants place the really large and really small orders, just to confuse the other side and obtain favorable quotes. A difference in quotation of the fourth decimal place can mean thousands of dollars on a large order. It is rather like massive-stakes poker.

If the banker who has been called wants to sell pounds, he or she will quote on the side that is felt to be cheap for pounds, given this banker's feel of the market. For example, if the banker feels that other banks are selling pounds at $1.6120/£, he or she might quote $1.6118/£ as the selling price. In fact, the banker will quote the buying price and the selling price. Having considered the two-way price, the caller will state whether he or she wishes to buy or sell and the amount. Once the rate has been quoted, convention determines that it must be honored whatever the decision of the caller and the amount involved. The caller has about 1 minute to decide and it is fair game to change the rate after this time. Good judgment of the counterparty and good judgment of the direction of the market are essential in this billion-dollar game. It is important to be accurate and constantly in touch with events.

Delivery Dates and Procedures for Spot Exchange

Whereas bank notes of the major Western countries are exchanged for each other instantaneously over the bank counter, when U.S. dollars are exchanged in the interbank spot market with non-North American currencies, funds are not generally received until two business days after the initiation of the transaction. With the currencies of the North American continent, the Canadian dollar and the Mexican peso, delivery is slightly quicker, with an exchange providing value after one business day. This means there is a distinction between the value date and the initiation date of transactions. The distinction can be illustrated by an example.[4]

Suppose that a financial executive of an American corporation, Amcorp, calls his or her bank, Ambank National, a large currency-dealing bank in New York City, to buy £1 million. Suppose that the call is placed on Thursday, May 18, 1989, and that the British pounds are to be used to settle Amcorp's debt to Britcorp. Ambank will quote an exchange rate at which it will sell Amcorp the £1 million. If Amcorp approves of this rate, then the foreign exchange department of Ambank will request details for making payment in Britain. These details will include the bank at which Britcorp is to be paid and the account number.

The details provided by Amcorp to Ambank will typically be conveyed to the designated bank in Britain, Britbank, by sending a message on the day of ordering the pounds, May 18, via SWIFT. The SWIFT network has been available since 1977, and has grown so rapidly that it has virtually replaced the preexisting methods of conveying messages, namely the mail and telegraphic transfer. SWIFT uses satellite linkages, and transmits messages between banks in a standard format to minimize errors which can easily occur due to different languages and banking customs. SWIFT has been so successful that banks in just about every country, including the Soviet Union and other communist countries, have joined or applied to join.[5]

The spot exchange rate that is quoted by Ambank National on May 18 will be binding and will not be changed even if market conditions subsequently change. A confirmation of the order for £1 million at the agreed exchange rate—for example, $1.60 per pound—will be sent out to Amcorp on Thursday, May 18. Because of the intervening weekend, the value date, which is two business days later, is Monday, May 22, and on this day Ambank will debit Amcorp's account at the bank by $1.6 million. On the same day, May 22, Britbank will credit Britcorp's account by £1 million. The transaction is complete for the payer and payee, with Britcorp receiving the £1 million and Amcorp having paid the dollar equivalent, $1.6 million.

Our description of the transaction in the example is complete only for the payer and the payee. We have not yet described the settlement between the

---

[4] It is possible to send money for value sooner than two days outside of North America and one day within North America. However, this is somewhat more expensive than the normal spot rate.

[5] Since 1987, nonbanking financial institutions such as brokerage firms have also been given access to SWIFT.

banks. This settlement is necessary because Britbank needs to be compensated for the £1 million it has credited to Britcorp's account. In order to keep our example straightforward, we will first assume that the banks settle by maintaining accounts with each other called **correspondent accounts**. Later we will consider what happens when banks do not have a correspondent relationship.[6]

Bank Settlement via Correspondent Accounts

With Ambank having a correspondent account at Britbank, when Britbank credits Britcorp it will debit Ambank's account the same amount. That is, on May 22 Britcorp's account will be credited £1 million and Ambank's account will be debited £1 million. This is illustrated in the top half of Table 2.2. We see that Britcorp is paid merely by a change at Britbank as to who owns the deposit.[7] What happens at Ambank is that while Ambank's deposit at Britbank is reduced by £1 million, Ambank's liability to Amcorp, that is, Amcorp's deposit, is reduced by $1.6 million.

If the situation were the reverse, with Britcorp paying Amcorp $1.6 million, on May 18 Britbank would inform Ambank, its correspondent in the U.S., to credit Amcorp on May 22. Britbank's account at Ambank would be debited at the same time that Ambank credits Amcorp's account, as shown in the lower part of Table 2.2.

Banks that are active in the foreign exchange market do not enter the market to cover each and every order from customers. Rather, they allow themselves a degree of flexibility in each currency, and they enter the market only when their holdings exceed or are below what they have deemed acceptable. Banks are conservative and prefer to avoid being heavily exposed to foreign exchange risk. Exposure means that the bank will be affected if there is an unexpected change in exchange rates. As we shall see in Chapter 9, a bank is exposed if it has agreed to sell foreign exchange that it does not have, or has not yet sold foreign exchange that it has agreed to purchase.

While large banks that are active in the foreign exchange market enter the market only when they feel their exposure exceeds a comfortable level, smaller inactive banks generally avoid having any exposure at all. They will enter the market on each and every order from a customer to ensure that they have bought or sold in the market whatever they have agreed to supply to or

---

[6]The term "correspondent" is used because in the past banks mailed letters to each other to give instructions about whom to credit with what amount of money on which date. As we have just mentioned, this practice of sending letters has largely been superseded by the electronic messages of the SWIFT network.

[7]A deposit at a bank is the liability of the bank.

TABLE 2.2
TWO EXAMPLES OF BANK CLEARING WITH CORRESPONDENT ACCOUNTS

(a) Amcorp pays Britcorp £1 million

Britbank		
Assets	**Liabilities**	
	Britcorp	+£1,000,000
	Ambank	−£1,000,000
0		0

Ambank		
Assets		**Liabilities**
At Britbank −£1,000,000	Amcorp	−$1,600,000
−$1,600,000		−$1,600,000
(£1,000,000 @ $1.6 / £)		

(b) Britcorp pays Amcorp $1.6 million

Britbank		
Assets	**Liabilities**	
At Ambank −$1,600,000	Britcorp	−£1,000,000
−£1,000,000		−£1,000,000
($1,600,000 @ $1.6 / £)		

Ambank		
Assets		**Liabilities**
	Amcorp	+$1,600,000
	Britbank	−1,600,000
0		0

purchase from the customer. When a bank does enter the market and reaches agreement with another bank with which it does not have a correspondent relationship, the bank that has purchased foreign currency will have to pay the bank that has sold the foreign currency. This payment generally takes place via a **clearing house**. A clearing house is an institution at which banks keep funds which can be moved from one bank's account to another to settle interbank transactions.

When foreign exchange is trading against the U.S. dollar the clearing house that is used is called CHIPS, an acronym for the Clearing House Interbank Payments System. CHIPS is located in New York and, as we shall explain below, is a place in which banks hold U.S. dollar accounts. Currencies do also trade directly with each other without involving the dollar—for example, German marks for pounds, or Italian lire for Swiss francs. In these situations a European clearing house will be used. However, because the largest volume of transactions is settled in dollars, we consider how CHIPS works, although we can note that settlement between banks is similar in other financial centers.

Bank Settlement via CHIPS

CHIPS is a computerized mechanism at which banks hold U.S. dollar accounts to pay each other when buying or selling foreign exchange. The system is owned by the large New York clearing banks; has over 150 members, including the U.S. agencies and subsidiaries of many foreign banks; and handles over 100,000 transactions a day, worth together hundreds of billions of dollars.

We can see how CHIPS works by extending the situation considered earlier, of Amcorp initiating payment to Britcorp on May 18, with Britcorp being credited at Britbank two business days later, May 22, after the intervening weekend. The extension is to assume that immediately on agreeing to sell Amcorp £1 million, Ambank enters the interbank market to replenish its pound account at Britbank.

Let us suppose that after placing a few telephone calls to pound specialist banks particularly active in British sterling, Ambank finds the cheapest rate on pounds to be at UKbank. (Perhaps UKbank has just paid out U.S. dollars for a client and wants to replenish its dollar holdings.) On agreeing to buy £1 million from UKbank, Ambank gives instructions to deliver the pounds to its account at Britbank.[8] Ambank's payment to Britbank will be effected by Ambank entering into its CHIPS computer terminal its own code, that of UKbank, and the number of dollars to be paid. Similarly, UKbank enters its code, Ambank's code, and the number of dollars to be received. This is all done at the time the two banks agree on the purchase/sale, assumed to be the same day as Amcorp orders the pounds, May 18.

---

[8]The pounds will be moved from UKbank to Britbank as part of the normal settlement between banks provided by the clearing house in London.

CHIPS records the information received from Ambank and UKbank, and keeps track of other amounts to be paid or received by these banks and the many other CHIPS members. On the value date of the transaction, May 22, settlement reports are sent to all banks for net amounts to be paid or received on that day. These reports are sent to members' CHIPS terminals at 4:30 p.m., Eastern time. Assuming Ambank and UKbank have no dispute over the reports they receive, the debtor bank, in our case Ambank, must send instructions to the Federal Reserve Bank of New York by 5:30 p.m. to debit Ambank's account there, called its **escrow account**, and to credit the escrow account of UKbank. The instruction from Ambank is sent via Fedwire, a system used for settlement of domestic transactions. All transfers between escrow accounts are normally completed by 6:00 p.m. on the value date of the transactions.

Market Clearing and Exchange Brokers

With so many participating banks it may seem remarkable that the market for each currency *clears*, that is, supply equals demand. Of course, it must be the case that the markets clear, since currencies that banks want to sell are sold, and currencies banks want to buy are bought. However, the markets do not always clear by the banks making direct agreements between themselves. Rather, banks sometimes find it necessary to call in the services of foreign exchange brokers. The brokers find sellers when banks want to buy currencies, and buyers when banks want to sell currencies.[9]

The procedure for dealing with brokers is different from that of banks dealing with each other. A bank will call a broker and state how much foreign exchange it wants to buy or to sell and the rate at which it is willing to buy or sell. This means that it will not ask for a two-way market but will offer to buy or sell a given amount. The broker will communicate to other banks what rates and amounts are available, always showing the best quotes to the potential counter-parties. If the two sides of the market are consistent so that a bank will meet the exchange rate demanded by another bank, a trade will be made. Until an agreement has been struck, neither of the two parties knows the identity of the other. When the contract is made, the broker provides the names of the two parties and receives a fee from each of them. It is this fee which makes dealing via brokers more expensive than direct exchange and which therefore explains why larger banks try to make a market between themselves before engaging a broker's services.

The informal nature of the U.S. foreign exchange market, with direct bank dealing coexisting with brokered transactions, is similar to that of markets in

---

[9]Of course, markets would eventually clear even if there were no foreign exchange brokers, since at some exchange rate you can always buy or sell. The service offered by brokers is finding more satisfactory exchange rates for both banks in a transaction.

Canada, Britain, and many other countries. In France, Germany, and some other countries, including those in Scandinavia, the procedure is rather more formal, with bank representatives, including a representative of the central bank, meeting daily in the same room. Contracts are exchanged directly, although an informal market coexists in which many of the transactions occur. The formal meeting place provides official settlement exchange rates for certain transactions.

Retail versus Interbank Spot Rates

While it is only exchange rates between banks that are determined in the interbank market, exchange rates faced by banks' clients are based on these interbank rates. Banks charge their customers slightly more than the going interbank selling or **ask rate**, and pay their customers slightly less than the interbank buying or **bid rate**. The extent of the banks' markup or markdown from the going interbank rates depends principally on the size of the retail transactions. As we have said, banks might not actually enter the interbank market, especially for small transactions, using instead currency they already own or adding to the amount they own. However, banks still base their retail spot rates on the interbank rates, perhaps revising these once or twice each day for small transactions of up to a couple of thousand dollars, and telephoning the banks' own foreign exchange trading rooms before quoting on large transactions.

Conventions for Spot Exchange Quotations

In virtually every professional enterprise, especially in the realm of finance and economics, there are special conventions and a particular jargon. This is certainly true in the foreign exchange market, where practices in the quotation of exchange rates make the quotes difficult to interpret unless the jargon and conventions are well understood.

Let us concentrate on the spot exchange rates and consider Figure 2.1. The table quotes rates from *The Wall Street Journal* of May 19, 1989. These rates are the previous day's exchange rates, quoted toward the end of the trading day at 3:00 p.m., Eastern time. Since, as the table states, the rates are those charged by Bankers Trust Company of New York on sales of more than $1 million to other banks, the rates are wholesale interbank rates involving large drafts. As we have indicated, retail rates to corporate clients will generally be less favorable than these interbank rates.

Figure 2.1 gives rates in two ways—as the number of U.S. dollars per foreign unit, which is called **US\$ equivalent**, and as the number of units of foreign currency per US\$. To a close approximation, the figures in the second two columns are merely the reciprocals of the figures in the first two columns. The large New York banks, when dealing among themselves, quote most rates as currency per US$ and no longer use the alternative form. The convention of using currency per US$ dates from 1979, when New York went on what is known as **European terms**. For example, on May 18, 1989, the dollar would have been quoted as 6.6520 Swedish kronor (S.Kr 6.6520) or DM 1.9720.[10]

The table gives only the rates for selling and not for buying foreign exchange. It is customary for newspapers and even some dealers to quote only the banks' selling rates, but dealers will generally give two-way quotations. The selling rates of banks are called offer or ask rates. In order to obtain the buying or bid rates, the newspaper rates must be adjusted, and we must guess the amount of adjustment, since data for both sides of the market are not made available. If US$ equivalent quotations were used, bid rates would be below ask rates; that is, the U.S. bank would buy foreign currency for less U.S. dollars than the amount at which it would sell the foreign currency. For example, Bankers Trust might sell West German marks at $0.5070 each and buy them at $0.5065. In this case the buy or bid rate is below the ask or offer rate by $0.0005, or 5 points. A *point* refers to the last digit of the quotation. We must be careful, since four, five or six digits could be involved. For example, the Hong Kong dollar might have an ask or offer rate of $0.128592 and a bid rate of $0.128587; in this case, there is also a 5-point spread.

With quotations in US$ equivalent, we subtract points from the selling or ask rate to obtain the buying or bid rate. However, to obtain buying rates with the currency per US$ quotation, we *add* points to the selling rates. For example, we might guess that Bankers Trust had been buying German marks at DM 1.9725 per US$ while selling them at the quoted DM 1.9720 per US$. This 5-point spread for the bank on a $1 million two-way transaction in marks will provide an income of about $500. For large transactions the spread might be as small as 4 points or even 2 points. With the quotation given as the amount of currency per US$, the bank's selling or ask rate only *looks* as if it were below the buying or bid rate. Usually, if an institution sells below its buying prices, it will incur losses. Of course, the banks do profit from exchanging currencies, and this odd-looking price structure reflects the convention for rate quotation.

It is important that we distinguish between bid and ask exchange rates, even if it seems that the differences are so small as to be almost irrelevant. There are two reasons for this. Firstly, the bid-ask spread provides banks with their incomes from dealing in foreign exchange. For example, even if the banks charge only 0.0002 of the value of transactions, the revenue to the banks in New York on their transactions of over $100 billion each day is more than $20 million. This is not all profit, as some of this revenue merely moves between banks doing interbank transactions, and because banks face costs; but it does indicate the importance of spreads to banks. Second, spreads may seem small

---

[10]There is a major exception, the British pound, which is quoted in US$ equivalent, that is, dollars per pound.

EXCHANGE RATES

Thursday, May 18, 1989

The New York foreign exchange selling rates below apply to trading among banks in amounts of $1 million and more, as quoted at 3 p.m. Eastern time by Bankers Trust Co. Retail transactions provide fewer units of foreign currency per dollar.

Country	U.S. $ equiv. Thurs.	U.S. $ equiv. Wed.	Currency per U.S. $ Thurs.	Currency per U.S. $ Wed.
Argentina (Austral) ...	.009900	.009900	101.00	101.00
Australia (Dollar)	.7575	.7570	1.3201	1.3210
Austria (Schilling)	.07209	.07219	13.87	13.85
Bahrain (Dinar)	2.6518	2.6518	.37710	.37710
Belgium (Franc)				
Commercial rate	.02422	.02426	41.28	41.21
Financial rate	.02415	.02418	41.40	41.34
Brazil (Cruzado) ...	.917431	.917431	1.0900	1.0900
Britain (Pound)	1.6120	1.6150	.6203	.6191
30-Day Forward	1.6080	1.6110	.6218	.6207
90-Day Forward	1.6000	1.6020	.6250	.6242
180-Day Forward	1.5877	1.5889	.6298	.6293
Canada (Dollar)	.8385	.8396	1.1925	1.1910
30-Day Forward	.8364	.8377	1.1955	1.1937
90-Day Forward	.8333	.8345	1.2000	1.1983
180-Day Forward	.8298	.8308	1.2050	1.2036
Chile (Official rate) ...	.0040000	.0040000	250.00	250.00
China (Yuan)	.268672	.268672	3.7220	3.7220
Colombia (Peso)	.002739	.002739	365.00	365.00
Denmark (Krone)	.1303	.1304	7.6730	7.6650
Ecuador (Sucre)				
Floating rate	.001851	.001851	540.00	540.00
Finland (Markka)	.2277	.2280	4.3900	4.3850
France (Franc)	.1498	.1499	6.6720	6.6675
30-Day Forward	.1500	.1501	6.6662	6.6609
90-Day Forward	.1501	.1503	6.6590	6.6529
180-Day Forward	.1503	.1505	6.6520	6.6440
Greece (Drachma) ...	.005973	.005970	167.40	167.50
Hong Kong (Dollar) ...	.128592	.128592	7.7765	7.7765
India (Rupee)	.0623052	.0623052	16.05	16.05
Indonesia (Rupiah) ...	.0005665	.0005665	1765.00	1765.00
Ireland (Punt)	1.3750	1.3750	.72727	.72727
Israel (Shekel)	.5502	.5502	1.8175	1.8175
Italy (Lira)	.0006963	.0006968	1436.00	1435.00
Japan (Yen)	.007202	.007186	138.85	139.15
30-Day Forward	.007233	.007217	138.25	138.55
90-Day Forward	.007286	.007272	137.24	137.50
180-Day Forward	.007359	c007343	135.88	136.18
Jordan (Dinar)	1.8968	1.8968	.5272	.5272
Kuwait (Dinar)	3.4299	3.4299	.2915	.2915
Lebanon (Pound)	.001953	.001953	512.00	512.00
Malaysia (Ringgit) ...	.37023	.37140	2.7010	2.6925
Malta (Lira)	2.8490	2.8490	.3510	.3510
Mexico (Peso)				
Floating rate	.0004123	.0004123	2425.00	2425.00
Netherland(Guilder) .	.4500	.4546	2.2220	2.1995
New Zealand (Dollar) .	.6030	.6015	1.6583	1.6625
Norway (Krone)	.1404	.1408	7.1190	7.0995
Pakistan (Rupee)	.04911	.04911	20.36	20.36
Peru (Inti)	.0003904	.0003904	2561.00	2561.00
Philippines (Peso)	.047846	.047846	20.90	20.90
Portugal (Escudo)	.006250	.006250	160.00	160.00
Saudi Arabia (Riyal) ..	.2666	.2666	3.7500	3.7500
Singapore (Dollar)	.5116	.5116	1.9545	1.9545
South Africa (Rand)				
Commercial rate	.3698	.3716	2.7038	2.6908
Financial rate	.2410	.2424	4.1500	4.1250
South Korea (Won) ...	.0015006	.0015006	666.40	666.40
Spain (Peseta)	.008116	.008133	123.13	122.95
Sweden (Krona)	.1503	.1505	6.6520	6.6420
Switzerland (Franc) ..	.5672	.5681	1.7630	1.7600
30-Day Forward	.5682	.5691	1.7598	1.7570
90-Day Forward	.5701	.5710	1.7540	1.7512
180-Day Forward	.5729	.5735	1.7453	1.7435
Taiwan (Dollar)	.039139	.03921	25.55	25.50
Thailand (Baht)	.039093	.039093	25.58	25.58
Turkey (Lira)	.0004918	.0004918	2033.00	2033.00
United Arab(Dirham) ..	.2722	.2722	3.6725	3.6725
Uruguay (New Peso)				
Financial	.001837	.001837	546.00	546.00
Venezuela (Bolivar)				
Floating rate	.02631	.02631	38.00	38.00
W. Germany (Mark) ..	.5070	.5080	1.9720	1.9685
30-Day Forward	.5083	.5091	1.9670	1.9640
90-Day Forward	.5103	.5110	1.9595	1.9566
180-Day Forward	.5129	.5135	1.9475	1.9473
SDR	1.25585	1.26697	0.796273	0.789285
ECU	1.05166	1.07029	....	....

Special Drawing Rights (SDR) are based on exchange rates for the U.S., West German, British, French and Japanese currencies. Source: International Monetary Fund.

European Currency Unit (ECU) is based on a basket of community currencies. Source: European Community Commission.

c-Corrected.

FIGURE 2.1

Exchange rates on bank drafts: wholesale spot and forward rates. (Reprinted by permission of *The Wall Street Journal* © Dow-Jones & Company Inc., May 19, 1989. All Rights Reserved Worldwide) but can have a substantial effect on yields when the spreads are faced on investments made for only a short period. For example, if a company invests abroad for 1 month and must therefore buy the foreign currency today and sell it after 1 month, a 0.1 percent spread on buying and selling the foreign exchange, when put on an annual basis by multiplying by 12, involves an annualized cost of 1.2 percent. If the extra interest available abroad is smaller than 1.2 percent, the spread will eliminate the advantage. The shorter the period for which funds are moved, the more relevant bid-ask spreads on foreign exchange become.

DIRECT VERSUS INDIRECT EXCHANGE AND CROSS EXCHANGE RATES

Indirect Exchange and the Practice of Quoting against the Dollar

With approximately 150 currencies in the world, there are approximately $150 \times 149 = 22,350$ different exchange rates. This is because each of the 150 different currencies has an exchange rate against the remaining 149 currencies. Fortunately for the people who work in the foreign exchange market, many of these 22,350 exchange rates are redundant. The most obvious cause of redundancy is that once we know, for example, the price of dollars in terms of pounds, this immediately suggests knowing the price of pounds in terms of dollars. This reduces the number of relevant exchange rate quotations by one-half. However, there is another cause of redundancy: it is possible, for example, to compute the exchange rate between the German mark and British pound from the exchange rate between the mark and the dollar and the exchange rate between the pound and the dollar. Indeed, if there were no costs of transacting in foreign exchange, that is, no bid-ask spreads, with 150 currencies all 22,350 possible exchange rates could be computed from the 149 exchange rates of each currency versus the U.S. dollar.[11] Let us show why by beginning with the simple situation in which the only currencies are the German mark, the British pound, and the U.S. dollar.

The procedure we are going to use is to consider people wanting to exchange marks for pounds or pounds for marks. These exchanges can be made directly, or indirectly via the dollar. For example, it is possible to sell marks for dollars, and then sell these dollars for pounds. We will argue that for banks to attract business involving the direct exchange of marks and pounds, the exchange rate they offer cannot be inferior to the exchange rate implicit in indirect exchange via the U.S. dollar.[12] We will see that when there are no foreign exchange

[11]The reason why transaction costs are relevant will be made clear later.
[12]As we shall see, banks in Britain and Germany do indeed quote direct exchange rates between the mark and pound, and the pound and mark. Furthermore, these rates are at least as favorable as the implicit rates calculated from rates vis-à-vis the dollar.

transaction costs, the constraint of competing with indirect exchange will force banks to quote a direct exchange rate between the mark and pound that is exactly equal to the implicit indirect exchange rate via the dollar. This means that, if there are no transaction costs, we can find all possible exchange rates by taking appropriate exchange rates versus the dollar. When there are transaction costs, we will see that direct exchange rates are not always those that are implicit in rates against the dollar. However, we will see that in that case there are limits within which direct quotations can move, set by exchange rates versus the dollar.

Zero Foreign Exchange Transaction Costs

Let us begin by defining the spot exchange rate between the dollar and pound as $S(\$/£)$. That is:

$S(\$/£)$ is the number of U.S. dollars per British pound in the spot exchange market. More generally, $S(i/j)$ is the number of units of currency i per unit of currency j in the spot exchange market.

First, consider a person who wants to go from marks to pounds. In terms of Figure 2.2, this is characterized by the heavily shaded arrow along the base of the triangle between DM and £. If a bank is to attract business selling pounds for marks, the exchange rate it offers directly between the mark and pound must be no worse than could be achieved by going indirectly from the mark to the dollar and then from the dollar to the pound. In terms of Figure 2.2 the indirect route involves traveling from DM to £ via $, that is, along the heavily shaded arrows from DM to $, and then from $ to £.

If the person buys pounds directly for marks, the number of pounds received per mark is $S(£/DM)$ pounds, the spot number of pounds per mark, as shown on the side of the triangle in Figure 2.2 with the arrow pointing from DM to £. If instead the indirect route is taken from DM to £ via $, then on the first leg of the exchange, that from DM to $, each German mark buys $S(\$/DM)$ dollars. Then, on the second leg, that from $ to £, each of these $S(\$/DM)$ dollars buys $S(£/\$)$ pounds. Therefore, from the two legs, $S(\$/DM) \cdot S(£/\$)$ pounds are received for each mark.[13]

As we have said, a bank offering to exchange German marks directly for pounds at $S(£/DM)$ pounds per German mark must offer at least as large a number of pounds as via the indirect route. That is, for the bank's exchange rate to be effective in attracting business it must be such that

$$S(£/DM) \geq S(\$/DM) \cdot S(£/\$) \tag{2.1}$$

---

[13] It is worth noting that the units of measurement follow the usual rules of algebra. That is, $(\$/DM) \times (£/\$) = £/DM$, with the dollar signs canceling.

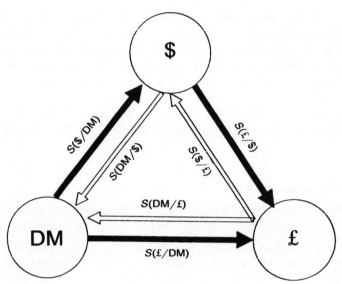

FIGURE 2.2
Direct versus indirect exchange: zero transaction costs.

Let us next consider a person who wants to exchange pounds into marks. This person can go from £ to DM directly along the unshaded leftward pointing arrow in Figure 2.2. This would result in $S(DM/£)$ marks for each pound. Alternatively they can go from £ to DM indirectly along the unshaded arrows, going from £ to $, and then from $ to DM. This route gives $S($/£)$ dollars for each pound, and then each of these dollars buys $S(DM/$)$ marks. Therefore, the number of marks received per pound from the indirect route is $S($/£) \cdot S(DM/$)$.

A bank posting an exchange rate for converting pounds into marks must offer at least as many marks as would be obtained by using the indirect route via the U.S. dollar. That is, for the bank to attract business, the exchange rate must satisfy

$$S(DM/£) \geq S($/£) \cdot S(DM/$). \tag{2.2}$$

We can compare the inequality (2.2) with the inequality (2.1) by noting that in the absence of transaction costs, by definition,

$$S(£/DM) = \frac{1}{S(DM/£)}, \quad S(£/$) = \frac{1}{S($/£)}, \quad \text{and} \quad S($/DM) = \frac{1}{S(DM/$)}$$

$$\tag{2.3}$$

That is, for example, if there are 0.25 pounds per mark, there are 4 marks per pound. Using equations (2.3) in inequality (2.1) gives

$$\frac{1}{S(DM/£)} \geq \frac{1}{S(DM/\$)} \cdot \frac{1}{S(\$/£)} \qquad (2.4)$$

Inverting both sides of the inequality (2.4), and therefore necessarily reversing the inequality, gives

$$S(DM/£) \leq S(DM/\$) \cdot S(\$/£) \qquad (2.5)$$

The inequality (2.5) is consistent with (2.2) only if the equalities rather than the inequalities hold. That is, the ability to choose the best way to go from marks to pounds and from pounds to marks ensures that

$$S(DM/£) = S(\$/£) \cdot S(DM/\$) \qquad (2.6)$$

Equation (2.6) tells us we can compute the exchange rate between marks and pounds from the pound-dollar and mark-dollar exchange rates. For example, if there are 1.5 dollars per pound and 2.0 marks per dollar, there are 3.0 marks per pound. What we have shown in deriving Equation (2.6) is why this is so. In summary, the reason is that there is always the possibility of indirect exchange via the dollar in going from marks to pounds or from pounds to marks. However, we recall that so far we have assumed zero transaction costs.

The exchange rate $S(DM/£)$ is a **cross rate**. More generally, cross rates are exchange rates directly between currencies when neither of the two currencies is the U.S. dollar. For example, $S(Can\$/£)$, $S(¥/Can\$)$, $S(¥/DM)$, $S(DM/SFr)$ are all cross rates. What we have derived in Equation (2.6) generalizes for any cross rate as

$$S(i/j) = S(i/\$) \cdot S(\$/j) \qquad (2.7)$$

Of course, since $S(i/\$) = 1/S(\$/i)$ and $S(\$/j) = 1/S(j/\$)$, we can also compute the cross rate $S(i/j)$ from exchange rates vis-à-vis the dollar via:

$$S(i/j) = \frac{S(i/\$)}{S(j/\$)}$$

$$S(i/j) = \frac{S(\$/j)}{S(\$/i)} \qquad (2.8)$$

$$S(i/j) = \frac{1}{S(\$/i)} \cdot \frac{1}{S(j/\$)}$$

Typically, the rule for calculating cross rates in Equation (2.7), and its corollaries in Equation (2.8), are derived from **triangular arbitrage**, which involves a different line of argument than is employed above. We can use Figure 2.2 to explain the difference between triangular arbitrage and the argument we employed.

Triangular arbitrage is based upon the notion that if you started with $1, and went from $ to £ to DM and then back to $ in Figure 2.2, you could not end up with more than $1 from this triangular journey or there would be an **arbitrage profit**. Similarly, you would not be able to take the reverse route, and go from $ to DM to £ and back to $, and end up with more than $1 if you started with $1. This argument based on triangular arbitrage gives the correct result when there are no transaction costs. However, it gives an inaccurate answer when there are transaction costs, for the following reason.

The choice of direct versus indirect exchange of currencies that we employed in deriving Equation (2.6) involves selecting between one (direct) transaction and two (indirect) transactions. This means just one extra transaction cost when taking the indirect route rather than the direct route. On the other hand, triangular arbitrage is based on three transactions, and hence three transaction costs—for converting $ to £, for converting £ to DM, and converting DM to $. There are also three transaction costs for the reverse arbitrage. The approach we have taken, which may be called **one-way arbitrage**, gives a narrower permissible bid-ask spread for a cross-rate transaction than is found by triangular arbitrage. In a market where a few points translate into millions of dollars, it is important we derive the correct permissible spread, and this requires one-way arbitrage, not the more circuitous triangular arbitrage.[14]

Nonzero Foreign Exchange Transaction Costs

Defining the Costs of Transacting   As we have already noted, in reality the price that must be paid to buy a foreign currency is different from the price at which the currency can be sold. For example, the U.S. dollar price a person must pay a bank for a German mark—the bank's ask price—will exceed the U.S. dollar price received from the sale of a German mark—the bank's bid price. In addition, the buyer or seller of a currency might have to pay a lump-sum fee or commission on each transaction. For our purpose, we can think of both the bid-ask spread and the exchange dealer's fee as two parts of the total cost of transacting. They both provide revenue for dealers in foreign currencies and cause those who need to exchange currencies to lose in going

---

[14] Transaction costs become especially important in the context of **interest arbitrage**, which is covered in Chapters 7 and 8.

back and forth. Let us define buy and sell rates:

$S(\$/\text{ask}\pounds)$ is the price that must be *paid to the bank* to buy one pound with dollars. It is the bank's offer or ask rate on pounds. $S(\$/\text{bid}\pounds)$ is the number of dollars *received from the bank* for the sale of pounds for dollars. It is the bank's bid rate on pounds.[15]

Because of transaction costs, we must be careful when taking the inverse of an exchange rate. When there are transaction costs, instead of writing

$$S(\$/\pounds) = \frac{1}{S(\pounds/\$)}$$

as in equations (2.3), we must write[16]

$$S(\$/\text{ask}\pounds) \equiv \frac{1}{S(\pounds/\text{bid}\$)} \quad \text{and} \quad S(\$/\text{bid}\pounds) \equiv \frac{1}{S(\pounds/\text{ask}\$)}$$

More generally,

$$S(i/\text{ask}j) \equiv \frac{1}{S(j/\text{bid}i)} \quad \text{and} \quad S(i/\text{bid}j) \equiv \frac{1}{S(j/\text{ask}i)} \qquad (2.9)$$

Figure 2.3 shows the exchange rates when going from DM to $ to £ when transaction costs are included. If a person were to buy pounds directly with German marks they would receive $S(\pounds/\text{bidDM})$ pounds from the bank; this is what the bank bids for German marks in terms of pounds, as is shown along the horizontal darkly shaded arrow in Figure 2.3. If instead the person goes indirectly from DM to $ to £ along the darkly shaded arrows, on the first leg each mark buys $S(\$/\text{bidDM})$ dollars; this is the bank's buying or bid rate for marks in terms of dollars. On the second leg, each dollar buys $S(\pounds/\text{bid}\$)$ pounds—the bank's buying or bid rate on dollars for pounds. Therefore, the indirect route gives $S(\$/\text{bidDM}) \cdot S(\pounds/\text{bid}\$)$ pounds per mark.

The bank's direct quote for $S(\pounds/\text{bidDM})$ will not be accepted by customers if it gives less pounds than the indirect route. This requires

$$S(\pounds/\text{bidDM}) \geq S(\$/\text{bidDM}) \cdot S(\pounds/\text{bid}\$) \qquad (2.10)$$

---

[15] Instead of writing $S(\$/\text{ask}\pounds)$ we could write $S(\text{bid}\$/\text{ask}\pounds)$, because if a bank is offering to sell pounds for dollars, it is offering to buy dollars for pounds; these are two sides of the same transaction. Similarly, instead of writing $S(\$/\text{bid}\pounds)$ we could write $S(\text{ask}\$/\text{bid}\pounds)$. We need label only one currency because, for example, if we are talking of the bank's ask rate for pounds in terms of dollars, $S(\$/\text{ask}\pounds)$, we know this is also the bank's bid rate on dollars. That is, once we have stated what is done with one currency, stating what is done with the other currency is redundant.

[16] These rules follow immediately from the extended notation in the previous footnote.

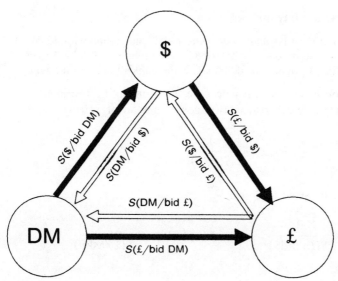

FIGURE 2.3
Direct versus indirect exchange: nonzero transaction costs.

Next, consider a person wanting to exchange pounds for German marks, the reverse of the previous situation. They can exchange directly as along the unshaded arrow in Figure 2.3, receiving $S(DM/bid£)$ marks per pound—the rate the bank pays for, or bids on, pounds. Alternatively, they can exchange via the dollar receiving $S(\$/bid£) \cdot S(DM/bid\$)$ marks per pound; this is seen from the two unshaded arrows from £ to $ and from $ to DM in Figure 2.3. The direct rate will attract business only if it gives at least as many marks per pound as buying marks indirectly. Therefore, for the direct exchange rate to attract business it is required that

$$S(DM/bid£) \geq S(\$/bid£) \cdot S(DM/bid\$) \tag{2.11}$$

By using the equations (2.9) in the inequality (2.10) we have

$$\frac{1}{S(DM/ask£)} \geq \frac{1}{S(DM/ask\$)} \cdot \frac{1}{S(\$/ask£)} \tag{2.12}$$

Taking reciprocals, and therefore reversing the inequality in (2.12), gives

$$S(DM/ask£) \leq S(DM/ask\$) \cdot S(\$/ask£) \tag{2.13}$$

By comparing the inequalities (2.11) and (2.13), we find what we do and do not know about cross rates when there are transaction costs. We no longer know exactly what the cross rates are from rates against the dollar. Instead, we know the smallest number of marks a bank can offer on pounds— given by inequality (2.11). We also know the maximum number of marks it can ask for a pound—given by inequality (2.13). However, we do not know where in between these limits the actual direct exchange rates are. The exact bid and ask cross rates depend on the competition between banks for direct exchange between the currencies. If there is a lot of competition because there is a lot of business, the range of

$$S(\text{DM}/\text{bid}\$) \cdot S(\$/\text{bid}\pounds) \le S(\text{DM}/\pounds) \le S(\text{DM}/\text{ask}\$) \cdot S(\$/\text{ask}\pounds) \quad (2.14)$$

will be small, perhaps on the order of the size of the bid-ask spread between the dollar and one of these foreign currencies. If there is little competition, the range in inequality (2.14) could be quite large, perhaps as much as double the size of the above bid-ask spread.

What do we learn from the above? We learn that when going from one foreign currency to another, for example, from Canadian dollars to pounds or from Mexican pesos to Japanese yen, it pays to call a number of banks. The worst you could find are exchange rates as unfavorable as on two separate transactions, going into and out of the U.S. dollar. Generally you will find a better situation. Different banks may have quite different direct quotes according to whether or not they are market makers in the direct exchange you are considering, and you might as well find the best deal.

Another thing we have learned is that, if there were no transaction costs, we could find all the possible exchange rates between n currencies from $n - 1$ exchange rates, those against the U.S. dollar. However, since in reality there *are* transaction costs, the situation is very different. Not only are there $2(n - 1)$ rates against the U.S. dollar, that is, a bid and an ask for each rate, but there are also a number of other bid and ask rates for direct exchanges. The major currencies of OECD countries trade directly against each other with, for example, quotations in Britain for direct purchase or sale of Canadian dollars, German marks, French francs, Japanese yen, and so on. In Tokyo there are quotes in yen for purchasing pounds, Canadian dollars, and so on. There are consequently far more than $2(n - 1)$ different quoted exchange rates.

It is worth pointing out that there is no rule that exchange rates should all be expressed only against the dollar in order to obtain other exchange rates. Any currency would do from a conceptual point of view. However, as a practical matter, it is important that the chief currency for determining other rates be one that is widely traded and held. At the beginning of the twentieth century, the pound sterling was heavily used, but after the 1944 Bretton Woods Agreement (which is described in the Addendum), the dollar emerged as the standard for stating other currencies' values. We might also note that it is possible to find all exchange rates even without knowing the values of currencies against an nth currency. Instead, we can use the values of currencies against a commodity such as gold, or even against a purely international money such as Special Drawing Rights (SDRs), which are also described in the Addendum.

The conditions we have derived are valid not only for conventional or spot exchange rates, but also for forward exchange rates, which are explained in the next chapter. That is, if we replaced the $S(i/j)$'s in this chapter with forward exchange rates, everything would still be valid.

SUMMARY

1 The bid-ask spread on foreign bank notes is high because of inventory costs and the risks of note handling. Bank notes are exchanged at a retail and at a wholesale level.

2 The spot foreign exchange market is the market in which bank drafts are exchanged. In this market, currencies are received in bank accounts one or two business days after they are ordered.

3 The interbank foreign exchange market consists of a complex network of informal linkages between banks and foreign exchange brokers. These links are also international. When banks are dealing with each other, they quote two-way exchange rates. Intentions are revealed only after rates have been quoted. When banks deal with a foreign exchange broker, they state their intentions, and the broker looks for a counterparty. A number of European countries maintain a formal market.

4 Banks settle between themselves on the same day their customers receive and pay for foreign exchange. Messages between banks are sent via SWIFT.

5 Banks use clearing houses like CHIPS to clear balances between themselves if they do not maintain correspondent accounts directly with each other.

6 Exchange rates are generally quoted in European terms, that is, in units of foreign currency per U.S. dollar. Newspapers generally quote only selling rates. When exchange rates are quoted in European terms, we must add points to selling rates to obtain buying rates. The British pound is still quoted in U.S. terms.

7 Transaction costs in the form of bid-ask spreads on exchange rates are important because they can greatly influence the return on short-term foreign investments. They also provide a large income for banks.

8 In the absence of transaction costs, cross exchange rates between currencies other than the U.S. dollar can be obtained from exchange rates vis-à-vis the U.S. dollar.

9 In the absence of transaction costs, the many possible cross exchange rates between n different currencies can be obtained by just knowing the $n - 1$ values of the currencies against the remaining nth currency. Any standard will do for measurement.

10 In the presence of transaction costs, we cannot compute cross rates precisely from rates versus the dollar. Instead, we can compute a range within which cross rates must be quoted.

QUESTIONS

1 Do you think that because of the costs of moving bank notes back to their country of circulation, buying bank notes could sometimes be cheaper than buying bank drafts? Could there be a seasonal pattern in exchange rates for bank notes? [*Hint*: Think of

what is involved in shipping U.S. dollars arising from Americans spending summers in Europe versus European vacationing in America.]

2 How can companies that issue and sell traveler's checks charge a relatively low fee? How do they profit?

3 Compute the percentage spread on South African rands and Canadian dollars from Table 2.1. Why do you think the spread on Canadian dollars is lower?

4 What steps are involved in settling a purchase made in Britain with a credit card issued by a U.S. bank? How do you think the spread between rates used in credit-card payments compares with that for foreign bank notes?

5 Does the use of U.S. dollars as a vehicle currency put U.S. banks at an advantage for making profits? Why do you think the U.S. dollar has become a common vehicle currency?

6 Why do you think that banks give two-way rates when dealing with each other? Why don't they state their intentions as they do when dealing with foreign exchange brokers?

7 Check a recent business newspaper or the business page for spot exchange rates. Form an $n \times n$ exchange-rate matrix by computing the cross rates, and check whether $S(\$/\pounds) = 1/S(\pounds/\$)$ and so on.

8 Complete the following exchange-rate matrix. Assume that there are no transaction costs.

Currency sold	Currency purchased				
	$	£	S Fr	DM	¥
$	1	2.0	0.6	0.5	0.005
£		1			
S Fr			1		
DM				1	
¥					1

BIBLIOGRAPHY

Aliber, Robert Z. (ed.): *The Handbook of International Financial Management*, Dow Jones Irwin, Homewood, Ill., 1989.

Deardorff, Alan V.: "One-Way Arbitrage and Its Implications for the Foreign Exchange Markets," *Journal of Political Economy*, April 1979, pp. 351–364.

Einzig, Paul: *A Textbook on Foreign Exchange*, St. Martin's, London, 1969.

Grubel, Herbert G.: *International Economics*, Richard D. Irwin, Homewood, Ill., 1977, Chapter 10.

Krugman, Paul: "Vehicle Currencies and the Structure of International Exchange," *Journal of Money, Credit and Banking*, August 1980, pp. 513–526.

Kubarych, Roger M.: *Foreign Exchange Markets in the United States*, Federal Reserve Bank of New York, 1978.

Reihl, Heinz, and Rita M. Rodriguez: *Foreign Exchange Markets*, McGraw-Hill, New York, 1977.

Syrett, William W.: *A Manual of Foreign Exchange*, 6th ed., Pitman, London, 1966.

CHAPTER 3

FORWARD, FUTURES, AND OPTION MARKETS

It would be difficult to overstate the importance of the **forward**, **futures**, and **option markets** for foreign exchange. Indeed, a financial manager of a firm with overseas interests may find himself or herself as much involved with these markets as with the spot market. The forward, futures, and option foreign exchange markets are valuable for hedging risks arising from changes in exchange rates when importing, exporting, borrowing, or investing. These markets are also used by speculators. This chapter explains the nature of these extremely important markets, while a later chapter, Chapter 10, shows how they can be used to hedge or speculate.

FORWARD EXCHANGE

What Is Forward Foreign Exchange?

We have already indicated in the previous chapter that there is a market for forward exchange that exists alongside the market for spot exchange. Because the 1- or 2-day delivery period for spot transactions is so short, when comparing spot rates with forward exchange rates we can usefully think of spot rates as exchange rates for undelayed transactions. On the other hand, forward exchange rates involve an arrangement to delay the exchange of currencies until some future date. A useful working definition is:

> The forward exchange rate is the rate that is contracted today for the delivery of a currency at a specified date in the future, at a price agreed upon today.

If we look back at Figure 2.1 on p. 38, we note that for Britain, Canada, France, Japan, Switzerland, and West Germany, we are given exchange rates for

30-day, 90-day, and 180-day forwards. Although they are not quoted in the table, forward rates can also be found for other currencies and for other maturities. Forward exchange contracts are drawn up between banks and their clients, and frequently involve two banks. The market does not have a physical being but instead is similar to the spot market, being an informal arrangement of banks and brokers linked by telephone and Telex.

Figure 2.1 tells us that on May 18, 1989, a client dealing in over $1 million in bank draft form could have purchased spot Japanese yen from Bankers Trust at $0.007202/¥. This would have meant delivery of the yen to the client's account on May 22, 1989, two business days after the order. If, however, this client wanted to have the yen in about 30 days rather than "immediately," then it would have been necessary to pay $0.007233, which is $0.000031/¥ or 31 points more than the rate for spot delivery. In a similar way, Figure 2.1 gives the exchange rate for the delivery of British pounds in 30 days as $1.6080/£. This is a lower value of the British pound (that is, more pounds per U.S. dollar) than the spot rate of $1.6120/£.

Forward Exchange Premiums and Discounts

When we must pay more for forward delivery than for spot delivery of a foreign currency, as we do in the case of the Japanese yen in Figure 2.1, we say that the foreign currency is at a **forward premium**. When we can pay less for forward delivery than for spot delivery, as we do in the case of the British pound in Figure 2.1, we say that the forward currency is at a **forward discount**.[1]

In order to provide a definition of forward premiums and discounts, let us first express the forward exchange rate in terms similar to those used for the spot rate:

$F_n(\$/£)$ is the n-year forward exchange rate of dollars to pounds. More generally, $F_n(i/j)$ is the n-year forward exchange rate of currency i to currency j.

For example, in Figure 2.1, $F_{1/4}(\$/£) = \$1.6000/£$, and $F_{1/2}(\$/£) = \$1.5877/£$. With the help of the definition of the forward rate we can define the n-year forward exchange premium or discount of pounds versus dollars, on an annual basis, as[2]

$$\text{Premium/Discount(£ vs. \$)} = \frac{F_n(\$/£) - S(\$/£)}{nS(\$/£)} \qquad (3.1)$$

[1] Some people would say that when the spot Canadian dollar is worth less than a U.S. dollar, as it is in Figure 2.1, it is at a discount. This is totally different from a forward discount. Indeed, the Canadian dollar could be at a forward premium while it is *at a discount against the U.S. dollar*. Conventions are hard to change, so the reader is warned to be careful of the misleading common use of terms.

[2] More generally, the n-year premium/discount of currency i versus currency j is

$$\text{Premium/Discount}(i \text{ vs. } j) = \frac{F_n(j/i) - S(j/i)}{nS(j/i)}$$

Note that for the premium of i versus j, the j and i are reversed in the exchange-rate terms.

When the value of the expression (3.1) is positive, the pound is at a forward premium vis-à-vis the dollar. This is because the pound costs more for forward delivery than for spot delivery. When (3.1) is negative, the pound is at a forward discount vis-à-vis the dollar. In this case the pound is cheaper to buy forward than to buy spot. In the event that the forward rate and spot rate are equal, we say that the forward currency is **flat**.

Forward premiums and discounts are put into annual terms by dividing by n because this is invariably the way interest rates are quoted, and it is useful to be able to compare interest rates and forward premiums in these same terms. Often, forward premiums and discounts are also put in percentage terms by multiplying by 100. Using the values in Figure 2.1, we find that the expression (3.1) is negative and equal to -0.0298 or 2.98 percent for the 1-month annualized forward pound discount. That is,

$$\text{Premium}/\text{Discount}(\pounds \text{ vs. } \$) = \frac{1.6080 - 1.6120}{\frac{1}{12} \times 1.6120} = -0.0298$$

This is a discount on the pound versus the dollar, because the pound costs approximately 3 percent (per annum) less for forward delivery than for spot delivery. Table 3.1 gives the forward premiums and discounts for all forward currencies quoted in Figure 2.1.

When the pound is at a forward discount against the dollar, this is precisely the same as saying that the dollar is at a forward premium against the pound. Clearly, when pounds cost less for forward delivery than for spot delivery against dollars, dollars must cost more against pounds. Indeed, the n-year annualized forward premium/discount of the dollar versus the pound is

$$\text{Premium}/\text{Discount}(\$ \text{ vs. } \pounds) = \frac{F_n(\pounds/\$) - S(\pounds/\$)}{nS(\pounds/\$)} \tag{3.2}$$

which from Figure 2.1 gives an annualized premium (since the value is positive) of $+0.0290$ or 2.90 percent on the 1 month, or $n = \frac{1}{12}$ year, forward contract.[3]

The fact that most currencies are quoted in European terms (number of units of foreign currency per U.S. dollar rather than the other way around) does not affect our definition of premiums or discounts. The n-year annualized premium/discount of, for example, the dollar versus the German mark is

$$\text{Premium}/\text{Discount}(\$ \text{ vs. } DM) = \frac{F_n(DM/\$) - S(DM/\$)}{nS(DM/\$)} \tag{3.3}$$

[3]There is a small difference between the numerical value of the pound-versus-dollar discount and the numerical value of the dollar-versus-pound premium, that is, -2.98 versus 2.90. This is because of bid-ask spreads and because of the base-selection problem in taking percentage differences.

TABLE 3.1
PREMIUM (+) OR DISCOUNT (−) PERCENTAGES ON FORWARD EXCHANGE
VIS-À-VIS U.S. DOLLAR

		Forward period		
Currency	Prem./ disc.	30	90	180 days
Pound sterling	£ disc.	− 2.98	− 2.98	− 3.01
	US$ prem.	+ 2.90	+ 3.03	+ 3.06
Canadian dollar	Can$ disc.	− 3.01	− 2.48	− 2.08
	US$ prem.	+ 3.02	+ 2.52	+ 2.10
French franc	Fr prem.	+ 1.60	+ 0.80	+ 0.67
	US$ disc.	− 1.04	− 0.78	− 0.60
Japanese yen	¥ prem.	+ 5.17	+ 4.67	+ 4.36
	US$ disc.	− 5.19	− 4.64	− 4.28
Swiss franc	S Fr prem.	+ 2.12	+ 2.05	+ 2.01
	US$ disc.	− 2.18	− 2.04	− 2.01
German mark	DM prem.	+ 3.08	+ 2.60	+ 2.33
	US$ disc.	− 3.04	− 2.54	− 2.48

This table is derived from Figure 2.1 using the formula Premium / Discount (i vs. j) = $\{[F_n(j / i) - S(j / i)] / nS(j / i)\} \times 100$, where n is the number of years forward. The discounts / premiums on the U.S. dollar (bottom row of each pair) do not precisely equal the negatives of the forward exchange premiums / discounts (top row) because of the base-selection problem in computing percentage differences and because of bid-ask spreads.

Forward premiums and discounts are known by other names. Frequently, the term **spot-forward spread** or just **forward spread** is used. Some market traders refer to premiums or discounts as forward **pickups** or **markdowns**. We shall stick with "premiums" and "discounts." These terms will be understood by almost everyone who deals in the forward market.

Varieties of Forward Exchange Contracts

It is easy to see from Figure 2.1 that forward exchange quotations are common in a limited number of currencies—those that are most heavily traded. This was clearly shown in a survey of 123 New York banks by the Federal Reserve Bank of New York in March 1986. The percentages of overall turnover activity in the major currencies are given in Table 3.2, which shows that over 94 percent of the turnover activity is in the six currencies in which most international trade is conducted, and for which forwards are quoted in Figure 2.1. Even on the heavily traded currencies the forward exchange quotations in Figure 2.1 are provided only for specific and rather short periods. The table, however, hides the variety of dates and features that appear on different forward exchange contracts.

The 30-day, 90-day, and 180-day quotations in Figure 2.1 are for interbank transactions, and banks do tend to deal among themselves in terms of these

TABLE 3.2
THE IMPORTANCE OF DIFFERENT CURRENCIES IN THE NEW YORK FOREIGN
EXCHANGE MARKET

Currency	Turnover, %
German mark	34.2
Japanese yen	23.0
British pound	18.6
Swiss franc	9.7
Canadian dollar	5.2
French franc	3.6
Dutch guilder	1.4
All other	4.3

Source: Survey by the Federal Reserve Bank of New York, March 1986.

"even" dates. However, when dealing with their customers, banks will draw up contracts for periods of a couple of days up to a number of years, and these periods do not have to be in even multiples of 30 or anything else. On May 18, 1989, a corporate buyer of sterling might well want to take delivery of pounds on February 22, 1990, to meet a sterling obligation that will come due on that date. Forward currency is bought or sold for the value date, February 22, 1990, and that is the day that usable funds will be obtained. Since for most currencies the spot market value date is already 2 business days in the future, the shortest forward contracts are for a period of 3 days.

Sometimes buyers and sellers of forward exchange are not precisely sure when they will need their foreign currency or when they will receive it. For example, a U.S. importer may know that he or she must pay a British producer 30 days after delivery of the goods, but the exact day of delivery may not be known; delivery might be "toward the end of June." To take care of this, banks will also sell forward exchange with some flexibility, allowing buyers to take delivery of foreign exchange on any day during the last 10 days of the contract period, or according to some other flexible scheme. Flexibility will cost the buyer a little more, the exchange rate being the most unfavorable for the customer during the period of possible delivery. However, it will relieve the buyer of considerable worry in case he or she needs the foreign currency before the contracted forward date, or has to take delivery of the foreign exchange before the contracted date of forward sale of the foreign currency.

Conventions in Quoting Forward Exchange

The conventions used in quoting forward rates need explanation, since there are two different methods in common use. Forward currencies are quoted both **outright** and as **swaps**. Outright quotations are similar in form to spot-exchange-rate quotations; they involve the rate of exchange expressed as so many units of one currency for another. European terms—the number of foreign units per dollar—are used for the same currencies that have European-term spot-rate quotations. Let us first deal with outright quotations and ask what you would have heard if you had called Bankers Trust on May 18, 1989, for forward quotations, and the bank had given you the rates in outright form.

An outright quotation on 30-day British sterling could have been given as 1.6070/80. This means that the bank will buy sterling (sell dollars) at $1.6070/£ and sell sterling (buy dollars) at a price 10 points higher, or $1.6080/£. Again, as in the spot market, when the bank quotes its buying and selling rates in the interbank market, it will stand ready to either buy or sell, and the inquirer does not have to specify beforehand what he or she intends to do. Because the first two decimal places could well be assumed to be already known, the outright quotation could be just 70/80. A 30-day quote on German marks, because European terms are used, could be 1.9670/80 or merely 70/80. This means that the bank will sell marks (buy dollars) at DM 1.9670/$, and buy marks (sell dollars) at the lower mark value of DM 1.9680/$.[4]

When forward rates are quoted in swap rather than outright form, the person who calls a bank will be given the spot exchange rate and an amount in points which must be either added to or subtracted from the spot rate to obtain the forward rate. The need to add or subtract depends on the nature of the swap quotation, which in turn depends on whether the foreign exchange is at a premium or a discount. Experience tells banks and their clients what is meant by each quotation. We can learn by examples.

A person who calls Bankers Trust and is given the quotation for forward sterling in terms of swaps would hear "Spot 1.6110/20; 30-day 45 over 40; 90-day 130 over 120; 180-day 258 over 243." We can write this as follows:

Spot	30-day	90-day	180-day
1.6110 / 20	45 / 40	130 / 120	258 / 243

These quotations correspond to the values in Table 3.3. The reader will observe that the swaps provide the same selling rates as those that are quoted outright in Figure 2.1 and that spreads become larger as we move forward.

Table 3.3 is obtained by subtracting the swap points from the spot bid and offer quotations. We subtract because on May 18, 1989, sterling was at a forward discount against the dollar. If sterling had been at a premium, the swap points would have been added. You might well wonder how you are supposed to know whether there is a premium or discount on sterling. Often the bank will

---

[4] We note that the lower number precedes the higher number in quotations for both sterling and the mark, even though sterling is quoted in U.S. dollar equivalent and the mark is quoted in European terms. What this means is that for sterling, the first number is the bank's bid on sterling in terms of dollars, while for the mark and all other currencies the first number is the bank's bid on the dollar in terms of the foreign currency.

TABLE 3.3
BIDS AND OFFERS ON STERLING
(U.S. dollars / £ sterling)

Type of exchange	Bank buys / bids	Bank sells / offers
Spot	1.6110	1.6120
30-day	1.6065	1.6080
90-day	1.5980	1.6000
180-day	1.5852	1.5877

tell. If it does not, it is possible to determine this from the order of the swap points. For example, if the bank quotes sterling as

Spot	30-day	90-day	180-day
1.6110 / 20	10 / 15	25 / 35	60 / 75

that is, with forward swap points having lower numbers before the obliques than after the obliques, the client should know that sterling is at a premium and add the swap points. This is because bank spreads always increase on more distant forwards, and this is what happens when we add swap points to obtain Table 3.4. If we had subtracted rather than added the swap points, we would have made the bank's buying and selling rates move toward each other at more distant forwards, which is never the case. We learn to add when the order of swap points is ascending.

The same rule of adding swap points when the order of swap points is ascending and subtracting swap points when they are descending applies whether exchange rates are quoted in U.S. dollar equivalent or as foreign currency per U.S. dollar. However, in the case of the foreign currency per U.S. dollar quotation used today for currencies other than the British pound, adding points means that the foreign currency is at a forward discount; there will be more foreign currency per dollar for forward than for spot delivery. This means that

TABLE 3.4
BIDS AND OFFERS ON STERLING
(U.S. dollars / £ sterling)

Type of exchange	Bank buys / bids	Bank sells / offers
Spot	1.6110	1.6120
30-day	1.6120	1.6135
90-day	1.6135	1.6155
180-day	1.6170	1.6195

with foreign currency per U.S. dollar quotation an ascending order of swap points means the foreign currency is at a forward discount, and a descending order means the foreign currency is at a forward premium. This is the opposite to the situation with U.S. dollar equivalent quotation. Clearly, it is necessary for foreign currency traders to think quickly and accurately. Nevertheless, mistakes do occasionally occur, and banks honor their agreements.

The piece of paper constituting the forward contract gives the agreed-upon forward exchange rate in outright terms. In addition to the exchange rate, the contract contains the following information:

1 Name of the primary party
2 Name of the counterparty
3 Value date
4 Total dollar value of contract
5 Specifics for delivery of foreign exchange and dollars, including details of location, bank accounts, and so on

The majority of forward contracts do not exist as outright agreements but instead take the form of swaps. According to the 1986 survey conducted by the Federal Reserve Bank of New York, spot transactions made up 64 percent of bank foreign exchange turnover in the 123 commercial banks surveyed, swaps made up 30 percent, and only 6 percent were outright forward agreements. The two different methods of quoting forward rates that we have described correspond to these two types of agreements. The outright agreements, generally between banks and nonbank customers, are for a straightforward purchase or sale of a forward currency. Swaps, which could be between banks or between a bank and a large corporation, involve two exchanges.[5]

We can define swaps as follows:

A foreign exchange swap is an agreement to both buy and sell foreign exchange at prespecified contracted exchange rates, where the buying and selling are separated in time.

The most common form of swap is to have the original exchange as a spot exchange and the second exchange as a forward exchange. Indeed, this is the reason the method of adding points to the spot rate to obtain the forward rate is called a **swap quotation**. Such swaps are called **spot-forward swaps** where the trader buys (sells) on the spot market while simultaneously selling (buying) on the forward market, hence reversing the original exchange. When the reversal is on adjacent days, the term **rollover** is used. Large banks also do **forward-for-ward swaps**, which involve buying and selling with the offsetting contracts both being forward exchange agreements.

Swaps are very valuable to those who are investing or borrowing abroad. For example, a person who invests in a foreign treasury bill can use a spot-forward

---

[5]While swap agreements will invariably be quoted in swap form, outright agreements could also conceivably be quoted in swap form. Conventions for quoting rates must be distinguished from the forms of contract even though there is close correspondence.

swap to avoid foreign exchange risk. The investor sells forward the maturity value of the bill at the same time as the spot foreign exchange is purchased. Since a known amount of the investor's local currency will be delivered according to the forward contract, no uncertainty from exchange rates is faced. In a similar way, those who borrow in foreign money markets can buy forward the foreign currency needed for repayment at the same time they convert the borrowed foreign funds on the spot market. The value of swaps to international investors and borrowers helps explain their popularity.

While valuable to investors and borrowers, the swap is not very useful to importers and exporters. Payments and receipts in international trade are frequently delayed. However, it is an outright forward purchase of foreign exchange that is valuable to the importer, not a swap. Similarly, the exporter needs to make an outright forward sale of foreign exchange. This is not, however, the place to present the details of these uses of forward exchange or the details of the value of forward exchange to borrowers and investors. That must wait until Part 4.

Swaps are popular with banks because it is difficult to avoid risk while trading in specific future days with so many markets to worry about—there are different markets for each future day. On some days a bank will be **long** in foreign exchange, which means that it has agreed to purchase more foreign currency than it has agreed to sell, or already holds more than it wants. On other days, it will be **short**, having agreed to sell more than it had agreed to buy. If, for example, bank A considers itself long on current holdings of British pounds (because it holds more than it wants) and short on 30-day forwards (because of net forward sales) it will find another bank, bank B, in the reverse position. Bank A will sell pounds spot and buy pounds forward, and bank B will do the opposite. In this manner, both banks can balance their spot versus forward positions while economizing on the number of transactions that will achieve this. The use of only even-dated contracts leaves some exposure to remaining long and short positions from day to day. These are then covered with rollover swaps. In this way swap agreements allow the banks to exchange their surpluses and shortages of individual currencies to offset spot and forward trades with their customers. It should be no surprise that matching customer trades with appropriate swaps is a complex and dynamic problem.[6]

Why Forward Spreads Widen with Increased Maturity

We have noted that the bid-ask spreads on forward exchange contracts increase as the maturity of the contract lengthens. In fact, as we pointed out, examining

---

[6]The reader is referred to the many other accounts of this dynamic market. *Foreign Exchange Markets in the United States*, by Roger Kubarych (Federal Reserve Bank of New York, 1978) is an excellent source which replaces the classic account, *The New York Foreign Exchange Market*, written by Alan Holmes and Francis Schott and published in 1965 by the same bank. Other valuable sources include Paul Einzig, *A Dynamic Theory of Forward Exchange*, Macmillan, London, 1966; Raymond G. Connix, *Foreign Exchange Today*, revised ed., Wiley, New York, 1980.

the spreads to see if they increase with contract maturity is a way of checking calculations of outright forward rates from swap quotations. The reason banks take larger spreads on longer-maturity contracts is not, as some people seem to think, that longer-maturity contracts are riskier to the banks because there is more time during which spot exchange rates might change. As we have seen, banks tend to balance their forward positions by the use of swaps and rollovers, and since they can simultaneously buy and sell forward for every maturity, they can avoid losses from changes in exchange rates during the terms of forward contracts; what the banks gain (lose) on forward contracts to sell they lose (gain) on offsetting forward contracts to buy. Rather, the reason spreads increase with maturity is the increasing **thinness** of the market as forward maturity increases.

Increasing thinness means smaller volumes of activity, which in turn means greater difficulty offsetting positions in the interbank forward market after taking orders to buy or sell forward; since banks state their market and are then obligated if their bid or ask is accepted, they often have to enter the market immediately themselves to help offset the position they have just taken. The difficulty of offsetting longer-maturity forward contracts makes them riskier than shorter-maturity contracts, but the extra risk involves uncertainty about the price of an offsetting forward contract immediately after quoting, rather than uncertainty about the path of the spot exchange rate during the maturity of the forward contract.

CURRENCY FUTURES

What Is a Currency Future?

Unlike forward exchange contracts, which are bought and sold by banks and trade in the interbank market, currency futures are bought and sold on the floor of a futures exchange. Currency futures began trading in the International Monetary Market (IMM) of the Chicago Mercantile Exchange in 1972; since then many other markets have opened.[7]

Currency futures are standardized contracts that trade like conventional commodity futures. In order for a market to be made in currency futures contracts, it is necessary to have only a few value dates. At the Chicago IMM, there are four value dates of contracts—the third Wednesday in the months of March, June, September, and December. Contracts are traded in whole units—£62,500, Can $100,000, and so on. This enables the traders to keep track of prices and to buy and sell in terms of numbers of contracts. The currencies that are traded, along with their contract sizes, are shown in Table 3.5.

Both buyers and sellers of currency futures enter into futures contracts with a contract clearing corporation rather than with each other. In doing this, it is necessary to post a **margin** and pay a fee. The margin is posted in a margin

---

[7]Currency futures were the first financial futures to trade on the IMM. Today, currency futures are also traded on the COMEX commodities exchange in New York, on the American Board of Trade, and on exchanges outside the United Sates.

TABLE 3.5
THE MARKET FOR CURRENCY FUTURES

Japanese yen (IMM) — ¥ 12.5 million; dollars per yen (.00)

Date	Open	High	Low	Settle	Open Interest
June	0.7203	0.7249	0.7191	0.7226	65,451
Sept	0.7283	0.7283	0.7270	0.7304	4,248
Dec.	07355	0.7385	0.7340	0.7380	702
Mar. 90	· · ·	· · ·	· · ·	0.7453	170

West German mark (IMM) — DM 125,000; dollars per mark

Date	Open	High	Low	Settle	Open Interest
June	.5062	.5109	.5045	.5080	68,213
Sept	.5084	.5137	.5060	.5107	4,274
Dec.	.5115	.5150	.5115	.5133	608

Canadian dollar (IMM) — Can$100,000; dollars per Canadian dollar

Date	Open	High	Low	Settle	Open Interest
June	.8360	.8370	.8353	.8364	20,416
Sept	.8317	.8324	.8312	.8320	2,056
Dec.	.8283	.8290	.8280	.8283	640
Mar. 90	.8250	.8250	.8250	.8250	99
June	· · ·	· · ·	· · ·	.8221	556

British pound (IMM) — £62,500; dollars per pound

Date	Open	High	Low	Settle	Open Interest
June	1.6054	1.6174	1.6010	1.6102	25,596
Sept	1.5920	1.6044	1.5880	1.5976	1,447
Dec.	1.5820	1.5910	1.5820	1.5872	166

Swiss franc (IMM) – SFr 125,000; dollars per franc

Date	Open	High	Low	Settle	Open Interest
June	.5673	.5709	.5660	.5685	41,601
Sept	.5694	.5735	.5681	.5712	2,933
Dec.	.5717	.5762	.5717	.5745	182

Australian dollar (IMM) — Aus$100,000; dollars per Australian dollar

Date	Open	High	Low	Settle	Open Interest
June	.7521	.7560	.7505	.7535	2,413
Sept	.7375	.7410	.7370	.7390	328

account with a member of the exchange to ensure all deals are honored. The margin must be supplemented if the equity position falls below a certain level, called the **maintenance level**. For example, the IMM's required minimum margin on sterling is currently $2000 per contract, and its maintenance level is $1500. This means that if the market value of the contract falls more than $500, the full amount of the decline in value must be added to the margin account. Falls in contract values which leave more than $1500 of equity do not require action. Increases in the value of a contract are added to the margin account and can be withdrawn. Margin adjustment is done on a daily basis and is called **marking to market**.

In contrast to the situation with futures contracts, banks require no margin from their larger clients for forward exchange contracts. They will, however, generally reduce the client's existing line of credit. For example, if a bank has granted a client a $1 million line of credit and the customer trades $5 million forward, the bank is likely to reduce the credit line by, perhaps, $500,000, or 10 percent of the contract. For a customer without a credit line, the bank will require that a margin be established within a special account. The procedure for maintaining the margin on a forward contract depends on the bank's relationship with the customer. Margin may be **called**, requiring supplementary funds to be deposited in the margin account, if a large, unfavorable movement in the spot exchange rate occurs. In deciding whether to call for supplementing margin accounts, banks consider the likelihood of their customers honoring forward contracts. The banks exercise considerable discretion, which is in sharp contrast to the formal daily marking to market of the futures market.

Margin accounts, whether held with a futures exchange member or with a bank, generally earn interest and therefore do not represent an opportunity cost. As with the situation for margin maintenance, banks are frequently very flexible about what is accepted as margin, and will hold stocks, bonds, and other instruments to ensure customers honor contracts.

Unlike the case for forward contracts, when the buyer of a futures contract wants to take delivery of the foreign currency, the currency is bought at the going spot exchange rate at the time of delivery. What happens is perhaps best described by considering an example.

Suppose a futures contract buyer needs pounds in August, and buys a September British pound futures contract.[8] In August, when the pounds are needed, the contract is sold back to the exchange, and the pounds are bought on the spot exchange market at whatever exchange rate exists on the day in August when the pounds are wanted. Most of the foreign exchange risk is still removed in this situation, because if, for example, the pound has unexpectedly increased in value from the time of buying the futures contract, there will be a gain in the margin account. This gain will compensate for the higher than expected spot exchange rate in August. However, not all exchange rate risk is removed,

---

[8]Alternatively, a June contract might be purchased and delivery of the pounds taken. The pounds could then be held at interest until needed.

because the amount in the margin account will not in general exactly compensate for the unexpected movement in the spot exchange rate. The remaining risk is due to unpredictable variations in interest rates earned on the margin account which leave some uncertainty in the amount which is in the account; interest rates might, for example, have been low when there was a large amount in the margin account, and high when there was little in the account, so that the margin account incompletely compensates for the unexpected change in the exchange rate. This risk due to variability in interest rates is called **marking-to-market risk**, and makes futures contracts riskier than forward contracts for which there is no marking to market.

Even in the very rare circumstance that delivery is taken on the maturity date of a futures contract, there is still marking-to-market risk.[9] What happens is that on the date of delivery, the value of the futures contract is what the foreign currency is worth at the going spot exchange rate. However, the amount in the margin account is not in general an exact compensation for any unexpected change in the spot exchange rate. This is again due to movements in interest rates. We see that a problem with futures in comparison with forwards is that futures contracts leave some risk when used as a hedging vehicle, whereas forwards do not.

Another problem with using futures contracts as a hedging vehicle is that the contract size will not in general correspond exactly to a firm's needs. For example, if a firm needs £50,000, the closest it can come is to buy one £62,500 contract. On the other hand, forward contracts with banks can be written for any desired amount. The flexibility in values of forward contracts and their lower risk makes them preferable to futures contracts for importers, exporters, borrowers, and lenders who wish to precisely hedge foreign exchange risk and exposure. Currency futures are more likely to be preferred by speculators because gains on futures contracts can be taken as cash by selling the contracts back to the exchange. As we have mentioned, with forward contracts it is necessary to buy an offsetting contract for the same maturity to lock in a profit, and then to wait for maturity before settling the contracts and taking the gain. For example, if pounds are bought forward in May for delivery in December, and by August the buyer wants to take a gain, in August it is necessary to sell pounds forward for December, and then wait for the two contracts to mature in December to collect the gain.[10]

Table 3.5 shows that in the Chicago IMM, futures exchange rates are quoted in U.S. terms—as so many dollars per foreign currency unit. Forward rates, which are set in the interbank market, are quoted in European terms. **Open interest** refers to the number of outstanding contracts. The statistics on open interest indicate that most of the activity is in the nearest maturity contracts.

---

[9]Statistics from the IMM show that fewer than 1 percent of futures contracts result in delivery. See *Currency Trading for Financial Institutions*, International Monetary Market, Chicago, 1982.

[10]Banks will sometimes offer to pay gains out early by discounting what is to be received. This is done to make forward contracts more competitive with futures as a speculative vehicle.

The Link between the Futures and Forward Markets

The market for currency futures is small compared with the market for forwards. A daily volume of over $4 billion in currency futures is not very common, but in the forward market the trading volume can exceed 20 times this amount. Despite the large difference in the sizes of the two markets, there is a mutual interdependence between them; each one is able to affect the other. This interdependence is the result of the action of arbitragers who take offsetting positions in the two markets when prices differ. The most straightforward type of arbitrage involves outright forward and futures positions.[11]

If, for example, the 3-month forward buying price of pounds were $1.6000/£ while the selling price on the same date on the Chicago IMM were $1.6020/£, an arbitrager could buy forward from a bank and sell futures on the IMM. The arbitrager would make $0.0020/£, so that on each contract for £62,500, he or she could make a profit of $125. However, we should remember that since the futures market requires maintenance or marking to market as daily contract prices vary, the arbitrage involves risk which can allow the futures and forward rates to differ. It should also be clear that the degree to which middle exchange rates on the two markets can deviate will depend very much on the spreads between buying and selling prices. Arbitrage will ensure that the ask price of forward currency does not significantly exceed the bid price of currency futures and vice versa. However, the prices can differ a little due to marking-to-market risk. We should also note that the direction of influence is not invariably from the rate set on the larger forward market to the smaller futures market. When there is a move on the Chicago IMM that results in a very large number of margins being called, the scramble to close positions with sudden buying or selling can spill over into the forward market.

CURRENCY OPTIONS

What Is a Currency Option?

Forward exchange and currency futures contracts must be exercised. It is true that currency futures can be sold back to the futures exchange and that forward contracts can be offset by going into a reverse agreement with a bank. However, all outstanding forward contracts and currency futures must be honored by both parties on the delivery date. That is, the bank and its customers, or the futures exchange and those holding outstanding futures, must settle. There is no option allowing a party to settle only if it is to that party's advantage.

Unlike forward and futures contracts, **currency options** give the buyer the opportunity, but not the obligation, to buy or sell the foreign currency at a preagreed exchange rate in the future. That is, as the name suggests, the buyer

---

[11]We can note that even without any arbitrage, the rates for forward contracts and currency futures will be kept in line by users of these markets choosing between them if the rates differ. This is analogous to one-way arbitrage in determining cross rates in Chapter 2.

of an option contract purchases the option or right to exchange currencies at the exchange rate stated in the contract if this is to the option buyer's advantage, but to allow the option to expire without exchanging currencies if it would be better to use the spot exchange rate.

Characteristics of Currency Option Contracts

The types of currency option contracts that have been devised and the terminology used in describing the different types of contracts can be described with the help of Figure 3.1. This gives details of the currency options trading on the Philadelphia Exchange.[12]

Figure 3.1 shows that options trade on a number of leading currencies. Contract amounts are listed next to the names of the currencies with, for example, 50,000 Australian dollars or 31,250 British pounds per contract.[13] The numbers in the first column, below the name of the currency, give the spot exchange rate in U.S.-dollar-equivalent terms. The second column, which is headed "Strike Price," gives the exchange rate at which the option is **written**, also quoted in U.S.-dollar-equivalent terms. The **strike price** gives the exchange rate at which the option buyer has the right to buy or sell the foreign currency, and is also known as the **exercise price**. We can see that on each currency there are options at numerous strike prices with gaps of 1 cent on the Australian dollar, $2\frac{1}{2}$ cents on the British pound, and so on. When a new set of options is introduced as an old set expires, the new options are written at the rounded-off value of the going spot exchange rate, and at a slightly higher and slightly lower exchange rate. New strike prices are subsequently introduced if the spot rate changes by a large amount.

Whether the option gives the buyer the right to buy or the right to sell the foreign currency is identified by whether the option is listed in one of the columns headed "Calls" or one of the columns headed "Puts." A **call option** gives the buyer the right to buy the foreign currency at the strike price or exchange rate on the option, and a **put option** gives the buyer the right to sell the foreign currency at the strike price.

Figure 3.1 provides details for contract maturity dates in May, June, and September. Options trade on a 9-month cycle. They expire on the Saturday before the third Wednesday of the month, for settlement on the third Wednesday of the month. That is, option holders must notify the exchange that they wish to exercise their options before the Saturday, and receive or deliver the foreign currency on the following Wednesday. The delivery on options corresponds with the delivery on futures, although, as with futures, delivery rarely occurs.

---

[12]Currency options also trade on the Chicago IMM as well as on a number of foreign exchanges. However, Chicago IMM currency options are options on futures contracts, and are therefore different from Philadelphia options, which are on spot exchange.

[13]The contract sizes on the Philadelphia Exchange are half those of the currency futures and futures option contracts trading on the Chicago IMM.

OPTIONS
PHILADELPHIA EXCHANGE

Option & Underlying	Strike Price	Calls—Last			Puts—Last		
		May	Jun	Sep	May	Jun	Sep
50,000 Australian Dollars-cents per unit.							
ADollr	...68	s	r	r	s	r	0.27
75.75	...70	s	r	r	s	r	0.60
75.75	...71	s	r	r	s	r	0.81
75.75	...72	s	r	3.52	s	r	1.14
75.75	...75	s	r	r	s	0.97	r
75.75	...76	s	0.69	r	s	1.53	3.06
75.75	...77	s	0.41	r	s	1.93	r
75.75	...78	s	0.18	0.61	s	2.47	r
75.75	...79	s	0.12	0.46	s	3.92	5.43
75.75	...80	s	r	0.33	s	4.47	r
31,250 British Pounds-cents per unit.							
BPound	157½	s	r	r	s	0.85	r
161.31	.160	s	2.70	4.40	s	1.70	3.95
161.31	162½	s	1.72	r	s	3.00	r
161.31	.165	s	0.78	r	s	4.85	r
161.31	167½	s	0.37	r	s	6.70	r
161.31	.170	s	0.14	1.05	s	9.80	10.70
161.31	172½	s	r	r	s	12.22	r
31,250 British Pounds-European Style.							
161.31	.165	s	r	2.10	s	r	r
50,000 Canadian Dollars-cents per unit.							
CDollr	...80	s	r	r	s	r	0.07
83.83	...81	s	r	r	s	r	0.17
83.83	...82	s	1.80	r	s	r	0.39
83.83	82½	s	r	1.35	s	r	r
83.83	...83	s	0.86	r	s	0.13	0.70
83.83	83½	s	r	r	s	0.30	r
83.83	...84	s	0.24	r	s	r	r
83.83	84½	s	r	r	s	0.92	r
62,500 West German Marks-cents per unit.							
DMark	.. 48	s	r	r	s	r	0.31
50.68	...49	s	r	r	s	0.15	0.54
50.68	...50	s	1.25	1.80	s	0.38	0.95
50.68	...51	s	0.62	1.38	s	0.70	1.32
50.68	...52	s	0.30	0.99	s	1.45	1.95
50.68	...53	s	0.10	0.54	s	2.30	2.43
50.68	...54	s	r	0.40	s	3.26	r
50.68	...55	s	0.02	0.26	s	r	r
50.68	...58	s	r	0.05	s	r	r
62,500 West German Marks-European Style.							
50.68	...50	s	1.15	r	s	r	r
50.68	...53	s	0.10	r	s	r	r
6,250,000 Japanese Yen-100ths of a cent per unit.							
JYen	... 69	s	r	r	s	r	0.43
71.97	...70	s	r	r	s	0.16	0.56
71.97	...71	s	1.55	r	s	0.38	1.02
71.97	...72	s	0.88	r	s	0.73	r
71.97	...73	s	0.49	1.56	s	1.21	1.69
71.97	...74	s	0.25	r	s	2.14	r
71.97	...75	s	0.10	0.84	s	3.10	r
71.97	...76	s	r	r	s	4.00	4.12
71.97	...77	s	r	0.41	s	5.00	r
71.97	...80	s	r	0.13	s	r	r
6,250,000 Japanese Yen-European Style.							
71.97	...73	s	0.60	r	s	1.14	r
71.97	...75	s	0.10	r	s	2.75	r
62,500 Swiss Francs-cents per unit.							
SFranc	...54	s	r	r	s	0.09	0.40
56.72	...55	s	r	r	s	r	0.66
56.72	...56	s	r	1.97	s	0.49	r
56.72	...57	s	0.73	1.55	s	1.02	1.43
56.72	...58	s	0.33	1.12	s	r	r
56.72	...59	s	0.15	0.86	s	2.53	2.68
56.72	...60	s	r	0.56	s	3.40	3.26
56.72	...61	s	r	r	s	4.14	r
62,500 Swiss Francs-European Style.							
56.72	...56	s	r	r	s	r	0.95
56.72	...57	s	r	1.50	s	r	1.48
56.72	...59	s	r	0.82	s	r	r

Total call vol.	23,721	Call open int.	470,724
Total put vol.	46,033	Put open int.	420,841

r—Not traded. s—No option offered.
Last is premium (purchase price).

FIGURE 3.1
Foreign currency option premiums. (Reprinted by permission of *The Wall Street Journal* © Dow Jones & Company Inc., May 19, 1989. All Rights Reserved Worldwide.)

If we read down the table, we see that quotations for "European Style" option contracts with a limited number of strike prices are given for several currencies. The term European style has nothing to do with European terms for quotation; rather, it has to do with when the option buyer can exercise, that is, buy or sell the currency at the strike price. **European options** can be exercised only on the maturity date of the option. They cannot be exercised before that date.

The alternative to the European option is the **American option**. The majority of options, those given above the headings "European Style," and given where it is not declared otherwise, are American options. American options offer buyers more flexibility in that they can be exercised on any date up to and including the maturity date of the option. Buyers would therefore pay no more for a European option than for an American option.

If we compare the spot exchange rates shown in the first column with the strike prices, we see that for each currency there are options with higher and lower strike exchange rates than the spot exchange rate. A call option that gives the buyer the right to buy a currency at a strike exchange rate that is below the spot exchange rate is said to be **in the money**. This is because the option holder has the right to buy the currency for less than it would cost in the spot market. A call option with a strike price that is above the spot exchange rate is said to be **out of the money**. This is because the option holder would find it cheaper to buy the foreign currency on the spot market than to exercise the option.

The fact that a call option might be out of the money does not mean the option has no value. As long as there is a possibility that the spot exchange rate might move above the strike price during the maturity of the option, people will be willing to pay for the option contract.

A put option that gives the buyer the right to sell the foreign currency is said to be in the money when the strike exchange rate is higher than the spot exchange rate. This is because the option holder has the right to sell the currency for more than it could be sold on the spot market. A put option is out of the money when the strike exchange rate is lower than the spot exchange rate. This is because the option holder wanting to sell foreign exchange immediately would be better off not to exercise the option, but rather to sell at the spot exchange rate. As with call options, the fact that a put option is out of the money does not mean it has no value. It has value as long as there is a possibility that the spot rate might move below the strike exchange rate during the life of the option.

The extent to which an option is in the money is called its **intrinsic value**. For example, with the spot exchange rate of $1.6131/£, the intrinsic value of the British pound June 160 call option is $161.31 - 160.00 = 1.31$ cents per pound. That is, the intrinsic value is how many cents per pound would be gained by exercising the option immediately. As can be seen from Figure 3.1, the market value of the pound June 160 call option is higher than its intrinsic value; for June maturity the option is priced at 2.70 cents per pound, and for September it is priced at 4.40 cents per pound. This is because there may be an even larger gain for exercising the option during the remainder of its life. While call options have intrinsic value when the strike price is below the spot exchange rate, put options have intrinsic value when the strike price exceeds the spot exchange rate.

The amount paid for the option on each unit of foreign currency—for each British pound or for each Canadian dollar or the like—is called the **option premium**. This premium can be considered to consist of two parts, the intrinsic value if there is any, and the **time value** of the option. The time value is the part of the premium that comes from the possibility that, at some point in the future, the option might have higher intrinsic value than at that moment. When an option is **at the money**, which occurs when the strike price exactly equals the spot rate, all of the option premium is the option's time value. For example, the Japanese yen June 72 call option has a time value of approximately 0.88 cents per hundred yen because the strike price approximately equals the spot rate.

Quotation Conventions and Market Organization

Option dealers quote a bid and an ask premium on each contract, with the bid being what buyers are willing to pay, and the ask being what sellers want to be paid. Of course, a dealer must state whether a bid or ask premium is for a call or put, whether it is for an American or European option, the strike price, and the month the option expires.

As we have said, the premium is the amount paid for each unit of foreign exchange. For example, it is the number of cents per Australian dollar or per British pound. In order to find the price of a contract, it is necessary to multiply the premium by the number of units of foreign currency represented by a contract. For example, because there are £31,250 per Philadelphia contract on pounds, a June $162\frac{1}{2}$ call option that costs 1.72 cents per pound costs the buyer 31,250 × 1.72 cents = $537.50 per contract. However, dealers in the market quote option premiums rather than the U.S. dollar price for an option contract, leaving option buyers to work out how much has to be paid for each contract.

After the buyer has paid for the option contract, he or she has no financial obligation. Therefore, there is no need to talk about margins for option *buyers*. The person selling the option is called the **writer**. The writer of a call option must stand ready, when required, to sell the currency to the option buyer at the strike price. Similarly, the writer of a put option must stand ready to buy the currency from the option buyer at the strike price. The commitment of the writer is open throughout the life of the option for American options, and on the maturity date of the option for European options. The option exchange guarantees that option sellers honor their obligations to option buyers, and therefore requires option *sellers* to post a margin. On the Philadelphia Exchange, this is 130 percent of the option premium plus a lump sum to a maximum of $2,500, depending on the extent the option is in or out of the money.[14]

---

[14] For more details on margins see *Foreign Currency Options: The Third Dimension to Foreign Exchange*, Philadelphia Stock Exchange, undated.

As in the case of futures contracts, an exchange can make a market in currency options only by standardizing the contracts. This is why option contracts are written for specific amounts of foreign currency, for a limited number of maturity dates, and for a limited number of strike exchange rates. The standardization allows buyers to resell contracts prior to maturity. It also allows writers to offset their risks more readily because, for example, the writer of a call option can enter the market as a buyer of a call option to limit losses or to lock in gains.[15]

Determinants of the Market Values of Currency Options

The factors that influence the price of an option are:

Intrinsic Value   As we have said, the premium on an option can be considered to be made up of the time value and the intrinsic value. (We recall that the intrinsic value is the extent to which the spot rate exceeds the strike price on a call option, and the extent to which the strike price exceeds the spot rate on a put option. Alternatively, it is what the option would be worth if it had to be exercised immediately.) Therefore, the more the option is in the money, (that is, the higher is the intrinsic value), the higher is the option premium.

Volatility of the Spot or Futures Exchange Rate   *Ceteris paribus*, the more volatile is the underlying exchange rate, the greater is the chance that an option will be exercised to the benefit of the buyer and to the cost of the seller.[16] That is, the higher is the volatility of the underlying exchange rate, the greater is the possibility that it will at some time exceed the strike exchange rate of a call, or be below the strike exchange rate of a put. Consequently, buyers will pay more for an option, and sellers will demand more, if the volatility of the exchange rate is higher.

Philadelphia options give the buyer the option to buy or sell spot foreign exchange. Therefore, it is the volatility of the spot exchange rate that determines the value of Philadelphia options. Chicago IMM options are on foreign currency futures contracts rather than on spot exchange. That is, Chicago IMM options give the buyers the option to buy or sell IMM currency future contracts. Therefore, it is the price and volatility of IMM futures contracts that determines

---

[15]The ways that options can be used for hedging and speculating are described in Chapter 10.

[16]The effects of volatility and the other influences listed here on stock options have been described by Fisher Black and Myron Scholes, "The Pricing of Options and Corporate Liabilities," *Journal of Political Economy*, May/June 1973, pp. 637–659. The effects of volatility and other factors on currency options have been described by Mark B. Garman and Steven W. Kohlhagen, "Foreign Currency Option Values," *Journal of International Money and Finance*, December 1983, pp. 231–237, and by J. Orlin Grabbe, "The Pricing of Call and Put Options on Foreign Exchange," *Journal of International Money and Finance*, December 1983, pp. 239–253.

the value of an IMM currency option. However, because the spot exchange rate is the principal factor affecting futures contract prices, it is still the volatility of the spot rate that matters. (We might note that on the Chicago IMM, whether options are in the money or out of the money depends on the strike price versus the futures price, not the strike price relative to the spot exchange rate.)

Length of Period to Expiration The longer the maturity period of the option, the greater is the chance that at some time the exchange rate will move above the strike price of a call or below the strike price of a put. Therefore, *ceteris paribus*, the longer the period to expiration, the higher the option premium a buyer is prepared to pay, and the higher the option premium a seller wants to be paid.

American or European Option Type The greater flexibility of American than European options means buyers will not pay more for a European option than for an American option of the same maturity. (Recall that American options can be exercised at any time before the expiry date, while European options can be exercised only on the expiry date.) Indeed, for a given strike price, exchange rate volatility and period to expiration, American options are typically more valuable than European options.

Interest Rate on Currency of Purchase The higher the interest rate on the currency paid for an option, the lower is the present value of the exercise price. A higher interest rate consequently has the same effect on an option as does a lower exercise price, namely, it increases the market value of a call and reduces the market value of a put.[17]

The Forward Premium/Discount or Interest Differential Because of very different rates of inflation, balances of trade, and so on, there can be trends in exchange rates that are to an extent predictable. For example, the foreign exchange values of currencies of countries with very rapid inflation tend to decline. *Ceteris paribus*, the greater the expected decline in the foreign exchange value of a currency, the higher is the value of a put option in that currency because there is a greater chance the put option will be exercised. Similarly, the more a currency is expected to increase in value—because of low inflation, consistently good international trade performance, and so on—the higher is the value of a call option on that currency. Again, this is because, *ceteris paribus*, the more the currency is expected to increase in value, the more likely it is that a call option will be worth exercising.

---

[17]This is because other things are assumed constant as the interest rate changes. See John C. Cox and Mark Rubinstein, *Options Markets*, Prentice-Hall, Englewood Cliffs, N.J., 1985, p. 35.

For reasons that will be made clear later, currencies that are expected to decline in value tend to trade at a forward discount, while currencies expected to increase in value tend to trade at a premium.[18] Indeed, the more a currency is expected to decline/increase in value, the larger the forward discount/premium tends to be. It follows that the greater the forward discount on a currency, the higher the value of a put option and the lower the value of a call option on that currency. Similarly, the greater the forward premium, the higher the value of a call option and the lower the value of a put option on the currency.[19]

An alternative way of stating the effect of expected decreases or increases in exchange rates on the value of options is in terms of interest rates. Countries with currencies that are expected to decline in value tend to have high interest rates relative to other countries. (Such high rates are necessary to compensate foreign investors for the expected decline in exchange rates.) Therefore, put options tend to be worth more when interest rates are higher than elsewhere; the relatively high interest rates suggest an expected decline in the value of the currency, and a consequently increased chance that a put will be exercised. Similarly, call options tend to be worth more when interest rates are lower than elsewhere, because relatively low interest rates suggest an expected increase in the currency's value, and consequently an increased chance the call will be exercised.

Other Types of Options

Well before options began trading on formal exchanges in 1981, there had been an active **over-the-counter option** market in Europe, the options being written by large banks.[20] Indeed, the over-the-counter option market remains larger than that of the formal option exchanges.

Many of the over-the-counter options written by banks are contingent upon such outcomes as whether a corporate takeover bid is accepted. That is, the buyer of the option purchases the opportunity to buy a foreign currency at a given strike exchange rate if the takeover occurs. An example of such an over-the-counter option is the option on sterling that was purchased in 1979 by the U.S. insurance broker, Marsh and McLennan Company. Marsh and McLennan made a cash and share offer for C.T. Bowring and Company, a member of Lloyds of London, that required Marsh and McLennan to pay £130 million if the offer was accepted. Rather than take a chance on the exchange rate that might prevail on the takeover settlement date, Marsh and McLennan wanted to buy a call option for £130 million that it could exercise only if its

---

[18]This is explained in Chapter 10.

[19]There is an arbitrage relation between option prices and the forward exchange rate that can be used to find the effects we have only intuitively described. See Cox and Rubinstein, *ibid.*, pp. 59–61.

[20]Currency options had also been traded in an unorganized fashion in the United States until this was ruled illegal. See David Babbel, "The Rise and Decline of Currency Options," *Euromoney*, September 1980, pp. 141–149.

TABLE 3.6
FORWARDS, FUTURES, AND OPTIONS COMPARED

	Forward contracts	Currency futures*	Currency options†
Delivery discretion	None.	None.	Buyer's discretion. Seller must honor if buyer exercises.
Maturity date	Any date.	Third Wednesday of March, June, Sept., or Dec.	Saturday before third Wednesday of March, June, Sept., or Dec. for settlement on third Wednesday.
Maximum length	Several years.	12 months.	9 months.
Contracted amount	Any value.	£62,500, Can$100,000, etc.	£31,250, Can$50,000, etc.
Secondary market	Must offset with bank.	Can sell via exchange.	Can sell via exchange.
Margin requirement	Informal, often line of credit or 5 – 10% on account.	Formal fixed sum per contract, e.g. $2000. Daily marking to market.	No margin for buyer who pays for contract. Seller posts 130% of premium plus lump sum varying with intrinsic value.
Contract variety	Swap or outright form.	Outright.	Outright.
Guarantor	None.	Futures Exchange.	Option-clearing corporation.
Major users	Primarily hedgers.	Primarily speculators.	Hedgers and speculators.

*Based on Chicago IMM contracts.
†Based on Philadelphia Stock Exchange contracts which are on spot foreign exchange. IMM options are on futures, and contracted amounts equal those on future contracts.

takeover effort did succeed.[21] Bankers Trust agreed to provide an option which could be exercised on´or before June 15, 1980, 6 months after the original agreement. The takeover bid did succeed and the option was duly exercised.

The reason why the over-the-counter market coexists alongside the formal options market is that options that trade on option exchanges are not perfectly suited for contingencies such as whether a takeover bid is accepted, whether an

[21]This interesting case is described in "March and McLennan Insures Takeover Exposure with Call Provision," Business International, Money Report, June 13, 1980.

export contract is signed, and so on. Exchange-traded options are imperfectly suited for such contingencies because, even though the option buyer can choose whether to exercise, the decision to exercise is contingent upon what happens to exchange rates rather than on whether the deal is consummated.[22]

DIFFERENCES BETWEEN FORWARDS, FUTURES, AND OPTIONS: A SUMMARY

While forwards, futures, and options can all be used both to reduce foreign exchange risk and to purposely take foreign exchange risk (that is, to hedge and speculate), the differences between forwards, futures, and options make them suitable for different purposes. An explanation of which type of contract would be most appropriate in different circumstances must wait until we have dealt with many other matters, including further ways of hedging and speculating, so that at this point we can do little more than list the differences between forwards, futures, and options. This is done in Table 3.6. The table notes the primary users of the markets as well as the institutional differences between forwards, futures, and options. The reasons the different markets have different primary users are to some extent self-evident, and are covered more fully in Chapter 10.

SUMMARY

1 Forward exchange contracts allow the purchase or sale of foreign exchange at a future date at a precontracted exchange rate. Forward contracts are written by banks and trade in the interbank market.

2 Forward contracts can be made for any value date, but rarely extend more than a few years forward. Bankers tend to concentrate on even dates (30 days, 90-days, 180 days) when trading among themselves.

3 A forward premium exists when forward foreign exchange is more expensive than spot foreign exchange. A forward premium on foreign currency means a forward discount on domestic currency.

4 Forward exchange rates are quoted outright and as swaps. Swap quotations involve the spot rate, and the swap points to be added or subtracted depending on whether there is a forward premium or discount.

5 Swaps involve a double exchange—usually a spot exchange reversed by a forward exchange. They are heavily traded between banks in even-dated form so that the banks can keep down their foreign exchange exposure in an efficient manner.

---

[22]An option that is contingent upon completion of a takeover might be cheaper than a traditional exchange-traded option. This is because the writer of a call contingent on completion of a takeover does not deliver foreign exchange if the foreign currency increases in value but the takeover is not completed. That is, there are outcomes where the takeover-contingent option writer does not lose, but where the writer of an exchange option would lose; an exchange call option will be exercised if the option has value on the options exchange, even if the takeover is not completed. Banks that write over-the-counter customized options frequently reinsure on an option exchange, so it is the bank rather than the option buyer that gains when the foreign currency increases in value but the takeover offer is rejected. The bank gains because it reinsures by buying an exchange-issued call option to cover the call it has written, and the exchange call increases in value without the need to deliver the foreign currency if the takeover offer is rejected.

6 Swaps are particularly valuable to international borrowers and investors. They are not so valuable to importers and exporters.

7 Currency futures are traded in specialized markets in numbers of standard contract units. Margins are posted and maintained.

8 Forward exchange and futures contracts are not options. All outstanding contracts must be honored.

9 Currency options give buyers the right or opportunity, but not the obligation, to buy or sell foreign exchange at a preagreed exchange rate, the strike exchange rate. Call options give the buyer the right to purchase the foreign currency at the strike exchange rate, and put options give the buyer the right to sell the foreign currency at the strike exchange rate.

10 American options allow the buyer to exercise at any time during the maturity of the option, while European options allow the buyer to exercise only on the expiry date of the option.

11 The value of an option depends on the extent to which it is in the money, that is, the option's intrinsic value, and also on the volatility of the underlying exchange rate, the length of time to expiration, the interest rate on the currency paid for the option, and the forward exchange premium or discount. Alternatively, the value of the option depends on the interest differential, which, like the forward premium or discount, reflects the expected path of the exchange rate.

12 An over-the-counter customized options market coexists with the exchange-based currency options. Over-the-counter options are written by banks.

QUESTIONS

1 Using the spot rates in Figure 2.1 and the currency futures prices in Table 3.5, compute the premiums or discounts on the foreign-currency futures for Canada and Japan for 90 days and 180 days. How do they compare with the forward premiums given in Table 3.1 over comparable periods?

2 Why do banks quote only even-dated forward rates, for example, 30-day rates and 90-day rates, rather than uneven-dated rates? How would you prorate the rates of uneven-dated maturities?

3 Compute the outright forward quotations from the following swap quotations of Canadian dollars in European terms:

Spot	30-day	90-day	180-day
1.1910 / 15	10 / 9	12 / 10	15 / 12

4 When would spreads widen quickly as we move forward in the forward market? Select two sets of actual quotations from a volatile time and from a stable time.

5 Could a bank that trades forward exchange ever hope to balance the buys and sells of forward currencies for each future date? How do swap contracts help?

6 Why do banks operate a forward exchange market in only a limited number of currencies? Does it have to do with the ability to balance buy orders with sell orders, and is it the same reason why they rarely offer contracts of over 2 years?

7 Why is the "open interest" smaller on the September contracts than on the June contracts in Table 3.5?

8 Why do you think that futures markets were developed when banks already offered forward contracts? What might currency futures offer which forward contracts did not?

9 Do you think that limits on daily price movements for currency futures would make these contracts more or less risky or liquid? Would limitation on price movement make the futures contracts difficult to sell during highly turbulent times?

10 How could arbitrage take place between forward exchange contracts and currency futures? Would this arbitrage be unprofitable only if the futures and forward rates were exactly the same?

11 Does the need to hold a margin make forward and futures deals less desirable than if there were no margin requirements? Does your answer depend on the interest paid on margins?

12 How does a currency option differ from a forward contract? How does the option differ from a currency future?

13 Suppose a bank sells a call option to a company making a takeover offer where the option is contingent on the offer being accepted. Suppose the bank reinsures on an options exchange by buying a call for the same amount of foreign currency. Consider the consequences of the following four outcomes or "states":

(a) The foreign currency increases in value, and the takeover offer is accepted.
(b) The foreign currency increases in value, and the takeover offer is rejected.
(c) The foreign currency decreases in value, and the takeover offer is accepted.
(d) The foreign currency decreases in value, and the takeover offer is rejected.

Consider who gains and who loses in each state, and the source of gain or loss. Satisfy yourself why a bank that reinsures on an option exchange might charge less for writing the takeover-contingent option than the bank itself pays for the call option on the exchange. Does this example help explain why a bank-based over-the-counter market coexists with a formal option exchange market?

BIBLIOGRAPHY

Borensztein, Eduardo R., and Michael P. Dooley: "Options on Foreign Exchange and Exchange Rate Expectations," *IMF Staff Papers*, December 1987, pp. 643–680.

Einzig, Paul A.: *The Dynamic Theory of Forward Exchange*, 2d ed., Macmillan, London, 1967.

Garman, Mark B., and Steven W. Kohlhagen: "Foreign Currency Option Values," *Journal of International Money and Finance*, December 1983, No. 3, pp. 231–237.

Giddy, Ian H.: "Foreign Exchange Options," *The Journal of Futures Markets*, Summer 1983, No. 2, pp. 143–166.

Grabbe, J. Orlin: "The Pricing of Call and Put Options on Foreign Exchange," *Journal of International Money and Finance*, December 1983, No. 3, pp. 239–253.

International Monetary Market of the Chicago Mercantile Exchange: *The Futures Market in Foreign Currencies*, Chicago Mercantile Exchange, Chicago, undated.

International Monetary Market of the Chicago Mercantile Exchange: *Trading in International Currency Futures*, Chicago Mercantile Exchange, Chicago, undated.

International Monetary Market of the Chicago Mercantile Exchange: *Understanding Futures in Foreign Exchange*, Chicago Mercantile Exchange, Chicago, undated.

Kubarych, Roger M.: *Foreign Exchange Markets in the United States*, Federal Reserve Bank of New York, 1978.

Philadelphia Stock Exchange: *Understanding Foreign Currency Options: The Third Dimension to Foreign Exchange*, Philadelphia Stock Exchange, undated.

TWO

THE BALANCE OF PAYMENTS AND EXCHANGE-RATE DETERMINATION

Part 2, consisting of Chapters 4 and 5, uses a supply-and-demand framework to explain what it is that makes exchange rates change. In courses in which students have a background in the determination of exchange rates, Part 2 can be omitted without loss of continuity.

Chapter 4 describes why the balance-of-payments account can be considered as a listing of the reasons for a currency being supplied and demanded. The chapter explains that all positive or credit items give rise to a demand for a currency, and all negative or debit items give rise to a supply of a currency. After explaining the basic principles of balance-of-payments accounting, each major entry in the account is examined to provide an understanding of what factors can make each entry increase or decrease, and thereby change the exchange rate. This introduces the student to how such factors as inflation, interest rates, foreign debt, political risk, and expectations about future values of these factors can affect exchange rates. The purpose of the chapter is to provide a framework for thinking about why exchange rates change.

Chapter 4 includes a brief account of the different interpretations of the balance of payments with fixed and flexible exchange rates. It is shown that with flexible exchange rates the balance of payments is achieved without any official buying or selling of currencies by governments, whereas with fixed exchange rates there are changes in official foreign exchange reserves. The chapter also shows how to interpret imbalances in the current- and capital-account components of the balance of payments. This is illustrated by comparing a country's balance' of payments account to the income statement of a firm. The chapter concludes with a discussion of a country's net indebtedness, and a brief account of recent developments in the balance of payments and indebtedness of the United States.

Chapter 5 builds the supply-and-demand picture of exchange rates that is suggested by the balance-of-payments account. This involves deriving the supply curve for a country's currency from that country's demand curve for imports, and the demand curve for a country's currency from that country's supply curve for exports. Using the knowledge about balance-of-payment entries developed in Chapter 4, it is shown what makes the currency supply and demand curves shift, and therefore what makes exchange rates change. It is also shown, however, that a currency supply curve can slope downward rather than upward as might normally be expected, and that if this happens, exchange rates can be unstable. The chapter explains that the conditions resulting in an unstable foreign exchange market are the same conditions that result in the so-called J curve. (A J curve occurs, for example, when a depreciation makes a country's balance of trade worse, rather than better as would normally be expected.)

The possibility of exchange-rate instability or of a J curve is included because of the increased volatility of exchange rates in the 1980s and because the U.S. and its trading partners appear to have exhibited J curves in recent years. Because of the contemporary relevance of instability and the J curve, Chapter 5 includes a short mathematical appendix in which exchange-rate stability conditions are derived.

The emphasis throughout Part 2 is on the determination of exchange rates when they are flexible, meaning that they are determined by the forces of supply and demand. Only the barest of details of fixed exchange rates are described. Those students who are interested in the workings of the various fixed-exchange-rate systems that have been tried, such as the gold standard and the Bretton Woods standard, can read the Addendum to the book. Part 2 should, however, provide sufficient coverage of the international financial environment for students without background in the determination of exchange rates and whose principal interest is international financial management. Where a more complete coverage of international financial markets and the international economic environment is appropriate, the Addendum can be read immediately after Part 2.

4

THE BALANCE OF INTERNATIONAL PAYMENTS

THE BALANCE OF PAYMENTS AS A RECORD OF SUPPLY AND DEMAND

As with the price of any commodity, the price of a country's currency depends on the supply of and demand for that currency, at least when exchange rates are determined in a free, unregulated market.[1] It follows that if we know the factors behind the supply of and demand for a currency, we also know what factors influence exchange rates. Any factor increasing the demand for the currency will, *ceteris paribus*, increase the foreign exchange value of the currency, that is, cause the currency to **appreciate**. Similarly, any factor increasing the supply of the currency will, *ceteris paribus*, reduce the foreign exchange value of the currency, that is, cause the currency to **depreciate**.[2] Clearly then, there is considerable interest in maintaining a record of the factors behind the supply and demand of a country's currency. That record is maintained in the balance-of-payments account. Indeed, we can think of the balance-of-payments account as an itemization of the factors behind the demand and supply of a currency.

Of course, the motivation for publishing the balance-of-payments account is not a desire of government statisticians to maintain a record of the factors behind the supply of and demand for a currency. Rather, the account is published to report the country's international performance in trading with

---

[1] When exchange rates are fixed, they are still determined by supply and demand, but there is an official supply or demand at the fixed exchange rate to keep rates fixed. Fixed exchange rates are discussed in the Addendum.

[2] When exchange rates are fixed and it is decided to fix the exchange rate at a lower value, the exchange is said to have been **devalued**. When the exchange rate is refixed at a higher value it is said to have been **revalued**.

other nations. However, reporting on a country's international trading performance involves measurement of all the reasons why a currency is supplied and demanded. This is what makes the balance-of-payments account such a handy way of thinking about what should be considered in the theory of exchange rates, the topic of the next chapter. This chapter shows why the balance-of-payments account can be thought of as a list of items behind the supply of and demand for a currency. We begin by examining the principles guiding the structure of the balance-of-payments account and the interpretation of the different items that are included. We then consider the different ways that balance can be achieved between supply and demand. As we shall see, the balance-of-payments account is designed to always balance, but the way that it is balanced tells us how well a country is doing in its transactions with other countries.

PRINCIPLES OF BALANCE-OF-PAYMENTS ACCOUNTING

Determining Credit and Debit Entries

The guiding principles of balance-of-payments accounting come from the purpose of the account, namely to record the flow of payments between the residents of a country and the rest of the world during a given time period. The fact that the balance of payments records the flow of payments during a given time period makes the account dimensionally the same as the national-income account—a **flow** of so much per year or per calendar quarter—and indeed, the part of the balance-of-payments account that records the values of exports and imports appears in the national-income account.

Balance-of-payments accounting uses the system of **double-entry bookkeeping**, which means that every debit or credit in the account is also represented as a credit or debit somewhere else. An easy way of seeing how this works is to take a couple of straightforward examples.

Suppose that an American corporation sells $2 million worth of U.S.-manufactured jeans to Britain, and that the British buyer pays from a U.S. dollar account that is kept in a New York bank. We will then have the double entry:

	Million dollars (Credits +; debits −)
Export (of jeans)	+2
Foreign assets in the U.S.: U.S. bank liabilities	−2

We can think of the export of the American jeans as resulting in a demand for dollars, and the payment with dollars at the New York bank as resulting in a supply of dollars. The payment reduces the liability of the U.S. bank, which is an asset of the British jeans buyer. We see that the balance-of-payments account shows the flow of jeans and the flow of payments.

As a second example, suppose that an American corporation purchases $5 million worth of denim cloth from a British mill, and that the British mill puts the $5 million it receives into a bank account in New York. We then have the double entry:

	Million dollars (Credits +; debits −)
Imports (of cloth)	−5
Foreign assets in the U.S.: U.S. bank liabilities	+5

We can think of the U.S. import of cloth as resulting in a supply of dollars, and the deposit of money by the British mill as resulting in a demand for dollars. The deposit of money increases U.S. bank liabilities and the assets of the British mill. In a similar way, every entry in the balance of payments will appear twice.

With the balance of payments, a record is maintained of *all* transactions that affect the supply of or demand for a currency in the foreign exchange markets. There is just as much demand for dollars when non-Americans buy U.S. jeans as there is when they are buying U.S. stocks, bonds, real estate, bank balances, or businesses, and all of these transactions must be recorded.

Since all sources of potential demand for dollars by foreigners or supply of dollars to foreigners are included, there are many types of entries. We need a rule for determining which are credits and which are debits. The rule is that any international transaction that gives rise to a demand for U.S. dollars is recorded as a credit in the U.S. balance of payments, and the entry takes a positive sign. Any transaction that gives rise to a supply of dollars in the foreign exchange market is recorded as a debit, and the entry takes a negative sign. A more precise way of expressing this rule is with the following definition:

> Credit transactions represent demands for U.S. dollars, and result from purchases by foreigners of goods, services, goodwill, financial and real assets, gold, or foreign exchange from Americans. Credits are recorded with a plus sign. Debit transactions represent supplies of U.S. dollars, and result from purchases by Americans of goods, services, goodwill, financial and real assets, gold, or foreign exchange from foreigners. Debits are recorded with a minus sign.[3]

The full meaning of our definition will become clear as we study the U.S. balance of payments in Table 4.1.[4] Let us consider each item and the factors that influence them.

[3] The item with the least obvious meaning in this definition is "goodwill." As we shall explain later, goodwill consists of gifts and foreign aid. In keeping with the double-entry bookkeeping system, the balance-of-payments accountant assumes that gifts and aid buy goodwill for the donor from the recipient. In the accountant's jargon, purchases and sales of goodwill are "unilateral transfers."

[4] The format of Table 4.1 has been in use since June 1976. Before then, a number of payments balances were given, including "basic balance," "official reserves transactions balance," "balance on current and long-term capital," and "liquidity balance," as well as those still included. Because of the demonetization of gold and the move to flexible exchange rates, it was decided to omit several balances. For a full list of reasons for the changes, see "Report of the Advisory Committee on the Presentation of the Balance of Payments Statistics," in U.S. Department of Commerce, *Survey of Current Business*, June 1976, pp. 18–25. We give a summary of the actual table by combining some entries.

TABLE 4.1
SUMMARY FORMAT OF THE U.S. BALANCE OF PAYMENTS, 1ST QUARTER, 1988
(U.S. International Transactions, Seasonally Adjusted)*

Line (credits, +; debits, −)			Billions of dollars
1 Exports of goods and services			+119
2 Goods / merchandise		+75	
3 Services		+44	
4 Imports of goods and services			−156
5 Goods / merchandise		−111	
6 Services		−45	
7 Unilateral transfers (net)			−3
8 U.S. government		−3	
9 Private		0	
10 U.S. assets abroad (net)			+9
11 Official reserves		+2	
12 U.S. government assets other than official reserves		−1	
13 U.S. private assets		+8	
14 Direct investment	−5		
15 Foreign securities	−4		
16 U.S. non-bank assets	0		
17 U.S. bank assets	+17		
18 Foreign assets in the U.S. (net)			+28
19 Foreign official		+25	
20 Other foreign assets in U.S.		+3	
21 Direct investment	+10		
22 U.S. securities	+9		
23 U.S. non-bank liabilities	0		
24 U.S. bank liabilities	−16		
25 Allocation of SDRs			0
26 Statistical discrepancy			+3
Memoranda:			
27 Balance of (merchandise) trade (lines 2 + 5)			−36
28 Balance of goods and services (lines 1 + 4)			−37
29 Balance on current account (lines 1 + 4 + 7)			−40
30 Increase in U.S. official reserve assets (line 11)			+2
31 Increase in foreign official reserve assets in U.S. (line 19)			+25

*Numbers are rounded so that additions are correct.
Source: Survey of Current Business, June, 1988.

Balance-of-Payments Entries and the Factors That Influence Them

Exports of Goods and Services   In order for overseas buyers to pay for U.S. goods and services which are invoiced in dollars, the overseas buyers must purchase dollars. In the rarer event that U.S. exports of goods and services are invoiced in foreign currency, it is the American exporter that will purchase dollars when selling the foreign currency.[5] In either case U.S. exports give rise to a demand for U.S. dollars in the foreign exchange market, and are recorded with a plus sign. While many of the same factors which affect the exports of goods also affect the export of services, there are some differences between goods and services. Therefore, we will consider them separately.

U.S. exports of goods, which are also referred to as **merchandise exports**, include wheat and other agricultural commodities, aircraft, computers, automobiles, and so on. The factors affecting these exports and hence the demand for U.S. dollars include:

1 *U.S. prices versus the prices of comparable goods abroad.* If inflation in the United States exceeds inflation elsewhere then, *ceteris paribus*, U.S. goods become less competitive, and the quantity of exports will decline. U.S. inflation therefore tends to reduce the demand for U.S. dollars.[6] The particular products that the U.S. exports also depend on U.S. versus foreign prices. Products that are relatively cheap in the U.S. because the U.S. has a comparative advantage in production or low demand by consumers are exported, while products that are relatively expensive in the U.S. because the U.S. has a comparative disadvantage or high demand are imported.

2 *Foreign incomes.* When foreign buyers experience an increase in their real incomes, the result is an improvement in the export market for American raw materials and manufactured goods. *Ceteris paribus*, this increases U.S.exports, and therefore also increases the demand for dollars.

3 *Foreign import duties and quotas.* Higher foreign import tariffs and lower **quotas**—the quantity of imports permitted into a country—as well as higher foreign **nontariff trade barriers** such as quality requirements and red tape, reduce U.S. exports.

4 *The foreign exchange value of the U.S. dollar.* For a particular level of domestic and foreign prices of internationally traded goods, the higher the foreign exchange value of the dollar, the higher are U.S. export prices, and the lower is the quantity of U.S. exports.[7] This means that U.S. exports depend on the exchange rate, while at the same time the exchange rate depends on U.S. exports.

Alongside exports of goods are exports of services. These service exports are sometimes called **invisibles**. U.S. service exports include spending by foreign tourists in the United States. Service exports also include overseas earnings of

[5]If the foreign buyer of a U.S. good or service pays with foreign currency which the U.S. exporter chooses to hold rather than sell, there are two entries in the balance of payments, the value of the export, and an increase in U.S. residents' holdings of foreign assets. In this case the U.S. export is considered to give rise to a demand for U.S. dollars, and the increased U.S. residents' holdings of foreign currency is considered to give rise to an equal increase in the supply of U.S. dollars.

[6]The *value* of exports could, however, increase because the reduced *quantity* of exports comes as a result of higher prices. As we shall show in the next chapter, values increase from higher prices when demand is inelastic so that the quantity of exports falls less than export prices increase.

[7]U.S. export prices are higher in foreign currency if the exchange rate for the dollar is higher, even if U.S. export prices are unchanged in terms of dollars. Therefore, the lower *quantity* of U.S. exports means a lower U.S. dollar *value* of exports, irrespective of the elasticity of demand.

U.S. banks and insurance companies, engineering, consulting, and accounting firms; overseas earnings of U.S. holders of patents; overseas earnings of royalties on books, music, and movies; overseas earnings of U.S. airlines and shipping, courier, and freight services; and similar items. These service exports give rise to a demand for U.S. dollars when the foreign tourists buy U.S. currency, when the U.S. banks repatriate their earnings, and so on. U.S. earnings on these "performed service" exports respond to the same factors as affect exports of goods—U.S. prices versus foreign prices, incomes abroad, restrictions on trade, and exchange rates.

There is a second category of service exports that is quite different from the performed services such as travel or consulting. This is the earnings U.S. residents receive from past investments made abroad, which can come in the form of interest on bills and bonds, dividends on stocks, rent on property, and profits on operating businesses. Sometimes these various sources of investment income are, for convenience, simply referred to as **debt service**. By debt-service exports we mean the interest, dividends, rents, and profits that U.S. residents earn abroad. These earnings are derived from past foreign investments and therefore depend principally on the amount Americans have invested abroad in the past. Debt-service exports also depend on the rates of interest and sizes of dividends, rents, and profits earned on these past foreign investments.

U.S. Imports of Goods and Services   U.S. imports of goods or merchandise include such items as oil, automobiles, TVs, clothing, wine, coffee, and so on. U.S. imports respond to the same factors that affect exports, the direction of response being reversed. *Ceteris paribus*, U.S. imports of goods are higher when U.S. prices are higher relative to foreign prices, when U.S. tariffs are lower, when U.S. import quotas are higher, and when the U.S. dollar is higher in the foreign exchange markets.[8] U.S. imports of performed services (such as American tourists' spending abroad, American use of foreign banks and consulting firms, American use of foreign patents, airlines, and shipping, and purchases of foreign movies and books) also depend on relative prices, U.S. incomes, U.S. import restrictions, and exchange rates. In the case of U.S. debt-service imports, the principal relevant factor is past foreign investments in U.S. government and private securities such as U.S. stocks and bonds, and past foreign investments in U.S. real estate and operating businesses. Debt-service imports also depend on the rates of return foreigners earn on past investments in the U.S.

Until 1985, the United States earned more on its investments abroad than foreigners earned on U.S. investments. That is, U.S. debt-service exports exceeded U.S. debt-service imports. This was because until that time, U.S. investment abroad exceeded foreign investment in the United States. Because of considerable borrowing by the U.S. from overseas lenders, and because of

---

[8]As in the case of inflation and exports, we should really distinguish between *quantity* and *value* of trade. A higher U.S. dollar could reduce the *value* of U.S. imports even if it increases the *quantity* of U.S. imports. This occurs if the demand for imports is inelastic. We discuss this in Chapter 5 in the context of the phenomenon of the J curve.

considerable foreign investment in the U.S., especially in the late 1970s and early 1980s, in 1985 the U.S. went from being a net creditor nation to a net debtor nation. Indeed, in a matter of only a couple of years after 1985, the U.S. became the largest debtor on earth. This has meant that the U.S. has become a net payer of debt service abroad.

Table 4.1 shows that on the goods side of trade, the U.S. ran a large deficit in the first quarter of 1988. U.S. exports of goods amounted to $75 billion during the quarter, while U.S. imports of goods amounted to $111 billion. This is a **balance-of-trade deficit** of $36 billion. This is shown on line 27 of Table 4.1, where it is referred to as the **balance of merchandise trade**.

On the service side, U.S. exports were $1 billion smaller than U.S. imports. Behind the $1 billion service deficit was a surplus on U.S. earnings on patents and royalties, consulting and so on, but a deficit on debt service. This is a reflection of the U.S. indebtedness. When the $1 billion service deficit is added to the trade deficit we find that the U.S. had a **balance of goods and services** that was in deficit by $37 billion. This is shown on line 28 of Table 4.1.

Unilateral Transfers   Unilateral transfers include such items as foreign aid, nonmilitary economic development grants, and private gifts or donations. These items are called *unilateral* transfers because, unlike the case of other items in the balance of payments where the item being traded goes in one direction and the payment goes in the other direction, in the case of gifts and aid there is a flow in only one direction, the direction of payment. However, unilateral transfers must be included somewhere in the account because the receipt of a gift or aid gives rise to a demand for the country's currency in the same way as the export of goods and services.[9] Similarly, gifts or aid to foreigners give rise to a supply of the country's currency in the same way as the import of goods and services. What the balance of payments accountant therefore does is include unilateral transfers as if the donor were buying goodwill from the recipient. That is, the granting of aid is considered as a purchase or import of goodwill, a debit entry under unilateral transfers, and the receipt of aid is considered a sale or export of goodwill, a credit entry. By including transfers as a trade in goodwill, we preserve double-entry bookkeeping, since the payment for or receipt from the transfer, which will appear elsewhere in the account, will be matched by the transfer item itself.

The value of unilateral transfers depends both on a country's own generosity and on the generosity of its friends. It also depends on the number of expatriates who send money to relatives or receive money from relatives. Poorer countries, from which large numbers typically leave for job opportunities elsewhere, receive net earnings on unilateral transfers. India and Pakistan, for example, receive net inflows on transfers. Richer countries—such as the United

---

[9]If the gift or aid must be spent in the donor country, so that the money never leaves the country, the gift or aid appears elsewhere in the account. In this case it is as if the donor country had an export which automatically matched the transfer.

States, Canada, Britain, and Australia—which have foreign aid programs and have taken immigrants generally have net outflows on transfers.

When we compute the subtotal up to and including unilateral transfers we obtain the **balance of payments on current account**. That is, the balance of payments on current account consists of exports and imports of goods and services, plus net unilateral transfers: lines 1, 4, and 7 in Table 4.1. The current account is in deficit by $40 billion, as shown on line 29. The reason why the balance of payments on current account is reported is that it shows how much the country will have to borrow or **divest**—sell off its past investments—to finance a current-account deficit, or how much the country must lend or invest if it has a current-account surplus. Borrowing or divesting is necessary if a country has a deficit in its current account, because it is necessary to pay for the extent that it is buying from abroad or giving away more than it earns or receives from abroad. Similarly, lending or investing must occur if the country has a current-account surplus, since what the country earns and does not spend or give away is not destroyed, but is loaned or invested in other countries. In summary:

> The current account of the balance of payments is the result of the export and import of goods, services, and goodwill (or unilateral transfers). A deficit in the current account must be financed by borrowing from abroad or by divestment of foreign assets, while a surplus must be loaned abroad or invested in foreign assets.

A country can finance a current-account deficit by selling to foreigners the country's bills, bonds, stocks, real estate, and operating businesses. A country can also finance its deficit by selling off its previous investments in foreign bills, bonds, stocks, real estate, and operating businesses, that is, via divestment. Before we examine how the U.S. financed its $40 billion current-account deficit in Table 4.1, we should recall that there is nothing to distinguish the demand for a country's currency when foreigners buy its financial and real assets, from when foreigners buy the country's goods and services; a check or draft for the country's currency must be purchased whatever is being bought. Similarly, a country's currency is supplied in the same way whether residents of a country are buying foreign financial or real assets or are importing goods and services. Of course, different factors influence the purchase and sale of financial and real assets than influence the purchase and sale of goods and services, and as we shall see, there are different long-run implications of trade in assets than of trade in goods and services; today's trade in stocks, bonds, real estate, and businesses affects *future* flows of dividends, interest, rents, and profits.

U.S. Assets Abroad (Net)   There are several components to this item, which are best considered separately. We see from Table 4.1 that between these components the U.S. financed $9 billion of its $40 billion current-account deficit.

The first subcomponent of U.S. assets abroad is **official reserves**. Official reserves are liquid assets held by the U.S. Federal Reserve and the Department of the Treasury. These liquid assets include gold, foreign currency in foreign banks, and balances at the International Monetary Fund (IMF), including balances of Special Drawing Rights (SDRs).[10] We see in line 11 of Table 4.1 that there is a positive entry of $2 billion for changes in official reserves. The positive sign means a demand for U.S. dollars because the U.S. Federal Reserve or Treasury sold gold, foreign currency, or balances held at the IMF. Whatever is sold, the U.S. is divesting itself of assets and is demanding U.S. dollars. This is done when the U.S. Government wishes to prop up the dollar in the foreign exchange market. The main influence on the size of the official reserve entry is the extent to which the U.S. Government wishes to influence exchange rates. The harder the Government is trying to support the dollar, the larger the positive entry. When the U.S. Government wishes to reduce the foreign exchange value of the dollar, the Fed or Treasury is instructed to buy gold, foreign exchange, or SDRs with dollars, and there is then a supply of U.S. dollars and a negative entry under official reserves.

The next item under the heading U.S. Assets Abroad (Net) is "U.S. government assets other than official reserves," line 12 of Table 4.1. This item shows new loans and loan repayments involving the U.S. Government and foreign governments. When the U.S. Government makes a foreign loan or repays a loan, this item shows a negative entry because there is a supply of dollars. When the U.S. Government borrows from foreign governments, there is a positive entry and a demand for dollars. In the first quarter of 1988, a net supply of dollars shows under this heading, indicating the U.S. Government made new loans or repaid old ones. As with the official reserve entry, a major factor influencing the size of this item is U.S. Government efforts to influence the foreign exchange value of the dollar.

After the two entries reflecting U.S. Government activity are four items which together constitute "U.S. private assets abroad." These entries show the extent to which U.S. private firms and individuals have made investments in foreign bills, bonds, stocks, real estate, and so on, or have divested themselves of such investments by selling assets purchased in the past.

The first subcategory of U.S. private assets is **direct investment**. By definition, direct investment by Americans occurs when the ownership is sufficiently extensive to give Americans a measure of control. Government statisticians have chosen the level of 10 percent or more ownership of a company's voting shares to constitute control. Original as well as incremental investments where 10 or more percent ownership is involved are considered direct investment (or divestment when funds are brought home). A typical example of direct investment would be the building of a factory in a foreign country by a U.S. multinational corporation. Line 14 of Table 4.1 shows that there was a supply of $5 billion of U.S. currency to the foreign exchange market from U.S. direct investment

---

[10]The IMF and SDRs are discussed in the Addendum. For current purposes we need note only that the IMF is a place where many countries hold funds for financing balance-of-payments deficits, and SDRs are one of the forms of funds countries hold.

during the reporting period. This supply of U.S. dollars adds to the supply of dollars from the deficit in the current account. This means that further down the balance-of-payments account there must be entries showing the U.S. borrowing and/or divestment that is financing the current-account deficit and U.S. direct investment abroad.

Direct investment depends on the expected return from investing in plant and equipment, real estate, and so on in foreign countries relative to the opportunity cost of shareholder capital. This expected return must be sufficient to compensate for the unavoidable risk of the direct investment.[11] Expected returns abroad may be high if foreign wage rates are low, if raw materials are cheap, if corporate taxes are low, if borrowing rates are low—perhaps because of subsidized loans—and so on. The risk of overseas direct investment includes both business and political risks.

It should be pointed out that amounts that appear as direct investments may be really more in the nature of speculation. On numerous occasions in the 1970s and 1980s, U.S.-based multinationals which expected falls in the value of a currency moved funds into stronger currencies by extending credit to subsidiaries or branches, or by reducing or increasing remittances from them.

The next private investment item is titled "foreign securities." This shows the supply of and demand for U.S. dollars from the purchase or sale by U.S. residents of foreign stocks and bonds.[12] When U.S. residents add to their holdings of these assets, there is a supply of dollars and a negative entry in the balance of payments account. When U.S. residents sell these assets and repatriate the proceeds, there is a demand for dollars and a positive entry. Line 15 shows that during the first quarter of 1988 U.S. residents moved about $4 billion into foreign stocks and bonds. This is yet a further supply of dollars, adding to the supply from direct investment and the deficit in the current account.

The amount of foreign security investment depends on the difference in expected returns between foreign stocks and bonds and domestic stocks and bonds, and on relative risks. The expected return on a foreign security depends on the expected dividend on the stock or interest on the bill or bond, the expected change in the security's local currency market value, and the expected change in the exchange rate. Because funds flow between countries until the expected returns in different locations are equal, the advantage that exists for investing in a particular location will be more obvious from statistics in the balance-of-payments account on the amounts flowing than from statistics on yields.[13] In addition to the difference between expected returns abroad and expected returns at home, U.S. residents' purchases of foreign securities depend

[11] Because the opportunity cost of capital includes the chance of investing at home rather than abroad, direct investment can also be considered to depend on expected returns at home versus expected returns abroad. The details of factors affecting direct investment are described in Chapter 15.

[12] Of course, when a U.S. resident holds 10 percent or more of the voting stock of a foreign company, the flow of U.S. dollars for stocks appears as direct investment.

[13] This point is made, for example, by Fischer Black in "The Ins and Outs of Foreign Investment," *Financial Analysts Journal*, May-June 1978, pp. 1–7.

on diversification benefits from foreign investment. We shall discuss these benefits in Chapter 13.

The next two items, shown in lines 16 and 17, give the supply and demand of U.S. dollars due to short-term lending abroad. Line 16 gives lending by nonbank firms, including credits extended by U.S. firms in commercial transactions, where the receivables on the credits are assets of U.S. firms. A negative entry means an increase in outstanding loans and credits during the reporting period, and a consequent supply of dollars. A positive entry means a reduction in outstanding loans and credits, and a demand for dollars from repayment. There was little reported supply of or demand for U.S. dollars from this source during the first quarter of 1988.

Line 17 shows the change in the amount loaned to foreign borrowers by U.S. banks. The large positive entry for this item tells us that U.S. banks reduced their lending abroad during the reporting period. This occurred partly because U.S. banks' dollar claims on their own offices abroad declined, and partly because of loan repayments by foreign borrowers.[14] A reduction of U.S. bank claims on their own offices abroad occurs when the banks find it more profitable to make dollar loans in the U.S. than to make dollar loans in the **Eurodollar market**.[15] The main reason why banks find it more profitable to lend in the U.S. than abroad is higher interest rates in the U.S. than in the Eurodollar market. Even a small interest-rate advantage can move a vast amount of money between nations. The speed with which the money can move is so rapid that funds moved between banks and bank offices has been called "hot money." This money needs only an internal bank reallocation, or an order sent via SWIFT if the money is moving between unrelated banks. The effect on exchange rates can be as fast as the money itself can move, which in turn is as fast as a satellite signal. For this reason, changes in interest rates can cause very large, sudden changes in exchange rates.

Foreign Assets in the U.S. (Net) The next set of items in the balance of payments, those on lines 18 to 24, are the same as those described above and shown in lines 11 to 17, but give the supply of and demand for U.S. dollars due to borrowing, lending, investment, and divestment by foreigners rather than U.S. residents. The entry "foreign official assets" gives the increase or decrease of U.S. dollar assets held by foreign governments in the U.S. We see from the large positive entry that there was a large demand for U.S. dollars due to dollar buying of foreign governments. This occurred as part of a cooperative effort of

---

[14]U.S. bank credits to their own offices abroad were reduced in part because in February 1988, the U.S. Government imposed restrictions on the transfer of funds to Panama in order to restrict the medium of exchange in that country. See Russel C. Kreuger, "U.S. International Transactions, First Quarter 1988," *Survey of Current Business*, U.S. Department of Commerce, June 1988, pp. 28–37.

[15]Eurodollars are U.S.-dollar-denominated bank deposits held in banks located outside the U.S. The U.S.-dollar loans that appear in line 17 are made out of these deposits. The reasons for the emergence of the Eurodollar market are given in Chapter 11.

the governments of the leading industrial nations to prop up the value of the dollar. The principal factor determining the size of this item is the extent to which foreign governments are committed to the stabilization of exchange rates.

When exchange rates are fixed, central banks buy whatever amount of dollars is necessary to prevent the dollar from falling. When exchange rates are flexible or floating, as they have been since the early 1970s, governments are not supposed to buy or sell foreign currencies at all, instead leaving exchange rates to be determined by the forces of supply and demand. What then do we make of the positive entry on line 19, as well as the positive entry for U.S. official reserve holdings on line 11? The answer is that exchange rates were not completely flexible in 1988. Rather, there was an effort to stabilize exchange rates, a so-called **dirty float**. If exchange rates had been truly flexible, there would have been no buying or selling of U.S. dollars by the U.S. or foreign governments, and lines 11 and 19 would have been zero.

Line 21 shows the amount of direct investment made by foreigners in the U.S. As with U.S. direct investment abroad, this is determined by the expected rate of return on the direct investment relative to the shareholders' opportunity cost of capital, and the amount of unavoidable risk of the investment. The expected rate of return is a function of market opportunities in the U.S., including the possibility of facing quotas and other forms of protectionism if the direct investment is not made. We find a substantial demand for U.S. dollars from direct investment by foreigners in the U.S. during the reporting period. This helps finance the current account deficit, but means profit repatriation within the debt-service component of *future* current accounts.

Line 22 shows purchases of U.S. securities by overseas investors, and is positive when foreigners increase their U.S. investments, and negative when they divest. We see a substantial increase in foreign holdings of U.S. stocks and bonds during the reporting period, augmenting the demand for dollars by foreign governments and for direct investment. The principal factors influencing foreign investment in U.S. stocks, bonds, and other securities are U.S. versus foreign yields, and expected future changes in exchange rates. The higher are U.S. versus foreign yields and the more the dollar is expected to increase in value, the greater is the demand for U.S. securities and dollars. The expected change in exchange rates tends to be reflected in the forward exchange premium or discount. Therefore, we can also think of the demand for U.S. securities as depending on yield advantages, plus the forward premium of discount on the U.S. dollar. We might note that a large number of U.S. Government bills and bonds issued to finance a large U.S. fiscal deficit helped to fuel the demand for dollars during the first quarter of 1988.

Line 23 shows no effect of nonbank credits and the like on the demand for dollars. However, line 24 shows a large supply of dollars due to U.S. bank liabilities. U.S. bank liabilities consist of deposits by foreigners in U.S. banks. We see that deposits were withdrawn during the reporting period. This could have occurred because of fear of an expected decline in the value of the U.S.

dollar, or because foreign investors preferred to shift their dollars from U.S. bank accounts into U.S. securities.[16]

Allocation of Special Drawing Rights (SDRs)   In line 25 of Table 4.1 we find an entry "allocation of SDRs." The specific details of SDRs, or Special Drawing Rights, are left to our discussion of alternatives to flexible exchange rates in the Addendum. However, we can say here that SDRs are reserves created by the International Monetary Fund (IMF) and allocated, when they are approved by a sufficient number of IMF members, by making ledger entries in the countries' accounts at the IMF. In 1988, the United States did not receive any SDRs. When SDRs are allocated, they appear as a positive entry, as would any other inflow of unilateral transfers.

Statistical Discrepancy   Until 1976 the **statistical discrepancy** was called "errors and omissions", which gives a better idea of its meaning. The discrepancy exists because of errors in estimating many of the items in Table 4.1. Errors might appear because of differences between the time that entries are made for the current account and the time that the associated payments appear elsewhere in the balance of payments account. It is customary for the U.S. Department of Commerce to collect data on exports and imports of goods and services from customs agents; the data on these current account items are reported as the goods cross the border or as the services are rendered. The payments for these goods or services, which are financial flows, appear only afterward. This may be in a subsequent report of the balance-of-payments statistics.

Another reason for errors is that many entries are estimates. For example, data on travel expenditures are estimated from questionnaire surveys of a limited number of travelers. The average expenditure discovered in a survey is multiplied by the number of travelers. A further reason for measurement error is that illegal transactions, which affect foreign exchange supply and demand despite their illegality, do not explicitly enter the accounts. We can therefore have flows of funds without any associated measured flows of goods or services. Finally, we can have unreported flows of capital. Indeed, some researchers believe that the capital account contains a greater measurement error than the current account. This is deduced from the observation by econometricians that the statistical discrepancy fits the theory of short-term capital flows rather well.

An obvious question is how the balance-of-payments accountant knows the size of the statistical discrepancy, since, by definition, it is due to inaccurate data. The answer is that due to the use of double-entry accounting principles, all the entries in the account must add to zero. (We saw this at the beginning of

---

[16] We might also imagine that foreigners moved funds out of U.S. banks because of higher interest rates elsewhere. However, this does not seem likely in light of the positive entries in lines 17 and 22.

the chapter where every positive entry is matched by a negative entry). If the balance-of-payments entries do not sum to zero, errors must have been made equal to the extent to which the sum of entries differs from zero. If you check by adding the numbers in the far-right column of Table 4.1, but excluding the statistical discrepancy, you will see they add to −$3 billion. Since the sum should have been zero, there must have been $3 billion of positive entries that were overlooked. Therefore we enter $3 billion as the statistical discrepancy.

The fact that the balance of payments must sum to zero means that it is subtotals such as the balance on current account that are of interest. Furthermore, the fact that the overall balance is zero can provide very useful insights into, for example, why a country has a current account deficit.

IMPLICATIONS OF THE BALANCE-OF-PAYMENTS ACCOUNTING IDENTITY

Interpreting the Accounts with Fixed and Flexible Rates

We can offer an interesting explanation of why a country can run a current-account deficit if we consider the following accounting identity:

$$B_c + \Delta R + B_k + \varepsilon \equiv 0 \qquad (4.1)$$

Here B_c is the balance of payments on current account, which is the sum of lines 1, 4, and 7 in Table 4.1. The next term, ΔR, is the change in official reserves of both the U.S. and foreign governments, that is, the sum of line 11 and line 19. The next term, B_k, is the sum of all the remaining entries in the balance of payments except the statistical discrepancy.[17] B_k is the **balance of payments on capital account**. Several forms of capital-account balances were omitted from the accounts, on the recommendation of the Advisory Committee on the Presentation of the Balance of Payments Statistics, despite the strong objection of some members of the committee.[18] The balance of payments on capital account, B_k, is the net result of all the borrowing, lending, investment, and divestment of nonbank firms, banks, and individuals, as estimated by the balance-of-payments accountant. The final term, ε, is the statistical discrepancy. In summary:

$$B_c = \text{balance on current account}$$

$$\Delta R = \text{changes in official reserves}$$

$$B_k = \text{balance on capital account}$$

$$\varepsilon = \text{statistical discrepancy}$$

---

[17]This means that B_k is the sum of lines 12, 13, 20, and 25.

[18]See "Report of the Advisory Committee on the Presentation of the Balance of Payments Statistics," in U.S. Department of Commerce, *Survey of Current Business*, June 1976, p. 25.

Equation (4.1) is a fundamental balance-of-payments identity. It is useful to consider the implications of this identity separately for fixed and flexible exchange rates.

Flexible Rates We have said that if exchange rates are truly flexible, there cannot be any changes in official reserves because central banks do not buy or sell currencies and gold. This means that if exchange rates are truly flexible,

$$B_c + B_k + \varepsilon \equiv 0$$

Assuming that we can calculate balances without error, this means

$$B_c \equiv -B_k \tag{4.2}$$

Equation (4.2) says that with flexible exchange rates, the correctly measured current-account deficit/surplus is exactly equal to the correctly measured capital-account surplus/deficit. It is Equation (4.2) that is behind the view of many economists that the large U.S. current-account deficits of the 1980s were the result of too much foreign borrowing. Let us consider this view.

Some people tend to think that the direction of causation runs from the current account to the capital account. They would argue that having a deficit in the current account from spending more abroad than is earned from abroad causes a country to have to borrow abroad or divest itself of assets. This suggests a direction of causation from B_c to B_k. However, an equally valid way to view the situation is that an inflow of capital, such as occurs when the U.S. Government sells its bills and bonds to foreign lenders to finance the U.S. fiscal deficit, forces the country to run a deficit in the current account equal to the import of capital. Indeed, flexible exchange rates are the mechanism that ensures a current-account deficit results from the capital imports. What happens is that the demand for dollars resulting from the foreign purchases of bills and bonds increases the value of the dollar, thereby reducing U.S. exports and increasing U.S. imports, causing a current-account deficit.

> With flexible exchange rates, the correctly measured current-account deficit/surplus equals the correctly measured capital-account surplus/deficit. It is equally valid to consider a current-account deficit/surplus to be the cause of, or to be caused by, a capital-account deficit/surplus.

Fixed Rates When exchange rates are fixed, there is no simple link between the correctly measured current and capital accounts as in Equation (4.2). However, we can still use the fundamental accounting identity in Equation (4.1) to reach some important conclusions.

If we again assume the current and capital account balances are correctly measured, we can rearrange Equation (4.1) to state

$$\Delta R \equiv -(B_c + B_k)$$

This tells us that when exchange rates are fixed, as they were for most currencies during the so-called Bretton Woods era from 1944 to 1973, the increase/decrease in official reserves equals the combined surplus/deficit in the current and capital accounts.[19] Indeed, the mechanism for fixing exchange rates ensured that this happened. If a country had a combined deficit on its current and capital accounts, the net excess supply of the country's currency would have forced down its exchange rate if the government did nothing. Only by buying an amount of its currency equal to the excess supply could the country keep its exchange rate from falling. That is, governments had to demand whatever excess amounts of their currencies were supplied if they were to prevent their exchange rates from falling. Similarly, governments had to supply whatever excess amounts of their currencies were demanded if they were to prevent their exchange rates from increasing. Therefore, ΔR had to be equal and opposite in sign to the combined balance on current and capital account, $B_c + B_k$.

Long-Run versus Short-Run Implications of Payments Imbalances

Flexible Rates   If $B_c + B_k = 0$, but B_c is large and negative and B_k is large and positive, the country is likely to run into trouble eventually. This is because with B_c negative and B_k positive a country is paying for its excess of imports over exports of goods, services, and goodwill by borrowing abroad or divesting itself of investments made in the past. This is acceptable in the short run, but not in the long run, because B_c includes debt service. If the country is borrowing or divesting, the size of debt service will grow in the future, and so therefore will the deficit on current account. That is, if B_c is negative and B_k is positive, then B_c will become more negative in the future via the additional payments of interest, dividends, rents, and profits. This will make it necessary to borrow or divest more, thereby making B_c even more negative in the future, and so on to catastrophe.

Fixed Rates   If $B_c + \Delta R + B_k = 0$ with $B_c + B_k$ negative and ΔR positive, this means the government is buying up its own currency to offset the net excess supply due to the current- plus capital-account deficits. The government buys its own currency by selling gold and foreign exchange reserves. This can occur in the short run if the government has a large stock of reserves. However, eventually reserves will run out. Official reserves can sometimes be borrowed from foreign governments, but the debt service due to borrowing causes higher future current-account deficits, requiring even more borrowing, still higher future current-account deficits, and so on. Eventually the country is likely to run out of credit.

What we discover is that one must not allow anything but temporary deficits in the current account, or a country is likely to fall deeper and deeper into debt.

[19]The Bretton Woods fixed-exchange-rate system is described in more detail in the Addendum.

With fixed exchange rates, it is possible to have a deficit in the combined current and capital accounts, but again, if this is not temporary, the country will run out of reserves and eventually fall into debt.

The Firm versus the Economy: An Analogy

We can illustrate the importance of correcting imbalances of payments by considering an analogous situation of imbalances in the current and capital accounts of an individual firm. This analogy also helps us push our understanding of the balance of payments a little further.

The analogous account to the balance of payments on current account for the firm is the firm's income statement. In the case of the firm, the credit entries are revenue from sales and earnings on past investment such as interest received on bank accounts. The debit entries are the firm's payments for wages, salaries, rent, raw materials, equipment, and entertainment/advertising—the buying of goodwill—plus interest and dividend payments. If the firm has a surplus on its income statement, it can add to its investments or build up a reserve in the bank against possible losses in the future. If the firm has a deficit in its income statement, it must borrow, raise more equity, or divest itself of assets purchased in the past.

In the case of a surplus, the addition to investments means higher future earnings and, *ceteris paribus*, ever larger future surpluses in its income statements. In the case of borrowing or divesting to cover losses, the extra debt or reduced income base of assets suggests even larger future losses. However, when we consider an individual firm, we recognize that having payments that exceed receipts is acceptable when it occurs because the firm is updating or otherwise improving its capital stock. This situation is acceptable because the firm is increasing its potential to generate future revenue or reducing its future costs of production. Provided the investment is a good investment, the extra revenue or saving in production costs will service any added debt incurred in making the investment. Therefore, having a deficit in the income statement, the analogous account to the current account of the balance of payments, is not necessarily a matter of concern. It depends on whether the deficit is the result of current operating and debt costs exceeding current revenue, or whether the deficit results from capital investment.

It follows from what we have just said that it is not necessarily bad for a country to have a current-account deficit and a capital-account surplus. If the country is borrowing from abroad to finance the building of important infrastructure, the development of natural resources such as oil, the purchase of state-of-the-art robots, construction equipment, and so on, then an excess of imports over exports in the current account may be due to the import of capital equipment. This is far healthier than a trade balance from importing consumer goods such as VCRs, expensive wine, clothing, and automobiles. Indeed, if the imported capital offers a return in excess of future interest or dividend payments incurred in financing the capital, this is a very healthy and sustainable

TABLE 4.2

INTERNATIONAL INVESTMENT POSITION OF THE UNITED STATES, DECEMBER 31, 1987

(Billions of dollars)

U.S. government assets:				Foreign official assets		283
Official reserves	46			Foreign private assets:		
Other assets	88			Direct investment	262	
Total government assets		134		U.S. securities:		
U.S. private assets:				Treasury securities	78	
Direct investment	309			Bonds, excluding		
Foreign securities				Treasury securities	171	
Bonds	91			Stocks	173	
Stocks	56			Total		422
Total		147		Liabilities of U.S. nonbanks		29
Assets of U.S. nonbanks		30		Liabilities of U.S. banks		540
Assets of U.S. banks		548		Total foreign private		
Total private assets		1034		assets		1253
				U.S. net investment position		−368
Total U.S. assets abroad		1168		Total foreign assets in the U.S.		1168

Source: U.S. Department of Commerce, *Survey of Current Business*, June, 1988.

situation. We see that we need to know the composition of the current-account deficit as well as whether the account is in deficit.[20] Unfortunately, no accounting distinction is made between the import of capital goods and the import of consumer goods. Both appear in the current account and contribute to a deficit even though they have very different implications for future living standards and financial viability.

THE NET INTERNATIONAL INVESTMENT POSITION

The capital account of the balance of payments presents the record of the *flows* of funds into and out of the United States. Capital inflows result from the sale of financial and real assets, gold, and foreign exchange to foreigners. Outflows result from the purchase of these assets from foreigners. The inflows and outflows are added to and subtracted from *stocks* of outstanding international assets and liabilities. The account that shows the stocks of assets and liabilities is called the **net international investment position** account. Table 4.2 gives the international investment position of the United States at the end of 1987.[21]

When capital leaves the United States for investment overseas, it is added to U.S. assets abroad. The debit that appears in the balance of payments therefore corresponds to an increase in the value of U.S. assets in Table 4.2. Similarly, when capital flows into the United States, the credit that appears in the balance of payments corresponds to an increase in U.S. liabilities to foreigners in

[20]This point has been made by K. Alec Chrystal and Geoffrey E. Wood, "Are Trade Deficits a Problem?," Federal Reserve Bank of St. Louis *Review*, January/February 1988, pp. 3–11.

[21]U.S. government publications usually show assets and liabilities in a column format rather than in the balance-sheet format shown here.

Table 4.2. However, while there is a close correspondence between the balance-of-payments account and the net international investment position, that correspondence is imperfect. For example, the change in the stock of U.S. direct investment from one year to the next as shown by the net international investment positions for the two successive years will not equal the amount of U.S. direct investment occurring during the period. This is because the stock of direct investment is also affected by unrepatriated earnings, realized changes in market values, and changes in exchange rates. These factors make the international investment position change from year to year in a way that is not completely explained by the balance of payments.

The imperfect link between the balance-of-payments account and the account showing the net international investment position has been used by some writers to argue that the U.S. is not really as large a debtor nation as is indicated in Table 4.2.[22] It is claimed that because the U.S. made its investments abroad many years ago, while foreign investments in the U.S. are relatively recent, U.S. assets are undervalued, at least in comparison with foreign assets held in the U.S. This is because capital gains are not recognized until they are realized. This gives some idea of the difficulty of going between the balance of payments and the net international investment position, and also of judging a country's situation.

It should go without saying that in order to judge the solvency of a country, the net international investment position should be consulted rather than the balance of payments. Table 4.2 shows a negative value of $368 billion for the U.S. net investment position. [By comparison, Brazil and Mexico had debts of a little over $100 billion at the end of 1987, but of course, also much smaller gross domestic products (GDPs) than the U.S.] The payments on this excess of liabilities over assets produce the net debt-service deficit of the United States that appears in the current account of the balance of payments.

Perhaps the most important item in the net international investment position for judging solvency is the reserve position of the central bank. This position is very important during times of fixed exchange rates or dirty floats for judging how long a country can influence exchange rates. A central bank can defend its currency as long as it has sufficient reserves. If, for example, a central bank can afford many years of substantial deficits with its stock of reserves, a devaluation —an official reduction in the fixed exchange rate—can be considered unlikely. On the other hand, if reserves will meet existing deficits for only a few months, a devaluation is quite possible.

OBJECTIVES OF ECONOMIC POLICY

Even when it is pointed out that a trade deficit can be healthy if it is due to importing capital equipment that increases future output and exports, it is difficult for many people to avoid thinking that it is still better to try to achieve

---

[22]See, for example, K. Alec Chrystal and Geoffrey E. Wood, "Are Trade Deficits a Problem?," *op. cit.*

trade surpluses than trade deficits. This presumption that trade surpluses are an appropriate policy objective has a long history, being the opinion of a diverse group of writers of the sixteenth, seventeenth, and eighteenth centuries known as **mercantilists**. The mercantilists believed that trade surpluses were the objective of trade because, during that time, surpluses resulted in increased holdings of gold, the medium of exchange against which internationally traded products were exchanged. Today, a version of mercantilism is that trade surpluses are an appropriate objective because they result in accumulations of foreign assets, as reflected in the net international investment position. This seems so eminently reasonable that it is worth asking why indefinitely running trade surpluses is not a good policy objective.

Consider what it means to have a trade surplus, with merchandise exports exceeding imports, and to have this surplus continue indefinitely. It means that a country is producing more goods for foreigners to enjoy than foreign countries produce for the country's own residents. But why should one country manufacture goods for the pleasure of another in excess of what it receives in return? No, indefinite surpluses mean a country is living below its means. The country could enjoy more of its own production and still keep trade in balance.

Just as surpluses mean a country is living below its means, deficits mean a country is living above its means. A deficit means enjoying the products and resources of other nations in excess of the products the country provides for others. This is marvelous as long as a country can get away with it, but as with individuals or firms that live beyond their means, a day of reckoning eventually comes when the credit runs out. This makes continuous deficits as undesirable as continuous surpluses. Indeed, in the case of deficits the situation is not easily sustainable.

In order to live within its means, a country does not need to balance its trade each and every year. Rather, it can have temporary surpluses and temporary deficits that on average leave its trade balanced.

Temporary trade surpluses followed by temporary trade deficits, or temporary deficits followed by temporary surpluses, are a very different matter than continuous surpluses or deficits. During temporary trade surpluses, the country increases its holdings of foreign assets such as stocks, bonds, real estate, operating businesses, and so on. The income on these foreign assets allows the country to run trade deficits in the future without the country slipping into debt; interest, dividend, and other earnings in the current account can offset the merchandise deficit. Even if there is an overall current account deficit because interest, dividends, and other "invisibles" do not fully offset the trade deficit, a country can sell off some of its past investments without becoming a debtor nation.

When a country has a trade surplus, it is saving, that is, acquiring foreign assets which can add to future income or which can be sold to finance future spending. It follows that indefinitely running trade surpluses is analogous to a family saving, and neither themselves nor their descendants ever dissaving. Saving is a reasonable choice for people who are patient, but only if it means that at some point in the future they or their descendants enjoy the benefits of past saving by consuming more than they earn. That is, it is appropriate to save sometimes, and dissave sometimes, as long as on average over a long interval of time the savings are approximately equal to the dissavings. Similarly, it is appropriate to sometimes have trade deficits and sometimes have trade surpluses. The objective of economic policy should be to aim to have balanced trade over a long period, perhaps as long as a decade or more.[23]

What we have said is important because people tend to look at relatively short periods of trade statistics and become seriously alarmed without considering the trade pattern of earlier years, or the likely trade pattern of future years. Such alarm was voiced, for example, in the 1980s at the large U.S. trade deficits and corresponding large Japanese trade surpluses. Few people stopped to recall that in the 1970s the situation was the reverse, with the U.S. running trade surpluses, and Japan, importing expensive oil and other resources, running trade deficits. This is not to suggest that the situation in the 1980s was desirable. It does, however, warn us to take a long-term perspective.

SUMMARY

1 The balance-of-payments account is a record of the flow of payments between the residents of one country and the rest of the world in a given period. Entries in the account that give rise to a demand for the country's currency—such as exports and asset sales—are identified by a plus sign. Entries giving rise to a supply of the country's currency are identified by a minus sign. Therefore, we can think of the balance-of-payments account as a record of supply of and demand for a country's currency.

2 The balance of payment account is based on double-entry bookkeeping. Therefore, every entry has a counterpart entry elsewhere in the account, and the account must balance. What is important, however, is *how* it balances. Anything tending to increase the size of positive entries, such as higher exports or increased sales of bonds to foreigners, will cause the account to balance at a higher exchange rate.

3 Credit entries in the balance of payments result from purchases by foreigners of a country's goods, services, goodwill, financial and real assets, gold, and foreign exchange. Debt entries result from like purchases from abroad by a country's residents.

4 The current account includes trade in goods and services and unilateral transfers. The goods or merchandise component alone gives the balance of trade as the excess of exports over imports. If exports exceed imports, this component is in surplus, and if imports exceed exports, it is in deficit. Services include not only performed services, but also debt service—the flow of interest and dividend payments. Unilateral transfers are flows of money not matched by any other physical flow, and double-entry

---

[23]The conclusion that an appropriate objective of policy is to balance the current account on average by borrowing sometimes and lending at other times is supported by the gain from consumption smoothing that is described in Appendix 1.2. In that appendix, it is shown that there is a gain in expected utility from borrowing and lending.

bookkeeping requires that we have an offsetting flow that can be marked down as goodwill.

5 A current-account deficit can be financed by selling a country's bills, bonds, stocks, real estate, or businesses. It can also be financed by selling off previous investments in foreign bills, bonds, stocks, real estate, or businesses. A current account surplus can be invested in foreign bills, bonds, stocks, real estate, or businesses. The principal factors influencing investments in financial and real assets are rates of return in one country versus elsewhere, and the riskiness of the investments.

6 Purchases and sales of financial and real assets result in a supply of or demand for a country's currency in the same way as purchases and sales of goods and services.

7 Changes in official holdings of gold, Special Drawing Rights, and foreign exchange occur when governments intervene in the foreign exchange markets to influence exchange rates. When exchange rates are truly flexible, changes in official reserves are zero.

8 Since all entries in the balance of payments should collectively sum to zero, the balance-of-payments accountant can determine the amount of the errors that were made. This is called the statistical discrepancy.

9 With flexible exchange rates, the correctly measured deficit/surplus in the current account equals the correctly measured surplus/deficit in the capital account. With fixed exchange rates, the combined increase/decrease in official reserves of the domestic and foreign governments is equal to the combined surplus/deficit of the correctly measured current and capital accounts.

10 The balance-of-payments account is analogous to a firm's income statement. Deficits are equivalent to corporate losses and can be financed by selling bonds, new equity, or divestment of assets. If there is a net outflow from a firm or country due to acquiring new capital, this need not be unhealthy. Unfortunately, the balance-of-payments account does not distinguish imports of capital goods from imports of consumption goods.

11 The international investment position is a record of the stock of foreign assets and liabilities. It is relevant for determining the likelihood of a currency devaluation.

12 It is not a good idea to run persistent deficits or persistent surpluses in the balance of trade. Rather, a country should balance its trade on average over the long run.

QUESTIONS

1 Since gold is a part of official reserves, how would the balance-of- payments statistics show the sale of domestically mined gold to the country's central bank? What happens if the mining company sells the gold to foreign private buyers?

2 Can all countries collectively enjoy a surplus, or must all surpluses and deficits cancel against each other? What does gold mining and creation of paper reserves (such as SDRs) at the IMF mean for the world's balance?

3 Under what conditions would inflation increase the value of exports?

4 Even if inflation did increase the value of exports, would the balance of trade and the exchange rate necessarily improve from inflation that is higher than in other countries?

5 How do we know that an exogenous increase in exports will cause a currency to appreciate even though the balance of payments is always zero? How does your

answer relate to the law of supply and demand whereby supply equals demand even after demand has increased?

6 What is the difference between the immediate and the long-run effect of the sale of bonds to foreigners?

7 What is the difference between the immediate and the long-run effect of direct investment by foreigners when the direct investment is in a heavily export-oriented activity such as oil exploration? Would it make any difference if the industry into which direct investment occurred were involved in the production of a good the country previously had been importing?

8 If the balance of payments of Alaska were prepared, what would it look like? How about the balance of payments of New York City? What do you think the net investment position of these entities will be? Should we worry if Alaska is in great debt?

9 If the overall level of interest rates in all countries went up, how would this affect the balance of payments of the U.S. as a net debtor nation?

10 Which item(s) in the balance-of-payments account, Table 4.1, would be most affected by an expected appreciation of the U.S. dollar, and how would the item(s) and the current spot value of the dollar be affected by the expected appreciation? Do you believe that the higher expected future value of the U.S. dollar could increase the spot value immediately?

BIBLIOGRAPHY

Baldwin, Robert E.: "Determinants of Trade and Foreign Investment: Further Evidence," *Review of Economics and Statistics*, Fall 1979, pp. 40–48.

Bame, Jack J.: "Analyzing U.S. International Transactions," *Columbia Journal of World Business*, Fall 1976, pp. 72–84.

Caves, Richard E., and Ronald W. Jones: *World Trade and Payments: An Introduction*, 4th ed., Little Brown, Boston, 1984, Chapter 5.

Chrystal, K. Alec and Geoffrey E. Wood: "Are Trade Deficits a Problem?," Federal Reserve Bank of St. Louis *Review*, January/February 1988, pp. 3–11.

Cooper, Richard N.: "The Balance of Payments in Review," *Journal of Political Economy*, August 1966, pp. 379–395.

Grubel, Herbert G.: *International Economics*, Richard D. Irwin, Inc., Homewood, Ill., 1977, Chapter 13.

Heller, H. Robert: *International Monetary Economics*, Prentice-Hall, Englewood Cliffs, N.J., 1974, Chapter 4.

Kemp, Donald S.: "Balance of Payments Concepts—What Do They Really Mean?," Federal Reserve Bank of St. Louis *Review*, July 1975, pp. 14–23.

Mundell, Robert A.: "The Balance of Payments," in David Sills (ed.), *International Encyclopedia of the Social Sciences*, Crowell-Collier and Macmillan, New York, 1968. Reprinted as Chapter 10 in Robert Mundell, *International Economics*, Macmillan, New York, 1968.

"Report of the Advisory Committee on the Presentation of the Balance of Payments Statistics," in U.S. Department of Commerce, *Survey of Current Business*, June 1976, pp. 18–25.

Salop, Joanne and Erich Spitaller: "Why Does the Current Account Matter?," in International Monetary Fund, *Staff Papers*, March 1980, pp. 101–134.

Stern, Robert M.: *The Balance of Payments: Theory and Economic Policy*, Aldine, Chicago, 1973, Chapter 1.

Stern, Robert M., et al.: *The Presentation of the U.S. Balance of Payments: A Symposium*, Essays in International Finance, no. 123, International Finance Section, Princeton University, Princeton, N.J., August 1977.

Wilson, John F.: *The Foreign Sector in the U.S. Flow of Funds Account*, International Finance Discussion Papers, Board of Governors of the Federal Reserve System, no. 239.

CHAPTER 5

THE DETERMINATION
OF EXCHANGE RATES

In the previous chapter we explained that when exchange rates are flexible, as they are for most major currencies today, they are determined by the forces of supply and demand.[1] In this chapter we consider these forces of supply and demand by deriving the supply and demand curves for a currency and using them to explain what makes exchange rates vary. As we might expect, this involves consideration of the effects of items listed in the balance-of-payments account on the slopes and positions of the supply and demand curves.[2] However, as we shall see, in the case of currencies there is no assurance that the supply-and-demand situation will have the form that is familiar from the applications of supply and demand in other markets. In particular, there is no assurance that the supply curve of a currency will be upward sloping.

The possibility that a currency supply curve slopes downward is not a mere curiosity with little practical relevance. Rather, it is a realistic possibility that is critical to explaining why foreign exchange markets may be unstable. This possibility is of considerable interest because of the volatility of exchange rates in recent years, as was shown vividly in Figure 1.5. It is also of interest because

---

[1] When exchange rates are fixed, as they are in the European Monetary System, and as they were under the gold standard and under the Bretton Woods Standard, they are also determined by supply and demand. The difference between fixed and flexible rates is that with fixed rates there is official demand or supply at the fixed rate, and this is adjusted to ensure that the exchange rate stays at or near the chosen rate. The determination of fixed exchange rates under a variety of fixed-rate systems is explained in the Addendum.

[2] The explanation of exchange rates based on the balance-of-payments account emphasizes *flow* demands and supplies of a currency. In the Addendum we describe theories of exchange rates which emphasize *stock* demands and supplies.

101

the condition for exchange-rate instability is the same as that for the so-called "J curve" whereby, for example, a depreciation of a currency worsens rather than improves a country's balance of trade. Considerable attention has been given to the J curve since a massive depreciation of the U.S. dollar during 1985–1988 was observed to accompany a worsening of the U.S. trade deficit. The cause of the J curve and of exchange-rate instability can be understood via the central economic paradigm of supply and demand.

The traditional approach to supply and demand is to begin by explaining why the supply and demand curves slope the way they do, and then to consider the effects of shifts of the curves. Our approach here is the same. Of course, in the case of exchange rates we write the exchange rate (the price of a country's currency expressed in terms of some other currency) on the vertical axis. In order to establish the slopes of the supply and demand curves for currencies, we consider the effects of exchange rates on the values of imports and exports. This is analogous to considering the effect of price on supply and demand. We then show that all other factors in the balance-of-payments account can be considered as shifting the supply or demand curves, with effects on exchange rates that depend on the slopes of the curves.

IMPORTS, EXPORTS, AND EXCHANGE RATES

Deriving a Currency's Supply Curve

As with supply curves in general, the supply curve of a currency shows the amount of that currency supplied on the horizontal axis, and the price of the currency, given by the exchange rate, on the vertical axis. However, when we draw the supply curve of a currency, we do not plot *quantities* on the horizontal axis as we do with normal supply curves—so many bushels of wheat or automobiles produced per month. Rather, we plot *values* on the horizontal axis —so many British pounds or German marks supplied per month. Values involve the multiplication of prices and quantities, and respond differently than do quantities. Indeed, as we shall show, it is the fact that values are on the horizontal axis that explains why the currency supply curve can easily slope downward rather than upward with respect to the foreign exchange value of the currency.

The supply curve of a currency is derived from a country's demand for imports. This is because when paying for imports that are invoiced in foreign currency, the country's residents must sell their currency for the needed foreign exchange, and when imports are invoiced in domestic currency, the foreign recipient of the currency sells it. In either case, imports result in the country's currency being supplied.[3] The amount of the currency supplied is

---

[3] If imports are invoiced in the importer's currency, and the foreign recipient of the currency chooses not to sell it, we still consider that the currency is supplied via imports. This is matched, however, by a demand for the currency in the capital account.

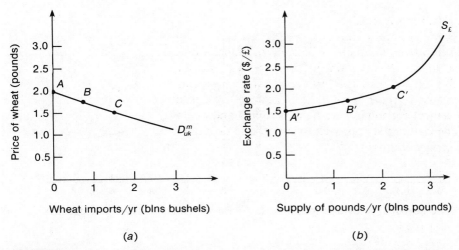

(a)   (b)

FIGURE 5.1
DERIVING THE SUPPLY OF POUNDS. A currency is supplied in the course of paying for imports. If we limit consideration to goods and services, the supply of a currency equals the value of imports. We find the currency supply curve by taking each possible exchange rate and finding the price of imports at that exchange rate. We then calculate the value of imports from the demand curve for imports by multiplying the price and the quantity of imports. We then plot the value of imports against the exchange rate at which it occurs.

equal to the value of imports. Let us see how we can plot the value of currency supplied against the exchange rate by considering British imports of wheat.

We can derive the supply curve of pounds by computing the value of British wheat imports at each exchange rate. This involves multiplying the pound price of wheat at each exchange rate by the quantity of wheat imported. The product is the number of pounds Britain spends on wheat imports, and therefore also gives the number of pounds supplied to the foreign exchange market. Let us suppose that the world price of wheat is \$3/bushel, that wheat is traded without tariffs or other restrictions, and that Britain buys such a small proportion of global wheat output that the world price of wheat is not influenced by Britain's imports.

At an exchange rate of \$1.5/£ the pound price of wheat is \$3 ÷ (\$1.5/£) = £2 per bushel. Figure 5.1a shows that at £2 per bushel the British import demand for wheat is zero, point A.[4] The supply of pounds is therefore zero at the exchange rate \$1.5/£. This is shown by point A' on the supply curve of pounds, $S_£$, in Figure 5.1b. If the exchange rate is \$1.7/£, the pound price of wheat is \$3 ÷ (\$1.7/£) = £1.76 per bushel. Figure 5.1a shows that at this price wheat imports are approximately 0.75 billion bushels, point B. The supply of pounds at exchange rate \$1.7/£ is therefore £1.76 × 0.75 billion = £1.32 billion per year.

---

[4]That is, at £2/bushel Britain's production of wheat equals Britain's consumption of wheat so that Britain is self-sufficient at this price. At wheat prices above £2/bushel, with higher British wheat supply and lower demand, we would expect Britain to be a wheat exporter.

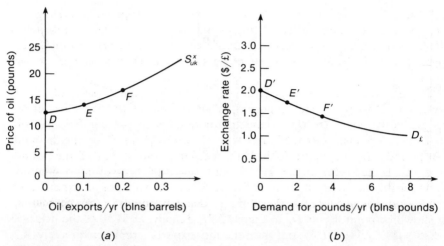

FIGURE 5.2
DERIVING THE DEMAND FOR POUNDS. A country's currency is demanded in the course of foreigners buying that country's exports. If we limit consideration to goods and services, the demand for a currency equals the value of exports. We find the currency demand curve by taking each possible exchange rate and finding the price of exports at that exchange rate. We then calculate the value of exports from the supply curve for exports by multiplying the price by the quantity of exports. We then plot the value of exports against the exchange rate at which it occurs.

This supply of pounds is plotted against the exchange rate $1.7/£ in Figure 5.1b, point B' on $S_£$ in Figure 5.1b.[5] Similarly, at the exchange rate $2/£ the pound price of wheat is $3 ÷ ($2/£) = £1.5 per bushel. Figure 5.1a shows imports of 1.5 billion bushels at this price, point C, which involves an expenditure of £1.5 × 1.5 billion = £2.25 billion. This gives point C' on $S_£$ in Figure 5.1b. By continuing in this way we can construct the supply curve of pounds, which in this case happens to slope upward for its entire length.[6]

Deriving a Currency's Demand Curve

The demand curve for a currency shows the value of the currency that is demanded at each possible exchange rate. Because the need to buy a country's currency stems from the need to pay for the country's exports, the currency's demand curve is derived from the country's export supply curve, which shows the quantity of exports at each price of exports.

Figure 5.2a shows the supply curve of British exports. For simplicity of reference we assume that Britain exports only oil. The demand for pounds to

---

[5]We see that we are calculating the *area* under D^m_{UK} in Figure 5.1a, and plotting this as the *distance* along the horizontal axis in Figure 5.1b.

[6]We consider the condition for a downward-sloping currency supply curve, and the implications of such a curve, later in the chapter.

pay for Britain's oil exports is equal to the value of oil exports. Therefore, in order to construct the demand curve for pounds we must calculate the value of exports at each exchange rate. Let us suppose that the world price of oil is $25 per barrel and that Britain has no effect on this price when it changes its oil exports.

If we begin with an exchange rate of $2/£, the pound price of oil is $25 ÷ $2/£ = £12.5 per barrel. Figure 5.2a shows that at £12.5 per barrel oil exports are zero, point D.[7] The demand for pounds to pay for Britain's oil exports is therefore also zero at $2/£. This is shown by point D' on the demand curve of pounds, $D_£$, in Figure 5.2b. If the exchange rate is $1.8/£ the pound price of oil is $25 ÷ $1.8/£ = £13.89 and oil exports are approximately 0.1 billion barrels per year, point E in Figure 5.2a. The value of oil exports and demand for pounds at $1.8/£ is therefore £13.89 × 0.1 billion = £1.389 billion. This is shown by point E' on $D_£$ in Figure 5.2b. Finally, at $1.50/£ the price of oil is $25 ÷ $1.5/£ = £16.67 per barrel, and exports are approximately 0.2 billion barrels—point F in Figure 5.2a. Therefore, the demand for pounds at $1.50/£ is £16.67 × 0.2 billion = £3.33 billion per year—point F' in Figure 5.2b.

THE EQUILIBRIUM EXCHANGE RATE

If we plot the supply and demand curves for pounds in the same figure, as in Figure 5.3, we can find the exchange rate that equates the value of exports and imports, and hence that equates the supply and demand of the country's currency resulting from these activities. We see that equality of supply and demand occurs at an exchange rate of approximately $1.75/£. It is clear from Figure 5.3 that an exogeneous increase in the value of exports at each exchange rate, which will shift the demand curve for pounds to the right, will, with the slopes of curves shown, result in an increase in the value of the pound. Such an increase in the value of exports could occur as a result of a higher world price of oil or an increase in the quantity of oil exported at each oil price. It is also clear from the figure that an exogenous increase in the value of imports at each exchange rate, which will shift the supply curve of pounds to the right, will result in a decrease in the value of the pound. This could result from a higher world price of wheat or an increase in the quantity of wheat imported at each price.

The price of exports relative to the price of imports is called the **terms of trade**. The terms of trade are said to improve when the price of exports increases relative to the price of imports. Our description of Figure 5.3 makes it clear that the pound will appreciate in value as a result of an improvement of Britain's terms of trade. The pound will also appreciate if the quantity of exports increases relative to the quantity of imports. This could happen, for

---

[7]That is, at £12.5/barrel Britain's production of oil equals Britain's consumption of oil, so that the country is exactly self-sufficient. At prices below £12.5/barrel, with higher domestic demand and lower supply, Britain would presumably be an oil importer.

example, if Britain steps up production of oil at each oil price. It could also happen if Britain has a good wheat harvest and therefore imports less wheat at each exchange rate.

We know from the description of the balance-of-payments account in Chapter 4 that there are many factors behind the supply and demand curves for a country's currency in addition to the factors which affect imports and exports. Let us consider how these other factors influence exchange rates by examining how they shift the supply and demand curves for pounds in Figure 5.3.

OTHER INFLUENCES ON A CURRENCY'S SUPPLY AND DEMAND

Imports and exports of performed services such as tourism, banking, consulting, engineering, and so on, respond to exchange rates in the same way as imports and exports of merchandise. Therefore, the currency supply and demand curves derived from the supply and demand curves for performed services look like those in Figure 5.3. The currency supply curve from importing services can be added to that from importing merchandise, and the currency demand curve from exporting services can be added to that from exporting merchandise. This has the effect of shifting $S_£$ and $D_£$ in Figure 5.3 to the right.[8] Clearly, if exports of performed services exceed imports of performed services, then the currency demand curve is shifted more than the currency supply curve and the exchange rate is higher than in Figure 5.3. On the other hand, if imports of performed services exceed exports, then the supply of currency is increased more than the demand and the exchange rate is lower than in Figure 5.3.

The supply of and demand for a currency from imports and exports of debt service—payments and receipts of interest, dividends, rents, and profits—do not respond to exchange rates in the same manner as the currency supply and demand from imports and exports of merchandise or performed services. Debt-service payments and receipts are largely determined by past investments and the rates of return on these investments. Therefore, we might consider debt-service payments and receipts as being independent of exchange rates.[9] However, as in the case of performed services, we can simply add the value of earnings from debt-service exports to the currency demand curve, and the value

[8]We can think of the currency supply and demand curves due to performed services as being "horizontally added" to the currency supply and demand curves from imports and exports of merchandise. Horizontal addition involves the addition of quantities demanded and supplied at each price, and the plotting of the resulting quantities against the prices at which they occur. With supply and demand curves for currencies from services sloping the same way as currency supply and demand curves from merchandise, the horizontally added curves will be flatter than the individual curves that are added. For example, if the demand for pounds from British purchases of wheat and the demand for pounds from British purchases of overseas vacations are both downward sloping, the sum of the two curves will be flatter than either curve from which it is constructed.

[9]Exchange rates do affect the domestic currency value of a given amount of foreign currency receipts or payments. However, this is an effect of translating foreign into domestic currency, and is very different from the effects of exchange rates on merchandise and performed services which result from an effect on competitiveness.

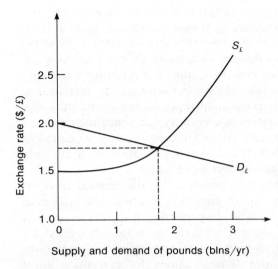

FIGURE 5.3
THE EQUILIBRIUM EXCHANGE RATE FROM IMPORTS AND EXPORTS. The equilibrium exchange rate is that at which the supply of and demand for the currency are equal. Factors other than the value of imports and exports shift the currency supply and demand curves and thereby change the equilibrium exchange rate.

of payments from debt-service imports to the currency supply curve.[10] It should be apparent that the higher are debt-service exports relative to debt service imports, the higher is the exchange rate. It follows that, *ceteris paribus*, the more a country's residents have invested abroad in the past, the higher is the country's exchange rate.

Transfers can easily be accommodated in the supply-and-demand model of exchange rates. We add the amount of transfers received from abroad to a currency's demand curve and the amount sent abroad to the supply curve. Clearly, net inflows of transfers tend to increase the value of a currency and net outflows tend to reduce it. Transfers depend on a country's need for help or its ability to help others. Transfers also depend on the number of residents sending funds to relatives abroad or receiving funds from relatives abroad.

Foreign investment in a country represents a demand for the country's currency when that investment occurs.[11] Therefore, a foreign investment in a country, whether it be direct investment, portfolio investment, or additions to bank deposits of nonresidents, shifts the currency demand curve to the right. Similarly, investment abroad by a country's residents represents a supply of the country's currency and shifts the currency supply curve to the right. Therefore, net inflows of investment tend to increase a currency's exchange rate and net outflows tend to reduce it.

---

[10] If the values of debt-service exports and imports are independent of the exchange rate, the addition of these items to the currency supply and demand curves involves simple parallel rightward shifts of the curves. However, if there is a translation effect from converting at different exchange rates, the shifts of currency supply and demand curves are not parallel.

[11] Of course, in all future periods when interest or dividends are paid, or profits and rents are repatriated, there is a supply of the country's currency.

The amount of investment flowing into or out of a country depends on rates of return in the country relative to rates of return elsewhere, as well as on relative risks. *Ceteris paribus*, increases in a country's interest rates or expected dividends cause an increase in demand for that country's currency from increased foreign investment, and a decrease in supply of that country's currency from a decrease in residents' investment abroad.[12] Consequently, increases in interest rates or expected dividends cause a currency to appreciate, and vice versa. Similarly, an expected appreciation of a country's currency increases the attractiveness of investments in that country and thereby causes the country's currency to appreciate. That is, expected future appreciation of a currency causes an immediate appreciation, just as with other assets.

All the conclusions we have reached have assumed that the demand curve for a currency slopes downward and the supply curve slopes upward. It is time to show why this assumption may not be valid. In particular, it is time to see why the supply curve of a currency may slope downward, and what this implies for exchange rates. There are implications both for the stability of exchange rates and for the way shifts in supply and demand curves for currencies affect exchange rates. Let us begin by considering the implications for stability, which, as we have said, are particularly important in light of the volatility of exchange rates in recent years.

THE STABILITY OF EXCHANGE RATES

The curve in Figure 5.3 that might not slope the way we normally assume is the supply curve for pounds. The curve is derived from the British demand for imports.

Figure 5.4*a* shows two demand curves for imports. The import demand curve labeled $D_{UK}^m(\eta_m > 1)$ is the import demand curve drawn in Figure 5.1*a*. It is labeled with $\eta_m > 1$ in parentheses because it is an elastic curve. That is, the quantity of imports increases by a greater percentage than the price of imports declines. The currency supply curve derived from $D_{UK}^m(\eta_m > 1)$ is $S_\pounds(\eta_m > 1)$. This is the same supply curve for pounds as shown in Figure 5.1*b*. The currency supply curve obtained from an elastic demand for imports is seen to slope upward.

Figure 5.4*a* also shows an inelastic curve demand for imports, $D_{UK}^m(\eta_m < 1)$. It is inelastic in that a reduction in the price of imports causes a smaller percentage increase in the quantity of imports than the percentage reduction in price. We can derive the supply curve for pounds that is associated with the inelastic demand curve for imports by considering a number of possible exchange rates, computing the price and quantity of imports at each of these exchange rates, and then plotting the values of imports against the associated

---

[12] One of the variables assumed to be constant and therefore included in the *ceteris paribus* is the price level, so that changes in interest rates and returns are real changes. We consider the effects of changes in the price level on exchange rates in Chapter 6.

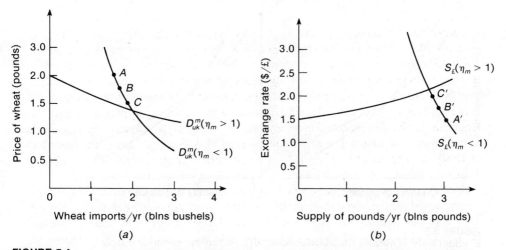

FIGURE 5.4
CURRENCY SUPPLY AND IMPORT ELASTICITY. When the demand for imports is elastic, that is, $\eta_m > 1$, the supply curve of the currency slopes upward. When the demand for imports is inelastic, that is, $\eta_m < 1$, the supply curve of the currency slopes downward. The downward slope occurs because depreciation raises import prices and reduces the quantity of imports, but the *value* of imports increases. This occurs when the percentage reduction in quantity imported is less than the percentage increase in price of imports.

exchange rates; recall that it is the *value* of imports that is the *quantity* of currency supplied. Let us again assume that the imported product, wheat, costs $3 per bushel.

At an exchange rate $1.5/£ the pound price of wheat is $3 ÷ $1.5/£ = £2.0 per bushel, and according to the inelastic demand curve $D_{UK}^m(\eta_m < 1)$ Britain imports 1.5 billion bushels at this price, point A in Figure 5.4*a*. The supply of pounds, which equals the value of imports, is therefore £2.0 × 1.5 billion = £3 billion at the exchange rate $1.5/£. This gives point A' in Figure 5.4*b*. At $1.7/£ the pound price of wheat is $3 ÷ $1.7/£ = £1.76 per bushel, and at this price Britain imports 1.6 billion bushels, point B in Figure 5.4*a*. Therefore, the supply of pounds at the exchange rate $1.7/£ is £1.76 × 1.6 million = $2.82 billion. This gives point B' in Figure 5.4*b*. Similarly, at $2/£ wheat costs $3 ÷ $2/£ = £1.5 and Britain imports 1.7 billion bushels, point C. Therefore, the supply of pounds at the exchange rate $2/£ is £1.5 × 1.7 billion = £2.55 billion, point C' in Figure 5.4*b*. We find that when the demand for imports is inelastic, the supply curve of the country's currency slopes downward. The reason is that when demand is inelastic the amount spent on a product decreases with decreases in the price of the product. The price of imports decreases with increases in the foreign exchange value of the importer's currency. Therefore, if the demand for imports is inelastic, then the higher the exchange rate, the less is spent on imports, and so the lower is the supply of the currency. We discover that all that is necessary for a downward-sloping currency supply curve is inelastic import demand. This could easily occur. Therefore, let

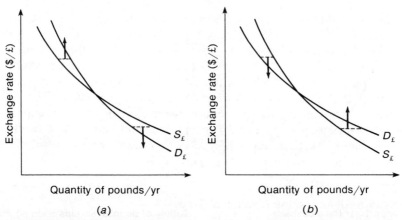

FIGURE 5.5
STABILITY OF FOREIGN EXCHANGE MARKETS. When the currency supply curve slopes downward, foreign exchange markets may be unstable. They are unstable if the currency demand curve is steeper than the supply curve, that is, the demand curve cuts the supply curve from above.

us consider the consequences of inelastic demand for imports and the associated downward sloping currency supply curve.

Figure 5.5 shows two situations in which the currency supply curve slopes downward. In the situation in Figure 5.5a the demand curve for pounds is steeper than the supply curve, but in Figure 5.5b the situation is the reverse. Let us consider the stability of the exchange rate in Figures 5.5a and b by allowing the exchange rate to deviate slightly from its equilibrium value where supply equals demand. In particular, let us consider whether market forces are likely to push the exchange rate back to equilibrium.

In Figure 5.5a a small decline in the exchange rate below equilibrium will result in an excess supply of pounds. This will push the value of the pound even lower, causing an even larger excess supply, and so on. Similarly, in Figure 5.5a a small increase in the exchange rate above equilibrium will result in an excess demand for pounds. This will push the value of the pound even higher, cause an even larger excess demand, and so on. We find that the equilibrium exchange rate in Figure 5.5a is unstable. Small shocks to exchange rates can result in substantial movements in exchange rates when the demand and supply curves for a currency have the configuration in Figure 5.5a.

Figure 5.5b has a downward-sloping supply curve of pounds just as in Figure 5.5a, but here the demand curve for pounds is flatter than the supply curve. In this case a small decline in the value of the pound below the equilibrium exchange rate causes an excess demand for pounds. This pushes the exchange rate back to equilibrium. Similarly, a small increase in the exchange rate above the equilibrium causes an excess supply of pounds. This pushes the exchange rate back down to equilibrium. The equilibrium in Figure 5.5*b* is therefore stable.

Consideration of Figures 5.5*a* and *b* allows us to conclude that having a downward-sloping currency supply curve is not sufficient to cause an unstable foreign exchange market. A relatively flat or elastic currency demand curve can offset the destabilizing nature of a downward-sloping supply curve. For an unstable market it is necessary to have a downward-sloping currency supply curve and a relatively steep or inelastic currency demand curve. A sufficient condition for instability is that the supply curve slopes downward and the demand curve is steeper at equilibrium than the supply curve.[13]

Unstable Exchange Rates and the Balance of Trade

Because the possibility of unstable exchange rates is of considerable interest, we should not leave the matter until we have a solid intuitive understanding of why it can occur. Such an understanding can be obtained by examining how exchange rates affect the balance of trade.

A depreciation increases the price of imports in terms of domestic currency. This reduces the quantity of imports, but does not necessarily reduce the value of imports. If import demand is inelastic, the higher price of imports more than offsets the lower quantity, so that the value of imports is higher. This means that if import demand is inelastic, a depreciation can worsen the balance of trade. (Recall that the balance of trade is the *value* of exports minus the *value* of imports.)

Even when more is spent on imports after a depreciation, the balance of trade is not necessarily worsened. This is because a depreciation makes exports cheaper in terms of foreign currency, and this increases the quantity and value of exports. The *value* of exports unambiguously increases with the quantity of exports because exports are not made cheaper in domestic currency. Indeed, if anything the stronger demand for exports can cause an increase in domestic-currency prices of exports. It follows that even if depreciation increases the value of imports, the balance of trade is worsened only if the value of exports increases less than the value of imports.

The preceding argument can be directly related to Figure 5.5. If import demand is inelastic, a depreciation of the pound, which is a movement down the vertical axis, causes an increase in the value of imports and hence in the supply of pounds; the pound supply curve slopes downward. This on its own does not cause instability, for the same reason it does not necessarily worsen the balance of trade, namely, that the depreciation also increases the value of exports and hence the demand for pounds. The foreign exchange market is unstable only if

[13]A more precise statement of the condition for stability of the foreign exchange market is derived in Appendix 5.1. This condition is known as the **Marshall-Lerner condition** and is stated directly in terms of the import and export elasticities of demand, which are determinants of the slopes of the currency supply and demand curves.

the value of exports does not increase sufficiently to compensate for inelastic import demand, just as depreciation worsens the balance of trade only if exports do not sufficiently increase to compensate for increased imports.

Short-Run versus Long-Run Trade Elasticities and the J Curve

A worsening of the balance of trade following a depreciation of a currency may be temporary. Similarly, instability in exchange rates may be only a short-run problem. Because the consequences of the trade balance worsening with depreciation and of exchange-rate instability are far more serious if they persist, it is well worthwhile considering why they may be temporary problems. Our consideration leads us to the J curve. The J curve has taken on such importance in the second half of the 1980s that it has moved out of the textbooks into the columns of the popular press.[14]

It takes time for people to adjust their preferences towards substitutes. Therefore, it is generally believed that demand is more inelastic in the short run than in the long run. This belief is particularly strong for the elasticity of demand for imports, because the demand curve for imports is derived from the difference between the demand curve for a product in a country and the domestic supply curve of the product; with both supply and demand more inelastic in the short run than the long run, the difference between supply and demand is *a fortiori* more inelastic in the short run.[15] That is, after a depreciation and consequent increase in import prices, a country's residents might continue to buy imports both because they have not adjusted their preferences toward domestically produced substitutes (an inelastic demand curve) and because the domestic substitutes have not yet been produced (an inelastic domestic supply curve). Only after producers begin to supply what was previously imported and after consumers decide to buy **import substitutes** can import demand fully decline after a depreciation. Similarly, exports expand from a depreciation only after suppliers are able to produce more for export and after foreign consumers switch to these products.

If import demand and export supply are more inelastic in the short run than the long run, we may find a depreciation worsening the balance of trade in the short run, but subsequently improving it. That is, the time path of changes in the balance of trade might look like that shown in Figure 5.6a. The figure assumes that a depreciation occurs at time 0, and that because people temporarily spend more on imports, and because exports do not sufficiently increase, the trade balance worsens. Only later, when import and export elasticities increase, does the balance of trade turn around and eventually improve. Because of the shape of the time path followed by the trade balance in Figure 5.6a the

---

[14]The J curve was also a topic of discussion in Britain after a 1967 sterling devaluation was followed by a worsening trade balance.

[15]The demand curve for imports is derived from the demand curve for a product and the domestic supply curve in Appendix 6.1.

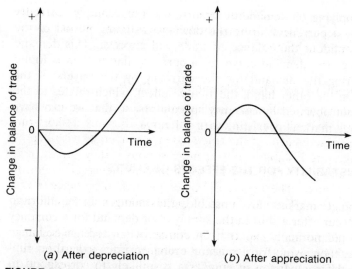

(a) After depreciation   (b) After appreciation

FIGURE 5.6

THE J CURVE. The J Curve describes the balance of trade after a depreciation or appreciation. The time path of the trade balance looks like a "J" if the elasticities of demand for imports and supply of exports are smaller in the short run than the long run.

phenomenon of a worsening and subsequent improvement of the trade balance after a depreciation is known as the **J-curve effect**.

Figure 5.6*b* shows what might happen after an *appreciation* of the exchange rate if import demand is more inelastic in the short run than in the long run. The figure shows that after an appreciation at time 0, the decline in import prices could reduce spending on imports. If exports do not decrease as much as the value of imports declines, the balance of trade will improve—not what one would normally expect to follow an appreciation. However, over time, as the import demand becomes more elastic, the quantity of imports increases more than the price declines, and/or exports decrease sufficiently for the balance of trade to worsen. In the case of an appreciation we find that the balance of trade follows the path of an inverted J.

What we have shown is that the J curve occurs under the very same conditions as instability of exchange rates. When import demand and export supply are sufficiently inelastic we have both unstable exchange rates and a temporary worsening/improvement of the balance of trade after a currency depreciation/appreciation, and when the trade balance turns around, stability returns to foreign exchange markets.

Before leaving the question of the J curve and instability of exchange rates, we should make it clear that foreign exchange markets can be stable even if imports and exports are extremely inelastic. This is because there are numerous other reasons for supplying or demanding a currency. For example, currency speculators might buy a currency during the downward-sloping period of the J curve if they are confident the balance of trade will improve. This demand from speculators makes the demand curve for a currency flatter than is found merely from considering the demand for the currency by the buyers of the country's exports.[16] On the other hand, the J-curve effect, which relates to the balance of trade, is not obviated by currency speculators, so that we can have stable foreign exchange markets coexisting with a J curve.

IMPLICATIONS OF INSTABILITY FOR THE EFFECTS OF SHIFTS IN CURVES

When foreign exchange markets are unstable, the changes in equilibrium exchange rates that occur after a shift in the supply of or demand for a currency are not what one would normally expect.[17] Of course, when foreign exchange markets are unstable, there is no force pushing exchange rates toward equilibrium. Consequently, the comparison of equilibria is unlikely to correspond to the changes in exchange rates that actually occur after a shift in demand or supply. Nevertheless, it is useful to consider what happens to equilibrium exchange rates after a shift in currency supply or demand, because this illustrates the importance of having sufficiently large trade elasticities for foreign exchange markets to function properly.

Figure 5.7 shows an unstable foreign exchange market because the supply and demand curves for pounds have the same configuration as in Figure 5.5a. With the initial supply and demand curves $D_£^1$ and $S_£^1$, the initial exchange rate is at S_1. Let us suppose that, as a result of a higher demand for or price of oil or any other factor, there is an increase in the demand for pounds from $D_£^1$ to $D_£^2$. That is, assume that, for whatever reason, there is a higher demand for pounds at each exchange rate.[18] As the figure shows, the new equilibrium exchange rate after the increase in the demand for pounds is at a depreciated pound, S_2 rather than S_1. That is, a higher demand for a currency reduces its value, or at least its equilibrium value, which is not what one would usually predict.

The reason for the strange response of the exchange rate in Figure 5.7 is that after an increase in the demand for pounds, for equilibrium to be restored it is necessary to have more pounds being supplied. If import demand is inelastic, this happens after a depreciation of the pound. This is because a depreciation increases the price of imports, and if the quantity of imports decreases by less than the price increases, as happens with inelastic demand, then more pounds

---

[16] The question of whether speculators are likely to stabilize or destabilize exchange rates is addressed in the Addendum. The Addendum also considers the effects of portfolio adjustments on exchange rates.

[17] The comparison of equilibria resulting from shifts in supply or demand is called **comparative statics**.

[18] Other factors that might cause such a rightward shift in the demand for pounds include higher British versus foreign interest rates, a reduction in perceived risks in direct investment in Britain, or any other factor increasing the size of a credit item in Britain's balance-of-payments account.

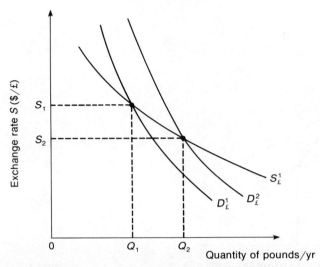

FIGURE 5.7
THE EFFECT OF AN INCREASED CURRENCY DEMAND WITH
MARKET INSTABILITY. When the currency supply curve slopes
downward and is cut from above by the demand curve, an
increase in demand causes a depreciation of the equilibrium
exchange rate, which is not what one would normally expect.
Of course, with such a configuration of supply and demand
the foreign exchange market is unstable, and so there is
doubt whether equilibrium exchange rates will be observed.

are supplied. Of course, with unstable markets there is little reason to expect
the exchange rate to find the new equilibrium. Nevertheless, S_2 is an equilibrium exchange rate in that, if it is attained, the supply of and demand for
pounds are equal. If we considered a decrease in demand for pounds because of
lower oil prices or lower British versus foreign interest rates, we would find that
this would cause the pound to appreciate, not the outcome one might have
predicted.

Figure 5.8 shows the effect of an increase in the supply of pounds on the
exchange rate. This might come about as a result of an increase in the price of
wheat, assumed to be Britain's import, lower British versus foreign interest
rates, or anything that would increase the size of debit items in Britain's
balance-of-payments account. As Figure 5.8 shows, the increased supply of
pounds, meaning a rightward shift in the supply curve from $S_£^1$ to $S_£^2$, results in
an appreciation of the pound from S_1 to S_2. This is not what would normally be
expected to result from increased spending on imports or lower British interest
rates. The reason for the conclusion is as follows.

An appreciation of the pound reduces import prices in Britain, and with
inelastic demand for imports, this reduces the value of imports; the quantity of
imports increases by less than the decrease in the price of imports. This

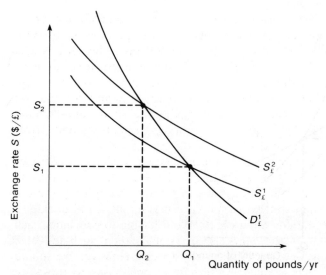

FIGURE 5.8
THE EFFECT OF AN INCREASED CURRENCY SUPPLY WITH
MARKET INSTABILITY. When a currency supply curve slopes
downward and is cut from above by the demand curve, an
increase in currency supply causes an appreciation in the
equilibrium exchange rate, the reverse of what one would
normally expect. Of course, with such a configuration of
currency supply and demand curves we might not observe
equilibrium exchange rates.

reduction in the value of imports brought about by an appreciation of the pound
cancels some of the effect of the assumed higher pound supply that caused the
rightward shift of $S_\pounds$. The appreciated pound also reduces the value of Britain's
exports by increasing their prices to foreign buyers.[19] The reduction in the
quantity of pounds demanded, plus the reduction in quantity of pounds supplied, both being brought about by the appreciation of the pound, offsets the
initially assumed increased supply of pounds. That is, equilibrium after an
increase in the supply of pounds is restored by an appreciation of the pound,
just as Figure 5.8 shows.

The unexpected consequences of shifts in currency supply and demand
curves with unstable foreign exchange markets are not, as we said earlier in this
chapter, a mere curiosity with little practical significance. This is because we
have not generated the conclusions by assuming, for example, that people buy a
higher quantity of imports at higher import prices. That is, we have not assumed
the demand for imports slopes *upward*. Rather, we have assumed only that

---

[19]We assume the pound price of exports is not affected by the pound appreciation, so that the
reduction in the *quantity* of Britain's exports results in a reduction in the *value* of Britain's exports
and hence in the number of pounds demanded.

import demand is *inelastic* This inelastic slope of the demand for *imports* is sufficient to cause the supply curve of the *currency* to slope downward. With sufficiently inelastic export supply this can cause market instability. It can also cause the strange effects of shifts in currency supply and demand curves we have just described. The reason for these unusual possibilities in the case of foreign exchange markets is that when we deal with currency supplies and demands we have values, not quantities, on the horizontal axis of the supply-and-demand diagram, and values which are obtained by multiplying quantities and prices behave very differently than quantities.

While exchange-market instability and unusual effects of shifts in currency supplies and demands are realistic possibilities, in what follows we assume exchange rates are stable. This is done to allow us to avoid being drawn into a taxonomy of possibilities when shifts occur in currency supplies and demands. That is, the assumption of stability allows us to avoid having to conclude, each time an event occurs, that if the markets are stable, then such-and-such happens, and if they are unstable, something else happens. However, we should remember as we proceed that there are alternative conclusions to those we reach. For example, when we show in the next chapter that a currency depreciates if a country's price level increases by more than the price level in other countries, we should bear in mind that the opposite would occur with sufficiently inelastic demand for imports and supply of exports.

SUMMARY

1 Flexible exchange rates are determined by supply and demand.
2 We can construct the supply curve for a currency from a country's demand curve for imports. The currency supply curve slopes downward if the demand for imports is inelastic. This is because depreciation raises the price of imports in domestic currency more than it reduces the quantity of imports. In this way depreciation increases the *value* of imports, meaning a downward-sloping supply curve for the currency.
3 We can construct the demand curve for a currency from the country's supply curve of exports. The currency demand curve always slopes downward. This is because depreciation increases the quantity of exports, and leaves export prices in domestic currency either unchanged or higher. Therefore, depreciation unambiguously increases the value of exports.
4 The effect of any item in the balance-of-payments account on the exchange rate can be determined by identifying how it shifts the currency supply or currency demand curve.
5 If import demand is inelastic, so that the currency supply curve slopes downward, the foreign exchange market may be unstable. Instability occurs when the currency demand curve is steeper than the supply curve.
6 Because import demand elasticities are smaller in the short run than in the long run, instability is more likely in the short run than in the long run.
7 The same conditions that cause short-run instability and long-run stability result in a J curve.
8 When foreign exchange markets are unstable, shifts in currency supply and demand curves have counterintuitive effects on equilibrium exchange rates. For example, an

increase in demand for a currency causes a depreciation in the equilibrium exchange rate. Of course, if markets are unstable, there is no reason why the actual exchange rate should equal the equilibrium exchange rate. The odd predictions are the result of having values and not quantities on the horizontal axis of the currency supply-and-demand diagram.

QUESTIONS

1 Assume that the foreign-currency amount of interest and dividend earnings from abroad is fixed. Show how the horizontal addition of debt-service exports to a currency's demand curve will appear when consideration is given to the effect of exchange rates on the translated values of interest and dividend earnings.
2 Are debt-service imports as likely to be affected by exchange rates as are debt-service exports? [*Hint*: It depends on the currency of denomination of debt-service earnings and payments.]
3 What is the slope of the currency supply curve when the demand for imports is unit-elastic, that is, equal to 1.0?
4 What is the intuitive explanation for the fact that a decrease in demand for a currency can cause it to appreciate if import and export demand are sufficiently inelastic?
5 How can speculators cause a stable foreign exchange market even when the economy is moving along the downward-sloping part of a J curve?

BIBLIOGRAPHY

Alexander, Sidney S: "The Effects of a Devaluation on the Trade Balance," *IMF Staff Papers*, April 1952, pp. 263–278. Reprinted in Richard E. Caves and Harry G. Johnson (eds.), *AEA Readings in International Economics*, Richard D. Irwin, Homewood, Ill., 1968.
Harbeler, Gottfried: "The Market for Foreign Exchange and the Stability of the Balance of Payments: A Theoretical Analysis," *Kyklos*, Fasc. 3, 1949, pp. 193–218. Reprinted in Richard N. Cooper (ed.), *International Finance*, Penguin, Baltimore, 1969.
Heller, H. Robert: *International Monetary Economics*, Prentice-Hall, Englewood Cliffs, N.J., 1974, Chapter 6.
McKinnon, Ronald I.: *Money in International Exchange: The Convertible Currency System*, Oxford Univ. Press, 1979.
Mundell, Robert A.: *International Economics*, Macmillan, New York, 1968, Chapter 1.
Pippenger, John E.: *Fundamentals of International Finance*, Prentice-Hall, Englewood Cliffs, N.J., 1984, Chapter 5.

APPENDIX 5.1: The Condition for Stability in Foreign Exchange Markets

Let us consider the case of the stability of $S(\$/£)$, assuming for simplicity only two countries, the United States and the United Kingdom. The demand for pounds is equal to the value of British exports. We can write this as $p_x \cdot Q_x(S \cdot p_x)$, where p_x is the pound price of British exports, Q_x is the quantity of British exports, and S is the spot exchange rate of dollars per pound, $S = S(\$/\pounds)$. That is, the value of pounds demanded is the price of exports multiplied by the quantity of exports, where the quantity depends on the dollar price of British exports, $S \cdot p_x$; the dollar price is relevant to the U.S. buyer of British exports. The supply of pounds is equal to the value of British imports. We can write this as $(p_m/S) \cdot Q_m(p_m/S)$, where p_m is the U.S. dollar price of British imports and Q_m is the quantity of British imports. That is, the value of pounds supplied is the pound price of imports (p_m/S) multiplied by the quantity of British imports, where the quantity of imports depends on p_m/S. [Recall that since S is the exchange rate $S(\$/\pounds)$, dividing by S puts the dollar price of imports into British pounds. The pound price of British imports is what is relevant to the British buyer.]

We can write the excess demand for pounds, E, as

$$E = p_x \cdot Q_x(S \cdot p_x) - \frac{p_m}{S} \cdot Q_m\left(\frac{p_m}{S}\right) \tag{5A.1}$$

If we assume a perfectly elastic supply of exports and imports then we can assume that p_x and p_m remain unchanged as the quantities of exports and imports vary with the exchange rate.[20] With this assumption we can differentiate Equation (5A.1) to obtain

$$\frac{dE}{dS} = p_x \cdot \frac{dQ_x}{d(Sp_x)} \cdot \frac{d(Sp_x)}{dS}$$

$$- \frac{p_m}{S} \cdot \frac{dQ_m}{d(p_m/S)} \cdot \frac{d(p_m/S)}{dS} - Q_m \cdot \frac{d(p_m/S)}{dS}$$

or

$$\frac{dE}{dS} = p_x \cdot \frac{dQ_x}{d(Sp_x)} \cdot p_x + \frac{p_m}{S} \cdot \frac{dQ_m}{d(p_m/S)} \cdot \frac{p_m}{S^2} + \frac{p_m Q_m}{S^2}$$

Multiplying and dividing the first two terms to form elasticities, we have

$$\frac{dE}{dS} = \left(\frac{Sp_x}{Q_x} \cdot \frac{dQ_x}{d(Sp_x)}\right) \cdot \frac{p_x Q_x}{S} + \left(\frac{p_m/S}{Q_m} \cdot \frac{dQ_m}{d(p_m/S)}\right) \cdot \frac{p_m Q_m}{S^2} + \frac{p_m Q_m}{S^2} \tag{5A.2}$$

We can define the elasticity of demand for exports, η_x, and the elasticity of demand for imports, η_m, as follows:[21]

$$\eta_x = -\left(\frac{Sp_x}{Q_x} \cdot \frac{dQ_x}{dSp_x}\right) \quad \text{and} \quad \eta_m = -\left(\frac{p_m/S}{Q_m} \cdot \frac{dQ_m}{d(p_m/S)}\right)$$

[20]Stability conditions can be derived without assuming perfectly elastic supply of exports and imports, but only at the expense of considerable additional complexity. See Miltiades Chacholiades, *Principles of International Economics*, McGraw-Hill, New York, 1981, pp. 386–387, or Joan Robinson, "The Foreign Exchanges," in Joan Robinson, *Essays in the Theory of Employment*, Macmillan, London, 1939.

[21]In this appendix we use the foreign elasticity of *demand* for exports, whereas in the main text we use the domestic elasticity of *supply* of exports. We can use the foreign elasticity of demand here because we are assuming only two countries. We could have assumed two countries in the text and then used the two elasticities of demand as we do here. However, the approach in the text is more general, because it uses the demand for the currency irrespective of who buys the country's exports.

We note that these elasticities are defined in terms of the currencies in which buyers are paying for their purchases, that is, exports from Britain are defined in terms of dollar prices $S \cdot p_x$, and imports into Britain are defined in terms of pound prices p_m/S. Using these definitions in Equation (5A.2) gives

$$\frac{dE}{dS} = -\eta_x \cdot \frac{p_x Q_x}{S} - \eta_m \cdot \frac{p_m Q_m}{S^2} + \frac{p_m Q_m}{S^2}$$

where we have defined the elasticities as positive. If the foreign exchange market started from a position of balance, then

$$p_x Q_x = \frac{p_m Q_m}{S}$$

That is, the pound value of British exports equals the pound value of British imports. This enables us to write

$$\frac{dE}{dS} = -(\eta_x + \eta_m - 1) \cdot \frac{p_x Q_x}{S} \qquad (5A.3)$$

The stability of the foreign exchange market requires that as the value of the pound goes up (S increases), the excess demand for pounds must fall (E falls). Similarly, it requires that as the pound falls in value (S goes down), the excess demand for pounds must rise (E goes up). This means that for stability, E and S must move in opposite directions ($dE/dS < 0$). That is,

$$\frac{dE}{dS} = -(\eta_x + \eta_m - 1) \cdot \frac{p_x Q_x}{S} < 0 \qquad (5A.4)$$

We know that $p_x \cdot Q_x/S$ is positive. Therefore, stability of the foreign exchange market requires that

$$\eta_x + \eta_m - 1 > 0$$

or

$$\eta_x + \eta_m > 1 \qquad (5A.5)$$

We discover that for stability, the average elasticity of demand must exceed 0.5. For exchange-rate instability,

$$\eta_x + \eta_m < 1$$

When $\eta_x + \eta_m = 1$, the market is metastable, staying wherever it is. The condition (5A.5) is generally known as the Marshall-Lerner condition, after Alfred Marshall and Abba Lerner, who independently discovered it.

Because demand elasticities are generally smaller in the short run than in the long run, foreign exchange markets might be unstable in the short run, but eventually return to stability. However, if there are speculators who realize that stability occurs in the long run, the foreign exchange market may be stable in the short run even if the Marshall-Lerner condition does not hold.

PART THREE

THREE

INTERNATIONAL MANIFESTATIONS OF THE LAW OF ONE PRICE

Part 3 explains the nature of, and limitations of, two relationships that are international manifestations of the so-called law of one price. The first of these relationships occurs in the commodities markets, where the law of one price states that, when measured in a common currency, freely traded commodities should cost the same everywhere. An extension of this relationship is the principle of purchasing-power parity (PPP). The second relationship occurs in the money markets, where the law of one price states that, when measured in a common currency, interest yields and borrowing costs should be the same everywhere. This relationship is known as the interest parity principle.

Chapter 6 begins by explaining the law of one price as it applies to an individual commodity such as gold or wheat. In this context the law of one price states that the dollar cost of every commodity should be equal everywhere. This means that when prices are measured in local currency, the ratio of, for example, the dollar price of wheat in the U.S. and the pound price of wheat in Britain should be the exchange rate of dollars for pounds. If not, commodity arbitrage would occur. It is shown, however, that shipping costs, tariffs, and quotas can result in deviations from the law of one price.

Chapter 6 also explains the extension of the law of one price to goods and services in general. The extension gives rise to the PPP principle, which states that the ratio of the dollar price of a bundle of goods and services in the U.S. to the pound price of the same bundle in Britain should be the exchange rate of the dollar for the pound.

When considered as a relationship over time, PPP becomes a link between the change in exchange rates and the difference between inflation rates:

currencies of countries with rapid inflation will depreciate vis-à-vis currencies of countries with slow inflation. Chapter 6 explains the nature of this link, and why it might be broken. It is also shown that PPP in its relative or dynamic form over time can be derived by considering commodity speculation as well as commodity arbitrage. An appendix to the chapter shows PPP also follows from applying the principles of supply and demand to exchange rate determination. This means that PPP could appear even if there were no commodity arbitrage or commodity speculation.

In the context of the money market, which is the market in which short-term securities are traded, the law of one price states that the dollar rates of return and dollar costs of borrowing will be the same everywhere. If this were not so, there would be interest arbitrage. This involves borrowing in one country/currency and lending in another country/currency, with foreign exchange risk hedged on the forward exchange market. The effect of interest arbitrage is to make it irrelevant where a person invests or borrows. The relationship between interest rates and exchange rates whereby it is irrelevant in which country/currency a person invests or borrows is called the covered interest parity condition. This condition is explained in Chapter 7, along with the way that the forward exchange market can be used to eliminate exchange rate risk and exposure when engaging in interest arbitrage.

The covered interest parity condition is derived with the assumptions that there are no transaction costs, political risks of investing abroad, taxes which depend on the country/currency of investment or borrowing, or concerns over the liquidity of investment. Chapter 8 describes the effects of dropping these assumptions. In the course of this, it is shown how to decide on where to invest or borrow when transaction costs, taxes, and other "frictions" are present. It is shown that it can pay to shop around for investment and borrowing opportunities.

THE PURCHASING-POWER PARITY PRINCIPLE

Of the many influences on exchange rates mentioned in Part 2, one factor is considered to be particularly important for explaining changes in exchange rates over the long run. That factor is inflation. In this chapter we examine the theory and the evidence for a long-run connection between inflation and exchange rates. This connection has become known as the **purchasing-power parity** (PPP) **principle**. An entire chapter is devoted to this principle because it plays an important role in foreign exchange risk and exposure, and many other topics covered in the remainder of this book.

The PPP principle, which was popularized by Gustav Cassell in the 1920s, is most easily explained if we begin by considering the connection between exchange rates and the local currency prices of an individual commodity in different countries.[1] This connection between exchange rates and commodity prices is known as the **law of one price**.[2]

The Law of One Price

Virtually every opportunity for profit will catch the attention of an entrepreneur somewhere in the world. One type of opportunity that will rarely be missed is

---

[1] See Gustav Cassell, *Money and Foreign Exchange after 1914*, Macmillan, London, 1923, and Gustav Cassell, "Abnormal Deviations in International Exchange," *Economic Journal*, December 1918, pp. 413–415.

[2] It is possible to obtain PPP by applying market-efficiency arguments to financial markets, and by applying the principles of supply and demand to goods markets. The derivation of PPP from market efficiency is explained in the main body of the text of this chapter, and the derivation using supply and demand is explained in an appendix.

the chance to buy an item in one place and sell it in another for a profit. For example, if you found that gold or copper was priced at a particular dollar price in London and that the price was simultaneously higher in New York, you would buy the metal in London and ship it to New York for sale. Of course, it takes time to ship physical commodities, and so at any precise moment, prices might differ a little between markets. Transportation costs are also involved. But if there is enough of a price difference, people will begin to take advantage of it by buying commodities in the cheaper market and then shipping them to and selling them in the more expensive market.

People who buy in one market and sell in another are known as **commodity arbitragers**. Through their actions commodity arbitragers remove any profitable opportunities that may exist. They force up prices in low-cost countries and reduce prices where they are high. Normally arbitragers cease their activities only when all profitable opportunities have been exhausted, which means that except for the costs of moving goods around, including any tariffs that might be involved, prices of the same product in different markets are equal.[3]

In fact, prices of commodities should be the same in different countries even if there is no direct commodity arbitrage between countries themselves. This is because outside buyers will select the lowest price. For example, even if there were no arbitrage of wheat between Canada and the United States, the prices would need to be the same; otherwise, outside buyers would not buy from the more expensive supplier. Shipping costs between Canada and the United States set a maximum on the possible price difference between the countries, but the actual price difference is generally smaller than this maximum. For example, if Canadian and U.S. ports used to export wheat are the same distance away from Soviet receiving ports, differential shipping costs will not result in different selling prices. Similarly, even when there are tariffs, if they apply equally to both potential sources, they cannot cause price differences.[4]

When prices in different countries are expressed in the *same* currency, the outcome of commodity market arbitrage—that particular commodity prices are everywhere equal—is easily seen. For example, we observe, as in Table 6.1, that dollar prices of an ounce of gold in London, Paris, Frankfurt, Zurich, and New York are very similar. But what does it mean to have arbitrage ensure that prices are the same when they are expressed in different foreign currencies? The answer follows from the law of one price, which states that in the absence of frictions such as shipping costs, tariffs, and so on, the price of a product stated in a common currency such as the U.S. dollar is the same in every country.[5] For example, because the dollar equivalent of the price of wheat in Britain is $S(\$/\pounds) \cdot p_{UK}^{wheat}$, where p_{UK}^{wheat} is the pound price of wheat in Britain,

---

[3]We exclude quality considerations, dependability of continuous supply, and other political factors as well. We also exclude credit conditions and special deals that may be part of a contract.

[4]In the terminology of Chapter 2, one-way arbitrage creates a tighter link between prices in different countries than does traditionally discussed arbitrage.

[5]As we have just said, even in the presence of shipping costs and tariffs, the law of one price might still hold.

TABLE 6.1

GOLD PRICES IN DIFFERENT CENTERS
(Thursday, May 18, 1989, by Associated Press)
Prices of commodities tend to be similar in different
countries. If they are not, profitable arbitrage can occur.

London:	Morning fixing	$371.90
	Afternoon fixing	370.00
Paris:	Afternoon fixing	371.65
Frankfurt:	Fixing	371.76
Zurich:	Late fixing: bid	370.50
	ask	371.00
New York:	Handy & Herman (only daily quote)	370.00
New York:	Engelhard (only daily quote) fabricated	371.28

Source: *The New York Times*, May 19, 1989 (© by The
New York Times Company. Reprinted by permission).

the law of one price states that

$$p_{US}^{wheat} = S(\$/£) \cdot p_{UK}^{wheat} \qquad (6.1)$$

When the law of one price does not hold, commodity arbitragers will profit from the opportunity and thereby help restore the equality. For example, if $p_{US}^{wheat} = \$4$ per bushel, $p_{UK}^{wheat} = £2.5$ per bushel, and $S(\$/£) = 1.70$, then an arbitrager could take $400,000 and buy 100,000 bushels of wheat in the United States. If this is sent to Britain it will fetch £250,000, which at the going exchange rate will give the arbitrager £250,000 × $1.7/£ = $425,000 for an initial outlay of $400,000. However, this arbitrage will not remain profitable, because the rush to exploit the opportunity of buying wheat in the U.S. for sale in Britain will increase the U.S. price of wheat and lower the British price of wheat until wheat prices satisfy Equation (6.1).

Absolute Form of the PPP Condition

If Equation (6.1) were to hold for each and every good and service, and we computed the cost of the same basket of goods and services in Britain and the U.S., we would expect to find that

$$P_{US} = S(\$/£) \cdot P_{UK} \qquad (6.2)$$

Here, P_{US} and P_{UK} are the costs of the basket of goods and services in the U.S. in dollars, and in Britain in pounds. Equation (6.2) is the **absolute form of the purchasing-power parity condition**. The condition in this form can be rearranged to give the spot exchange rate in terms of the relative costs of the basket in the two countries, namely,

$$S(\$/£) = \frac{P_{US}}{P_{UK}} \tag{6.3}$$

For example, if the basket costs \$1000 in the U.S. and £600 in Britain, the exchange rate according to Equation (6.3) should be \$1.67/£.

The PPP condition in the absolute form in Equation (6.2) or (6.3) offers a very simple explanation for changes in exchange rates. However, it is difficult to test the validity of PPP in the form of Equations (6.2) or (6.3), because different baskets of goods are used in different countries for computing price indexes. This means that even if the law of one price holds for each individual good, price indexes, which depend on the weights attached to each good, will not conform to the law of one price.[6] Statisticians use weights appropriate to their own countries so as to be able to calculate their countries' rates of inflation. For this reason an alternative form of the PPP condition, the **relative form of PPP**, which is stated in terms of rates of inflation, can be very useful.

The Relative Form of PPP

In order to state PPP in its relative form let us define the following:

$\dot{S}(\$/£)$ is the percentage change in the spot exchange rate over a year, and $\dot{P}_{US}$ and $\dot{P}_{UK}$ are the percentage changes in the price levels in the U.S. and Britain over a year. That is, $\dot{P}_{US}$ and $\dot{P}_{UK}$ are the U.S. and British annual rates of inflation.

If the PPP condition holds in its absolute form at some moment in time, that is,

$$P_{US} = S(\$/£) \cdot P_{UK} \tag{6.2}$$

then at the end of 1 year, for PPP to continue to hold it is necessary that

$$P_{US}(1 + \dot{P}_{US}) = S(\$/£) \cdot \left[1 + \dot{S}(\$/£)\right] \cdot P_{UK}(1 + \dot{P}_{UK}) \tag{6.4}$$

The left-hand side of Equation (6.4) is the price level in the U.S. after 1 year, written as the price level in the U.S. at the beginning of the year, multiplied by 1 plus the U.S. annual rate of inflation. Similarly, the right-hand side of Equation (6.4) shows the spot exchange rate at the end of 1 year as the rate at the beginning of the year multiplied by 1 plus the rate of change in the spot

---

[6]Different baskets are used for constructing price indexes in different countries because tastes and needs differ. For example, people in cold, northern countries consume more heating oil and less olive oil than people in more temperate countries. A more detailed explanation of why different baskets of commodities mean PPP may not hold even if the law of one price holds for every individual commodity is given later in the chapter along with other reasons why PPP does not hold.

exchange rate. This is multiplied by the price level in Britain after 1 year, written as the price level at beginning of the year multiplied by 1 plus the British annual rate of inflation.

Taking the ratio of Equation (6.4) to Equation (6.2) by taking the ratios of the left-hand sides and of the right-hand sides gives by cancellation

$$\left(1 + \dot{P}_{US}\right) = \left[1 + \dot{S}(\$/£)\right] \cdot \left(1 + \dot{P}_{UK}\right) \tag{6.5}$$

Equation (6.5) can be rearranged into

$$1 + \dot{S}(\$/£) = \frac{1 + \dot{P}_{US}}{1 + \dot{P}_{UK}}$$

or

$$\dot{S}(\$/£) = \frac{1 + \dot{P}_{US}}{1 + \dot{P}_{UK}} - 1 \tag{6.6}$$

Alternatively, Equation (6.6) can be written as

$$\dot{S}(\$/£) = \frac{\dot{P}_{US} - \dot{P}_{UK}}{1 + \dot{P}_{UK}} \tag{6.7}$$

Equation (6.7) is the PPP condition in its relative or dynamic form. We note that the relative form is necessary but not sufficient for PPP in its absolute form, Equation (6.2), to hold.

To take an example, if the United States experiences inflation of 10 percent ($\dot{P}_{US} = 0.10$) and Britain 15 percent ($\dot{P}_{UK} = 0.15$), then the dollar price of pounds should fall at a rate of 4.3 percent, because

$$\dot{S}(\$/£) = \frac{\dot{P}_{US} - \dot{P}_{UK}}{1 + \dot{P}_{UK}} = \frac{0.10 - 0.15}{1.15} = -0.043, \text{ or 4.3 percent}$$

If the reverse conditions hold, with the United States having higher inflation, then $\dot{S}(\$/£)$ is positive, and the dollar falls in value against sterling by 4.5 percent:

$$\dot{S}(\$/£) = \frac{0.15 - 0.10}{1.10} = 0.045, \text{ or 4.5 percent}$$

Both values are close to the 5 percent obtained from taking an approximation of Equation (6.7) and writing instead

$$\dot{S}(\$/£) = \dot{P}_{US} - \dot{P}_{UK} \tag{6.8}$$

What the PPP condition in this approximate form says is that the movement in the exchange rate is equal to the difference between inflation rates. Equation (6.8) is a good approximation whenever the foreign inflation rate is moderate.

An Alternative Derivation of PPP

The PPP condition, which we have derived from arbitrage considerations, can also be derived by considering the behavior of speculators.[7] In order to do this let us define the *expected* rates of change of the spot exchange rate and prices in the U.S. and Britain as follows:

$\dot{S}^*(\$/£)$ is the market's overall annual expected percentage change in the spot exchange rate, and $\dot{P}^*_{US}$ and $\dot{P}^*_{UK}$ are the market's annual expected rates of inflation in a common basket of commodities in the U.S. and Britain.[8]

The expected return in terms of dollars from buying and holding the bundle of commodities in the U.S. is $\dot{P}^*_{US}$, the U.S. expected rate of inflation in this bundle of commodities.[9] The expected return *in terms of dollars* from buying and holding the same bundle of commodities in Britain is $\dot{P}^*_{UK} + \dot{S}^*(\$/£)$. This is because there are two components to the expected *dollar* return from holding commodities in Britain, namely

1 the expected change in commodity prices in British pounds, and
2 the expected change in the dollar value of the pound.

If we ignore risk, then if markets are efficient, the expected returns to buying and holding the bundle of commodities in the two countries will be driven to equality and we therefore have

$$\dot{P}^*_{US} = \dot{P}^*_{UK} + \dot{S}^*(\$/£)$$

or

$$\dot{S}^*(\$/£) = \dot{P}^*_{US} - \dot{P}^*_{UK} \tag{6.9}$$

Equation (6.9) is the relative form of the PPP condition written in terms of expected rates of change. For expectations to be rational the expectations of

---

[7]This approach to the PPP condition has been suggested by Richard Roll, "Violations of PPP and their Implications for Efficient Commodity Markets," in Marshall Sarnat and George Szegö (eds.): *International Finance and Trade*, Ballinger, Cambridge, Mass., 1979. An alternative derivation of the PPP condition, showing it to be the natural result of applying the principles of supply and demand to exchange rates and commodity prices, is given in the appendix to this chapter.

[8]Of course, in reality different people are likely to hold different expectations about the change in the spot exchange rate and commodity prices. It is traditional in finance to ignore this problem of heterogeneous expectations, and to assume for simplicity that speculators have homogeneous expectations.

[9]We do not include costs of storage because, although the presence of storage costs will reduce expected returns in the U.S. and Britain, if storage costs are similar in the two countries they will cancel.

variables should on average equal realized rates of change, so that there are no persistent biases.[10] That is, if expectations are rational, then on average $\dot{S}^*(\$/£)$, $\dot{P}^*_{US}$, and $\dot{P}^*_{UK}$ should equal the actual rates of change in these variables, so that for Equation (6.9) to hold, it is necessary that Equation (6.8) also hold on average over a long period of time. We see that speculation, in conjunction with expectations being rational, means that the PPP condition in its relative form holds on average.

If PPP held in its relative form (6.8), we would be able to explain short-run changes in exchange rates from short-run differences in inflation rates. If, instead, PPP held in its relative form (6.9), then by arguing that on average over a long interval of time the expected and actual change are equal, we would be able to explain long-run changes in exchange rates from long-run differences in inflation rates. Unfortunately, PPP does not fit the data very well. This is because, as we saw in Chapters 4 and 5, there are many factors other than commodity prices which influence exchange rates, and these other factors can dominate inflation, at least in the short run. However, rather than simply dismiss the PPP condition as an explanation of exchange rates, let us consider the evidence in more detail to see whether there are circumstances under which PPP gives useful predictions.

The Empirical Evidence on PPP

A major problem in testing the validity of the PPP condition is the need to use accurate price indexes for the measurement of $\dot{P}_{US}$ and $\dot{P}_{UK}$ or the inflation rates for the countries being studied. Price indexes cover many items, and what is happening to relative prices within an index is not revealed.

In an effort to use as specific a set of prices as can be obtained and to avoid index-number problems, J. David Richardson employed data on prices of narrowly classified industrial items in the U.S. and Canada.[11] The classifications are as specific as "cement," "animal feeds," "bakery products," "chewing gum," and "fertilizers." That is, Richardson examined the law of one price rather than the PPP condition. Clearly, if the law of one price does not hold between the U.S. and Canada, there is not much hope for the PPP condition, especially between countries further apart and more different in the contents of price indexes than are the U.S. and Canada.

Richardson estimated an equation similar to that in Equation (6.8) for several commodity groups, and found that it did not fit the data well in most commodity categories. Richardson's results suggest that even the law of one price is violated, at least in its relative form.

---

[10] The lack of bias in expectations if expectations are rational is one of the conditions of rationality described by John F. Muth, "Rational Expectations and the Theory of Price Movements," *Econometrica*, July 1961, pp. 315–335.

[11] J. David Richardson, "Some Empirical Evidence on Commodity Arbitrage and the Law of One Price," *Journal of International Economics*, May 1978, pp. 341–351.

A possible explanation of Richardson's results on the law of one price is the differential pricing of the same object in different countries by multinational firms. Such differential pricing, with higher prices charged where demand is more inelastic, is predicted by the theory of discriminating monopoly. Firms with monopoly power may be able to prevent arbitragers from taking advantage of price differences by withholding supply from any outlets for the monopolists' products where there is cooperation with arbitragers.[12] This possibility is supported by the observation that where there is little or no opportunity for price discrimination, as in the case of commodity markets, the law of one price does appear to hold in the long run although not in the short run.[13]

Irving Kravis and Richard E. Lipsey extensively studied the relationship between inflation rates and exchange rates using different price indexes.[14] They used the "GNP implicit deflator" (which includes prices of all goods and services in the GNP), the consumer price index, and the producer price index. They also took care to distinguish between goods that enter into international trade (tradable goods) and those that do not (nontradable goods). They discovered, using these many prices and price indexes, that there were departures from purchasing-power parity. They concluded, "As a matter of general judgement we express our opinion that the results do not support the notion of a tightly integrated international price structure. The record . . . shows that price levels can move apart sharply without rapid correction through arbitrage."[15] They did find that PPP holds more closely for tradable goods than for nontradable goods, but the departures from PPP even over relatively long periods were substantial even for traded goods.

Hans Genberg concentrated on testing to see whether PPP holds more precisely when exchange rates are flexible rather than fixed.[16] The most important aspects of his conclusion can be seen by comparing the two columns in Table 6.2. The table gives the average deviations, in percentages, from an estimated PPP condition. The estimates show departures from PPP for each country with its combined trading partners. The importance of each partner is judged by the share of that partner in the country's export trade. The PPP condition is then statistically fitted between the country, for example, Belgium, and the weighted average of its trading partners. The table shows, for example, that for the United States from 1957 to 1976, the actual difference between the inflation rate in the United States and the inflation rate in its (weighted) trading

---

[12] Substantial evidence supports the discriminating-monopoly argument. See Peter Isard, "How Far Can We Push the 'Law of one Price'?," *American Economic Review*, December 1977, pp. 942–948.

[13] See Aris A. Protopapadakis and Hans R. Stoll, "The Law of One Price in International Commodity Markets: A Reformulation and Some Formal Tests," *Journal of International Money and Finance*, September 1986, pp. 335–360.

[14] Irving B. Kravis and Richard E. Lipsey, "Price Behavior in the Light of Balance of Payments Theories," *Journal of International Economics*, May 1978, pp. 193–246.

[15] *Ibid.*, p. 216.

[16] Hans Genberg, "Purchasing Power Parity under Fixed and Flexible Exchange Rates," *Journal of International Economics*, May 1978, pp. 247–267.

TABLE 6.2
AVERAGE ABSOLUTE DEVIATIONS FROM PPP
(In Percent)
There are larger departures from PPP for the years
1957 – 1976, which include a period of flexible exchange
rates. However, this could be because conditions
were more volatile during the 1967 – 1976 period.

	1957 – 1966	1957 – 1976
United States	1.2	3.8
United Kingdom	0.5	3.8
Austria	1.3	2.0
Belgium	1.4	2.1
Denmark	1.3	2.0
France	2.5	3.0
Germany	1.3	2.7
Italy	1.2	5.8
Netherlands	0.5	1.7
Norway	0.9	2.9
Sweden	0.7	1.4
Switzerland	0.7	5.8
Canada	2.0	3.3
Japan	1.9	3.8
Average	1.2	3.2

Source: Hans Genberg, "Purchasing Power Parity under Fixed and Flexible Exchange Rates," *Journal of International Economics*, North-Holland Publishing Company, May 1978, p. 260.

partners differed from the exchange rate change by, on the average, 3.8 percent per annum.

The second column of Table 6.2 includes the flexible exchange rate period which began in 1973. We find from the average deviations from PPP given at the bottom of the table that the addition of the flexible period makes the deviations increase. The implication is that there were greater violations during the flexible years, 1973 to 1976.[17]

Niels Thygesen has summarized the results of a study by the Commission of the European Communities, which set out to discover how long it takes for inflation rates to restore PPP after exchange rates have been artificially changed by the government to gain competitiveness for exports.[18] The idea is that a devaluation should raise the rate of inflation until PPP is restored. This could

[17]Genberg also discovered that most of the departures from PPP resulted from movements in exchange rates rather than from changes in price levels. This supports Richardson's conclusion. See also Mario Blejer and Hans Genberg, "Permanent and Transitory Shocks to Exchange Rates: Measurement and Implications for Purchasing Power Parity," unpublished manuscript, International Monetary Fund, 1981.

[18]Niels Thygesen, "Inflation and Exchange Rates: Evidence and Policy Guidelines for the European Community," *Journal of International Economics*, May 1978, pp. 301–317.

come about via higher import prices and consequent wage demands setting off reactions elsewhere in the economy. Using economic models of Britain and Italy, the study concluded that it took 5 to 6 years for inflation differentials to restore the PPP condition. However, Thygesen also observed that 75 percent of the return to PPP was achieved within 2 years.

Another study that examined how long it takes for PPP to be restored after being disturbed is that of John Hodgson and Patricia Phelps.[19] They used a statistical model that allows lags and discovered that differential inflation rates precede the change in exchange rates with a lag of up to 18 months. A similar conclusion was reached by William Folks, Jr., and Stanley Stansell.[20] Their purpose was to forecast changes in exchange rates, and they discovered that exchange rates do adjust to relative inflation rates, but with a long lag.

A conclusion different from that of Hodgson and Phelps and of Folks and Stansell was reached by Richard Rogalski and Joseph Vinso.[21] They chose a flexible-exchange-rate period, 1920 to 1924, and studied relative inflation for six countries.[22] Rogalski and Vinso concluded that there is no lag. This, they claim, is what would be expected in an efficient market, because relative inflation rates are publicly available information and should therefore be reflected in market prices such as exchange rates. This question of efficiency in the spot exchange rate has been tackled by Jacob Frenkel and Michael Mussa, who argue that even if we do observe departures from PPP, this does not imply that foreign exchange markets are inefficient. Exchange rates, they show, move like stock and bond prices. Indeed, Frenkel and Mussa find average monthly variations in exchange rates to be more pronounced than the variation of stock prices.[23] This is not itself evidence of efficiency, which refers more to the pattern of departures from PPP over time.[24]

[19]John A. Hodgson and Patricia Phelps, "The Distributed Impact of Price-Level Variation on Floating Exchange Rates," *Review of Economics and Statistics*, February 1975, pp. 58–64.

[20]William R. Folks, Jr., and Stanley R. Stansell, "The Use of Discriminant Analysis in Forecasting Exchange Rate Movements," *Journal of International Business Studies*, spring 1975, pp. 33–50.

[21]Richard J. Rogalski and Joseph D. Vinso, "Price Level Variations as Predictors of Flexible Exchange Rates," *Journal of International Business Studies*, spring 1977, pp. 71–81.

[22]This period was also studied by Jacob A. Frenkel, not because exchange rates were flexible but because the inflationary experience was so extreme. See Jacob A. Frenkel, "Purchasing Power Parity: Doctrinal Perspective and Evidence from the 1920's," *Journal of International Economics*, May 1978, pp. 169–191.

[23]Jacob Frenkel and Michael Mussa, "Efficiency of Foreign Exchange Markets and Measures of Turbulence," Working Paper 476, National Bureau of Economic Research, Cambridge, Mass., 1981.

[24]There have been numerous other studies of PPP which we have not mentioned. These studies include Hali J. Edison and Jan Tore Klovland, "A Quantitative Reassessment of the Purchasing Power Parity Hypothesis: Evidence from Norway and the United Kingdom," International Finance Discussion Paper Number 231, Board of Governors of the Federal Reserve, October 1983; David T. King, "The Performance of Exchange Rates in the Recent Period of Floating," *Southern Economic Journal*, April 1977, pp. 1582–1587, Moon H. Lee, *Purchasing Power Parity*, Marcel Decker, New York, 1976; Lawrence H. Officer, "The Purchasing Power Theory of Exchange Rates, *Staff Papers*, International Monetary Fund, March 1976, pp. 1–60; and Louka T. Papaefstratiou, *The Reemergence of the Purchasing Power Parity Doctrine in the 1970s*, Special Papers in International Economics, No. 13, Princeton University, December 1979.

Our survey of the empirical evidence and the conclusion that violations of PPP do occur should come as no surprise. Anyone who has traveled extensively and knows about prices abroad will probably feel that purchasing-power parity rarely occurs. There are countries that are notoriously expensive, and they appear to stay this way over long periods. This proves, without any formal empirical evidence, that there are serious departures from PPP, at least in the absolute or static form, where price levels rather than inflation rates are compared. There are two major reasons that we can offer as to why this can occur.

Reasons for Departures from PPP

Restrictions on Movement of Goods   It is obvious that prices can differ between two markets by up to the cost of transportation without commodity-market arbitrage taking place. Clearly, if it costs $0.50 per bushel to ship wheat between the United States and Britain, the price difference must exceed $0.50 in either direction before arbitrage will occur. This means a possible deviation from the absolute form of purchasing-power parity for wheat that spans a full dollar.[25] Tariffs and quotas will have a similar effect. If one country has, for example, a 15-percent import duty, prices within the country will have to move more than 15 percent above those in the other before it pays to ship and cover the duties that are involved.

The effect of duties is different from the effect of transportation costs. Duties do not have a symmetrical effect. As a result of duties, prices can move higher only in the country which has the import duties. But whether it be transportation costs or duties that must be paid, they explain departures from PPP only in its absolute or static form. Once the maximum price difference from shipping costs and duties has been reached, the PPP principle in its relative or dynamic form should explain movements through time that push against the maximum price difference. For example, suppose that prices at existing exchange rates are already 25 percent higher in one country because of a 15-percent import duty and 10-percent transportation costs. If that country has an inflation rate that is 10 percent higher than the inflation rate in another country, its exchange rate will have to fall, on the average, by 10 percent to prevent commodity arbitrage.

Quotas, which are limits on the amounts of different commodities that can be imported, generally mean that price differences can become quite sizable, because commodity arbitragers are limited in their ability to narrow the gaps. Like import duties, they provide a reason for persistent departures from PPP.

Price Indexes and Nontraded Outputs   We have already observed in describing the work of Irving Kravis and Richard E. Lipsey that many of the items that

---

[25]As we mentioned, however, competitive pressures for similar prices to third countries equidistant from Britain and the United States will keep prices in a narrower range than would result from direct arbitrage between Britain and the United States.

are included in the commonly used price indexes do not enter into international trade. We cannot, therefore, invoke the notion of commodity arbitrage to create an equivalent of Equation (6.1) for these items. Most difficult to arbitrage between countries are immovable items such as land and buildings; highly perishable commodities such as fresh milk, vegetables, eggs, and some fruits; and also services such as hotel accommodations and repairs. These "untraded" items can allow departures from PPP to persist when we measure inflation from conventional market-bundle price indexes.

To some extent, a tendency toward parity even in untraded items can be maintained by the movement of the buyers instead of the movement of the items themselves. For example, factories and office complexes can be located where land and rent are cheap. Vacationers can travel to places where holidays are less expensive. The movement of *buyers* tends to keep prices in different countries in line with each other.

The relative prices of traded versus nontraded outputs will not differ greatly between countries if *producers* within each country can move into the production of the nontraded outputs when their prices are very high. Consequently, if comparative advantages do not differ significantly between nations (that is, the nations have similar relative efficiencies in producing different goods), the relative prices of traded versus nontraded items will be kept similar between countries by the prospective movement of domestic producers. But if the prices of traded goods satisfy PPP, then so will the prices of nontraded items if they move with the prices of traded goods. However, we do require that the producers can move between traded and nontraded goods, which is frequently very difficult. And even when producers can move, the price adjustment can take a very long time, during which departures from PPP can persist.[26]

We should note that even if the price of each individual good were equalized between countries, price *indexes* could differ if the importance of each item in the indexes of different countries also differs. This will happen if the populations of different countries have different tastes. That is, with different baskets of goods in different countries because people buy different products, PPP will not hold even though the law of one price holds for every item. In order to see this, suppose that beef has twice the weighting in the U.S. price index that it has in the British price index, but that fish has half the weighting. If beef prices increase by 25 percent and fish prices increase by 10 percent in both countries, so that the law of one price holds from year to year, the U.S. price index will increase by more than the British price index; the U.S. price index weighs the more rapidly inflating item more heavily, and vice versa. What we find is that even if the law of one price holds exactly for every item, PPP may not.

[26] Mario Blejer and Ayre Hillman have provided a formal model with the costs of commodity arbitrage allowing temporary departures from PPP. See their article "A Proposition on Short-Run Departures from the Law of One Price: Unanticipated Inflation, Relative Price Dispersion, and Commodity Arbitrage, *European Economic Review*, January 1982, pp. 51–60.

Statistical Problems of Evaluating PPP*

It has been suggested that the difficulty finding empirical support for PPP may be due to the statistical procedures that have been used.[27] We can indicate the problems with the statistical procedures by examining the bases for judging empirical support for PPP.

Most tests of PPP are based on estimates of a regression equation that in the context of the dollar-pound exchange rate can be written

$$\dot{S}(\$/£) = \beta_0 + \beta_1(\dot{P}_{US} - \dot{P}_{UK}) + \mu \qquad (6.10)$$

where μ is the *ex ante* regression error. It is argued that if PPP is valid, then in estimates of Equation (6.10), β_0 should be close to zero, β_1 should be close to 1.0, and the *ex post* regression errors should be small.[28] This is because in such a case the regression equation reduces to Equation (6.8). The statistical problems that can result in incorrect rejection of PPP are:

1 *Errors in measuring the inflation differential $\dot{P}_{US} - \dot{P}_{UK}$.* It is a characteristic of the regression methodology that errors in the measurement of explanatory variables bias regression coefficients toward zero.[29] This means that if the inflation differential is poorly measured because of the problem of different baskets being used in each country, then we could find the estimated β_1 to be smaller than 1.0 even if the true β_1 is exactly equal to 1.0.

2 *Simultaneous determination of the variables $\dot{S}(\$/£)$ and $\dot{P}_{US} - \dot{P}_{UK}$.* It is another characteristic of the regression methodology that if the direction of causation goes from inflation to exchange rates and vice versa, then failure to use simultaneous-equation methods biases coefficient such as β_1, again usually toward zero.[30] In the case of PPP, causation does go both ways because changes in exchange rates affect inflation and inflation causes changes in exchange rates.[31]

---

*Sections marked with an asterisk can be omitted on first reading without loss of continuity.

[27] The statistical problems have been surveyed by John Pippenger, "Arbitrage and Efficient Markets Interpretations of Purchasing Power Parity: Theory and Evidence," *Economic Review*, Federal Reserve Bank of San Francisco, Winter 1986, pp. 31–48.

[28] Small errors mean that the equation fits well. The "goodness of fit" measure that is usually used is the R^2 statistic, which gives the fraction of the variation in the dependent variable, $\dot{S}(\$/£)$, that is explained by the explanatory variable(s), in this case, $\dot{P}_{US} - \dot{P}_{UK}$.

[29] This occurs however many explanatory variables are included. See Maurice D. Levi, "Errors in the Variables Bias in the Presence of Correctly Measured Variables," *Econometrica*, September 1973, pp. 985–986, and Maurice D. Levi, "Measurement Errors and Bounded OLS Estimates," *Journal of Econometrics*, September 1977, pp. 165–171.

[30] This bias exists if common factors affect $\dot{P}_{US} - \dot{P}_{UK}$ and $\dot{S}(\$/£)$. See Maurice D. Levi, "World-Wide Effects and Import Elasticities," *Journal of International Economics*, May 1976, pp. 203–214.

[31] Researchers who have tried to overcome the statistical problems have tended to support PPP as a long-run condition. For example, by considering only the trends in variables seen after removing "noise" in the data, Mark Rush and Steven Husted show PPP holds for the U.S. dollar versus other currencies. See Mark Rush and Steven Husted, "Purchasing Power Parity in the Long Run" *Canadian Journal of Economics*, February 1985, pp. 137–145 Similarly, by considering many countries concurrently over many periods, Craig Hakkio achieves a similar effect, and is unable to reject PPP. Craig S. Hakkio, "A Re-examination of Purchasing Power Parity: A Multi-Country and Multi-Period Study," *Journal of International Economics*, November 1984, pp. 265–277.

SUMMARY

1 The law of one price states that a commodity will have the same price in terms of a common currency in every country. The law follows from commodity arbitrage, which involves buying in the cheapest country if prices are different.

2 It follows from the law of one price that the dollar price of a commodity in the U.S. equals the pound price of the commodity in Britain multiplied by the spot exchange rate of dollars per British pound. Deviations from this relationship can be caused by shipping costs.

3 The principle of purchasing-power parity (PPP) is the extension of the law of one price to prices of a basket of goods. In its absolute form, PPP says that the dollar price of a basket of goods in the U.S. is the pound price of the basket in Britain, multiplied by the exchange rate of dollars per pound.

4 In its relative form, PPP says that the rate of change of the exchange rate is equal to the difference between inflation rates.

5 Speculation and efficient markets also produce the relative form of the PPP conditions in terms of expected values.

6 Empirical support or the PPP condition is weak, although there is some evidence it may hold in the long run.

7 The reasons the law of one price and PPP do not hold include transportation costs, tariffs, quotas, and the fact that there are goods and services that are nontradable. PPP may not hold even if the law of one price holds for every item because of different weights for different items in different countries' price indexes.

8 The fact that empirical evidence does not support PPP may be due to statistical difficulties.

QUESTIONS

1 Why might the law of one price hold even in the presence of import tariffs?

2 Why might there be departures from PPP even if the law of one price holds for every commodity?

3 If speculators are risk-averse, could this affect the accuracy of the link between the expected change in the exchange rate and the difference between expected inflation rates?

4 In predicting the change in exchange rate due to differences in inflation from the approximate PPP condition in Equation (6.8) rather than the precise condition in Equation (6.7), does it matter if the rate of inflation is high? In other words, is the accuracy of the approximate PPP condition negatively affected by the level of inflation?

5 Why is it easier to test the relative than the absolute form of PPP?

BIBLIOGRAPHY

Balassa, Bela: "The Purchasing-Power Parity Doctrine: A Re-Appraisal," *Journal of Political Economy*, December 1964, pp. 584–596. Reprinted in Richard N. Cooper (ed.): *International Finance: Selected Readings*, Penguin Books, Middlesex, U.K., 1969.

Dornbusch, Rudiger and Dwight Jaffee: "Purchasing Power Parity and Exchange Rate Problems: Introduction" and the papers included in "Purchasing Power Parity: A Symposium," *Journal of International Economics*, May 1978, pp. 157–351.

Gaillot, Henry J.: "Purchasing Power Parity as an Explanation of Long-Term Changes in Exchange Rates," *Journal of Money, Credit and Banking*, August 1970, pp. 348–357.

Lee, Moon H.: *Purchasing Power Parity*, Marcel Decker, New York, 1976.

Officer, Lawrence H.: "The Purchasing Power Theory of Exchange Rates: A Review Article," *Staff Papers*, International Monetary Fund, March 1976, pp. 1–60.

Pippenger, John: "Arbitrage and Efficient Market Interpretations of Purchasing Power Parity: Theory and Evidence," *Economic Review*, Federal Reserve Bank of San Francisco, Winter 1986, pp. 31–48.

Roll, Richard: "Violations of PPP and their Implications for Efficient Commodity Markets," in Marshall Sarnat and George Szegö (eds.): *International Finance and Trade*, Ballinger, Cambridge, Mass., 1979.

Shapiro, Alan C.: "What Does Purchasing Power Parity Mean?" *Journal of International Money and Finance*, December 1983, pp. 295–318.

APPENDIX 6.1: PPP and the Principles of Supply and Demand

In the text we "derived" the law of one price by noting that commodity arbitrage would occur if the dollar equivalent prices were not equal everywhere. We stated that the accuracy with which the law of one price holds is limited by shipping costs, quotas, and other limitations on the movement of goods and services.[32] We generalized the law of one price into the PPP condition, but noted in doing so that problems in calculating price indexes allow deviations from PPP to exist even if the law of one price holds for every item. We also derived a version of PPP in the text by considering efficient commodity speculation. This version was stated in terms of expectations, and it was noted that since expected inflation and exchange rates are equal to actual inflation and exchange rates only on average, speculation produces PPP only on average.[33] In short, there were lots of caveats in the text in coming up with the PPP condition.

In this appendix we demonstrate that it is not necessary to invoke either arbitrage or speculation to produce the PPP condition. We show that PPP is the perfectly natural outcome of the effect of inflation on the supply of and demand for currencies in the foreign exchange market. That is, even if arbitrage and speculation were very seriously limited by the factors we have listed, or even if arbitrage and speculation were prohibited, shifts in currency supply and demand curves from inflation would still produce the PPP condition. This means that PPP is an outcome of considering inflation within the supply-and-demand framework of exchange rates described in Chapter 5. However, to obtain PPP we first have to explain the derivation of the import demand and export supply curves that we merely assumed in Chapter 5.

---

[32] We pointed out that shipping costs between countries sets a maximum on price deviations because buyers who are equidistant to different suppliers will tend to drive suppliers' prices to equality despite costly shipping between the suppliers.

[33] Furthermore, we ignored risk when equating expected dollar returns.

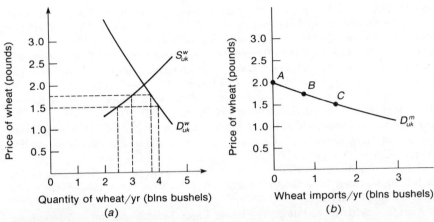

FIGURE 6A.1
DERIVING THE DEMAND FOR IMPORTS. The quantity of imports demanded at each price is the excess of the quantity of the product that is demanded over the quantity of the product produced in the country. That is, it is the horizontal distance between the country's demand curve for the product and its supply curve.

DERIVING THE IMPORT DEMAND CURVE

Figure 6A.1*a* shows the demand for wheat in Britain, D_{UK}^w, and the quantity of wheat British farmers supply at each price, S_{UK}^w. If Britain can take the world price of wheat as given, whether Britain is an importer or exporter of wheat depends on the world price of wheat translated into pounds. For example, if the world price of wheat is equivalent to £1.5/bushel, Britain produces 2.5 billion bushels per year and consumes 4 billion bushels per year, so that imports are 1.5 billion bushels per year. At £2.0 per bushel Britain is self-sufficient, producing and consuming 3.5 billion bushels per year, and at prices above £2.0 per bushel Britain is a wheat exporter.[34]

If we consider only pound prices of wheat below £2 per bushel, where Britain is a wheat importer, we can plot the British demand curve for imports by selecting different pound prices and measuring the distance between D_{UK}^w and S_{UK}^w at each price. These distances, which are the quantities of wheat imported at each price, are plotted against the prices at which they occur. By doing this we obtain the British import demand curve D_{UK}^m shown in Figure 6A.1*b*. This is the import demand curve that we took as our starting point in Figure 5.1*a*.

DERIVING THE CURRENCY'S SUPPLY CURVE

As we showed in the previous chapter, the supply curve for pounds is determined from the value of imports at each exchange rate. Assuming wheat is the only import, this involves multiplying the pound price of wheat at each exchange rate by the quantity of

---

[34]Strictly speaking, production minus consumption is equal to exports plus the addition to inventory.

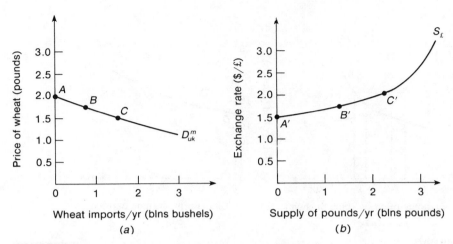

FIGURE 6A.2
DERIVING THE SUPPLY OF POUNDS. The currency supply curve is derived from the import demand curve by taking each possible exchange rate and finding the price of imports at that exchange rate. We then calculate the value of imports as the price of imports multiplied by the quantity of imports, and plot the value of imports against the exchange rate at which it occurs.

wheat imported. The result is the number of pounds supplied to the foreign exchange market at each exchange rate. Assuming that the world price of wheat is \$3/bushel, we can construct the supply curve of pounds, $S_£$, in Figure 6A.2b. This is the same as curve $S_£$ in Figure 5.1b.

DERIVING THE SUPPLY OF EXPORTS

Curves D_{UK}^0 and S_{UK}^0 in Figure 6A.3a show respectively British oil demand and supply at different oil prices. We can construct the export supply curve from D_{UK}^0 and S_{UK}^0 by considering different pound prices of oil, and computing the excess of quantity supplied over quantity demanded at each price. For example, at £12.50 per barrel oil consumption equals oil production, so that exports are zero. This is point D on the export supply curve, S_{UK}^x, shown in Figure 6A.3b. At £14 per barrel oil consumption is 0.2 billion barrels and production is 0.3 billion barrels, so that exports are 0.1 billion barrels. This is point E in Figure 6A.3b. Proceeding in this way, we obtain the supply curve of exports, S_{UK}^x, that we merely assumed in Figure 5.2a.

We explained in the text that the demand for pounds to pay for Britain's oil exports is equal to the *value* of oil exports. Assuming that the world price of oil is \$25 per barrel and considering different exchange rates, we derive the demand curve for pounds, $D_£$, in Figure 6A.4b, which is the same as $D_£$ in Figure 5.2b.

When we plot the supply and demand curves for pounds in the same figure as we did in Figure 5.3, we find that the exchange rate that equates the supply of and demand for pounds before inflation has occurred. Let us now consider the effect of inflation.

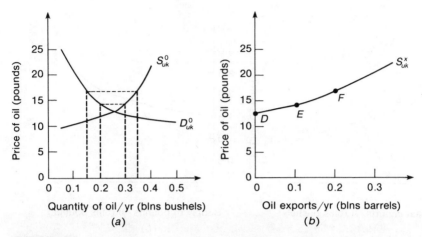

FIGURE 6A.3
DERIVING THE SUPPLY OF EXPORTS. The quantity of exports supplied at each price is the excess of the quantity of the product that is supplied over the quantity demanded in the country. That is, it is the horizontal distance between the country's supply curve of the product and its demand curve.

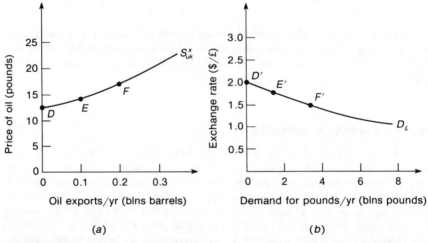

FIGURE 6A.4
DERIVING THE DEMAND FOR POUNDS. The currency demand curve is derived from the export supply curve by considering different exchange rates and finding the price of exports at each exchange rate. We then calculate the value of exports as the price of exports multiplied by the quantity of exports, and plot the value of exports against the exchange rate at which it occurs.

INFLATION, IMPORT DEMAND, AND EXPORT SUPPLY

Let us assume that Britain experiences a 25-percent inflation. If all prices and wages in Britain increase 25 percent during a year, the British demand curves for wheat and oil at the end of the year will be 25 percent higher than at the beginning of the year. That is, they are shifted vertically upward by 25 percent. This is because with all prices and wages higher by the same amount, real incomes and relative prices are unchanged. Therefore, after the 25-percent inflation the same quantities of goods are purchased at prices 25 percent higher than before inflation.

At the same time as the British demand curves for wheat and oil shift upward, so do the supply curves of wheat and oil. The easiest way of thinking about why this occurs is to recall that the supply curves for competitive firms are their marginal cost curves.[35] If all wages and prices increase 25 percent, the marginal costs are 25 percent higher, and therefore so are the supply curves. We can reach the same conclusion if we think of supply as being set to equate marginal cost and marginal revenue. At any given output the marginal cost is 25 percent higher after inflation, and therefore if the marginal revenue is also 25 percent higher from the demand curve shifting up 25 percent, there is no reason to change output; marginal cost still equals marginal revenue.

The left-hand diagrams in Figure 6A.5 show the supply and demand curves for wheat and oil before and after 25-percent inflation. The supply and demand curves before inflation are identified by P_0, the price level at the beginning of the year, and those after inflation are identified by P_1, the price level at the end of the year.

The right-hand diagrams in Figure 6A.5 show the demand for imports and supply of exports before and after 25-percent inflation. As before, P_0 signifies the curve before inflation, and P_1 after inflation. We recall that the demand for imports and supply of exports are obtained by selecting different prices and calculating the difference between domestic supply and demand at each price. For example, before inflation, the demand for imports of wheat was zero at £2/bushel. After inflation, it is zero at £2.50/bushel. That is, the intercept of $D_{UK}^m(P_1)$ with the price axis is 25 percent higher than the intercept of $D_{UK}^m(P_0)$. Since the slopes of the supply and demand curves for wheat are the same before and after inflation, the slope of the demand curve for wheat imports is the same before and after inflation. Therefore, we find that $D_{UK}^m(P_1)$ is above $D_{UK}^m(P_0)$ by 25 percent, not only at the intercept with the price axis, but at every other quantity of imports. Similarly, the supply curve of oil exports intercepts the price axis at £12.50 before inflation, because this is where domestic oil supply equals demand. After inflation the intercept is at a price 25 percent higher. Because the slopes of the supply and demand curves for oil are the same before and after inflation, the slope of the export supply curve is the same before and after inflation. Therefore, as in the case of the demand curve for imports, the supply curve of exports shifts upwards 25 percent at every quantity.

We can employ Figure 6A.5 to show how inflation affects currency supply and demand curves and hence exchange rates. There are different effects according to whether inflation occurs only in Britain or in Britain and elsewhere, and so we consider these situations in turn.

---

[35]The individual competitive firm's short-run supply curve is that firm's marginal cost curve, and the competitive industry's short-run supply curve is the horizontal sum of all existing firms' marginal cost curves. Long-run supply curves which consider newly entering firms also shift up by the rate of inflation, because inflation also increases the marginal costs of new firms.

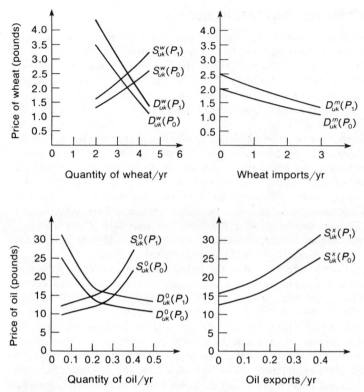

FIGURE 6A.5
INFLATION IN RELATION TO SUPPLY AND DEMAND. Inflation in all
prices and incomes shifts demand and supply curves vertically
upward by the amount of inflation. Thus the demand curve for imports
and supply curve of exports also shift vertically upward by the amount
of inflation.

INFLATION IN ONLY ONE COUNTRY

Figure 6A.6a shows the supply and demand curves for pounds that are implied by the
demand curve for imports and supply curve of exports when inflation of 25 percent
occurs in Britain but not in the U.S. The curves labeled $S_£(P_0)$ and $D_£(P_0)$ are those
existing before inflation, and are the same supply and demand curves for pounds used in
Figure 5.3. The curves labeled $S_£(P_1)$ and $D_£(P_1)$ are the supply and demand curves for
pounds after 25-percent inflation in Britain but not elsewhere. The derivation of $S_£(P_1)$
and $D_£(P_1)$ is based on the following somewhat lengthy reasoning.

Because inflation occurs only in Britain, we can take the U.S. dollar prices of wheat
and oil as unchanged. Considering first the supply curve of pounds, we know from Figure
6A.5 that the same quantity of wheat is imported after inflation as before inflation if the
pound price of wheat is increased 25 percent; this follows immediately from the fact that
$D^m_{UK}(P_1)$ is 25 percent higher than $D^m_{UK}(P_0)$. When the same quantity of wheat is

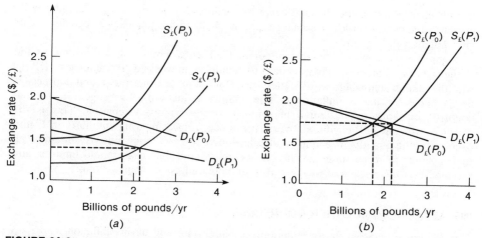

FIGURE 6A.6
INFLATION AND EXCHANGE RATES. With inflation in one country only (part *a*), the same quantity of exports is sold after a depreciation of the country's currency equal to the rate of inflation. The same *quantity* sold at the higher prices means the *value* of exports is higher by the rate of inflation. This means the currency demand curve shifts down in proportion to the inflation rate and to the right by the same proportion. The same argument applies to currency supply. Therefore the exchange rate of the inflating country depreciates by its rate of inflation. When inflation also occurs elsewhere (part *b*), the same *quantities* are imported and exported at the same exchange rates at the postinflation prices. Therefore, the *values* of imports and exports are higher by the rate of inflation at each exchange rate. That is, the currency supply and demand curves shift to the right in proportion to the rate of inflation, and the exchange rate is unaffected.

imported at a price that is 25 percent higher, the supply of pounds, which is the pound price of imports multiplied by the quantity of imports, is also 25 percent higher. The change in exchange rate that will achieve a 25-percent-higher pound price and a corresponding 25-percent-higher supply of pounds is a 25-percent depreciation of the pound. This follows because the dollar price of wheat is unchanged. That is, at an exchange rate that is 25 percent lower, the pound price of wheat is 25 percent higher and the quantity of imports is unchanged. Therefore, at an exchange rate that is 25 percent lower there is a 25-percent-higher supply of pounds. This means that inflation of 25 percent shifts the supply curve for pounds downward and to the right by 25 percent, so that points on $S_£(P_1)$ are 25 percent below and to the right of corresponding points on $S_£(P_0)$.

The reasoning behind the effect of inflation on the demand for pounds is similar to the reasoning behind its effect on the supply of pounds. Figure 6A.5 shows that the same quantity of oil is exported after inflation as before inflation if the pound price of oil increases by 25 percent; $S^x_{UK}(P_1)$ is 25 percent above $S^x_{UK}(P_0)$. Because the dollar price of oil is unchanged, to achieve a 25-percent-higher oil price we need a 25-percent pound depreciation. Therefore, at a 25-percent-lower exchange rate in Figure 6A.6*a* we have a 25-percent-higher pound price of oil and the same quantity of oil exports. This represents a 25-percent increase in the demand for pounds. Therefore, the effect of inflation is to shift each point on the demand curve for pounds downward and to the right by 25 percent; at a 25-percent-lower exchange rate the demand for pounds is 25 percent higher after inflation than before.

Figure 6A.6a shows the supply and demand curves for pounds shifted downward and to the right by 25 percent. If we compare the equilibrium where $S_£(P_1)$ intersects $D_£(P_1)$ with the equilibrium where $S_£(P_0)$ intersects $D_£(P_0)$, we see that the pound depreciates by 25 percent. That is, inflation in one country reduces the exchange rate of that country's currency by the same percentage as the country's inflation. This is the conclusion of the PPP condition. We also can see from comparing equilibria in Figure 6A.6a that the quantity of pounds traded also increases by 25 percent. We should recall that in order to reach these conclusions we considered only exports and imports, and assumed that *all* prices and wages in Britain increased by the same amount.

INFLATION ALSO IN OTHER COUNTRIES

The difference between having inflation only in Britain and having inflation in Britain and elsewhere is that in the latter case we must allow for increases in the dollar prices of the imported and exported products. Let us assume inflation outside Britain is also 25 percent, so that the dollar prices of wheat and oil increase to $3.75/bushel and $31.25/barrel.

Let us consider first the supply curve of pounds. We know from our earlier discussion and from Figure 6A.5 that the quantity of wheat imports after inflation is the same as before inflation if the pound price of wheat increases by the amount of inflation, that is, 25 percent. When the price of wheat increases from $3/bushel to $3.75/bushel, the pound price of wheat increases by 25 percent if the exchange rate is unchanged. That is, at the same exchange rate as before there is a 25 percent increase in the pound price of wheat and the same quantity of wheat imports. It follows that at the same exchange rate the supply of pounds is 25 percent higher after inflation than before inflation. This is due to an unchanged quantity of imports and a 25 percent higher price. That is, the supply curve of pounds is shifted 25 percent to the right at every exchange rate. This is shown in Figure 6A.6b, where $S_£(P_1)$ is at a 25-percent-higher quantity of pounds at each exchange rate.

Considering the demand for pounds, we note that, as before, oil exports are the same after inflation as before inflation if the pound price of oil is 25 percent higher. This was seen in Figure 6A.5. When the price of oil increases 25 percent from $25/barrel to $31.25/barrel, the pound price of oil increases 25 percent if the exchange rate is unchanged. That is, at the same exchange rate the pound price of oil is 25 percent higher and the quantity of oil exported is unchanged. This means that at the same exchange rate the quantity of pounds demanded to pay for oil is 25 percent higher after inflation than before inflation. We discover that inflation in Britain and elsewhere shifts $D_£$ to the right by the rate of inflation. That is, at each exchange rate $D_£(P_1)$ is at a 25-percent-higher quantity of pounds than $D_£(P_0)$.

Comparing the two equilibria in Figure 6A.6b, we see that when inflation occurs at the same rate in Britain and elsewhere, the exchange rate remains unchanged, just as is predicted by the PPP condition. We see we can reach the implications of the PPP condition without invoking arbitrage or speculation, both of which face limitations.

CHAPTER 7

INTEREST PARITY

The purchasing-power parity condition, which was the subject of the previous chapter, applies to the goods market. There is an important parallel condition that applies to the securities market. This is the **interest parity condition**. It states that in the absence of frictions, the dollar rates of return on security investments, or the dollar costs of borrowing, will be equal in different countries.[1] In this chapter we derive the interest parity condition and show its connection to the purchasing-power parity condition. In the following chapter we consider the frictions that must be absent for the interest parity condition to hold.

Our approach to deriving the interest parity condition is to begin by explaining how to make short-term investment and borrowing decisions in the international context. We then show how shopping around for the highest investment yield or lowest borrowing cost pushes yields and costs in different countries/currencies towards equality, thereby resulting in the interest parity condition.

As we proceed, and indeed for the remainder of the book, it will be useful at a number of points to develop concepts by referring to a specific example. For this purpose, we shall consider a manufacturing company that makes denim clothing, primarily jeans; the company is called Aviva Corporation.

Aviva Corporation is headquartered in the United States but has sales and a reputation for its denim clothing in many different countries. It buys denim

---

[1]The frictions that must be absent include restrictions on the movement of capital, transaction costs, taxes, and risk. These frictions play an analogous role to the frictions that must be absent for PPP to hold, namely, restrictions on the movement of goods, transportation costs, tariffs, and risk.

cloth wherever it finds the best price, and it competes with other U.S. and foreign producers of denim clothing. Primarily production is in the United States, but Aviva will consider opening plants elsewhere if this is particularly advantageous. Aviva has uneven cash flows; therefore, on some occasions it has surplus funds to invest, and on other occasions it needs to borrow.

Short-term borrowing and investment take place in the money market. This is the market that deals in securities with maturities of less than 1 year. Because there are forward contracts with money-market maturities, the money market deserves special treatment. Forward contracts allow money-market borrowers and lenders to avoid foreign exchange risk.[2] We will start by asking where Aviva should invest.

THE INVESTMENT AND BORROWING CRITERIA

Determining the Currency of Investment

Suppose that a firm like Aviva Corporation has some funds that it wishes to place in the money market for a period of 3 months. Perhaps it has received a major payment but can wait before paying for a large investment in new equipment. The firm could place these funds in its own domestic money market at an interest rate that can be discovered simply by calling around for the going rates on, for example, commercial paper or treasury bills. Alternatively, it could invest in foreign securities. Should it buy money market securities at home or abroad?

Many countries have well-developed money markets in which instruments such as treasury bills are traded and in which the default risks are small. It might well be possible in some of these markets to obtain interest yields that are higher than those available at home. Simply placing funds in the foreign-currency-denominated securities could, however, involve the firm in foreign exchange risk. If, for example, the value of the foreign currency in which Aviva's treasury bills are denominated happens to fall unexpectedly during the period before maturity, then there will be a foreign exchange loss when the bills mature and are converted back into dollars. Of course, exchange rates could also move the other way so that gains are made, but the uncertainty of the direction of exchange-rate movements might keep many risk-averse firms from investing abroad, even if foreign interest rates are appreciably higher. However, as we shall see, the existence of the forward exchange market makes avoiding foreign currency issues on the grounds of extra foreign exchange risk completely unjustified.

---

[2]Foreign exchange risk is discussed in some detail in Chapter 9. For the time being we note only that it is the uncertainty in asset/liability values or income flows due to unexpected changes in exchange rates. Risk can exist even if values of assets/liabilities or income flows are not uncertain in terms of a particular currency if there is instead uncertainty in the prices of what people buy. This type of risk is called **inflation risk**. We assume that people are not concerned with inflation risk.

It is possible for a firm like our Aviva Corporation to invest in a foreign-currency money-market instrument without incurring any foreign exchange risk. In other words, it is possible to avoid being affected at all by changes in exchange rates. All that is required is the sale on the forward market of the foreign-currency proceeds from the investment. Let us see how an exchange-risk-free investment decision is made. We will select for our example 3-month rather than full-year securities to make clear the need to keep exchange-rate movements and interest rates in comparable annualized terms.

Aviva knows that if it invests in the U.S. money market for 3 months, each dollar will provide

$$\$\left(1 + \frac{r_{US}}{4}\right)$$

where r_{US} is the annualized interest rate, and division by 4 gives the 3-month return.[3] The interest rate is in decimal form, and so an 8-percent rate means that $r_{US} = 0.08$.

Suppose that Aviva considers the British money market and that the spot dollar/sterling exchange rate, in the conventional U.S. terms of quotation, is $S(\$/£)$. The exchange rate $S(\$/£)$ gives the number of dollars per pound sterling, and so for \$1 our firm will obtain $1/S(\$/£)$ in British pounds, assuming that there are no transaction costs. If the annualized British interest rate on 3-month commercial paper is r_{UK}, then for every dollar sent to Britain, our firm will receive after 3 months the number of pounds, $1/S(\$/£)$, that was invested (the principal) plus the 3-month interest on this, which is $r_{UK}/4$. That is, it will receive

$$£\frac{1}{S(\$/£)} \cdot \left(1 + \frac{r_{UK}}{4}\right) \tag{7.1}$$

For example, if $S(\$/£) = 1.6120$ and $r_{UK} = 0.1244$, then each dollar invested in Britain will produce

$$£\frac{1}{1.6120}\left(1 + \frac{0.1244}{4}\right) = £0.6396$$

This certain number of pounds represents an uncertain number of dollars, but a forward contract can offer a complete hedge and guarantee the number of dollars that will finally be received.

If, at the time of buying the 3-month commercial paper in Britain, Aviva sells forward the amount of pounds to be received at the maturity of the security, that is, the amount in (7.1) or £0.6396 in our example, then the number of

---

[3]Later we allow for compound interest in computing returns. However, division by 4 is expositionally more convenient than taking the fourth root to find the 3-month return, and because we do the same for U.S. and for other countries' interest rates, the simplification does not affect our conclusions.

dollars that will be obtained is set by the forward contract. After 3 months, Aviva will deliver the British pounds and will receive the number of dollars stated in the forward exchange agreement. If, for example, the 3-month forward exchange rate at the time of buying the commercial paper is $F_{1/4}(\$/£)$ in the conventional U.S. terms, then we must multiply (7.1) by this amount to get the number of dollars received for each pound sold forward. We will obtain

$$\$\frac{F_{1/4}(\$/£)}{S(\$/£)} \cdot \left(1 + \frac{r_{\text{UK}}}{4}\right). \tag{7.2}$$

For example, if $F_{1/4}(\$/£) = 1.6000$, then the number of pounds from (7.1), £0.6396, will provide $\$1.6000 \times 0.6396 = \$1.02336$ when sold forward for dollars. This is the number of dollars received after 3 months, or $\frac{1}{4}$ year, for each original dollar sent to the London money market. This means an annual rate of return of

$$4\left(\frac{1.0234 - 1.0000}{1.0000}\right) = 0.0936, \text{ or } 9.36\%$$

It is important to remember that the number of dollars given in (7.2) is a certain amount. The purchase of the spot pounds, the British security, and the forward sale of the British pounds take place at the same time, and so there is no doubt about the number of dollars that will be received. If the exchange rate changes before the security matures, that will make no difference. The exchange rate to be used is already set in the terms of the forward contract, which is part of the swap of pounds for dollars. In terms of our example, it is guaranteed that $\$1.0234$ will be received.

It is now a simple matter to express the rule for deciding where to invest. The U.S. firm should invest in the domestic money market, rather than in the British market, over a 3-month period whenever[4]

$$\left(1 + \frac{r_{\text{US}}}{4}\right) > \frac{F_{1/4}(\$/£)}{S(\$/£)} \cdot \left(1 + \frac{r_{\text{UK}}}{4}\right)$$

If this inequality holds, there is more to be gained from investing in the domestic money market than from investing in the British money market. There is more to be gained from investing in the British market whenever the reverse inequality holds. Only if

$$\left(1 + \frac{r_{\text{US}}}{4}\right) = \frac{F_{1/4}(\$/£)}{S(\$/£)} \cdot \left(1 + \frac{r_{\text{UK}}}{4}\right) \tag{7.3}$$

---

[4]When exchange rates are in European terms, the forward and spot rates must be inverted, and subsequent deduction gives results which are more difficult to interpret. This is left as an exercise at the end of the chapter.

should the firm be indifferent, since the same amount will be received from a dollar invested in either money market.[5]

We can convert Equation (7.3) into a more meaningful equality if we subtract the amount $1 + r_{UK}/4$ from both sides:

$$\left(1 + \frac{r_{US}}{4}\right) - \left(1 + \frac{r_{UK}}{4}\right) = \frac{F_{1/4}(\$/£)}{S(\$/£)}\left(1 + \frac{r_{UK}}{4}\right) - \left(1 + \frac{r_{UK}}{4}\right)$$

With cancelation and rearrangement we obtain

$$r_{US} = r_{UK} + 4\left(\frac{F_{1/4}(\$/£) - S(\$/£)}{S(\$/£)}\right)\left(1 + \frac{r_{UK}}{4}\right) \tag{7.4}$$

We will interpret this below, but before we do, we can note that part of the second right-hand term in Equation (7.4) involves the multiplication of two small numbers, the forward pound premium and $r_{UK}/4$. The product will frequently be very small. For example, if the forward premium is 5 percent and British interest rates are 10 percent, the cross-product term from Equation (7.4) will be 0.00125 (0.05 × 0.025), or only $\frac{1}{8}$ percent. In order to interpret Equation (7.4), we might therefore temporarily drop the term formed from this product (which means dropping the $r_{UK}/4$) and write it to an approximation as follows:

$$r_{US} = r_{UK} + 4\left(\frac{F_{1/4}(\$/£) - S(\$/£)}{S(\$/£)}\right) \tag{7.5}$$

The second right-hand term in Equation (7.5) is the annualized (because of the 4) forward premium on pounds. A firm should be indifferent about investing at home or investing abroad if the home interest rate equals the foreign rate plus the annualized forward exchange premium/discount on the foreign currency. The firm should invest at home when the domestic interest rate exceeds the sum of the foreign rate plus the foreign exchange premium/discount, and it should invest abroad when the domestic rate is less than this sum. We discover that a mere comparison of interest rates is not sufficient. In order to determine where to invest, we must add the foreign interest rate to the forward premium or discount. Using the terminology of the previous chapter, we must add the foreign interest rate to the cost of the spot-forward swap of pounds for dollars, where this swap is put in annualized terms.

---

[5]In more general terms, Equation (7.3) can be written as

$$\frac{F}{S} = \frac{1 + r}{1 + r_f}$$

where the form of the exchange-rate quotation and the annualization are assumed to be understood. The term r_f is the foreign interest rate.

TABLE 7.1
EXCHANGE RATES AND INTEREST RATES IN DIFFERENT MARKETS*

New York	London			Toronto		
r_{US}	r_{UK}	$S(\$/£)$	$F_{1/4}(\$/£)$	r_C	$S(\$/\text{Can }\$)$	$F_{1/4}(\$/\text{Can }\$)$
9.20	12.44	1.6120	1.6000	11.88	0.8385	0.8333

	Covered yield†		
9.20%	9.37%		9.33%

*Interest rates on commercial paper.

†Covered yields are computed as $r_j + 4\left(\dfrac{F_{1/4}(\$/j) - S(\$/j)}{S(\$/j)}\right)\left(1 + \dfrac{r_j}{4}\right).$

The difference between Equation (7.4) and Equation (7.5) is that in Equation (7.4) we include the forward exchange premium on the principal invested in Britain *and* the forward exchange premium on the interest earned. In the approximate form (7.5) we consider the forward premium on the principal but not on the interest.

An Example

Suppose that Aviva Corporation faces the exchange-rate and money-market situation shown in Table 7.1 and has $10 million to invest for 3 months. Where should it place its funds?

If we compute

$$r_j + 4\left(\frac{F_{1/4}(\$/j) - S(\$/j)}{S(\$/j)}\right)\left(1 + \frac{r_j}{4}\right)$$

for each market j, we obtain the annualized yields given in the bottom line of Table 7.1. The market with the highest yield in this example is London.

The differences in yields are smaller, in general, than the differences in interest rates, with the discounts on the British pound and Canadian dollar compensating for the higher interest rates in London and Toronto than in New York. If Aviva invests $10 million for 3 months in London, it will receive $10,000,000 · (1 + 0.0937/4) = $10,234,250 without incurring any foreign exchange risk. If the management of Aviva had not looked abroad and had kept the $10 million in New York, the corporation would have received $10,000,000 · (1 + 0.9200/4) = $10,230,000. Thus Aviva will receive a reward of $4250 over 3 months for doing its homework and investing in London.

Determining the Country from Which to Borrow

Imagine that Aviva Corporation needs to borrow for a period of 3 months. If the annualized interest rate for domestic borrowing is r_{US}, then the required repayment after 3 months is the principal plus interest, or

$$\$\left(1 + \frac{r_{US}}{4}\right) \tag{7.6}$$

for each dollar borrowed.

If Aviva has access to the British money market, and if the going spot exchange rate is $S(\$/\pounds)$, then borrowing \$1 means borrowing $1/S(\$/\pounds)$ in pounds. For example, at the exchange rate $S(\$/\pounds) = 1.6120$, borrowing \$1 means borrowing £0.6203. If the annualized interest rate is r_{UK}, then for each dollar borrowed Aviva must repay

$$\pounds\frac{1}{S(\$/\pounds)}\left(1 + \frac{r_{UK}}{4}\right) \tag{7.7}$$

For example, if $r_{UK} = 0.1300$ (the 3-month annualized borrowing rate), Aviva must repay £0.6405. Without a forward exchange contract the number of dollars this would represent when Aviva repays its debt is uncertain. With a forward exchange contract the risk is eliminated.

Suppose that Aviva buys forward the amount of pounds in (7.7) at the price $F_{1/4}(\$/\pounds)$. When the debt is repaid, Aviva will receive the required number of pounds on a forward contract for which it must pay

$$\$\frac{F_{1/4}(\$/\pounds)}{S(\$/\pounds)}\left(1 + \frac{r_{UK}}{4}\right) \tag{7.8}$$

The firm should borrow abroad whenever (7.8) is less than (7.6), that is, when

$$\left(1 + \frac{r_{US}}{4}\right) > \frac{F_{1/4}(\$/\pounds)}{S(\$/\pounds)}\left(1 + \frac{r_{UK}}{4}\right)$$

This inequality says that Aviva should borrow in Britain when the dollar amount to be repaid is lower in Britain than in the United States. The borrowing decision criterion is seen to be just the reverse of the investment criterion.

Borrowing and Investing for Arbitrage Profit

Imagine a firm that can borrow funds in its own money market and/or in foreign money markets, as can a large corporation or bank. Suppose that it can borrow for 3 months in New York at an annualized interest rate of r_{US}. Thus for each dollar it borrows, it must repay $1 + r_{US}/4$ dollars. The firm can take each borrowed dollar and buy $1/S(\$/\pounds)$ pounds. If this is invested at r_{UK} per annum and if the resulting receipts are sold forward, the firm will receive

$$\$\frac{F_{1/4}(\$/\pounds)}{S(\$/\pounds)}\left(1 + \frac{r_{UK}}{4}\right)$$

Note that because of the forward cover there is no exchange risk and that the company has begun with no funds of its own. Borrowing in New York and simultaneously investing in London will result in a profit if the number of dollars received from the British investment exceeds the repayment on the U.S. loan, that is, if

$$\left(1 + \frac{r_{US}}{4}\right) < \frac{F_{1/4}(\$/\pounds)}{S(\$/\pounds)}\left(1 + \frac{r_{UK}}{4}\right)$$

The reverse activity, borrowing in London and investing in New York, will be profitable if the reverse inequality holds. As long as either inequality holds, it pays to borrow in one market and lend, or invest, in the other. This is known as **covered interest arbitrage**.

It should be no surprise that the potential for covered interest arbitrage helps guarantee that little opportunity for profit remains and that investors and borrowers will be relatively indifferent with regard to choosing a market. This is clear, for example, from the similarity of yields in Figure 7.1.

THE INTEREST PARITY CONDITION

We have determined that 3-month investors and borrowers would be indifferent between the United States and Britain if

$$\left(1 + \frac{r_{US}}{4}\right) = \frac{F_{1/4}(\$/\pounds)}{S(\$/\pounds)} \cdot \left(1 + \frac{r_{UK}}{4}\right). \tag{7.9}$$

More precisely, if we allow for compound interest, as we should for long-term investing and borrowing, investors and borrowers will be indifferent between the U.S. and Britain for investing and borrowing when

$$(1 + r_{US})^n = \frac{F_n(\$/\pounds)}{S(\$/\pounds)} \cdot (1 + r_{UK})^n. \tag{7.10}$$

When Equation (7.10) holds, interest arbitrage is not profitable. Equation (7.10) is the **interest parity condition**. When this condition holds, there is no advantage to borrowing or investing in any particular market or from covered interest arbitrage.

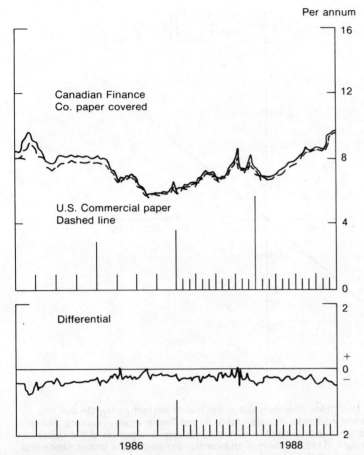

Per annum

FIGURE 7.1
THE SIMILARITY OF COVERED YIELDS. (From "Selected Interest
and Exchange Rates," *Weekly Series of Charts*, Board of Governors,
Federal Reserve System, December 27, 1988.)

The interest parity condition can be considered the money-market equivalent
of the law of one price, and follows from money-market efficiency. A straightforward demonstration of why the condition holds can be made by using a
graphical analysis.

Interest Parity: A Graphical Presentation

We can represent interest parity by using the framework of Figure 7.2. The
annualized sterling premium is drawn on the vertical axis, and the annualized
interest advantage of the United States versus Britain is drawn along the
horizontal axis. The section above the origin represents a sterling forward

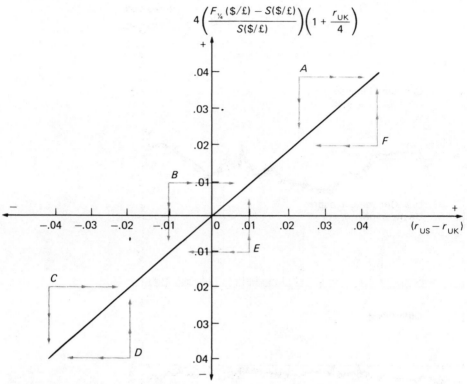

FIGURE 7.2
THE INTEREST PARITY DIAGRAM. The diagonal is the line of interest parity. On that line, investors and borrowers are indifferent between the U.S. and British money markets. Above and to the left of the line there is an incentive to invest in Britain and borrow in the United States. Below and to the right of the line there is an incentive to invest in the United States and borrow in Britain. In situations off the interest parity line, forces are at work pushing us back toward it.

premium, and the section below the origin represents a sterling forward discount. To the right of the origin there is a U.S. interest advantage, and to the left there is a U.S. interest disadvantage.

Interest parity, as expressed in Equation (7.9) or Equation (7.4), can be written as

$$r_{US} - r_{UK} = 4\left(\frac{F_{1/4}(\$/£) - S(\$/£)}{S(\$/£)}\right)\left(1 + \frac{r_{UK}}{4}\right) \qquad (7.11)$$

If the same scale is used on the two axes in Figure 7.2, this parity condition is represented by the 45-degree line. This line traces the points where the two sides of our equation are indeed equal.

Suppose that instead of having the equality in (7.11) we have the following inequality:

$$r_{US} - r_{UK} < 4\left(\frac{F_{1/4}(\$/£) - S(\$/£)}{S(\$/£)}\right)\left(1 + \frac{r_{UK}}{4}\right) \qquad (7.12)$$

This condition means, for example, that any sterling premium more than compensates for any U.S. interest advantage. Thus:

1 Covered investment in Britain yields more than in the United States.
2 Borrowing in the United States is cheaper than covered borrowing in Britain.

It also means that it is profitable for an interest arbitrager to borrow in the United States and make a covered investment in Britain. Since this act of covered interest arbitrage involves both borrowing in the cheaper market and investing in the higher-yielding market, we can concentrate on the combined rather than the separate effects of borrowing and investing.

The incentive in (7.12) to borrow in the United States and make a covered investment in Britain means an incentive to

1 borrow in the United States, perhaps by issuing and selling a security—and thus tend to raise r_{US},
2 buy spot sterling with the borrowed dollars—and thus raise $S(\$/£)$,
3 buy a British security—and thus lower r_{UK},
4 sell the sterling proceeds forward for U.S. dollars—and thus lower $F_{1/4}(\$/£)$.

The inequality in (7.12) can be represented in Figure 7.2 by points such as A, B, and C that are above and to the left of the 45-degree line. The character of these points is summarized in Table 7.2. At point B, for example, U.S. interest rates are lower than British rates, and at the same time the U.S. dollar is at a forward discount. For both reasons there is an advantage to moving funds from the United States into the British money market. The covered margin or advantage of doing this is the interest differential plus what we loosely call the

TABLE 7.2
POINTS OFF THE INTEREST PARITY LINE*

	Point					
	A	**B**	**C**	**D**	**E**	**F**
Interest differential	+.02	−.01	−.04	−.02	+.01	+.04
Forward premium†	−.04	−.01	+.02	+.04	+.01	−.02
Covered margin	−.02	−.02	−.02	+.02	+.02	+.02

*U.S. advantage = +; U.S. disadvantage = −.
†This is the forward premium multiplied by $1 + r_{UK}/4$.

forward pound premium, for a total of 2 percent. In terms of Equation (7.12), the inequality holds because the left-hand side is negative (-0.01) and the right-hand side is positive ($+0.01$). The interest arbitrage, in each of the four steps we have distinguished, will tend to restore interest parity by pushing the situation at B back toward the parity line. The same thing will occur at every other point, and we should show why.

Consider the situation at point A, where there is an incentive to borrow in the United States and invest in Britain. The extra borrowing in the United States to profit from the arbitrage opportunity will put upward pressure on U.S. interest rates. If the borrowing is through money-market instruments, efforts to sell them will reduce their prices. For a given coupon or par value, this will raise their yield. We will find r_{US} increasing. The increase in r_{US} can be represented in Figure 7.2 as a force pushing to the right of A, toward the interest parity line.

The second step in interest arbitrage requires the spot sale of the U.S. dollars for British sterling. This will help bid up the spot price of the sterling; that is, $S(\$/£)$ will increase. For any given value of $F_{1/4}(\$/£)$, this will lower the value of

$$\frac{F_{1/4}(\$/£) - S(\$/£)}{S(\$/£)}$$

This is shown in Figure 7.2 by an arrow pointing downward from A, toward the interest parity line.

The pounds that were purchased will be used to invest in a British security. If there are enough extra buyers, the price of the security will increase, and the yield will decrease, that is, r_{UK} will fall. This will mean an increase in $r_{US} - r_{UK}$, which is shown by an arrow that points to the right from A. Again, the movement is back toward the parity line.

Covering the funds moved abroad, which involves the forward sale of sterling, will lower $F_{1/4}(\$/£)$. For any given value of $S(\$/£)$, there will be a lower value of $[F_{1/4}(\$/£) - S(\$/£)]/S(\$/£)$. Thus there is a second force that will also push downward from A and toward the parity line. We can observe, of course, that since all four steps of the arbitrage will occur simultaneously, all the forces shown by the arrows will work simultaneously.

Since points B and C, like point A, indicate profitable opportunities to borrow in the United States and invest in Britain, there will also be changes in interest and exchange rates at these two points, as revealed by the arrows. For example, at point C the interest rate in the United States is 4 percent lower than in the United Kingdom, and there is a 2-percent annual discount on pounds. This will encourage arbitrage flows toward the United Kingdom. As before, there will be borrowing in the United States, and hence an increase in r_{US}; spot purchases of pounds, which will raise $S(\$/£)$; investment in Britain, which will lower r_{UK}; and forward sales of pounds, which will lower $F_{1/4}(\$/£)$. Indeed, at any point above the interest parity line, these forces, shown by the arrows emanating from A, B, and C in Figure 7.2, will be at work. We find that if we are off the interest parity line and above it, the market forces that are set up force us back down toward the line.

Below the interest parity line, forces push us back up. At points such as D, E, and F, interest arbitragers will wish to borrow in the British money market and invest in the U.S. market. For example, at point E, U.S. interest rates are 1 percent higher than U.K. rates, *and* the dollar is at a 1-percent forward premium. Thus the U.S. money market has a 2-percent advantage. This will cause arbitragers to sell British securities, lowering their price and raising r_{UK}. This is shown in Figure 7.2 by an arrow that points to the left. The arbitragers will then sell sterling for dollars, lowering $S(\$/£)$ and causing a movement upward, toward the line. They will also purchase U.S. securities, lowering r_{US} and causing a second movement toward the left. Hedging by buying sterling forward for dollars will raise the forward premium on sterling: $[F_{1/4}(\$/£) - S(\$/£)]/S(\$/£)$. This means that again there will be an upward pressure and movement toward the line, since the forward premium is the primary component on the vertical axis.

We find that above the interest parity line, flows of funds from the U.S. to the U.K. push us back toward it, and below the line, flows of funds from the U.K. to the U.S. also push us back toward it. The amount of adjustment in the interest rates vis-à-vis spot or forward exchange rates depends on the "thinness" of the markets. The spot exchange market and the securities markets are generally more active than the forward market. It is likely, therefore, that a large part of the adjustment toward interest parity will take place in the forward rate. As a result, the actual paths followed from points such as A or E back toward the parity line will lie closer to the vertical arrows than to the horizontal ones. We can therefore think of the forward premium as being determined by the interest differential.[6]

COMBINING PPP AND INTEREST PARITY

The Uncovered-Interest-Parity Condition

Equation (7.10) is the condition for hedged or covered interest parity because it involves the use of the forward market. It can be argued that a very similar unhedged-interest-parity condition should also hold. This follows because, as we shall see later, up to the level of a very small risk premium, speculation will make the forward exchange rate equal to the expected future spot rate.[7] That is, if we define $S_n^*(\$/£)$ by

$S_n^*(\$/£)$ is the expected spot exchange rate between the dollar and the pound in n years' time,

---

[6] Indeed, covered interest parity holds so closely that brokers frequently compute forward premiums from interest differentials.

[7] This is shown in Chapter 10. We shall see there that the risk premium varies over time and is empirically insubstantial.

then it follows that to a close approximation

$$S_n^*(\$/£) = F_n(\$/£). \tag{7.13}$$

Substituting Equation (7.13) into Equation (7.10) allows us to say that, to a close approximation, uncovered interest parity should hold in the form

$$(1 + r_{US})^n = \frac{S_n^*(\$/£)}{S(\$/£)}(1 + r_{UK})^n \tag{7.14}$$

Equation (7.14) can be put in a different form by noting that by definition

$$S_n^*(\$/£) \equiv S(\$/£) \cdot (1 + \dot{S}^*)^n \tag{7.15}$$

where $\dot{S}^*$ is the average annual expected rate of change of the exchange rate. Substituting Equation (7.15) into Equation (7.14) and canceling $S(\$/£)$ gives

$$(1 + r_{US})^n = (1 + \dot{S}^*)^n \cdot (1 + r_{UK})^n \tag{7.16}$$

Taking the nth root of both sides and expanding the right-hand side gives

$$1 + r_{US} = 1 + \dot{S}^* + r_{UK} + \dot{S}^* \cdot r_{UK}. \tag{7.17}$$

Assuming $\dot{S}^*$ and r_{UK} are small compared to 1, the interaction term $\dot{S}^* \cdot r_{UK}$ will be very small, allowing us to write to a close approximation

$$r_{US} - r_{UK} = \dot{S}^*. \tag{7.18}$$

That is, the interest differential should approximately equal the expected rate of change of the spot exchange rate.

The Expectations Form of PPP

We recall from Chapter 6 that the expected dollar return from holding commodities in the U.S. is $\dot{P}_{US}^*$, that is, the expected U.S. rate of inflation. Similarly, we recall that the expected dollar return from holding commodities in Britain is $\dot{P}_{UK}^* + \dot{S}^*$ because there are expected changes both in the pound prices of commodities and in the dollar value of the pound.[8] We have seen that if we ignore risk, the rates of return from holding commodities in the two countries

[8]We assume no holding costs, or that holding costs are equal in the two countries.

will be driven to equality by speculators until[9]

$$\dot{P}^*_{US} - \dot{P}^*_{UK} = \dot{S}^*(\$/£) \tag{6.9}$$

Equation (6.9) is the PPP condition in terms of expectations.

The Interrelationship of the Parity Conditions

If we take the PPP condition in its expectations form (6.9), and compare it with the interest parity condition (7.18), we can note a clear similarity. We have

$$\dot{P}^*_{US} - \dot{P}^*_{UK} = \dot{S}^*(\$/£) \tag{6.9}$$

$$r_{US} - r_{UK} = \dot{S}^*(\$/£) \tag{7.18}$$

The right-hand sides of these two equations are equal. It follows that the left-hand sides are likewise equal. This means that

$$r_{US} - r_{UK} = \dot{P}^*_{US} - \dot{P}^*_{UK} \tag{7.19}$$

By rearranging this equation, we get

$$r_{US} - \dot{P}^*_{US} = r_{UK} - \dot{P}^*_{UK} \tag{7.20}$$

What we have on the two sides of this equation are the market interest rates less the expected rates of inflation in the two countries. The interest rate minus the expected inflation rate is the expected "real" rate of interest, popularized principally by Irving Fisher. As a result, Equation (7.20) could be dubbed the **Fisher-open condition.**[10]

The conventional Fisher condition, or **Fisher equation**, involves only an individual country. Irving Fisher suggested that in each country, such as the United States and Britain, we should find nominal interest rates equal to the

[9] In Chapter 6 we attributed this version of PPP to Richard Roll, "Violations of PPP and Their Implications for Efficient Commodity Markets," in Marshall Sarnat and George Szëgo (eds.): *International Finance and Trade*, Ballinger, Cambridge, Mass., 1979. We could also derive Equation (6.9) by arguing that departures from PPP in its relative form, Equation (6.8), are random and on average equal to zero. Therefore, even though we know that in general the actual exchange rate will not change by the difference between actual inflation rates, the expected value of the change in the exchange rate, that is, $\dot{S}^*$, should equal the difference between the expected rates of inflation. Indeed, if the deviations from Equation (6.8) are truly random and unrelated from period to period, Equation (6.9) should hold precisely.

[10] Generally, economists refer to Equation (7.18), not Equation (7.20), as the Fisher-open condition. However, since Fisher spoke of real interest rates as actual rates minus the expected inflation rate, Equation (7.20) would be more appropriately so called. Equation (7.18) should perhaps be called the "interest-open" condition, where "open" means "open economy." For accounts of the Fisher-open condition, we can cite Robert Aliber and Clyde Stickney, "Accounting Measures of Foreign Exchange Exposure: The Long and Short of It," *The Accounting Review*, January 1975, pp. 45–57, and Ian Giddy, "An Integrated Theory of Exchange Rate Equilibrium," *Journal of Financial and Quantitative Analysis*, December 1976, pp. 883–892.

expected real interest rate, which he assumed was constant, plus the expected rate of inflation, that is,

$$r_{US} = \rho_{US} + \dot{P}_{US}^* \quad \text{and} \quad r_{UK} = \rho_{UK} + \dot{P}_{UK}^* \tag{7.21}$$

where ρ_{US} and ρ_{UK} are the expected real interest rates in the United States and Britain, and $\dot{P}_{US}^*$ and $\dot{P}_{UK}^*$ are, as before, the expected rates of inflation in the two countries.[11]

By comparing the Fisher equation in (7.21) with the Fisher-open condition in (7.20), we can immediately see that the two sides of Equation (7.20) are the expected real rates of interest in the two countries. In other words, the Fisher-open condition is the condition that the expected real rates of interest are equal in different countries. From purchasing-power parity and interest parity we have been able to derive an equality between expected real rates of return in different countries. We say expected because ρ_{US} and ρ_{UK} are the observed or nominal interest rates less the *expected* inflation rates, which are never known, unlike actual or *ex post* inflation rates, which can be calculated after the inflation has occurred.

The equality of expected real interest rates can be considered as having an independent existence, one that does not have to be derived from PPP and interest parity. It follows from investors allocating their funds to where real returns are highest. The real return is computed after movements in exchange rates are considered or after adjustment for forward hedging. This yield from abroad is adjusted for expected inflation in the investor's country. Investing according to the highest expected yield will tend to reduce the marginal available returns where funds are sent—because of the greater supply of funds created. It will also tend to raise returns in the countries from which the funds are taken—because of the reduced supply of funds. The flow of funds will continue until the expected *ex ante* real returns in different countries are equalized. Thus the equality $\rho_{US} = \rho_{UK}$ itself follows directly.[12]

If we write the *ex ante* forms of the variants of the interest parity, purchasing-power parity, and Fisher-open conditions all together, that is,

$$\begin{aligned}
\text{"interest parity":} \quad & r_{US} - r_{UK} = \dot{S}^*(\$/£) \\
\text{PPP:} \quad & \dot{P}_{US}^* - \dot{P}_{UK}^* = \dot{S}^*(\$/£) \\
\text{Fisher-open:} \quad & r_{US} - \dot{P}_{US}^* = r_{UK} - \dot{P}_{UK}^*
\end{aligned}$$

[11] See Irving Fisher, *The Theory of Interest*, A. M. Kelley, New York, 1965.

[12] The relationship between security yields in different countries can be extremely complex because of taxes, regulations, currency risks, citizens' tastes, and so on. The problem has been tackled by F. L. A. Grauer, R. H. Litzenberger, and R. E. Stehle, "Sharing Rules and Equilibrium in an International Capital Market under Uncertainty," *Journal of Financial Economics*, June 1976, pp. 233–256, and Fisher Black, "International Capital Market Equilibrium with Investment Barriers," *Journal of Financial Economics*, December 1974, pp. 337–352. Few data exist on real rates in different countries. See, however, Robert Z. Aliber, "Real Interest Rates in a Multicurrency World," unpublished paper, University of Chicago.

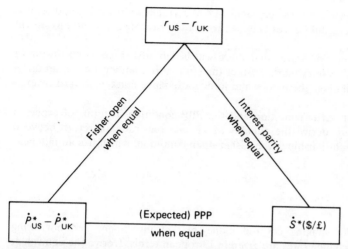

FIGURE 7.3
THE INTERDEPENDENCE OF EXCHANGE RATES, INTEREST
RATES, AND INFLATION RATES. Interest parity, purchasing-power
parity, and the Fisher-open condition are related. They can be
derived from each other.

we find that we can derive any one from the other two. This is left as an
end-of-chapter problem for the reader. The conditions are shown in Figure 7.3,
where we have used the Fisher-open condition as it appears in Equation (7.19).
Each side of the triangle in Figure 7.3 represents a condition. The figure helps
make it clear why satisfying any two conditions will mean that the remaining
condition is satisfied.

Because each of the three parity conditions along the sides of Figure 7.3 can
be derived from the other two, any one condition must be correct if the other
two are correct. For example, if we believe expected real returns are equal and
that interest parity holds precisely, we are implicitly accepting that PPP in its
expectations form also holds precisely.

SUMMARY

1 Forward exchange markets allow short-term investors and borrowers to avoid foreign
exchange risk.

2 An investor should be indifferent with respect to investing at home or abroad when the
domestic interest rate equals the foreign rate plus the annualized forward exchange
premium or discount. The investor should invest at home when the domestic rate
exceeds the other two, and invest abroad when the domestic rate is lower than the
other two.

3 A borrower should borrow abroad when the domestic interest rate exceeds the foreign
rate plus the forward foreign exchange premium or discount, and borrow at home
when the domestic interest rate is lower than the foreign interest rate plus the forward
foreign-exchange premium or discount.

4 Covered interest arbitrage involves borrowing in one currency to invest in another. It is profitable when there are differences between covered borrowing costs and investment yields.

5 The interest parity condition states that there will be no advantage to borrowing or lending in one country's money market rather than in that of another. Forces set up by interest arbitragers will move the money and foreign exchange markets toward covered interest parity.

6 The unhedged-interest parity condition and the PPP condition in terms of expected inflation can be used to derive the equality of *ex ante* real rates of return between countries. This latter relationship is the Fisher-open condition, which has an independent rationale.

QUESTIONS

1 Derive the criteria for making covered money-market investment and borrowing decisions when the exchange rates are given in European terms. Derive the equivalent of Equation (7.5).

2 You have been given the following information:

r_{US}	r_{UK}	$S(\$ / \pounds)$	$F_{1/4}(\$ / \pounds)$
15%	16%	2.000	1.995

where r_{US} = annual interest on 3-month U.S. commercial paper
         r_{UK} = annual interest on 3-month U.K. commercial paper
         $S(\$ / \pounds)$ = number of dollars per pound, spot
         $F_{1/4}(\$ / \pounds)$ = number of dollars per pound, 3-month forward

On the basis of the precise criteria:

a Where would you invest?
b Where would you borrow?
c How would you arbitrage?
d What is the profit from interest arbitrage per dollar borrowed?

3 a Use the data in Question 2 and the precise formula on the right-hand side of Equation (7.4) to compute the yield on investment in Britain. Repeat this, using the approximate formula on the right-hand side of Equation (7.5).

b Compare the error between the precise formula and the approximate formula in **a** above with the error in the situation where r_{US} = 5 percent, r_{UK} = 6 percent, and $S(\$ / \pounds)$ and $F_{1/4}(\$ / \pounds)$ are as above.

c Should we be more careful to avoid the use of the "interest plus premium or minus discount" approximation in Equation (7.5) at higher or at lower interest rates?

d If the interest rates and the forward rate in Question 2 are for 12 months, is the difference between Equation (7.4) and Equation (7.5) greater than when we are dealing with 3-month rates?

4 Derive the equivalent of Table 7.1 where all covered yields are against sterling rather than dollars. This will require computing appropriate cross spot and forward rates.

5 Draw a figure like Figure 7.2 to show what interest arbitrage will do to the interest-rate differentials and the forward premiums at points A to F in the table below. If all the

adjustment to interest parity occurs in the forward exchange rate, what will $F_{1/12}(\$/\pounds)$ be after interest parity has been restored?

	A	B	C	D	E	F
$S(\$/\pounds)$	1.6200	1.6200	1.6200	1.6200	1.6200	1.6200
$F_{1/12}(\$/\pounds)$	1.6220	1.6150	1.6220	1.6150	1.6180	1.6120
r_{US}(1 month), %	8.00	8.00	8.00	8.00	8.00	8.00
r_{UK}(1 month), %	10.00	9.00	8.00	7.00	6.00	5.00

6 Write down the expectation form of PPP, the uncovered-interest-parity condition, and the Fisher-open condition. Derive each one from the other two.

BIBLIOGRAPHY

Aliber, Robert, Z., and Clyde P. Stickney: "Accounting Measures of Foreign Exchange Exposure: The Long and Short of It," *The Accounting Review*, January 1975, pp. 44–57.

Giddy, Ian H.: "An Integrated Theory of Exchange Rate Equilibrium," *Journal of Financial and Quantitative Analysis*, December 1976, pp. 883–892.

Huang, Roger D.: "Expectations of Exchange Rates and Differential Inflation Rates: Further Evidence on Purchasing Power Parity in Efficient Markets," *Journal of Finance*, March 1987, pp. 69–79.

Kubarych, Roger M.: *Foreign Exchange Markets in the United States*, Federal Reserve Bank of New York, New York, 1978.

CHAPTER 8

WHY COVERED INTEREST DIFFERENCES PERSIST

In reality, interest parity holds very closely, but it does not hold precisely. This is apparent from, for example, the covered interest differentials shown in Figure 7.1. The failure to achieve exact covered interest parity occurs because in actual financial markets there are:

1 transaction costs,
2 political risks,
3 potential tax advantages to foreign exchange gains versus interest earnings,
4 liquidity differences between foreign securities and domestic securities.

In this chapter we explain how these factors contribute to departures from interest parity. Later, in Chapter 12, we show that these same factors also influence cash management.

TRANSACTION COSTS AND INTEREST PARITY

The cost of transacting in the foreign exchange market is reflected in the bid-ask spread when buying or selling foreign exchange. The bid-ask spread represents the cost of two foreign exchange transactions, a purchase and a sale of foreign currency. That is, if a person buys and then immediately sells a foreign currency, the cost of these two transactions is the difference between the buying and selling prices of the foreign currency, which is the bid-ask spread. Covered investment and borrowing abroad both involve two foreign exchange transaction costs—one on the spot market and the other on the forward market—that are not faced when borrowing or investing at home. These two transaction costs discourage foreign investment and borrowing.

Interest arbitrage also involves two foreign exchange transaction costs, since the borrowed currency is sold spot and then bought forward. However, there are additional transaction costs of interest arbitrage due to interest-rate spreads. This is because even within the same country the borrowing interest rate is likely to exceed the investment interest rate.[1] Let us be specific about the foreign exchange and borrowing-investment transactions costs, and reformulate the borrowing, investing, and interest arbitrage criteria derived in the previous chapter to allow explicitly for transaction costs. As in Chapter 2, let us define $S(\$/\text{ask£})$ and $F_n(\$/\text{ask£})$ as the spot and n-year forward exchange rates for buying pounds with dollars, and $S(\$/\text{bid£})$ and $F_n(\$/\text{bid£})$ as the spot and forward exchange rates when selling pounds for dollars. Let us also define r_{US}^I and r_{UK}^I as the interest rates earned on investments in the two countries, and r_{US}^B and r_{UK}^B as the interest rates on borrowing.

Investment, Borrowing, and Arbitrage Criteria, Including Transaction Costs

Investment Criterion with Transaction Costs An investment in British securities by a holder of U.S. dollars requires a spot purchase of pounds The pounds must be bought at the offer or ask rate, $S(\$/\text{ask£})$, so that $1 will buy

$$£\frac{1}{S(\$/\text{ask£})}$$

This initial investment will grow in n years at r_{UK}^I to[2]

$$£\frac{1}{S(\$/\text{ask£})}\left(1 + r_{UK}^I\right)^n$$

This can be sold forward at the buying or bid rate on pounds, $F_n(\$/\text{bid£})$, giving a U.S. investor, after n years,

$$\$\frac{F_n(\$/\text{bid£})}{S(\$/\text{ask£})}\left(1 + r_{UK}^I\right)^n$$

The proceeds from $1 invested in the U.S. for n years are $\$(1 + r_{US}^I)^n$.

---

[1] The borrowing-lending spread can be considered as a transaction cost in the same way that we consider the bid-ask spread a transaction cost, namely, it is the cost of borrowing and then immediately lending the borrowed funds.

[2] From this point on we use the correct compound-interest-rate formulations of the investment, borrowing, and arbitrage criteria. We previously used an approximation with 3-month securities—dividing interest rates by 4—for expositional convenience; the approximation allowed us to write $r_{US} - r_{UK}$ more simply in terms of the annualized forward premium/discount.

Therefore, the rule for a holder of U.S. dollars is to invest in Britain whenever

$$\frac{F_n(\$/\text{bid}£)}{S(\$/\text{ask}£)}\left(1 + r_{\text{UK}}^I\right)^n > \left(1 + r_{\text{US}}^I\right)^n \tag{8.1}$$

and to invest in the United States when the reverse inequality holds.

If we had ignored foreign exchange transaction costs, then instead of the condition (8.1) we would have written the criterion for investing in Britain as

$$\frac{F_n(\$/£)}{S(\$/£)}\left(1 + r_{\text{UK}}^I\right)^n > \left(1 + r_{\text{US}}^I\right)^n \tag{8.2}$$

In comparing the conditions (8.1) and (8.2) we can see that because transaction costs ensure that $F_n(\$/\text{bid}£) < F_n(\$/£)$ and $S(\$/\text{ask}£) > S(\$/£)$, where $F_n(\$/£)$ and $S(\$/£)$ are the middle exchange rates (that is, the rates half way between the bid and ask rates), the condition for advantageous investment in Britain is made less likely by transaction costs on foreign exchange. That is, the left-hand side of (8.1), which includes transaction costs, is smaller than the left-hand side of (8.2). However, because both interest rates are investment rates, transaction costs on securities represented by a borrowing-lending spread have no bearing on the decision, and do not discourage foreign versus domestic investment.

Borrowing Criterion with Transaction Costs   When a U.S. borrower raises U.S. dollars by borrowing pounds, the borrowed pounds must be sold at the pound selling rate, $S(\$/\text{bid}£)$. For each \$1 the U.S. borrower wants he or she must therefore borrow

$$£\frac{1}{S(\$/\text{bid}£)}$$

The repayment of this number of borrowed pounds after n years at r_{UK}^B per annum is

$$£\frac{1}{S(\$/\text{bid}£)}\left(1 + r_{\text{UK}}^B\right)^n$$

This number of pounds can be bought forward at the buying rate for pounds, $F_n(\$/\text{ask}£)$, so that the number of dollars paid in n years for borrowing \$1 is

$$\$\frac{F_n(\$/\text{ask}£)}{S(\$/\text{bid}£)}\left(1 + r_{\text{UK}}^B\right)^n$$

Alternatively, if \$1 is borrowed for n years in the U.S. at r_{US}^B per annum, the repayment in n years is

$$\$\left(1 + r_{\text{US}}^{B}\right)^{n}$$

The borrowing criterion that allows for foreign exchange transaction costs is that a borrower should obtain dollars by borrowing British pounds (that is, via a swap) whenever

$$\frac{F_{n}(\$/\text{ask£})}{S(\$/\text{bid£})}\left(1 + r_{\text{UK}}^{B}\right)^{n} < \left(1 + r_{\text{US}}^{B}\right)^{n} \tag{8.3}$$

Because $F_{n}(\$/\text{ask£}) > F_{n}(\$/£)$ and $S(\$/\text{bid£}) < S(\$/£)$, the condition (8.3) is more unlikely than the condition without transaction costs on foreign exchange. We find that the incentive to venture abroad for investment or for borrowing is reduced by the consideration of foreign exchange transaction costs.

Unlike the situation with investment, where borrowing-lending spreads are irrelevant, in the case of borrowing, venturing abroad may be discouraged by borrowing-lending spreads. This is because lenders may well charge foreign borrowers more than they charge domestic borrowers because they consider loans to foreigners to be riskier. For example, the markup over the prime interest rate for a U.S. borrower in the U.S. might be smaller than the markup over prime for the same U.S. borrower in Britain. This may be due to greater difficulty in collecting on loans to foreigners, or to difficulty in transferring information on creditworthiness of borrowers between countries.

Arbitrage Criterion with Transaction Costs   Consider first the interest arbitrage consisting of borrowing dollars, buying pounds, investing in pound securities, and selling the pounds forward for dollars to repay the U.S. dollar loan. Each dollar borrowed will buy

$$£\frac{1}{S(\$/\text{ask£})}$$

because the pounds must be bought at the ask rate. When invested in Britain, this will become after n years

$$£\frac{1}{S(\$/\text{ask£})}\left(1 + r_{\text{UK}}^{I}\right)^{n}$$

This number of pounds can be sold forward at $F_{n}(\$/\text{bid£})$, the bid rate on pounds, so that the dollar receipts from the investment are

$$\$\frac{F_{n}(\$/\text{bid£})}{S(\$/\text{ask£})}\left(1 + r_{\text{UK}}^{I}\right)^{n}$$

This must be compared with the dollar repayment on the n-year loan in the U.S. used to finance the investment, which is $\$(1 + r_{US}^B)^n$. Therefore, the criterion for this arbitrage is to proceed if

$$\left(1 + r_{US}^B\right)^n < \frac{F_n(\$/\text{bid}\pounds)}{S(\$/\text{ask}\pounds)} \left(1 + r_{UK}^I\right)^n \tag{8.4}$$

Examination of the arbitrage condition (8.4) shows it is made less likely to hold as a result of all transaction costs. First, the borrowing rate r_{US}^B is on the high side of the interest-rate spread, while the investment rate r_{UK}^I is on the low side, and yet the left-hand side must be smaller than the right for profitable arbitrage. Second, $F_n(\$/\text{bid}\pounds)$ is on the low end of the exchange-rate range and $S(\$/\text{ask}\pounds)$ is on the high end, thereby reducing the value of the right-hand side of (8.4), and yet this must be larger than the left-hand side for profitable interest arbitrage. Therefore, not unexpectedly, transaction costs discourage this covered interest arbitrage.

It is a natural extension of the condition (8.4) to write that the reverse interest arbitrage to that above, namely borrowing in the U.K. and investing in the U.S., is profitable if

$$\frac{F_n(\$/\text{ask}\pounds)}{S(\$/\text{bid}\pounds)} \left(1 + r_{UK}^B\right)^n < \left(1 + r_{US}^I\right)^n \tag{8.5}$$

Examination of (8.5) shows that this arbitrage is also discouraged by transaction costs. This follows because r_{UK}^B is on the high side of the borrowing-lending spread while r_{US}^I is on the low side, and yet the left-hand side of (8.5) must be smaller than the right-hand side. Similarly, $F_n(\$/\text{ask}\pounds)$ is on the high side of the spread and $S(\$/\text{bid}\pounds)$ is on the low side, thereby raising the left-hand side of (8.5), the side that must be smaller for profitable arbitrage.

Interest Disparity and Transaction Costs

The extent to which the interest parity condition is violated because of transaction costs has been studied by numerous researchers.[3] It has generally become recognized that transaction costs do not substantially contribute to the deviations from interest parity that have been observed. A major reason for this

---

[3]The extensive literature on transaction costs and interest parity includes Mohsen Bahmani-Oskooee and Staya P. Das, "Transaction Costs and the Interest Parity Theorem," *Journal of Political Economy*, August 1985, pp. 793–799; William H. Branson, "The Minimum Covered Interest Differential Needed for International Arbitrage Activity," *Journal of Political Economy*, December 1969, pp. 1029–1034; Phillipe Callier, "One Way Arbitrage, Foreign Exchange and Securities Markets: A Note," *Journal of Finance*, December 1981, pp. 1177–1186; Kevin Clinton, "Transaction Costs and Covered Interest Arbitrage: Theory and Evidence," *Journal of Political Economy*, April 1988, pp. 358–370; Alan V. Deardorff, "One-Way Arbitrage and Its Implications for the Foreign Exchange Markets," *Journal of Political Economy*, April 1979, pp. 351–364; Jacob A. Frenkel and Richard M. Levich, "Covered Interest Arbitrage: Unexploited Profits?," *Journal of Political Economy*, April 1975, pp. 325–338; Frank McCormick, "Covered Interest Arbitrage: Unexploited Profits? Comment," *Journal of Political Economy*, April 1979, pp. 411–417; and Stephen F. Overturf, "Risk, Transaction Charges, and the Market for Foreign Exchange Services," *Economic Inquiry*, April 1982, pp. 291–302. This list is by no means exhaustive.

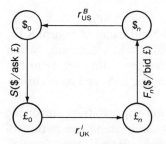

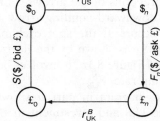

U.S. borrowing − U.K. investment   U.K. borrowing − U.S. investment

(*a*) Round-trip covered interest arbitrage

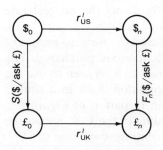

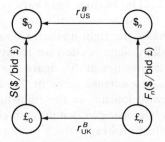

Spot dollars to future pounds   Future pounds to spot dollars

(*b*) One-way covered interest arbitrage

FIGURE 8.1
ONE-WAY AND ROUND-TRIP INTEREST ARBITRAGE. Round-trip interest
arbitrage which is illustrated in (*a*) involves going along all four sides of the
diagram at the interest rates and exchange rates that are shown. The
presence of four transaction costs allows for large deviations from interest
parity. One-way interest arbitrage which is illustrated in (*b*) involves
comparing two alternative ways of going from one corner to the other. Either
route involves two transaction costs, but since these are for the same types
of transactions, they do not cause deviations from interest parity.

recognition is the realization that one-way interest arbitrage overcomes some of
the transaction costs that are involved in the foreign exchange and securities
markets. We can explain the nature of one-way interest arbitrage and how it
influences the interest parity theorem by contrasting one-way and **round-trip
arbitrage**.[4] This is done in Figure 8.1

Part *a* of Figure 8.1 illustrates round-trip covered interest arbitrage. The four
corners of the diagram show current dollars ($\$_0$), current pounds, ($\pounds_0$), future
dollars ($\$_n$), and future pounds ($\pounds_n$). The arrows drawn between the corners of
the diagram show the interest rates or exchange rates when going between the

[4]The term "round-trip" was suggested by Richard Levich.

corners in the directions of the arrows. For example, when going from $\$_0$ to $£_0$ as shown by the downward-pointing arrow in the left-hand panel of Figure 8.1a, the transaction occurs at the spot exchange rate, $S(\$/ask£)$. Similarly, when going from $\$_n$ to $\$_0$ as shown by the horizontal leftward-pointing arrow in the left-hand panel of Figure 8.1a, it involves borrowing in the U.S. and so occurs at the U.S. borrowing rate, r_{US}^B.

The left-hand diagram in part a shows the round-trip arbitrage involving borrowing in the U.S and investment in Britain. To understand the nature of this arbitrage we begin at corner $\$_n$. The top leftward-pointing arrow from $\$_n$ shows the interest rate on U.S. borrowing which gives immediate dollars, $\$_0$, in return for paying dollars back in the future, $\$_n$. The left downward-pointing arrow shows the spot exchange rate at which the borrowed dollars are exchanged into pounds; the pounds must be purchased, so the spot rate is the ask rate for pounds. The bottom rightward-pointing arrow shows the interest rate earned on the British investment which converts today's pounds, $£_0$, into future pounds $£_n$. Finally, the right upward-sloping arrow shows the forward exchange rate at which the dollars needed for repaying the U.S. loan are purchased. The counterclockwise journey in this figure from $\$_n$ and back to $\$_n$ is seen to use the interest rates and exchange rates in the arbitrage condition (8.4). In a similar way, the clockwise journey in the right-hand diagram in part a of Figure 8.1, which involves borrowing in Britain with covered lending in the U.S., shows the round-trip interest arbitrage which gives rise to the arbitrage condition (8.5).

If the maximum possible size of deviations from covered interest parity due to transaction costs were determined by the potential to engage in round-trip covered interest arbitrage, the deviations could be considerable. This is because for round-trip interest arbitrage to be profitable it is necessary to overcome the transaction costs in the foreign exchange markets and the borrowing-lending spread on interest rates. Let us attach some numbers to see the size of deviations that might result. We shall use transactions costs faced by the lowest-cost arbitragers, such as the banks, since it is they who are likely to act first and preclude others from profiting from interest arbitrage.

Let us assume a potential interest arbitrager can borrow for 1 year at $\frac{1}{4}$ percent above his or her investment rate, and can borrow a sufficient amount to reduce the spot and forward transaction costs both to only $\frac{1}{10}$ percent. In this situation, it is necessary that the interest parity deviation calculated using interest rates and exchange rates that exclude transaction costs would have to exceed approximately $\frac{1}{2}$ percent for profitable arbitrage. This is because it is necessary to earn $\frac{1}{4}$ percent to cover the borrowing-investment spread, and another $\frac{1}{5}$ percent to cover the two transaction costs, those for the spot and forward exchange transactions. This is illustrated in Figure 8.2. We can interpret the interest rates on the horizontal axis as the midpoints in both countries between the borrowing and lending rates, and the exchange rates as the midpoints between the bid and ask rates.

We show a band around the interest parity line within which round-trip interest arbitrage is unprofitable. This band has a width of approximately $\frac{1}{2}$ percent on either side of the interest parity line, as is seen, for example, along

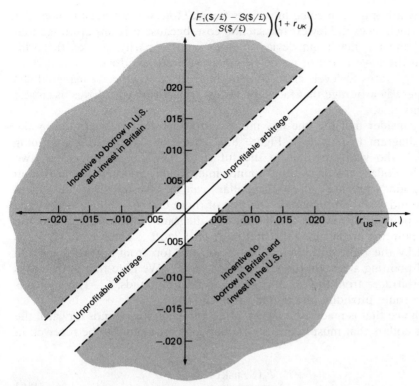

FIGURE 8.2
INTEREST PARITY IN THE PRESENCE OF TRANSACTION COSTS, POLITICAL
RISK, OR REQUIRED LIQUIDITY PREMIUMS. Interest parity might not hold
exactly because of transaction costs, political risk, and liquidity preference. This
means interest rates and exchange rates may not plot on the interest parity line.
Rather, they may be somewhere within a band around the line; only outside this
band are the covered yield differences enough to overcome the costs or risks of
covered interest arbitrage. However, the band is narrow because there are some
participants for whom the costs and risk of arbitrage are unimportant or
irrelevant. For example, transaction costs are irrelevant for one-way arbitragers.

the horizontal axis around the origin. The band reflects the fact that arbitrage
must cover the $\frac{1}{2}$ percent lost in transaction costs. Above and to the left of the
band it is profitable to borrow in the U.S. and make covered investment in
Britain, and to the right of the band it is profitable to do the reverse.[5]

---

[5]If interest rates were for 3 months rather than 1 year, the band would be considerably wider.
Even if the borrowing-lending spread remained at $\frac{1}{4}$ percent and the foreign exchange transaction
costs remained at $\frac{1}{10}$ percent, the band would be more than one full percent on either side of the
interest parity line. The reason for this is that the costs of buying spot and selling forward are
incurred within a 3-month period, and when annualized are effectively 4 times larger. With
$\frac{1}{5}$ percent lost in 3 months, it is necessary for the interest arbitrage to generate $\frac{4}{5}$ percent to cover
foreign exchange costs, plus $\frac{1}{4}$ percent to cover the borrowing-lending spread. Of course, if we were
dealing with 1-month or shorter arbitrage the potential deviations from interest parity would be
even larger.

One-way arbitrage can come in various forms. However, we need to consider only that which faces the lowest transaction cost, because it is this arbitrage that will determine the maximum deviation from interest parity; just as the arbitrager with the lowest cost of round-trip interest arbitrage drives interest rates and exchange rates to levels closest to the interest parity line, so it is that the form of one-way arbitrage that faces the lowest transaction cost drives us closest to the parity line.

Let us consider first the one-way interest arbitrage that is illustrated by the left-hand diagram in part b of Figure 8.1. This shows an arbitrager holding dollars ($\$_0$) who wants pounds in the future ($£_n$).[6] The arbitrager has two choices. The dollars can be sold for pounds immediately and invested in Britain until the pounds are needed, or the dollars can be invested in the U.S. and forward pounds can be purchased. The first of these choices is illustrated by the downward-pointing arrow on the left of the diagram from $\$_0$ to $£_0$ and the rightward-pointing arrow along the bottom from $£_0$ to $£_n$. The second choice is illustrated by the rightward-pointing arrow on the top from $\$_0$ to $\$_n$ and the downward-pointing arrow on the right from $\$_n$ to $£_n$. We note that both routes take the arbitrager from today's dollars, $\$_0$, to future pounds, $£_n$. The choice is to pick the route providing the pounds at lower cost.

If the choice that is made is to invest in the U.S. and buy pounds forward, the number of dollars that must be invested today for each pound to be received in n years is

$$\$\frac{F_n(\$/\text{ask}£)}{\left(1 + r_{\text{US}}^I\right)^n} \tag{8.6}$$

If the other choice is made, that is, to buy pounds immediately and invest in Britain for n years, the number of dollars that must be spent per pound is

$$\$\frac{S(\$/\text{ask}£)}{\left(1 + r_{\text{UK}}^I\right)^n} \tag{8.7}$$

In the same way that we saw that there are forces pushing interest rates and exchange rates to the interest parity line, we can see that there are forces making the amounts in (8.6) and (8.7) equal to each other. For example, if (8.7) gives a lower cost per pound than (8.6), there will be spot purchases of pounds and funds invested in Britain. These actions increase $S(\$/\text{ask}£)$ and reduce

---

[6]The use of the term "arbitrager" in this context stretches the usual meaning of the term, because we have assumed that dollars are already held, and that there is already a need for pounds in the future. Without engaging in excessive semantics we can note that the essence of what our "arbitrager" is doing is judging which of two ways of going from current dollars to future pounds is the cheaper. This choice of the preferred route is the same type of choice met in deriving cross exchange rates in Chapter 2. The term "arbitrage" comes from "arbitrate," which means "choose." However, a reader who still objects to the term "arbitrager" can substitute his or her own term; the conclusion is the same whatever word we use.

r_{UK}^I. At the same time the lack of forward pound purchases will reduce $F_n(\$/ask£)$, and the capital outflow from the U.S. will increase r_{US}^I. The choice between alternatives therefore drives them to the same cost, that is,

$$\frac{F_n(\$/ask£)}{\left(1 + r_{US}^I\right)^n} = \frac{S(\$/ask£)}{\left(1 + r_{UK}^I\right)^n} \tag{8.8}$$

We can rewrite (8.8) as

$$\left(1 + r_{US}^I\right)^n = \frac{F_n(\$/ask£)}{S(\$/ask£)}\left(1 + r_{UK}^I\right)^n \tag{8.9}$$

If the transaction costs in the spot and forward foreign exchange markets were the same, then Equation (8.9) would plot as a 45-degree line through the origin in the interest parity diagram, Figure 7.2. This is because we have investment interest rates on both sides of the equation, and we have ask exchange rates for forward and spot transactions.[7] This means that if spot and forward transaction costs were equal, the choice we have described would drive us all the way to the interest parity line even though there are transaction costs. The reason this happens is that the only decision is how to buy pounds, spot or forward. Therefore, the transaction costs will be paid whatever the choice. Similarly, investment interest rates are earned if the choice is to buy pounds spot or forward, the only difference being where the interest is earned.

Another one-way interest arbitrage is illustrated by the lower right-hand diagram in Figure 8.1b. The choice in this case is between two ways of going from £$_n$ to $\$_0$, namely either going from £$_n$ to £$_0$ by borrowing pounds, and then from £$_0$ to $\$_0$ via the spot market, or going from £$_n$ to $\$_n$ via the forward market, and from $\$_n$ to $\$_0$ by borrowing dollars.[8]

If the route that is taken from £$_n$ to $\$_0$ is to borrow pounds and sell them spot for dollars, the number of dollars received immediately for each pound that must be repaid in n years is

$$\$ \frac{S(\$/bid£)}{\left(1 + r_{UK}^B\right)^n} \tag{8.10}$$

---

[7]That is, because both exchange rates are ask rates, the exchange rates in the numerator and denominator of Equation (8.9) are both on the high side of the bid-ask spread. To the extent that transaction costs in the spot and forward markets are equal, they cancel. Similarly, because the interest rates on the two sides of Equation (8.9) are investment rates, they are both on the low side of the borrowing-lending spread. The spread component again cancels.

[8]A U.S. exporter who is to receive pounds and who needs to borrow dollars is interested in going from £$_n$ to $\$_0$. This will become clear when we examine hedging in Chapter 10.

The alternative route provides

$$\$ \frac{F_n(\$/\text{bid}£)}{\left(1 + r_{US}^B\right)^n} \tag{8.11}$$

The choice between the alternatives will drive exchange rates and interest rates until

$$\frac{S(\$/\text{bid}£)}{\left(1 + r_{UK}^B\right)^n} = \frac{F_n(\$/\text{bid}£)}{\left(1 + r_{US}^B\right)^n}$$

that is,

$$\left(1 + r_{US}^B\right)^n = \frac{F_n(\$/\text{bid}£)}{S(\$/\text{bid}£)}\left(1 + r_{UK}^B\right)^n \tag{8.12}$$

Again, if the forward and spot transaction costs are equal, this is the interest parity line; we have borrowing interest rates on both sides, and both exchange rates are bid rates.[9]

In fact, of course, forward exchange transaction costs are higher than spot costs, so that Equation (8.9) and Equation (8.12) might differ a little from the interest parity line drawn without transaction costs. However, the departures will be much smaller than those obtained from consideration of round-trip arbitrage. This is because round-trip interest arbitrage involves the borrowing-investment interest-rate spread and the foreign exchange transaction costs of buying spot and selling forward, or of buying forward and selling spot; see, for example, the arbitrage conditions (8.4) and (8.5). On the other hand, one-way arbitrage does not involve interest-rate spreads, and foreign exchange transaction costs are faced whatever the choice.

The one-way arbitrage we have described produces the interest parity line or at most a narrow band around the line, because we have established situations where the arbitrager has in any case to buy/sell foreign exchange and to invest/borrow. An alternative one-way arbitrage is a choice between buying/selling forward on the one hand, and buying/selling spot and using the money markets on the other hand.[10] For example an arbitrager could buy pounds forward, or alternatively could borrow dollars, buy pounds spot, and invest the pounds in Britain. Either way the arbitrager receives pounds in the future and has to deliver dollars. This is illustrated in Figure 8.3a, where the

---

[9]In the case of borrowing there may be a departure from interest parity if foreign borrowers are viewed as riskier than domestic borrowers. We met this point earlier with round-trip arbitrage.

[10]This is the more usual one-way arbitrage considered in explaining why transaction costs are not important. For example, see Deardorff, *op. cit.*

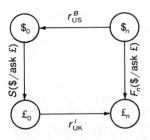

(a) Pounds needed in future

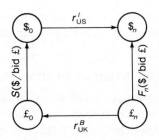

(b) Need to short pounds

FIGURE 8.3
A MORE ROUNDABOUT ONE-WAY ARBITRAGE. We can reduce the band around the interest parity line by considering whether to use the forward market or the spot market plus money markets. This choice, however, involves one transaction versus three transactions, and is likely to leave larger deviations from interest parity than some other one-way arbitrage choices.

arbitrager can go from $\$_n$ to $£_n$ via the forward market (the downward-pointing arrow on the right-hand side), or by borrowing in the U.S. (the upper leftward-pointing arrow), buying pounds spot with the borrowed dollars (the left-hand downward-pointing arrow), and investing in the U.K. (the lower rightward-pointing arrow). This one-way arbitrage does make foreign exchange transaction costs irrelevant, or at least less relevant, because it involves ask rates in either case. However, it does not avoid the borrowing-lending spread. It does not, therefore, take us as close to the interest parity line as the arbitrage we considered. We reach the same conclusion if we consider the reverse forward exchange of $£_n$ for $\$_n$ versus the alternative of borrowing pounds, using these to buy dollars spot, and investing the dollars. This is illustrated in Figure 8.3b; it again gives a line further from the interest parity line than the one-way arbitrage we described.

An alternative way of concluding that the deviations from interest parity as a result of transaction costs are small is to consider the choice faced by third-country borrowers and investors. For example, if Japanese or German investors and borrowers are looking for the best place to invest or borrow, they will drive the situation between the U.S. and Britain to the interest parity line. This is because the Japanese or Germans pay foreign exchange costs wherever they invest or borrow, and compare investment rates in the two countries or borrowing rates in the two countries.[11] For this reason, or because of the presence of one-way arbitrage, we can expect deviations from interest parity to be too small for round-trip arbitrage to ever occur. Indeed, the presence of one-way arbi-

[11] This assumes that cross exchange rates of pounds for yen or pounds for marks do not have a larger bid-ask spread than direct yen-dollar or mark-dollar exchange rates. When cross-exchange-rate spreads are larger, dollar investments and borrowing will be favored.

trage and third-country investors and borrowers suggests that transaction costs are probably not a cause of deviations from interest parity.[12]

POLITICAL RISKS AND INTEREST PARITY

Another factor that has been cited as an explanation of why interest parity may not precisely hold is that foreign securities face political risk. Political risk involves the uncertainty that while funds are invested in a foreign country, they may be frozen or they may become inconvertible into other currencies, or they may be confiscated. Even if such extremes do not occur, investors might find themselves facing new or increased taxes in the foreign country. Generally, the investment that involves the least political risk is at home. If funds are invested abroad, to the risk of tax or other changes at home is added the risk of changes in another political jurisdiction. It is, of course, possible that for investors in some countries, it is politically less risky to send funds abroad. This will be true if investors thereby avoid restrictions or taxes at home. Investing in Switzerland is an example of reducing the potential for risk by moving funds abroad. In these circumstances, a foreign investment might be made even at a covered interest disadvantage. In general, however, we would expect a premium from a foreign investment versus a domestic investment when funds are moved abroad.

In diagrammatic terms, political risk creates a band like that shown in Figure 8.2. Only in an area beyond a certain positive covered differential is there an incentive to invest abroad.[13] This band does not have to be of equal width on the two sides of the interest parity line if one country is viewed as riskier than the other. For example, if we refer back to Figure 7.1, we see that Canadian yields are generally a little higher than U.S. yields, even when forward hedging is included. This can be attributed to U.S. investors viewing Canada as politically more risky than Canadians view the U.S., thereby causing a larger political-risk premium on Canadian securities than on U.S. securities.

As in the case of transaction costs, third-country investors might force interest rates and exchange rates onto the interest parity line even if investors in, for example, the U.S. and Britain perceive foreign investment as riskier than investment at home. For example, if Japanese investors view the U.S. and Britain as equally risky politically from their perspective, then they will drive the U.S.-British interest rates and exchange rates onto the interest parity line. Of course, this will encourage U.S. and British investors to keep funds at home,

---

[12] The arguments we have given for transaction costs to be a minor or irrelevant reason for deviation from interest parity can be supplemented by an argument advanced by Kevin Clinton, *op. cit.* Clinton argues that by buying and selling swaps, banks have greatly reduced foreign exchange transaction costs. (Swaps, as we saw in the quotation of forward rates in Chapter 3, are ordinarily spot purchases plus forward sales, or vice versa, although they can also involve two maturities of forwards.) Swaps are transactions between the corners in Figure 8.1 and 8.3 that run directly along the diagonals. This means round-trip arbitrage can be performed with low transaction costs.

[13] Of course, political risk does not create a band via the borrowing decision.

because neither is receiving compensation for the risk of investing in the other country.

TAXES AND INTEREST PARITY

If taxes are the same on domestic and on foreign investment and borrowing, then the existence of taxes will make no difference in our investment and borrowing criteria or the interest parity line. Taxes will cancel out when yield comparisons are made. However, if the tax rates depend on the country in which funds are invested or borrowed, the interest parity condition will be affected. There are two ways in which taxes could conceivably affect the parity condition. One way involves withholding taxes, and the other way involves differences between the tax rate on income and that on capital gains.

Withholding Taxes

One might think that a potential cause of higher taxes on foreign earnings than on domestic earnings, and hence a band around the interest parity line, is the foreign-resident withholding tax. A withholding tax is a tax applied to foreigners at the source of their earnings. For example, if a Canadian resident were to earn $100 in the United States, the payer of that $100 would be required to deduct, as tax, a percentage of earnings (for example, 15 percent). Similarly, the earnings of U.S. residents in Canada might be subject to a withholding tax. Withholding taxes, however, are unlikely to offer a reason for a band around the interest parity line.

As long as the rate of withholding is less than or equal to the tax rate that would be applied to the earnings at home, domestic withholding tax credits will offset the tax withheld. For example, suppose that a resident of the United States pays the equivalent of $15 on $100 of interest or dividends earned in Canada, and the total tax payable on the $100 in the United States is $25. The Internal Revenue Service (IRS) will grant the U.S. resident a $15 credit on taxes paid to the taxing authority in Canada. Only an additional $10 will be payable in the United States. The investor ends up paying a total of $25, which is the same as he or she would have paid on $100 earned at home. Complete or full withholding tax credit leaves no incentive to choose domestic securities rather than foreign securities. Only if withholding tax credits are less than the amounts withheld will there be a reason to keep money at home.[14] This means that the interest parity condition is in general not affected, and we have no band around the parity line as a result of withholding taxes.

---

[14] Even when full credit is obtained, interest earnings are lost on the funds withheld in comparison with what might have been earned if taxes had been paid at home at the end of the tax period. This should, however, be a relatively small consideration except when interest rates are high.

Capital Gains versus Income Taxes*

Taxes can affect the investment and borrowing criteria and the interest parity condition if investors effectively pay lower tax rates on foreign exchange earnings than on interest earnings.[15] This can be the tax situation faced by investors who only infrequently buy or sell foreign exchange. This is because such investors can obtain capital-account treatment of their foreign exchange gains or losses; gains and losses are normally given capital-account treatment if they are not part of the "normal conduct of business."[16] If the tax rate on capital gains is lower than that on ordinary income, this affects the slope of the interest parity line. Let us see how, by considering a U.S. investor who pays a lower effective tax rate on capital gains than on interest income.

Let us write the U.S. investor's tax rate on capital gains as τ_k and the U.S. tax rate on income as τ_y, and let us assume that for this particular investor, $\tau_y > \tau_k$. Since all interest earnings are considered as income, after paying taxes and ignoring transaction costs the U.S. investor will receive from each dollar invested at home for 1 year

$$1 + (1 - \tau_y)r_{\text{US}} \tag{8.13}$$

That is, the investor will lose a fraction τ_y of the interest earned. If he or she instead invests in Britain, then before taxes the U.S. dollar receipts will be

$$\frac{F_1(\$/£)}{S(\$/£)}(1 + r_{\text{UK}}) = \left(\frac{F_1(\$/£) - S(\$/£)}{S(\$/£)}\right)(1 + r_{\text{UK}}) + (1 + r_{\text{UK}})$$

We have expanded the total return into the earnings from exchange rates—the first term on the right-hand side—and the principal plus interest. After taxes, if capital gains taxes are paid even on hedged foreign exchange earnings, the investor will receive only $1 - \tau_y$ of the interest and $1 - \tau_k$ of the gain from the forward premium, that is,

$$1 + (1 - \tau_y)r_{\text{UK}} + (1 - \tau_k)\left(\frac{F_1(\$/£) - S(\$/£)}{S(\$/£)}\right)(1 + r_{\text{UK}}) \tag{8.14}$$

We have used the income tax rate τ_y, since all interest, whatever the source, is subject to that rate.

---

*Sections marked with an asterisk can be omitted on first reading without loss of continuity.

[15]Even where the tax rate on realized capital gains is the same as on ordinary income, as is the case in the U.S., the *effective* tax rate on capital gains is lower if capital gains can be deferred, or if there are capital losses against which the capital gains can be taken. In many countries the *actual* tax rate on capital gains is lower than that on ordinary income.

[16]For the conditions for capital-account treatment of foreign exchange earnings, see Martin Kupferman and Maurice Levi, "Taxation and the International Money Market Investment Decision," *Financial Analysts Journal*, July/August 1978, pp. 61–64.

We can show the effect of taxes in terms of the graphical presentation of interest parity if we proceed the same way as we did when we included transaction costs. The U.S. investor for whom we have assumed $\tau_y > \tau_k$ will be indifferent between investing in the United States or in the United Kingdom if (8.13) and (8.14) are equal, which requires that

$$r_{US} - r_{UK} = \frac{1 - \tau_k}{1 - \tau_y} \left(\frac{F_1(\$/\pounds) - S(\$/\pounds)}{S(\$/\pounds)} \right)(1 + r_{UK}) \qquad (8.15)$$

In comparing Equation (8.15) with the equation for the interest parity line in Figure 8.2, which is

$$r_{US} - r_{UK} = \left(\frac{F_1(\$/\pounds) - S(\$/\pounds)}{S(\$/\pounds)} \right)(1 + r_{UK})$$

we see that differential taxes add $(1 - \tau_k)/(1 - \tau_y)$ to the front of the forward premium/discount term. When the capital gains tax rate is lower than the income tax rate,

$$\frac{1 - \tau_k}{1 - \tau_y} > 1$$

For example, if $\tau_k = 0.10$ and $\tau_y = 0.25$, then

$$\frac{1 - \tau_k}{1 - \tau_y} = 1.20$$

This means that the line of indifference for investors who face lower taxes on foreign exchange earnings than on interest income is flatter than the 45-degree interest parity line in Figure 8.2.

While some investors may enjoy a lower tax rate on foreign exchange than on interest earnings, banks and other major players will not; such investors, for whom international investment is a normal business, pay the same tax on interest and foreign exchange earnings. For this reason we can expect interest rates and exchange rates to remain on the 45-degree interest parity line; banks will take positions until the situation is on the line. This implies that those investors who do pay lower taxes on foreign exchange earnings than on interest income may find valuable **tax arbitrage** opportunities. For example, suppose interest rates and exchange rates are such that interest parity holds precisely on a before-tax basis with the values

$$r_{US} = 12\%$$
$$r_{UK} = 8\%$$
$$\left(\frac{F_1(\$/\pounds) - S(\$/\pounds)}{S(\$/\pounds)} \right)(1 + r_{UK}) = 4\%$$

For a U.S. investor for whom $\tau_y = 0.25$ and $\tau_k = 0.10$, U.S. investments yield $(1 - \tau_y)r_{US} = 9\%$ after tax, while British investments yield after tax

$$\left(1 - \tau_y\right)r_{UK} + \left(1 - \tau_k\right)\left(\frac{F_1(\$/£) - S(\$/£)}{S(\$/£)}\right)(1 + r_{UK}) = 9.6\%$$

The British investment will be preferred on an after-tax basis even though interest parity holds exactly on a before-tax basis. More generally, if covered interest parity holds on a before-tax basis, investors with favorable capital gains treatment will prefer investments denominated in currencies trading at a forward premium. It is a natural extension of our argument to show that in the same tax situation, borrowers will prefer to denominate borrowing in currencies at a forward discount.[17]

LIQUIDITY DIFFERENCES AND INTEREST PARITY

The liquidity of an asset can be judged by how quickly and cheaply it can be converted into money. For example, when a domestic asset such as a 90-day security is sold before maturity after only 50 days, domestic security selling transaction costs must be paid that would not have been incurred had the security been held to maturity. If, however, a covered foreign 90-day investment is sold after only 50 days, there are more than security selling costs to be faced. This should be explained carefully.

The brokerage costs for selling the foreign asset are likely to be virtually the same as those for selling the domestic security. However, we face transaction costs when we convert on the spot exchange market the foreign exchange received from the sale of the security. These costs would have not been faced had the asset been held to maturity and the proceeds converted according to the original forward contract. Further, when an asset is sold prior to maturity and the funds are brought home, there is still the matter of honoring the original forward contract to sell the foreign exchange at the maturity of the foreign investment. If cash managers want to avoid the foreign exchange risk that would be faced by leaving the original forward contract in effect, they must cover their position. In our example, if there is a 90-day forward contract and the funds are brought home after only 50 days, the cash manager should buy a new forward exchange contract for 40 days. This purchase of forward foreign exchange will nullify the sale of foreign exchange that was part of the original covered investment. At the conclusion of the full 90-day period, the foreign exchange that was originally sold will be obtained from that bought 40 days previously.

The extra spot and forward exchange transaction costs from the premature sale of a foreign investment require an initial covered advantage of foreign

---

[17]This is because the high interest rates they pay are tax-deductible. For more on taxes and interest parity see Maurice Levi, "Taxation and 'Abnormal' International Capital Flows," *Journal of Political Economy*, June 1977, pp. 635–646.

investment to make the initial investment worthwhile. There is hence another reason for a band around the parity line. The amount of extra required return and hence the potential width of the band depend on the likelihood that the funds will be needed early and on whether these funds can be borrowed by using the original covered investment as a guarantee. Since the required extra return depends on the *likelihood* that the funds will be needed, it is clear that this liquidity consideration is different from the transaction costs consideration discussed earlier, which involved *known* amounts of transaction costs. Liquidity does relate to transaction costs, but these are *expected* costs. Clearly, if it is known that funds will not be required, or if it is known that the foreign investment can be used as the guarantee or security for borrowing funds, no foreign yield premium is required. The more uncertainty there is concerning future needs and alternative sources of short-term financing, the higher will be the premiums that should be required before venturing into foreign money markets. This will mean wider bands around the interest parity line.[18]

As in the case of transaction costs and political risk, the choice by third-country investors of which country to invest in should be symmetrical. That is, if there is the same probability of needing to liquidate investments from either country and the same transaction costs if liquidation occurs, liquidity preference should not cause deviations from interest parity.

Effect of the Reasons for Interest Disparity on Investment and Borrowing Decisions

Each investor or borrower must evaluate yields and borrowing costs from his or her own perspective. This means using exchange rates that include transaction costs and appropriate tax rates, and then comparing yield or borrowing-cost differences with the difference the investor or borrower believes is necessary to compensate for the risk or illiquidity that is faced. What we have argued in this chapter suggests that except for banks, transaction costs are likely to work toward keeping investing and borrowing at home. Withholding taxes are likely to matter only if withholding rates are higher than domestic tax rates, but differential taxes on interest income versus capital gains could induce investors with favorable capital gains treatment to place funds in currencies that trade at a forward premium.[19] As for political risk, this will create yield and cost differences that are not exploitable for those facing the political risk, although the differences may be exploitable by others.[20] A similar conclusion applies to

---

[18] It might be felt that movements in asset values because of changes in market interest rates also affect the liquidity of domestic investment versus foreign investment. Although the reason is not obvious, this view is not, in general, correct, because relative interest-rate movements should be offset by exchange-rate movements, which are all related according to the interest parity condition.

[19] This opportunity exists even if interest parity holds exactly on a before-tax basis, as will happen as a result of actions of banks for which tax rates on interest and capital gains are equal.

[20] Those that can exploit differences are third-country investors for whom the political risks are similar, and borrowers for whom political risks are irrelevant. Borrowers will tend to borrow in the low-risk countries because covered interest costs there can remain lower than elsewhere.

liquidity premiums. That is, to the extent that interest parity does not hold because foreign investments are less liquid, those investors for whom liquidity is not relevant can enjoy a higher yield. We can see that it can pay to shop around when investing or borrowing, but it all depends on the specific circumstances of the investor or borrower.

SUMMARY

1 Because there is a difference between bid and ask exchange rates and between borrowing and investing interest rates, we must use the correct exchange rates and interest rates in evaluating where to invest or borrow.
2 If round-trip arbitrage were the only force moving exchange rates and interest rates toward interest parity, the deviations could be relatively large. This is because it would be necessary to be compensated in the covered interest differential for foreign exchange transaction costs and borrowing-lending spreads on interest rates.
3 One-way arbitrage involves choosing between alternative ways of going from current dollars/pounds to future pounds/dollars. Because the choices involve the same transaction costs whichever route is taken, one-way arbitrage should drive markets very close to covered interest parity.
4 Third-country investors or borrowers who face the same transaction costs whichever country they choose for borrowing or investment should also drive markets very close to covered interest parity.
5 Political risks can also cause deviations from interest parity and allow a band around the interest parity line, because investors from each country need compensation for the greater risk of investing in the other country. However, if investors outside the two countries view the countries as equally risky politically, they will drive markets to interest parity.
6 Withholding taxes do not affect the interest parity condition. For those who face differential taxes on income versus capital gains, the relevant interest parity line has a different slope, but since many firms pay the same tax on interest and foreign exchange gains, interest disparity should not result from differential taxes.
7 Covered foreign investments are less liquid than domestic investments because extra exchange transaction costs are met on liquidating foreign securities. The liquidity relates to expected rather than actual transaction costs.
8 Each investor or borrower must evaluate opportunities from his or her own perspective of transaction costs, taxes, political risks, and liquidity concerns. There can well be advantages from shopping around.

QUESTIONS

1 Suppose that as the money manager of a U.S. firm you face the following situation:

r_{US}^{B}	9.0%
r_{US}^{I}	8.0%
r_{C}^{B}	10.5%
r_{C}^{I}	9.5%
$S(\text{Can\$}/\text{ask\$})$	1.2400
$S(\text{Can\$}/\text{bid\$})$	1.2350
$F_1(\text{Can\$}/\text{ask\$})$	1.2600
$F_1(\text{Can\$}/\text{bid\$})$	1.2550

Here, r_{US}^B and r_{US}^I are the 1-year interest rates at which you can respectively borrow and invest in the U.S., and r_C^B and r_C^I are the 1-year borrowing and investing interest rates in Canada.

a If you had funds to invest for 1 year, in which country would you invest?

b If you wished to borrow for 1 year, from which country would you borrow?

2 Suppose that you face the situation in Question 1, except that the effective tax rate on interest income is 50 percent, and the effective tax rate on capital gains is 30 percent. Where would you wish to invest?

3 Assuming that there are a large number of third-country borrowers and investors, do you think that political risk will cause larger deviations from interest parity than are caused by transaction costs?

4 If banks are as happy to advance loans that are secured by domestic money-market investments as they are to advance loans secured by similar foreign covered money-market investments, will firms prefer local investments on the grounds of liquidity? How does the importance that should be attached to liquidity relate to the probability that cash will be needed?

5 Use the framework of Figure 8.2 to show how the band of unprofitable arbitrage when one-way arbitrage occurs compares to the band when only round-trip arbitrage occurs.

6 Why might a borrower want to borrow in a currency that is at a forward discount if that borrower faces a higher tax rate on income than on capital gains?

BIBLIOGRAPHY

Bahmani-Oskooee, Mohsen, and Satya P. Das: "Transaction Costs and the Interest Parity Theorem," *Journal of Political Economy*, August 1985, pp. 793–799.

Branson, William H.: "The Minimum Covered Interest Differential Needed for International Arbitrage Activity," *Journal of Political Economy*, December 1969, pp. 1029–1034.

Clinton, Kevin: "Transaction Costs and Covered Interest Arbitrage: Theory and Evidence," *Journal of Political Economy*, April 1988, pp. 358–370.

Deardorff, Alan V.: "One-Way Arbitrage and Its Implications for the Foreign Exchange Markets," *Journal of Political Economy*, April 1979, pp. 351–364.

Frenkel, Jacob A., and Richard M. Levich: "Covered Interest Arbitrage: Unexploited Profits?," *Journal of Political Economy*, April 1975, pp. 325–338.

Levi, Maurice D.: "Taxation and 'Abnormal' International Capital Flows," *Journal of Political Economy*, June 1977, pp. 635–646.

Llewellyn, David T.: *International Financial Integration: The Limits of Sovereignty*, Macmillan, London, 1980.

Officer, Lawrence H., and Thomas D. Willet: "The Covered-Arbitrage Schedule: A Critical Survey of Recent Developments," *Journal of Money, Credit and Banking*, May 1970, pp. 247–257.

FOREIGN EXCHANGE
RISK AND EXPOSURE
AND THEIR MANAGEMENT

Part 4 explains the nature of exchange-rate exposure and the difference between exposure and risk. It also describes the different techniques that are available for managing exposure and risk.

Chapter 9 begins by defining foreign exchange exposure. It is shown that from a U.S. perspective, exposure can be considered as the slope of a line drawn between changes in the dollar values of assets, liabilities, or operating incomes on the one hand, and unanticipated changes in exchange rates on the other. This description of exposure is shown to apply whatever the number of exchange rates that might be relevant. It is explained that domestic as well as foreign assets, liabilities, and operating incomes can be exposed to unanticipated changes in exchange rates. Similarly, it is shown that exchange-rate risk, which is defined as the variability in dollar values of assets, liabilities, or operating incomes due to unanticipated changes in exchange rates, is faced on domestic as well as foreign assets, liabilities, and operating incomes.

After defining exchange-rate exposure and risk and explaining what they depend upon, Chapter 9 describes U.S. international accounting principles, and how well, or poorly, corporate accounts reflect the gains or losses resulting from changes in exchange rates when a firm is exposed. The gains or losses which show up in the accounts, and which are called translation gains or losses, are compared with the theoretically correct amounts, which are called real changes in exchange rates. The real change in exchange rates is distinguished from exposure and from the translation effects that appear in accounts. Comparisons are made for financial and real assets, and for liabilities.

Chapter 9 contains two appendices which help to distinguish exchange-rate exposure from exchange-rate risk. The first appendix does this in terms of statistical measures; the second uses some geometry.

With exposure and risk defined, Chapter 10 turns to how they can be reduced or avoided, that is, how to hedge. After explaining why a firm might want to hedge its exposure (a matter which is more complex than might first appear), Chapter 10 describes a number of hedging techniques. These include forwards, futures, options, swaps, and invoicing procedures. The chapter also considers how to purposely create risk and exposure so as to speculate. Conditions are described for deciding on the best way to speculate. The effects of both hedging and speculative techniques are described graphically and vividly in terms of payoff profiles.

FOREIGN EXCHANGE RISK AND EXPOSURE

Even though foreign exchange risk and exposure have been central issues of international financial management for many years, a considerable degree of confusion remains about their nature and measurement. For example, it is not uncommon to hear the term "foreign exchange exposure" used interchangeably with the term "foreign exchange risk" when in fact they are conceptually completely different. (Foreign exchange risk is related to the variability of domestic-currency values of assets, liabilities, or operating incomes due to unanticipated changes in exchange rates, whereas foreign exchange exposure is what *is* at risk.) This chapter is devoted to clarifying the nature and measurement of risk and exposure, as well as to explaining the factors contributing to them. Because the effects of changes in exchange rates that appear in accounting statements may differ from the real economic effects, we also examine U.S. accounting principles and their implications for exposure.

THE NATURE OF EXCHANGE-RATE RISK AND EXPOSURE

Definition of Foreign Exchange Exposure

Foreign exchange exposure can be defined in the following way:

> Foreign exchange exposure is the sensitivity of the real domestic currency value of assets, liabilities, or operating incomes to unanticipated changes in exchange rates.[1]

---

[1]Exposure is defined this way in Michael Adler and Bernard Dumas, "Exposure to Currency Risk: Definition and Measurement," *Financial Management*, summer 1984, pp. 41–50. See also Christine R. Hekman, "Measuring Foreign Exchange Exposure: A Practical Theory and its Application," *Financial Analysts Journal*, September/October 1983, pp. 59–65; and Lars Oxelheim and Clas G. Wihlborg, *Macroeconomic Uncertainty: International Risks and Opportunities for the Corporation*, Wiley, New York, 1987.

Several features of this definition are worth noting.

First, we notice that exposure is a measure of the *sensitivity* of domestic currency values. That is, it is a description of the *extent* or *degree* to which the home currency value of something is changed by exchange rate changes. Second, we notice that it is concerned with *real domestic currency values*. By this we mean, for example, that from a U.S. perspective exposure is the sensitivity of real—that is, inflation-adjusted—U.S. dollar values of assets and so on, to changes in exchange rates. Third, we notice that exposure can exist on assets and liabilities, or on the operating incomes of firms. Since the values of assets and liabilities are so much at a particular moment in time, and the values of operating incomes are so much per period of time, we see that exposure exists on stocks and flows. Fourth, we notice that we have not qualified the list of exposed items by describing them as being *foreign* assets, and so on. This is because, as we shall see, unanticipated changes in exchange rates can affect domestic as well as foreign assets, liabilities, and operating incomes. Finally, we notice that the definition refers only to *unanticipated* changes in exchange rates. This is because markets compensate for changes in exchange rates that are anticipated. Consequently, it is only to the extent that exchange rates change by more or less than had been expected that there will be gains or losses on assets, liabilities, or operating incomes.

Exposure as a Regression Slope

We can further clarify the definition of foreign exchange exposure at the same time as we describe how it can be calculated by considering Figures 9.1a and b. The horizontal axis in both figures shows unexpected changes in exchange rates, $\Delta S''(\$/\pounds)$, with these being positive to the right of the origin and negative to the left of the origin. Positive values of $\Delta S''(\$/\pounds)$ are unanticipated appreciations of the pound, and negative values are unanticipated depreciations of the pound. The vertical axis of each figure shows the changes in the real values of assets, liabilities, or operating incomes, in terms of a reference currency, which for a U.S. firm is the U.S. dollar. We can interpret ΔV as the change in the real value of particular individual assets, liabilities, or operating incomes, or as the change in the real value of a collection of assets, liabilities, or operating incomes. As we have said, ΔV is in real terms, and so it is adjusted for U.S. inflation.[2]

When there is an unanticipated change in an exchange rate, there will be an accompanying change in the dollar value of, for example, a foreign-currency bank account, real-estate investment, stock, bond, or loan. Of course, factors other than exchange rates may also influence the dollar values of these items, and so we cannot always predict with certainty how dollar values will change

---

[2]Of course, inflation itself is unknown and contributes to uncertainty. However, because of the difficulty of dealing with uncertain inflation, this problem is usually ignored in discussions of exposure. Furthermore, because it is difficult to keep track of real values in the context of examples of exposure, in much of what follows we ignore the level of inflation as well as uncertainty about inflation. However, this is done only for expositional convenience, and does not imply that the level of inflation or uncertainty about inflation is unimportant.

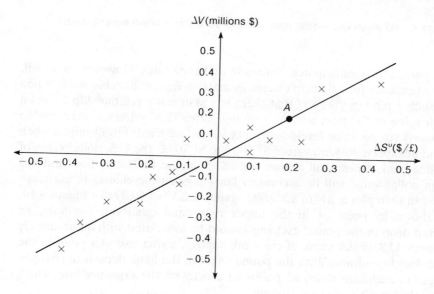

(a) Exposure line for "foreign" assets

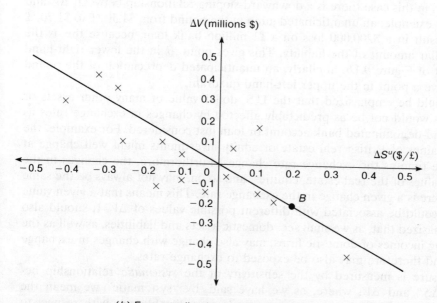

(b) Exposure line for "foreign" liabilities

FIGURE 9.1

EXPOSURE AS THE SLOPE OF A REGRESSION LINE. Each unanticipated change in the exchange rate will be associated with a change in the dollar value of an asset, liability, or operating income. The unanticipated change in the exchange rate can be plotted against the associated change in dollar value. Because other factors also affect values, the same $\Delta S^u(\$/\pounds)$ will not always be associated with the same ΔV. However, there may be a systematic relationship between $\Delta S^u(\$/\pounds)$ and ΔV. For example, unanticipated pound appreciations may typically be associated with higher dollar values of pound-denominated assets and lower dollar values of pound-denominated liabilities, the former implying an upward-sloping scatter and the latter a downward-sloping scatter.

189

with any particular unanticipated change in exchange rates. However, there will often be a tendency for values to change in more or less predictable ways. When there is such a tendency we say that there is a **systematic relationship** between the dollar value of the item and the exchange rate. This systematic relationship is particularly strong when foreign-currency values are fixed. For example, when the pound unexpectedly jumps from $1.50/£ to $1.70/£, the U.S. dollar value of a £1 million bank deposit will change from $1.5 million to $1.7 million, and this change in dollar value will be accurately known, given the change in exchange rate. We can then plot a ΔV of $200,000 against a ΔS^u of $0.2/£ in Figure 9.1$a$. This is shown by point A in the upper right-hand quadrant. Similarly, an unexpected drop in the pound exchange would be associated with an accurately known lower U.S. dollar value of the bank deposit, giving rise to a point in the lower left-hand quadrant. With the pound value of the bank deposit unchanged by changes in exchange rates, all points sit exactly on the **exposure line**, which for the bank deposit is upward sloping.

If we consider a pound-denominated bank loan instead of a bank deposit, the effect of unanticipated changes in exchange rates is again accurately known. However, in this case there is a downward-sloping relationship between ΔV and ΔS^u. For example, an unanticipated jump in the pound from $1.50/£ to $1.70/£ would result in a $200,000 loss on a £1 million bank loan, because this is the extra dollar amount of the liability. This gives point B in the lower right-hand quadrant of Figure 9.1b. Similarly, an unanticipated depreciation of the pound would give a point in the upper left-hand quadrant.

It should be emphasized that the U.S. dollar value of many other assets or liabilities would not be as predictably affected by changes in exchange rates as the pound-denominated bank account or loan just considered. For example, the pound values of British real estate or equity investments might well change at the same time as the exchange rate changes. Furthermore, the changes in the pound values of the real estate, equities, and so on, may not always be the same when there is a given change in the exchange rate. This means that a given value of ΔS^u could be associated with different possible values of ΔV. It should also be emphasized that, as we shall see, domestic assets and liabilities, as well as the operating incomes of domestic firms, may also change with changes in exchange rates, and therefore may also be exposed to exchange rates.

Exposure is measured by the sensitivity of the *systematic* relationship between ΔS^u and ΔV, where, as we have said, by "systematic" we mean the tendency for ΔV to change in a more or less predictable way with respect to ΔS^u. That is, by "systematic relationship" we mean the way ΔS^u and ΔV are *on average* related to each other. Of course, because the actual ΔV associated with a given ΔS^u is not always the same, the equation which describes the relationship between ΔV and ΔS^u must allow for random errors. Such an equation is a **regression equation**, which, for exposure to the dollar-pound exchange rate for which $\Delta S^u = \Delta S^u(\$/£)$, takes the form

$$\Delta V = \beta_0 + \beta_1 \Delta S^u(\$/£) + \mu \qquad (9.1)$$

Here β_0 and β_1 are the **regression coefficients**. The regression coefficient β_0 is the constant in the equation, and shows how much ΔV changes on average when $\Delta S^u(\$/\pounds) = 0$. The other regression coefficient β_1, describes the systematic relation between ΔV and $\Delta S^u(\$/\pounds)$. That is, β_1 describes the tendency for ΔV and $\Delta S^u(\$/\pounds)$ to be related. The term μ is the random error in the relationship, and is called the **regression error**. The role of μ is to allow the value of ΔV to be less than perfectly predictable for a given $\Delta S^u(\$/\pounds)$.[3]

The item of most interest in Equation (9.1) is β_1. This is because β_1 describes the sensitivity of the systematic relation between unanticipated changes in exchange rates, $\Delta S^u(\$/\pounds)$, and changes in the values of assets and so on, ΔV. That is, β_1 is the sensitivity measure we have called foreign exchange exposure.[4] Because β_1 is the slope of the line described by Equation (9.1) we can redefine exposure as follows:

> Foreign exchange exposure is the slope of the regression equation which relates changes in the real domestic currency value of assets, liabilities, or operating incomes to unanticipated changes in exchange rates.

Let us consider how we might estimate β_1.

Estimating Exposure

As we have seen, we can plot the values of ΔV and associated ΔS^u's on a graph such as Figure 9.1. Of course, to do this we would have to know how much of the actual changes in exchange rates were unanticipated, and also be able to measure the changes in the real dollar values of assets, and so on. However, this may not be as difficult as one might think. In particular, the unanticipated changes in exchange rates may be judged from looking back at forward exchange rates, which are predictions of future spot exchange rates, and subtracting the forward rates from the actual exchange rates.[5] Similarly, dollar values of assets and liabilities may be apparent in stock and bond prices.[6] After we have plotted the values of the ΔV's and associated ΔS^u's, we can fit a line to the scatter of points.

Of course, if the values of ΔV are affected only by the values of ΔS^u, as in the examples of the British pound bank deposit and bank loan, the observed ΔV's and ΔS^u's would all sit exactly along a line. Then, exposure is deduced

---

[3]Normally, subscripts are placed on ΔV, $\Delta S^u(\$/\pounds)$, and μ to identify the particular observations on these variables we are considering. The observations could be for different periods of time, or for different potential situations at a given moment in time.

[4]This means that exposure can be defined in the terms used to define the slope coefficient of a regression. Those readers with a background in statistics will realize that this means that by definition the exposure is $\text{cov}(\Delta V, \Delta S^u)/\text{var}(\Delta S^u)$. This definition, and some of the implications of writing exposure in this way, are explored in Appendix 9.1. See also Adler and Dumas, *op. cit.*, and Oxelheim and Wihlborg, *op. cit.*

[5]The reason why forward rates can be considered to proxy for expected future spot rates is explained in Chapter 10.

[6]The effects on operating incomes are likely to be much more difficult to measure. This is discussed in Chapter 18.

from joining the points and measuring the slope of the resulting line. However, for other assets, liabilities, incomes, and payments, there is noise in the relation, so the points describing ΔV's and associated ΔS^u's will look like the scatters in Figure 9.1a and b. When this happens we must use statistical procedures to fit the line .and find the systematic relationship. One such procedure is **ordinary least squares**, which finds the line through the scatter of points that minimizes the value of the sum of squared distances of the points from the line. The distances are squared so that both positive and negative deviations of actual observations from the line are counted as positive.[7]

Once we have fitted a line to the scatter of observations on ΔV's and associated ΔS^u's, we have estimates of the regression coefficients. If the estimated line passes through the origin, as in Figure 9.1a and b, we shall find β_0 to be insignificantly different from zero, and can then ignore this constant term.

Our estimate of exposure is the estimated value of β_1. However, before we consider questions such as how accurate this estimate is, and how closely ΔV is related to ΔS^u, we should consider the units of measurement of exposure, β_1. We shall find that exposure is measured in units that make good sense.[8]

Units of Measurement of Exposure

If ΔV is measured in U.S. dollars, as it will be if we are measuring exposure from a U.S. perspective, and if ΔS^u is measured in dollars per pound, then exposure, that is, β_1, must be measured in pounds. This is because in terms of units of measurement, Equation (9.1) involves $\$ = \beta_1 \cdot (\$/£)$, so that $\beta_1 = \$ \div (\$/£) = £$.

The fact that exposure is measured in units of the foreign currency is most appropriate, as can be seen by reconsidering our examples involving pound-denominated bank deposits and loans. In the case of bank deposits, when the exchange rate unexpectedly changes from $1.50/£ to $1.70/£, a £1 million bank deposit is worth $200,000 more. That is, assuming $\beta_0 = 0$ and $\mu = 0$ in Equation (9.1),

$$\$200,000 = \beta_1 \cdot \$0.20/£.$$

or

$$\beta_1 = \$200,000 \div \$0.20/£ = £1,000,000$$

We find that exposure is £1 million. This is the amount that is at risk to

---

[7]Ordinary least-squares estimation methods are described in most introductory statistics textbooks and all econometrics textbooks.

[8]It is beyond the scope of this book to consider the possibility of bias in estimates of β_1. Bias will occur if there is a systematic relation between ΔS^u and the regression error μ.

unanticipated changes in exchange rates.[9] In a similar way, exposure on a £1 million bank loan is calculated from the fact that a loss of $200,000 is made when $\Delta S^u = \$0.20/\pounds$, so that

$$-\$200,000 = \beta_1 \cdot \$0.20/\pounds$$

or

$$\beta_1 = \$200,000 \div \$0.20/\pounds = -\pounds1,000,000$$

In the case of the slope being negative we say the item has a **short exposure**, whereas when the slope is positive we say the item has a **long exposure**. However, because *a priori* we do not know whether ΔS^u will be positive or negative, we sometimes drop the negative sign and say the exposure is, for example, £1 million, whether the exposure is on a bank deposit or bank loan.

In the case of bank deposits and loans the pound amounts are unchanged as the exchange rate changes. However, what do we do if, at the same time as exchange rates change, there is a change in the pound value of an asset or liability? Or what do we do if there are many exchange rates changing at the same time? It is in these situations that the definition of exposure in terms of slope coefficients of a regression line comes to the fore. Indeed, when we consider these more complex situations, we find out why even assets, liabilities, and operating incomes that appear to be entirely domestic may in fact be exposed to exchange rates and subject to exchange-rate risk.

Exposure When Local Currency Values Vary with Unanticipated Changes in Exchange Rates

Suppose a piece of British real estate has a market value of £1 million when the exchange rate is $\$1.80/\pounds$. Let us suppose that inflation subsequently occurs, and is reflected both in the value of the real estate and in the exchange rate. In particular, let us suppose the inflation causes the pound to depreciate to $\$1.60/\pounds$, and the property value to increase to £1.125 million. In this case the dollar value of the real estate before inflation has occurred is

$$\$1.80/\pounds \times \pounds1 \text{ million} = \$1.8 \text{ million}$$

and after the inflation has occurred it is

$$\$1.60/\pounds \times \pounds1.125 \text{ million} = \$1.8 \text{ million}$$

We see that with the assumed numbers there is no change in the dollar value of the British real estate.

---

[9]In this example and the examples that follow we assume that U.S. inflation is zero, so that the real change in value equals the nominal change in value.

In terms of Equation (9.1), if all the assumed change in exchange rate is unanticipated, what we have is $\Delta V = 0$ and $\Delta S^u = -\$0.20/\pounds$, so that

$$0 = \beta_0 + \beta_1(-\$0.20/\pounds) + \mu \tag{9.2}$$

If β_0 and μ are both zero, then the only way Equation (9.2) can hold is if $\beta_1 = 0$. That is, if the pound value of the British real estate and the exchange rate of the pound change systematically as in the example, the real estate is not exposed. The reason is that the change in the exchange rate exactly compensates for the change in the pound value of the real estate.

Of course, we have constructed a special case in this example, and on selecting different numbers we would have found the real estate to be exposed to unanticipated changes in exchange rates. For example, if the real estate systematically increased in value from £1 million to £1.0625 million with the depreciation of the exchange rate from $\$1.80/\pounds$ to $\$1.60/\pounds$, then

$$\Delta V = (\$1.60/\pounds) \times \pounds1.0625 \text{ million} - (\$1.80/\pounds) \times \pounds1.00 \text{ million}$$
$$= -\$0.10 \text{ million}$$

Assuming β_0 and μ are zero, the exposure given by Equation (9.1) is β_1 from

$$-\$0.10 \text{ million} = \beta_1 \cdot (-\$0.20/\pounds)$$

i.e.,

$$\beta_1 = \pounds500,000$$

That is, if this outcome occurred systematically, then the exposure on the British real estate would be only half its market value. Similarly, if the value of the real estate happened to decrease systematically from £1 million to £0.9375 million with the same change in the exchange rate, then

$$\Delta V = (\$1.60/\pounds) \times \pounds0.9375 \text{ million} - (\$1.80/\pounds) \times \pounds1.00 \text{ million}$$
$$= -\$0.3 \text{ million},$$

and the exposure is given by

$$-\$0.3 = \beta_1(-\$0.20/\pounds),$$

i.e.,

$$\beta_1 = \pounds1.50 \text{ million.}$$

That is, the exposure on the £1 million British real estate is 50 percent larger than the value of the real estate itself.[10]

---

[10] In reality it is unlikely that the pound value of the real estate would systematically decline when the pound depreciates if the depreciation is due to inflation. However, as we shall see later, stocks may well be exposed more than their market value.

Exposure against Numerous Exchange Rates

When many different exchange rates can affect ΔV, as when ΔV is the value of a firm that holds assets and liabilities in many countries and currencies, or earns incomes in many countries and currencies, we can use an extension of Equation (9.1) to estimate exposure. For example if ΔV could conceivably be influenced by the exchange rates of the dollar versus the British pound, German mark, Japanese yen, French franc, and so on, we can use the **multiple regression equation**

$$\Delta V = \beta_0 + \beta_1 \Delta S^u(\$/\pounds) + \beta_2 \Delta S^u(\$/DM)$$
$$+ \beta_3 \Delta S^u(\$/\yen) + \beta_4 \Delta S^u(\$/Fr) + \mu \qquad (9.3)$$

Each slope coefficient gives exposure to the associated foreign currency. For example, β_2 gives the sensitivity of ΔV to unanticipated changes in the U.S. dollar value of the German mark. As in the case of exposure to only one exchange rate, the coefficients are all measured in units of the foreign currency. Furthermore, as in the case of exposure to only one currency, the coefficients all depend on the tendency for ΔV to be associated with the ΔS^u for each exchange rate.

Exposure on "Domestic" Assets, Liabilities, and Operating Incomes

It might seem that from a U.S. perspective, such items as U.S. treasury bills and bonds, U.S. corporate stocks and bonds, and operating incomes from businesses in the United States are not exposed to exchange rates. After all, we do not have to multiply foreign-currency values of such items by an uncertain exchange rate in order to compute their U.S. dollar values. The reality is, however, that all these items may well be exposed to exchange rates. This is because their U.S. dollar values may be systematically affected by exchange rates, even though we do not have to do any **translation** into dollar terms. Let us see why exposure might exist by considering first the case of U.S. bonds.

Suppose that when the U.S. dollar falls vis-à-vis other leading currencies, the Federal Reserve typically tries to reduce the dollar's depreciation by increasing interest rates. Such a policy is known as "leaning against the wind," and there is substantial evidence that it is practiced.[11] When interest rates increase, the market values of bonds decline. If the relationship between exchange rates and interest rates is systematic, the U.S. holders of U.S. bonds are exposed to exchange rates. This is the case because they lose when the dollar unexpectedly depreciates, and they gain when it appreciates.

[11]For example, see Bruno Solnik, "Using Financial Prices to Test Exchange Rate Models: A Note," *Journal of Finance*, March 1987, pp. 141–149. Solnik shows that exchange rates and interest rates are negatively related, which suggests that central banks increase interest rates when their currencies are depreciating.

Our definition of exposure in terms of the slope of a regression line confirms that U.S. holders of U.S. bonds are indeed exposed if the Federal Reserve systematically leans against the wind. This is because in such a case we have, referring back to Equation (9.1), that when, for example, $\Delta S''(\$/£)$ is large and positive because of a depreciation of the dollar, ΔV is typically large and negative. Therefore, there is a negative association between $\Delta S''(\$/£)$ and ΔV, which produces a negative slope β_1. Furthermore, the larger the impact of an unanticipated dollar depreciation on U.S. interest rates and bond prices, the greater is the exposure. Similarly, if U.S. stock prices systematically decline as U.S. interest rates increase, then the Federal Reserve's policy of leaning against the wind will expose U.S. stocks too. That is, a depreciating dollar will mean lower stock prices. This means that from a non-U.S. perspective, U.S. stocks are exposed more than their market value. This follows because the combined effect of a depreciating dollar and a declining dollar value of U.S. stocks is a more substantial decline in the foreign-currency values of U.S. stocks than the decline in their dollar values.

While stock prices in general might decline when the U.S. dollar unexpectedly depreciates, some stocks may benefit from the dollar depreciation. In particular, stocks of U.S. export-oriented firms might increase in value because the cheaper dollar makes the firms more competitive in foreign markets. Indeed, since a dollar depreciation makes imports to the U.S. more expensive, some U.S. firms which sell exclusively in the U.S. market, but which compete against imports, may also gain from a depreciation. If the extra profitability of the U.S. export-oriented and import-competing firms shows up in higher stock prices, then these stocks are exposed. In this case there is a positive association between ΔV and $\Delta S''$.[12]

Estimation Difficulties

Unfortunately, the calculation of exposure is not as straightforward as our definition might suggest. This is because exposure changes over time. Consequently, we cannot collect values of ΔV and relevant $\Delta S''$'s over a period of time and fit an equation like Equation (9.3).[13] Instead, it is necessary to employ other techniques such as an analysis of possible scenarios. This involves the generation of values of ΔV which might occur for different $\Delta S''$'s. For example, possible values of ΔV and $\Delta S''(\$/£)$ might be generated for different rates of inflation. A regression line can then be fitted to the generated data. As might be surmised, this is a rather lengthy process.

[12]As we mentioned earlier, because the effects on operating incomes show up in the future, the exposure of export-oriented and import-competing firms is different from the exposure on assets and liabilities, which shows up as gains or losses only at the time changes in exchange rates occur. Of course, market values of publicly-traded export-oriented and import-competing firms should change immediately, converting operating exposure into asset exposure.

[13]One of the results of fitting a line which assumes constant coefficients when they are in fact variable is low t statistics. The t statistic is a measure of the accuracy of estimation of regression coefficients.

Definition of Foreign Exchange Risk

In the important article in which they define exposure in the way we have done in this chapter, Michael Adler and Bernard Dumas define foreign exchange risk in terms of the variance of unanticipated changes in exchange rates.[14] That is, they define exchange-rate risk in terms of the unpredictability of exchange rates as reflected by the variance of ΔS^u, that is, $\text{var}(\Delta S^u)$.

While Adler and Dumas's definition makes it clear that unpredictability is paramount in the measurement of exchange-rate risk, this author prefers a different focus on variability. The definition of **exchange-rate risk** we shall use is:

Foreign exchange risk is measured by the variance of the domestic-currency value of an asset, liability, or operating income that is attributable to unanticipated changes in exchange rates.

The principal difference between the definition used in this book and that of Adler and Dumas is that the definition used here focuses on the unpredictability of values of assets, liabilities, or operating incomes due to uncertainty in exchange rates, not on the uncertainty of exchange rates themselves. This difference in definitions can have important consequences. For example, according to our definition, an asset is not subject to exchange-rate risk if its value does not depend on exchange rates, even though exchange rates might be extremely volatile. According to our definition, volatility in exchange rates is responsible for exchange-rate risk only if it translates into volatility in real dollar values of assets, liabilities, or operating incomes. This makes exchange-rate risk dependent on exposure as well as on $\text{var}(\Delta S^u)$. Let us see why this is so by reconsidering the regression equation (9.1).

Equation (9.1) makes it clear that changes in the values of assets, liabilities, or operating incomes depend both on exchange rates and on other factors, with the effect of the non-exchange-rate factors captured by the term μ. We can isolate the effect of exchange rates from the effect of other factors if we define the variable

$$\Delta \hat{V} = \beta_0 + \beta_1 \Delta S^u(\$/\pounds) \tag{9.4}$$

$\Delta \hat{V}$ is the change in value of an asset, liability, or operating income *that is due to the exchange rate*. That is, we have partitioned the total change in value, ΔV, into that due to changes in exchange rates, $\Delta \hat{V}$, and that due to other influences, μ; this follows by relating Equation (9.4) to Equation (9.1), giving

$$\Delta V \equiv \Delta \hat{V} + \mu \tag{9.5}$$

[14] Michael Adler and Bernard Dumas, *op. cit.* We might note that because the probabilities of outcomes are not known, it would be more appropriate to refer to exchange-rate *uncertainty* rather than to *risk*. However, because it has become customary to use the term risk, we will also use this term.

With ΔV so partitioned, we can explain how our definition of exchange-rate risk relates to exchange-rate exposure and to the definition of risk due to Adler and Dumas.

Our definition of exchange-rate risk as the variance of the values of assets, liabilities, or operating incomes due to unanticipated changes in exchange rates is a definition in terms of $\text{var}(\Delta\hat{V})$, where $\Delta\hat{V}$ is as defined in Equation (9.4). Applying standard statistical procedures to Equation (9.4), we have[15]

$$\text{var}(\Delta\hat{V}) = \beta_1^2\,\text{var}(\Delta S^u) \tag{9.6}$$

Equation (9.6) shows that risk as we have defined it depends on foreign-exchange exposure. This is because β_1 appears on the right-hand side of Equation (9.6). However, exchange-rate risk also depends directly on $\text{var}(\Delta S^u)$, the variance of unanticipated changes in exchange rates, which is the risk measure used by Adler and Dumas.

Equation (9.6) makes it clear that exchange-rate risk requires both exposure and unpredictability of exchange rates. Exposure on its own does not mean exchange-rate risk if exchange rates are perfectly predictable. Similarly, unpredictability of exchange rates does not mean exchange-rate risk for items that are not exposed. Equation (9.6) shows that exchange-rate risk is proportional to exposure squared, and proportional to the variance of unanticipated changes in exchange rates.[16]

EXPOSURE, RISK, AND THE PARITY RELATIONSHIPS*

With exchange-rate risk and exposure now defined and compared, we can consider how the amounts of risk and exposure on particular items are related to PPP and interest parity. This will allow us to clarify several features of risk and exposure that we have alluded to, but not so far systematically explored.

Exposure, Risk, and Interest Parity

Interest parity, the focus of the previous two chapters, can be summarized in the U.S.-British context by Equation (7.10):

$$(1 + r_{\text{US}})^n = \frac{F_n(\$/£)}{S(\$/£)} \cdot (1 + r_{\text{UK}})^n \tag{7.10}$$

The right-hand side of Equation (7.10) gives the hedged dollar receipts to a U.S. investor on an n-year British interest-bearing security. Clearly, if the British

---

[15] See Johnston, ibid., or any introductory textbook in statistics.

[16] In Appendix 9.2 to this chapter we show the connection between exchange-rate risk and exposure within a geometrical framework.

*Sections marked with an asterisk can be omitted on first reading without loss of continuity.

security is hedged and held to maturity, unanticipated changes in exchange rates can have no effect on the dollar value of the security. That is, the hedged British security is not exposed and faces no foreign exchange risk. Indeed, this is why the return equals that on U.S. securities.[17] However, the lack of exposure and risk on the British security is only because the security is combined with a forward contract, and because both the security and forward contract are held to maturity.

When a foreign-currency-denominated security is not hedged with a forward contract or may be sold before maturity, the security is exposed and subject to exchange-rate risk, irrespective of interest parity. Indeed, the presence or absence of interest parity has no bearing even on the amount of exchange-rate risk or exposure. This can be seen if we reconsider the definitions of these terms.

We have defined exposure as the slope coefficient in the regression equation

$$\Delta V = \beta_0 + \beta_1 \Delta S^u(\$/\pounds) + \mu \tag{9.1}$$

If there is an unanticipated change in the exchange rate, the change in the dollar value of, for example, an unhedged interest-bearing British security depends on:

1 the effect of the exchange rate on the pound value of the security, and
2 the effect of the exchange rate on the translation of the pound value of the security into dollars.

If the pound value of the security does not systematically change with unanticipated changes in exchange rates, the only effect of ΔS^u on ΔV is via the translation of the pound value into dollars. This is the same situation as is faced on a British pound bank deposit, which is affected only via the translation of pounds into dollars and, as we saw earlier in this chapter, has an exposure equal to its face value. We find that if the pound value of a British security does not systematically vary with unanticipated changes in exchange rates, its exposure equals its face value, whatever the interest rate that is earned on the security.

If interest parity were to influence the amount of exposure or risk on a British interest-bearing security, it would have to have an implication for the change in the pound value of the security after unanticipated changes in exchange rates. For example, if interest parity implied that pound values of British securities systematically increased in proportion to unanticipated depreciations of the pound against the U.S. dollar, British securities would not be exposed; the higher pound value would compensate for the depreciated currency to leave ΔV, which is measured in dollars, unaffected by $\Delta S^u(\$/\pounds)$.[18]

---

[17] We recall that exposure and risk are in terms of the effects on *real* dollar values, and since exchange rates can affect prices of what security holders purchase, there can still be risk and exposure. In this chapter we abstract from this difficult issue.

[18] If the effect were not just systematic but always occurred, there would be no foreign exchange *risk* either.

However, there is no such implication of interest parity for exposure. While interest parity does suggest that *anticipated* changes in exchange rates are compensated for in interest differentials, there is no compensation for *unanticipated* changes in exchange rates.[19] With no implication of interest parity for a systematic effect of $\Delta S^u(\$/£)$ on the pound value of British interest-bearing securities, there is no implication for exposure.[20]

Interest parity also has no implication for exchange-rate risk, which we have measured by

$$\text{var}(\Delta \hat{V}) = \beta_1^2 \cdot \text{var}(\Delta S^u) \tag{9.6}$$

This is because it has no implications for the exposure β_1 or for the variability of unanticipated changes in exchange rates, $\text{var}(\Delta S^u)$.

Exposure, Risk, and Purchasing-Power Parity

Whereas there are no implications of unhedged interest parity for exposure and risk, the situation is quite different for purchasing-power parity. In the case of PPP there are implications for exposure and risk on real assets such as real estate and equities, the prices of which can systematically vary with exchange rates.[21] There are also implications of PPP for exposure and risk on the operating incomes of export-oriented, import-competing, and import-using firms. It is useful to consider the implications of PPP for real assets separately from those for operating incomes.

PPP and Real-Asset Exposure   We can explore the implications of PPP for risk and exposure of real assets such as real estate and equities by referring to the example involving British real estate discussed earlier in this chapter. The essential features of the example are summarized in the top two rows of Table 9.1. The table shows a British real-estate investment that has a value of £1 million in period zero when the exchange rate is $1.80/£, and has a value of £1.125 million one period later when the exchange rate is $1.60/£. As the table shows, these numbers imply that the dollar value of the real estate is unchanged and equal to $1.8 million despite the change in exchange rate. We pointed out earlier that if this situation systematically occurred the real-estate investment would not be exposed. What we did not point out earlier is what might cause the numbers to behave as they do in Table 9.1, causing an exposure of zero.

[19]As we saw in Chapter 8, the interest differential is closely related to the *anticipated* change in the spot rate.

[20]Of course, while interest parity does not imply anything about a systematic relationship between $\Delta S^u(\$/£)$ and the pound value of British securities, this does not mean there is no systematic relationship between $\Delta S^u(\$/£)$ and the pound value of British securities. For example, if the Bank of England systematically leans against the wind, British security prices will decline as $\Delta S^u(\$/£)$ decreases.

[21]Assets without a fixed face value, such as real estate and equities, are sometimes referred to as **noncontractual assets**, while assets with a fixed face value, such as bills and bonds, are referred to as **contractual assets**. A bank loan or corporate bond is a **contractual liability**.

TABLE 9.1
PPP AND REAL-ASSET VALUES

Time	£ value, millions	$S(\$/£)$	$ value, millions
0	1.000	1.80	1.80
1	1.125	1.60	1.80
2	1.286	1.40	1.80
3	1.500	1.20	1.80
4	1.800	1.00	1.80

We recall from Chapter 6 that in its relative form PPP can be written as

$$\dot{S}(\$/£) = \frac{\dot{P}_{US} - \dot{P}_{UK}}{1 + \dot{P}_{UK}} \tag{6.7}$$

where the dots over variables mean rates of change. The numbers in Table 9.1 would occur if British real-estate prices followed the overall British rate of inflation, and this rate were 12.5 percent, while U.S. inflation was zero. In such a case we have from Equation (6.7)

$$\dot{S}(\$/£) = \frac{0.0 - 0.125}{1.125} = -0.1111$$

This rate of change of the exchange rate would mean that if in period zero the exchange rate was $1.80/£, then in period 1 it would be 11.11 percent lower than in period zero. That is, if PPP is to hold, the exchange rate in period 1 must be

$$(\$1.80/£) \cdot (1 - 0.1111) = \$1.60/£$$

We can see that the numbers in Table 9.1 would occur if PPP held precisely in an ex post sense, and if the pound value of the British real estate precisely followed the British rate of inflation. In such a situation there is zero exposure. There is also no foreign exchange risk if PPP always holds *ex post*. That is so because the dollar value of the asset is the same whatever happens to the exchange rate; any change in exchange rate is precisely offset by the change in the pound value of the asset.

In reality, two empirical facts force us to reconsider the absence of exposure and risk on real assets such as real estate. These two facts are:

1 As we saw in Chapter 6, PPP does not hold, at least in the short run.
2 Any individual real-estate investment, or even real estate in general, will not usually change in value by the overall rate of inflation.

Let us consider the implications of each of these facts.

If the deviations from PPP are random in the sense that exchange rates are sometimes higher and sometimes lower than their PPP values, but on average equal their PPP values, then the exposure is still zero, just as if PPP always held. The reason for this can be explained by referring back to Figure 9.1. It is clear from this figure that we shall find the same slope on a fitted regression equation between ΔV and ΔS^u whether all observations fit exactly on the regression line, or they are as likely above as below the line. In the event that PPP holds exactly *ex post*, all the observations will sit exactly along the horizontal axis, because ΔV is always zero. This gives an exposure of zero. In the event that deviations from PPP occur, but are random with a zero mean, the observations will be above and below the horizontal axis because ΔV is sometimes positive and sometimes negative. However, the estimated exposure line will still sit exactly along the horizontal axis. Again the exposure is zero.

If PPP holds only on average, the variations in the domestic currency values of assets or liabilities will, *ceteris paribus*, be higher than if PPP always holds exactly. This is because the deviations from PPP will contribute to variations in the values of assets and liabilities. That is, if PPP holds on average, var(ΔV) will be higher *ceteris paribus* than if PPP holds at all times. However, the variations in ΔV due to departures from PPP are not attributable to changes in exchange rates. Rather, they are due to other factors affecting ΔV, which themselves contribute to deviations from PPP. That is, while random deviations from PPP contribute to var(ΔV), the total variance in ΔV, they do not affect var($\Delta \hat{V}$), the variance in ΔV due to unanticipated changes in exchange rates. This confirms with what we would conclude from Equation (9.6), namely, that when there is no exposure, so that $\beta_1 = 0$, there is no exchange-rate risk, irrespective of whether $\beta_1 = 0$ because PPP always holds or because PPP holds on average.

The second fact we mentioned is that individual asset prices do not in general change at a country's overall rate of inflation. As with random PPP violations, this does not change exposure if, on average, individual asset prices move at the rate of inflation; there is no change in the systematic relationship between ΔS^u and ΔV. What is affected by individual asset prices moving differently than overall inflation is the total amount of risk. Added to the risk caused by PPP deviations is a **relative-price risk**. This risk is not, however, due to exchange-rate changes, and so, while it adds to total risk, it does not add to exchange-rate risk.

PPP and Operating Exposure   As we have mentioned, there are implications of PPP for the exposure of operating incomes of export-oriented, import-competing, and import-using firms. This type of exposure is not surprisingly called **operating exposure**, and the risk is called **operating risk**. In particular, operating exposure is the sensitivity of operating income to unanticipated changes in exchange rates. Similarly, operating risk is the variance of operating income directly attributable to unanticipated changes in exchange rates.

Operating risk and exposure involve the effects of exchange rates on the current and future profitability of firms. We should be careful to distinguish operating risk and exposure from the effects of exchange rates on the dollar values of foreign currency accounts receivable and payable. Accounts receivable and payable are fixed-face-value, short-term assets and liabilities, and have risk and exposure like those of foreign-currency bank accounts and loans. On the other hand, operating incomes do not have fixed face values. Indeed, as we shall see, operating exposure depends on such factors as the elasticity of demand for imports or exports, the fraction of input prices that depend on exchange rates, the flexibility of production to respond to exchange-rate-induced changes in demand, and the reference currency for computing operating incomes.[22]

We can show how different operating risk and exposure are from risk and exposure on assets and liabilities, as well as show the relevance of PPP for operating risk and exposure, by considering the case of a U.S. exporter selling to Britain. Let us consider under what conditions the profit or operating income of the exporter is systematically affected by exchange rates.[23]

Let us denote the dollar profits of the U.S. exporting firm by π; then from the definition of profits as revenue minus costs we can write

$$\pi = S(\$/£)p_{UK}q - C_{US}q$$

or

$$\pi = [S(\$/£)p_{UK} - C_{US}]q \tag{9.7}$$

Here p_{UK} is the pound price of the U.S. firm's export good in Britain, and C_{US} is the (constant) per-unit U.S. dollar production cost of the export. The product, $S(\$/£)p_{UK}$, is the export sales price of the company's product in dollars, and so the difference between $S(\$/£)p_{UK}$ and C_{US} is the dollar profit ("markup") per unit sold. By multiplying this difference by the total quantity of sales, q, we get the U.S. exporter's total profit in dollar terms, or π.

In order to see the conditions under which changes in exchange rates will raise or lower a U.S. exporter's profits, we will write the annual rates of change in exchange rates and profits as $\dot{S}$ and $\dot{\pi}$. As before, the dot over a variable signifies a rate of change. Let us assume that the market selling price of the company's product in the United Kingdom grows at the British general rate of inflation, which we have written as $\dot{P}_{UK}$. Let us also assume that the production cost of the product, which is made in the United States, grows at the general rate of inflation in the United States, $\dot{P}_{US}$. For the given output level q, we can write the U.S. exporter's profit at the end of the year as follows:

$$\pi(1 + \dot{\pi}) = [S(\$/£)p_{UK}(1 + \dot{S})(1 + \dot{P}_{UK}) - C_{US}(1 + \dot{P}_{US})]q \tag{9.8}$$

---

[22] The reasons why these factors influence operating risk and exposure are explained in Chapter 18.

[23] The case of a U.S. importer is a natural extension of that of a U.S. exporter, and is left as an exercise for the reader.

Equation (9.8) is obtained from Equation (9.7) merely by replacing π with $\pi(1 + \dot{\pi})$, $S(\$/£)$ with $S(\$/£)(1 + \dot{S})$, and so on.

Subtracting Equation (9.7) from Equation (9.8) gives

$$\dot{\pi} = \left\{ S(\$/£)p_{UK}\left[\dot{S}(1 + \dot{P}_{UK}) + \dot{P}_{UK}\right] - C_{US}\dot{P}_{US}\right\}q/\pi$$

Profits will grow after, for example, a depreciation or devaluation of the dollar (when $\dot{S}$ is positive) if $\dot{\pi} > 0$, that is, if

$$S(\$/£)p_{UK}\left[\dot{S}(1 + \dot{P}_{UK}) + \dot{P}_{UK}\right] - C_{US}\dot{P}_{US} > 0$$

If the devaluation or depreciation takes place when the profits are zero $[S(\$/£)p_{UK} = C_{US}]$, we can rewrite this as

$$S(\$/£)p_{UK}\left[\dot{S}(1 + \dot{P}_{UK}) + \dot{P}_{UK} - \dot{P}_{US}\right] > 0$$

Since $S(\$/£)$ and p_{UK} are positive, a devaluation or depreciation of the dollar will raise a U.S. exporter's profits if

$$\dot{S} > \frac{\dot{P}_{US} - \dot{P}_{UK}}{1 + \dot{P}_{UK}} \tag{9.9}$$

and reduce profits if

$$\dot{S} < \frac{\dot{P}_{US} - \dot{P}_{UK}}{1 + \dot{P}_{UK}} \tag{9.10}$$

Comparison of the inequalities (9.9) and (9.10) with the relative form of PPP in Equation (6.7) shows that for effects on profits to occur, that is for there to be operating exposure, it is necessary to have *ex post* violations of PPP. The intuitive explanation of this is that for the U.S. exporter's product to gain in competitiveness in Britain from a dollar depreciation, it is necessary for the product's price to fall vis-à-vis prices of competing British goods. This requires that the depreciation exceed the extent that U.S. prices are increasing faster than British prices. For example, if U.S. prices are increasing by 8 percent and British prices are increasing by 6 percent, it is necessary for the dollar depreciation to exceed 2 percent for the U.S. exporter's competitiveness to be improved by the depreciation.

Consideration of the inequalities (9.9) and (9.10) tells us that if PPP always held, and the assumptions we made in deriving these equations are correct, there is no operating risk or exposure. Similarly, as with assets and liabilities, if PPP is violated, but deviations from PPP as are likely to be positive as be negative and on average are equal to zero, there is still no exposure. In terms of

Figure 9.1, in this situation we have a scatter of observations around the horizontal axis with, for example, positive ΔS^u's associated with some positive ΔV's and some negative ΔV's, depending on whether PPP is violated positively or negatively. However, the *systematic* relationship between ΔV and ΔS^u is zero, just as it is when all observations are along the horizontal axis. Again, as with assets and liabilities, random deviations from PPP add to the total operating risk, but do not add to exchange-rate risk, which is the variation in operating income due to unanticipated changes in exchange rates. That is, when PPP holds only as a long-run tendency, the firm faces greater risk than when PPP always holds exactly, but this added risk is due to the factors causing the deviations from PPP, not to the exchange rate.

In the course of deriving the inequalities (9.9) and (9.10) we assumed that the market selling price of the U.S. exporter's product in Britain grows at the overall British rate of inflation, and that the cost of production grows at the overall U.S. rate of inflation. If these assumptions are invalid at every moment, but are valid on average, there is still no exposure, provided of course that PPP holds, at least on average.[24] However, violation of the assumptions does add a relative price risk to any risk from random deviations from PPP. This conclusion is very similar to that reached for real assets.

While operating risk and exposure and real-asset risk and exposure relate similarly to PPP, these two types of risk and exposure are completely different in nature. Indeed, gains and losses from operating risk and exposure have a different dimension to those from real-asset exposure, and from exposure on any type of asset or liability. Operating gains and losses have the dimension of flows, with profit changes occurring by so much *per month* or *per year*, that is, over a period of time. On the other hand, asset and liability gains or losses have the dimension of stocks, occurring at the moment of the change in exchange rates. This dimensional difference between operating risk and exposure, and the risk and exposure of assets and liabilities, real or not, manifests itself in corporate financial accounts.

Because the flow of gains or losses from changes in exchange rates on operating income occur over time, they show up in current and future income statements of the firm. However, gains or losses on assets and liabilities show up in balance sheets after they accrue, and in income statements only during the period of time when they are realized. That is, the balance sheets show foreign exchange gains or losses on assets and liabilities as they accrue, but show them in income statements only when the assets or liabilities are liquidated. The situation has not always been this way, and it is well worth taking the time to consider U.S. international accounting principles, past and present. This will help us clarify what is meant by foreign exchange gains and losses accruing and being realized.

---

[24] By the assumptions being valid "on average" we mean that there is no systematic difference between the rate of change of the product's price and British inflation, and no systematic difference between the rate of change in production costs and U.S. inflation.

U.S. INTERNATIONAL ACCOUNTING PRINCIPLES

It will help in understanding past and present U.S. international accounting principles to distinguish between **translation risk** and **translation exposure** on the one hand, and **transaction risk** and **transaction exposure** on the other hand. From a U.S. perspective, translation risk is the uncertainty of real U.S. asset or liability values *appearing in financial statements*, where this uncertainty is due to unanticipated changes in exchange rates. Similarly, translation exposure is the sensitivity of real U.S. dollar asset or liability values *appearing in financial statements*, with respect to unanticipated changes in exchange rates. On the other hand, transaction risk is the uncertainty of realized U.S. dollar asset or liability values *when the assets or liabilities are liquidated*, due to unanticipated changes in exchange rates. Similarly, transaction exposure is the sensitivity of realized U.S. dollar values of assets or liabilities *when the assets or liabilities are liquidated*, with respect to unanticipated changes in exchange rates.

Until 1982, the United States used an accounting standard generally known as FASB 8.[25] Under FASB 8 a company was required to show all foreign exchange translation gains or losses (those from converting foreign assets or liabilities into dollar amounts) in the current-period income statement. Different treatment was given to current operating receipts and expenditures and financial assets/liabilities on the one hand, and to fixed or real assets on the other hand. This was referred to as a temporal distinction, and the rules were as follows:

1 Revenues and expenses from foreign entities (overseas operations) were translated at the average exchange rate prevailing during the period, except for asses valued on a historical basis such as depreciation. These assets were translated at historical exchange rates. Financial assets and liabilities were translated at the average exchange rate during the period.

2 Other assets, primarily fixed or real assets, were translated at historical exchange rates. Historical costs were used in terms of local (foreign) currency.

What FASB 8 therefore required was that if local currency values were measured at current cost, they were to be translated at current exchange rates, and if they were measured at historical cost, they were to be translated at historical exchange rates.

The FASB 8 accounting procedure required that all translation adjustments had to appear in the income statement. This made income appear highly volatile and caused numerous corporate treasurers to take permanently hedged positions to prevent adverse shareholder reaction. The procedure which has

---

[25]See *Statement of Financial Accounting Standards*, *No. 8*, Financial Accounting Standards Board, Stamford, Conn., October 1975. The accounting system which replaced the FASB 8 system is described in *Statement of Financial Accounting Standards*, *No. 52—Foreign Currency Translation*, Financial Accounting Standards Board, Stamford, Conn., December 1981.

replaced FASB 8 is called FASB 52, and this involves two principal changes:

1 The **functional currency** is selected for the subsidiary. This is the primary currency of the subsidiary. For example, a British subsidiary of a U.S. parent firm will declare that the pound is its functional currency. Any foreign-currency income of the subsidiary (for example, marks or francs earned by the British subsidiary) is translated into the functional currency according to the FASB 8 rules. After this, all amounts are translated from the functional currency into dollars at the current exchange rate.

2 Translation gains and losses are to be disclosed and accumulated in a separate account showing shareholders' equity. Only when foreign assets or liabilities are liquidated do they become transaction gains or losses and appear in the income statement.

The rule on using current exchange rates on all items is relaxed when there is extremely high inflation in the country whose currency is being translated. Extremely high inflation means a cumulative amount of over 100 percent during the preceding 3 years. If this condition is met, the temporal distinction used in FASB 8 still applies. This means that in circumstances of extreme inflation, current exchange rates are used for current-cost items such as financial assets and liabilities, and historical rates are used for historical-cost items.

The best way to illustrate the effects of these accounting procedures is to take examples. However, before we consider these examples it is useful to define the concept of real changes in exchange rates. This is because our examples show not only the implications of U.S. accounting principles for translation and transaction gains and losses, but also the extent to which the accounts accurately reflect what has really happened to exchange rates.

REAL CHANGES IN EXCHANGE RATES

Definition of the Real Change in Exchange Rates

We can define the **real change in exchange rates** in this way:

The real change in exchange rates is the change that produces a difference between the overall rate of return on domestic versus foreign assets/liabilities or in the profitability of export-oriented, import-using, or import-competing firms.

As we proceed, we shall see that in order for real changes in exchange rates to occur there must be *ex post* departures from interest parity or PPP. As we have seen, these departures are also necessary for there to be exchange-rate risk. Furthermore, just as exchange-rate risk can exist without exposure, so real changes in exchange rates can occur without exposure; the real changes in exchange rates could be random with no systematic effects on returns of assets, liabilities, or operating income. However, this is as far as the analogy goes. The real change in exchange rates is a measure of how much *any particular change in exchange rates* has affected rates of return or operating incomes. On the other hand, exchange-rate risk is a measure of the volatility of asset or liability values or operating incomes due to *the many possible exchange-rate values that could occur*. Therefore, while the sources of exchange-rate risk and of real changes in exchange rates are the same, they are measures of very different phenomena.[26]

Financial Assets and Liabilities and Real Changes in Exchange Rates

Suppose that Aviva Corporation, which we introduced in Chapter 7, has invested in British bonds. Let us assume that these are long-term bonds. Clearly, a depreciation of the British pound will decrease the dollar value of these financial securities when they are translated (that is, converted into dollars) at the new exchange rate. But would we want to consider Aviva as being worse off by holding sterling bonds rather than dollar-denominated bonds? Alternatively, would an appreciation of the pound make Aviva better off?

A depreciation of a currency that is compensated for in terms of higher interest yields on financial assets should not be considered a real depreciation from the point of view of these assets. For example, if the pound fell in value against the dollar by 10 percent but British interest rates were 10 percent higher than those in the United States, the firm would be no worse off from British than from U.S investments. According to our definition of a real change in exchange rates, that is, a change which affects the rate of return on foreign versus domestic assets, we might therefore define the real change for financial assets held for a year as follows:

$$\text{Real proportional change in } (\$/\pounds) = \frac{S_1(\$/\pounds) - S(\$/\pounds)}{S(\$/\pounds)} - (r_{US} - r_{UK})$$

$S_1(\$/\pounds)$ is the actual spot rate at year end, and r_{US} and r_{UK} refer to interest earnings during that year. The definition consists of the actual proportional increase in the value of the pound minus the extent to which higher interest rates in the United States have compensated for this.

Because translation gains are made on the interest earned in Britain as well as on the principal, a more precise definition is

(Real proportional change in $\$/\pounds$)

$$= \frac{S_1(\$/\pounds) - S(\$/\pounds)}{S(\$/\pounds)}(1 + r_{UK}) - (r_{US} - r_{UK}) \quad (9.11)$$

---

[26] Indeed, the units of measurement are different. We measure real changes in exchange rates in percent, whereas exchange-rate risk has the dimension of the variance of dollar values, which is in units of dollars squared.

The real change of $/£ shown in (9.11) is equal to the deviation from *ex post* unhedged interest parity, which can be seen as follows.

Each dollar a U.S. investor invests in Britain will buy $1/S(\$/£)$ of British pounds, which will produce after 1 year

$$£\frac{1}{S(\$/£)}(1 + r_{UK})$$

If the British investment is not hedged by selling the pounds forward, the pounds will be sold at the following year's spot rate, $S_1(\$/£)$, giving

$$\$\frac{S_1(\$/£)}{S(\$/£)}(1 + r_{UK})$$

The return from the unhedged British security is therefore

$$\frac{S_1(\$/£)}{S(\$/£)}(1 + r_{UK}) - 1$$

The difference between this return and the U.S. return, which is the *ex post* departure from interest parity, is

$$\frac{S_1(\$/£)}{S(\$/£)}(1 + r_{UK}) - (1 + r_{US})$$

On subtracting and adding $1 + r_{UK}$ this gives

$$\frac{S_1(\$/£) - S(\$/£)}{S(\$/£)}(1 + r_{UK}) + (1 + r_{UK}) - (1 + r_{US})$$

or

$$\frac{S_1(\$/£) - S(\$/£)}{S(\$/£)}(1 + r_{UK}) - (r_{US} - r_{UK}) \qquad (9.12)$$

Comparison of (9.12) with (9.11) shows that for a real change in the exchange rate for financial securities we need an *ex post* departure from unhedged interest parity.

Financial Assets and Liabilities and Financial Statements

In order to describe how U.S. international accounting principles show translation gains or losses on financial assets and liabilities, and to illustrate the definition of the real change in exchange rates, suppose that in the previous year Aviva had placed $1 million in a U.S. long-term bond yielding 12 percent

(r_{US} = 0.12), and $1 million in a British long-term bond yielding 20 percent (r_{UK} = 0.20). Suppose that last year the spot rate was $S(\$/£) = 2.0$ and that during the year the pound depreciates or is devalued to $S_1(\$/£) = 1.8$.

The actual pound depreciation or devaluation is 10 percent. However, interest rates make up for some of this. The real depreciation of the pound given by Equation (9.11) is computed as follows:

$$\text{(Real change in \$/£)} = \frac{1.8 - 2.0}{2.0}(1.20) - (-0.08) = -0.04$$

The negative value means a real depreciation of the pound of 4 percent, which is a real appreciation of the dollar. The 10 percent decline in the value of the pound is not fully compensated by the higher British interest rate.

In terms of the financial accounts, after placing $1 million in the U.S. bond for 1 year, there will be $120,000 in interest appearing in the income statement, and if interest rates do not change, there is no change in the value of financial assets. This is shown in Table 9.2a.

Placing $1 million in Britain at the initial exchange rate $S(\$/£) = 2.0$ means investing £500,000. At r_{UK} = 0.20, this will earn £100,000. At the exchange rate of $1.8/£, the £100,000 will be translated into $180,000 of income.

The £500,000 British asset is worth only $900,000 at the rate of $1.8/£. Since the initial value was $1 million, there is a translation loss of $100,000. Under FASB 8 this would have appeared in the income account, but with the FASB 52 accounting procedure it will appear separately. This is shown in the second row of Table 9.2a. Under FASB 8 the declared income on the British bond would have been $180,000 − $100,000 = $80,000 with $S(\$/£) = 1.8$, and under the FASB 52 system, which has replaced FASB 8, there is a declared income of $180,000 if the translation loss is not realized, that is, if the bond is not sold.

Under FASB 8, there is a relative loss on the British bond of $40,000 ($80,000 − $120,000 = − $40,000), or 4 percent of the original investment compared with the $120,000 in earnings from the U.S. bond. In the same way, when using the FASB 52 procedure and combining the shareholder equity account with income, we have an absolute income on British bonds of $180,000 − $100,000 = + $80,000. Compared with the $120,000 that would have been earned on the U.S. bond, this involves a relative loss of $40,000. The real depreciation or devaluation of 4 percent found from both the FASB 8 procedure and the FASB 52 procedure agrees with what we found in the definition, Equation (9.11). But we note that with the FASB 52 accounting procedure, we must include shareholder equity effects if we are to make the correct judgment of the real change in the exchange rate.

If the exchange rate after a year of investment had moved to $S_1(\$/£) = 1.8667$, then the real change in the exchange rate would have been zero, since the definition, Equation (9.11), tells us that

$$\frac{1.8667 - 2.0}{2.0}(1.20) - (-0.08) = 0.0$$

TABLE 9.2
EARNINGS ON DOMESTIC VERSUS FOREIGN ASSETS

(a) Financial assets

	Interest earnings	Translation gain or loss	Declared Income, FASB 8	Declared Income, FASB 52
U.S. bond	+$120,000	—	+$120,000	+$120,000
$S_1(\$/£) = 1.8000$	+$180,000	−$100,000	+$80,000	+$180,000
$S_1(\$/£) = 1.8667$	+$186,667	−$66,667	+$120,000	+$186,667
$S_1(\$/£) = 1.9000$	+$190,000	−$50,000	+$140,000	+$190,000

(b) Real assets

	Rental or profit income	Translation gains			Income plus *declared* translation gains			Income plus actual translation gains		
		FASB 8	FASB 52	Correct method	FASB 8	FASB 52	Correct method	FASB 8	FASB 52	Correct method
$S_1(\$/£) = 1.8000$	+$50,000	0	−$100,000	+$44,000	+$50,000	+$50,000	+$94,000	+$50,000	−$50,000	+$94,000

This result occurs because the end-of-year exchange rate of $1.8667/£ is the rate that produces *ex post* unhedged interest parity.[27]

In terms of the entries in the financial accounts, $1 million in Britain at $S(\$/£) = 2.0$ is £500,000, which as before earns £100,000. At $S_1(\$/£) = 1.8667$, this is worth a total of $186,667. The translation loss at this realized exchange rate is $66,667 [$1,000,000 − ($1.8667/£ × £500,000)]. If we use FASB 52, this gives total earnings of $120,000 ($186,667 − $66,667) if we are careful to aggregate the appropriate interest earnings from the income account and the foreign exchange loss that is given in the shareholder equity account. FASB 8 provides the same answer. We obtain the same earnings at home as abroad, $120,000, and the actual fall in the value of the pound means no real change in the exchange rate.

If the pound falls in actual value by only 5 percent to $S_1(\$/£) = 1.9$, then the £100,000 in earnings from Britain will be worth $1.9/£ × £100,000 = $190,000, and the translation loss will be $50,000 [$1,000,000 − ($1.9 × 500,000)]. The total earnings are therefore $140,000 ($190,000 − $50,000) if we are careful to include all earnings. This is $20,000 more than the earnings from the U.S. bond. Even though the pound has fallen in value, the overcompensation in the British interest rate is a real gain from the British bond of 2 percent. This will be found as the real percentage change in the exchange rate from the definition, Equation (9.11), but we again note that if our accounts are to give the correct result, they must be integrated so that equity effects are added to income earned.

Judging the borrowing decision, which means judging financial liabilities, is the reverse of judging the investment decision, and we must reverse the interpretation of Equation (9.11). When borrowing is unhedged, real borrowing costs are the same at home and abroad as long as the depreciation in the value of the foreign currency is compensated for by higher interest payments. There is an *ex post* real gain from borrowing abroad instead of at home if the realized depreciation of the foreign currency is more than the extra interest rate that is paid abroad versus at home. There is a loss from borrowing abroad rather than at home if the realized depreciation of the foreign currency is less than the extra interest rate paid abroad versus at home. These effects are shown both by FASB 8 and FASB 52, provided we integrate the shareholder equity account with FASB 52.

Real Assets and Real Changes in Exchange Rates

If real-asset prices have risen at the rate $\dot{P}_{US}$ and the real rate of return (in the form of, for example, rental income or dividends on the assets) has been ρ_{US},

---

[27]With $r_{UK} = 0.20$, $r_{US} = 0.12$, and $S(\$/£) = 2.0$ we can rearrange the interest parity condition

$$S_1(\$/£) = S(\$/£)\frac{1 + r_{US}}{1 + r_{UK}}$$

to find $S_1(\$/£) = 1.8667$.

then the overall rate of return on each dollar of real assets held at home is

$$\rho_{US} + \dot{P}_{US} \tag{9.13}$$

Each dollar placed abroad in real assets that rose with inflation at $\dot{P}_{UK}$ with a rent or dividend rate of ρ_{UK} will produce, when translated at the new realized exchange rate $S_1(\$/£)$, dollar receipts of

$$\$\frac{S_1(\$/£)}{S(\$/£)}\left(1 + \rho_{UK} + \dot{P}_{UK}\right) \tag{9.14}$$

This is because the original dollar will purchase £$\{1/S(\$/£)\}$ of British real assets, on which there is a rental or dividend of ρ_{US} and inflation of $\dot{P}_{UK}$, and which is translated back into dollars at $S_1(\$/£)$. The rate of return on the dollar invested in the British real asset is therefore

$$\frac{S_1(\$/£)}{S(\$/£)}\left(1 + \rho_{UK} + \dot{P}_{UK}\right) - 1 \tag{9.15}$$

According to our definition of the real change in the exchange rate as the change causing a difference between the overall return on domestic versus foreign investments, from (9.15) minus (9.13) we have

(Real proportional change in $\$/£$)

$$= \left(\frac{S_1(\$/£)}{S(\$/£)}\left(1 + \rho_{UK} + \dot{P}_{UK}\right) - 1\right) - \left(\rho_{US} + \dot{P}_{US}\right) \tag{9.16}$$

By adding and subtracting $\dot{P}_{UK}$ this can be written as

(Real proportional change in $\$/£$) $= \dfrac{S_1(\$/£)}{S(\$/£)}\left(1 + \dot{P}_{UK}\right) - \left(1 + \dot{P}_{UK}\right) + \dot{P}_{UK}$

$$+ \frac{S_1(\$/£)}{S(\$/£)}\rho_{UK} - \rho_{US} - \dot{P}_{US}$$

which by combining terms gives

(Real proportional change in $\$/£$) $= \dfrac{S_1(\$/£) - S(\$/£)}{S(\$/£)}\left(1 + \dot{P}_{UK}\right)$

$$-\left(\dot{P}_{US} - \dot{P}_{UK}\right) - \left(\rho_{US} - \frac{S_1(\$/£)}{S(\$/£)}\rho_{UK}\right) \tag{9.17}$$

Examination of Equation (9.17) shows that if rental or dividend yields in the U.S. or Britain are equal when we include the translation gain/loss in the British yield, that is, if $\rho_{US} = [S_1(\$/£)/S(\$/£)]\rho_{UK}$, then Equation (9.17) becomes

$$(\text{Real proportional change in } \$/£) = \dot{S} \cdot (1 + \dot{P}_{UK}) - (\dot{P}_{US} - \dot{P}_{UK}) \quad (9.18)$$

where $\dot{S} = [(S_1(\$/£) - S(\$/£))]/S(\$/£)$, the proportional change in the exchange rate. A comparison of Equation (9.18) with the relative form of PPP in Equation (6.7) shows that real changes in exchange rates on real assets require *ex post* deviations from PPP. We recall that this conclusion also applies to real changes in exchange rates for the profitability of export-oriented, import-using, or import-competing firms; as we saw in our discussion of operating exposure, a change in profitability requires *ex post* departures from PPP.

Real Assets and Financial Statements

When we examine the financial accounts in order to judge the performance of domestic versus foreign real investments, we are up against even more problems than we face with financial assets and liabilities. With financial assets and liabilities we can obtain the correct judgment as long as we are sure to include both income and the separate shareholder-equity effect within total earnings. With real assets this is not sufficient. Indeed, by including shareholder-equity effects as they are measured with the FASB 52 accounting procedure, we might distort the picture even more than by leaving these effects out of the calculations. These points are by no means obvious, so we will show them by taking an example.

Suppose that in the previous year, $1 million was invested in U.S. real assets that provided a 5-percent real rate of return, and $1 million was invested in British real assets which provided a 5.5556-percent real rate of return. Suppose that over the previous year, inflation in the United States was 10 percent, and inflation in Britain was 16 percent, with fixed- or real-asset market prices and general prices moving at the same rates. Suppose that in the previous year the exchange rate was $2.0/£ and that by the end of the year it was $1.8/£. We have

$$\rho_{US} = 0.0500 \qquad \rho_{UK} = 0.05556 \qquad \dot{P}_{US} = 0.10 \qquad \dot{P}_{UK} = 0.16$$

$$S(\$/£) = 2.0 \quad \text{and} \quad S_1(\$/£) = 1.8$$

What we want to know from the example is what we will find in a company's accounts.

The actual pound depreciation or devaluation is 10 percent. However, the higher inflation in asset values in Britain has made up for some of this. The real pound depreciation (dollar appreciation) against which to judge the measured accounting effects is calculated with Equation (9.17), which gives

$$\text{(Real proportional change in \$/£)} = \frac{1.8 - 2.0}{2.0}(1.16) - (-0.06)$$

$$-\left(0.05 - \frac{1.8}{2.0}0.05556\right)$$

$$= -0.056, \text{ or } -5.6\%$$

Since the change is negative, we call it a real pound depreciation. It is lower than the actual depreciation because the actual fall has been partially compensated by higher rates of return and higher inflation in the market value of British real assets. But what will the different accounting procedures show?

In terms of the financial accounts, the $1 million in the U.S. real assets earned a return of $\rho_{US} \times \$1,000,000 = \$50,000$. In addition, the 10-percent inflation in the United States raised the dollar value of the real assets by $100,000, which is a "gain" to the company even if it does not show in accounts until it is realized.

The $1 million sent to Britain at $S(\$/£) = 2.0$ had an initial value of £500,000. At $\rho_{UK} = 0.05556$, the £500,000 earned $\rho_{UK} \times \pounds500,000 = \pounds27,778$. When translated into U.S. dollars at the current exchange rate $S_1(\$/£)$, as current earnings, this £27,778 becomes $1.8/£ \times \pounds27,778 = \$50,000$ in the income statement. This is true no matter what accounting procedure is used. The $50,000 is shown as the first item in Table 9.2b. Translation gains and losses—those resulting from converting foreign-asset values into units of domestic currency—require more careful treatment than real rental or dividend returns.

Let us first consider the translation gains or losses that would have appeared with FASB 8. We recall that FASB 8 required that the historical values of real assets had to be translated at historical exchange rates and that any changes in these values had to be declared in the income statement. Only in special circumstances will this procedure provide the correct answer, and in this case it will not. The historical real-asset market value of the British real asset is £500,000, and the historical exchange rate is $S(\$/£) = 2.0$. This gives a balance-sheet entry of $2.0/£ \times \pounds500,000 = \$1,000,000$. Since the original cost is also $1,000,000, there is no exchange gain or loss. The current income, as for all the procedures we are comparing, is $50,000 when $S_1(\$/£) = 1.8$, and so the declared income, which is the sum of the current income and the translation loss (of zero), is $50,000. This is shown with the FASB 8 entries in Table 9.2b and is the same as the *declared* income on the U.S. real asset, but smaller than the true income.

Under the FASB 52 procedure which has replaced FASB 8, the income on the British real asset is still $50,000. However, with FASB 52, the values of real assets are translated at current exchange rates, but historical costs are used for the value of the assets in units of the local currency. The current exchange rate is $S_1(\$/£) = 1.8$, and the historical cost is £500,000, and so the value is recorded as $900,000. There is a translation loss of $100,000 from the original $1 million value of the British real asset. This is excluded from current income and goes only into the separate shareholder equity account, and so the declared income with FASB 52 is the same as with the FASB 8 procedure, and it is the same as domestic income.[28] However, if exchange rates do not return to the previous levels before the British real asset is sold, the $100,000 will appear as income when it becomes a transaction loss, showing a loss of $50,000 ($50,000 − $100,000 = −$50,000).

The correct method for handling foreign real assets uses the current exchange rate and the current market value of assets. This is different from the FASB 52 procedure and the older FASB 8 procedure. We note that by the year end, the initial £500,000 invested in the British real asset has increased with 16-percent inflation to £580,000. At the current exchange rate of $S_1(\$/£) = 1.8$, this is translated into $1,044,000 on the balance sheet, and so there is a translation gain of $44,000. If this is included as income, the total earnings from Britain are $50,000 + $44,000 = $94,000, compared with the total return from U.S. fixed assets of $150,000. The relative loss from the change in exchange rates is $56,000 ($94,000 − $150,000 = −$56,000), which is 5.6 percent of the original investment, the same as the real percentage change in exchange rates computed with Equation (9.17). This correct result is in contrast with the outcomes of FASB 8 and FASB 52, which show no loss in the income statement in relation to declared U.S. income. When the shareholder-equity effect is included with FASB 52 and the total return from the British real asset is compared with the total return from the U.S. asset, we have a relative loss on the British asset of $200,000 (−$50,000 − $150,000 = −$200,000). No matter how we look at it, we cannot obtain the correct picture from the new FASB 52 procedure or the old FASB 8 procedure. We shall not do so until we use a current-cost, current-exchange-rate translation procedure.

The Relevance of Translation Exposure

Assuming that there are no adverse tax implications, the fact that the effects of changes in exchange rates appearing in financial statements are not always the true economic effects should not influence the value of a firm. This is because shareholders should be able to see through the veil of financial statements to the true economic effects. Therefore, if a firm decides to hedge it should hedge against exposure as measured by β_1 in Equation (9.1), rather than hedge translation exposure. However, as we shall see in the next chapter, there are

[28]Our treatment is valid for countries which do not suffer from extreme inflation and for which the straightforward forms of FASB 52 rules apply. Countries with extreme inflation (over 100 percent in three years) continue to use the temporal distinction found in FASB 8 and will have accounts like those shown for FASB 8 rather than for FASB 52.

arguments that suggest that firms should not bother to hedge their exposure whatever way it is measured.

SUMMARY

1 From a U.S. perspective, foreign exchange exposure is the sensitivity of the real U.S. dollar value of assets, liabilities, or operating incomes with respect to unanticipated changes in exchange rates.
2 Exposure can be measured by the slope coefficient(s) in a regression equation relating the real change in the dollar value of assets, liabilities, or operating incomes to unanticipated changes in exchange rates.
3 There is exposure only if there is a systematic relationship between dollar values of assets, liabilities, or operating incomes, ΔV, and unanticipated changes in exchange rates, ΔS^u. That is, for exposure to exist, dollar values must on average change in a particular way vis-à-vis unanticipated changes in exchange rates.
4 Exposure on, for example, a British pound-denominated bank account is measured in pounds.
5 Normally there is noise in the relationship between domestic currency values and unanticipated changes in exchange rates. However, the size of exposure of, for example, a pound-denominated bond is still the face value of the bond if the noise is random and on average equal to zero.
6 When exposure exists against numerous currencies, it can be measured from the slope coefficients in a multiple regression.
7 Domestic-currency-denominated assets can be exposed to exchange rates if, for example, unanticipated depreciations of the country's currency cause its central bank to increase interest rates.
8 Foreign exchange risk is measured by the variance of the domestic-currency value of an asset, liability, or operating income that is due to unanticipated changes in exchange rates.
9 Foreign exchange risk is positively related to both exposure and the variance of unanticipated changes in exchange rates.
10 When a foreign-currency-denominated security is not hedged with a forward exchange contract, it is exposed and subject to exchange-rate risk, irrespective of whether interest parity holds.
11 If individual asset values do not always change by the overall rate of inflation for a country, but on average change at the rate of inflation, exposure is still zero if PPP holds on average. With random departures from PPP there is an added source of risk, but this is part of the total risk, not the foreign exchange risk.
12 The sensitivity of operating income to changes in exchange rates is called operating exposure, and the variance of operating income due to unanticipated changes in exchange rates is called operating risk.
13 If PPP always holds exactly and market prices and production costs always move in line with overall inflation, there is no exchange-rate exposure or exchange-rate risk. If PPP holds only on average and prices and production costs move on average at the overall rate of inflation, there is still no exchange-rate exposure or risk, but there is greater risk.
14 Asset and liability exposure and risk show up in a company's balance sheet, whereas operating exposure and risk show up in its income statement.

15 Translation risk and exposure have to do with how asset and liability values appear in financial accounts. Transaction risk and exposure have to do with asset or liability values when the assets or liabilities are liquidated.

16 The real change in exchange rates is the change that produces a difference between the overall rate of return on domestic versus foreign assets/liabilities, or in the profitability of export-oriented or import-competing firms. There are no real changes in exchange rates on financial assets and liabilities only if interest parity always holds *ex post*, and there are no real changes in exchange rates for real assets or operating income only if PPP always holds *ex post*.

17 FASB 8 used historical costs and historical exchange rates if assets were valued at historical costs, as with real assets. The FASB 52 procedure uses historical costs and current exchange rates, but puts translation gains or losses in a separate account.

18 Both FASB 8 and FASB 52 produce incorrect measures of real changes in exchange rates for real assets.

QUESTIONS

1 In what sense is the sign of the slope coefficient which measures exposure relevant, and in what sense is it irrelevant?

2 How can exposure exceed the face value of a foreign-currency-denominated asset or liability?

3 Would it make sense to add a firm's exposures in different currencies at the spot exchange rate to obtain a measure of the firm's aggregate exposure, and if not, why not?

4 What is the problem in using $\text{var}(\Delta S^u)$ as a measure of foreign exchange risk?

5 Redo the analysis in the text for measuring the effect of exchange-rate changes on an exporter, so that it applies to an importer instead. Assume that the importer competes with local producers of similar goods, and that production costs and prices move with inflation.

6 Redo the analysis of the effect of exchange-rate changes on an exporter by allowing the quantity sold, q, to change with the exchange rate instead of holding it constant. Use calculus to make the problem easier, and note that p_{UK} and q should be at profit-maximization levels in every period. [This is a very difficult question.]

7 Would the distinction between real and actual changes in exchange rates be important if inflation and interest rates were everywhere the same and were also small?

8 Suppose you had invested $500,000 for 6 months in the United States and in Italy and interest rates and exchange rates turn out to be as follows:

r_{US}	r_{IT}	$S(\$/\text{Lit})$	$S_{1/2}(\$/\text{Lit})$
15%	28%	0.0010	0.0009

$S(\$/\text{Lit})$ is the exchange rate when the investment was made, and $S_{1/2}(\$/\text{Lit})$ is the actual rate 6 months later.

a Was foreign investment a good idea?

b What would appear under FASB 8 as foreign income?

c What values will appear in the income account and the shareholder equity account with the FASB 52 accounting procedure?

d What value of $S(\$/\text{Lit})$ would create equal returns for domestic and foreign investment?

9 Suppose you had invested $1 million in U.S. fixed assets and in Italian fixed assets under the following conditions:

ρ_{US}	ρ_{IT}	$\dot{P}_{US}$	$\dot{P}_{IT}$	$S(\$/\text{Lit})$	$S_1(\$/\text{Lit})$
2%	4%	10%	25%	0.00100	0.00085

Assume that fixed-asset prices in local currency have kept pace with prices in general.

a Which investment yielded higher returns over the year?

b What would appear in an FASB 8 income statement for foreign investment income?

c What will appear in the income statement and the shareholder equity account under the FASB 52 procedure?

d What should appear as income?

e Why do both your answer to **b** and your answer to **c** (where income and shareholder equity are aggregated) disagree with your answer to **d**?

10 What has been the real change between 1982 and 1989 in the value of the dollar against the pound on bonds? Use quotations of 1989 and 1982 spot rates and 1982 government bond interest rates in Britain and the United States. What has been the real change in the exchange rate for dollars against pounds with regard to the international competitiveness of U.S. versus British manufacturers? What has been the real change in exchange rates for stocks, assuming that these are real assets and that earnings are as given from price earnings ratios and that stock price are as given from New York and London stock-exchange indexes?

11 Redo the analysis in the text of a real change in exchange rates for financial liabilities instead of assets. Describe how declining value of a currency retires debt.

12 Use Figure 9A.1 in Appendix 9.2 to show the effects of varying the slope of the exposure line for the probability distribution of $\Delta\hat{V}$. Also, show the effect of varying $\text{var}(\Delta S^u)$ on the probability distribution of $\Delta\hat{V}$ for a given exposure line.

BIBLIOGRAPHY

Adler, Michael, and Bernard Dumas: "Exposure to Currency Risk: Definition and Measurement," *Financial Management*, summer 1984 pp. 41–50.

Carsberg, Bryan: "FAS #52—Measuring the Performance of Foreign Operations," *Midland Corporate Finance Journal*, summer 1983, pp. 48–55.

Flood, Eugene Jr., and Donald R. Lessard: "On the Measurement of Operating Exposure to Exchange Rates: A Conceptual Approach," *Financial Management*, spring 1986, pp. 25–37.

Garner, C. Kent, and Alan C. Shapiro: "A Practical Method of Assessing Foreign Exchange Risk," *Midland Corporate Finance Journal*, fall 1984, pp. 6–17.

Hekman, Christine R.: "Measuring Foreign Exchange Exposure: A Practical Theory and its Application," *Financial Analysts Journal*, September/October 1983, pp. 59–65.

Robert E. Hoskin: "The Effects of the FASB-52 Translation Mandate on Financial Measures of Corporate Success," unpublished manuscript, Fuqua School of Business, February 1985.

Hodder, James E., "Exposure to Exchange-Rate Movements," *Journal of International Economics*: November, 1982, pp. 375–386.

Jorion, Philippe: "The Exchange Rate Exposure of U.S. Multinationals," unpublished manuscript, Columbia University, February 1986.

Korsvold, Pal E.: "Managing Strategic Foreign Exchange Exposure of Real Assets," presented at European Finance Association meetings, Madrid, September 1987.

Lessard, Donald R., and David Sharp: "Measuring the Performance of Operations Subject to Fluctuating Exchange Rates," *Midland Corporate Finance Journal*, fall 1984, pp. 18–30.

Levi, Maurice D., and Joseph Zechner: "Foreign Exchange Risk and Exposure," in Robert Z. Aliber (ed.), *Handbook of International Financial Management*, Richard Irwin–Dow Jones, New York, 1989.

Miller, Martin A.: *Comprehensive GAAP Guide*, Harcourt Brace Jovanovich, New York, 1989.

Oxelheim, Lars, and Clas G. Wihlborg: *Macroeconomic Uncertainty: International Risks and Opportunities for the Corporation*, Wiley, New York, 1987.

Shapiro, Alan C., "Defining Exchange Risk," *The Journal of Business*, January 1977, pp. 37–39.

_____, "What Does Purchasing Power Parity Mean?" *Journal of International Money and Finance*, December 1983, pp. 295–318.

Solnik, Bruno: "International Parity Conditions and Exchange Risk" *Journal of Banking and Finance*, August 1978, pp. 281–293.

_____, *Statement of Financial Accounting Standards No. 52—Foreign Currency Translation*, Financial Accounting Standards Board, Stamford, Conn., December 1981.

Wyman, Harold E.: "Analysis of Gains and Losses from Foreign Monetary Items: An Application of Purchasing Power Parity Concepts," *The Accounting Review*, July 1976, pp. 545–558.

APPENDIX 9.1: The Statistical Measurement of Exchange-rate Risk and Exposure

In this appendix we explore a little further the statistical dimensions of risk and exposure. This is done both to clarify the nature of risk and exposure, and to provide a simple way of judging how important foreign exchange risk is relative to other risks that a company faces.

In the main part of the chapter we defined exposure as the slope β_1 of the regression equation

$$\Delta V = \beta_0 + \beta_1 \Delta S^u(\$/£) + \mu \tag{9.1}$$

The slope coefficient β_1 can be written as

$$\beta_1 = \frac{\text{cov}(\Delta V, \Delta S^u)}{\text{var}(\Delta S^u)} \tag{9A.1}$$

where $\text{cov}(\Delta V, \Delta S^u)$ is the covariance between ΔV and ΔS^u, and $\text{var}(\Delta S^u)$ is the variance of unanticipated changes in exchange rates.[29] The definition of the regression coefficient makes it clear that when ΔV does not covary systematically with ΔS^u, the exposure is zero. This is the conclusion we reached in the example giving rise to Equation (9.2), in which the value of British real estate in U.S. dollars is unaffected by the exchange rate. It is also clear from the definition of the regression coefficient that the more ΔV changes systematically with ΔS^u, the greater is the exposure.

While exposure is defined in terms of the slope coefficient, risk was defined as $\text{var}(\Delta \hat{V})$, where

$$\Delta \hat{V} = \beta_0 + \beta_1 \Delta S^u (\$/£) \qquad (9.4)$$

That is, exchange-rate risk is judged by the variance of the change in the dollar value of an asset, liability or operating income, due only to unanticipated changes in exchange rates. The remainder of the total risk faced by a company is the result of other influences, which are captured by the term μ in Equation (9.1).[30] That is, total risk is judged by $\text{var}(\Delta V)$, where ΔV is given in Equation (9.1).

The connection between total risk and exchange-rate risk can be shown by noting that because

$$\Delta V \equiv \Delta \hat{V} + \mu \qquad (9.5)$$

then

$$\text{var}(\Delta V) = \text{var}(\Delta \hat{V}) + \text{var}(\mu) + 2\,\text{cov}(\Delta \hat{V}, \mu) \qquad (9A.2)$$

Using the definition of $\Delta \hat{V}$ in Equation (9.4), $\text{cov}(\Delta \hat{V}, \mu)$ can be written as

$$\text{cov}(\Delta \hat{V}, \mu) = \beta_1 \text{cov}(\Delta S^u, \mu) \qquad (9A.3)$$

It is an assumption of regression analysis that explanatory variables such as ΔS^u are not correlated with the error term, so that $\text{cov}(\Delta S^u, \mu) = 0$. If this assumption is valid, then from Equation (9A.3) $\text{cov}(\Delta \hat{V}, \mu) = 0$, and so Equation (9A.2) becomes

$$\text{var}(\Delta V) = \text{var}(\Delta \hat{V}) + \text{var}(\mu) \qquad (9A.4)$$

We can see from Equation (9A.4) that the total risk of an asset, liability, or operating income consists of its exchange rate risk, $\text{var}(\Delta \hat{V})$, and the risk due to non-exchange-rate factors, $\text{var}(\mu)$.

The relative importance of exchange-rate risk can be judged by the size of $\text{var}(\Delta \hat{V})$, the variance of value due to exchange rates, relative to $\text{var}(\Delta V)$, the total variance due to

---

[29] The formula for calculating regression coefficients can be found in most statistics and econometrics textbooks. For example, see John Johnston, *Econometric Methods*, 3d ed., McGraw-Hill, New York, 1984.

[30] This is not the place to deal with the question of how much either risk matters, the answer to which depends on the extent to which risk is systematic or diversifiable, and on the risk aversion of shareholders. Such matters are taken up in Chapter 13.

exchange-rate and non-exchange-rate factors. The ratio

$$\frac{\text{var}(\Delta \hat{V})}{\text{var}(\Delta V)}$$

plays an important role in statistics and econometrics, where it is known as R^2.

The R^2 statistic, which is an output of just about every available regression package, gives the fraction of overall variance of a dependent variable such as ΔV, that is explained by the explanatory variables. If we limit the explanatory variables to exchange rates, then the resulting R^2 gives the fraction of total variance due to exchange rates. It is clear that R^2 is bounded by zero and 1.0. When $R^2 = 0$ exchange rates contribute none of the total risk, and when $R^2 = 1$ they are responsible for all the risk.

We can conclude that if exposure can be assumed to be nearly constant over time, a firm can estimate the historical relationship between changes in its share price and relevant ΔS^u's. Management should be interested in both the resulting estimates of regression coefficients and the R^2 statistic. If the regression coefficients are insignificantly different from zero, the firm is not exposed. If in addition $R^2 = 0$, none of the risk the firm faces is due to exchange rates. On the other hand, if there are regression coefficients that differ from zero, the firm might consider paying attention to exposure. The amount of attention paid to managing exposure relative to managing the other risks faced by the firm should depend on R^2 in a regression containing only exchange rates.

APPENDIX 9.2: Exchange-Rate Risk Versus Exposure: A Geometrical Exposition

We can sharpen our understanding of foreign exchange risk and exposure by considering Figure 9A.1. This figure is an extension of Figure 9.1, with ΔV measured on the vertical axis and ΔS^u on the horizontal axis. Where Figure 9A.1 differs from Figure 9.1 is first in the addition of $\Delta \hat{V}$ on the vertical axis, and second in the addition of a third dimension in which probabilities of possible values of ΔS^u, ΔV, and $\Delta \hat{V}$ are measured. Let us see how Figure 9A.1 can clarify the distinction between exchange-rate risk and exposure, and also graphically indicate the importance of exchange-rate risk versus total risk.

In Figure 9.1, where only ΔV is measured on the vertical axis, the observations of ΔV and ΔS^u are not in general exactly on the exposure line. This is because ΔV is influenced by both exchange rates and other factors. However, the observations of $\Delta \hat{V}$ and ΔS^u do sit exactly on the exposure line. This is because $\Delta \hat{V}$ is the change in value of assets, liabilities, or operating incomes due to unanticipated changes in exchange rates. It follows that the exposure line can be interpreted either as the fitted line between the scatter of observations of ΔV and ΔS^u, or as the line giving precise values of $\Delta \hat{V}$ for each ΔS^u. Whichever interpretation we apply, it is the slope of this line that is the measure of exposure.

The probabilities of different possible values of ΔS^u are given from the probability distribution—drawn in the shape of a **bell curve**—which has its base on the horizontal axis measuring ΔS^u, and its height on the axis labeled Prob ΔS^u. This is the bell curve which is projected towards the reader in the horizontal plane, the height of which gives the probabilities of associated ΔS^u's. The variance of this probability distribution is

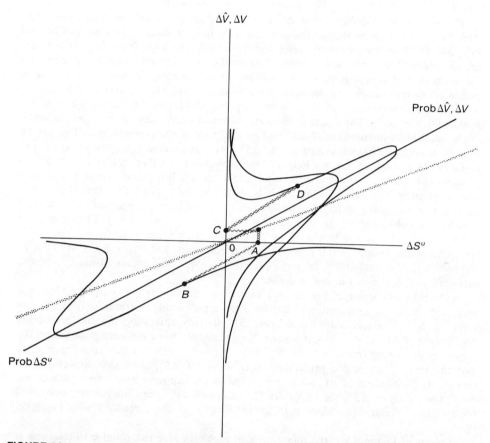

FIGURE 9A.1
THE GEOMETRY OF RISK AND EXPOSURE. Exposure is measured by the slope of the line fitted between ΔV and ΔS^u. This line gives the values of $\Delta \hat{V}$ for each ΔS^u. The probability distribution of ΔS^u is shown by the bell curve with its base along the ΔS^u axis and height along the Prob ΔS^u axis. We can find the probability of each $\Delta \hat{V}$ associated with each ΔS^u by using the exposure line *EE*. For example, the probability of ΔS^u given by distance *OA* is *AB*, and this is the same probability as that of $\Delta \hat{V}$ given by distance *OC*. The probability distribution of $\Delta \hat{V}$ is given by the more compact of the two bell curves with bases measured on the $\Delta \hat{V}, \Delta V$ axis and heights on the Prob $\Delta \hat{V}, \Delta V$ axis. The broader of these two bell curves gives the probability distribution of ΔV. The steeper the exposure line, the larger are the values of $\Delta \hat{V}$ associated with given ΔS^u's, and therefore the greater is var($\Delta \hat{V}$). The relative importance of exchange-rate risk can be judged from the relative dispersions of the $\Delta \hat{V}$ and ΔV distributions.

var(ΔS^u). The greater is var(ΔS^u), the more disperse is the curve. The dispersion of the probability distribution of ΔS^u is the geometrical representation of the risk measure suggested by Adler and Dumas.[31]

[31]Adler and Dumas, *op. cit.*

The probability distributions of $\Delta\hat{V}$ and ΔV are shown by the two bell curves with their bases measured on the vertical axis and their heights measured on the axis labeled Prob $\Delta\hat{V}$, ΔV. These are the bell curves which are projected away from the reader in the vertical plane. The dispersions of these two curves, as described by their variances, are the measures of exchange-rate risk and total risk we have described. Total risk is measured by the variance of the more disperse bell curve, which shows probabilities of ΔV's, and exchange-rate risk is measured by the more compact curve, which shows probabilities of $\Delta\hat{V}$'s. The shape of the more compact curve depends both on the shape of the probability distribution of ΔS^u and on the slope of the exposure line. This can be seen by selecting particular points on the ΔS^u axis. For example, the probability of ΔS^u equal to OA is distance AB, the height of the probability distribution above A. If ΔS^u is given by OA, then $\Delta\hat{V}$, the change in value due to the unanticipated change in exchange rate, is given by the exposure line. This is shown by point C on the vertical axis; this point is found by going up to the exposure line at A and then going across to the vertical axis. The probability of the $\Delta\hat{V}$ at point C is the same as the probability of the associated value of ΔS^u. That is, the height of the probability distribution of $\Delta\hat{V}$ above point C is the same as the height of the probability distribution of ΔS^u above point A. That is, distance CD, the probability of $\Delta\hat{V}$ equal to distance OC, equals distance AB, the probability of ΔS^u equal to distance OA.

A careful examination of Figure 9A.1 shows that the steeper is the exposure line, the more disperse is the distribution of $\Delta\hat{V}$ for a given probability distribution of ΔS^u; each value of ΔS^u is associated with a larger $\Delta\hat{V}$, thereby spreading out the probability distribution of $\Delta\hat{V}$. That is, *ceteris paribus*, the greater the foreign exchange exposure, the greater is the foreign exchange risk. Similarly, it can be seen by examining Figure 9A.1 that the more disperse the probability distribution of ΔS^u, the more disperse is the probability distribution of $\Delta\hat{V}$ for a given slope of the exposure line; *ceteris paribus*, the larger the values of ΔS^u, the larger are the values of $\Delta\hat{V}$, spreading out the associated probabilities. These conclusions correspond directly to those reached with Equation (9.6).

In terms of Figure 9A.1, the importance of exchange-rate risk relative to total risk is judged by the dispersion of the probability distribution of $\Delta\hat{V}$ relative to the probability distribution of ΔV. As was also clear from Equation (9A.2), the closer the variance of $\Delta\hat{V}$ is to that of ΔV, the more important is foreign exchange risk relative to total risk.[32]

---

[32]The difference between the dispersions of the two probability distributions depends on how closely the exposure line fits the actual observations of ΔS^u and ΔV. The closer the observations are to the fitted line, the less important are the non-exchange-rate factors, reflected in Equation (9.1) by μ, and the closer is the distribution of $\Delta\hat{V}$ to that of ΔV.

CHAPTER 10

HOW TO HEDGE AND SPECULATE

With foreign exchange risk and exposure defined, we can now consider how they can be reduced or avoided. That is, we can consider the techniques that are available for hedging, or covering, risk and exposure. We can also describe the techniques for purposely engaging in risk and exposure in order to speculate. In the course of examining these techniques we can consider what it is that determines whether to hedge or to speculate. Let us begin by considering hedging.

HEDGING

Before going into the details of *how* a firm can hedge we should ask *whether* a firm should hedge. We shall see that while there are reasons for a firm to hedge, the issue is not as straightforward as it might initially appear.

Whether to Hedge: Managerial Hedging versus Shareholder Hedging

It is usually argued that the objective of management is to maximize the wealth of the company's shareholders. However, even though hedging reduces or even eliminates exchange-rate risk, and lower risk is valued by shareholders, it does not pay for a firm to hedge exchange-rate risk if shareholders can reduce this risk themselves for the same or lower cost; shareholders will not value risk reduction they can achieve as or more effectively themselves. This is particularly relevant because shareholders may be residents of different countries and have different risk perspectives.[1] However, several arguments have been advanced

---

[1] If PPP holds the residence of shareholders should not matter provided tastes are similar; with PPP the same bundle of goods should cost the same in different countries.

which suggest that managers rather than shareholders should hedge foreign exchange exposure. These arguments include:

1 A stable before-tax corporate income results in a higher average after-tax income than a volatile income of the same average value if corporate tax rates are progressive. This is because with progressive tax rates more taxes are paid in high-income periods than are saved in low-income periods.[2]

2 It may be difficult for shareholders to determine the amount of exposure in each currency that exists at any particular moment. Furthermore, even if the overall exposure is known, the share of this facing an individual shareholder may be so small that forward or swap hedging by the shareholder is impractical.[3]

3 Marketing of a company's product may be helped by a stable corporate income if buyers want assurance that the company will stay in business to service its product and supply parts.

4 Corporate employees may be frightened away by volatile corporate earnings, which might suggest less job security. Alternatively, those that accept employment might demand higher salaries to compensate for the employment uncertainty.

5 Bankruptcy costs constitute a higher reduction in corporate value when earnings are more volatile. It may be that suppliers of capital will demand higher returns to cover the expected bankruptcy costs.

6 Loan repayments can sometimes be triggered when earnings fall below a stated low level.

7 Internal allocation of marketing or R & D budgets may depend on managers knowing the profit centers within a company. Leaving hedging to shareholders reduces the quality of information available to managers, because incomes of different divisions of the company can be a mixture of foreign exchange gains and losses and of operating income.[4]

8 There are hedging techniques involving selecting the currency of invoicing and buying inputs in markets or currencies of exports that are available to the firm, but not to its shareholders.

---

[2] This and some of the other reasons given here for why managers rather than shareholders should hedge can be found in René Stulz and Clifford W. Smith, "The Determinants of Firms' Hedging Policies," *Journal of Financial and Quantitative Analysis*, December 1985, pp. 391–405, and Alan C. Shapiro, "Currency Risk and Relative Price Risk," *Journal of Financial and Quantitative Analysis*, December 1984, pp. 365–373.

[3] This impracticality is manifest in the large bid-ask spreads on small swap and forward transactions: a shareholder whose share of exposure is $100 might face a bid-ask spread fifty times that of the company whose exposure is, say, over $1 million, if the shareholder can find cover at all. We should note, however, that shareholders have ways of hedging other than using forward contracts and swaps. For example, they can hold a portfolio of shares in import- and export-oriented companies. If shareholders can select an alternative to the swap or forward markets, higher spreads are not a reason for firms rather than their shareholders to hedge.

[4] Of course, firms can calculate the profitability of different divisions "as if" they had hedged. However, this requires maintaining a lot of data on foreign currency inflows and outflows as well as on forward exchange rates.

Let us assume that for one or more of these reasons it is the firm that should hedge. Before evaluating the techniques that are available for this purpose, let us give the problem a context by considering the hedging decision of importers and exporters, dealing first with the source of their risk and exposure.

The Source of Risk and Exposure for Importers and Exporters

Importing and exporting firms can face significant exposure because of settlement delays when their trade is denominated in a foreign currency. An importer, for example, does not normally receive a product immediately after ordering it. Often, the product must first be produced, and this takes time. After production is completed, the goods must be shipped, and this again takes time. And after delivery, it is customary for the vending firm to grant the importer a short period of trade credit. As a result of all these delays the importer may not be required to pay until 6 months, a year, or even a couple of years after the order has been placed. Yet the price of a product is generally agreed on at the time of ordering.

If an importer agrees on a price that is stated in the vendor's currency, the importer faces exposure on the account payable if steps are not taken to hedge it. Alternatively, if the price that is agreed upon is stated in the importer's currency, the exporter faces exposure on the account receivable if nothing is done to hedge it.[5] The exposure is due both to the delay between agreeing on the price and settling the transaction, and to the price being in terms of a foreign currency. However, the exposure can be hedged in various different ways. Let us begin by considering hedging via the forward market.

Hedging via the Forward Market

Suppose that Aviva Corporation, which we introduced in Chapter 7, has placed an order with a British denim-cloth manufacturer for £1 million of fabric to be delivered in 2 months. Suppose also that the terms of agreement allow for 1-month trade credit after delivery, so that the sterling payment is due in 3 months.

One alternative open to Aviva is to buy £1 million forward for delivery on the settlement date. This will eliminate all uncertainty about the dollar cost of the denim. However, before Aviva can decide if forward hedging is a good idea, it must consider the cost. This can then be compared with the benefit of making the dollar cost certain. Let us therefore consider the cost and benefit of forward hedging.

---

[5]Exposure exists if the import or export price is stated in any currency other than that of the importer or exporter. The frequent practice of stating prices in a major international currency such as the U.S. dollar means the importer and exporter can both face exposure if neither is an American firm.

The Cost of Forward Hedging If a firm does not hedge, there will be a gain or loss vis-à-vis hedging. However, this gain or loss is known only *ex post*. The relevant cost in deciding whether to hedge is not this *ex post* actual cost, but rather the *expected* cost. The expected cost of forward hedging is equal to the known cost of foreign currency if it is bought forward, minus the expected cost of the foreign currency if it is bought spot. That is, in the context of our example, the expected cost of buying pounds 3 months forward versus waiting and buying the pounds at the unknown future spot rate is

$$\text{Expected cost of hedging £ payables} \equiv F_{1/4}(\$/\text{ask£}) - S^*_{1/4}(\$/\text{ask£})$$

where $S^*_{1/4}(\$/\text{ask£})$ is the expected future spot cost of buying pounds in 3 months' time.[6]

As we shall again mention later in this chapter, *if speculators are risk-neutral, and there are no transaction costs*, speculators will buy pounds forward when

$$F_{1/4}(\$/£) < S^*_{1/4}(\$/£) \tag{10.1}$$

This is because there is an expected gain from selling the pounds in the future at a higher spot price than will be paid when taking delivery of the pounds under the forward contract.[7] If a sufficient number of people are prepared to speculate in this way, the forward price of the pound will increase if the inequality (10.1) momentarily holds until $F_{1/4}(\$/£)$ is no longer less than $S^*_{1/4}(\$/£)$. Similarly, if

$$F_{1/4}(\$/£) > S^*_{1/4}(\$/£) \tag{10.2}$$

risk-neutral speculators will sell pounds forward and expect to gain by buying pounds spot when it is time to deliver the pounds on the forward contract. If a sufficient number of speculators sell forward whenever the inequality (10.2) momentarily holds, $F_{1/4}(\$/£)$ will decline until it does not exceed $S^*_{1/4}(\$/£)$.

With speculation occurring whenever the inequality (10.1) or (10.2) holds, and with this speculation forcing the forward rate toward the expected future spot rate, we find that risk-neutral speculation and zero transaction costs ensure

$$F_{1/4}(\$/£) = S^*_{1/4}(\$/£) \tag{10.3}$$

---

[6] If we were instead to consider the expected cost of hedging pound receivables, the expected cost of hedging would be $F_{1/4}(\$/\text{bid£}) - S^*_{1/4}(\$/\text{bid£})$. We note that at this stage we can think of all speculators as having the same expectations, so that individual speculators' expectations are also market expectations.

[7] Of course, there is risk in this speculation because the actual future spot rate will not in general equal the expected rate, but we are assuming risk neutrality. We are also at this stage ignoring transaction costs of *buying* pounds forward and *selling* them spot.

That is, with risk-neutral speculation and zero transaction costs the expected cost of hedging is zero.[8]

It is clear that for there to be an expected cost of hedging, one or both of the assumptions made in arriving at Equation (10.3) must be invalid. These assumptions were

1 speculators are risk-neutral, and/or
2 there are no transaction costs.

As it turns out, only the transaction-cost assumption is relevant for the existence of an expected net cost of hedging. Let us see why.

Risk Premiums on Forward Contracts   If speculators are risk averse, they may not buy forward when the inequality (10.1) holds or sell forward when (10.2) holds. This is because with risk aversion, speculators will require an expected return for taking risk. This expected return is equal to the difference between $F_{1/4}(\$/£)$ and $S^*_{1/4}(\$/£)$. That is, risk aversion may result in a **risk premium** in the forward exchange rate; the risk premium is equal to the expected cost of hedging, assuming zero transaction costs.

Of course, there is no reason *a priori* why the need for a risk premium would result in the inequality (10.2) holding rather than (10.1). The situation that prevails depends on how the forward market is imbalanced without any speculation occurring. For example, if forward purchases and sales of pounds from the combined hedging activities of importers, exporters, borrowers, investors, and interest arbitragers results in a net excess demand for forward pounds, then speculators will have to be drawn in to be sellers of forward pounds; otherwise the forward exchange market will not be in equilibrium. In this case speculators will need an expected return from selling pounds, causing the inequality (10.2) to be an equilibrium situation; with speculators selling pounds forward for more than the expected future spot value of the pound, speculators collect a forward risk premium.[9] However, the presence of such a risk premium is irrelevant for the hedging decision, for the following reason.

If there is an expected cost of hedging when buying pounds forward because $F_{1/4}(\$/£) > S^*_{1/4}(\$/£)$, the risk premium earned by the speculators who sell pounds forward must be appropriate for the risk they take; otherwise more speculators would enter the market to sell pounds forward. If the hedgers who *buy* pounds forward have the same risk concerns as the speculators who *sell* them pounds forward, the hedgers receive a benefit that equals the expected cost. That is, the risk premium is paid by hedgers when buying pounds forward

[8]This has given rise to the view that forward hedging is a "free lunch." See André F. Perold and Evan C. Shulman, "The Free Lunch in Currency Hedging: Implications for Policy and Performance Standards," *Financial Analysts Journal*, May-June 1988, pp. 45–50.
[9]The nature of the forward-market equilibrium, with speculators earning a premium for taking up imbalances in the forward market from the activities of hedgers, is described in Maurice Levi, "Spot versus Forward Speculation and Hedging: A Diagrammatic Exposition," *Journal of International Money and Finance*, April 1984, pp. 105–109.

because this reduces risk to the hedger, just as it adds to the risk of the speculator. This means that if a company's shareholders are typical in their attitude to the pound, the risk premium paid to buy (or sell) pounds forward comes with an offsetting benefit. That is, the presence of the forward risk premium is irrelevant in deciding whether to use the forward market.

Transaction Costs in Forward versus Spot Exchange Markets Whereas the presence of a risk premium is irrelevant to the forward-hedging decision, this is not the case for transaction costs. This is because transaction costs constitute an expected cost of hedging. This cost arises because the bid-ask spreads on forward exchange are larger than that on spot exchange.[10] This means that even if in the absence of transaction costs

$$F_{1/4}(\$/£) = S^*_{1/4}(\$/£) \tag{10.3}$$

(that is, there is no risk premium), it would still be the case that

$$F_{1/4}(\$/\text{ask}£) > S^*_{1/4}(\$/\text{ask}£)$$

That is, transaction costs make the forward price of pounds higher than the expected future spot price. At the same time, we would expect transaction costs to result in

$$F_{1/4}(\$/\text{bid}£) < S^*_{1/4}(\$/\text{bid}£)$$

That is, the number of dollars received from selling pounds forward will be less than the expected number of dollars to be received from waiting and selling the pounds spot.

While the larger spread on forward than on spot transactions does mean an expected cost of forward hedging, this expected cost is small. There are two reasons for this. First, the transaction cost of (for example) buying pounds forward versus waiting and buying them spot is only the *difference* between the two transaction costs; a transaction cost is paid to buy the pounds whatever method is employed. Second, this difference between forward and spot transaction costs is small, because banks that buy and sell forward can readily hedge

---

[10] It can be argued that the bid-ask spread is larger on forward than on spot transactions because forward trading is riskier than spot trading, thereby basing the risk-premium and transaction-cost arguments both on the same source. However, in principle we might distinguish two types of risk. One risk is that faced by speculators who maintain open positions over time, the open positions being needed to balance the aggregate supply of, and demand for, forward exchange. (The mirror image of the imbalance of forward contracts absorbed by speculators consists of the net holdings of forward contracts by hedgers.) The other type of risk is that of banks accepting orders for forward purchases/sales, and trying to remain balanced at each moment in time. The former risk will cause what we have called a risk premium, while the latter will cause a larger bid-ask spread on forward than on spot transactions. Of course, both risks are related to uncertainty in exchange rates, and differ only in the period of time over which the risk is faced.

their positions. That is, the bid-ask spread on forward exchange is not due to the risk of changes in exchange rates over the maturity of the forward contract. Rather, it is due to the risk of changes in exchange rates *while covering a position the bank has taken.* This risk is higher in forward than in spot markets because forward markets are thinner.[11] However, the market for short maturity contracts is almost as deep as the spot market, and so the spreads on forward contracts used for hedging importers' and exporters' receivables and payables are only slightly higher than those on spot transactions.

The Benefit of Forward Hedging   What we have found is that the possibility of a risk premium on forward contracts is irrelevant because the expected cost of hedging is matched by a benefit, and that transaction costs constitute only a small cost of hedging via forward exchange. That is, there is an expected cost of buying or selling forward rather than waiting and buying or selling spot, but it is a very small cost. But how about the benefit of buying or selling forward? As we have explained, there are several benefits of forward hedging which are enjoyed if management hedges.[12] For example, forward hedging reduces taxes if tax rates are progressive, reduces expected bankruptcy costs, has marketing and hiring benefits, and can improve information on profit centers. These benefits accrue because hedging reduces the volatility of receipts and payments. Let us show how forward hedging reduces volatility within the context of our example of Aviva having agreed to pay £1 million in 3 months.

If Aviva does not hedge its £1 million account payable in 3 months, the dollar cost of the pounds will depend on the realized spot exchange rate at the time of settlement. The possible payments resulting from remaining unhedged are shown in the top line of Table 10.1. If instead of being unhedged Aviva decides to buy forward at $1.50/£, the cost of the pounds is $1.5 million whatever happens to the spot rate by the time of settlement. This is shown on the second line of Table 10.1. Comparing the certain payment of $1.5 million via the forward contract with the uncertain payment if Aviva waits and buys pounds spot, we see that *ex post* it is sometimes better to hedge, and sometimes better not to hedge. However, since the gains from hedging versus not hedging equal the losses from hedging versus not hedging, on average the cost of the pounds is the same.[13] Let us make this our base case against which to compare alternative ways of hedging. Let us consider next hedging via the currency futures market.

---

[11] This was mentioned in Chapter 3.

[12] Of course, if shareholders (or management) hedge they reduce risk, but we cannot count this as a benefit to compare with the transaction cost of forward hedging, because, as we have just explained, the value of the benefit of reduced risk exactly equals the size of the risk premium in the forward rate that is paid for hedging. That is, we cannot count risk reduction as a benefit to shareholders or managers unless we also count the risk premium as an equal cost.

[13] The average of $1.3 million, $1.4 million, $1.5 million, $1.6 million, and $1.7 million, with equal probabilities of all outcomes, equals $1.5 million. Of course, this outcome is the result of assuming a zero expected hedging cost in determining the forward rate.

TABLE 10.1
DOLLAR PAYMENTS ON £1-MILLION ACCOUNTS PAYABLE
USING DIFFERENT HEDGING TECHNIQUES

Technique	Dollar payment, millions				
	Rate* = 1.3	1.4	1.5	1.6	1.7 $/£
Unhedged	1.3	1.4	1.5	1.6	1.7
Forward £ purchase @$1.5 / £	1.5	1.5	1.5	1.5	1.5
Futures £ purchase @$1.5 / £	1.5 ±	1.5 ±	1.5 ±	1.5 ±	1.5 ±
$1.50 / £ call option @$0.06 / £	1.36	1.46	1.56	1.56	1.56
$1.40 / £ call option @$0.12 / £	1.42	1.52	1.52	1.52	1.52
$1.60 / £ call option @$0.02 / £	1.32	1.42	1.52	1.62	1.62

*Realized future spot exchange rates.

Hedging via the Futures Market

The consequence of using futures contracts to hedge foreign exchange exposure is similar to that of using forward contracts. However, the fact that there is marking to market in futures exchanges makes it necessary to note a minor difference.[14]

If Aviva decides to hedge its pound payables exposure in the futures market and buys £1 million of futures contracts, it is necessary to post a margin. If subsequent to buying the futures contracts the price of these contracts declines, it is necessary to add to the margin account.[15] Alternatively, if the futures price increases, the margin account is credited by the amount gained. This addition or subtraction to the margin account is done on a daily basis, and is, as we have said, called marking to market. What marking to market means is that if, for example, the pound increases in value more than had been anticipated in the original pricing of the futures contract, at the maturity of the contract the margin account will include the value of the unanticipated increase in the value of the pounds represented by the futures contracts, as well as the original margin.

The gain that is made by buying pound futures contracts rather than waiting to buy spot pounds is the amount in or taken from the margin account minus what was originally placed in the account. This gain can be put towards buying the pounds on the spot market. As we saw in Chapter 3, the net result of paying the higher than anticipated spot rate for the pounds, and the compensation of the gain from the futures contracts, is to end up paying approximately the same for the pounds as if a forward rather than futures contract had been purchased. For example, if, in the pricing of the futures contracts for £1 million that Aviva purchased, the expected future spot exchange rate had implicitly been $1.5/£, and it turns out at the maturity date of the futures contracts that the actual spot

---

[14]The nature of marking to market is discussed in Chapter 3.
[15]As we mentioned in Chapter 3, on each contract of £62,500 on the Chicago IMM it is necessary to post $2000, and to supplement the margin only if it falls below $1500.

rate is $1.7/£, then Aviva will find it has gained about $200,000 in its margin account. Aviva will, of course, have to pay $1.7 million for the £1 million pounds it needs, rather than $1.5 million that would have been paid with a forward contract. However, after the compensating gain in the margin account Aviva will be paying only approximately $1.5 million, the same as if the pounds had been purchased on the forward market. On the other hand, if the expected future spot rate had been $1.5/£, but the actual spot rate ended up at $1.3/£, Aviva would find it had contributed $200,000 to its margin account which had been taken by the futures exchange.[16] Aviva would then buy the required £1 million for $1.3 million at the going spot rate, making the total cost of pounds $1.5 million. We find that whatever happens to the spot rate, Aviva pays approximately $1.5 million for its £1 million. The difference between using the forward and futures markets is that in the forward market all the payment is made at the end, whereas with the futures market some of the payment or compensation for the payment is made before the pounds are eventually bought at the spot rate.

Because interest rates vary over time, it is possible that the amount in the margin account at the maturity of the futures contract, or the amount paid into the account and lost, does not bring the eventual price of the £1 million to exactly $1.5 million. For example, if interest rates are low when the margin account has a large amount in it, and high when the margin account is close to the maintenance level, it could be that slightly more than $1.5 million is paid for the pounds. Alternatively, varying interest rates could make the eventual cost of the pounds slightly less than $1.5 million. This is the marking-to-market risk of futures contracts discussed in Chapter 3. Because of this risk, in Table 10.1 we write the cost of the £1 million when using the futures market as $1.5 ± million.

Hedging via the Option Market

If Aviva buys call options on pounds that mature on the payment date for the denim at a strike price of $1.50/£, the options will be exercised if the spot rate for the pound ends up above $1.50/£. The options to buy pounds will not be exercised if the spot rate for the pound is below $1.50/£, because it will be cheaper to buy the pounds at the spot rate; the option has no value. Table 10.1 shows the result of buying £1 million of $1.50/£ strike-price call options if the option premium, that is, the option price, is $0.06/£. At this option premium the cost of the option for £1 million is £1 million × $0.06/£ = $60,000. Let us examine the entries in Table 10.1 for the $1.50/£ call option to see how the entries are obtained.

If the realized spot rate at the time of payment is $1.30/£, then the $1.50/£ strike-price call option will not be exercised, and the pounds will be bought spot for $1.3 million. However, $60,000 has been paid for the option, and so we can think of the pounds as having a total cost of $1.36 million, as

[16]This $200,000 is, of course, shifted into the margin accounts of those who sold pounds forward.

shown in Table 10.1.[17] Similarly, if the spot rate ends up at $1.40/£, the total cost of the pounds including the option premium is $1.46 million. If the spot rate is the same as the strike rate, both $1.50/£, then Aviva will be as well off to exercise as to buy spot, and in either case the total cost of pounds is $1.56 million. If the spot rate ends up at $1.60/£ or $1.70/£, Aviva will exercise and pay the call rate of $1.50/£, bringing the total cost of pounds to $1.56 million.

It is clear from examining Table 10.1 that the benefit of buying a call option on the pound when there is a pound payable is that it puts a ceiling on the amount that is paid for the pounds, but allows the option buyer to benefit if the exchange rate ends up below the spot rate. It can similarly be demonstrated that if a firm has a receivable in pounds it can buy a put option and ensure that a minimum number of dollars is received for the pounds, and yet the firm can still benefit if the dollar value of the pound ends up higher than the strike rate.

Let us suppose that instead of buying a call option at a strike price of $1.50/£, Aviva buys one at a strike price of $1.40/£, which, if the spot rate at the time of buying the option is above $1.40/£, is an in-the-money option. Table 10.1 shows the effect of buying this option if it costs $0.12/£.

Aviva will not exercise the $1.40/£ call option if the eventually realized spot rate is $1.30/£. Instead, it will buy the pounds spot for $1.3 million. Adding the $0.12/£ × £1 million = $120,000 price of the option gives a total cost of £1 million, equal to $1.42 million. At a realized spot rate of $1.40/£ Aviva will be indifferent between exercising or buying spot. Either way the pounds will cost $1.52 million, including the cost of the option. At $1.50/£ and above, the $1.40/£ call option will be exercised, and whatever the spot rate happens to be, the cost of the pounds is $1.40 million. When we include the amount paid for the option, this brings the cost to $1.52 million.

If Aviva chooses a $1.60/£ call option—which, if the spot rate of the pound at the time it is purchased is below this value, is an out-of-the-money option—and if the option premium is $0.02/£, then the effect is as shown on the bottom line of Table 10.1. These values are obtained in a similar fashion to those for the other options, recognizing that the option is exercised only when the spot rate ends up above $1.60/£.

A comparison of the effects of the different-strike-price options and of these versus forwards and futures can be made by looking along each row in Table 10.1. We can see that with the exposure of a payable in pounds, the out-of-the-money option (that with a strike price of $1.60/£) turns out to have been best if the pound ends up at a low value, but the in-the-money option (that with a strike price of $1.40/£) is best if the pound ends up at a high value. The at-the-money option is somewhere in between. All options are better than forwards and futures if the pound ends up very low, but options are worse if the

---

[17]Our description is directly applicable to options on spot exchange, such as those trading on the Philadelphia Stock Exchange. We note that for simplicity we exclude the opportunity cost of forgone interest on the payment for the option contract.

pound ends up high. If the pound ends up at its expected value, \$1.50/£, having used forwards or futures is *ex post* a little cheaper than having used options: the option premium is avoided.

Hedging via Borrowing and Lending: Swaps

In the discussion of interest disparity in Chapter 8 we pointed out that it is possible to use borrowing, investing, and the spot exchange market to achieve the same result as by using the forward market. For example, Aviva can hedge its import of £1 million of denim fabric with payment due in 3 months by borrowing dollars, buying pounds spot with the dollars, and investing the pounds for 3 months in a pound-denominated security.[18] If this is done, then in 3 months Aviva owes a known number of dollars on its dollar loan, and receives a known number of pounds, just as with a forward contract. Let us consider the cost of hedging via borrowing and lending so that we can compare it with the cost of the forward market. We will use the notation introduced in Chapter 8, and will be careful to distinguish between borrowing and lending interest rates, and bid versus ask exchange rates.

For every £1 Aviva wants in n years' time, where $n = \frac{1}{4}$ in our particular example, the company must purchase

$$\pounds \frac{1}{\left(1 + r^I_{UK}\right)^n} \tag{10.4}$$

on the spot market. Here r^I_{UK} is the interest rate the pounds will earn—the pound investment rate—in the chosen pound-denominated security. For example, if $r^I_{UK} = 0.12$, then if Aviva buys £970,874 immediately and invests it at 12 percent, it will receive £1 million in 3 months. The dollar cost of the spot pounds in (10.4) is

$$\$S(\$/\text{ask}\pounds) \cdot \frac{1}{\left(1 + r^I_{UK}\right)^n} \tag{10.5}$$

where $S(\$/\text{ask}\pounds)$ is the cost of buying pounds spot from the bank. If the number of dollars in (10.5) has to be borrowed, then in n years Aviva will have to pay for each pound it receives

$$\$S(\$/\text{ask}\pounds) \cdot \frac{\left(1 + r^B_{US}\right)^n}{\left(1 + r^I_{UK}\right)^n} \tag{10.6}$$

where r^B_{US} is Aviva's U.S. dollar borrowing rate.[19]

---

[18] We say "pound-denominated security" rather than "British security" because, as we shall see in the next chapter, pound-denominated securities are available outside Britain in the offshore currency market. Indeed, the borrowing of dollars to buy the pounds may also occur in the offshore currency market, where the market for dollars is called the Eurodollar market.

[19] If Aviva does not have to borrow, but already has the dollars, we use Aviva's opportunity cost of dollars, r^I_{US}, in place of r^B_{US}.

We should recall that this hedging technique involves:

1 borrowing, if necessary, at home,
2 buying the foreign exchange on the spot market,
3 investing the foreign exchange,
4 repaying the domestic debt.

Clearly, if the value in (10.6) is the same as the forward exchange rate for buying the pounds n years ahead, $F_n(\$/\text{ask}£)$, then Aviva will be indifferent to the choices of buying forward and going through this borrowing-investment hedging procedure. Indifference between these two hedging methods therefore requires that

$$S(\$/\text{ask}£)\frac{\left(1 + r_{US}^B\right)^n}{\left(1 + r_{UK}^I\right)^n} = F_n(\$/\text{ask}£) \qquad (10.7)$$

We recognize Equation (10.7) as one of the forms of the interest parity condition. We find that when interest parity holds, an importer should not care whether he or she hedges by buying forward, or by borrowing domestic currency and investing in the needed foreign currency.

Borrowing and investing can also be used by an exporter to hedge foreign exchange exposure. The exporter does the reverse of the importer. For example, if Aviva is to receive foreign currency for its jeans, it can sell it forward. Alternatively, it can:

1 borrow in the foreign currency that is to be received,
2 sell the borrowed foreign currency spot for dollars,
3 invest or otherwise employ the dollars at home,
4 repay the foreign debt with its export earnings.

Since the foreign debt will be repaid with the foreign exchange proceeds on its exports, Aviva will not have any foreign exchange exposure or risk. The amount borrowed should be such that the amount needed to repay the debt is equal to the export revenues that are to be received. If, for example, payment is due in n years, Aviva should borrow

$$£\frac{1}{\left(1 + r_{UK}^B\right)^n}$$

for each pound it is due to receive; this will leave Aviva owing £1 in n years. This number of pounds will be exchanged for

$$\$S(\$/\text{bid}£) \cdot \frac{1}{\left(1 + r_{UK}^B\right)^n}$$

which if invested in the U.S. will produce

$$\$S(\$/\text{bid£})\frac{\left(1 + r_{US}^{I}\right)^{n}}{\left(1 + r_{UK}^{B}\right)^{n}} \tag{10.8}$$

at the time that payment for the jeans is received. The alternative is to sell the foreign exchange receipts on the forward market at $F_n(\$/\text{bid£})$. Clearly, an exporter will be indifferent between (1) using the forward market and (2) borrowing at home and investing abroad when $F_n(\$/\text{bid£})$ equals the expression (10.8), that is, when a version of interest parity holds. The borrowing and lending procedure is something called a **swap** and is the money-market equivalent of the customized currency swaps we shall meet later.

Hedging via Currency of Invoicing

While it is usually a simple matter to arrange hedging via forwards, futures, options, or swaps, we should not overlook an obvious way for importers or exporters to avoid exposure, namely by invoicing trade in their own currency.[20] For example, if Aviva can negotiate the price of its denim cloth in terms of U.S. dollars, it need not face any foreign exchange risk or exposure on its imports. Indeed, in general, when business convention or the power that a firm holds in negotiating its purchases and sales results in agreement on prices in terms of the home currency, the firm that trades abroad will face no more risk and exposure than the firm with strictly domestic interests. However, even when trade can be denominated in the importer's or exporter's local currency, only part of the risk and exposure is resolved. For example, an American exporter who charges for his or her products in U.S. dollars will still find the level of sales dependent on the exchange rate, and hence faces operating exposure and risk. This is because the quantity of exports depends on the price the foreign buyer must pay, and this is determined by the rate of exchange between the dollar and the buyer's currency. Therefore, even when all trade is in local currency, some foreign exchange exposure—operating exposure—will remain.

Of course, only one side of an international deal can be hedged by stating the price in the importer's or exporter's currency. If the importer has his or her way, the exporter will face the exchange risk and exposure, and vice versa.

When there is international bidding for a contract, it may be wise for the company calling for bids to allow the bidders to state prices in their own currencies. For example, if Aviva invites bids to supply it with denim cloth, Aviva may be better off allowing the bids to come in stated in pounds, marks, and so on, rather than insisting on dollar bids. The reason is that the bidders

---

[20] The fact that this method has been overlooked became clear from a survey of firms conducted by Business International. See "Altering the Currency of Billing: A Neglected Technique for Exposure Management," *Money Report*, Business International, January 2, 1981, pp. 1–2.

cannot easily hedge, because they do not know if their bids will succeed. (They can use options, but option contracts from option exchanges are contingent on future spot exchange rates rather than the success of bids, and so are not ideally suited for the purpose.) When all the bids are in, Aviva can convert them into dollars at the going forward exchange rates, choose the cheapest, and then buy the appropriate foreign currency at the time it announces the successful bidder. This is a case of asymmetric information, where the buyer can hedge and the seller cannot, and where the seller may therefore add a risk premium to the bid. When the *seller* is inviting bids, as when equipment or a company is up for sale, the seller knows more than the buyer, and so bidding should be in the buyer's currency.

So far we have considered situations in which all of the exposure is faced by the importer or the exporter. However, another way of hedging, at least partially, is to mix the currencies of trade.

Hedging via Mixed-Currency Invoicing

If the British mill were to invoice its denim at £1 million, Aviva would face the exchange exposure. If instead Aviva agreed to pay, for example, $1.5 million, then it would be the British mill that accepted the exposure. In between these two extreme positions is the possibility of setting the price at, for example, £500,000 plus $750,000. That is, payment could be stated partly in each currency. If this were done and the exchange rate between dollars and pounds varied, Aviva's exposure would involve only half of the funds payable—those that are payable in pounds. Similarly, the British mill would face exposure on only the dollar component of its receivables.

The mixing of currencies in denominating sales contracts can go further than a simple sharing between the units of currency of the importer and exporter. It is possible, for example, to express a commercial agreement in terms of a **composite currency unit**—a unit that is formed from many different currencies. A prominent composite unit is the Special Drawing Right, or SDR. This unit is constructed by taking a weighted average of the major world currencies. Another officially maintained currency unit is the European Currency Unit (ECU), which consists of an average of the exchange rates of the EEC countries. Besides the official SDR and ECU units, there are private **currency baskets**, or **cocktails**, which are also designed to move smoothly. They are formed by various weighted averages of a number of different currencies.

The composite currency units will reduce risk and exposure because they offer some diversification benefits. However, they cannot eliminate risk and exposure as can a forward contract, and they themselves can be difficult to hedge forward. It is perhaps because of this that cocktails and baskets are not as common in denominating trade, where forward, futures, options, and swaps are frequently available, as they are in denominating long-term debt, where these other hedging techniques are not as readily available.

A large fraction of the world's trade is, by convention and for convenience, conducted in U.S. dollars. This is an advantage for American importers and exporters in that it helps them avoid exchange-rate exposure. However, when the U.S. dollar is used in an agreement between two non-American parties, *both* parties experience exposure. This situation occurs often. For example, a Japanese firm may purchase Canadian raw materials at a price denominated in U.S. dollars. Often both parties can hedge, for example, by engaging in forward exchange contracts. The Japanese importer can buy and the Canadian exporter can sell the U.S. dollars forward against their own currencies. In the case of some of the smaller countries where foreign business is often expressed in dollar terms, there may not be regular forward, futures, option, or swap markets in the country's currency. However, the denomination of trade in U.S. dollars might still be seen as a way of reducing exposure and risk if the firms have offsetting business in the dollar, or view the dollar as less volatile in value than the currency of either party involved in the trade.

Hedging via Selection of Supplying Country: Sourcing

A firm that can invoice its inputs in the same currency as it sells its goods can offset foreign-currency payables against receivables. This type of hedging practice is called **sourcing**. For example, Aviva Corporation might buy its denim cloth in the currencies in which it sells its jeans. If about one-half of the wholesale value of jeans is the value of the material, then on each pair of jeans the firm has only about one-half of the foreign exchange exposure of the jeans themselves. Aviva could buy the denim in the various currencies in rough proportion to the volume of sales in those currencies.

The risk-reducing technique of buying inputs in the currencies in which outputs are sold has a clear disadvantage: Aviva should buy its denim where the material is cheapest, and it should not pay more for its cloth just to avoid foreign exchange exposure. However, after an input source has been chosen at the best price, there will be some automatic hedging occurring in that currency. For example, if Aviva settles on buying its denim in Britain because the cloth is cheapest there, the total value of the jeans that it sells in that market should be netted against its denim purchases.

Now that we have explained the different techniques that are available for hedging exposure, we can consider their different consequences. This can be done most easily by examining **payoff profiles**, which show graphically the rewards and/or costs of selecting different methods of hedging.

Payoff Profiles of Different Hedging Techniques

Forward Profile As before, let us assume the expected future spot rate is $1.50/£. Then the difference between the realized spot rate and this expected rate is the unanticipated change in the exchange rate, which we have previously written as ΔS^u.

When the expected spot rate for 3 months ahead is $1.50/£, and the spot rate indeed turns out to be $1.50/£, if Aviva has bought pounds forward at

TABLE 10.2
PAYOFFS FROM DIFFERENT HEDGING TECHNIQUES

	ΔV, millions of \$				
ΔS^u(\$/£)	Forward contract	Futures contract	At-the-money option	In-the-money option	Out-of-the-money option
−0.2	−0.2	−0.2 ±	−0.06	−0.12	−0.02
−0.1	−0.1	−0.1 ±	−0.06	−0.12	−0.02
0	0.0	0.0 ±	−0.06	−0.02	−0.02
0.1	0.1	0.1 ±	0.04	0.08	−0.02
0.2	0.2	0.2 ±	0.14	0.18	0.08

\$1.50, the forward contract has a value of zero. Let us write this as $\Delta V = 0$, where we can think of ΔV as the gain or loss by having purchased the forward contract. If instead of \$1.50/£, the realized spot rate happens to be \$1.70/£, Aviva's forward contract to buy £1 million at \$1.50/£ is worth \$0.2/£ × £1 million = \$0.2 million. Then we can write ΔV as \$0.2 million. Alternatively, if for example, the realized spot rate is \$1.30/£, then Aviva's \$1.50/£ contract has a negative value of −\$0.2/£ × £1 million = −\$0.2 million, because forward contracts, unlike options, must be honored. These and other values of ΔV are shown against the realized spot rates that bring them about in the first column of Table 10.2.

The values of ΔV and ΔS^u for the £1-million forward contract at \$1.50/£ are plotted against each other in the left-hand panel of Figure 10.1a. We find an upward-sloping line because the forward contract has positive value when the pound experiences unanticipated appreciation ($\Delta S^u > 0$) and negative value when the pound experiences unanticipated depreciation ($\Delta S^u < 0$).

The middle panel of Figure 10.1a shows the underlying exposure for the £1-million account payable. The exposure is represented by a line with negative slope, showing a loss if the pound unexpectedly appreciates, and a gain if the pound unexpectedly depreciates.

The right-hand panel of Figure 10.1a shows the effect of hedging pound receivables with a forward purchase of pounds. The figure is obtained by adding the two ΔV's from the left-hand and middle panels at each ΔS^u. We find that the combination of a forward purchase of pounds and the underlying payables exposure produces a line with a zero slope. That is, the forward contract eliminates exposure on the account payable. Figure 10.1a is an example of how to use payoff profiles to see the effect of different hedging techniques.

Futures Profile Table 10.2 shows the gains or losses on futures contracts to purchase £1 million at different unanticipated changes in the exchange rate. We see, for example, that if the future spot rate had been expected to be \$1.50/£, but the realized rate turns out to be \$1.30/£, that is, ΔS^u(\$/£) = −0.2, then by buying £1 million via pound futures Aviva will find that it has lost approximately

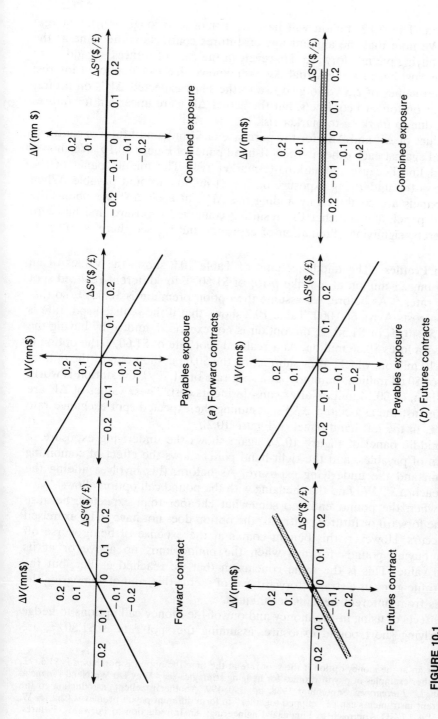

FIGURE 10.1
PAYOFF PROFILES, PAYABLES EXPOSURE, AND RESULTING EXPOSURE WITH FORWARD AND FUTURES CONTRACTS.

$0.2 million. This $0.2 million will have been moved through Aviva's margin account. We note that the amount lost on futures contracts is the same as the loss from buying pounds forward. However, in the case of futures we add $\pm$ to the amount lost because the actual ΔV is unknown due to volatility of interest rates. Other values of ΔS^u also give rise to the same expected ΔV's on futures contracts as on forward contracts, but the actual ΔV's are uncertain for futures contracts, due to marking-to-market risk.

The values of ΔV and ΔS^u for the purchase of £1 million of futures contracts are plotted against each other in the left-hand panel of Figure 10.1*b*. We show a broadened line because of marking-to-market risk. The middle panel of the figure shows the underlying exposure on the £1-million account payable. When the two panels are combined by adding the ΔV's at each ΔS^u we obtain the right-hand panel. We see that the resulting combined exposure line has zero slope, thereby signifying elimination of exposure, but we see there is still risk.

Option Profiles   The middle-column of Table 10.2 shows the values of an option to buy £1 million at a strike price of $1.50/£ for different realized spot exchange rates.[21] As before, we assume the option premium is $0.06/£, so that the option costs Aviva $60,000. Table 10.2 shows that if the realized spot rate is $1.30/£, $1.40/£, or $1.50/£, the option is not exercised, and so by buying the option Aviva loses $0.06 million. At a realized spot rate of $1.60/£ the option is worth $0.10 million, which, after subtracting the $0.06 million cost of the option, is a gain of $0.04 million. Similarly, at a spot rate of $1.70/£ the option is worth $0.20 million, or $0.14 million after considering its cost. These values of ΔV are plotted against the associated ΔS^u's, assuming the expected spot exchange rate is $1.50/£, in the left-hand panel of Figure 10.2*a*.

The middle panel of Figure 10.2*a* again shows the underlying exposure of £1 million of payables, and the right-hand panel shows the effect of combining the option and the underlying exposure. As before, this involves adding the ΔV's at each ΔS^u. We find that hedging with the pound call option allows Aviva to gain when the pound ends up somewhat cheaper than expected, because unlike the forward or futures contracts, the option does not have to be exercised if this occurs. However, this benefit comes at the expense of being worse off than on buying pounds forward when the pound ends up above or at its expected value. This is the same conclusion that we reached earlier, but the payoff profile gives us a straightforward way of seeing this, and of comparing the outcomes from different hedging techniques.[22]

The effects of using in-the-money and out-of-the-money call options to hedge an underlying short pound exposure, assuming the spot rate is $1.50/£, are

---

[21] This is an at-the-money option if the spot rate at the time the option is purchased is $1.50/£.

[22] For other examples of payoff profiles for hedging strategies see "Why Do We Need Financial Engineering?," *Euromoney*, September 1988, pp. 190–199. Another excellent introduction to the ways different instruments can be "clipped together" to form different payoff profiles is Charles W. Smithson, "A LEGO Approach to Financial Engineering: An Introduction to Forwards, Futures, Swaps, and Options," *Midland Corporate Finance Journal*, winter, 1987, pp. 16–28.

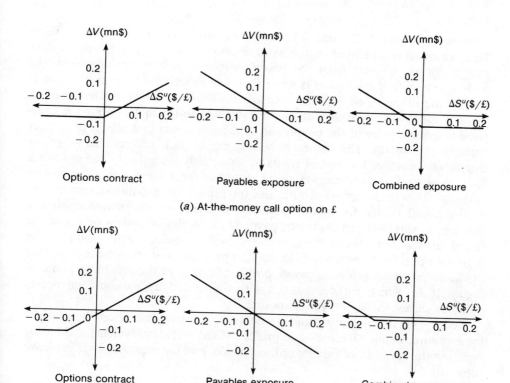

(a) At-the-money call option on £

(b) In-the-money call option on £

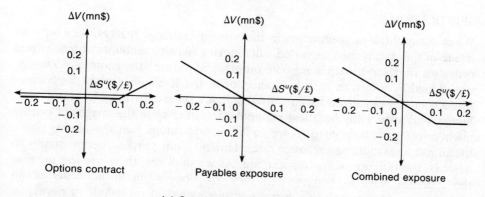

(c) Out-of-the-money option on £

FIGURE 10.2
PAYOFF PROFILES FROM OPTION HEDGES.

described in Figure 10.2*b* and *c*. These graphs are based on the values in Table 10.2, which were obtained in the same fashion as the values for the at-the-money option. We see from the payoff profiles that both options allow the hedger to benefit if the pound is lower than was expected. However, the gain is less for the in-the-money option, because this is more expensive. On the other hand, if the pound unexpectedly appreciates, the in-the-money option is exercised at a lower price of the pound and so there is a gain that offsets the higher price of the option. The choice between options with different strike prices depends on whether the hedger wants to insure only against very bad outcomes for a cheap option premium (by using an out-of-the money option) or against anything other than very good outcomes (by using an in-the-money option).

The payoff profile for swaps is exactly the same as for forward contracts, because, as with forward contracts, payment or receipt of dollars occurs in the future at the time the pounds are received or paid.[23] For example, the borrowing of dollars combined with the spot purchase and investment of pounds produces an upward-sloping payoff profile like that in the left-hand panel of Figure 10.1*a*, which when combined with the underlying exposure on pound payables leaves Aviva with zero exposure.

Hedging via denominating trade in domestic currency eliminates the underlying exposure, giving a flat exposure profile. Mixed-currency invoicing and buying inputs in the currency of exports reduce the slope of the exposure line, but leave some risk.

SPECULATION

When many think of speculators in the foreign exchange market, they have an image of quiet, tidy men in vested suits moving massive amounts of money and providing themselves with handsome profits. The phrase "the gnomes of Zurich" was coined by a former British Chancellor of the Exchequer when his country faced what he perceived as an outright attack on its currency by those ever-hungry and apparently heartless manipulators. In spite of the images of evil we might have, it can be argued, as we do in the Addendum, that speculators play a useful role in stabilizing exchange rates. However, our purpose here is simply to describe the different ways to speculate. As we shall see, these are the same as the different ways to hedge when they are done without the offset of an underlying exposure such as a foreign-currency account receivable or payable.

---

[23] In principle, swaps can be arranged with borrowing and investment for periods of time shorter than the maturity of foreign-currency accounts receivable or payable. For example, Aviva might borrow dollars from a U.S. bank at a variable interest rate linked to the prime rate, or roll its pounds over in very short-term British securities. This will eliminate exposure, but it does not eliminate risk. In particular, it leaves risk due to volatility in interest rates. In this situation the payoff profile for the swap is similar to that of a futures contract.

Speculating via the Forward Market

Speculating without Transaction Costs   If we write a speculator's expected spot exchange rate in n years as $S_n^*(\$/\pounds)$, then, as we indicated at the beginning of this chapter, if the speculator is risk-neutral, he or she will want to buy pounds n years forward if [24]

$$F_n(\$/\pounds) < S_n^*(\$/\pounds)$$

For example, if $F_1(\$/\pounds) = 1.5500$ and the speculator thinks that in 1 year the spot rate will be $\$1.5550/\pounds$, that is, that $S_1^*(\$/\pounds) = 1.5550$, then the speculator will buy pounds forward at the forward rate, $F_1(\$/\pounds) = 1.5500$, in the hope of selling each of the purchased pounds at $\$1.5550/\pounds$. The expected profit is $\$0.005$ per pound purchased, or $\$5000$ per $\pounds1,000,000$. On the other hand, as we saw earlier in this chapter, the risk-neutral speculator will want to sell pounds n years forward if

$$F_n(\$/\pounds) > S_n^*(\$/\pounds)$$

For example, if $F_1(\$/\pounds) = 1.5500$, and the speculator thinks the spot rate will be $\$1.5420$, that is, $S_1^*(\$/\pounds) = 1.5420$, then the speculator will sell forward for $F_1(\$/\pounds) = 1.5500$ in the hope of being able to buy the pounds spot when making delivery on the forward contract at the lower rate of $\$1.5420/\pounds$. The expected profit is then $\$0.008$ per pound sold forward, or $\$8000$ per $\pounds1,000,000$.

As we stated earlier in this chapter, if the speculator is not risk-neutral, he or she will not buy or sell forward unless the expected return is sufficient for the systematic risk that the speculator faces. This risk depends on the covariances of the exchange rate with other assets and liabilities the speculator holds. Because most exchange-rate risk is probably diversifiable and therefore unsystematic, the risk premium which determines the extent that $F_n(\$/\pounds)$ is below or above $S_n^*(\$/\pounds)$ before speculation occurs is likely to be very small. This is confirmed by the empirical evidence which is discussed in Chapter 12.

When a speculator buys pounds forward and has no other exposure in the pound, his or her exposure is that shown in the left-hand panel of Figure 10.1a. That is, the speculator creates an exposure line with an upward slope. If the forward rate that is paid when buying pounds is the *market's* expected future spot rate—which assumes no risk premium—the speculator will gain when the actual spot rate ends up higher than the market anticipated, and vice versa.[25] We see that exposure means facing an exposure line of nonzero slope. The speculator will want to create an upward slope by buying pounds forward if he

---

[24] We should distinguish the *individual speculator's* expected future spot rate from the *market's* expected future spot rate. In this section of this chapter and in some later chapters, expected future spot rates are those of the individual speculator. The occasions when this is the interpretation of $S_n^*(\$/\pounds)$ will be made clear.

[25] We recall that $S_n^*(\$/\pounds)$ is the individual's expected spot rate.

or she thinks that $\Delta S^u(\$/£)$, the unanticipated change in the spot rate, will be positive, and will want to create a downward slope by selling pounds forward if he or she thinks that $\Delta S^u(\$/£)$ will be negative.

Speculating with Transaction Costs When there are transaction costs in the spot and the forward foreign exchange market, a risk-neutral speculator will buy pounds n years forward when

$$F_n(\$/\text{ask£}) < S_n^*(\$/\text{bid£}) \tag{10.9}$$

That is, the speculator will buy forward if the buying price of the forward pound is less than his or her expected future spot selling price of the pound. Clearly, the expected movement of the exchange rate has to be sufficient to cover two transaction costs, one being half the forward spread and the other being half the spot spread. Similarly, the risk-neutral speculator will sell pounds n years forward if

$$F_n(\$/\text{bid£}) > S_n^*(\$/\text{ask£}) \tag{10.10}$$

The remarks about risk premiums and the nature of the exposure line created by forward speculation that were made in the context of zero transaction costs also apply when transaction costs exist.

Speculating via the Futures Market

The decision criteria for the futures market are, not surprisingly, essentially the same as those for the forward market. That is, the risk-neutral speculator buys pound futures if he or she believes the future spot price when selling pounds will exceed the current futures buying rate [the inequality (10.9)]. The risk-neutral speculator sells pound futures when the reverse is the case [the inequality (10.10)]. However, there are two small differences between the decision to buy futures and to buy forwards, namely:

1 Because of marking-to-market risk on futures, if speculators are risk-averse they might want a larger gap between the futures price and the expected future spot price to compensate for the extra risk. That is, there is risk from unanticipated changes both in the spot exchange rate [movement along the $\Delta S^u(\$/£)$ axis in Figure 10.1b] and in the interest rate [noise around the exposure line in Figure 10.1b].

2 Futures contracts are rarely held to their maturity, and the speculator may therefore be comparing today's futures exchange rate, not with the eventual spot rate, but with an expected futures exchange rate for a date prior to the futures contract's maturity.

The consequence of speculation by buying a futures contract on the pound is shown by the left-hand panel in Figure 10.1b. The result of selling a futures contract would be a downward-sloping exposure line, also including fuzziness due to risk from uncertain interest rates.

Speculating via the Option Market

A speculator will buy an option if the expected payoff exceeds the cost of the option by enough to compensate the speculator for the opportunity cost of money paid for the option. Of course, positive payoffs occur only if an option is in the money, and an option could move into the money at different times during its maturity and by different amounts. Furthermore, each of the different extents of being in the money occurs with a different probability. This means that to calculate the expected payoff the different possible outcomes must be weighted by the probabilities of these outcomes. This is obviously a very difficult calculation.[26] Rather than go into the specifics of calculating an option's value, let us intuitively explain what might induce a speculator to buy an option that has been priced in the market.

Clearly, a speculator will buy an option if he or she values the option at more than its market price. This may occur if the speculator believes that the option will be in-the-money with a higher probability than the market in general believes. For example, a speculator my buy a call option on the pound with a strike price of $1.60/£ if he or she believes the probability of the pound moving above $1.60/£ is higher than the probability attached to this eventuality by the market in general. Similarly, a speculator may buy a put option at $1.40/£ if he or she believes the probability of the pound moving below this rate is higher than the probability attached to this eventuality by the market.

The exposures created by buying call options at the money, in the money, and out of the money are shown by the payoff profiles in the left-hand panels of Figure 10.2a, b, and c. It is clear from examining these profiles and comparing them with those for speculating via forward or futures contracts in Figure 10.1 that options will appeal to speculators who wish to limit their maximum possible loss to the price of the option.[27]

A speculator who is prepared to accept the possibility of large losses can sell, or **write**, currency options. If the speculator writes a call option on the pound, she or he gives the buyer the right to buy the pound at the strike price, and if the speculator writes a put option, she or he gives the buyer the right to sell the pound at the strike price.

The exposure created by writing an at-the-money call option on the pound is shown in Figure 10.3. The figure shows that if the dollar value of the pound

---

[26]The reader who is interested in how currency options are valued is referred to Nahum Biger and John Hull, "The Valuation of Currency Options," *Financial Management*, spring 1983, pp. 24–28, or Mark Garman and Steven Kohlhagen, "Foreign Currency Option Values," *Journal of International Money and Finance*, December, 1983, pp. 231–237.

[27]Options can be combined with other options, forward and futures contracts, cash positions, and so on, which means that numerous other profiles are possible. Some of these are shown in Smithson, *op. cit.*

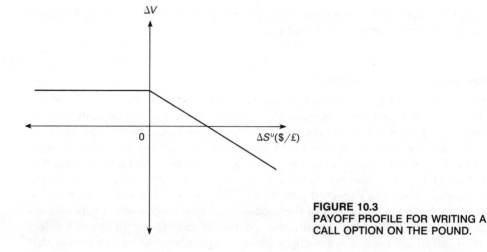

FIGURE 10.3
PAYOFF PROFILE FOR WRITING A
CALL OPTION ON THE POUND.

ends up below the strike exchange rate, signified by $\Delta S^u(\$/£)$ being negative, then the buyer does not exercise and so the option writer receives the option premium given by the height of the horizontal segment of the payoff profile. However, if the pound ends up above its strike rate, so that the option is in the money, the option is exercised and the speculator must deliver the pounds.[28] If the option ends up only slightly in the money, the premium might cover the extent to which the option is in the money, but as the profile shows, if the pound moves much higher than the market had expected, the speculator stands to lose very heavily. Clearly, option writing is a very risky speculative strategy unless, as usually is the case, the speculator creates offsetting exposure via other options, forwards, futures, or holding of currencies against which options are written.

Speculating via Borrowing and Lending: Swaps

We saw earlier in this chapter and in Chapter 8 that by borrowing in the U.S., buying pounds spot, and investing in Britain, it is possible to achieve essentially the same objective as buying pounds forward. That is, at maturity, dollars are paid on the U.S. loan, and pounds are received from the British investment.

For each pound a speculator wants to have in n years, he or she must invest in pounds today

$$£\frac{1}{\left(1 + r_{UK}^I\right)^n}$$

where r_{UK}^I is the return earned in Britain. The cost of buying this number of

---

[28]Options are not generally exercised, so when an option is in the money it is usually more a matter of the option writer settling up with the buyer via the option exchange.

pounds on the spot market so as to have £1 in n years is

$$\$\frac{S(\$/\text{ask}£)}{\left(1 + r_{\text{UK}}^{I}\right)^{n}}$$

If the speculator borrows the money at r_{US}^{B}, the number of dollars that must be repaid on the loan is

$$\$S(\$/\text{ask}£) \cdot \frac{\left(1 + r_{\text{US}}^{B}\right)^{n}}{\left(1 + r_{\text{UK}}^{I}\right)^{n}} \tag{10.11}$$

In summary, the amount in Equation (10.11) is the dollar amount to be paid in n years to receive £1 in n years.

A risk-neutral speculator would use the borrowing-lending technique to speculate in favor of the pound if[29]

$$S(\$/\text{ask}£) \cdot \frac{\left(1 + r_{\text{US}}^{B}\right)^{n}}{\left(1 + r_{\text{UK}}^{I}\right)^{n}} < S_{n}^{*}(\$/\text{bid}£) \tag{10.12}$$

where $S_{n}^{*}(\$/\text{bid}£)$ is the number of dollars the speculator expects to be able to sell the pounds for in n years' time. That is, the speculator will borrow in the U.S., buy pounds spot, and invest in pound securities if he or she thinks the pounds to be received can be sold spot in n years for more dollars than he or she owes on the dollar loan.[30]

The exposure line from the long pound speculation we have described is, not surprisingly, the same as if pounds had been bought forward. Therefore, the exposure is as shown in the left-hand panel of Figure 10.1a.

Speculating via Not Hedging Trade

While it might not seem like speculation, when a firm has foreign currency receivables or payables and does *not* hedge these by one of the procedures we have described, that firm is speculating. By not hedging an exposure, the firm accepts an exposure just as if there were no underlying exposure and the firm used one of the techniques for speculating that we have described. For example, a U.S. exporter that invoices in pounds and does nothing to hedge the exposure is speculating in favor of pounds. This should seem obvious after what we have

[29] If forwards are also available, the forward market would be used instead if

$$F_{n}(\$/\text{ask}£) < S(\$/\text{ask}£) \cdot \left(1 + r_{\text{US}}^{B}\right)^{n}/\left(1 + r_{\text{UK}}^{I}\right)^{n}$$

[30] The criterion for speculating against the pound by borrowing pounds, buying dollars spot, and investing in dollar securities is left as an exercise for the reader.

said in this chapter, because it should be clear that speculation is synonymous with having an exposure line with nonzero slope. Yet despite the obvious fact that not hedging foreign-currency receivables or payables means speculating, it is remarkable how many firms, when asked if they use the forward, futures, option or swap markets to hedge their trade, say, "Oh no! We do not speculate!" As we have seen, in fact they are unwittingly speculating by not using these markets to hedge exposure.

Speculating on Exchange-Rate Volatility

It is possible to speculate, not on whether an exchange rate will unexpectedly increase or on whether it will decrease, but rather on the possibility that the exchange rate will change by an unexpectedly large amount in either direction. That is, it is possible to speculate on the exchange rate being volatile, not on the exchange rate moving in a particular direction. One way to speculate on volatility is to simultaneously buy a call option and a put option at the same strike price. Then, if the value of the foreign currency increases substantially, the call can be exercised for a good profit, and if it decreases substantially, the put can be exercised. Such a speculative strategy is called a **straddle**.[31]

SUMMARY

1 There are several reasons why hedging should be performed by the firm rather than its shareholders. These include progressive corporate taxes, scale economies in hedging transactions, marketing and employment benefits, lower expected bankruptcy costs, and better internal information.

2 An importer or exporter faces exposure and risk because of delay between agreeing on a foreign currency price and settling the transaction.

3 The expected cost of hedging is the difference between the forward exchange rate and the expected future spot rate.

4 The decision to use forward hedging does not depend on there being a forward risk premium. However, if the bid-ask spread on forward transactions exceeds that on spot transactions, there is an expected cost of forward hedging.

5 The bid-ask spread on short-maturity forward transactions does not substantially exceed that on spot transactions, so that the expected cost of forward hedging is small. Because there are several benefits of forward hedging, it generally pays to use the forward market.

6 Futures-market hedging achieves essentially the same result as forward hedging. However, with futures the foreign exchange is bought or sold at the spot rate at maturity, and the balance of receipts from selling a foreign currency or cost of buying a foreign currency is reflected in the margin account. Because interest rates vary, the exact receipt or payment with futures is uncertain.

7 Foreign-currency accounts payable can be hedged by buying a call option on the foreign currency, and accounts receivable can be hedged by buying a put option on

---

[31]There are too many speculative strategies to describe in this book. The reader who is interested in other possibilities should read Smithson, *op. cit.*

the foreign currency. Options set a limit on the worst that can happen from unfavorable exchange-rate movements without preventing enjoyment of gains from favorable exchange-rate movements.

8 An importer can hedge with a swap by borrowing in the home currency, buying the foreign-currency spot, and investing in the foreign currency. Exporters can hedge with a swap by borrowing in the foreign currency, buying the home-currency spot, and investing in the home currency.

9 Foreign exchange exposure can be eliminated by invoicing in domestic currency. Exposure can be reduced by invoicing in a mixture of currencies or by buying inputs in the currency of exports.

10 Payoff profiles provide a graphical comparison of the consequence of using different techniques for hedging or speculating.

11 The techniques for speculation are the same as those used for hedging. Any forward, futures, swap, or option position without underlying exposure is a speculative position.

12 Doing nothing when there is exposure is speculating.

QUESTIONS

1 In what sense are the forward risk premium and the bid-ask spread on forward contracts both related to risk? Does the fact that the bid-ask spread is always positive, and yet the forward risk premium can be positive or negative, suggest that the nature of the risk behind them is different?

2 Suppose that you were importing small electric transformers, that delivery from all suppliers would take approximately 6 months, and that you faced the situation shown in the table below:

	United States	Canada	Great Britain	France	Germany
Local cost	$20,000	Can$22,000	£10,000	Fr 82,000	DM 38,000
$S(\$/j)$	1	0.84	2.00	0.20	0.50
$S^*_{1/2}(\$/j)$	1	0.82	2.05	0.19	0.52
$F_{1/2}(\$/j)$	1	0.83	2.02	0.21	0.54
$S_{1/2}(\$/j)$	1	0.80	2.00	0.23	0.51

a Where would you buy if you decided on forward hedging?

b Where would you buy if you decided on being unhedged [and you did not know $S_{1/2}(\$/j)$ for another 6 months]?

c If you were a speculator, in which currencies would you go long and in which would you go short?

d What is the profit/loss from your chosen speculations per million units of foreign exchange?

e If you knew that your own expected future spot rates were also the market's expected spot rates, could you deduce from the table if there is a forward risk premium?

3 Assume that you are importing German transformers and that you face the following:

r_{US}^B	12%
r_{GY}^I	8%
$S(\$/askDM)$	0.5000
$F_{1/2}(\$/askDM)$	0.5100

a How would you hedge? Would you buy German marks forward or would you borrow, buy spot, and invest in Germany for 6 months?

b Would it make any difference in your choice of hedging technique if you already had dollars that were earning 10 percent?

4 Suppose that as the money manager of a U.S. firm you faced the following situation:

r_{US}^B	9.0%
r_{US}^I	8.0%
r_C^B	10.5%
r_C^I	9.5%
$S(Can\$/ask\$)$	1.2400
$S(Can\$/bid\$)$	1.2350
$F_1(Can\$/ask\$)$	1.2600
$F_1(Can\$/bid\$)$	1.2550

Here, r_{US}^B and r_{US}^I are the 1-year interest rates at which you can respectively borrow and invest in the U.S., and r_C^B and r_C^I are the 1-year borrowing and investing interest rates in Canada.

a If you had funds to invest for 1 year, in which country would you invest?

b If you wished to borrow for 1 year, in which country would you borrow?

c What is it that induces you to borrow and invest in the same country?

d If you needed Canadian dollars in 1 year and were not holding U.S. dollars, would you buy forward or use a swap?

e If you needed Canadian dollars in 1 year and already had some U.S. dollars, would you buy forward or use a swap?

f Suppose that *your* expectations of the buying and selling prices of the U.S. dollar vis-à-vis the Canadian dollar are $S_1^*(Can\$/ask\$) = 1.2575$ and $S_1^*(Can\$/bid\$) = 1.2525$ respectively. Would you want to speculate via the forward market if you were risk-neutral?

g Would a forward speculation dominate a swap speculation?

5 Show the payoff profile for a pound receivable matched by an at-the-money put option on the pound.

6 Draw the payoff profile from simultaneously buying a put and a call option on the pound at the same strike rate. Why is this speculation profitable only if volatility is unexpectedly large?

7 If you thought the pound would increase by a very large amount, would you buy an in-the-money, at-the-money, or out-of-the money option?

8 Derive the criterion comparable to that in the inequality (10.12) whereby a risk-neutral speculator would speculate against the pound by borrowing pounds, buying dollars, and investing in dollar securities.

BIBLIOGRAPHY

Khoury, Sarkis J., and K. Hung Chan: "Hedging Foreign Exchange Risk: Selecting the Optimal Tool," *Midland Corporate Finance Journal*, winter 1988, pp. 40–52.

Levi, Maurice: "Spot versus Forward Speculation and Hedging: A Diagrammatic Exposition," *Journal of International Money and Finance*, April 1984, pp. 105–109.

Perold, André F., and Evan C. Shulman: "The Free Lunch in Currency Hedging: Implications for Investment Policy and Performance Standards," *Financial Analysts Journal*, May-June 1988, pp. 45–50.

Smithson, Charles W.: "A LEGO Approach to Financial Engineering: An Introduction to Forwards, Futures, Swaps, and Options," *Midland Corporate Finance Journal*, winter 1987, pp. 16–28.

Stulz, René, and Clifford W. Smith: "The Determinants of Firms' Hedging Policies," *Journal of Financial and Quantitative Analysis*, December 1985, pp. 391–405.

SHORT-TERM
FINANCIAL MARKETS
AND MANAGEMENT

Part 5 describes the nature of short-term international financial markets, that is, markets in which borrowing and investing for terms of up to 1 year take place. Part 5 also considers the international dimensions of cash management, which is intricately involved with these short-term financial markets.

Chapter 11 describes the Eurocurrency market, which is the market in which funds are deposited in banks and borrowed from banks in currencies of denomination that are not those of the countries in which the banks are located. For example, there is a market for U.S. dollar bank deposits and loans in London, and a market for Japanese yen deposits and loans in New York. We explain why the Eurocurrency market developed, and the process by which banks create Eurocurrency deposits and loans. The chapter concludes with a discussion of the organizational structure of international banking, and an explanation of why banking has become so multinational in scope. We see the important role played by regulations, as well as some of the risks faced by banks as a result of their multinational scale of operations.

With the institutional dimensions of short-term international financial markets described, Chapter 12 turns to the management of liquidity in these markets. After explaining the numerous advantages of managing cash centrally, the chapter examines the details of two actual international cash management systems that have been devised and operated.

Active cash management is potentially more rewarding if foreign exchange and/or money markets are inefficient in the sense that they do not reflect all available information. This is because in inefficient markets there can be abnormally high returns to gathering or buying information for determining speculative actions. Because of this link between market efficiency and cash management, Chapter 12 ends with a discussion of the ways researchers have examined whether markets are efficient, and the nature of their findings. This involves explanations of statistical analyses, as well as a consideration of the performance of forecasting services. We show that while it cannot be proven that markets are efficient, the evidence suggests that, given the risk involved in international financial speculation, cash management should be oriented toward avoiding exchange-rate exposure.

CHAPTER 11

EURODOLLARS, EUROCURRENCIES, AND MULTINATIONAL BANKING

Currencies have leaped beyond their traditional boundaries, so that today it is possible to write checks in U.S. dollars against bank accounts in Tokyo, or to write checks in Japanese yen against bank accounts in New York. Indeed, bank accounts in different currencies exist side by side in just about every financial center, so that in, for example, London, we find bank accounts in dollars, yen, marks, francs, and every other major currency. Similarly, it has become possible to arrange loans in U.S. dollars in Hong Kong or in marks in Madrid. The growth rate of these so-called **Eurocurrency** deposits and loans has been nothing short of startling, and is part of the increased globalization of financial markets in general and of the banking industry in particular.[1]

Spearheading the growth of Eurocurrencies was the appearance of **Eurodollars** in the 1950s. Despite several decades of study of the causes and consequences of the emergence of Eurodollars, there are few topics in international finance that have attracted as much controversy and disagreement. The most important parts of this disagreement center on the extent banks can create Eurodollars, and the danger Eurodollar creation involves. We shall attempt to give a balanced view of these issues, and shall also explain the many aspects of Eurodollars and Eurocurrencies on which there is consensus. Then we shall describe the nature of the banks which deal in the Eurocurrency market. However, before we begin, we should define what we mean by Eurodollars and Eurocurrencies.

---

[1]The existence of foreign-currency bank deposits and loans outside of Europe in such centers as Singapore, Sydney, Tokyo, Manila, and Hong Kong has prompted some to use the more general term **offshore currencies** rather than Eurocurrencies. We will stay with the latter term, which is still commonly used.

TABLE 11.1
SIZE OF EUROCURRENCIES AND EURODOLLARS

Year	Gross Eurocurrency* bank deposits, billions of dollars	Eurodollars as % of total
1970	115	81
1975	480	78
1980	1578	76
1985	2846	75
1987	3999	70

*Gross deposits include interbank deposits.
Source: Morgan Guarantee Trust Co., *World Financial Markets*, various issues.

THE EURODOLLAR AND EUROCURRENCY MARKETS

What Are Eurodollars and Eurocurrencies?

Here is a short, accurate definition:

A Eurodollar deposit is a U.S.-dollar-denominated bank deposit outside the United States.

Hence a dollar-denominated bank deposit in Barclays Bank in London or in Citibank in Singapore is a Eurodollar deposit, while a dollar deposit in Barclays or Citibank in New York is not.[2] Eurocurrency deposits are a generalization of Eurodollars and include other externally held currencies. For example, a Euromark deposit is a mark-denominated bank deposit held outside Germany, and a Eurosterling deposit is a sterling deposit held outside Britain.

The total value of Eurocurrency deposits and the proportion of these that are Eurodollar deposits are shown in Table 11.1. As the table makes clear, the Eurocurrency market has grown rapidly, and while shrinking as a proportion of all Eurocurrencies, Eurodollars remain the dominant form.

The Differences between Eurocurrency Yields

Table 11.2 gives the Eurocurrency rates that were offered in London on May 19, 1989. There were similar quotations of rates on dollars, sterling, and so on in other money markets, such as Frankfurt, Paris, Zurich, Tokyo, and New York.[3] The existence of the Eurocurrency market means that in making hedged or covered investment and borrowing decisions such as those described in Chapter 7, there is no need to go to the different currency centers to arrange deals. For

---

[2] The Singapore market is also referred to as the Asiadollar market. Currencies other than dollars are not heavily traded in Asia.

[3] British pound interest-rate quotations in London allow comparison with deposits denominated in other currencies. They are, however, no more a Eurocurrency than an American's U.S. dollar deposit in a New York bank is a Eurodollar.

TABLE 11.2
EUROCURRENCY YIELDS IN LONDON, SPOT AND FORWARD RATES, AND COVERED DOLLAR YIELDS

	U.S. dollar	Canadian dollar	British pound	Belgian (financial) franc	French franc	German mark	Italian lira	Dutch guilder	Swiss franc	Japanese yen
Eurocurrency yields										
1 month	9.6250	12.1875	12.5000	8.1250	8.5625	6.5000	11.8750	7.0000	7.3125	4.8750
3 months	9.5625	12.0000	12.7500	8.3125	8.7500	6.8125	11.7500	7.1250	7.3750	4.9375
6 months	9.5625	11.6875	12.8125	8.3125	8.8750	7.0625	11.5000	7.5625	7.3125	5.0933
12 months	9.5625	11.5000	12.8125	8.3750	9.0000	7.1875	11.7500	7.6875	7.3125	n / a
Exchange rates										
Spot rate	1.0	1.1899	1.6190	41.12	6.6620	1.9655	1432.50	2.2140	1.7525	138.55
1 month forward	1.0	1.1925	1.6154	41.05	6.6558	1.9605	1435.00	2.2090	1.7490	137.96
3 months forward	1.0	1.1972	1.6071	40.98	6.6480	1.9520	1440.30	2.2005	1.7429	136.92
6 months forward	1.0	1.2024	1.5947	40.86	6.6390	1.9415	1448.00	2.1900	1.7334	135.51
12 months forward	1.0	1.2106	1.5752	40.65	6.6245	1.9225	1462.50	2.1705	1.7155	132.90
Covered yields in U.S. terms										
1 month	9.6250	9.5446	9.8039	10.1851	9.6883	9.5770	9.7637	9.7320	9.7285	10.0278
3 months	9.5625	9.4878	9.7162	9.7074	9.1308	9.6260	9.5202	9.6227	9.6188	9.7582
6 months	9.5625	9.4868	9.6183	9.6380	9.5986	9.6221	9.2360	9.8372	9.5968	9.6943
12 months	9.5625	9.5935	9.7605	9.6280	9.6170	9.5849	9.4577	9.8457	9.6270	n / a

Source: The Harris Bank, Weekly Review, May 19, 1989.

Percent per annum

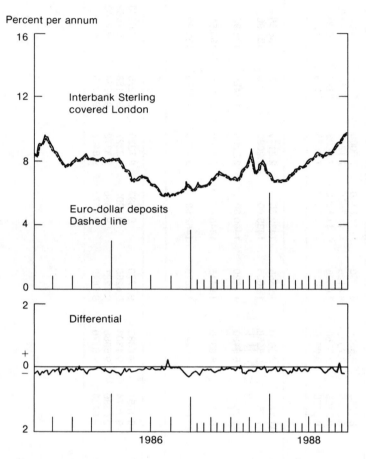

1 percent on differential scale = 2 percent on rate scale

FIGURE 11.1
EURODOLLAR YIELDS VERSUS COVERED STERLING YIELDS. (From
Selected Interest Rates and Exchange Rates, Weekly Series of
Charts, Board of Governors, Federal Reserve System, December 27,
1988.)

example, an American investor could compare covered 3-month yields on
dollars, sterling, marks, yen, and various other currencies in London and
arrange for investment or borrowing in the currency of his or her choice in that
market. Moreover, as we shall see later in this chapter, the multinational nature
of banks means that this American, dealing in London in foreign currencies,
could easily be trading with an American bank. The larger U.S., British,
Japanese, French, German, and Swiss banks, along with many others, maintain
sizable operations in the larger money-market Eurocurrency centers.

It should be no surprise that with different Eurocurrencies available within
the same jurisdiction, the covered yields or costs are very similar. This is readily

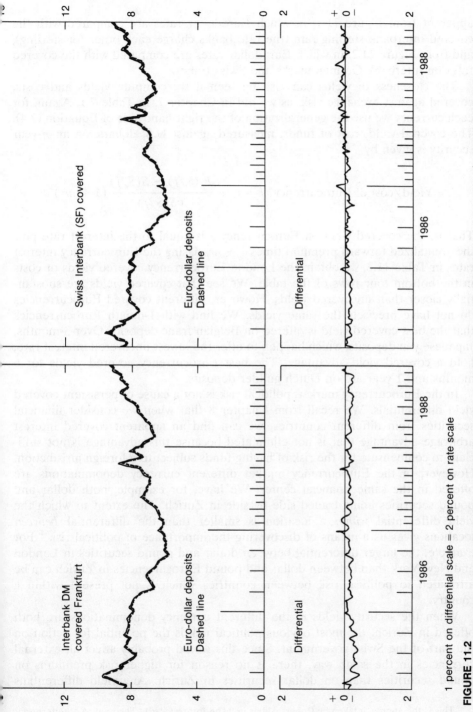

FIGURE 11.2
EURODOLLAR RATES VERSUS COVERED RATES ON INTERBANK GERMAN MARKS AND SWISS FRANCS. (From *Selected Interest Rates and Exchange Rates*, Weekly Series of Charts, Board of Governors, Federal Reserve System, December 27, 1988.)

apparent from Figure 11.1, in which Eurodollar rates are compared with the covered interbank sterling rate (the rate banks charge each other for sterling), and from Figure 11.2, in which Eurodollar rates are compared with the covered rates on interbank German marks and Swiss francs.

The closeness of yields can also be seen if we compute yields and costs, covered against exchange risk, as we did in Chapter 7, in Table 7.1. Again, for each currency we use the generalization of the right-hand side of Equation (7.4). The covered yield/cost of funds, measured against U.S. dollars, on an n-year security is given by

$$\text{Yield/cost of Eurocurrency, } j = r_j + \frac{F_n(\$/j) - S(\$/j)}{nS(\$/j)}(1 + nr_j)$$

That is, the covered yield on Eurocurrency j is equal to the interest rate plus the annualized forward premium times $1 + nr_j$. Using the Eurocurrency interest rates in Table 11.2, we obtain the London Eurocurrency covered yields or costs in the bottom four rows of the table. We see that covered yields are substantially closer than uncovered yields. However, different covered Eurocurrencies do not have precisely the same yields. We find with 1-month Eurocurrencies that the best covered yield is offered on Belgian franc deposits. Over-3-months, Japanese yen deposits, which happen to offer the lowest uncovered interest rate, hold a covered yield advantage. The best Eurocurrency covered yields for 6 months and 1 year are on Dutch guilder deposits.

In the Eurocurrency market, political risk is not a cause of persistent covered yield differentials. We recall from Chapter 8 that when we consider financial securities from different countries, we can find an apparent covered interest arbitrage advantage that is not eliminated because this advantage is not sufficient to compensate for the risk of having funds subject to a foreign jurisdiction. However, in the Eurocurrency market different currency denominations are offered in the same financial center. We have, for example, both dollar and pound securities being traded side by side in Zurich. The extent to which the yield differential *within* a location is smaller than the differential *between* locations gives us a means of discovering the importance of political risk.[4] For example, the larger differential between dollar and pound securities in London and New York than between dollar and pound Eurocurrencies in Zurich can be attributed to political risk between countries which is not present within a country.

When the security yields in the different currency denominations are both offered in Zurich, the most obvious political risk is the potential for action on the part of the Swiss government. Since this would probably affect all external currencies in the same way, there is no reason for higher risk premiums on pound securities than on dollar securities in Zurich. Any yield differentials

---

[4]This is the approach taken by Robert Aliber in "The Interest Parity Theorem: A Reinterpretation," *Journal of Political Economy*, December 1973, pp. 1451–1459.

should not, therefore, result from political risks. By comparing market-quoted covered yield differentials, we can see how important the political risks happen to be. Not surprisingly, perhaps, they are not substantial between Eurocurrency deposits denominated in the more important currencies.

Why Did Eurodollar Deposits Develop?

In order to explain why Eurodollars developed and why later other Eurocurrencies developed, we must explain why holders of U.S. dollars preferred to keep them in banks located outside the United States rather than in banks in the United States. We must also explain why borrowers of U.S. dollars arranged their loans with banks located outside the United States rather than with banks in the United States.

The original establishment of Eurodollar accounts is usually credited to the Soviet Union, although in reality its role was probably rather small.[5] During the 1950s, the Soviet Union found itself selling gold and some other products in order to earn U.S. dollars. These dollars were to be used to purchase grain and other western products, many of which came from the United States. What was the Moscow Narodny bank to do with its dollars between the time they were received and the time they would be needed? Of course, banks in New York were willing to take them on deposit. This, however, was generally unacceptable to the Soviets because of the risk that the dollars might be frozen if the cold war became hotter. Also, placing dollars in New York banks would have meant that the Soviet government was "making loans" to capitalist banks, which would channel the funds to other capitalist enterprises. So instead of using New York banks as the place of deposit for their dollars, the Soviets made their dollars available to banks in Britain and France. The British and French banks took the Soviet-earned dollars and invested them at interest. This partly involved making loans in the United States by buying U.S. treasury bills, private commercial and financial paper, and so on.[6] With the interest earned on these investments, the banks in Europe were able to pay interest on the Soviet deposits.

As intriguing as the covert Soviet role in the creation of Eurodollars may sound, in reality the development and expansion of the Eurocurrency market had its roots in more overt events. We can classify these events as affecting the supply of deposits moving to the Eurodollar market or affecting the demand for loans from Eurodollar banks.

The Supply of Eurodollar Deposits During the 1960s and 1970s, U.S. banks and other deposit-taking institutions were subject to limitations on the maximum interest rates they could offer on deposits. The most notable of these

---

[5]See especially Gunter Dufey and Ian Giddy, *The International Money Market*, Prentice-Hall, Inc., Englewood Cliffs, N.J., 1978.

[6]The truth, therefore, is that the Soviet government was, via British and French banks, making loans to the U.S. government, defense manufacturers, and so on.

limitations came from the U.S. Federal Reserve Board's Regulation Q. Banks in London and other centers were not subject to such interest limitations, and so were able to pay more on U.S. dollar deposits than U.S. banks could. With higher interest rates offered on dollars deposited in London and other financial centers than in the United States, there was an obvious incentive to deposit dollars outside the United States. Many U.S. banks opened overseas offices to receive these funds. Most restrictions were removed after the mid-1970s, but to the extent that limitations were effective before that time, they contributed to the flow of dollars abroad. The dollars placed abroad to avoid U.S. interest ceilings on deposits were reinvested, often back in the United States.

The supply or availability of Eurodollar deposits also grew from the advantage for U.S. banks in moving operations overseas to avoid Federal Reserve Regulation M. This regulation required the keeping of reserves against deposits. Until 1969, this regulation did not apply to deposits of overseas branches of U.S. banks (and since 1978 this regulation has not applied to such deposits). Since reserves mean idle funds, the cost of operations overseas was reduced vis-à-vis the cost of operations in the United States. This encouraged U.S. banks to move some of their depositors' accounts, including the accounts of many Americans, to the relatively unregulated overseas market, principally to London and other large European financial centers. Also, the absence of reserve requirements and other troublesome Federal Reserve regulations, such as the need to pay for deposit insurance on deposits held in the U.S., has allowed U.S. banks operating overseas to offer higher interest rates on dollar deposits.[7] This is revealed in Figure 11.3, which shows that most of the time Eurodollar deposits offer a higher interest rate than comparable certificates of deposit (CDs) in the United States.

Since the late 1960s, growth in Eurodollars has come from sources other than Federal Reserve and U.S. government regulations. For example, Eurodollars are more convenient than dollars that are in the United States. Europeans and other non-Americans have uneven cash flows in U.S. dollars. On some occasions they have inflows of dollars, and on others they have outflows. They could, of course, sell the dollars for their home currency when their inflows are large and repurchase dollars with the home currency when outflows are large. However, this involves transaction costs, and there is the potential for exchange risk. Alternatively, they could leave their dollars in banks in the United States. However, this means dealing with bankers who are thousands of miles away and unfamiliar with the customers' problems. It is easier to keep the dollars in a bank with offices close by which can respond quickly to the customers' needs. Therefore, the Eurocurrency market has expanded at a rapid rate. The convenience of Eurodollars is, of course, augmented by the higher yields on them.

---

[7]Banks operating in tax havens such as the Cayman Islands and Netherlands Antilles had an additional advantage of paying low corporate income taxes. This allowed them to cover operating costs with a lower spread between deposit and lending rates.

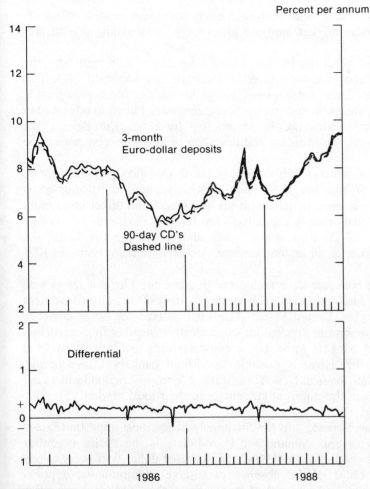

Percent per annum

3-month
Euro-dollar deposits

90-day CD's
Dashed line

Differential

1986   1988

FIGURE 11.3
EURODOLLAR VERSUS U.S. INTEREST RATES. (From *Selected Interest
Rates and Exchange Rates*, Weekly Series of Charts, Board of Governors,
Federal Reserve System, December 27, 1988.)

The Demand for Eurodollar Loans   Eurodollars could have developed without a local desire to borrow the funds left on deposit, but the banks would have
been required to recycle their Eurodollar holdings back into the U.S. money
market. However, as a result of limitations in the 1960s and 1970s on obtaining
loans within the United States that did not apply overseas, a demand for U.S.
funds outside the United States was created. This encouraged the growth of
Eurodollars on the asset side of banks' balance sheets. The controls and
restrictions on borrowing funds in the United States for reinvestment abroad
began with a voluntary restraint program in 1965. This was followed by manda-

tory controls in 1968. These controls forced many borrowers to seek sources of loans in the Eurodollar market, and the loans were often arranged with U.S. banks.

Another regulation affecting foreign demand for Eurodollar loans was the U.S. interest equalization tax, introduced in 1963 and in effect until 1974. This was a tax on U.S. residents' earnings on foreign securities. To encourage U.S. residents to lend to foreign borrowers, the foreigners were forced to offer higher yields in order to cover this tax. By channeling funds via Eurodollars, the interest equalization tax was avoided, and this allowed lower interest rates to be offered.

With deposits going abroad to escape Regulation Q, banks going aboard to escape Regulation M and the U.S. Federal Reserve, and borrowing going abroad to escape the interest equalization tax and credit and direct investment controls, the Eurodollar market expanded very rapidly. Furthermore, despite the removal of most of the regulations, taxes, and controls in the 1970s, the Eurodollar market grew at an annual average rate of 17 percent between 1975 and 1988.

Considerations of convenience affected the demand for Eurodollars as well as the supply of Eurodollars. Taking Eurodollar loans is often more convenient than taking loans in the United States. The same is true for other currency loans; it is more convenient to arrange for them locally instead of in a currency's home market. Local bankers know the creditworthiness and talents of local borrowers in a way that is rarely possible for distant bankers. Consequently, instead of taking dollar loans in New York, sterling loans in London, and so on, borrowers take loans in the different currencies in their local market.

The Role of Narrow Spreads   In the final analysis, the most important factor affecting the supply of and demand for Eurodollars is the desire of dollar depositors to receive the highest yield and the desire of dollar borrowers to pay the lowest cost. Because of the absence of reserve requirements, deposit-insurance requirements, and other costly regulations, the Eurobanks can offer higher yields on dollar deposits than can U.S. banks. At the same time, the Eurobanks can charge lower borrowing costs. The lower interest rates on loans are made possible by the absence of severe regulations and by the sheer size and number of informal contacts among the Eurobanks. These factors are important advantages in making large loans. Higher rates to depositors and lower costs to borrowers mean operating on narrower spreads. Nevertheless, the Eurobanks are left with profits because of their lower costs. While the growth of the Eurodollar market is best attributed to the ability of the Eurobanks to operate on a narrow spread, this has not always been the accepted explanation.

The Role of U.S. Deficits   During the early period of development of the Eurodollar market, the market's growth was often attributed to the U.S. trade deficits occurring at the time. A trade deficit means that dollars are being received and accumulated by non-Americans. This did not, however, have much to do with the expansion of Eurodollar deposits. The dollars being held by non-Americans could have been placed in banks within the United States or invested in U.S. financial securities. Eurodollar deposits will grow only if the dollars are kept in overseas banks. Similarly, the Eurodollar market will not disappear if the United States runs trade surpluses. We need the reasons given above, such as convenience and liberal regulations, for the Eurodollar market to exist. As long as banks located outside the United States offer greater convenience and smaller spreads than banks within the United States, they will continue to prosper.

The same factors that are behind the emergence and growth of the Eurodollar market are behind the emergence and growth of the markets in other Eurocurrencies. For example, Japanese-yen deposits and loans are found in London and New York because British and American businesses have found it more convenient to make yen deposits and arrange yen loans locally than in Japan, and because banks in London and New York can avoid restrictions faced by banks in Tokyo. The restrictions that are avoided by operating overseas vary from country to country, and have generally become less important in recent years with the global trend towards the deregulation of banking. The role of convenience has increased as a result of the growth in importance of international trade versus domestic trade. As more trade comes to be denominated in the Japanese and European currencies, we can expect more deposits and loans to be denominated in these currencies in the Eurocurrency market.

Determination of Eurocurrency Interest Rates

Eurocurrency interest rates cannot differ much from rates offered on similar deposits in the home country. For example, as we have indicated, the rate offered to Eurodollar depositors is slightly higher than in the United States, and the rate charged to borrowers is slightly lower. Each country's market interest rates influence the Eurocurrency interest rates, and vice versa, as they are all part of an integrated money market. The total supply of each currency in this well-integrated market, together with the total demand, determines the rate of interest. As a practical matter, however, each individual bank bases its rates on the rates it observes in the market.

The interest rates charged to borrowers of Eurocurrencies are based on London Interbank Offer Rates (LIBOR) in the particular currencies. LIBOR rates are those charged in interbank transactions (that is, when banks borrow from each other) and are the base rates for nonbank customers. LIBOR rates are calculated as the averages of the lending rates in the respective currencies of six leading London banks. Borrowers are charged on a "LIBOR-plus" basis, with the premium based on the creditworthiness of the borrower. With borrowing maturities of over 6 months, a floating interest rate is charged. Every 6 months or so, the loan is rolled over, and the interest rate is based on the current LIBOR rate. This reduces the risk to both the borrower and the lender (the bank) in that neither will be left with a long-term contract that does not reflect the current interest costs. For example, if interest rates rise after the credit is extended, the lender will lose the opportunity to earn more interest for only 6 months. If interest rates fall after a loan is arranged, the borrower will lose the opportunity to borrow more cheaply for only 6 months. With the lower interest-rate risk, credit terms frequently reach 10 years.

Different Types of Eurocurrency Instruments

Eurocurrency deposits are primarily conventional term deposits, which are bank deposits with a fixed term, such a 30 days or 90 days. The interest rate is fixed for the term of a deposit, and this keeps the maturity of deposits short.

Not as important as any of the Eurocurrency denominations shown in Table 11.2, but nevertheless of some importance, are the Eurocurrency deposits denominated in Special Drawing Rights (SDRs). SDRs were originally introduced as central-bank reserve assets by the International Monetary Fund, and they have already been briefly described in Chapter 4. SDR term deposits were first offered by Chemical Bank in London. Like the bulk of other Eurodeposits, SDR-denominated deposits are mostly nonnegotiable term deposits.

A relatively small proportion of the liabilities of Eurobanks are not term deposits, but instead take the form of certificates of deposit (CDs). Unlike Eurocurrencies in the form of term deposits, the CDs are negotiable instruments that can be traded in a secondary market. This makes the CDs more liquid than term deposits, which have a penalty on early withdrawal. In the case of Eurodollars approximately 20 percent of Eurobank liabilities are CDs, the balance being conventional term deposits. Since 1981, some London-based banks have offered SDR-denominated CDs as well as conventional deposits. The banks that first offered the SDR-denominated CDs were Barclays Bank International, Chemical Bank, Hong Kong and Shanghai Bank, Midland Bank International, National Westminster Bank, and Standard Chartered Bank.[8]

An expansion of Eurocurrency operations within the United States has been made possible by rules allowing the establishment of international banking facilities (IBFs). The IBFs are, in effect, a different set of accounts with an existing bank; they date back to late 1981. The facilities can accept foreign-currency deposits and are exempt from both U.S. reserve requirements and insurance premiums on deposits as long as the deposits are used exclusively for making loans to foreigners. Two days' notice for withdrawals is required. These facilities compete with the Eurocurrency banks operating within Europe and have brought some of the offshore business back to the United States.

[8]See Business International, "Slimmed-Down SDR Makes Comeback; Techniques Include Opening Up Market for Negotiable SDR CDs," *Money Report*, January 16, 1981.

Eurobanks generally remain well hedged. They accept deposits in many different currencies, and they also have assets in these same currencies. When they balance the two sides of their accounts with equal volumes and maturities of assets and liabilities in each denomination, they are perfectly hedged and therefore unaffected by changes in exchange rates. Sometimes it is difficult to balance the maturities of assets and liabilities, and until 1981 this situation involved the Eurobanks in risk. However, since the end of 1981 the Eurobanks have been able to avoid risk from unbalanced maturities by using the Eurodollar futures market at the International Monetary Market operated by the Chicago Mercantile Exchange. Since the early 1980s banks have also been able to use the Eurodollar futures markets of the Chicago Board of Trade, the New York Futures Exchange, the London International Financial Futures Exchange, the Singapore Monetary Exchange, and an exchange in Bermuda. It is worthwhile to explain the risk from unbalanced maturities and the way this can be avoided with Eurodollar futures.

Suppose that a bank accepts a 3-month Eurodollar deposit of $1 million on March 1 at 9 percent and at the same time makes a Eurodollar loan for 6 months at 10 percent. In June, when the 3-month deposit matures, the Eurobank must refinance the 6-month loan for the remaining 3 months. If by June the deposit rate on 3 month Eurodollars has risen above 10 percent, the spread on the remaining period of the loan will become negative. To avoid this risk, on March 1, when making the 6-month loan, the bank could sell a 3-month Eurodollar future for June. (On the International Monetary Market in Chicago, contracts are traded in $1 million denominations for March, June, September, and December.) If by June the Eurodollar rates have gone up, the bank will find that it has made money on the sale of its Eurodollar future. This follows because, as in the bond market, purchases of interest-rate futures provide a profit when interest rates fall, and sales (short positions) provide a profit when interest rates rise. The profit made by the Eurobank in selling the Eurodollar future will offset the extra cost of refinancing the 6-month Eurodollar loan for the remaining 3 months.

Eurobanks perform "intermediation" when they convert Eurocurrency deposits into, for example, commercial loans. This term is used because the banks are intermediaries between the depositors and the borrowers. If the two sides of the Eurobankers' accounts are equally liquid—that is, if the IOUs they purchase are as marketable as their Eurocurrency deposits—then according to the view of some researchers, the Eurobanks have not created any extra liquidity or "money."[9] However, it could happen that the original foreign currency that was deposited in a Eurobank is redeposited in other Eurobanks before finding its way back to the home country. In this way we can have a total of Eurocurrency deposits that is a multiple of the original deposit. Before demonstrating how we

---

[9] This is the view in Jurg Niehans and John Hewson, "The Euro-Dollar Market and Monetary Theory," *Journal of Money, Credit and Banking*, February 1976, pp. 1–27.

can have a **Eurocurrency multiplier** we should state that this remains a topic of considerable controversy, and there is even some dispute over whether Eurodollar multipliers can be defined at all.[10]

Redepositing and Multiple Eurocurrency Expansion

Let us construct a situation in which multiple expansion of Eurodollars does occur. Assume that a British exporter, Britfirm A, receives a $100 check from an American purchaser of its products and that this check is drawn against a U.S. bank. This is an original receipt of dollars in Europe. Assume that Britfirm A does not need the dollars immediately but that it will need them in 90 days. The $100 is held in Britfirm A's account in a British bank as a dollar term deposit—a Eurodollar. The British bank will, after accepting the check from Britfirm A, send the check to the U.S. bank with which it deals. The British bank will be credited with $100.

The $100 deposit in the British bank probably will not be removed during the term of the deposit, since removing it would involve a substantial interest penalty for Britfirm A. The British bank will therefore look for an investment vehicle that approximately matches the term of Britfirm A's deposit. Suppose that the British bank decides to maintain a cash reserve of 2 percent with an American bank and discovers a British firm, Britfirm B, which wishes to borrow the remaining $98 for 90 days to settle a payment with an Italian supplier, Italfirm A. The British bank will give to Britfirm B a check for $98 drawn against the British bank's account at the U.S. bank and payable to Italfirm A. We have the situation in the top part of Table 11.3. (If the dollars are loaned to a U.S. borrower, as they could well be, the effects end here with the British bank merely intermediating, that is, serving as go-between for the depositor and the borrower.)

On receiving the check from Britfirm B, Italfirm A will deposit it in its account at an Italian bank, which will in turn send it for collection to the United States. If the Italian bank deals with the same U.S. bank as the British bank, all that will happen in the United States is that $98 will be removed from the British bank's account and credited to the Italian bank's account. The British bank's account with the U.S. bank will be reduced to $2. The British bank's account will have the entries shown in Table 11.3; it will show the $100

---

[10]The controversy began after the publication of Milton Friedman's article "The Euro-Dollar Market: Some First Principles" (*Morgan Guarantee Survey*, October 1969, pp. 4–14, reprinted with clarifications in *Review*, Federal Reserve Bank of St. Louis, July 1971, pp. 16–24). Friedman treated the Eurodollar multiplier as a conventional domestic banking multiplier, and this prompted a criticism from Fred H. Klopstock ("Money Creation in the Euro-Dollar Market—A Note on Professor Friedman's Views," *Monthly Review*, Federal Reserve Bank of New York, January 1970, pp. 12–15). The controversy expanded with the publication of Niehans and Hewson's paper (see note 9 above). Gunter Dufey and Ian H. Giddy have introduced a variety of multipliers (*The International Money Market*, Prentice-Hall, Englewood Cliffs, N.J. 1978). We will use the conventional multiplier and treat the question in the conventional way, as does Herbert G. Grubel in *International Economics*, Richard D. Irwin, Homewood, Ill., 1977.

TABLE 11.3
CHANGE IN BALANCE SHEETS FROM $100 OF PRIMARY DEPOSITS

Bank	Assets		Liabilities	
British	Deposit in U.S. bank Loan to Britfirm B	+$ 2.00 +$ 98.00 +$100.00	Term deposit of Britfirm A	 +$100.00 +$100.00
Italian	Deposit in U.S. bank Loan to Italfirm B	+$ 1.96 +$ 96.04 +$ 98.00	Term deposit of Italfirm A	 +$ 98.00 +$ 98.00
Dutch	Deposit in U.S. bank Loan to Dutchfirm B	+$ 1.92 +$ 94.12 +$ 96.04	Term deposit of Dutchfirm A	 +$ 96.04 +$ 96.04
Canadian	Deposit in U.S. bank Loan to Canafirm B	+$ 1.88 +$ 92.24 +$ 94.12	Term deposit of Canafirm A	 +$ 94.12 +$ 94.12

Eurodollar deposit offset by a $2 reserve and a $98 IOU. (If the British and Italian banks maintain reserves at different U.S. banks, the outcome will be the same after U.S. interbank clearing.) We see that the clearing of Eurodollars takes place in New York, with the banks in the United States merely showing different names of depositors after Eurodollars have been transferred. Originally, they showed the owner of the dollars who paid Britfirm A. Afterward, the U.S. banks showed the British bank and then the Italian bank as the depositor. Since only the names change, nothing happens inside the United States to increase or decrease the number of loans.

After Italfirm A deposits the check in the Italian bank, the Italian bank will have a $98 deposit at the U.S. bank to offset its Eurodollar liability to Italfirm A. Like its British counterpart, it will not leave the funds idle. Let us suppose that it maintains 2 percent, or $1.96, in the U.S. bank, and lends the balance of $96.04 to Italfirm B. The loan will be effected by the Italian bank drawing a check for $96.04 against its U.S. bank account on behalf of Italfirm B. We assume that this check is made payable to Dutchfirm A.

If Dutchfirm A deposits the check in a Dutch Eurodollar term account, the Italian bank will be left with $1.96 in reserves in the U.S. bank. The Dutch bank will be credited with $96.04. We now assume that the Dutch bank keeps 2 percent of the $96.04 deposit, that is, $1.92, as a cash reserve, and lends the balance of $94.12 to Dutchfirm B by drawing a check on Dutchfirm B's behalf to Canafirm A. After Canafirm A deposits the check, the Dutch bank will have $1.92 in reserves, and the Canadian bank with which the check is deposited will have $94.12. If the Canadian bank lends Canafirm B 98 percent of this, or $92.24, and Canafirm B pays an American company that banks in the United States, then the process of Eurodollar creation will end. The Canadian bank will have its account in its U.S. bank reduced by $92.24 and will be left with 2 percent, or $1.88, against its Eurodollar deposit of $94.12. The books are balanced, and every bank is in its desired position of having a 2-percent reserve backing its Eurodollar deposit, with the remaining 98 percent out as loans. By the time the Eurodollar creation comes to an end, there is a total of $100.00 + $98 + $96.04 + $94.12, or $388.16, in Eurodollars. The original deposit of $100 has grown 3.8816 times, and this might be called the Eurodollar multiplier vis-à-vis the original $100 base. However, the $388.16 in Eurodollars vis-à-vis *the reserves still remaining in Eurobanks*—that is, $2 + $1.96 + $1.92 + $1.88, or $7.76, gives a **deposit ratio** of 50. That is, $388.16 is 50 times the remaining dollar reserves of $7.76. This is what we would expect with a reserve ratio of 0.02, since each $1 of reserves supports $50 of deposits.

The interesting magnitude is not the deposit ratio but rather the multiplier, which is the expansion on the base of the original deposit. Only if there are no leakages back to the United States will the multiplier be as large as the deposit ratio. If funds deposited in the Euromarket are loaned back in the United States at the outset, the leakage is immediate and the Eurobank is merely intermediating. The rate of leakage depends on how extensively U.S. dollars are used for settling payments between parties outside the United States. The more any currency is used between offshore parties, the larger the multiplier is likely to be.

When dollar loans offered by commercial banks outside the United States are made to central banks, a leakage back to the United States is almost certain to occur. Central banks tend to hold their dollars in U.S. banks or place them in U.S. treasury bills. This will drain any extra dollar reserves back into the U.S. banking system. However, when many central banks kept dollars at the Bank for International Settlements (BIS) in Basle, Switzerland, in the 1960s, the leakage did not occur. The BIS frequently reinvested in the Eurodollar market and thus contributed to the expansion of Eurodollars.

Estimates of the value of the Eurodollar multiplier vary. As we have seen, the value of the multiplier depends on the definition and on the speed with which funds return to the United States. Fred Klopstock estimates that the leakage back to the United States is so rapid that the multiplier is about 1.05 to 1.09. Alexander Swoboda gives a value of about 2.00, which is close to the estimates of Boyden Lee. John Hewson and Eisuke Sakakibara find a range of 3 to 7, whereas John Makin has produced estimates from 10.31 to 18.45.[11] Clearly,

---

[11] These estimates are found in Boyden E. Lee, "The Eurodollar Multiplier," *Journal of Finance*, September 1973, pp. 867–874; John Hewson and Eisuke Sakakibara, "The Eurodollar Multiplier: A Portfolio Approach," *IMF Staff Papers*, July 1974, pp. 307–328; Fred H. Klopstock, "Money Creation in the Euro-Dollar Market—A Note on Professor Friedman's Views," *Monthly Review*, Federal Reserve Bank of New York, January 1970, pp. 12–15; John H. Makin, "Demand and Supply Functions for Stocks of Eurodollar Deposits: An Empirical Study," *Review of Economics and Statistics*, November 1972, pp. 381–391; and Alexander K. Swoboda, *The Eurodollar Market: An Interpretation*, Essays in International Finance, no 64, Princeton University Press, Princeton, N.J., 1968.

the larger estimates must refer to deposits-to-reserve ratios rather than to the multiplier and are incorrect as multiplier estimates.

INTERNATIONAL BANKING

Organizational Features of International Banking

In our example showing how Eurodollars are created, we did not specify the ties that banks in different countries maintain with each other. Banks are linked in numerous formal and informal ways; for example, there are correspondent accounts and fully owned foreign banks. We briefly mentioned correspondent accounts in Chapter 2. The relative importance of foreign branches and some other forms of foreign-bank organization in New York City are shown in Figure 11.4, and the overall growth and importance of foreign banks in the U.S. is shown in Figure 11.5. We should describe the other popular forms of banking organizations, and why banks have become such large multinational operations.

Correspondent Banking An informal linkage between banks in different countries is set up when banks maintain correspondent accounts with each other. Large banks have correspondent relationships with banks in almost every country in which they do not have an office of their own. The purpose of maintaining foreign correspondents is to facilitate international payments and collections for customers. The term "correspondent" comes from the mail or cable communications that the banks used to use for settling customer accounts. Today, these communications have largely been replaced by SWIFT messages, and the settling between banks occurs via CHIPS.[12] For example, if Aviva wants to pay a Canadian supplier, it will ask its U.S. bank, which will communicate with its Canadian correspondent bank via SWIFT. The Canadian bank credits the account of the Canadian firm, while Aviva's bank debits Aviva's account. The U.S. and Canadian banks then settle through CHIPS.

Correspondent banking allows banks to help their customers who are doing business abroad, without having to maintain any personnel or offices overseas. This relationship is primarily for settling customer payments, but it can extend to providing limited credit for each other's customers and to setting up contacts between local businesspeople and the clients of the correspondent banks.

Resident Representatives In order to provide their customers with help from their own personnel on the spot in foreign countries, banks open overseas business offices. These are not banking offices in the sense of accepting local deposits or providing loans. The primary purpose of these offices is to provide information about local business practices and conditions, including the credit-

---

[12]SWIFT and CHIPS were discussed in Chapter 2. For more on how correspondent banking has been rationalized and reorganized through these message and bank-settlement systems see "On Correspondent Banking," *Euromoney*, December 1988, p. 115.

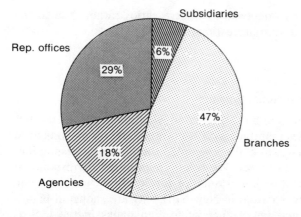

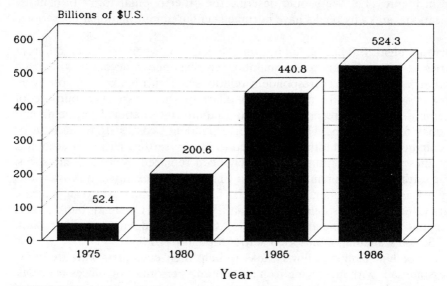

FIGURE 11.4
THE FORMS OF FOREIGN-BANK OPERATIONS IN NEW YORK.
Source: Computed from *International Bankers' Directory*, First 1986 edition, Rand-McNally, Chicago, 1986.

FIGURE 11.5
TOTAL ASSETS OF U.S. BRANCHES OF FOREIGN BANKS. *Source:* U.S. Department of Commerce, Bureau of the Census, *Statistical Abstract of the United States*, 1988.

worthiness of potential customers and the bank's clients. The resident representatives will keep in contact with local correspondent banks and provide help when needed. Representative offices are generally small; they have the appearance of an ordinary commercial office rather than a bank.

Bank Agencies An agency is like a full-fledged bank in every respect except that it does not handle ordinary deposits. The agencies deal in the local money markets and in the foreign exchange markets, arrange loans, clear bank drafts and checks, and channel foreign funds into financial markets. Agencies are common in New York; for example, Canadian and European banks keep busy offices there, with perhaps dozens of personnel dealing in the short-term credit markets and in foreign exchange. Agencies will also often arrange long-term loans for customers, but they deal primarily on behalf of the home office to keep it directly involved in the important foreign financial markets.

Foreign Branches Foreign branches are operating banks like local banks, except that the directors and owners tend to reside elsewhere. Generally, foreign branches are subject to both local banking rules and the rules at home, but because they can benefit from loopholes, the extra tier of regulations is not necessarily onerous. The books of a foreign branch are incorporated with those of the parent bank, although the foreign branch will also maintain separate books for revealing separate performance, for tax purposes, and so on. The existence of foreign branches can mean very rapid check clearing for customers in different countries, because the debit and credit operations are internal and can be initiated by a telephone call. This can offer a great advantage over the lengthy clearing that can occur via correspondents. The foreign branch also offers bank customers in small countries all the service and safety advantages of a large bank, which the local market might not be able to support.

There would probably be far more extensive foreign branch networks of the large international banks were it not for legal limitations imposed by local governments to protect local banks from aggressive foreign competition. Great Britain has traditionally been liberal in allowing foreign banks to operate and has gained in return from the reciprocal rules that are frequently offered. On the other hand, until the 1980 Bank Act was passed, the opening of foreign bank subsidiaries within Canada was prohibited, and branches of foreign banks are still not allowed. The United States selectively allows foreign banks to operate. The regulation and supervision of foreign banks within the United States is provided for in the International Banking Act of 1978. This act allows the U.S. Comptroller of the Currency to grant foreign banks a license to open branches (or agencies). The foreign banks can open wherever state banking laws allow them to. The banks are restricted to their declared "home state" and are subject to federally imposed reserve requirements when they are federally chartered.[13] They have access to services of the Federal Reserve and can borrow from its discount window. Since 1980, the foreign banks that accept retail deposits have been required to provide deposit insurance for customers. Between December 31, 1975, and December 31, 1987, the number of foreign banks in the United States grew from 79 to 246, and their assets rose from $38 billion to $463 billion. The foreign banks are relatively more important in providing commercial and industrial loans than in other investment activities,

---

[13] Foreign as well as domestic banks can, however, operate outside their declared home states by establishing Edge Act subsidiaries. These are discussed later in this chapter.

and by December 1989 they were responsible for more than 20 percent of the business in this area.

Foreign Subsidiaries and Affiliates A foreign *branch* is part of a parent organization that is incorporated elsewhere. A foreign *subsidiary* is a locally incorporated bank that happens to be owned either completely or partially by a foreign parent. Foreign subsidiaries do all types of banking, and it may be very difficult to distinguish them from an ordinary locally owned bank except perhaps by the name.

Foreign *subsidiaries* are controlled by foreign owners, even if the foreign ownership is partial. Foreign *affiliates* are similar to subsidiaries in being locally incorporated and so on, but they are joint ventures, and no individual foreign owner has control (even though a *group* of foreign owners might have control).

Consortium Banks Consortium banks are joint ventures of the larger commercial banks. They can involve a half dozen or more partners from numerous countries. They are primarily concerned with investment, and they arrange large loans and underwrite stocks and bonds. Consortium banks are not concerned with taking deposits, and they deal only with large corporations or perhaps governments. They will take equity positions—part ownership of an investment —as well as make loans, and they are frequently busy arranging takeovers and mergers. Table 11.4 shows the ownership structure of a typical large consortium bank.

Edge Act and Agreement Corporations While U.S. banks can participate in investment-bank consortia and may operate branches overseas, they cannot themselves have equity—direct ownership—in foreign banking subsidiaries. However, because of a 1919 amendment to the Federal Reserve Act initiated by Senator Walter Edge, U.S. banks are able to establish subsidiaries for doing business "abroad." These subsidiaries, which are federally chartered, can have

TABLE 11.4
A LARGE MULTINATIONAL CONSORTIUM BANK

International Commercial Bank, PLC	
Members:	
Hong Kong & Shanghai Bank Co.	22.0%
Irving Trust Co.	22.0%
First National Bank of Chicago	22.0%
Commerzbank AG	12.0%
Credit Lyonnais	11.0%
Banco di Roma International SA	11.0%
Total assets, December 31, 1987: £881 million	

Source: Polk's Bank Directory, 1988.

equity in foreign banks and are known as **Edge Act corporations**. They profit both from holding stock in subsidiaries overseas and by engaging in investment banking, that is, borrowing and investing. Edge Act corporations engage in almost all the activities of banking: accepting deposits, making loans, exchanging currencies, selling government and corporate securities, and so on. They can invest in equity, while domestic banks are not allowed to.[14] A major impetus to the growth of Edge Act corporations has been that they enable a bank to open an office outside of its home state. The International Banking Act of 1978 allows *foreign* banks to open Edge Act corporations and accept deposits directly related to international transactions. There is no longer a rule that states that foreign-bank-owned Edge Act corporations will be permitted only if the directors of these corporations are U.S. citizens. These changes in the International Banking Act were made to put foreign and U.S. banks on a more equal footing.

Agreement corporations are a little different from Edge Act corporations. The authority to establish agreement corporations dates from a 1916 amendment to the Federal Reserve Act. This allows banks which are members of the Federal Reserve System to enter into an agreement with that organization to engage in international banking. Agreement corporations, unlike Edge Act corporations, can be chartered by a state government, and they can only engage in international banking, not in general investment activities. There are only a handful of agreement corporations as of 1989.

U.S. International Banking Facilities (IBFs) We have already mentioned international banking facilities (IBFs) in connection with the Eurodollar market. Since 1981, U.S. banks, Edge Act corporations, foreign commercial banks through branches and agencies in the U.S., savings and loan associations, and mutual savings banks have been allowed by the Board of Governors of the Federal Reserve System to establish IBFs as adjunct operations.[15] The motive for this permission is to allow banks in the U.S. to participate in the lucrative Eurocurrency market. IBFs are not subject to domestic banking regulations, including reserve requirements and interest ceilings, and escape some local and state taxes. IBFs can accept deposits only from non-Americans and with a minimum size of $100,000. Withdrawals are also subject to a $100,000 minimum. Deposits cannot be withdrawn without at least 2 days' notice. However, overnight deposits can be offered to overseas banks, other IBFs, and the IBF's parent bank. Funds obtained by IBFs cannot be used domestically; they must be used overseas. To ensure that U.S.-based companies and individuals satisfy this requirement, borrowers must sign a statement when they begin taking loans. By the end of 1988 well over 500 IBFs had been established, the majority in New York and California.

---

[14] In February 1988, the Federal Reserve Board made an exception when it allowed U.S. banks to swap loans to governments of heavily indebted developing countries into equity investments. This was done to help the debtor countries and the U.S. banks deal with the third-world debt crisis.
[15] For more on IBFs see K. Alec Chrystal, "International Banking Facilities," *Review*, Federal Reserve Bank of St. Louis, April 1984, pp. 5–11.

TABLE 11.5
THE WORLD'S 20 LARGEST BANKS, 1988

Rank	Bank and head office	Capital ($ millions)	Staff	Assets ($ millions)
1	National Westminster, London	10,907	111,000	178,505
2	Barclays, London	10,545	118,410	189,368
3	Citicorp, New York	9,864	89,000	203,827
4	Fuji Bank, Tokyo	9,018	14,542	327,765
5	Credit Agricole, Paris	8,740	73,938	214,382
6	Sumitomo Bank, Osaka	8,550	16,516	334,654
7	Dai-Ichi Kangyo Bank, Tokyo	8,481	18.663	352,533
8	Mitsubishi Bank, Tokyo	8,200	14,296	317,760
9	Industrial Bank of Japan, Tokyo	8,155	5,342	261,479
10	Sanwa Bank, Tokyo	7,567	14,337	307,392
11	Union Bank of Switzerland	6,715	20,872	110,760
12	Bank of China, Peking	6,620	33,240	150,372
13	Deutsche Bank, Frankfurt	6,460	54,769	170,808
14	Japan Development, Tokyo	6,430	1,074	64,960
15	Mitsubishi Trust, Tokyo	6,342	6,390	205,962
16	Swiss Bank Corp, Basle	6,055	17,477	102,466
17	Bank of Tokyo, Tokyo	5,913	13,223	171,399
18	Lloyds Bank, London	5,867	75,000	93,800
19	J.P. Morgan, New York	5,838	14,000	82,651
20	Banque Nationale de Paris	5,567	58,595	196,955

Source: The Banker, July 1989.

Why Banking Has Become Multinational

Through the opening of representative offices, agencies, and branches, and through the acquisition or establishment of subsidiaries, banking has become among the most multinational of industries. For example, large banks such as National Westminster, Barclays, Citicorp, and Fuji Bank have operations in as many or more countries than industrial giants such as GM, IBM, Shell, and Sony.[16] There are special reasons for the multinational nature of banking, among them the importance of timely and accurate information about money and foreign exchange market development, and about the quality of borrowers. Let us consider the role of information as well as some other factors contributing to the multinational nature of banking.[17]

[16]The world's 20 largest banks are shown in Table 11.5. A glance at the table reveals a very different ranking by size of capital than by size of assets. For example, when ranked by assets, the largest five banks are Japanese, whereas when ranked by capital only one Japanese bank is in the top five. This difference reflects different capital adequacy standards in different countries.

[17]For empirical evidence on the importance of some different factors for the evolution of multinational banking see Michael A. Goldberg, Robert W. Helsley, and Maurice D. Levi, "On the Development of International Financial Centers," *The Annals of Regional Science*, February 1988, pp. 81–94. A more general treatment of the factors contributing to the growth of MNCs is contained in Chapter 16.

Market Information It might seem that with the rapid dissemination of information via modern subscription services such as Reuters and Dow Jones News Services, which flash up prices and recent developments on video screens at the speed of light, there is no need to have operations in expensive money centers such as London and New York. However, it is one thing to be plugged into the latest developments, but quite another to be able to interpret or even anticipate events. For being able to interpret what is happening and to get a sense of where markets are going there is nothing like having personnel on the spot where the big markets and events are unfolding. For this reason we find a vast number of foreign banks with offices in the large money-market centers, especially London and New York. Many of these offices may not be profitable on their own, but by acting as eyes and ears for their parent banks, they improve the profitability of overall operations.

Borrower Information When making loans abroad, banks could in theory take the word of a foreign bank such as a correspondent about the financial stability of a borrower, or send bank personnel to the borrower's country and review the borrower's finances on the spot. It can, however, be cheaper and more efficient to maintain local offices to gather "street talk," not only at the time of making a loan, but afterwards when the borrower's circumstances may suddenly deteriorate.

The importance of reliable information about borrowers has played a significant role in banking history, and in particular, in the relative success of early family banking houses. For example, it was no accident that the Rothschild bank did so well in the nineteenth century, after the founder, Mayer Rothschild of Frankfurt, posted his sons in the capitals of Europe. Mayer Rothschild could trust the reports coming from his sons about the quality of sovereign borrowers in a way that banks without "in house" overseas representation could not. Thus in competition with banks with less reliable information, family banking houses such as the Rothschilds, Warburgs, and others did extremely well. Indeed, we can meaningfully consider the family banking houses of Europe as the precursors of today's multinational banks, their success being based on the same factors.[18]

Serving Clients Profit-maximizing banks do not open overseas offices merely to provide services for clients. Usually, correspondents could do most of what an overseas office can do to serve customers. However, it may be better for a bank to serve its domestic customers in their foreign operations than to allow its

---

[18]The House of Rothschild in particular knew the value not just of information about borrowers, but also about events which could affect financial markets. For example, by using pigeons, runners, horsemen, and rowers, Nathan Rothschild, the London-based member of the Rothschild family knew before others that the Duke of Wellington had defeated Napoleon in the fields of Waterloo in 1815. Rothschild capitalized on his superior information by *selling* British bonds. This triggered panic selling, because it was known that Rothschild was the first in London to know the outcome of the battle. Rothschild profited by employing others to buy the heavily discounted bonds before word finally arrived that Wellington had won.

customers to develop strong ties with foreign banks or competing domestic banks that do have overseas offices. Some overseas banking offices may therefore follow the trade of domestic clients for strategic reasons rather than to earn from the services provided to clients.

Of course, it may be that the services that are provided by overseas banking offices *are* profitable. For example, the handling of collections and payments for domestic clients engaged in foreign trade can be lucrative and serve as reason for having an office, such as a representative office, in a country in which important clients are doing business. Indeed, for many banks the fees from services provided to customers that are connected to international trade have become an increasingly important component of their earnings. For example, the sale of letters of credit, the discounting of bills of exchange, the provision of collection services, and the conversion of currencies have become increasingly important in comparison with accepting deposits and making loans.

Custodial Services   One fee-for-service activity of multinational banks that is worth singling out is the provision of **custodial services**. These services are provided to clients who invest in securities overseas. Several large banks take possession of foreign securities for safekeeping, collect dividends or offer up coupons, and handle stock splits, rights issues, tax reclamation, and so on.[19] Banks also provide clients with reports on the status of their overseas investments, manage cash balances, and so on. It is clear that these services require that the banks have overseas offices.[20]

Avoiding Regulations   In the list of reasons banks have become so multinational we should not overlook the role of regulations. As we saw in our discussion of the evolution of the Eurocurrency market, banks have frequently moved abroad to avoid reserve requirements, deposit insurance, onerous reporting requirements, corporate taxes, interest-rate ceilings, and other hindrances to their operations. For example, many U.S. banks opened London and tax-haven offices to avoid U.S. regulations and taxes, and similarly, many Japanese banks have opened New York and London offices to avoid domestic restrictions and to exploit special opportunities. Indeed, over the years, the activities which are open to foreign banks have become more and more similar to those open to domestic banks. This is made clear in Table 11.6, which shows by the similarity of the "yes" and "no" entries for functions in different centers, that, with a few exceptions, there remains little discrimination between foreign and domestic banks in the important financial centers—New York, London, and Tokyo.

While overseas offices may make banks more profitable by avoiding domestic regulations, at the same time they make banks and the banking industry more

---

[19] We shall have more to say about custodial services in Chapter 14. In particular, we shall explain the trading of the claims the banks issue against the securities they hold.
[20] For a detailed account of the main players in the custodial service game, such as Chase Manhattan Bank with $85 billion of custodial assets and Citibank with $50 billion at the end of 1988, see "Global Custody; Speeding the Paperchase," special supplement to *Euromoney*, March 1989.

TABLE 11.6
ACTIVITIES OPEN TO DIFFERENT INSTITUTIONS IN DIFFERENT CENTERS

Activity	Location*	Permitted to[†]					
		U.S. bank holding co.	Japanese city bank	U.K. clearing bank	U.S. securities firm	Japanese securities firm	U.K. merchant bank
Banking license	NY	YES	YES	YES	S	S	S
	LO	YES	YES	YES	YES	YES	YES
	TO	YES	YES	YES	NO	NO	NO
Dealing in corporate securities	NY	NO	NO	NO	YES	YES	YES
	LO	YES	YES	YES	YES	YES	YES
	TO	S	NO	S	YES	YES	YES
Foreign-exchange dealing	NY	YES	YES	YES	YES	YES	YES
	LO	YES	YES	YES	YES	YES	YES
	TO	YES	YES	YES	NO	NO	NO
Dealing in U.S. treasuries	NY	YES	YES	YES	YES	YES	YES
	LO	YES	YES	YES	YES	YES	YES
	TO	NO	NO	NO	YES	YES	YES
Dealing in U.K. gilts	NY	NO	NO	NO	YES	YES	YES
	LO	YES	YES	YES	YES	YES	YES
	TO	NO	NO	NO	YES	YES	YES
Dealing in Japanese govt. bonds	NY	NO	NO	NO	YES	YES	YES
	LO	YES	YES	YES	YES	YES	YES
	TO	YES	YES	YES	YES	YES	YES
Trust bank	NY	YES	YES	YES	S	S	S
	LO	YES	YES	YES	YES	YES	YES
	TO	YES	NO	YES	NO	NO	NO
Account at the central bank	NY	YES	YES	YES	S	S	S
	LO	YES	YES	YES	YES	YES	YES
	TO	YES	YES	YES	YES	YES	YES

*NY = New York; LO = London; TO = Tokyo.
[†]YES = full license permitted; NO = not generally permitted; S = permitted only through special-purpose companies, such as a 50-percent-owned affiliate or a "near bank".
Source: E. Gerald Corrigan, "A Perspective on the Globalization of Financial Markets and Institutions," *Quarterly Review*, Federal Reserve Bank of New York, spring 1987, pp. 1–9.

vulnerable and subject to crisis. It is worthwhile considering the problems that have accompanied the multinationalization of banking.

The Problems of Multinational Banking

The failures of Franklin National Bank and Bankhaus Herstatt in 1974, both due to foreign exchange losses, provided early evidence that multinational banking can be risky business. Further evidence of the risk of multinational banking was provided by a subsequent string of failures and other crises, including major losses by the Union Bank of Switzerland, Westdeutsche Landesbank, and Lloyds International; the collapse of the Banco Ambrosiano in 1982; and the banking crisis of 1982–1983, which occurred after Mexico, Brazil, Argentina, and over 20 other borrowers announced they were unable to meet scheduled repayments on their debts.

The major cause of the risk of multinational banking is also a major cause of the development of multinational banking. In particular, the opening of overseas offices to avoid domestic regulations such as reserve requirements, reporting of asset positions, and payment for deposit insurance has at the same time made banks more vulnerable to deposit withdrawals. Furthermore, the acceptance of default and other risks from overseas lending has made banks' domestic depositors subject to greater risks. While there has been some easing of anxiety of depositors since the mid-1980s, it is worthwhile considering why the problem developed.[21]

Banking provides a country with jobs and prestige. Consequently, each country has an incentive to make its regulations just a little more liberal than other countries' and thereby attract banks from other locations. For example, if London can be a little less regulated than New York, it can gain at New York's expense. Then, if the Cayman Islands, Bermuda, the Netherlands Antilles, or Liechtenstein can be less regulated than London, they can gain at London's expense. The attractiveness of banking in this way drew more and more countries into competitive deregulation, special advantages being offered by Cyprus, Jersey, Gernsey, Malta, Madeira, Gibraltar, Monaco, the Isle of Man, and other new entrants. Traditional centers like London and New York were forced to respond to avoid losing their niche, creating a wave of financial deregulations in the 1980s that left more than a few regulators feeling extremely uneasy.

What is needed to prevent "deregulation wars" is international cooperation. Some efforts have been made in this regard. For example, the **Basle Committee** was established after the Herstatt and Franklin Bank failures for the purpose of "better co-ordination of the surveillance exercised by national authorities over the international banking system . . . ." This committee has had some success in sharing information on banks and their subsidiaries so that national regulators are more aware of difficulties before they trigger panics. However, despite improved information exchange via 1975 and 1983 **Concordat Agreements** among the Basle Committee members, no solution has been found to the natural tendency to compete for bank offices by progressive deregulation.

---

[21] The easing of anxiety about the stability of international banking has been brought about partly by a rescheduling of debt repayments of the major debtor countries, and partly by a large increase in the loan loss reserves set aside by creditor banks. The first bank to add massively to its loss reserves was Citibank in May 1987, and this was followed by a wave of appropriations by multinational banks to take care of bad third-world debts.

SUMMARY

1 Eurodollars are U.S.-dollar bank deposits held outside the United States. Included within the Eurodollar market are the Asiadollar market and other markets outside Europe. Eurocurrencies are bank deposits held outside the home countries of the currencies. The Eurocurrency market is also known as the offshore currency market. Eurocurrency markets allow investors and borrowers to choose among different currencies of denomination at the same location.

2 Eurocurrency yields are very close when covered for foreign exchange risk. They are more similar on different currencies than in different locations.

3 The commonly held view is that Eurodollars came into existence initially as the result of the preferences of Soviet holders of dollar balances. For safety and ideological reasons, they preferred to hold their dollars in Europe. Perhaps more important were the U.S. Federal Reserve System regulations on interest rates on deposits, and on holding reserves; these regulations encouraged a flow of dollars to Europe. The borrowing of these dollars was stimulated by credit and capital-flow restrictions in the United States. The convenience of holding deposits in and negotiating loans with local banks, as well as the lower spreads on Eurocurrencies from the absence of severe regulation, resulted in the later expansion of Eurodollars and other Eurocurrencies.

4 Eurocurrencies result in potential multiple expansions of bank deposits. The size of the multiplier depends on the speed with which funds leak to a currency's home market.

5 Banks can do business abroad via correspondents. They can also post representatives abroad to help clients. If they wish even greater involvement overseas, they can consider opening an agency, which does not solicit deposits, open a foreign branch, or buy or establish a subsidiary. Banks can venture abroad as part of a consortium. In the U.S., banks can establish an Edge Act subsidiary to invest in foreign subsidiary banks or otherwise invest outside the home state or abroad, or they can establish an international banking facility.

6 Banks are among the most multinational of firms. The benefits of being multinational include more timely and meaningful information on financial markets and events, better information on borrower quality, keeping clients from using other banks, earnings fees from custodial and other services, and avoiding onerous regulations.

7 The opening of overseas offices to avoid domestic regulations on required reserves, reporting assets, and paying deposit insurance premiums, has increased the riskiness of banks. That is, the major factors making banks multinational are also the major factors contributing to their riskiness.

8 Countries have to some extent competed with each other by progressively deregulating banking. Banking regulators have tended to match the deregulations of other countries to avoid losing banks, but as a result, banking has become more risky.

QUESTIONS

1 Since a person can open a Eurosterling account with dollars—by converting the dollars into pounds—or open a Eurodollar account with sterling, what yield differences can exist between different (forward-hedged) Eurocurrencies?

2 Why do you think Eurodollars are the major Eurocurrency? Does it have to do with the amount of business transacted in U.S. dollars?

3 Given the relatively extensive use of dollars in denominating sales contracts in international trade, are Eurodollar multipliers likely to be larger than multipliers for other Eurocurrencies? [*Hint:* Recall that the value of a multiplier has to do with the speed with which funds return to their home.]

4 a What is the Eurodollar creation from a deposit of $2 million when the Eurocurrency banks maintain a 5-percent reserve? Assume that the $2 million is deposited in a London office of Barclays Bank, which makes a loan to British Holdings Ltd., which uses the funds to pay for goods from British Auto Ltd., which in turn places the proceeds in Citibank in London. Assume that Citibank uses its extra dollars to make a loan to Aviva Corporation, which uses the dollars back in the United States.

  b Recompute the change in Eurodollars in a above, assuming instead that a 10-percent reserve is maintained.

  c Recompute the change in Eurodollars in a above with the 5-percent reserve, assuming that five banks are involved before leakage occurs.

  d What do you think is more important in affecting the size of the Eurodollar multiplier—the size of reserves or the time before a leakage occurs?

5 Give a reason (or reasons) why each of the following might open a Eurodollar account.

  a The government of Iran.

  b A U.S. private citizen.

  c A Canadian university professor.

  d A European-based corporation.

  e A U.S.-based corporation.

6 Does it make any difference to the individual bank that makes a loan whether the loaned funds will leak to the United States? In other words, does the individual bank lose the funds no matter who borrows the dollars?

7 What is the difference between a foreign branch, a foreign subsidiary, a foreign affiliate, and a foreign agency? Which types of foreign banking will make banks multinational?

8 If the object of U.S. banks moving overseas had been purely to help customers, could they have used only correspondent relationships and representative offices? Why then do you believe they have opened branches and purchased subsidiaries?

9 In what way does Table 11.6 suggest little discrimination against foreign financial firms? Can you find any apparent examples of discrimination?

10 Empirical evidence suggests banks tend to locate near importers rather than exporters. What do you think is responsible for this?

BIBLIOGRAPHY

Aliber, Robert Z.: "International Banking: A Survey," *Journal of Money, Credit and Banking*, Part 2, November 1984, pp. 661–678.

Baker, James C., and M. Gerald Bradford: *American Banks Abroad, Edge Act Companies and Multinational Banking*, Frederick A. Praeger, New York, 1974.

Bhattacharya, Anindya: *The Asian Dollar Market*, Frederick A. Praeger, New York, 1977.

Corrigan, E. Gerald: "Coping with Globally Integrated Financial Markets," *Quarterly Review*, Federal Reserve Bank of New York, winter 1987, pp. 1–5.

Debs, Richard A.: "International Banking," *Monthly Review*, Federal Reserve Bank of New York, June 1975, pp. 122–129.

Dufey, Gunter, and Ian Giddy: *The International Money Market*, Prentice-Hall, Englewood Cliffs, N.J., 1978.

Einzig, Paul A.: *The Euro-Dollar System*, 5th ed., St. Martin's Press, New York, 1973.

Freedman, Charles: "A Model of the Eurodollar Market," *Journal of Monetary Economics,* April 1977, pp. 139–161.

Friedman, Milton: "The Euro-Dollar Market: Some First Principles," *Morgan Guarantee Survey*, October 1969, pp. 4–44.

Henning, Charles N., William Pigott, and Robert H. Scott: *International Financial Management*, McGraw-Hill, New York, 1977.

Klopstock, Fred H.: "Money Creation in the Euro-Dollar Market—A Note on Professor Friedman's Views," *Monthly Review*, Federal Reserve Bank of New York, January 1970, pp. 12–15.

Lees, Francis A.: *International Banking and Finance*, John Wiley & Sons, New York, 1974.

McKenzie, George W.: *The Economics of the Euro-Currency System*, John Wiley & Sons, New York, 1976.

McKinnon, Ronald I.: *The Eurocurrency Market*, Essays in International Finance, no. 125, Princeton University Press, Princeton, N.J., 1977.

Ricks, David A., and Jeffrey S. Arpan: "Foreign Banking in the United States," *Business Horizons*, February 1976, pp. 84–87.

Robinson, Stuart W., Jr.: *Multinational Banking*, A. W. Sijthoff International, Leiden, The Netherlands, 1972.

CHAPTER 12

CASH MANAGEMENT AND MARKET EFFICIENCY

For most corporations, both the inflow and the outflow of funds are frequently uncertain. It is therefore important for companies to maintain a certain degree of liquidity. The amount of liquidity, as well as the form it should take, constitutes the topic of working-cash (or working-capital) management. Liquidity can take a number of forms, including coin and currency, bank deposits, overdraft facilities, and short-term readily marketable securities. These involve indifferent degrees of opportunity cost, in terms of forgone earnings available on less liquid investments. However, there are such highly liquid short-term securities in sophisticated money markets that virtually no funds have to remain completely idle. There are investments with maturities that extend no further than "overnight" or the next day, and there are overdraft facilities which allow firms to hold minimal cash balances. This makes part of the cash management problem similar to the problem of where to borrow and invest.

The objectives of effective working-capital management in an international environment are both to allocate short-term investments and cash-balance holdings between currencies and countries to maximize overall corporate returns and to borrow in different money markets to achieve the minimum cost. These objectives are to be pursued under the conditions of maintaining the required liquidity and minimizing any risks that might be incurred. The problem of having numerous currency and country choices for investing and borrowing, which is the extra dimension of international finance, is shared by firms with local markets and firms with international markets for their products. For example, a firm that produces and sells only within the United States will still have an incentive to earn the highest yield, or borrow at the lowest cost, even if that means venturing abroad to Eurocurrency or foreign money markets. There *are* additional problems faced by firms that have a multinational orientation of production and sales. These include the questions of local versus head-office management of working capital, and how to minimize foreign exchange transaction costs, political risks, and taxes. These are the questions we address in this chapter.[1] We will also describe some actual international cash management systems that have been devised.

If foreign exchange or money markets are not efficient, there is a possible additional objective of cash management, namely to attempt to take advantage of the inefficiencies.[2] Consequently, at the conclusion of the chapter we consider the evidence on market efficiency in the international context.

Let us begin our discussion of cash management by considering whether a company with receipts and payments in different countries and currencies should manage working capital locally or centrally. We shall see that there are a number of advantages to centralization of cash management, and only a few disadvantages.

INTERNATIONAL DIMENSIONS OF CASH MANAGEMENT

Advantages of Centralized Cash Management

Netting It is extremely common for multinational firms to have divisions in different countries, each having accounts receivable and accounts payable, as well as other sources of cash inflows and outflows, denominated in a number of currencies. If the divisions are left to manage their own cash, it can happen, for example, that one division is hedging a long pound position while at the same time another division is hedging a short pound position of the same maturity. This situation can be avoided by **netting**, which involves calculating the overall corporate position in each currency. This calculation requires some central coordination of cash management.

The benefit that is enjoyed from the ability to net cash inflows and outflows through centralized cash management comes in the form of reduced transaction costs. The amount that is saved depends on the extent that different divisions deal in the same currencies, and on the extent that different divisions have opposite positions in these currencies.[3] The benefit also depends on the length of the period over which it is feasible to engage in netting. This in turn depends on the ability to practice **leading** and **lagging**.

---

[1]Another important international cash management issue concerns whether to hedge or speculate, and how to hedge or speculate once a policy has been decided. These matters are not discussed in this chapter, because they were treated extensively in Chapter 10.

[2]As we shall see, the inefficiencies, if they exist, could take the form of interest-arbitrage opportunities or abnormal returns to currency speculation.

[3]Clearly, if all divisions are long in pounds, or all divisions are short in pounds, the transaction-cost advantage of centralized cash management exists only if there are economies of scale in transacting. Of course, there *are* in fact such economies of scale.

Leading and lagging involve the movement of cash inflows and outflows forward and backward in time so as to permit netting and achieve other goals.[4] For example, if Aviva has to pay £1 million for denim on June 10, and has received an order for £1 million of jeans from Britain, it might attempt to arrange payment for about the same date and thereby avoid exposure. If the payment for the jeans would normally have been after June 10 and the receivable is brought forward, this is called leading of the export. If the payment would have been before June 10 and is delayed, this is called lagging of the export. In a similar way imports can be led and lagged.

When dealing at arm's length, the opportunities for netting via leading and lagging are limited by the preferences of the other party. However, when transactions are between divisions of the same multinational, the scope for leading and lagging (for the purpose of netting and achieving other benefits such as deferring taxes) is considerable. Recognizing this, numerous governments regulate the length of credit and acceleration of settlement by putting limits on leading and lagging. The regulations vary greatly from country to country, and are subject to change, often with very little warning. If cash managers are to employ leading and lagging successfully, they must keep current with what is allowed.[5]

Currency Diversification When cash management is centralized it is possible not only to net inflows and outflows in each separate currency, but also to consider whether the company's foreign exchange risk is sufficiently reduced via diversification that one need not hedge all the individual positions. The diversification of exchange-rate risk results from the fact that exchange rates do not all move in perfect harmony. Consequently, a portfolio of inflows and outflows in different currencies will have a smaller variance of value than the sum of variances of the values of the individual currencies.[6] We can explain the nature of the diversification benefit by considering a straightforward example.

Suppose that in its foreign operations, Aviva buys its cloth in France and sells its finished garments in both France and Germany in the amounts shown below:

	Germany (DM)	France (Fr)
Denim purchase	0	8,000,000
Jeans sales	2,000,000	3,000,000

[4] Leading and lagging are practiced to defer income and thereby delay paying taxes, and to create unhedged positions in order to speculate; cash managers may delay paying out currencies they expect to appreciate, and accelerate paying out currencies they expect to depreciate. Leading and lagging are therefore used to hedge, speculate, and reduce taxes.

[5] The regulations governing leading and lagging are described each year by Business International in its *Money Report*. The large multinational accounting firms also publish the current regulations.

[6] For an account of the size of diversification benefits see Mark R. Eaker and Dwight Grant, "Cross-Hedging Foreign Currency Risk," Working Paper, University of North Carolina, August 1985.

The timing of payments for French denim and the timing of sales of jeans are the same. (Alternatively, we could think of the revenue from the export of jeans as receipts from foreign investments, and the payment for imports of cloth as repayment on a debt.)

One route open to Aviva is to sell forward DM 2 million and, after netting its French-franc position, buy forward Fr 5 million. Aviva would then be hedged against changes in exchange rates. An alternative, however, is to consider how the French franc and the German mark move vis-à-vis the dollar and hence between themselves. Let us suppose, simply to reveal the possibilities, that because France and Germany are both members of the European Monetary System, when the German mark appreciates vis-à-vis the dollar, generally the French franc does so also. In other words, let us suppose that the mark and the franc are highly positively correlated.

With net franc payables of Fr 5 million, mark receivables of DM 2 million, and spot exchange rates of, for example, $S(\$/DM) = 0.5$ and $S(\$/Fr) = 0.2$, the payables and receivables cancel out. The payable to France is $1 million at current rates, which is the same as the receivable from Germany. The risk is that exchange rates can change before payments are made and receipts are received. However, if the franc and the mark move together and the exchange rates become, for example, $S(\$/DM) = 0.55$ and $S(\$/Fr) = 0.22$, then payments to France will be $1,100,000, and receipts from Germany will also be $1,100,000. What will be lost in extra payments to France will be gained in extra revenue from Germany. We find in this case that Aviva is quite naturally unexposed if it can be sure that the currencies will always move together vis-à-vis the dollar.[7]

In our example, we have, of course, selected very special circumstances and values for convenience. In general, however, there is safety in large numbers. If there are receivables in many different currencies, then when some go up in value, others will come down. There will be some canceling of gains and losses. Similarly, if there are many payables, they can also cancel. Moreover, as in our example, receivables and payables can offset each other if currency values move together. There are many possibilities that are not obvious, but it should be remembered that although some canceling of gains and losses might occur, some risk will remain. A firm should use forward contracts or some other form of hedging if it wishes to avoid all foreign exchange risk and exposure. However, a firm with a large variety of small volumes of payables and receivables (that is, small volumes in many different currencies) might consider that all the transaction costs involved in the alternative forms of hedging are not worthwhile in

---

[7]If two different currencies move in opposite directions vis-à-vis the dollar, then natural hedging will exist with payables in both currencies or with receivables in both currencies, rather than with offsetting payables and receivables in the two currencies. We can note that positive comovement of exchange rates vis-à-vis the dollar will be very common. It will occur, for example, with the European currencies, which have fixed exchange rates between themselves. Because of this, when the mark is gaining vis-à-vis the dollar, generally the franc will also be gaining, as in our example. Negative comovement is much more difficult to rationalize than positive comovement.

view of the natural hedging from diversification. The determination of whether the diversification has sufficiently reduced the risk can only be made properly when cash management is centralized.

Pooling   Pooling occurs when cash is held as well as managed in a central location. The advantage of pooling is that cash needs can be met wherever they occur without having to keep precautionary balances in each country. Uncertainties and delays in moving funds to where they are needed require that some balances be maintained everywhere, but with pooling, a given probability of having sufficient cash to meet liquidity needs can be achieved with smaller cash holdings than if holdings are decentralized.[8] The reason pooling works is that cash surpluses and deficiencies in different locations do not move in a perfectly parallel fashion. As a result, the variance of total cash flows is smaller than the sum of the variances of flows for individual countries. For example, when there are large cash balance outflows in Belgium, it is not likely that there will also be unusually large outflows in Britain, the United States, France, Holland, Germany, and so on. If a firm is to have sufficient amounts in each individual country, it must maintain a large cash reserve in each. However, if the total cash needs are pooled in, for example, the United States, then when the need in Belgium is unusually high, it can be met from the central pool because there will not normally be unusually high drains in other countries at the same time.

Security Availability and Efficiency of Collections   All of the advantages of centralized cash management that we have mentioned so far, which are all particular aspects of economies of scale, would accrue wherever centralization occurs. However, if the centralization occurs in a major international financial center such as London or New York, there are additional advantages in terms of a broader range of securities that are available and an ability to function in an efficient financial system.

It is useful for a firm to denominate as many payments and receipts as its counterparties will allow in units of a major currency and to have bills payable in a financial center. Contracts for payment due to the firm should stipulate not only the payment date and the currency in which payment is to be made, but also the branch or office at which the payment is due. Penalties for late payment can help ensure that payments are made on time. The speed of collection of payments can be increased by using post-office box numbers wherever they are available. Similarly, if a firm banks with a large-scale multinational bank, it can usually arrange for head-office accounts to be quickly credited, even if payment is made at a foreign branch of the bank.

Disadvantages of Centralized Cash Management

Unfortunately, it is rarely possible to hold all cash in a major international financial center. This is because there may be unpredictable delays in moving

[8]This is shown in the appendix to this chapter.

funds from the financial center to other countries. If an important payment is due, especially if it is to a foreign government for taxes or to a local supplier of a crucial input, excess cash balances should be held where they are needed, even if these mean opportunity costs in terms of higher interest earnings available elsewhere. When the cash needs in local currencies are known well ahead of time, arrangements can be made in advance for receiving the needed currency, but substantial allowances for potential delay should be made. When one is used to dealing in North America, Europe, and other developed areas, it is too easy to believe that banking is efficient everywhere, but the delays that can be faced in banks in, for example, the Middle East and Africa can be exceedingly long, uncertain, and costly.

In principle it is possible to centralize the *management* of working capital even if some funds do have to be held locally. However, complete centralization of management is difficult because local representation is often necessary for dealing with local clients and banks. Even if a multinational bank is used for accepting receipts and making payments, problems can arise that can only be dealt with on the spot. Therefore, the question a firm must answer is the degree of centralization of cash management that is appropriate, and in particular, which activities can be centralized and which should be decentralized. The answer will generally involve a considerable amount of centralization, especially if the company works closely with a multinational bank.

If interest parity always held exactly, the cash management problem would be simplified in that it would then not matter in which currency or country a firm borrowed or invested. However, as we explained in Chapter 8, there are factors which do allow limited departures from interest parity to occur, at least from the perspective of any one borrower or lender. Let us consider what each of the factors discussed earlier—transaction costs, political risk, liquidity preference, and taxes—implies for working-capital management. We shall see that each factor has slightly different implications.

Transaction Costs, Political Risk, Liquidity Preference, Taxes, and Cash Management

Transaction costs are a reason for keeping funds in the *currency* that is received if the funds might be needed later in the same currency. For example, if a firm receives 2 million won in payment for sales from its subsidiary in South Korea, and needs approximately this quantity of won to meet a payment in a month or two, the funds should be left in Korean won—if expected yields are not sufficiently higher in other currencies to cover two sets of transaction costs.

Political risk is a reason to keep funds in the company's home *country* rather than in the country in whose currency the funds are denominated. This is because the home jurisdiction is generally the most friendly one. The reduction in political risk that results from moving funds home must, of course, be balanced against the extra costs this entails when the funds must later be converted back into the foreign currency. Between most developed countries, the transaction costs of temporarily moving funds home are likely to exceed the benefit from reduced political risk, and so cash balances should be maintained in the foreign countries. However, the political situation in some third-world countries might be considered sufficiently volatile that only minimal working balances should be maintained in those countries.

Liquidity considerations argue in favor of keeping funds in the currency in which they are *most likely* to be needed in the future. This might not be the currency in which the funds arrive or the company's home currency. The liquidity factor is hence different from transaction costs, which suggest that funds should be kept in the currency in which they arrive, and it is also different from political risk, which suggests that funds should be kept at home. We use words "most likely" because it is the uncertainty of cash flows that is responsible for the need to maintain liquidity. If inflows and outflows were *perfectly* predictable, a firm could arrange the maturities of long-term securities so that each security matures at the precise time the funds are needed. Complete certainty would do away with the so-called precautionary motive for holding money balances. However, even with uncertainty in the timing and amounts of cash inflows and outflows, extremely liquid money-market investments and overdraft facilities at banks have allowed firms to keep most of their funds in interest-bearing or money-market instruments.

Withholding taxes are a reason to avoid countries whose withholding rates exceed the investor's domestic tax rate, because in such a case it will not in general be possible to receive full withholding-tax credit. Lower taxes on foreign exchange gains than on interest income are a reason to invest in countries whose currencies are at a forward premium if the premium is treated as a capital gain.[9] However, for firms that are heavily involved in dealing in many countries, foreign exchange gains and interest earnings are likely to face the same tax rates. There is therefore little need to favor any particular market. The factors affecting the location of working capital are summarized in Table 12.1.

Examples of Cash Management Systems

It will be illustrative to end our discussion of cash management by considering the cash management systems of two U.S. multinational corporations. These systems illustrate how netting can be done, and how centralized cash management through a **currency center** can be effected.

Navistar International　Navistar International was formed in a reorganization of International Harvester, the farm and transportation equipment manufacturer. In 1969, the company established a netting system that works as follows:[10]

The netting system is based at a currency clearing center, located in a finance company in Switzerland. Prior to clearing foreign exchange, the Swiss finance

---

[9]This was explained in Chapter 8.

[10]See "Multilateral Netting System Cuts Costs, Provides Flexibility for International Harvester," *Money Report*, Business International, December 20, 1979.

TABLE 12.1
FACTORS AFFECTING WORKING-CAPITAL MANAGEMENT

Factor	Implication
Absence of forward markets	Keep funds in the currency received if an anticipated future need exists.
Transaction costs	Keep funds in the currency received.
Political risk	Move funds to the domestic market.
Liquidity requirements	Keep funds in the currency most likely to be needed in the future.
Taxes	Avoid high withholding taxes and keep funds in appreciating currencies.

company had been responsible for Eurocurrency financing, investment, and other transactions involving foreign currencies. The netting scheme works on a monthly cycle, as illustrated in Figure 12.1. By the 15th day of each month, all the participating subsidiaries have sent information to the currency clearing center on payables and receivables existing at that time in local currencies. The clearing center converts all amounts into dollar terms at the current spot exchange rate and sends information to those subsidiaries with net payables on how much they owe and to whom. These paying subsidiaries are responsible for informing the net receivers of funds and for obtaining and delivering the foreign exchange. Settlement is on the 25th of the month or the closest business day, and the funds are purchased 2 days in advance so that they are received on the designated day. Any difference between the exchange rate used by the Swiss center on the 15th and the rate prevailing for settlement on the 25th gives rise to foreign exchange gains or loses, and these are attributed to the subsidiary.

The original clearing system was for intracompany use and did not include outside firms. After a decade with this system, the company introduced a scheme for foreign exchange settlements for payments to outsiders. There are two different dates, the 10th and the 25th or the nearest business day, on which all foreign exchange is purchased by and transferred from the Swiss center. The payment needs are telexed to the center from the subsidiary more than 2 days before the settlement date, and the center nets the amounts of each currency so as to make the minimum number of foreign exchange transactions. The subsidiary which owes the foreign exchange settles with the clearing center by the appropriate settlement date. According to the company, netting can cut the total number of transactions with outsiders in half, saving the company transaction costs.

More flexibility is given to the cash management system by the use of interdivisional leading and lagging. If, for example, a subsidiary is a net payer, it may delay or lag payment for up to 2 months while compensating the net receiver at prevailing interest rates. Net receivers of funds may at their discre-

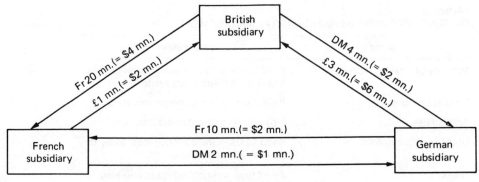

(a) Receivables and payables reported to currency center
before the 15th of month.

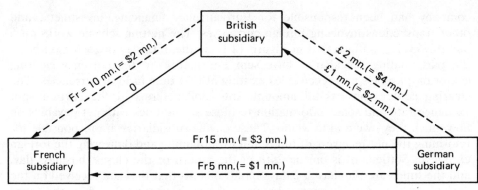

(b) Net payables/receivables (broken lines) and actual cash flows
(solid lines) made on the 25th of the month.

FIGURE 12.1
EXAMPLE OF NAVISTAR INTERNATIONAL'S FOREIGN EXCHANGE NETTING SYSTEM. It is
assumed that on the 15th of the month $S(DM / \$) = 2.0$, $S(£ / \$) = 0.5$, and $S(Fr / \$) = 5.0$.
Information on receivables and payables is provided for the Swiss currency center on or
before the 15th of the month. The currency center converts the amounts of foreign exchange
into dollars at the going exchange rate (as shown in part a) and evaluates the net amounts
owed between subsidiaries (as shown by the broken lines in part b). Rather than having the
German subsidiary pay the British subsidiary the equivalent of $4 million while the British
subsidiary in turn pays the French subsidiary $2 million, the German subsidiary will be
instructed to add $2 million onto what it pays the French subsidiary and to reduce what it pays
the British subsidiary by this amount. The British and French subsidiaries will receive no
instructions to pay anybody. The total number of transactions will be reduced from six to only
two. Transaction costs will be faced on only $5 million worth of transactions.

tion make funds available to other subsidiaries at interest. In this way the need to resort to outside borrowing is reduced; the Swiss clearing center serves to bring different parties together. The netting with leading and lagging has allowed the company to eliminate intracompany floats and reduce by over 80 percent the amount that otherwise would have been transferred.

Digital Equipment Itself an advanced information-processing company, Digital Equipment centralizes its cash management in two currency centers.[11] The cash positions of European subsidiaries are monitored and managed from the European headquarters in Geneva. Cash management for other subsidiaries is handled by the company's principal headquarters, which is in Acton, Massachusetts. The subsidiaries and appropriate headquarters communicate via Telex, and the movement of cash is facilitated by the use of a limited number of U.S. banks with offices in many countries. The cash management system works as shown in Figure 12.2.

Foreign exchange positions are established and adjusted on a weekly basis. Every Thursday, all subsidiaries send a report to the currency center at their headquarters. In their statements they give projected cash inflows and outflows in each foreign currency for the following week. They also give their bank-account positions. The foreign sales subsidiaries are generally net receivers of foreign exchange. On the following Monday the subsidiary borrows its antici-pated net cash inflow via an overdraft facility and transfers the funds to the headquarter's account at the same bank. For example, if the British sales subsidiary expects net receipts of £10 million and has no bank balance, it will call its banks for the best exchange rate. If the most favorable rate for buying dollars is $S(\$/£) = 2.0$, it will transfer $20 million to the Geneva currency center by borrowing £10 million and converting it into dollars. The selected bank—the one which offered the best rate on dollars—will debit the British subsidiary's account in London by £10 million and, on the same day, credit the Geneva headquarter's account with $20 million. The British subsidiary will pay the £10 million debt due to the overdraft as the receipts come in.

In order to ensure that it is able to make the same-day transfers and obtain the overdrafts, Digital maintains close ties with a limited number of multina-tional U.S. banks. The subsidiaries obtain funds only via overdrafts; they do not use other means of borrowing funds. Subsidiaries that are net users of foreign exchange instead of net receivers use the reverse procedure. The subsidiary reports its need for cash to the appropriate headquarters on Thursday, and beginning on the following Monday it uses overdraft lines as payments are met.

[11] An excellent account of Digital Equipment's centralized cash management system can be found in "How Digital Equipment's Weekly Cash Cycle Mobilizes Idle Funds," *Money Report*, Business International, January 30, 1981. A similar system that uses a currency center in London is operated by RCA. The company adapted a system available from Citibank for large clients which keeps track of currency needs and netting. For a full account, see "Standard Netting System Remodelled to Suit RCA's Own Needs, *Money Report*, Business International, July 13, 1979. Chase Manhattan's system is known as Infocash, and the netting and information system available from the international financial advisory firm Business International in known as Xmis.

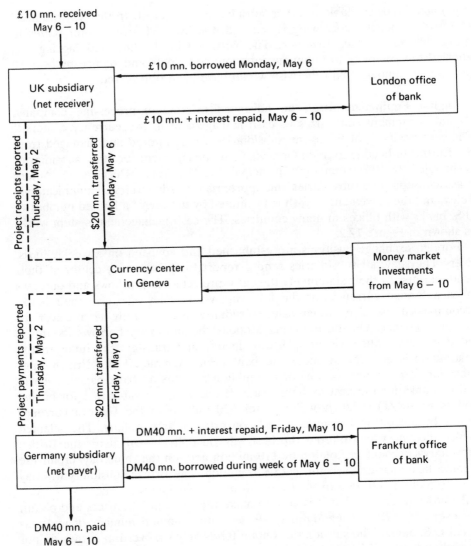

FIGURE 12.2
DIGITAL EQUIPMENT'S WEEKLY CASH CYCLE. We assume that the U.K. subsidiary is a net receiver of pounds and that the German subsidiary is a net payer of German marks. Both subsidiaries send their cash-flow projections to the currency center on Thursday, May 2. On the following Monday the U.K. subsidiary borrows its expected cash needs and then transfers the dollar equivalent to Geneva. [It is assumed that $S(\$ / £) = 2.0$.] The debt is repaid in the currency of borrowing during the week of May 6–10. The German subsidiary borrows marks during the week of May 6–10 as its payments fall due. On Friday, May 10, the Geneva currency center transfers the dollar equivalent to the subsidiary. [It is assumed that $S(\$ / DM) = 0.5$.] This is used to repay the overdraft on that day. During the week the currency center has $20 million to invest in the money market.

On the following Friday the subsidiary receives funds from the parent company to pay off the overdraft and make up for any unanticipated disbursements that have been made.

There are occasions when a subsidiary will receive more funds than it anticipated and transfers them to headquarters more than once a week. Alternatively, a subsidiary may face unprojected disbursements or late receipts. It will then use backup overdrafts. Similarly, a subsidiary may face unusually large payments. It will have to Telex its parent for extra funds. Digital uses post-office lock boxes in Canada and the United States in order to speed up the handling of receivables, and in Europe, Digital instructs customers to pay its bank directly rather than the local subsidiary itself. All investing or borrowing in currencies other than the U.S. dollar is hedged on the forward market to avoid foreign exchange risk.

Because the amount of cash handled by the two headquarters is so large, it can generally be invested more favorably than if each separate subsidiary placed it. Funds are invested in various money markets, including Eurodollars and dollar time deposits in the United States. The parent has the total amount of funds from its many subsidiaries to invest for a full week. A subsidiary will, however, repay the overdraft *during* the week. It follows that the interest costs on overdrafts are not as large as the interest earnings of the headquarters.

The major advantage of Digital Equipment's system is that there is no foreign exchange exposure for the subsidiary. This is because the payable on the overdraft is in the local currency, as is the receivable against which the funds have been borrowed. Local currency is paid out as it arrives. An additional advantage is that the currency centers handle large amounts of cash and can therefore get lower spreads when buying and selling foreign exchange. They can also take a broader perspective of investment and borrowing opportunities as well as enjoy the advantages of netting, currency diversification, pooling, and financial efficiency that we discussed earlier.

MARKET EFFICIENCY

Active cash management is potentially more useful if foreign exchange and money markets are inefficient than if they are efficient. This is because in an efficient market, by definition, there are no abnormal returns from gathering and using information when making borrowing and investment decisions, or taking positions in foreign exchange.[12] The abnormal return is the actual return minus the return that would be expected, given the level of risk, if all available information concerning the asset had been utilized. Excess returns are examined over time to determine whether, on the average, they are equal to zero and

---

[12] On the concept of market efficiency and the tests in the context of the stock market, see Eugene Fama, "Efficient Capital Markets: A Review of Theory and Empirical Work," *Journal of Finance*, June 1970, pp. 383–417.

serially uncorrelated.[13] Since we must specify the expected returns, tests of market efficiency are really joint tests of the model used to generate the expected returns and of market efficiency.

Efficiency can take on different meanings according to which type of information we wish to include in the set that is assumed to be available to decision makers. If information only on historical prices or returns on the particular asset is included, we are testing for **weak-form efficiency**. With all publicly known information included, we are testing for **semistrong efficiency**, and with all information, including that available to insiders, we are testing for **strong-form efficiency**. Because of central-bank involvement with foreign exchange rates, tests of the efficiency of exchange markets are not as straightforward as tests of the efficiency of stock markets. Nevertheless, some tests are possible.[14]

Efficiency of the Money Markets

If profits can consistently be made by interest arbitrage, then we are led to believe that the foreign exchange (or money) markets are inefficient. Profits are made when there are departures from interest parity, and so we can test for inefficiency by examining, for example,

$$\varepsilon = (r_{US} - r_{UK}) - \left[\frac{F_1(\$/\pounds) - S(\$/\pounds)}{S(\$/\pounds)} \right] \cdot (1 + r_{UK}) \qquad (12.1)$$

where ε is the interest disparity, and it is understood that the forward premium/discount is annualized. If ε is large enough to allow a profit to be made from interest arbitrage, we can claim that the foreign exchange market is inefficient. Tests by Jacob Frenkel and Richard Levich find some opportunity for earning a profit from interest arbitrage between countries even after adjusting for transaction costs.[15] However, this appearance of a potential profit could persist because of political risk of foreign versus domestic investments, liquidity differentials, taxes, or foreign exchange controls, and might not mean that an actual abnormal profit can be made.

Efficiency of Foreign Exchange Markets

Another aspect of efficiency in the international context concerns whether there is any abnormal bias in the forward exchange rate as a predictor of the expected

[13]By having no serial correlation we mean that excess returns in successive periods are not related to each other. If an excess return in one period means a likelihood of further excess returns in an adjacent or subsequent period, the excess returns are serially correlated.

[14]An excellent survey of the tests can be found in Richard Levich, "On the Efficiency of Markets for Foreign Exchange," in Rudiger Dornbusch and Jacob Frenkel (eds.), *International Economic Policy: Theory and Evidence*, Johns Hopkins Press, Baltimore, 1979. This section draws on Levich's survey.

[15]See Jacob Frenkel and Richard Levich, "Covered Interest Arbitrage: Unexploited Profits?," *Journal of Political Economy*, April 1975, pp. 325–338.

future spot rate. By an **abnormal bias** we mean a difference between the forward rate and the expected future spot rate that is inappropriate for the risk taken. (This difference between the forward rate and the expected future spot rate is the expected gain from speculation. Therefore, an abnormal bias means an abnormal return to speculation.)

A straightforward test of the existence of bias, albeit not of abnormal bias, stated in the context of the dollar-pound exchange rate, is to estimate over a period of time the regression equation

$$S_n(\$/£) = \beta_0 + \beta_1 F_n(\$/£) + \mu \tag{12.2}$$

Here, $S_n(\$/£)$ are the realized spot rates for the maturity dates of the forward contracts, β_0 and β_1 are coefficients that we wish to estimate, and μ is the statistical error.[16] The forward rate is said to be an unbiased predictor of the eventual spot rate if the estimate of β_1 is insignificantly different from unity, and if β_0 is zero. In such a case the realized spot exchange rate is on average what had been predicted by the forward rate.

Even if $\beta_1 = 1$ and $\beta_0 = 0$, so that the forward rate is an *unbiased* predictor of the future spot rate, this does not mean the forward rate is an *efficient* predictor. A semistrong efficient predictor, for example, is one that cannot be improved upon by considering any additional public information. A predictor might be unbiased because the spot rate is on average as predicted by the forward rate, and yet better predictions of the spot rate might be made by including additional information as explanatory variables in Equation (12.2). Of course, for $F_n(\$/£)$ to be an unbiased predictor of $S_n(\$/£)$, any excluded variables must have a zero average effect; otherwise the realized spot rates will be systematically higher or lower than the forward rates. However, even when the forward rate is an unbiased predictor, other additional explanatory variables in Equation (12.2) may help explain *when* or *by how much* the spot rate will be higher or lower than the forward rate implies.

One factor which might have a zero average effect on $S_n(\$/£)$ versus $F_n(\$/£)$, but which could help predict individual values of $S_n(\$/£)$, is a time-varying risk premium in the forward exchange rate. We pointed out in Chapter 10 that it is only if we assume that speculators are risk-neutral that[17]

$$F_n(\$/£) = S_n^*(\$/£)$$

If speculators are risk-averse, they may not, for example, buy pounds forward unless they can buy pounds for less than they believe they will be worth on the future spot market. The difference between the forward rate and the market's expected future spot rate is the risk premium. The risk premium could be for taking the risk of buying pounds forward of dollars, or for taking the risk of

---

[16] A regression equation of this form can be estimated for n equal to 1 month, 2 months, and so on.

[17] We abstract from transaction costs here.

buying dollars forward for pounds. Whether the risk premium is for buying the dollar or the pound depends on what other assets can be held by speculators and on the covariances between exchange rates and these other assets and inflation.[18] Sometimes speculators might want to be rewarded for being long in pounds, and at other times they might want to be rewarded for being short in pounds. That is, the risk premium may vary over time.

If we could measure the normal forward risk premium, and knew that other factors did not cause a systematic difference between the forward rate and expected future spot rate, we could test for efficiency of the forward market by extending Equation (12.2). We would instead estimate

$$S_n(\$/\pounds) = \beta_0 + \beta_1 F_n(\$/\pounds) - \beta_2 \phi_n(\$/\pounds) + \mu$$

where $\phi_n(\$/\pounds)$ is the n-period normal risk premium in the forward dollar exchange rate of the pound. The forward market would be considered efficient if $\beta_0 = 0$, $\beta_1 = 1$, and $\beta_2 = 1$ because then, on average,

$$S_n(\$/\pounds) = F_n(\$/\pounds) - \phi_n(\$/\pounds)$$

or

$$F_n(\$/\pounds) = S_n(\$/\pounds) + \phi_n(\$/\pounds)$$

That is the forward rate would equal the expected spot rate—which is proxied by the realized spot rate, which should on average equal the expected spot rate —plus the n-period forward risk premium. Unfortunately, we cannot apply this test, because it requires knowledge of the normal risk premium, and without a theory of what the premium should be, we have no measure of $\phi_n(\$/\pounds)$.

The empirical evidence suggests there is a risk premium in the forward rate, and that it does vary over time.[19] However, it appears that the risk premium is

---

[18] See Michael Adler and Bernard Dumas, "International Portfolio Choice and Corporate Finance: A Synthesis," *Journal of Finance*, June 1983, pp. 925–984.

[19] A by no means exhaustive list of papers reaching this conclusion includes Richard T. Baillie, Robert E. Lippens, and Patrick C. McMahon, "Testing Rational Expectations and Efficiency in the Foreign Exchange Market," *Econometrica*, May 1983, pp. 553–563; Eugene F. Fama, "Forward and Spot Exchange Rates," *Journal of Monetary Economics*, November 1984, pp. 320–338; Lars P. Hansen and Robert J. Hodrick, "Forward Exchange Rates as Optimal Predictors of Future Spot Rates: An Economic Analysis," *Journal of Political Economy*, October 1980, pp. 829–853; David A. Hsieh, "Tests of Rational Expectations and No Risk Premium in Forward Exchange Markets," *Journal of International Economics*, August 1984, pp. 173–184; Rodney L. Jacobs, "The Effect of Errors in the Variables on Tests for a Risk Premium in Forward Exchange Rates," *Journal of Finance*, June 1982, pp. 667–677; Robert A. Korajczck, "The Pricing of Forward Contracts for Foreign Exchange," *Journal of Political Economy*, April 1985, pp. 346–368; and Christian C. P. Wolff, "Forward Foreign Exchange Rates, Expected Spot Rates and Premia: A Signal-Extraction Approach," *Journal of Finance*, June 1987, pp. 395–406.

very small. For example, Jeffrey Frankel has considered the change in risk premium that would occur if there were an increase in the supply of dollar assets of 1 percent of global assets, which in 1989 would amount to an increase of almost $100 billion. Such an increase in dollar assets should make people less willing to hold dollars, thereby increasing the required forward premium on dollars. Frankel estimates that such a 1-percent increase would change the risk premium by 2.4 basis points, that is, by less than $\frac{1}{40}$ percent.[20] Moreover, the evidence for there being a significant risk premium at all was thrown into question by further research by Jeffrey Frankel and his coresearcher Kenneth Froot.[21] By considering exchange-rate predictions gathered in surveys of foreign exchange market participants, Frankel and Froot discovered that the predictions are biased. Consequently, the appearance of risk premiums from β_1 in Equation (12.2) that are different from unity may be due to biased expectations. Indeed, even some of those who originally identified a risk premium subsequently obtained evidence that casts some doubt on the model used to find it.[22]

A further way of testing market efficiency, and in particular of testing whether speculation offers an expected return, is to examine the forecasting performance of exchange-rate models. If markets are efficient, so that exchange rates reflect all available information, it should not be possible to make an abnormal return from speculating by following the models' predictions; forward and futures exchange rates, interest-rate differences between countries, and so on, should all reflect the models' predictions.

In a frequently cited paper Richard Meese and Kenneth Rogoff compared the forecasting performance of a number of exchange-rate models.[23] The models generally predicted well during the period of time over which they were estimated. That is, when using the estimated equations and the known values of the explanatory variables, these models predicted exchange rates that were generally close to actual exchange rates. However, when predicting outside the

---

[20]See Jeffrey A. Frankel, "In Search of the Exchange Risk Premium: A Six-Currency Test Assuming Mean-Variance Optimization," *Journal of International Money and Finance*, December 1982, pp. 255–274.

[21]Jeffrey A. Frankel and Kenneth A. Froot, "Using Survey Data to Test Some Standard Propositions Regarding Exchange Rate Expectations," *American Economic Review*, March 1987, pp. 133–153.

[22]Robert J. Hodrick and Sanjay Srivastava, "An Investigation of Risk and Return in Forward Foreign Exchange," *Journal of International Money and Finance*, April 1984, pp. 5–29. Other research that does not support the notion of a risk premium includes Bradford Cornell, "Spot Rates, Forward Rates and Exchange Market Efficiency," *Journal of Financial Economics*, August 1977, pp. 55–65; David L. Kaserman, "The Forward Exchange Rate: Its Determination and Behavior as a Predictor of the Future Spot Rate," *Proceedings of the American Statistical Association*, 1973, pp. 417–422; David Longworth, "Testing the Efficiency of the Canadian-U.S. Exchange Market under the Assumption of No Risk Premium, *Journal of Finance*, March 1982, pp. 43–49; and Alan C. Stockman, "Risk, Information and Forward Exchange Rates," in Jacob A. Frenkel and Harry G. Johnson (eds.), *The Economics of Exchange Rates: Selected Studies*, Addison-Wesley, Boston, 1978, pp. 159–178.

[23]Richard A. Meese and Kenneth Rogoff, "Empirical Exchange Rate Models of the Seventies: Do They Fit Out of Sample?," *Journal of International Economics*, February 1983, pp. 3–24.

estimation period, the models did a poorer job than a naive forecast that future spot rates equal current spot rates.[24] This is despite the fact that the out-of-sample forecasts—those made outside the estimation period—were made using actual realized values of explanatory variables. (In practice, forecasting would be based on forecast values of explanatory variables, adding to the forecast error.) This is the outcome we would expect with efficient markets, namely, that it is not possible to use any generally available model of exchange rates to make an abnormal return.

Another way of verifying whether forecasting models produce abnormal returns is to consider the record of exchange-rate forecasting services and to see whether they have performed better than using forward exchange rates as predictors of future spot rates. In an extensive examination of numerous services selling exchange-rate forecasts, Stephen Goodman found that, whereas the forward rate predicts the direction of change in exchange rates over 50 percent of the time, the forecasting services did so less than 50 percent of the time.[25] Richard Levich found the same for short-term forecasts, but discovered some gain from following the advice of forecasting services for predictions going beyond one year.[26] Longer-term predictions based on restoration of PPP have also been made with some degree of success by Robert Everett, Abraham George, and Aryeh Blumberg.[27] However, the useful predictions are accompanied by risk, making it unclear whether the return from following the forecasting services is a fair return for taking the associated risk.

What we learn from the various approaches to testing market efficiency is that the hypothesis cannot be rejected. While there may be some opportunities for profit in the foreign exchange and international money markets, this may be because of political risk, liquidity differentials, taxes, or foreign exchange controls. Similarly, while there may be expected returns to speculating in the forward market, they are small and come at the expense of taking risk. That is, risk premiums in forward exchange rates, if they exist at all, are small and may

---

[24] Because forward rates offer free estimates of future spot rates, the test of efficiency we would normally make is whether a model's predictions outperform the forward exchange rate, not whether the model's predictions outperform naive forecasts of future spot rates as being equal to current spot rates. Surprisingly, however, it has been shown that the current spot rate is a better predictor of the future spot rate than is the forward rate. Therefore, if the models do worse than predicting future spot rates from current spot rates, they do *a fortiori* worse than predicting future spot rates from current forward rates. See Thomas C. Chiang, "Empirical Analysis of the Predictors of Future Spot Rates," *The Journal of Financial Research*, summer 1986, pp. 153–162.

[25] Stephen H. Goodman, "No Better than the Toss of a Coin," *Euromoney*, December 1978, pp. 75–85.

[26] Richard Levich, "Analyzing the Accuracy of Foreign Exchange Advisory Services: Theory and Evidence," in Richard Levich and Clas Wihlberg (eds.), *Exchange Risk and Exposure: Current Developments in International Financial Management*, D. C. Heath, Lexington, Mass., 1980. Other papers that consider the value of different forecasting techniques include Arvind Mahajan, "Swaps, Expectations, and Exchange Rates," *Journal of Banking and Finance*, March 1986, pp. 7–20; and Richard J. Sweeney, "Beating the Foreign Exchange Market," *Journal of Finance*, March 1986, pp. 163–182.

[27] Robert M. Everett, Abraham M. George, and Aryeh Blumberg, "Appraising Currency Strengths and Weaknesses: An Operational Model for Calculating Parity Exchange Rates," *Journal of International Business Studies*, fall 1980, pp. 80–91.

merely compensate speculators for the risk that is taken. It follows that cash management should be oriented to maintaining the appropriate degree and form of liquidity, not to looking for abnormal profits from borrowing, investing, or currency speculation.

SUMMARY

1 Centralized cash management allows netting of long and short positions in each currency, where the positions are those of different divisions of a multinational firm. The scope for netting is enhanced by leading and lagging cash inflows and outflows.

2 Centralized cash management provides an ability to consider how systematic comovement of exchange rates provides diversification.

3 Centralization permits a broad view of investment and borrowing opportunities.

4 Centralized cash management also reduces the precautionary cash needs via pooling; funds can be moved from the central location to where they are needed.

5 Complete centralization is limited by the need to maintain local personnel to deal with unpredictable delays in moving funds between countries, and for dealing with local banks and clients.

6 The different reasons why interest parity may not hold have different implications for the management of working capital. In particular, transaction costs induce keeping funds in the currency in which cash arrives, political risk induces keeping funds at home, liquidity considerations induce holding currencies that are most likely to be needed, and taxes induce avoiding countries with very high withholding rates and holding appreciating currencies if facing favorable capital-gains treatment on foreign exchange gains.

7 Efficient cash management systems have been developed by several multinational corporations.

8 Foreign exchange and money markets cannot be considered efficient if there are opportunities to profit from riskless covered interest arbitrage.

9 Foreign exchange markets cannot be considered efficient if the forward exchange rate differs from the expected future spot rate by more than a normal risk premium. Unfortunately for judging efficiency, the normal risk premium is difficult to define, and varies over time.

10 Market efficiency can also be tested by seeing whether prediction models or forecasting services allow an abnormal return from speculating. However, again because we do not know the equilibrium risk premium, we cannot determine if returns are abnormal for the risk that is faced.

QUESTIONS

1 What is the connection between the gain from netting and the nature of long and short positions in different currencies of the different divisions of a multinational firm?

2 Which of the gains from centralization of cash management are related to foreign exchange transaction costs?

3 What are the differences and similarities between the gain from centralization of cash management via pooling, and the gain via diversification of different currencies?

4 Will allowance for comovement between currencies allow a firm to eliminate foreign exchange risk or foreign exchange exposure?

5 Why might we be suspicious that any apparent covered interest arbitrage opportunity must be due to not considering transaction costs, political risk, taxes, or liquidity?

6 What do the results of efficiency tests which suggest foreign exchange and money markets are efficient imply for cash management?

7 What is the difference between an unbiased predictor and an efficient predictor, and might we distinguish different levels of efficiency according to the information employed?

8 Why might foreign exchange markets be efficient even if you can make a positive return from following the advice of a forecasting service?

BIBLIOGRAPHY

Boothe, Paul, and David Longworth: "Foreign Exchange Market Efficiency Tests," *Journal of International Money and Finance*, June 1986, pp. 135–152.

Goodman, Stephen H.: "No Better than the Toss of a Coin," *Euromoney*, December 1978, pp. 75–85.

Hodrick, Robert J.: *The Empirical Evidence on the Efficiency of Forward and Futures Foreign Exchange Markets*, Harwood Academic Publishers, New York, 1988.

Koedijk, Kees G., and Mack Ott: "Risk Aversion, Efficient Markets and the Forward Exchange Rate," *Review*, Federal Reserve Bank of St. Louis, December 1987, pp. 5–8.

Levich, Richard M.: "On the Efficiency of Markets for Foreign Exchange," in Rudiger Dornbusch and Jacob A. Frenkel (eds.), *International Economic Policy: Theory and Evidence*, Johns Hopkins University Press, Baltimore, 1979.

APPENDIX 12.1: The Pooling Gain from Centralized Cash Management

In order to demonstrate the pooling gain from centralized cash management, we need to define some terms. Let us write the expected working-capital requirements for a multinational operating in the United States and the United Kingdom as W_{US}^* and W_{UK}^*. Let the standard deviations of anticipated cash needs be σ_{US} and σ_{UK}.

W_{US}^* and W_{UK}^* are the amounts, in terms of U.S. dollars, that are most likely to be needed at any time. Let us assume that a multinational wants to be 95 percent sure of having sufficient cash on hand in each country and that working-capital requirements for each country can be represented by a normal curve.

If cash is held separately in the two countries, then to be 95 percent sure of meeting needs in the United States, the multinational must hold as working capital this amount of dollars:

$$W_{US}^* + 1.64\sigma_{US}$$

We add $1.64\sigma_{US}$ to the most likely cash need because with a normal curve, 95 percent of the area under the curve falls to the left of 1.64 standard deviations.[28] Similarly, to be 95 percent sure of meeting needs in the United Kingdom, the company should hold this amount of dollars:

$$W^*_{UK} + 1.64\sigma_{UK}$$

The total need for cash with the localized holdings of working capital is the sum of the two separate needs:

$$(W^*_{US} + W^*_{UK}) + 1.64(\sigma_{US} + \sigma_{UK}) \tag{12A.1}$$

This should be compared with total cash requirements when the funds are centrally held —in London *or* in New York—and moved to where they are required.

If the multinational pools its working-cash balances, the most likely need is the sum of the separate needs:

$$W^*_{US} + W^*_{UK}$$

However, the standard deviation of the pooled needs is not the sum of the individual standard deviations. With total cash needs divided between the United States and the United Kingdom in the proportions θ_{US} and θ_{UK}, the standard deviation of the total need for working capital will be as follows.[29]

$$\sigma = \sqrt{\theta^2_{US} \cdot \sigma^2_{US} + \theta^2_{UK} \cdot \sigma^2_{UK}}$$

where

$$\theta_{US} = \frac{W^*_{US}}{W^*_{US} + W^*_{UK}} \quad \text{and} \quad \theta_{UK} = \frac{W^*_{UK}}{W^*_{US} + W^*_{UK}}$$

[28]This can be shown diagrammatically:

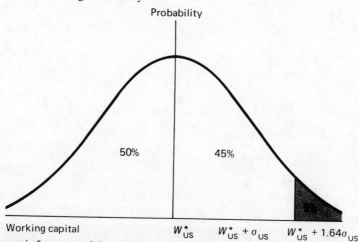

The shaded area is 5 percent of the total area, and so that area to the left of $W^*_{US} + 1.64\sigma_{US}$ is 95 percent of the area under the normal curve.

[29]This follows from the standard result in statistics for the variance of the sum of independent variables. It is shown in most if not all introductory statistics textbooks.

It is assumed for simplicity that cash needs in the two countries are mutually independent. The equation for the value of σ means that the multinational can be 95 percent sure of having sufficient cash by holding

$$(W_{US}^* + W_{UK}^*) + 1.64\sqrt{\theta_{US}^2 \cdot \sigma_{US}^2 + \theta_{UK}^2 \cdot \sigma_{UK}^2} \qquad (12A.2)$$

dollars in its central location.

For example, let us assume that

$$W_{US}^* = \$2.8 \text{ million} \qquad W_{UK}^* = \$5.2 \text{ million}$$

$$\sigma_{US}^2 = \$1.0 \text{ million} \qquad \sigma_{UK}^2 = \$1.8 \text{ milion}$$

Without pooled cash balances, the need—from Equation (12A.1)—for working capital is as follows:

$$(2.8 + 5.2) + 1.64(1.0 + 1.34) = \$11.84 \text{ million}$$

If cash is pooled, the working capital need—given by Equation (12A.2)—is as follows:

$$(2.8 + 5.2) + 1.64\sqrt{(0.35)^2 \times 1.0 + (0.65)^2 \times 1.8} = \$9.54 \text{ million}$$

We find that there are definite gains to be had from centralizing working capital and returning funds that are not immediately needed by local operations to a central pool that serves the cash needs of the countries.

LONGER-TERM FINANCIAL MARKETS AND MANAGEMENT

Part 6 focuses on the international dimensions of investing in stocks and bonds, and of raising capital via the issue of stocks, bonds, and some uniquely international forms of longer-term finance. We give separate treatment to stocks and bonds because the issues encountered with them are different from those encountered in the money markets and with direct investment.[1]

Chapter 13 explains the international financial aspects of stock and bond investments. It is shown how returns from foreign stocks can be decomposed into components due to dividends, to changes in local market values, and to changes in exchange rates. The decomposition of stock returns is used to show the effect of favorable tax treatment of capital gains on the international choice of equities. The chapter also pays considerable attention to the benefits of international portfolio diversification. It is shown that international diversification offers significant advantages over domestic diversification, despite uncertainty about exchange rates. An optional section is included on the international capital-asset pricing model. This model is used to compare the implications of internationally segmented and of integrated capital markets. Chapter 13 ends with a discussion of bond investments, again with a focus on tax and diversification issues.

Chapter 14 concentrates on the costs of raising capital by selling stocks and bonds, as well as by intercompany loans, credit swaps, and government and development-bank financing. The chapter also considers issues relating to the appropriate mix of sources of capital, that is, appropriate capital structure.

[1]Short-term money-market investment and borrowing have been discussed in Chapters 7, 8, 10, and 12. Direct investment, which occurs when the investor has a degree of control by owning more than 10 percent of voting shares, is discussed in Part 7.

The central issues with stocks and bonds are in which countries to sell them, and whether they should be sold by the parent or a subsidiary. With bonds an additional issue is the currency of denomination. The chapter includes a description of the different types of bonds which are encountered in the international bond market, including Eurobonds and multicurrency bonds. It is explained that issuing bonds denominated in foreign currency can increase or decrease exchange-rate exposure and risk. For example, a firm earning a particular currency, and therefore having a long exposure in that currency, will reduce its exposure and risk by dominating its bonds in the foreign currency.

Chapter 14 also explains the nature of two forms of financing that are uniquely international, namely, parallel loans and credit swaps, both of which are designed to circumvent foreign exchange controls. We also consider government and development-bank financing, which, when available, can offer considerable savings. The chapter concludes with a discussion of financial structure, including a consideration of whether an MNC should maintain is global financial structure in overseas subsidiaries, or should conform to local norms. A number of issues relating to financial structure are discussed, including using local debt to reduce political risk, and how agency costs can explain international variations in financial structure.

CHAPTER 13

PORTFOLIO INVESTMENT[1]

There are several aspects of portfolio investment which are unique to the international arena. These peculiarly international aspects have to do with the need to compare investment returns and risks in different countries, and with the benefits of international portfolio diversification. In this chapter we examine the composition of rates of return in different countries, and show how returns involve exchange-rate and local-market components. We also describe the effects of taxes and how international diversification offers special opportunities for reducing risk. The main body of the chapter concentrates on equity investments—those in the stock market—but the chapter concludes with a discussion of returns and risks on bonds.

EQUITY INVESTMENTS

Comparing Investments

A domestic investment in stocks provides a return in two forms: a dividend yield, and a change in market value of the stocks in terms of domestic currency. If we write ρ_{US}^* for the expected average annual dividend yield and e_{US}^* for the expected average annual rate of change in market value, then after n years the expected U.S. dollar value of a $1 investment in U.S. stocks when dividends are reinvested annually at the expected average annual rate ρ_{US}^* is[2]

$$\text{expected dollar value of U.S. stocks after } n \text{ years} = \$(1 + \rho_{US}^* + e_{US}^*)^n \quad (13.1)$$

---

[1]Direct investment, defined in Chapter 4 as being investment in which the investor has control, is discussed separately in Chapter 15.

[2]We note, in terms of the usual statistical notation, that we are not taking $E[(1 + \rho_{US} + e_{US})^n]$, which, because ρ_{US} and e_{US} are random variables, would involve the covariances between ρ_{US} and e_{US}. Rather we are taking $[1 + E(\rho_{US}) + E(e_{US})]^n$, where the averages $E(\rho_{US})$ and $E(e_{US})$ cannot have covariance and where, for brevity, we have used the notation $E(\rho_{US}) = \rho_{US}^*$, $E(e_{US}) = e_{US}^*$.

When a U.S. investor buys foreign stocks, the expected return takes three forms: an expected dividend yield, an expected change in local market value, and an expected change in the exchange rate. We can see how these different components of return affect the expected receipts from a $1 investment in British stocks for n years by first noting that $1 will purchase[3]

$$\pounds \frac{1}{S(\$/\pounds)}$$

If we write the expected average annual dividend yield in Britain as ρ^*_{UK}, and the expected average annual change in market value of the British stocks as e^*_{UK}, then the expected pound value of the investment after n years if dividends are reinvested at the expected average annual rate ρ^*_{UK} is

$$\pounds \frac{1}{S(\$/\pounds)}(1 + \rho^*_{UK} + e^*_{UK})^n$$

Assuming the entire amount is to be repatriated or valued at the end of n years, the expected U.S. dollar value of the British stocks is

expected dollar value of $1 of British stocks after n years

$$= \$ \frac{S^*_n(\$/\pounds)}{S(\$/\pounds)}(1 + \rho^*_{UK} + e^*_{UK})^n \quad (13.2)$$

where $S^*_n(\$/\pounds)$ is the expected spot exchange rate at the end of year n.[4]
We can simplify the expression (13.2) by noting that by definition

$$\frac{S^*_n(\$/\pounds)}{S(\$/\pounds)} \equiv (1 + \dot{S}^*)^n \quad (13.3)$$

where $\dot{S}^*$ is the expected average annual rate of change of the exchange rate. Substituting the identity (13.3) into the expression (13.2) gives

expected dollar value of $1 of British stocks after n years

$$= \$(1 + \dot{S}^*)^n(1 + \rho^*_{UK} + e^*_{UK})^n$$

[3]We ignore foreign exchange transaction costs when we consider long-term investments, because, unlike those for short-term money-market investments, transaction costs should not have a substantial effect on yields when averaged out over a long holding period.

[4]As with the expression (13.1), we are not taking the expected value of (13.2), which would involve covariances, but rather we have taken the expected average annual value of each component of return. Later, when considering the value investors attach to stocks, we do take expectations over portfolios of stocks and therefore consider covariances between components of return.

Ignoring issues of risk, from a U.S. investor's point of view the investment in British stocks will be a better investment than U.S. stocks when

$$(1 + \dot{S}^*)^n (1 + \rho^*_{UK} + e^*_{UK})^n > (1 + \rho^*_{US} + e^*_{US})^n \tag{13.4}$$

Taking the nth root of both sides gives

$$(1 + \dot{S}^*)(1 + \rho^*_{UK} + e^*_{UK}) > (1 + \rho^*_{US} + e^*_{US}) \tag{13.5}$$

The cross-product terms in the expansion of the left-hand side of (13.5) are small if $\dot{S}^*$, ρ^*_{UK}, and e^*_{UK} are small. Therefore, if we expand the two sides of (13.5) and drop the cross-product terms, we have that British stocks are a better investment if

$$1 + \dot{S}^* + \rho^*_{UK} + e^*_{UK} > 1 + \rho^*_{US} + e^*_{US}$$

or if

$$\dot{S}^* + \rho^*_{UK} + e^*_{UK} > \rho^*_{US} + e^*_{US} \tag{13.6}$$

The left-hand side of (13.6) is the approximate expected annual average return from British stocks, and the right-hand side is the approximate expected annual average return on U.S. stocks. The inequality (13.6) can be rearranged into

$$\dot{S}^* > (\rho^*_{US} - \rho^*_{UK}) + (e^*_{US} - e^*_{UK}) \tag{13.7}$$

We can see from (13.7) that British stocks may be a better investment even if they have a lower expected annual average dividend yield plus expected annual average rate of change in market value than U.S. stocks. This will occur when the expected annual average rate of appreciation of the pound more than compensates for the lower local expected return in Britain.

Comparing Equity Investments After Taxes

Some investors receive capital-gains tax treatment on changes in market values of stocks and on foreign exchange gains. Dividends are, however, almost invariably taxed as ordinary income whether they are earned at home or abroad. As in the case of money-market investments, when the different components of income face different tax rates in this way, the relative expected advantages of investments on an after-tax basis may differ from those based on before-tax returns. Indeed, it can be shown that when capital gains receive favorable tax treatment, investors will *ceteris paribus* prefer investments in strong-currency countries, that is, countries whose currencies are expected to appreciate.[5] In

---

[5]As mentioned in Chapter 8, even when the tax rate on capital gains is not lower than the tax rate on income, as in the United States, the ability to defer capital gains until realization means an effectively lower tax rate.

order to see this we can use the before-tax expected annual average returns in Britain and the U.S. on the two sides of the inequality (13.6) to write the approximate expected average annual after-tax returns to a U.S. investor on U.S. and British stocks as

expected after-tax annual average return on U.S. stocks

$$= (1 - \tau_y)\rho_{US}^* + (1 - \tau_k)e_{US}^*$$

expected after-tax annual average return on British stocks

$$= (1 - \tau_y)\rho_{UK}^* + (1 - \tau_k)(e_{UK}^* + \dot{S}^*)$$

Here, τ_y is the tax rate on dividend income from either country, and τ_k is the tax rate on capital gains. British stocks offer a higher after-tax expected annual average return if

$$(1 - \tau_y)\rho_{UK}^* + (1 - \tau_k)(e_{UK}^* + \dot{S}^*) > (1 - \tau_y)\rho_{US}^* + (1 - \tau_k)e_{US}^*$$

or if

$$\dot{S}^* > \frac{1 - \tau_y}{1 - \tau_k}(\rho_{US}^* - \rho_{UK}^*) + (e_{US}^* - e_{UK}^*) \tag{13.8}$$

Let us use the inequality (13.8) to show why, *ceteris paribus*, lower taxes on capital gains make investors prefer investments in strong-currency countries.

For simplicity let us assume $\dot{S}^* > 0$, that is, the pound is expected to appreciate. Let us also assume $\rho_{US}^* - \rho_{UK}^* > 0.$[6] Now let us compare the expected before-tax and after-tax returns from investing in Britain versus the U.S., namely the inequalities (13.7) and (13.8). We see that they differ only in having $(1 - \tau_y)/(1 - \tau_k)$ multiplying $\rho_{US}^* - \rho_{UK}^*$ in (13.8). If an investor faces lower tax rates on capital gains than on dividend income, that is, $\tau_k < \tau_y$, then

$$\frac{1 - \tau_y}{1 - \tau_k} < 1$$

This means that the right-hand side of (13.8) is smaller than that of (13.7). It follows that a given positive value of $\dot{S}^*$ is more likely to satisfy (13.8) than (13.7). That is, investment in Britain, assumed to be a strong-currency country because $\dot{S}^* > 0$, is more likely to be preferred on an after-tax basis—requiring (13.8) to hold—than on a before-tax basis—requiring (13.7) to hold.

---

[6]Taxes can have different effects according to whether a foreign currency is expected to appreciate or depreciate, and according to the expected composition of local market returns. Our purpose here is merely to illustrate one possibility.

The intuition behind our conclusion can be provided by a simple example. Suppose

$$\dot{S}^* = 0.09 \qquad \rho^*_{US} - \rho^*_{UK} = 0.06 \qquad e^*_{US} - e^*_{UK} = 0.04$$
$$\tau_y = 0.4 \qquad \tau_k = 0.2$$

Applying the inequality (13.7) shows that the U.S. stocks would have been preferred on a before-tax basis, because $0.09 < 0.06 + 0.04$. However, applying the inequality (13.8) shows that the British stocks would be preferred on an after-tax basis because $0.09 > 0.75 \times 0.06 + 0.04$, i.e., $0.09 > 0.085$. The reason for this conclusion is that investors prefer a dollar of capital gains to a dollar of dividend income.[7]

The Benefits of International Portfolio Diversification

Because of risk aversion, investors will trade off lower expected return for lower risk. It is a well-established proposition in portfolio theory that whenever there is imperfect correlation between returns on different securities, risk is reduced by maintaining only a portion of wealth in any asset. More generally, by selecting a portfolio according to expected returns and correlations between returns, an investor can achieve minimum risk for a given expected portfolio return, or maximum expected return for a given risk. Furthermore, *ceteris paribus*, the lower the correlations between returns, the greater are the benefits of portfolio diversification.[8]

Within an economy there is some degree of independence of asset returns, and this provides some diversification opportunities for investors who do not venture abroad. However, there is a tendency for the various segments of an economy to feel jointly the influence of overall domestic activity, and for asset returns to respond jointly to prospects for domestic activity and uncertainties about these prospects. This limits the independence of individual security returns, and therefore also limits the gains to be made from diversification within only one country. Because of different industrial structures in different countries, and because different economies do not trace out exactly the same business cycles, there are reasons for smaller correlations of expected returns between investments in different countries than within any one country. This means that foreign investments offer diversification benefits that cannot be enjoyed by investing only at home, and means, for example, that a U.S. investor

---

[7]This conclusion is the capital-market equivalent of the effect of taxes on money-market investments explained in Chapter 8. We might note that if expected after-tax yields are driven to equality by the choices made by those investors who enjoy favorable capital-gains-tax treatment, then those investors paying the same rate of tax on dividends as on capital gains will *ceteris paribus* prefer weak-currency investments.

[8]See Harry Markowitz, *Portfolio Selection: Efficient Diversification of Investments*, John Wiley & Sons, New York, 1959, and James Tobin, "Liquidity Preference as Behavior toward Risk," *Review of Economic Studies*, February 1958, pp. 65–86.

TABLE 13.1

CORRELATION COEFFICIENTS BETWEEN WEEKLY RETURNS ON MAJOR STOCK
MARKETS, 1980 – 1985

Country	France	Germany	Japan	Switzerland	U.K.	U.S.
Canada	0.247	0.274	0.267	0.326	0.472	0.722
France		0.132	0.167	0.203	0.266	0.205
Germany			0.363	0.393	0.341	0.300
Japan				0.294	0.390	0.337
Switzerland					0.266	0.297
U.K.						0.429

Source: Cheol S. Eun and Bruce G. Resnick, "Exchange Rate Uncertainty, Forward
Contracts, and International Portfolio Selection," *Journal of Finance,* March 1988, pp. 197 – 215.

might include British stocks as part of a portfolio, even if they offer lower
expected returns than U.S. stocks: the benefit of risk reduction might more than
compensate for lower expected returns.

Table 13.1 gives the correlations between weekly returns on the stock
markets of seven major countries as calculated by Cheol Eun and Bruce
Resnick.[9] While measured covariances will depend on the period chosen and on
whether the returns are weekly, monthly, or annual, it is clear from the table
that there is considerable independence between stock markets, the correlation
coefficients being well below 1.0. Correlations between markets calculated for
different time periods by other researchers also reveal substantial independence.[10] These calculated correlations suggest there should be clear gains from
international diversification of stock portfolios.

An indication of the size of the gains from including foreign stocks in a
portfolio has been provided by the research of Bruno Solnik.[11] Solnik computed
the risk of portfolios of *n* securities for different values of *n* in terms of the
variance of these portfolios. The variance of a portfolio was compared with the
variance of a typical stock, and—as expected—it was found that the risk
declines as more stocks are added. In addition, Solnik discovered that an
international portfolio of stocks from numerous markets has about half as much
risk as a portfolio of comparable size of only U.S. stocks. This result is shown in
Fig. 13.1. We see that the risk of U.S. stocks for portfolios of over about 20
stocks is approximately 20 percent of the risk of a typical security, whereas the
risk of a well-diversified international portfolio is only about 12 percent of the
risk of a typical security. When Solnik considered other countries which have far

[9]Cheol S. Eun and Bruce G. Resnick, "Exchange Rate Uncertainty, Forward Contracts and
International Portfolio Selection," *Journal of Finance*, March 1988, pp. 197–215.

[10]For example, see Donald Lessard, "World, Country, and Industry Relationships in Equity
Returns: Implications for Risk Reduction through International Diversification," *Financial Analysts
Journal*, January/February 1976, pp. 2–8, and Haim Levy and Marshall Sarnat, "International
Diversification of Investment Portfolios," *American Economic Review*, September 1970, pp. 668–675.

[11]Bruno H. Solnik, "Why Not Diversify Internationally Rather than Domestically?" *Financial
Analysts Journal*, July-August 1974, pp. 48–54.

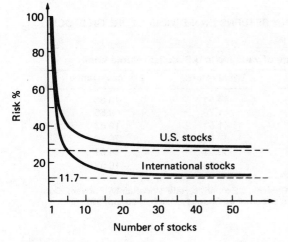

FIGURE 13.1
THE ADVANTAGES OF
INTERNATIONAL
DIVERSIFICATION. (From Bruno H.
Solnik, "Why Not Diversify
Internationally Rather than
Domestically?" *Financial Analysts
Journal,* July – August 1974,
pp. 48 – 54.)

smaller stock markets, he found that the gains from international diversification were, not surprisingly, much larger than for the U.S.[12] The gain from diversification through holding equities of different countries turned out to greatly exceed the gain through holding different equities within a single country.

While there are gains from international diversification because of the degree of independence between foreign and domestic stock returns, there is the possibility of added risk of unanticipated changes in exchange rates when foreign stocks are held. It is therefore important to consider whether the gains from imperfect correlation between stock returns more than compensates for the risk introduced by exchange rates. The extent to which holding foreign stocks increases risk from unanticipated changes in exchange rates depends on both the volatility of exchange rates and on the way exchange rates and stock returns are themselves related. The added risk from exchange rates also depends on whether stocks from only one foreign country, or from a number of different foreign countries, are added to a portfolio of domestic stocks.

Evidence on exchange-rate risk from investing in one country and from a group of countries has been provided by Eun and Resnick.[13] However, before we consider their evidence, we should show the way the volatility of returns on foreign stocks can be decomposed into the volatility of stock returns, the volatility of exchange rates, and the comovement of stock returns and exchange rates.

Let us write the expected dollar rate of return to a U.S. holder of British stocks as

$$\text{expected dollar return on U.K. stocks} = \dot{S}^* + R_{\text{UK}}^* \qquad (13.9)$$

[12] This is because in smaller countries there is less opportunity to diversify within the country than in larger countries.

[13] Eun and Resnick, *op. cit.*

TABLE 13.2
COMPOSITION OF U.S. DOLLAR WEEKLY RETURNS ON INDIVIDUAL FOREIGN STOCK
MARKETS, 1980 – 1985

Country	Percentage of variance in U.S. dollar returns from		
	Exchange rate	Local return	2 × covariance
Canada	4.26	84.91	10.83
France	29.66	61.79	8.55
Germany	38.92	41.51	19.57
Japan	31.85	47.65	20.50
Switzerland	55.17	30.01	14.81
U.K.	32.35	51.23	16.52

Source: Cheol S. Eun and Bruce G. Resnick, "Exchange Rate Uncertainty, Forward Contracts, and International Portfolio Selection," Journal of Finance, March 1988, pp. 197 – 215.

Here, R_{UK}^* is the expected return in terms of pounds, which consists of the expected dividend return plus the expected change in market value in pounds. The variance of the dollar return on U.K. stocks is[14]

$$\text{var}(\$ \text{ return on U.K. stocks}) = \text{var}(\dot{S}) + \text{var}(R_{UK}) + 2\,\text{cov}(\dot{S}, R_{UK}) \quad (13.10)$$

This expression shows that the variance of the U.S. dollar rate of return on British stocks can be decomposed into the variance of the dollar-pound exchange rate, the variance of the return on British stocks in pounds, and the covariance between the exchange rate and the return on British stocks.

Table 13.2 shows the percentage composition of the U.S. dollar return from holding the stock-market indexes of six foreign countries, when each market is held on its own. The first column gives $\text{var}(\dot{S})$ as a percentage of the variance of the dollar return from each foreign market, the second column gives $\text{var}(R)$ as a percentage of the variance of the dollar return, and the final column gives 2 times the covariance between the exchange rate and associated local return. We see that on its own the volatility in the exchange rate can contribute anything from less than 5 percent to over 50 percent of the volatility of dollar returns. We can also see that the covariance between exchange rates and local-currency returns contributes to the variance of U.S. dollar returns. That is, movements in exchange rates are reinforced by movements in local stock markets. For example, on average, when the pound is declining, so is the British stock-market index. This means that exchange rates add to the volatility both directly in being volatile themselves, and indirectly by being positively related to local stock-market returns.

The situation for a portfolio of stocks from different countries is essentially the same as that for stocks from an individual country. This is shown in Table

---

[14]$\dot{S}$ and R_{UK} are not average returns over a period of time, but rather are per-period returns which, because they are random variables, can have covariance.

TABLE 13.3
COMPOSITION OF WEEKLY U.S. DOLLAR RETURN ON AN EQUALLY WEIGHTED PORTFOLIO
OF SEVEN COUNTRIES STOCK MARKETS, 1980–1985

Percentage of variance in U.S. dollar return from		
Exchange rate	**Local return**	**2 × covariance**
32.20	42.88	24.92

Source: Cheol S. Eun and Bruce G. Resnick, "Exchange Rate Uncertainty, Forward Contracts, and International Portfolio Selection," *Journal of Finance*, March 1988, pp. 197–215.

13.3. The table shows the composition of the U.S. dollar returns from holding an equally weighted portfolio of the stock markets of seven countries: the U.S. and the six countries in Table 13.2. The contribution of exchange-rate volatility is that due to the volatility of each exchange rate and to the covariance between exchange rates. Similarly, the contribution of volatility of local returns is that due to the volatility of each stock market and to the covariance among stock markets. Finally, the contribution of the covariance is that due to the covariance between each exchange rate and each market return. We see from the table that the exchange rate contributes a substantial fraction of the volatility of dollar returns via the direct effect of the exchange-rate volatility itself, and via the indirect effect of positive covariance between exchange rates and local market returns. It would not appear that diversification among currencies has a substantial effect in reducing the *proportion* of risk attributable to changes in exchange rates.

With so much volatility directly or indirectly resulting from unanticipated changes in exchange rates, it is important to ask whether this cancels the benefits from international diversification attributable to the presence of some independence between stock-market returns in different countries. The answer is no. One reason is that it is possible to diversify internationally without adding exchange-rate exposure—by hedging in the forward market, by borrowing in the foreign currencies, or by using futures or currency options. The hedges would have to be based on the exposure in each currency, as given by regression coefficients according to Chapter 9.[15] A second reason international diversification is beneficial despite exchange-rate variability is that, even without hedging, the variance of the dollar return on an internationally diversified portfolio of stocks remains lower than the variance of the expected dollar return on holding the domestic stock market. This has been shown by Bruno Solnik, who compared the variance of returns on portfolios of U.S. stocks with the variance of

[15] It was explained in Chapter 9 that the exposure on a foreign stock depends on how the stock price covaries with the exchange rate, and consequently the exposure is not simply the market value of the stock. The appropriate hedge would have to take this into account. We should note that while exposure at any moment can be eliminated by hedging, it is not feasible to eliminate exposure. This is because the market value of foreign stocks varies, so that the hedge will not always be the correct amount, unless, of course, the hedge is changed continuously.

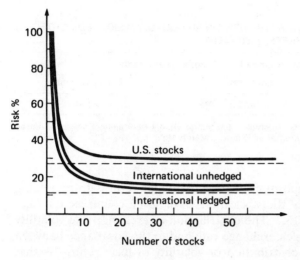

FIGURE 13.2
THE ADVANTAGES OF
INTERNATIONAL
DIVERSIFICATION WITH AND
WITHOUT EXCHANGE RISK.
(From Bruno H. Solnik, "Why Not
Diversify Internationally Rather
than Domestically?" *Financial
Analysts Journal*, July – August
1974, pp. 48 – 54.)

returns on internationally diversified portfolios, both when not hedging ex-change-rate exposure and when hedging on the forward market.[16] Different-sized portfolios of U.S. stocks and internationally diversified stocks were compared, with the results shown in Figure 13.2. This figure reveals that even though there is exchange-rate risk—given by the gap between the hedged and unhedged curves—it is still better to diversify internationally than to hold only U.S. stocks. It is clear that the gain from having independence of returns due to holding securities of different countries in a portfolio more than offsets any exchange-rate risk that this implies, even when not hedging. And of course, when hedged, the benefits from international portfolio diversification are even greater.

Many researchers other than Eun and Resnick, and Solnik, have studied the gains from international diversification, and while all agree on the existence of gains, they differ substantially in the estimated size of these gains. One major reason the estimates of gains are different is that some of the studies use past returns over different sample periods to form efficient, internationally diversi-fied portfolios, rather than using the distribution of future returns as is called for by the theory.[17] The problem introduced by using past returns and covari-ances for forming efficient diversified portfolios is that if, for example, the past return in Belgium was very high during the estimation period, Belgian stocks

---

[16]Solnik, *op cit*. We might note that Solnik's hedges on the international portfolios are not the optimal hedges as given by regression coefficients, but rather the value of the foreign stocks at the time of investment. Consequently, Solnick's results, if anything, are an understatement of the benefits of hedged international diversification.

[17]An **efficient portfolio** is one which is constructed to have maximum expected return for a given variance. The studies by Solnik and by Eun and Resnick are not based on efficient portfolios, and consequently are not subject to the problems we are about to describe.

will be heavily weighted in the internationally diversified portfolio.[18] This is the case even though it may have been just by chance that Belgian stocks did so well. It is then little surprise that the internationally diversified portfolio with its abnormally high proportion of high-return Belgian stocks outperforms the domestic portfolio when applied to past data. The problem is that there is an upward bias in the estimated benefits of international diversification due to. basing international portfolios on past returns rather than the distribution of future returns. This bias can be verified by taking the internationally diversified portfolio that is formed using past-return data during a given interval of time, and seeing how it performs out of sample, that is, over other intervals. The results of this type of test suggest that the benefits of international diversification have indeed been overestimated in many studies.[19]

In an attempt to partially overcome the problem of using past returns to construct portfolios for judging the gain from international diversification, Phillippe Jorion used statistical procedures which "shrink" past returns in different countries toward the mean return for all countries combined.[20] This means, for example, that if the observed past return for Belgium happened to have been very high, a realistic investor is assumed to expect a future return less than the past return, and somewhere between the past return for Belgium and the past average return for all countries combined. The results from Jorion's study show that the gains from international diversification in earlier studies have been greatly overstated. His conclusions are supported by the fact that the portfolios he constructed outperform portfolios based on unadjusted past returns when their returns are compared with out-of-sample data. Nevertheless, Jorion shows there is still some gain from international portfolio diversification.

One direct way of judging whether international diversification provides benefits is to examine the performance of those who have diversified internationally with those who have not; clearly, those diversifying internationally have had to put their portfolios to test outside any sample period used for forming portfolios. In this regard we can consider the performance of the Putnam Management Company with its internationally diversified portfolio.[21] This performance is shown in Table 13.4. Between March 24, 1971 and June 30, 1975, a higher return and a lower variance were experienced with the international portfolio than in the New York market. Putnam has shown that the indepen-

---

[18] Belgian stocks will receive high weighting if their return is high relative to the risk they contribute to the international portfolio. The risk is a function of the covariance between Belgian and other returns.

[19] See Phillippe Jorion, "International Diversification with Estimation Risk," *Journal of Business*, July 1985, pp. 259–278.

[20] Jorion, *op. cit.*

[21] See Gary F. Bergstrom, "A New Route to Higher Returns and Lower Risks," *Journal of Portfolio Management*, Autumn 1975, pp. 30–38. Of course, we must be careful in attaching significance to results for particular individual performances, because they might not be representative. That is, there might be a large number of poorly performing international portfolios. In addition, the variance of particular portfolios may not represent their risk. Estimates of risk should allow for covariance with the relevant market portfolio.

TABLE 13.4
INTERNATIONAL PORTFOLIO VERSUS NEW YORK MARKET, MARCH 24, 1971 – JUNE 30, 1975

Total international portfolio return	+30.8%
S & P 500 — total return	+11.6%
NYSE composite — total return	+8.4%
Standard deviation of international portfolio	2.0% per week
Standard deviation of NYSE composite	2.7% per week

Source: Gary F. Bergstrom, "A New Route to Higher Returns and Lower Risks," *Journal of Portfolio Management*, autumn 1975, pp. 30 – 38.

dence of the markets of different countries can be valuable in portfolio management.

International Capital Asset Pricing

The central international financial question concerning the pricing of assets, and hence their expected rates of return, is whether they are determined in an integrated, international capital market, or in local, segmented markets. If assets are priced in an internationally integrated capital market, expected yields on assets will be in accordance with the risks of the assets when they are held in an efficient, internationally diversified portfolio, such as the world market portfolio. This means that while in such a situation it is better to diversify internationally than not to, the expected yields on assets will merely compensate for their systematic risk when this is measured with respect to the internationally diversified world portfolio. That is, with internationally integrated capital markets the expected returns on foreign stocks will be appropriate for the risk of these stocks in an internationally diversified portfolio. There will be no "free lunches" from foreign stocks due to higher expected returns for their risk. On the other hand, if assets are priced in segmented capital markets, their returns will be in accordance with the systematic risk of their domestic market. This means that if an investor happens to have an ability to circumvent whatever it is that causes markets to be segmented, this investor will be able to enjoy special benefits from international diversification. It is consequently important for us to consider whether assets are priced in internationally integrated or in segmented capital markets. However before doing this it is useful to review the theory of asset pricing in a domestic context, because if we do not understand the issues in the simpler domestic context, we cannot understand the international dimensions of asset pricing.

The domestic variant of the **capital asset pricing model** (CAPM), familiar from the so-called beta analysis used in security selection, can be written as follows:[22]

$$R_j^* = R_f + \beta(R_m^* - R_f) \tag{13.11}$$

where

$$\beta = \frac{\text{cov}(R_j, R_m)}{\text{var}(R_m)} \tag{13.12}$$

and where

R_j^* = equilibrium or required expected return on security or portfolio j,

R_f = risk-free rate of interest,

R_m^* = expected return on the market portfolio,

$\text{cov}(R_j, R_m)$ = covariance between security j and the market m,

$\text{var}(R_m)$ = variance of the màrket portfolio.

The essential point of the CAPM is that a security or portfolio will offer an equilibrium expected rate of return, R_j^*, equal to the risk-free interest rate plus a risk premium that is linearly related to the risk that the asset or portfolio contributes to the market as a whole, $\text{cov}(R_j, R_m)/\text{var}(R_m)$. This is the risk which cannot be diversified away—**systematic risk**. If a security compensated for more than the systematic risk, it would be a bargain, and investors would buy it and combine it with other securities, causing the risk it contributes to be small relative to its contribution to the expected return. The buying of the security would raise its market price and lower its expected return until it was no longer a bargain, even within a diversified portfolio.

The implications of the CAPM for security of portfolio returns is illustrated graphically in Fig. 13.3. The figure shows the expected return on an asset or portfolio of assets, R_j^*, on the vertical axis. The degree of systematic risk, β, is measured on the horizontal axis. The figure shows a **securities-market line** which gives the expected rate of return that is offered for taking different amounts of systematic risk. For example, an asset with no systematic risk—one for which all risk can be eliminated by diversification—will offer only the risk-free rate of return. That is, when $\beta = 0$, as is seen from Equation (13.11) and in Figure 13.3, $R_j^* = R_f$. Similarly, an asset with the same systematic risk as the market will offer the same expected return as the market. That is, when $\beta = 1$, as is seen from Equation (13.11), $R_j^* = R_m^*$.

With the domestic variant of the CAPM explained, we can clarify the conclusion stated earlier about internationally integrated versus segmented markets. If assets are priced in internationally integrated capital markets, expected yields are given off the securities market line that is constructed with

---

[22] For the derivation of the capital asset pricing model, see William Sharpe, "Capital Asset Pricing: A Theory of Market Equilibrium under Conditions of Risk," *Journal of Finance*, September 1964, pp. 424–447. The model is explained in many finance textbooks and is only stated here.

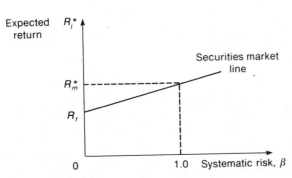

FIGURE 13.3
THE RELATIONSHIP BETWEEN
A SECURITY'S OR A
PORTFOLIO'S EXPECTED
RETURN AND SYSTEMATIC
RISK. Assets offer a higher
expected return for a greater
systematic risk, β. An asset or
portfolio with no systematic risk
will offer an equilibrium return of
the risk-free interest rate R_f,
while an asset or portfolio with
the same risk as the market will
offer an equilibrium return equal
to the expected return on the
market, R_m^*.

R_m^* equal to the expected return on the world market portfolio.[23] If this is the case, then by investing in foreign assets investors will not receive any abnormal return; the return is the amount required to compensate for the systematic risk of the asset in an internationally diversified portfolio.[24] On the other hand, if assets are priced in domestically segmented capital markets, their expected returns are given on the securities market line that is constructed with R_m^* equal to the expected *domestic* market return. If this is the case, then by diversifying internationally it might be possible to find foreign securities with expected returns above the (domestically oriented) securities market line—provided the investor can overcome the reasons for market segmentation.

There is an alternative way of viewing the implications of integrated versus segmented capital markets for the benefits of international diversification. This is based on the risk-return framework that is used frequently in the domestic context to describe diversification benefits.

Figure 13.4 shows the expected returns on the vertical axis, and the total risk, given by the standard error σ of expected returns, on the horizontal axis. The upward-sloping part of the curve, or **envelope**, gives the best combination of expected returns and risk that can be achieved with different portfolios; combinations along the envelope above the minimum σ are those of efficient portfolios. As before, R_f is the risk-free interest rate, and R_m^* is the expected return on the market portfolio; again as before, the interpretation of R_f and R_m^* depends on whether we are considering integrated or segmented capital markets. We note that R_m^* is the tangency point on a straight line drawn between the risk-free rate and the envelope of efficient portfolios' risks and returns. This line is the **capital market line**, which gives the expected returns and risks of combinations of the risk-free asset and the market portfolio. It is a well-known

[23] Of course, we cannot expect to include all assets such as human capital, real estate, and so on. See Richard Roll, "A Critique of the Asset Pricing Theory's Test; Part I: On Past and Potential Testability of the Theory," *Journal of Financial Economics*, March 1977, pp. 129–176.

[24] Indeed, by not investing internationally, investors will face more risk than is necessary.

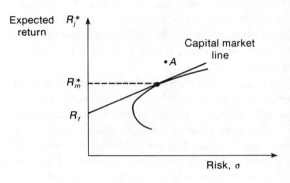

FIGURE 13.4
THE RELATIONSHIP BETWEEN EXPECTED RETURN AND TOTAL RISK. If assets are priced in segmented markets, it may be possible for an investor to enjoy a combination of expected return and risk above the capital market line *for a particular country* if the investor can overcome the causes of segmentation and diversify internationally. If assets are priced in internationally integrated capital markets, then by not diversifying internationally an investor will be accepting higher risk and / or lower return than necessary.

proposition in finance that an investor cannot do better than select such a combination and therefore be somewhere on the capital market line.

If capital markets are internationally integrated, then we can interpret R_f in Figure 13.4 as the (common) risk-free rate, and R_m^* as the expected world market return. That is, with integrated capital markets the international CAPM is merely an extension of the domestic CAPM where we reinterpret R_m^* as the expected world market return. Indeed, if the capital market is integrated, by not holding the world market portfolio the investor will be below the capital market line in Figure 13.4; the investor could reduce risk and increase expected return by holding the world portfolio. On the other hand, if capital markets are segmented, so that we can interpret R_m^* as the domestic market expected return, then by overcoming the obstacles to foreign investment an investor might be able to create a risk-return portfolio that is above the domestic capital market line. For example, the investor might be able to reach a point such as A and enjoy gains from international diversification, since these are not priced by the market.

Segmentation of capital markets can occur for a variety of different reasons. The most obvious cause of segmentation is the presence of legal barriers to foreign investment. These barriers can take the form of outright restrictions on investing abroad, or can involve higher rates of tax on income from foreign than from domestic investment. However, even if the majority of investors are subject to legal barriers, assets could still in principle be priced according to integrated markets. This is because some investors, such as giant multinational firms with operations in numerous countries, might be able to circumvent the legal barriers.

A slightly less obvious form of market segmentation occurs as a result of so-called **indirect barriers**.[25] Indirect barriers include the difficulty of finding and interpreting information about foreign securities and reluctance to deal

---

[25]Phillippe Jorion and Eduardo Schwartz, "Integration vs. Segmentation in the Canadian Stock Market," *Journal of Finance*, July 1986, pp. 603–616.

with foreigners. As with legal barriers, those who can overcome the indirect barriers through, for example, access to better information or freedom from xenophobia, might be able to enjoy abnormal returns by diversifying internationally. That is, those who can overcome the barriers might achieve a risk-return combination such as that at A in Figure 13.4.

When we interpret market segmentation in the more general terms of having different expected returns or risks according to where an investor lives, it becomes clear that as well as legal and indirect barriers, segmentation can arise because prices of what investors consume relative to the returns they earn change differently in different countries.[26] In such a case the buying power of returns would depend on where investors live. It turns out, however, that this cause of segmentation requires that PPP does not hold. This is because, for example, if PPP holds and investors in one country, say Canada, happen to earn a lower nominal return than investors elsewhere because of an appreciation of the Canadian dollar, then the lower nominal return to Canadians is compensated for by lower inflation in Canada; an appreciation of the Canadian dollar lowers prices in Canada.[27] It follows that if PPP holds, securities will be priced according to Equation (13.11) in which the market return is the global market return, provided of course there are no legal or indirect causes of segmentation.

When PPP does not hold, there is exchange-rate risk, and markets are segmented with different real rates of return for investors according to where they live; the changes in exchange rates will not be exactly offset by changes in prices. The effect of having exchange-rate risk for the asset pricing relationship in Equation (13.11) is to make the international CAPM more complex than a mere reinterpretation of the domestic CAPM.[28]

Evidence on whether securities are priced in an integrated or a segmented capital market has been provided by Phillippe Jorion and Eduardo Schwartz.[29] They began by noting that integration means expected returns depend only on international factors, and in particular the systematic risk of securities vis-à-vis the world market. That is, if markets are completely integrated, the R_j^*'s of different securities in Figure 13.3 should depend only on their β's calculated vis-à-vis the world market return. On the other hand, if markets are completely segmented, expected returns will depend on only domestic factors, and in particular the β's vis-à-vis the domestic market return. By isolating the international and domestic β's Jorion and Schwartz were able to show that domestic

---

[26] For an excellent account of this interpretation of segmentation see Michael Adler and Bernard Dumas, "International Portfolio Choice and Corporation Finance: A Synthesis," *Journal of Finance*, June 1983, pp. 925–984.

[27] The appreciation of the Canadian dollar means that to Canadians, there is a depreciation of the U.S. dollar, pound, yen, and so on. This would reduce the return on foreign securities to Canadians, but reduce the prices of imported products that Canadians buy.

[28] For accounts of the international CAPM in the presence of exchange rate risk due to deviations from PPP see Piet Sercu, "A Generalization of the International Asset Pricing Model," *Revue Française de Finance*, June 1980, pp. 91–135, and René Stulz, "A Model of International Asset Pricing," *Journal of Financial Economics*, December 1981, pp. 383–406. See also the excellent survey in Adler and Dumas (1983), *op cit.*

[29] Jorion and Schwartz, *op cit.*

factors are relevant for expected returns on Canadian securities, suggesting some degree of market segmentation.[30]

Jorion and Schwartz also separated out interlisted Canadian stocks—those trading simultaneously on both U.S. and Canadian stock exchanges—and found the same result, namely that returns are related to systematic risk vis-à-vis the Canadian market. This suggests that the segmentation is not attributable to reporting of information on Canadian stocks, because Canadian companies with shares trading on U.S. exchanges must report similar information to that reported by U.S. companies.

Limited further support for segmentation based on an examination of interlisted stocks has been provided by Gordon Alexander, Cheol Eun, and S. Janakiramanan.[31] They begin by stating that if markets are segmented, the listing of a security abroad should reduce the security's expected rate of return. This should come about as a result of a jump in the stock price at the time the market learns of the additional listing. They find evidence consistent with a lower expected return after overseas listing for their sample of non-Canadian firms. However, they do not detect the implied jumps in stock prices and find insignificant effects for Canadian firms.

An alternative, although even more indirect, way of testing whether markets are integrated or segmented is to see whether securities of companies that can overcome segmentation have returns more related to systematic risk vis-à-vis the international than vis-à-vis the domestic market. For example, if U.S. multinational corporations can invest in countries where private U.S. citizens cannot, then the returns on U.S. multinationals' securities should be more closely related to their β's vis-à-vis the international market than vis-à-vis the U.S. market, whereas returns on other U.S. securities should not. Indeed, the extent to which the U.S. multinationals' securities are priced according to international or domestic risk should depend on their international orientation, judged, for example, by the fraction of sales made overseas. One test of this was performed by Tamir Agmon and Donald Lessard, who found some weak indication that multinationals can achieve something investors cannot achieve themselves.[32] However, it has been pointed out that the U.S. market index itself contains

[30]It has been argued that, if investors in the different countries care about different measures of inflation, so that PPP cannot hold, then the pricing of domestic factors does not necessarily mean markets are segmented. See Mustafa N. Gultekin, N. Bulent Gultekin, and Alessandro Penati, "Capital Controls and International Capital Markets Segmentation: The Evidence from the Japanese and American Stock Markets," paper presented to European Finance Association Meetings, Madrid, 1987.

[31]Gordon J. Alexander, Cheol S. Eun, and S. Janakiramanan, "International Listings and Stock Returns: Some Empirical Evidence," *Journal of Financial and Quantitative Analysis*, June 1988, pp. 135–151.

[32]Tamir Agmon and Donald R. Lessard, "Investor Recognition of Corporate International Diversification," *Journal of Finance*, September 1977, pp. 1049–1056. The results of Agmon and Lessard disagree with those of Bertrand Jacquillat and Bruno Solnik, "Multinationals are Poor Tools for Diversification," *Journal of Portfolio Management*, winter 1978, pp. 8–12; H. L. Brewer, "Investor Benefits from Corporate International Diversification," *Journal of Financial and Quantitative Analysis*, March 1981, pp. 113–126; and A. J. Senschak and W. L. Beedles, "Is Indirect International Diversification Desirable?," *Journal of Portfolio Management*, winter 1980, pp. 49–57.

companies which earn a substantial fraction of their earnings overseas, so that the β's of securities vis-à-vis the U.S. market are not really measuring systematic risks vis-à-vis the domestic market. That is, the R_m^* for the U.S. market includes a substantial amount of the effect of international returns, so that studies comparing the use of R_m^* for an international index and a U.S. index understate the role of internationalization of investment by U.S. multinationals. When U.S. stock indexes are constructed in a way that removes the international returns in them, the results show a more significant benefit from the ability of multinational corporations to invest overseas.[33] This suggests that markets are segmented for the ordinary U.S. investor.

BOND INVESTMENTS

Domestic versus Foreign Bond Returns

In our discussion of money-market borrowing and investing in Chapter 7 we pointed out that the ability to choose between short-term securities denominated in different currencies would tend to force yields covered against exchange risk towards equality. That is, there is a tendency towards interest parity in the money market. If interest parity also holds in the bond market, it will not matter which countries' bonds are purchased. However, while the choice between bonds of different currencies of denomination does tend to move yields towards equality, in the case of bonds there are reasons why significant differences in yields may persist. Firstly, it is difficult if not impossible to hedge bond investments in the forward market; forward contracts with maturities of more than two years are rare, whereas bonds have maturities of 5 to 10 years or longer. Secondly, political risks are larger on bonds than on short-term money-market securities because it is difficult to forecast election outcomes and political trends over the longer terms of bonds. Thirdly, taxes can be extremely important in the bond decision, resulting in substantial differences in after-tax yields. Fourthly, liquidity considerations are more relevant on bonds than on money-market securities.[34]

While we have seen how bond yield differences can occur in our discussion of real changes in exchange rates in Chapter 9, we may well reconsider the issue here because for one thing, our discussion of real changes in exchange rates did not consider taxes. We also did not consider risk.

The expected (and actual) U.S.-dollar receipts from $1 invested for n years in an n-year-maturity U.S.-dollar-denominated compound-interest bond with

[33]See John S. Hughes, Dennis E. Logue and Richard J. Sweeney, "Corporate International Diversification and Market Assigned Measures of Risk and Diversification," *Journal of Financial and Quantitative Analysis*, November 1975, pp. 627–637.

[34]The reader will note that this list of reasons for interest disparity, namely, political risk, taxes and liquidity, was also met in the context of the money market in Chapter 8. The absence of the ability to hedge was not used in Chapter 8, because forward hedging is feasible in the money market.

coupons received and reinvested annually are[35]

$$\text{expected dollar receipts on U.S. \$ bond} = \$(1 + r_{US})^n \quad (13.13)$$

where r_{US} is the average annual compound U.S.-dollar interest rate. If \$1 is to be placed in a compound-interest British-pound-denominated bond, the first step is to purchase pounds. The \$1 will buy £$1/S(\$/£)$. This will become

$$\pounds \frac{1}{S(\$/£)}(1 + r_{UK})^n$$

after n years at r_{UK} per annum with coupons received and reinvested annually. If the expected exchange rate at the end of n years is $S_n^*(\$/£)$, the expected U.S.-dollar value of receipts on each original \$1 invested in the compound interest bond, when repatriated after n years is

$$\text{expected dollar receipts on pound bond} = \$\frac{S_n^*(\$/£)}{S(\$/£)}(1 + r_{UK})^n \quad (13.14)$$

If we write, as before,

$$\frac{S_n^*(\$/£)}{S(\$/£)} \equiv (1 + \dot{S}^*)^n \quad (13.3)$$

where $\dot{S}^*$ is the expected annual average rate of change of the exchange rate, we can say that pound-denominated compound-interest bonds offer a higher expected return if

$$(1 + \dot{S}^*)^n (1 + r_{UK})^n > (1 + r_{US})^n \quad (13.15)$$

Taking the nth root of both sides and rearranging gives

$$\dot{S}^* > \frac{1 + r_{US}}{1 + r_{UK}} - 1$$

or

$$\dot{S}^* > \frac{r_{US} - r_{UK}}{1 + r_{UK}} \quad (13.16)$$

Ignoring considerations of risk, if the inequality (13.16) holds, pound-denominated bonds will be preferred by a U.S. investor, and if the reverse inequality holds, then dollar-denominated bonds will be preferred.

---

[35]When the bond may not be held to maturity, there is an expected return/loss from expected changes in the market value of the bond that we do not consider here. We also ignore default risk.

If r_{UK} is small, we can write (13.16) to a close approximation as

$$\dot{S}^* > r_{US} - r_{UK}$$

or

$$\dot{S}^* + r_{UK} > r_{US} \tag{13.17}$$

We see that pound-denominated bonds offer a higher expected dollar return if the expected annual average exchange gain and interest rate on the British pound bond exceed the U.S.-dollar interest rate.

We can modify the inequality (13.17) in order to compare expected after-tax returns on bonds. If gains/losses from changes in exchange rates are taxed at the rate τ_k, and interest earnings are taxed at the rate τ_y, then pound-denominated bonds offer a higher expected return than U.S.-dollar bonds on an after-tax basis if

$$(1 - \tau_k)\dot{S}^* + (1 - \tau_y)r_{UK} > (1 - \tau_y)r_{US}$$

or

$$\dot{S}^* > \frac{1 - \tau_y}{1 - \tau_k}(r_{US} - r_{UK}) \tag{13.18}$$

As in the case of stocks, bonds denominated in strong currencies, that is, currencies for which $\dot{S}^* > 0$, are more likely to be preferred on an after-tax than on a before-tax basis if capital gains are taxed at a lower rate than interest income. This is because if, for example, the pound is a strong currency, then $r_{US} - r_{UK} > 0$. With $\tau_y > \tau_k$, we have $(1 - \tau_y)/(1 - \tau_k) < 1$. This means that the tax factor, $(1 - \tau_y)/(1 - \tau_k)$, increases the chance that the inequality (13.18) will hold.

Risk Considerations with Bond Investment

What we have said about stocks concerning risk and international diversification is relevant for bonds. For example, the variance in the domestic-currency value of a foreign-currency bond can be decomposed into the variance of the exchange rate, the variance of the local-currency market value, and (twice) the covariance between the exchange rate and the market value.[36] Similarly, markets will price bonds and thereby set their expected returns according to the risk the bonds contribute to an efficiently diversified portfolio. Indeed, as in the case of stocks, the expected returns on bonds will depend on whether bondholders

---

[36] The covariance will be positive if central banks "lean against the wind," raising interest rates in an effort to support their currency when it depreciates. This is because when this occurs, lower market prices of foreign currency denominated bonds typically occur when the foreign currency is depreciating.

diversify internationally or domestically, that is, on whether capital i. internationally integrated or segmented. Again, as with stocks, segmentatio. occur as a result of legal or indirect restriction on foreign investment, or as a result of (real) exchange-rate risk due to departures from PPP.

Our next task is to consider the other side of stock and bond returns, namely the cost of raising capital. In the next chapter we shall consider the costs of stock and bond capital along with the costs of other forms of capital and questions about capital structure.

SUMMARY

1 The expected return on domestic equities consists of the expected dividend return plus the expected change in market value. The expected return on foreign equities consists of the expected dividend return, the expected change in local market value, and the expected change in the exchange rate.

2 Currency appreciation can compensate for a lower foreign expected dividend return and change in market value.

3 When investors face different tax rates on capital gains versus dividend income, after-tax comparisons of returns differ from before-tax comparisons. With favored capital-gains-tax treatment, investors prefer investments in strong currencies, that is, currencies they expect will appreciate.

4 Because different countries' economic performances are not perfectly synchronized, and because there are other differences between nations such as in the types of industries they have, there are benefits from international diversification of portfolios beyond those of diversification within a single country. Therefore, investments in foreign countries might be made even if they offer lower expected returns than some domestic investments; the diversification benefits may more than compensate for lower expected returns.

5 The evidence shows considerable independence between different countries' stock returns, suggesting large gains from international diversification. Portfolios that are internationally diversified do indeed prove to have lower volatility than portfolios of domestic stocks of the same size.

6 Even if internationally diversified portfolios are not hedged against exchange-rate risk, they show lower volatility than domestically diversified portfolios. This is despite the fact that exchange rates are an important component of overall volatility of foreign stocks, both directly, and indirectly via their covariance with local market returns.

7 Many early studies of the gains from international diversification overstated the gains because they constructed portfolios on the basis of past actual returns rather than the distribution of future returns.

8 If assets are priced in internationally integrated capital markets, their returns are appropriate for their risk when combined with the world portfolio. Then, by not diversifying internationally and holding the world portfolio, an investor is accepting more risk than is necessary for a given expected return, or lower expected return than is necessary for a given risk.

9 If capital markets are segmented, those who can invest abroad can enjoy abnormal returns for the risk taken. This is because assets are priced only to compensate for the risk in internationally undiversified portfolios.

10 Multinational corporations' shares appear to be priced according to their systematic risk vis-à-vis an internationally diversified portfolio. Investors appear to value the ability of multinationals to invest abroad, overcoming the barriers which the investors themselves face on making overseas investments.

11 Foreign-currency-denominated bonds will be preferred to domestic-currency-denominated bonds if the expected appreciation of the foreign currency exceeds any interest advantage that may be provided by bonds denominated in the investor's own currency. With lower tax rates on capital gains than on interest, investors prefer strong-currency-denominated bonds.

12 The risk considerations on bonds are similar to those on stocks.

QUESTIONS

1 Using $\rho_{US}^* = 0.05$, $e_{US}^* = 0.08$, $\rho_{UK}^* = 0.04$, $e_{UK}^* = 0.06$, and $\dot{S}^* = 0.0280$, show how substantial is the difference between applying the approximate inequality (13.6) and applying the exact inequality (13.5) for judging foreign versus domestic investment.

2 Why does favorable tax treatment on capital gains increase the attractiveness of stocks from strong-currency countries?

3 If expected stock returns were equalized on an after-tax basis, and capital gains were taxed less than dividends, how would expected returns differ on a before-tax basis?

4 Why are the benefits from international diversification overstated if efficient portfolios are formed on the basis of past returns?

5 Why is it that there are gains from international diversification without hedging exchange-rate risk even though exchange rates contribute a substantial *proportion* of overall risk?

6 Could we judge whether markets are segmented or integrated by examining rules governing the international flow of capital?

7 Why can we consider capital markets to be segmented if PPP is violated?

8 How is the expected equilibrium return on bonds likely to vary with the covariance between the local-currency market value of bonds and the exchange rate?

BIBLIOGRAPHY

Adler, Michael, and Bernard Dumas: "Optimal International Acquisitions," *Journal of Finance*, March 1975, pp. 1–19.

_____: "International Portfolio Choice and Corporation Finance: A Synthesis," *Journal of Finance*, June 1983, pp. 925–984.

Agmon, Tamir, and Donald R. Lessard: "Investor Recognition of Corporate International Diversification," *Journal of Finance*, September 1977, pp. 1049–1055.

Cohen, Kalman, Walter Ness, Robert Schwartz, David Whitcomb, and Hitoshi Okuda: "The Determinants of Common Stock Returns Volatility: An International Comparison," *Journal of Finance*, May 1976, pp. 733–740.

Eun, Cheol S., and Bruce G. Resnick: "Exchange Rate Uncertainty, Forward Contracts, and International Portfolio Selection," *Journal of Finance*, March 1988, pp. 197–215.

Frankel, Jeffery A.: "The Diversifiability of Exchange Risk," *Journal of International Economics*, August 1979, pp. 379–393.

Grauer, Frederick L., Robert H. Litzenberger, and Richard E. Stehle: "Sharing Rules and Equilibrium in an International Capital Market under Uncertainty," *Journal of Financial Economics*, June 1976, pp. 223–256.

Hughes, John S., Dennis E. Logue, and Richard J. Sweeney: "Corporate International Diversification and Market Assigned Measures of Risk and Diversification," *Journal of Financial and Quantitative Analysis*, November 1975, pp. 627–637.

Jorion, Phillippe, and Eduardo Schwartz: "Integration vs. Segmentation in the Canadian Stock Market," *Journal of Finance*, July 1986, pp. 603–614.

Lessard, Donald R.: "World, Country, and Industry Relationships in Equity Returns: Implications for Risk Reduction through International Diversification," *Financial Analysts Journal*, January–February 1976, pp. 2–8.

Levy, Haim, and Marshall Sarnat: "International Diversification of Investment Portfolios," *American Economic Review*, September 1970, pp. 668–675.

Serçu, Piet: "A Generalization of the International Asset Pricing Model," *Revue Française de Finance*, June 1980, pp. 91–135.

Solnik, Bruno H.: "Why Not Diversify Internationally Rather than Domestically?," *Financial Analysts Journal*, July–August 1974, pp. 48–54.

————: "International Arbitrage Pricing Theory," *Journal of Finance*, May 1983, pp. 449–457.

Stultz, René: "A Model of International Asset Pricing," *Journal of Financial Economics*, December 1981, pp. 383–406.

CHAPTER 14

INTERNATIONAL ASPECTS OF LONG-TERM FINANCING

In this chapter we consider the international dimensions of medium- and longer-term financing.[1] We begin by explaining the central international financial issues involved in each of the major methods of raising capital. We consider the international aspects of raising capital via stocks, bonds, parallel loans between corporations, credit swaps between banks and corporations, and loans from host governments and development banks. We shall see the importance of exchange-rate risk, taxes, political risk, and issuance costs for the form of financing chosen. The chapter concludes with a discussion of the appropriate relative amounts of each type of financing, that is, the appropriate **financial structure**.

EQUITY FINANCING

The main international financial question concerning equity financing is in which country stocks should be issued. A second question concerns the legal vehicle that should be used for raising equity capital; should this be done by a subsidiary, and if so, where should this subsidiary be registered?

The Country in Which Shares Should Be Issued

Clearly, shares should be issued in the country in which the best price can be received, net of issuing costs. If for the time being we assume the costs of issue to be the same everywhere, the country in which the best price can be received

---

[1]Short-term financing, which involves raising funds for less than 1 year, was discussed in Chapters 11 and 12 as well as in our treatment of the interest parity theorem in Chapter 7.

for the shares is the country in which the cost of equity in terms of the expected rate of return is lowest. There is no concern about risk from the equity *issuer's* perspective, other than to the extent that through equity *buyer's* concern for systematic risk, the riskiness of shares issued affects the required expected rate of return and hence the price received for the shares; the required expected rate of return of shareholders is, of course, the expected rate of return paid by the firm.

It should be clear from our discussion of equity investment in the previous chapter that if capital markets are integrated the expected cost of equity capital will be the same in every country. That is, the expected return on the company's shares, R_j^*, given on the securities-market line in Figure 13.3, or from the international CAPM using the global market return R_m^* in (13.11), will be the same everywhere.[2]

If capital markets are segmented, the expected returns on the same security *could* be different in different markets. A company might then be able to receive more for its shares in some markets than in others. Of course, when a company's shares are listed simultaneously in different countries, the share price will have to be the same everywhere up to transaction costs of arbitrage. However, the cause of segmentation may prevent arbitrage. Furthermore, a company may not be considering simultaneous issue in different countries, but rather, the single country in which to float an issue.

Ceteris paribus, the higher are savings relative to investment, the lower is the cost of capital. This means, for example, that a country like Japan, which has a very high savings rate, should have a lower cost of capital than the U.S., which has a very low savings rate, provided investment opportunties are similar. Of course, if markets are integrated, we shall not see these different costs of capital, because those countries which would have had low costs of capital in segmented markets have outflows of capital until the rates of return are the same as elsewhere. Similarly, those countries which would have had high costs of capital with segmentation would have inflows of capital until their rates of return are the same as elsewhere.

Sometimes, as a result of capital-market segmentation, it can be advantageous to issue shares simultaneously in two or more countries' equity markets. Such share issues are called **Euroequity issues**. The scale of Euroequity issues has varied widely from year to year, reaching as high as $18 billion in 1987, before dropping below half this level in 1988. The idea for simultaneously floating equities in different countries' markets is based on the view that any one market can absorb only so much of a company's stock. This was the argument for the initial multicountry offerings of two Canadian multinationals, Alcan and Bell Canada Enterprises, which in 1983 simultaneously sold shares in Canada, the U.S., and Europe. It should be clear that for the rationale for

---

[2] We recall from the previous chapter that the expected average annual U.S. dollar rate of return on shares trading in, for example, Britain includes the expected appreciation of the pound as well as the expected change in the pound price of the shares and the expected dividend yield.

Euroequities to be valid there must be some market segmentation. If not, it would be possible for a company such as Alcan or Bell Canada to sell shares in Canada that would be as readily bought by Americans and Europeans as if the shares were sold on U.S. or European stock exchanges. Of course, as we pointed out in the previous chapter, segmentation could be caused by such a factor as differential reporting requirements. Then, it might well be that more shares can be sold to Americans by issuing the shares in the U.S. and therefore necessarily satisfying U.S. reporting rules. Indeed, it is probably because U.S. reporting rules are more stringent than those on stock exchanges in many smaller countries that so many foreign firms have found it necessary to list in the U.S. in order to tap the huge U.S. equity market; American and other nationals would otherwise be more wary about buying the stocks.

While some non-U.S. firms have listed on U.S. stock exchanges—mostly the New York Stock Exchange and the American Stock Exchange, which list numerous Canadian firms—the shares of many foreign firms trade indirectly as **American Depository Receipts** (ADRs). The idea of trading ADRs originated with the Morgan Guarantee Bank, but several other U.S. banks, including Citibank and the Bank of New York, have become involved. What happens is that the bank holds the foreign shares, receives dividends, reports, and so on, but issues claims against the shares it holds. These claims—the ADRs—then generally trade in the relatively unregulated over-the-counter market. This has the advantage for foreign firms of reducing listing fees and the information that they must report.

When we mentioned that the highest price a firm could obtain for its shares, net of issuance costs, is in the market with the lowest required rate of return, we assumed that the costs of issue are the same everywhere. The correct rule for where to issue shares is that they should be sold where the price *net of issue costs* is the highest.

In fact, issue costs do vary and can be an important consideration. The costs of underwriting can be several percent of the value of funds raised, and can vary significantly between financial markets. Generally, the lowest costs are faced in large equity markets such as that of the United States. This may explain why a substantial number of foreign companies have sold shares on the New York Stock Exchange and the American Stock Exchange. Indeed, as Figure 14.1 shows, there has been a substantial increase in the number of foreign shares listed on the New York Stock Exchange.

The Vehicle of Share Issue

A firm that has decided to issue shares abroad must decide whether to issue them directly, or to do so indirectly via a subsidiary located abroad. There is frequently a motive to use a specially established financing subsidiary to avoid the need to withhold tax on payments made to foreigners. For example, until 1984 many U.S. firms established subsidiaries in the Netherlands Antilles and other **tax havens** to avoid having to withhold 30 percent of dividend or interest income paid to foreigners. The U.S. financing subsidiaries took advantage of a

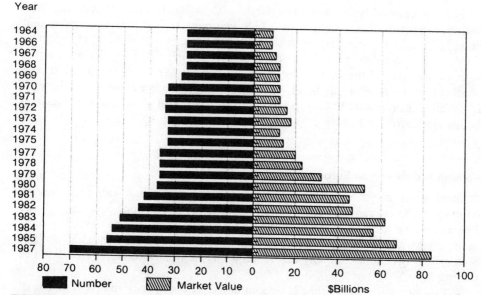

FIGURE 14.1
NUMBER AND SIZE OF FOREIGN SECURITIES LISTED ON THE NYSE. *Source:* New York Stock Exchange, *Fact Book,* issues for 1965 – 1988.

ruling of the U.S. Internal Revenue Service that if 80 percent or more of a corporation's income is earned abroad, then dividends and interest paid by the corporation are considered foreign and not subject to the need to withhold. The financing subsidiaries were known as **80-20 subsidiaries**. To the extent that foreign creditors or shareholders of U.S. companies could not receive full credit for taxes withheld, they would pay more for securities issued by U.S. 80-20 subsidiaries than for the securities of the parent company in the U.S.

In the case of U.S. firms, the need to use 80-20 subsidiaries ended in 1984 with the passage of the Deficit Reduction Act. Among other things this act of the U.S. Congress repealed the requirement for U.S. firms to withhold on income paid to foreigners, and meant that parent companies could sell securities directly. Therefore, in the U.S. the question of the vehicle of share issue is no longer a concern to the firm. However, this is not the case in every country, and tax havens are still used. The need to use subsidiaries in tax havens when raising capital is dependent on the specific tax rules in the parent company's home country.

BOND FINANCING

The same two issues arise with bond financing as with equity financing, namely:

1 the country of issue, and
2 the vehicle of issue.

However, an extra issue arises with bond financing, namely the *currency* of issue.

The currency of issue is not the same as the country of issue, although the two may coincide. For example, if a U.S. company sells a pound-denominated bond in Britain, the currency of issue is that of the country of issue. However, if a U.S. company sells a U.S.-dollar-denominated bond in Britain, the currency of issue is not that of the country of issue. In the former of these situations the bond is called a **foreign-pay bond**, or more briefly, a **foreign bond**; in the latter it is called a **Eurobond**. Let us provide a more general description of foreign bonds and Eurobonds.

Foreign Bonds versus Eurobonds

A foreign-pay bond, or foreign bond for short, is a bond sold in a foreign country in the currency of the country of issue. This currency is foreign to the issuer, whence the name. For example, a Canadian firm or a provincial government might sell a foreign bond in New York denominated in U.S. dollars. Similarly, a Brazilian company might sell a German-mark-denominated bond in Germany.

A Eurobond is a bond that is denominated in a currency that is not that of the country in which it is issued. For example, a U.S.-dollar-denominated bond sold outside of the United States—in Europe or elsewhere—is a Eurobond, a **Eurodollar bond**. Similarly, a sterling-denominated bond sold outside of Britain is a Eurobond, a **Eurosterling bond**. We see that Eurobonds are the long-term equivalent of Eurocurrency deposits and loans. A Eurobond differs from a foreign bond, which is sold in the country in whose currency it is issued.

Foreign bonds are usually sold by brokers in the country in which they are issued. Eurobonds are sold by international syndicates of brokers, because they are generally sold simultaneously in a number of countries. The syndicates will normally have a lead manager which underwrites the largest proportion of the issue, and a number of smaller members, although some syndicates have co-lead managers. Table 14.1 shows the names of the top 20 lead managers in the international bond market.

Selecting the Currency of Issue

Whether a firm issues a foreign bond, a Eurobond, or an ordinary domestic bond, it must decide on the bond's currency of denomination.[3] Of course, with foreign bonds the currency of denomination is that of the country of issue, so deciding on the currency of denomination is the same as deciding on the country of issue; with Eurobonds the currency and the country or countries of issue must both be decided.

---

[3] When a company issues a domestic bond, as when a U.S. firm sells a U.S.-dollar-denominated bond in the U.S., the company has consciously or unconciously decided on the currency of issue. In principle the U.S. firm could have denominated its bond in any of a number of currencies.

TABLE 14.1
TOP 20 LEAD MANAGERS IN THE INTERNATIONAL BOND MARKET, 1988

Rank	Bank / firm	Amount, millions of $	No. of issues	Share, %
1	CSFB / Credit Suisse	21,702.53	167	9.33
2	Nomura Securities	19,586.19	152	8.42
3	Deutsche Bank	12,401.19	88	5.33
4	Union Bank of Switzerland	11,364.35	117	4.88
5	Daiwa Securities	10,849.31	87	4.66
6	Merrill Lynch Capital Markets	10,219.61	55	4.39
7	Yamaichi Securities	8,690.31	71	3.74
8	Nikko Securities	8,277.73	69	3.56
9	JP Morgan Securities	7,967.81	41	3.42
10	Swiss Bank corp. Investment Banking	7,666.89	91	3.30
11	Banque Paribas	7,149.37	94	3.07
12	Salomon Brothers	7,088.82	44	3.05
13	Goldman Sachs International	6,310.53	38	2.71
14	SG Warburg	6,206.33	45	2.67
15	Bankers Trust International	6,029.30	50	2.59
16	Industrial Bank of Japan	5,824.65	54	2.50
17	Morgan Stanley International	5,286.78	44	2.27
18	Dresdner Bank	3,810.96	24	1.64
19	Commerzbank	3,483.34	31	1.50
20	Hambros Bank	2,676.35	46	1.15

Source: Euromoney, March 1989.

Suppose that Aviva is neutral to exchange-rate risk and is choosing between denominating a bond in pounds and in dollars.[4] For simplicity, let us assume all payments are made at maturity.[5] Writing r_{US} for the annual interest cost of a dollar-denominated bond, Aviva's eventual payment on a n-year bond per dollar raised is

$$\$(1 + r_{US})^n$$

Each $1 raised by selling a pound-denominated bond means raising £1/$S(\$/£)$. Assuming again that all payments are made at maturity, Aviva's

[4]Later we drop the assumption of risk neutrality, and show how having pound receivables can make pound borrowing *preferred* on grounds of foreign-exchange exposure and risk reduction.

[5]If we drop this assumption and allow for periodic coupons, the algebra is more complex but the conclusion is the same.

payment in terms of pounds per dollar raised on an n-year bond is

$$\pounds \frac{1}{S(\$/\pounds)} (1 + r_{UK})^n$$

where r_{UK} is the annual interest cost on a pound-denominated bond. The expected dollar cost of this payment is

$$\$ \frac{S_n^*(\$/\pounds)}{S(\$/\pounds)} (1 + r_{UK})^n$$

where $S_n^*(\$/\pounds)$ is the expected exchange rate at the end of year n.[6] Aviva will prefer floating the pound bond if

$$\frac{S_n^*(\$/\pounds)}{S(\$/\pounds)} (1 + r_{UK})^n < (1 + r_{US})^n \qquad (14.1)$$

Writing

$$S_n^*(\$/\pounds) \equiv S(\$/\pounds) \cdot \left[1 + \dot{S}^*(\$/\pounds)\right]^n$$

where $\dot{S}^*(\$/\pounds)$ is the expected average annual rate of change of the spot exchange rate, the inequality (14.1) becomes

$$\left[1 + \dot{S}^*(\$/\pounds)\right]^n (1 + r_{UK})^n < (1 + r_{US})^n$$

Taking the nth root of both sides, rearranging, and ignoring the cross-product term $\dot{S}^*(\$/\pounds) \cdot r_{UK}$, we have[7]

$$r_{UK} + \dot{S}^*(\$/\pounds) < r_{US} \qquad (14.2)$$

That is, if the inequality (14.2) holds, Aviva should denominate its bond in the pound rather than the dollar. (If Aviva sells a pound bond in Britain, the bond is a foreign bond, and if it sells the pound bond in some country other than Britain, it is a Eurosterling bond.) Alternatively, if interest rates and expected exchange rates are such that

$$r_{UK} + \dot{S}^*(\$/\pounds) > r_{US} \qquad (14.3)$$

Aviva should sell a U.S.-dollar-denominated bond, whether this be sold in the

---

[6] We use the expected future spot rate rather than the forward rate because forward cover may not be available for the maturity of a long-term bond. Of course, so far we have assumed Aviva is neutral to any exchange-rate risk involving the bond.

[7] As we have noted before, the cross-product term is typically very small.

U.S., making it an ordinary domestic bond, or outside the U.S., making it a Eurodollar bond.

For example, suppose as before that Aviva is risk-neutral and the borrowing costs and Aviva's expected change in the exchange rate are as follows:

r_{US}	r_{UK}	$\dot{S}*(\$ / £)$
10%	14%	−5%

That is, Aviva sees a higher borrowing cost for the firm on pound-denominated bonds, but also expects a decline in the foreign exchange value of the pound against the dollar of 5 percent per annum over the life of the bond. It would be advantageous to denominate in terms of pounds, assuming Aviva is not averse to risk involving exchange rates, because in the example

$$r_{US} > r_{UK} + \dot{S}*(\$/£)$$

Ex post, the actual exchange rate will often change by a considerable amount over the life of a bond, creating a potential for sizable gains or losses. In other words, actual changes can deviate markedly from the changes which had been expected by the firm. History is full of examples of currencies which have changed in value against the dollar by substantial amounts. Even some of the major currencies have moved considerably in value over a number of years. Relatively small annual changes in exchange rates build up into very large changes over the life of long-term bonds.

To show how great the mistake can be, we can examine the results of a survey by William R. Folks, Jr., and Josef Follpracht. These results are shown in Table 14.2. Folks and Follpracht examined the cost of a number of foreign-currency-denominated bonds issued by U.S.-based multinational firms over the period July 1969 to December 1972. The table allows us to compare the coupon rates with the eventual effective annual costs computed as of March 1976 or at the bonds' maturities. We can see that the appreciation of the German mark, Swiss franc, Dutch guilder, and Luxembourg franc made the borrowing costs of bonds considerably higher than the rates given by the coupons. We cannot tell whether the costs were high compared with the dollar rates that were available when the bonds were originally sold, but there is good reason to believe that they were. The only foreign-currency bond which turned out to be advantageous as of March 1976 was the pound-sterling bond. The fall in value of the pound sterling reduced the effective dollar repayment cost by over 2.7 percent per annum. The conclusion depends on where the examination ends, but it does show that what may appear to be a cheap debt may end up being expensive.

Because of the potential for large unanticipated costs when borrowing by issuing bonds in currencies that rapidly appreciate, some nontrivial advantage may be required before any added exposure by foreign-currency borrowing is considered worthwhile. In such a case, our criteria (14.2) and (14.3) need some

TABLE 14.2
COSTS OF FOREIGN-CURRENCY BONDS

Currency	Issue	Coupon rate, % / yr	Before-tax cost of borrowing % / yr
Deutsche mark	Studebaker-Worthington	$7\frac{1}{4}$	14.69
	International Standard Electric	7	12.31
	TRW	$7\frac{1}{2}$	12.38
	Tenneco	$7\frac{1}{2}$	12.33
	Tenneco	$7\frac{3}{4}$	12.77
	Kraftco	$7\frac{1}{2}$	12.27
	Continental Oil	8	15.83
	Transocean Gulf	$7\frac{1}{2}$	12.50
	Firestone	$7\frac{3}{4}$	11.83
	Philip Morris	$6\frac{3}{4}$	9.87
	Goodyear	$7\frac{1}{4}$	10.44
	Teledyne	$7\frac{1}{4}$	10.44
Swiss franc	Burroughs	$6\frac{1}{4}$	12.31
	Standard Oil (California)	$6\frac{1}{4}$	12.42
	Goodyear	7	13.69
	American Brands	$6\frac{1}{2}$	13.08
	Texaco	$6\frac{3}{4}$	13.37
	Cities Services	$7\frac{1}{4}$	19.27
Dutch guilder	General Electric	$8\frac{1}{4}$	20.08
	GTE	$8\frac{1}{4}$	19.44
	IBM	8	16.46
	Cities Service	8	17.65
	International Harvester	8	17.65
	Philip Morris	$7\frac{1}{2}$	12.67
	Sperry Rand	$6\frac{1}{2}$	10.44
	Holiday Inns	$6\frac{1}{2}$	10.62
	Teledyne	$6\frac{1}{4}$	10.27
	Standard Brands	$6\frac{1}{2}$	10.85
	Textron Atlantic	$6\frac{3}{4}$	11.21
Pound sterling	Amoco	8	5.29
Luxembourg franc	International Standard Electric	$6\frac{1}{2}$	7.85

Source: William R. Folks, Jr., and Josef Follpracht, "The Currency of Denomination Decision for Offshore Long-Term Debt: The American Experience," working paper, Center for International Business Studies, University of South Carolina, 1976.

modification. For example, if management determines that any added foreign exchange exposure and risk will be worth taking only with an expected 2-percent saving, we must revise (14.2) to the following:

$$r_{US} > r_{UK} + \dot{S}^*(\$/£) + 0.02 \tag{14.4}$$

Only when (14.4) holds will the expected borrowing cost be sufficiently lower in pounds to warrant borrowing in that currency. For example, if r_{US} is 10 percent, r_{UK} is 14 percent, and $S^*(\$/£)$ is -5 percent (a 5-percent-per-annum expected depreciation of the pound), then the exposure and risk of borrowing in pounds will not be warranted, for although the criterion (14.2) is met, the revised criterion (14.4) is not.

When foreign-currency bonds do add to exposure and risk, the required risk premiums will have to be established by management. During times of greater economic uncertainty and potential volatility in foreign exchange markets, higher premiums should generally be required to compensate for the greater risk. Borrowing in a foreign currency involves risk because the actual rate of change of the exchange rate, $\dot{S}(\$/£)$ in the dollar-pound case, will in general differ from the *ex ante* expectation, $\dot{S}^*(\$/£)$. If $\dot{S}(\$/£) > \dot{S}^*(\$/£)$, this will make the *ex post* borrowing cost greater than the *ex ante* cost.

For example, if as before we have $r_{US} = 10$ percent, $r_{UK} = 14$ percent, and $\dot{S}^*(\$/£) = -5$ percent, then by using the straightforward *ex ante* criteria in inequalities (14.2) and (14.3), we know that the U.S. borrower facing these particular conditions should borrow in pounds. Suppose that this is done and that *ex post* we discover that $\dot{S}(\$/£) = -2$ percent. The actual cost of borrowing in pounds will be

$$r_{UK} + \dot{S}(\$/£) = 0.14 - 0.02 = 0.12 \qquad \text{or 12 percent per annum}$$

Having borrowed in pounds will in retrospect turn out to have been a bad idea via-à-vis the 10-percent dollar interest rate.

In general, if it turns out that $\dot{S}(\$/£)$, the actual per annum change in the exchange rate, has been such that

$$r_{UK} + \dot{S}(\$/£) > r_{US}$$

then we know that borrowing in pounds was a mistake. We see that it is necessary to compare the actual, not the expected, per-annum change in the exchange rate with the interest differential. A management-determined risk premium such as the 0.02 premium we used in writing the revised criterion in inequality (14.4) will help to ensure that correct decisions are made. The larger the required premiums, the more often the decision will in retrospect appear correct, but larger premiums also mean missing many opportunities, and they will never guarantee *ex post* correct decisions.

Borrowing with Foreign-Source Income

There may be *less* foreign exchange exposure and risk involved in foreign currency than in domestic currency borrowing when the borrower is receiving income in foreign exchange and is facing a long exposure in the foreign currency. That is, foreign-currency receivables can require a *negative* premium when borrowing in foreign exchange because exposure is reduced. We have already pointed out in Chapters 9 and 12 that firms receiving foreign income can hedge by borrowing foreign funds in the money market. The point is even more valid with long-term borrowing and is extremely important for firms which have sizable foreign operations. When a steady and predictable long-term income is received in foreign currency, it makes sense to denominate some long-term payments in that same currency. The amount of debt that should be denominated in each foreign currency will depend on the size of income in that currency, and also on the extent that the firm's income is exposed. As we shall show in Chapter 18, the exposure depends on the elasticity of demand, the flexibility of production, the proportion of inputs that are imported, and so on. That is, it is not simply a matter of borrowing enough in a foreign currency so that debt payments match income in the currency.

An example of a situation where the sale of bonds denominated in foreign exchange will reduce foreign exchange exposure and risk involves a Canadian firm that sells Canadian resources in world markets at contracted amounts in U.S. dollars.[8] If lumber or coal is sold by the Canadian firm to, for example, the U.S. or Japanese market at prices stated in U.S. dollars, then the firm faces a long exposure in U.S. dollars, and it makes good sense for the firm to borrow in New York, Europe, or Canada in U.S. dollars. Then the repayments on the debt can come out of the firm's U.S.-dollar revenues. Alternatively, losses on the dollars earned after a U.S.-dollar depreciation are matched by a gain in the form of reduced debt when this is translated into Canadian dollars. Similarly, if an Australian manufacturer is selling to Japan in yen, it makes sense to borrow with yen-denominated bonds, or if a Venezuelan oil exporter is selling to Chile in dollars, it makes good sense to borrow by selling U.S.-dollar-denominated bonds in the Eurobond market or in the United States.

Currency Speculation and Tax Considerations

When bonds are denominated in a foreign currency for which there is no matching income stream, the firm is speculating: it has created an exposure. Firms may be tempted to denominate in currencies that they expect to appreciate by less than the bond buyers expect. That is, in the notation of the criteria (14.2) and (14.3), for the firm it may be that

$$r_{US} > r_{UK} + \dot{S}^*(\$/£),$$

[8]Virtually all natural-resource exports—oil, coal, gas, minerals, and lumber—are sold at U.S. dollar prices. This reduces the foreign exchange problem for U.S.-based firms that sell or buy natural resources.

TABLE 14.3
DISTRIBUTION OF CURRENCIES OF ISSUE OF FOREIGN BONDS PLUS EUROBONDS

Issue currency	Percentage of total				
	1984	1985	1986	1987	1988
U.S. dollar	62.8	54.0	53.9	38.8	41.7
Swiss franc	12.3	11.3	10.7	12.9	11.4
German mark	6.2	8.5	8.0	8.0	10.2
British pound	5.4	4.0	4.6	7.8	8.6
Japanese yen	5.5	9.1	10.4	13.7	8.4
Canadian dollar	2.1	1.6	2.3	3.4	5.6
E.C.U.	2.8	5.2	3.4	4.0	4.9
Australian dollar	0.3	1.6	1.5	4.9	3.3
French franc	—	1.9	1.7	1.3	1.3
Dutch guilder	1.7	1.3	1.3	1.1	1.3
Other	0.9	2.3	2.2	4.1	3.3
Total	100.0	100.0	100.0	100.0	100.0
	U.S.-dollar equivalent (billions)				
	113.9	191.4	233.4	169.8	204.2

Source: OECD *Financial Market Trends*, 1986, 1988.

whereas for the bond buyers the reverse inequality may hold. In this case we shall find firms willing to borrow in pounds, while at the same time bond buyers are prepared to buy pound bonds. With different lenders and borrowers having their own expectations of $\dot{S}^*(\$/£)$, and of changes in other exchange rates, it is little surprise that there are willing sellers and buyers of foreign-currency-denominated bonds, even though the buyers or the sellers, or both, may be speculating.

The suggestion that some speculation is occurring in the Eurobond and foreign bond markets is indicated by the statistics on currencies of denomination of bonds sold in the international bond markets in 1984 versus 1988. These statistics are shown in Table 14.3. The year 1984 was a year in which the U.S. dollar was viewed by many as very strong, having appreciated substantially during the previous four years. We see that in 1984, over 60 percent of the bonds sold in the international bond market—consisting of Eurobonds plus foreign bonds—were dominated in the U.S. dollar. Presumably, bond buyers were more confident than bond issuers were that the dollar would continue to appreciate. In 1985 the dollar began a rapid depreciation, falling 50 percent or more against some major currencies in the following two years. By 1988 the dollar had moved from being viewed as a strong currency to being viewed as a weak currency, while the Japanese yen and German mark had become highly desired because of their very rapid appreciations. Table 14.3 shows that between 1984 and 1988 dollar-denominated bonds declined from 62.8 to 41.7 percent of the total of bonds floated, while yen- and mark-denominated bonds both grew in importance. Presumably bond buyers in 1988 were less confident about the dollar than were bond issuers. The amount of the switching in the currencies of denomination suggests currency speculation, because it is highly unlikely that the currencies of incomes of firms issuing the bonds shifted as much as did the currencies of denomination of the bonds they issued.[9]

While the switching of currencies of denomination between 1984 and 1988 may have been due to changes in the balances of beliefs between bond buyers and issuers, it may also have been due to favorable tax treatment of capital gains versus interest income. As we saw in the previous chapter, bond buyers who pay a lower tax on capital gains than on ordinary interest income will prefer a dollar of capital gain from foreign-currency appreciation to a dollar of interest income. This induces them to buy bonds denominated in strong currencies, such as the dollar in 1984, or such as the yen or mark in 1988. On the other hand, bond issuers who can deduct the full cost of their bonds, including the interest paid and the foreign currency they must buy to make interest and principal payments, will be indifferent between interest rates and expected changes in exchange rate. This would cause the switching of denomination shown in Table 14.3, as can be seen by considering an example.

Suppose that

$$r_{US} = 12\% \qquad r_{JP} = 5\% \qquad \dot{S}^*(\$/\yen) = 6\%$$
$$\tau_k = 0.2 \qquad \tau_y = 0.4$$

where $\dot{S}^*(\$/\yen)$ is the expected appreciation of the yen by both bond issuers and buyers, r_{JP} is the interest rate on yen bonds, τ_k is the tax rate on foreign exchange gains of bond buyers, and τ_y is the tax rate on ordinary income, including interest, of both bond buyers and bond issuers. The after-tax expected returns from dollar and from yen bonds to bond buyers are

$$(1 - 0.4) \times 0.12 = 7.2\% \qquad \text{(dollar bonds)}$$
$$(1 - 0.4) \times 0.05 + (1 - 0.2) \times 0.06 = 7.8\% \qquad \text{(yen bonds)}$$

The buyers therefore prefer yen bonds to dollar bonds. However, to borrowers who can deduct the full cost of bond capital the after-tax costs are

$$(1 - 0.4) \times 0.12 = 7.2\% \qquad \text{(dollar bonds)}$$
$$(1 - 0.4) \times 0.05 + (1 - 0.4) \times 0.06 = 6.6\% \qquad \text{(yen bonds)}$$

The issuers therefore also prefer the yen bonds. We see that tax factors can explain the popularity of strong-currency-denominated bonds among bond buyers and sellers.

---

[9]It could also be due to changes in who was doing the borrowing, and to tax benefits as described below.

Other Bond-Financing Considerations

Issue Cost   Bond flotation costs are lower in some financial markets than in others. Because flotation costs are nontrivial, the differences in costs between financial markets can influence the country in which bonds are floated.[10] Firms should approach a number of bond underwriters situated in different countries before determining where to issue bonds. With markets in most of the European financial centers, as well as in Asia and North America, and with considerable variation in the flotation costs within and between these financial centers, the benefits of shopping around can be substantial.

Issue Size   Another factor bond issuers should consider when issuing bonds is the size of the issue relative to the sizes of issues handled in different markets. The New York and London capital markets can handle very large individual bond issues. In many of the other capital markets of the world, a $100 million bond issue would be considered large, and a $400 million bond issue would be huge. In New York or London, such issues are not uncommon. Indeed, the volume of funds handled by some of the bigger institutions such as the pension funds and insurance companies is such that these institutions can often buy an entire bond issue that is privately placed with them. The bond-issue size that the New York and London markets can handle and the lower costs of issuing bonds under private placement make New York and London attractive markets for large American and foreign borrowers, even when the interest cost of funds is a little higher than elsewhere.[11]

Multicurrency Bonds

Types of Multicurrency Bonds   Not all Eurobonds are denominated in a single currency. Rather, some Eurobonds are **multicurrency bonds**. A multicurrency bond gives the lender the right to request repayment in one or two or more currencies. The amounts of repayment are often set equal in value at the exchange rates in effect when the bond is issued. If, during the life of the bond, exchange rates change, the lender will demand payments in the currency that has appreciated the most or depreciated the least. This reduces the risk to the lender in that it can help him or her avoid a depreciating currency. It does, however, add to the borrower's risk.

A variant of the multicurrency Eurobond using special exchange rates is the **unit-of-account bond**, such as the European unit-of-account (EUA) bond. This

---

[10]Rodney Mills and Henry Terrell have shown that front-end fees on Eurobonds on an interest-equivalent basis account for an average of approximately 20 percent of one year's annual return, and vary between 9 percent and 43 percent. See Rodney H. Mills and Henry S. Terrell, "The Determination of Front-End Fees on Syndicated Eurocurrency Credits," International Finance Discussion Paper Number 250, Board of Governors of the Federal Reserve System, Washington, D.C., undated.

[11]The importance of transaction costs and the size of borrowing in encouraging Canadian borrowers to look at the United States capital market is examined by Karl A. Stroetmann in "The Theory of Long-Term International Capital Flows and Canadian Corporate Debt Issues in the United States," unpublished Ph.D. dissertation, University of British Columbia, 1974.

type of bond has a unit of account established as a reference unit. The exchange rates vis-à-vis the unit are changed only infrequently. These might be DM2.0 per EUA, £0.40 per EUA, and so on. The borrowers borrow a certain number of EUAs. Clearly, the funds will be taken in the currency that has the highest current market premium over the parity exchange rate within the unit. But what the borrowers gain in their option of taking the borrowed funds in the currency of choice is lost in making interest payments and repaying the principal. Here the lender has the option of selecting the currency; the lender will also take the currency at the highest premium vis-à-vis the parities of the unit of account.[12]

To take a straightforward situation, suppose that the EUA is defined only in German marks and sterling as DM2.00 per EUA and £0.50 per EUA and that a borrower sells EUA 1 million worth of bonds. Suppose that when the bonds are sold, there are DM 3.60 per pound. The borrower can take DM 2 million or £500,000 at his or her discretion. At DM 3.60/£, the DM 2 million will by £555,556, and so the borrower will take marks. Suppose that at the time of repaying the principal the spot rate is DM 5.00/£. The lender can receive either DM 2 million or £500,000. Since DM 2 million will buy only £400,000 at DM 5.0/£, the lender will take the £500,000. The same criterion will be used to select the currency for interest payments.

There are other multicurrency types of borrowing that are even more involved than borrowing with EUAs. There are units of account with currency components that are weighted by the volume of international trade, GNP, and so on, of the various countries. These include **currency cocktails** such as the SDR unit. The SDR is worth 0.42 U.S. dollars plus 0.19 German marks plus 0.15 Japanese yen plus 0.12 British pounds plus 0.12 French francs. Another cocktail is the **Eurco**.

Currency cocktails can offer significant savings. For example, in January 1981 the rate on a 5-year SDR-denominated bond offered by Nordic Investment Bank was approximately 11.5 percent, while at the same time the rate on a straight 10-year U.S.-dollar bond offered by Du Pont of Canada was 13.69 percent, and the rate on a 7-year bond offered by GM's offshore finance subsidiary, General Motors Acceptance Corporation (or GMAC) Overseas Finance N.V., was 12.87 percent. While the rates are not strictly comparable, the lower rate on the SDR bond shows that investors value the diversification of currency cocktails. They will be particularly desirable during unstable times. SDR-denominated bonds date back to 1975.[13]

The Rationale for Multicurrency Bonds Bond buyers can form their own multicurrency bond portfolios by combining different bonds, each of which is

---

[12] There are prescribed procedures for revising conversion rates between EUAs and the component currencies. Some of these have been described by Peter Lusztig and Bernhard Schwab in "Units of Account and the International Bond Market," *Columbia Journal of World Business*, spring 1975, pp. 74–79.

[13] For more on SDR bonds, see "Slimmed-Down SDR Makes Comeback: Techniques Include Opening Up Market for Negotiable SDR C.D.'s," *Money Report*, Business International, January 16, 1981.

denominated in a single currency. Because this is possible, it is worth asking why some firms have found it advantageous to issue multicurrency bonds. The answer must be that there are limitations faced by some bond buyers in forming their own portfolios. One possible limitation is that the total wealth they have to allocate to bonds is too small to achieve significant diversification, which in turn depends on there being economies of scale when buying bonds; if the costs do not increase as smaller amounts of bonds are bought, the bond buyers can form diversified portfolios of separate bonds as cheaply as buying multicurrency bonds. This size-of-wealth limitation may be a major consideration with bonds which are frequently sold only in very large minimum denominations, especially when the bonds are privately placed.

An example of multicurrency denomination of a lease contract rather than a bond involved the Australian carrier Qantas Airlines. In 1980 Qantas arranged to lease two Boeing 747s from an owner who was willing to accept multicurrency payment. The lease required payment in German marks, Dutch guilders, Australian dollars, and pounds sterling—all currencies that the airline received in its business. With this arrangement, Qantas could match the multicurrency nature of its income with the payments on the lease. If Qantas had bought rather than leased the planes, it could have matched the currencies of incomes and payments by financing the planes with a currency-cocktail Eurobond requiring repayment in the various currencies of income.

The Vehicle of Bond Issue

Whether the bond that is issued is a Eurobond, foreign bond, or domestic bond, and whether it is denominated in a single currency or in several currencies, a decision must be made either to issue the bond directly as a liability of the parent company, or to issue it indirectly through a financing subsidiary or some other subsidiary. As we mentioned when discussing equities, the advantage in using an 80-20 subsidiary (not having to withhold taxes) has been removed for U.S. corporations since the enactment of the Deficit Reduction Act in 1984. This has resulted in a general shift by U.S. corporations—but not non-U.S. corporations—away from issuing bonds through special financing subsidiaries. Nevertheless, U.S. companies still issue bonds via an operating subsidiary if they do not want the bonds to be an obligation of the parent company. However, because the parent is almost invariably viewed as less risky than subsidiaries, the reduction in the parent's liability must be traded off against the fact that the interest rates that must be paid are generally higher when having a subsidiary issue bonds.

BANK FINANCING, DIRECT LOANS, AND THE LIKE

So far we have examined international aspects of equity and bond financing. We have stated that gains on selling equity in one market rather than another or simultaneously in several markets—Euroequities—depend on markets being segmented. We have also stated that bonds may be sold in a foreign currency

TABLE 14.4
SOURCES OF FUNDS FOR SUBSIDIARIES

	Billions of dollars			Percentage		
From within the multinational enterprise			6.1			60
Internally generated by affiliate		4.7			46	
Depreciation	2.9			29		
Retained earnings	1.7			17		
From parent		1.4			14	
Equity	1.0			9		
Loans	0.5			5		
From outside the multinational enterprise			4.0			40
Loans		3.9			39	
Equity		0.2			2	
Total			10.1			100

Source: U.S. Department of Commerce, Office of Foreign Direct Investments, *Foreign Affiliate Financial Survey, 1966–1969*, July 1971, p. 34.

denomination in the country using that currency (foreign bonds) or in countries not using the denomination currency (Eurobonds). The ability to select the currency of issue can lower borrowing costs, but can introduce foreign exchange exposure and risk because forward markets are generally not available for hedging on bonds. However, a firm might actually reduce foreign exchange exposure and risk by borrowing in a foreign currency if it has an income in that currency.

A large part of the financing of foreign subsidiaries of MNCs involves neither bonds nor equity. According to a survey of foreign direct investors by the U.S. Department of Commerce, approximately half of the financing of U.S. based MNCs was generated inside the corporation.[14] The results of the survey are summarized in Table 14.4. If anything, the true percentage of internally generated funds is probably larger than the percentage shown because, according to a different survey by Sidney Robbins and Robert Stobaugh, lending and borrowing by different subsidiaries net out in the Commerce Department's financial survey.[15] Robbins and Stobaugh estimated that the total for outstanding loans was $14 billion. This amount is much larger than the amount quoted for loans outstanding to the parent companies in the Commerce Department's survey. We can note from Table 14.4 that subsidiaries raise little equity. The debt incurred by subsidiaries is almost 20 times the equity they themselves raise.

According to Robbins and Stobaugh, most MNCs prefer to use intracompany credit rather than discretionary loans. This is because credit requires less

[14]U.S. Department of Commerce, Office of Foreign Direct Investments, *Foreign Affiliate Financial Survey*, 1966–1969, July 1971. This study has not been revised, because the office that prepared it was eliminated; but the proportion of funds generated within the corporation has probably not changed greatly.

[15]Sidney M. Robbins and Robert B. Stobaugh, "Financing Foreign Affiliates," *Financial Management*, winter 1973, pp. 56–65.

documentation than a discretionary loan, and because there are potential gains from avoidance of withholding tax on credit advances, whereas withholding by the foreign government is likely on interdivisional loans.

Some of the earliest work in financing subsidiaries by Edith Penrose revealed a varying financial structure as MNCs' subsidiaries grew larger.[16] Penrose argued that after receiving initial help from the parent company, subsidiaries move onto an independent growth path using funds from retained earnings and local borrowing.

Some of the debt raised outside companies takes on a character which is peculiarly international. For example, only in the international arena do we find the so-called back-to-back or parallel loans.

Parallel Loans

A **parallel loan** involves an exchange of funds between firms in different countries, with the exchange reversed at a later date. For example, suppose that a U.S. company's subsidiary in Brazil needs cruzados while a Braziian company's subsidiary in the United States needs dollars. The Brazilian firm can lend cruzados to the U.S.-owned subsidiary in Brazil while it borrows an approximately equivalent amount of dollars from the U.S. parent in the United States.[17] After an agreed-upon term, the funds can be repaid. There is no exchange-rate risk or exposure for either firm, because each is borrowing and repaying in the same currency. Each side can pay interest within the country where funds are lent according to the going market rates.

The advantages of parallel loans over bank loans are that they can circumvent foreign exchange controls and that they help avoid banks' spreads on borrowing versus lending and on foreign exchange transactions. The problem with parallel loans is locating the two sides of the deals. As in other barter deals, the needs of the parties must be harmonious before a satisfactory contract can be achieved. While the banks might well know of financing needs which are harmonious, they have little incentive to initiate a deal which avoids their spreads. Consequently, a large portion of parallel loans are arranged by brokerage houses rather than banks.

Credit Swaps

A credit swap involves the exchange of currencies between a bank and a firm rather than between two firms. It is an alternative method of obtaining debt capital for a foreign subsidiary without sending funds abroad. In a credit swap

---

[16] Edith T. Penrose, "Foreign Investment and the Growth of the Firm," *Economic Journal*, June 1956, pp. 220–235. Reprinted in John H. Dunning, *International Investment*, Penguin Books, Harmonsworth, England, 1972.

[17] The loan agreement could just as well involve subsidiaries of the Brazilian and U.S. firms in a different country. For example, the U.S. firm might lend the Brazilian firm dollars in New York, while a German subsidiary of the Brazilian firm lends a German subsidiary of the U.S. firm German marks in Germany.

the parent makes funds available to a bank at home. For example, a U.S. firm may place U.S. dollars in an account in New York. The U.S. bank then instructs one of its foreign subsidiaries to lend foreign currency to a subsidiary of the parent that made the deposit. For example, an office of the U.S. bank in Rio de Janeiro might lend cruzados to a subsidiary of the U.S. firm operating in Brazil. As with parallel loans, the major advantage of credit swaps is that they allow firms (and banks) to circumvent foreign exchange controls. In addition, they allow the parent and subsidiary to avoid foreign exchange exposure: the parent deposits and receives U.S. dollars in our example, while the subsidiary borrows and receives Brazilian cruzados.

GOVERNMENT AND DEVELOPMENT-BANK LENDING

It is not at all uncommon for financing to be provided by governments or development banks. Because government and development-bank financing is generally at favorable terms, many corporations consider these official sources of capital before considering the issue of stock, the sale of bonds, loans from commercial banks, or parallel loans from other corporations.

Host governments of foreign investments provide financing when they believe projects will generate jobs, earn foreign exchange, or provide training for their workers. There are numerous examples of loans being provided to MNCs by the governments of, for example, Australia, Britain, Canada, and Spain, to attract manufacturing firms to make investments in their countries. Sometimes the state or provincial governments also offer financing, perhaps even competing with each other within a country to have plants built in their area. Several U.S. states have provided cheap financing and other concessions to induce Japanese and other foreign firms to establish operations. Canadian provincial and Australian state governments have also used special financing arrangements to attract investors.

Even though the governments of poorer countries do not usually have the means to offer concessionary financing to investors, there are a number of development banks which specialize in providing financing for investment in infrastructure, for irrigation, and similar projects. While this financing is usually provided to the host government rather than to corporations involved in the construction of the projects, the corporations are indirectly being financed by the development-bank loans to the host governments.

A leading provider of financial assistance is the **International Bank for Reconstruction and Development** (IBRD), commonly known as the **World Bank**. The World Bank, which was established in 1944, is not a bank in the sense of accepting deposits and providing payment services between countries. Rather, it is a lending institution that borrows from governments by selling them its bonds, and then uses the proceeds for development in undeveloped (or developing) nations. World Bank or IBRD loans have a maturity of up to 20 years. Interest rates are determined by the (relative low) cost of funds to the bank.

Many developing countries do not meet the conditions for World Bank loans, so in 1960 an affiliated organization, the **International Development Agency** (IDA), was established to help even poorer countries. Credits, as the loans are called, have terms of up to 50 years and carry to interest charges. A second affiliate of the World Bank is the **International Finance Corporation** (IFC). The IFC provides loans for private investments and takes equity positions along with private-sector partners.

OTHER FACTORS AFFECTING THE FINANCING OF SUBSIDIARIES

We have presented a number of international financial considerations affecting bond and equity decisions, and decisions involving bank loans, parallel loans, and credit swaps. There are, however, a number of other factors which can affect the financing decision. Frequently these are based on the politically sensitive nature of a large amount of foreign direct investment. Sometimes, however, they are based on concern for exchange-rate risk or on restrictions imposed by host governments. We shall quickly mention some of the more notable factors.

The freezing or seizing of assets by inhospitable governments should not be a worry to those who borrow abroad. Instead, it should be a concern to the investors whose assets are lost. It might therefore be thought that while political risks are important in the investment decision, they are relatively inconsequential in the borrowing decision. However, some firms may borrow abroad *because* they fear confiscation or expropriation. If assets are seized, these firms can refuse to repay local debts and thereby reduce their losses.

Not only are losses from actual confiscations reduced by having foreign debt, but even the probability of confiscation is reduced. Foreign host governments may prefer to avoid the anger of people at home who are holding the debt of a foreign corporation. A similar argument applies to having foreign holders of equity. The probability of expropriation may be reduced by having foreign private shareholders.[18] Unfortunately, it may be difficult to raise equity or even debt from local private sources.

Generally, the more financing is denominated in local currency, the lower the danger from changing exchange rates. This supports the use of debt. Reinforcing the tendency toward using debt is the greater political sensitivity with regard to repatriating income on equity than with regard to receiving interest on debts. However, offsetting the factors leading to more debt is the fact that if equity is kept small, profits can look unreasonably high on the equity invested in foreign operations. The profit rate on equity can be used in claims of exploitation by foreign governments.

---

[18]As we shall see in Chapter 16, the probability of expropriation may be increased by having foreign *public* shareholders, such as the host government, who stand to gain from expropriation.

Certain governments require that a minimum equity/debt ratio be maintained, while some banks also set standards to maintain the quality of debt.[19] According to Sidney Robbins and Robert Stobaugh, U.S. firms have generally kept their equity well above that required by local regulations.[20] However, this does not mean that local regulations are not binding. Firms may keep their equity higher than necessary as a cushion against any future need to borrow.

When earnings are retained abroad, U.S. corporations can postpone the payment of U.S. corporate income taxes and foreign withholding taxes. According to Walter Ness, the saving from the deferral of tax payments lowers the cost of equity capital for multinational corporations and induces the corporations to have a lower debt/equity ratio in financing foreign subsidiaries.[21] However, according to Ian Giddy and Alan Shapiro, the alternatives for repatriating income via pricing of intersubsidiary trades, royalties, and interdivisional fees override any advantage from deferred tax payments encouraging the use of equity capital.[22]

FINANCIAL STRUCTURE

Subsidiary or Parent Determination of Financial Structure

If the success or failure of an overseas subsidiary has little or no effect on the ability of the parent or other subsidiaries to raise capital, decisions of financial structure can be left to subsidiaries.[23] The subsidiaries can then weigh the various economic and political pros and cons of different sources of funds, and adopt a financial structure that is appropriate for their own local circumstances. However, if there are spillovers from the failure of a subsidiary which reduce the financing opportunities of the parent or its other subsidiaries, decisions of subsidiary financial structure should be made by the parent. Full consideration should be given to the implications of a default by one subsidiary for global operations. Because spillovers will exist if the parent is legally or morally bound to support subsidiaries, we should consider the evidence on corporate responsibility for subsidiary debt.

Survey evidence shows clearly that even when not bound by legal guarantees on subsidiary-incurred debt, parent firms rarely if ever admit they will allow a

---

[19]Restrictions on the amount of equity or debt can be handled in a linear-programming approach to financing. An example of this has been shown by Walter L. Ness, Jr., "A Linear Programming Approach to Financing the Multinational Corporation," *Financial Management*, winter 1972, pp. 88–100.

[20]Robbins and Stobaugh, *op. cit.*

[21]Walter L. Ness, Jr., "U.S. Corporate Income Taxation and the Dividend Remittance Policy of Multinational Corporations," *Journal of International Business Studies*, spring 1975, pp. 67–77.

[22]Alan C. Shapiro, "Financial Structure and the Cost of Capital in Multinational Corporations," *Journal of Financial and Quantitative Analysis*, June 1979, pp. 211–226; Ian H. Giddy, "The Cost of Capital in the Multinational Firm," unpublished paper, Columbia University, 1976.

[23]By financial structure we mean the composition of firm's sources of capital. That is, financial structure involves the amount of equity, versus bond debt, versus bank debt, versus credit swaps, and so on.

subsidiary to default. For example, in a survey by Robert Stobaugh, all twenty of the large MNCs in the sample, and all but one of the smaller MNCs, said they would not allow a subsidiary to default whatever the circumstances.[24] Similar responses were received in a later survey conducted by *Business International*.[25] This evidence suggests that multinationals realize that a default in a subsidiary will affect operations elsewhere. There is no other explanation for the almost universal willingness to support subsidiaries.

With a parent company having a *de facto* obligation to honor debt incurred by its subsidiaries, the parent must monitor its subsidiaries' debt/equity ratios as well as the corporation's overall debt/equity ratio. This does not, however, mean that a parent should keep its subsidiaries' debt/equity ratios equal to its own overall preferred debt/equity ratio. For example, subsidiaries facing high political risk and no ability to raise local equity capital should be allowed to take on relatively high debt loads. Similarly, subsidiaries in countries with relatively high tax savings from deducting interest but not dividend payments should be allowed to take on relatively large amounts of debt to exploit the tax shields debt provides. All the time, however, a parent company should make compensating adjustments to the capital structure of itself and its other subsidiaries so that the global debt/equity ratio is maintained at the level it deems appropriate.

Capital Structure in Different Countries

Financial structure varies greatly from country to country. This is seen clearly in Table 14.5 and in Figure 14.2. Possible reasons for the variations can be found in explanations of capital structure commonly advanced in a domestic context. These explanations hinge on the tax deductability of interest payments but not dividends, and on bankruptcy and agency costs.

Countries in which interest payments are deductible against corporate taxes will, *ceteris paribus*, have relatively high debt/equity ratios. However, if interest rates are particularly high *because* borrowers can deduct interest and lenders must pay tax on interest, this will militate against the advantage of debt.[26]

The risk and expected cost of bankruptcy increase with the amount of debt.[27] If expected costs of bankruptcy are lower in some countries than others,

---

[24] Robert B. Stobaugh, "Financing Foreign Subsidiaries of U.S.-Controlled Multinational Enterprises," *Journal of International Business Studies*, summer 1970, pp. 43–64.

[25] Business International, Money Report, "Policies of MNC's in Debt/Equity Mix," 1979.

[26] An account of the effect of differential tax shields that considers the role of both corporate and individual income tax rates has been provided by Moon H. Lee and Josef Zechner, "Debt, Taxes, and International Equilibrium," *Journal of International Money and Finance*, December 1984, pp. 343–355. Lee and Zechner point out that for there to be an advantage in debt, corporate relative to individual tax rates must be higher in one country than in other countries. This is because high individual tax rates on interest earnings push up interest rates and thereby reduce the attractiveness of debt. For debt to be attractive the corporate deductibility needs to be high relative to the extent interest rates are pushed higher by individual tax rates.

[27] The expected cost of bankruptcy depends on the probability that bankruptcy will occur as well as on legal and other costs if it does occur.

TABLE 14.5
FINANCIAL STRUCTURE IN DIFFERENT COUNTRIES*

Country	D / E	D / A
Australia	0.87 : 1	0.43 : 1
Canada	1.16 : 1	0.54 : 1
France	2.42 : 1	0.71 : 1
Germany	2.03 : 1	0.67 : 1
Italy	4.00 : 1	0.58 : 1
Japan	5.13 : 1	0.83 : 1
Netherlands	1.49 : 1	0.60 : 1
Saudi Arabia	1.63 : 1	0.62 : 1
Sweden	1.78 : 1	0.64 : 1
Switzerland	1.25 : 1	0.49 : 1
United Kingdom	1.36 : 1	0.58 : 1
United States	0.95 : 1	0.49 : 1

*D = total debt, E = shareholders' equity, A = total assets.
Source: *Money Report*, Business International, February 1, 1980, p. 41.

debt/equity ratios will *ceteris paribus* be higher in the countries with low expected bankruptcy costs. In countries where banks are both providers of debt and holders of companies' equity, the probability of bankruptcy is relatively low because the banks are likely to help in times of trouble. It follows that in countries such as Japan and Germany where banks hold considerable amounts of equity, debt/equity ratios are substantially higher than in countries such as the U.S. and Canada where banks provide considerable debt, but little or no equity.[28]

Lenders know that once they have made loans to firms, the managers of the firms will be more concerned with taking care of their own and their shareholders' well-being than with protecting the lenders' interests. This is one of the **agency costs** of debt, and because lenders are aware of this cost, they demand corresponding high interest rates on their loans. These high interest rates reduce typical debt/equity ratios. The greater is the agency cost of debt, the lower is the typical debt/equity ratio.

In countries such as Japan and Germany, where banks hold equity in the firms to which they make loans, agency costs are not as high as in countries such as the U.S. and Canada, where banks are providers of debt but provide little or no equity. This is because when banks hold equity they can indirectly represent their interest as creditors when, for example, casting their votes on corporate policy. Agency costs are even further reduced when banks hold directorships in

---

[28]Of course, the equity in the U.S. and Canada which keeps down companies' debt/equity ratios is provided through the stock markets rather than by commercial banks.

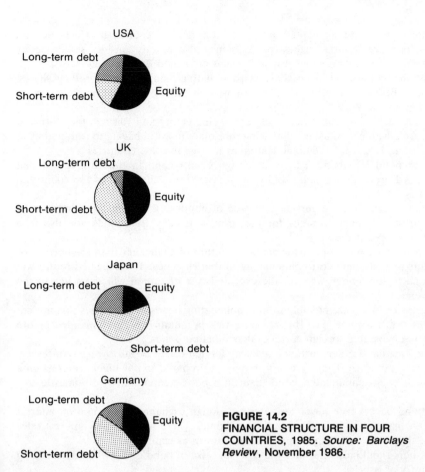

FIGURE 14.2
FINANCIAL STRUCTURE IN FOUR
COUNTRIES, 1985. *Source: Barclays*
Review, November 1986.

firms, because they can then very directly represent their interests as creditors when attending board meetings. The high degree of horizontal integration in Japan, where banks and manufacturers are frequently subdivisions of the same giant MNC, has greatly reduced agency costs, and this, combined with the reduced expected bankruptcy costs that also result from horizontal integration, probably explains Japan's very high debt ratios.

SUMMARY

1 If capital markets are internationally integrated, the costs of equity capital should be the same wherever the equity is sold. It follows that the total expected cost of equity capital, consisting of dividends plus changes in local market values plus changes in exchange rates, will be equal everywhere with integrated capital markets.

2 If capital markets are segmented, it pays to consider the country in which the firm can sell its shares for the highest price. It may also pay to consider selling equity simultaneously in several countries; such issues are called Euroequities.

3 Low issuance costs may make some markets better than others for selling shares. Generally, the costs of selling shares are lowest in the big financial markets such as London and New York.

4 Firms must decide on the best vehicle for issuing equity and raising other forms of capital. An advantage of using a financing subsidiary to avoid having to withhold taxes existed in the U.S. until 1984, and continues to exist in some countries.

5 A foreign bond is a bond sold in a foreign country and in the currency of that country. A Eurobond is a bond sold in a currency other than that of the country in which it is sold.

6 Firms must decide on the currency of issue of bonds. All foreign-pay bonds are by definition in a foreign currency for the firm, and many Eurobonds are also in a foreign currency for the firm.

7 When lenders are more optimistic about the future of a currency than are borrowers, borrowers may be tempted to denominate in that currency. The expected return will seem high to the lender, and yet the expected cost of capital will seem low to the bond issuer.

8 Large gains or losses are possible from denominating bonds in currencies that are not part of a firm's income. For this reason a risk premium may be demanded before speculating by issuing foreign-currency-denominated bonds.

9 When a firm has foreign-currency income, foreign-currency borrowing reduces exchange rate exposure. Therefore, a firm may be prepared to pay higher interest on a foreign-currency-denominated bond than on a bond denominated in domestic currency.

10 When bond buyers face lower tax rates on foreign exchange gains than on interest income, it may pay to issue strong-currency bonds. These will have low interest rates because they offer bond buyers part of their return as capital gain.

11 Bond issuers should also consider the costs and size of bond issues when determining the country of issue.

12 Bonds denominated in two or more different currencies, called multicurrency or currency-cocktail bonds, will appeal to lenders if there are costs associated with forming portfolios of bonds denominated in single currencies.

13 A substantial proportion of financing of overseas subsidiaries is provided from within multinational corporations.

14 Parallel loans are made between firms. They are particularly useful when there are foreign exchange controls.

15 Credit swaps are made between banks and firms. They are also a way of avoiding foreign exchange controls.

16 Political risk can be reduced by borrowing in countries in which investment occurs; this tends to increase debt/equity ratios of subsidiaries.

17 Because parent companies tend to honor subsidiaries' debts whether legally obligated to do so or not, parent companies should monitor subsidiaries' debt/equity ratios as well as their global debt/equity ratios. Nevertheless, parents should allow variations in debt/equity ratios between subsidiaries to take advantage of local situations.

18 If a country has a high debt/equity ratio, this can be because of high tax shields on debt or low bankruptcy or agency costs. The links between banks and corporations in

Japan, Germany and some other countries may explain the high debt/equity ratios in these countries.

QUESTIONS

1 Why might a firm want to issue shares simultaneously in a number of financial centers?

2 How can the availability of savings and the opportunities for investment influence the cost of capital in different countries?

3 Is a U.S. dollar bond sold by a British firm in the U.S. a foreign bond, or Eurobond? How about a pound bond sold by a British firm in the U.S.?

4 Why do Canadian firms borrow so heavily in U.S. dollars?

5 What does Table 14.3 suggest about the changes in beliefs of bond buyers and sellers concerning the Canadian dollar between 1985 and 1988? Might the amount of business foreign firms do in Canada also explain the change in popularity of Canadian dollar bonds?

6 How is the tax shield on debt mitigated by a high tax rate on interest earnings, thereby making debt/equity ratios in different countries depend on individual income versus corporate tax rates?

7 With $r_{US} = 12.50$ percent, $r_{UK} = 14.00$ percent, $S(\$/£) = 2.25$, and $S_{10}^*(\$/£) = 1.50$, where would you borrow? What is the total gain on each \$1 million borrowed from making the correct choice?

8 If $r_{US} = 12.50$ percent, $r_{UK} = 14.00$ percent, and $S(\$/£) = 2.25$, what must the actual exchange rate after 10 years, $S_{10}(\$/£)$, be in order to make borrowing in Britain a good idea?

9 Why does having an income in foreign currency reduce required borrowing risk premiums? What type of risk—translation/transaction risk or operating risk—is reduced?

10 What determines whether you would issue a Eurosterling bond or a sterling bond (that is, a foreign bond) in Britain?

BIBLIOGRAPHY

Brown, Robert L., "Some Simple Conditions for Determining Swap Feasibility," unpublished, Monash University, Australia, 1986.

Hodder, James E., "Hedging International Exposure: Capital Structure Under Flexible Exchange Rates and Expropriation Risk," unpublished, Stanford University, 1982.

Hodder, James E., and Lemma W. Senbet, "International Capital Structure Equilibrium," unpublished, Stanford University, 1988.

Lee, Moon, H., and Josef Zechner, "Debt, Taxes, and International Equilibrium," *Journal of International Money and Finance*, December 1984, pp. 343–355.

Lessard, Donald R., and Alan C. Shapiro, "Guidelines for Global Financing Choices," *Midland Corporate Finance Journal*, winter 1983, pp. 68–80.

Nauman-Etienne, Rudiger, "A Framework for Financial Decisions in Multinational Corporations—A Summary of Recent Research," *Journal of Financial and Quantitative Analysis*, November 1974, pp. 859–874.

Ness, Walter L. Jr., "A Linear Approach to Financing the Multinational Corporation," *Financial Management*, winter 1972, pp. 88–100.

Remmers, Lee, "A Note on Foreign Borrowing Costs," *Journal of International Business Studies*, fall 1980, pp. 123–134.

Shapiro, Alan C., "Financial Structure and the Cost of Capital in the Multinational Corporation," *Journal of Financial and Quantitative Analysis*, June 1978, pp. 211–226.

———, "The Impact of Taxation on the Currency-of-Denomination Decision for Long-Term Foreign Borrowing and Lending," *Journal of International Business Studies*, spring 1984, pp. 15–25.

Stonehill, Arthur, Theo Beekhuisen, Richard Wright, Lee Remmers, Norman Toy, Antonio Pares, Douglas Egan, and Thomas Bates: "Financial Goals and Debt Ratio Determinants: A Survey of Practice in Five Countries," *Financial Management*, autumn 1975, pp. 27–41.

Toy, Norman, Arthur Stonehill, Lee Remmers, Richard Wright, and Theo Beekhuisen: "A Comparative International Study of Growth, Profitability, and Risk as Determinants of Corporate Debt Ratios in the Manufacturing Sector," *Journal of Financial and Quantitative Analysis*, November 1974, pp. 875–886.

Wihlborg, Clas: "Economics of Exposure Management of Foreign Subsidiaries of Multinational Corporations," *Journal of International Business Studies*, winter 1980, pp. 9–18.

SEVEN

EVALUATION AND EXPLANATION OF FOREIGN DIRECT INVESTMENT

In this part of the book we consider the procedure that management should follow when deciding whether or not to make foreign direct investment. (As we saw when discussing the balance of payments, direct investment is investment where the investor has a measure of control, which for the balance-of-payments account is defined as 10 percent or more ownership of voting stock. A typical direct investment is the building or purchase of an overseas manufacturing plant.) We also discuss the reasons why direct foreign investments have been made, and the consequences of these investments.

A number of problems are faced in evaluating foreign investments that are not present when evaluating domestic investments. These extra problems include the presence of exchange-rate and country risks, the need to consider taxes at home and abroad, the issue of which country's interest rate to use as the base when selecting a discount rate, the problem posed by restrictions on repatriating income, the frequent need to account for subsidized financing, and so on. Chapter 15 presents a procedure for dealing with these and other problems. This is the capital budgeting method known as the **adjusted-present-value technique**. The investment-evaluating procedure is clarified by an extensive example.

Chapter 15 includes an appendix in which various topics in taxation are covered, some of which are relevant for the capital budgeting procedure used to evaluate foreign direct investments. The appendix offers a general overview of taxation in the international context, covering such topics as value-added tax—which is assuming increasing international importance—and withholding tax.

It is through direct foreign investment that some companies have grown into the giant multinational corporations whose names are known around the globe and are words in every major language—Sony, IBM, Shell, Ford, Nestlé, Mitsubishi, Citibank, and so on. Chapter 16 examines the various reasons that have been given for the growth of the MNC. The chapter also considers some special problems faced by the MNCs, including the need to set transfer prices of goods and services moving between corporate divisions, and the need to measure and monitor country risk. The difficulties in obtaining and using transfer prices are described, as are some methods of measuring country risk. Clarification is given of the differences between country risk and the two narrower concepts, political risk and sovereign risk. Methods for reducing or eliminating country risk are described.

Chapter 16 concludes with a discussion of the problems and benefits that have accompanied the growth of the MNC. This involves a discussion of the power of MNCs to frustrate the economic policies of host governments, and of the transfer of technology and jobs that are the results of the MNCs' foreign direct investments.

15

CAPITAL BUDGETING FOR FOREIGN DIRECT INVESTMENT

The massive multinational corporations (MNCs), whose names are household words in numerous languages and which have power that is the envy and fear of almost every government, grew by making direct investments overseas. The criterion used for making these direct investments will be presented here as we develop a principle of capital budgeting that can be used in evaluating foreign capital investments. In the international arena, capital budgeting involves complex problems that are not shared in a domestic context. These include, for example, the dependence of cash flows on capital structure because of cheap loans from foreign governments, exchange-rate risks, country risks, multiple tiers of taxation, and restrictions on repatriating income. We will show the conditions under which some of the more complex problems in the evaluation of overseas investments can be reduced to manageable size.

There are a number of approaches to capital budgeting for traditional domestic investments, including net present value (NPV), adjusted present value (APV), internal rate of return, and payback period. We shall use the APV technique, which has been characterized as a "divide and conquer" approach, for each difficulty is tackled as it occurs. This technique involves accounting separately for the complexities found in foreign investments as a result of such factors as subsidized loans and restrictions on repatriating income. Before we show how the difficulties can be handled, we shall give explanations of the difficulties themselves. Our explanations will show why the APV approach has been proposed for the evaluation of overseas projects rather than the traditional NPV approach, which is used extensively in evaluating domestic projects.

DIFFICULTIES IN EVALUATING FOREIGN PROJECTS[1]

Introductory textbooks in finance tend to advise the use of the NPV technique. The NPV is defined as follows:

$$NPV = -C_0 + \sum_{t=1}^{T} \frac{CF_t^*(1 - \tau)}{(1 + \bar{r})^t} \qquad (15.1)$$

where
$\quad C_0$ = project cost
$\quad CF_t^*$ = expected before-tax cash flow in year t
$\quad \tau$ = tax rate
$\quad \bar{r}$ = weighted average cost of capital
$\quad T$ = life of the project

The weighted average cost of capital, $\bar{r}$, is in turn defined as follows:

$$\bar{r} = \frac{E}{E + D}r^e + \frac{D}{E + D}r(1 - \tau)$$

where
$\quad r^e$ = equilibrium cost of equity reflecting only the systematic risk
$\quad r$ = before-tax cost of credit
$\quad E$ = total market value of equity
$\quad D$ = total market value of debt
$\quad \tau$ = tax rate

We see that the cost of equity and the cost of debt are weighted by the importance of equity and debt as sources of capital and that an additional adjustment is made to the cost of debt, since interest payments are generally deductible against corporate taxes. The adjustment of $1 - \tau$ gives the effective cost of debt after the fraction τ of interest payments has been saved from taxes. While not universally accepted, this NPV approach has enjoyed a prominent place in finance textbooks.[2]

There are two categories of reasons why it is difficult to apply the traditional NPV technique to overseas projects and why an alternative framework such as the adjusted-present-value technique is required. The first category of reasons involves the difficulties which cause cash flows—the *numerators* in NPVs—to be seen from two different perspectives: that of the investor's home country and

---

[1] Our account of the adjusted present value technique draws heavily on a paper by Donald Lessard: "Evaluating International Projects: An Adjusted Present Value Approach," in Donald R. Lessard (ed.), *International Financial Management: Theory and Application*, Warren, Gorham & Lamont, Boston, 2nd ed., 1985.

[2] For the traditional textbook account of the NPV approach with the weighted average cost of capital, see James C. Van Horne, *Financial Management and Policy*, 8th ed., Prentice-Hall, Englewood Cliffs, N.J., 1988. For an account of the alternative APV approach using an adjusted cost of capital, see Richard Brealey and Stewart Myers, *Principles of Corporate Finance*, 3rd ed. McGraw-Hill, New York, 1988.

that of the country in which the project is located.[3] The correct perspective is that of the investor's home country, which we assume to be well identified. The second category of reasons involves the degree of risk of foreign projects and the appropriate discount rate—the *denominator* of the NPV. We shall begin by looking at why cash flows differ between the investor's perspective and the perspective of the country in which the project is located; later we shall turn to the appropriate discount rate.

FACTORS AFFECTING INVESTORS' CASH FLOWS

Blocked Funds

If funds that are blocked or otherwise restricted can be utilized in a foreign investment, the project cost to the investor may be below the local project construction costs. From the investor's perspective there is a gain from activated funds equal to the difference between the face value of those funds and the present value of the funds if the next best thing is done with them. This gain should be deducted from the capital cost of the project to find the cost from the investor's perspective. For example, if the next best thing that can be done is to leave blocked funds idle abroad, the full value of the activated funds should be deducted from the project cost. Alternatively, if half of the blocked funds can be returned to the investor after the investor pays taxes or uses an internal funds transfer system, then half of the value of the blocked funds should be subtracted from the cost of the project.

Effects on the Sales of Other Divisions

From the perspective of the manager of a foreign project, the total value of cash flows generated by the investment is relevant. However, factories are frequently built in countries in which sales have previously taken place. If the multinational corporation exports to the country of the project from the home country or some other preexisting facility, only the increment in the MNC's corporate income is relevant. Sales will often decline or be lost in the absence of a project, and this is why the investment is made. Therefore, we must net out whatever income would have otherwise been earned by the multinational corporation in order to take care of the so-called synergy or interdependence between subsidiaries.

Remittance Restrictions

When there are restrictions on the repatriation of income, only those flows that are remittable to the parent are relevant from the MNC's perspective. This is

---

[3]Michael Adler has tackled the challenging problem of having no clear home base. See Michael Adler, "The Cost of Capital and Valuation of a Two-Country Firm," *Journal of Finance*, March 1974, pp. 119–132.

true whether or not the income is remitted. When remittances are legally limited, sometimes the restrictions can be circumvented to some extent by using internal transfer prices, overhead payments, and so on. If we include only the income which is remittable via legal and open channels, we will obtain a conservative estimate of the project's value. If this is positive, we need not add any more. If it is negative, we can add income that is remittable via illegal transfers, for example. The availability of this two-step procedure is a major advantage of the APV approach. A two-step procedure can also be applied to taxes.

Different Levels of Taxation

International taxation is an extremely complex subject that is best treated separately, as it is in Appendix 15.1. However, for the purpose of evaluating overseas direct investment, what matters is the total taxes paid, and not which government collects them, the form of taxes collected, the expenditures allowed against taxes, and so on. The essential point is that for a U.S.-based multinational, when the U.S. corporate tax rate is above the foreign rate, the effective tax rate will be the U.S. rate if full credit is given for foreign taxes paid. For example, if the foreign project is located in Singapore and the local tax rate for foreign-based corporations is 33 percent, while the U.S. corporate tax rate is 34 percent, then after the credit for foreign taxes paid is applied, only 1 percent will be payable in the United States. If, however, the project is located in Sweden and faces a tax rate of 52 percent, full credit will not be available, and the effective tax rate will be 52 percent. This means that when we deal with foreign projects from the investor's point of view, we should use a tax rate τ which is the higher of the home-country and foreign rates.

Taking τ as the higher of the tax rates at home and abroad is a conservative approach. In reality, taxes are often reduced to a level below τ through the appropriate choice of transfer prices, royalty payments, and so on. These techniques can be used to move income from high-tax countries to low-tax countries and thereby reduce overall corporate taxes. In addition, the payment of taxes can be deferred by leaving remittable income abroad, and so if cash flows are measured as all remittable income whether or not remitted, some adjustment is required, since the actual amount of taxes paid will be less than the cash-flow term suggests. The adjustment can be made to the cost of capital or included as an extra term in an APV calculation.[4]

---

[4]A method for valuing foreign investment that is based on net present value and the weighted average cost of capital that takes care of taxes has been developed by Alan C. Shapiro ("Financial Structure and the Cost of Capital in the Multinational Corporation," *Journal of Financial and Quantitative Analysis*, November 1978, pp. 211–226). In general, the NPV and APV approaches will be equivalent if they take care of all complexities. This has been shown by Lawrence D. Booth ("Capital Budgeting Frameworks for the Multinational Corporation," *Journal of International Business Studies*, fall 1982, pp. 113–123.) Preference for APV over NPV is based on the more explicit nature of allowance for complexities and the ability to use APV to see whether projects are profitable even before an allowance is made for complexities. If they are profitable before positive allowances are added, we know they will be profitable after the allowances are added.

Concessionary Loans

While governments do offer special financial aid or other kinds of help for certain domestic projects, it is very common for foreign investments to carry some sort of assistance. This may come in the form of low-cost land, reduced interest rates, and so on. Low-cost land will merely be reflected in project costs, but concessionary lending is more problematic in the NPV approach. However, with the APV technique we can add a special term to include the subsidy. This is particularly important in that the special concessionary loan will be available to the corporation but not directly to the shareholders. This will make the appropriate cost of capital for foreign investment projects differ from that for domestic projects, which is what happens in segmented capital markets.[5]

The various difficulties encountered in the evaluation of foreign projects can be incorporated within the APV approach, which we have not yet presented. We need not delay any longer.

THE ADJUSTED-PRESENT-VALUE TECHNIQUE

The APV for a foreign project can be written as follows.

$$\text{APV} = -S_0 K_0 + S_0 \text{AF}_0 + \sum_{t=1}^{T} \frac{(S_t^* \text{CF}_t^* - \text{LS}_t^*)(1 - \tau)}{(1 + \text{DR}_e)^t} + \sum_{t=1}^{T} \frac{\text{DA}_t \tau}{(1 + \text{DR}_a)^t}$$

$$+ \sum_{t=1}^{T} \frac{r_g \text{BC}_0 \tau}{(1 + \text{DR}_b)^t} + S_0 \left[\text{CL}_0 - \sum_{t=1}^{T} \frac{\text{LR}_t}{(1 + \text{DR}_c)^t} \right]$$

$$+ \sum_{t=1}^{T} \frac{\text{TD}_t^*}{(1 + \text{DR}_d)^t} + \sum_{t=1}^{T} \frac{\text{RF}_t^*}{(1 + \text{DR}_f)^t} \qquad (15.2)$$

where
S_0 = spot exchange rate, period zero
S_t^* = expected spot rate, period t
K_0 = capital cost of project in foreign currency units
AF_0 = restricted funds activated by project
CF_t^* = expected remittable cash flow in foreign currency units
LS_t^* = profit from lost sales, in dollars
τ = higher of U.S. and foreign corporate tax rates
T = life of the project

[5]Indeed, blocked funds, remittance restrictions, and different levels of taxation are also causes of market segmentation.

DA_t = depreciation allowances in dollar units
BC_0 = contribution of project to borrowing capacity in dollars
CL_0 = face value of concessionary loan in foreign currency
LR_t = loan repayments on concessionary loan in foreign currency
TD_t^* = expected tax savings from deferrals, intersubsidiary transfer pricing
RF_t^* = expected illegal repatriation of income
DR_e = discount rate for cash flows, assuming all-equity financing
DR_a = discount rate for depreciation allowances
DR_b = discount rate for tax saving on interest deduction from contribution to borrowing capacity
DR_c = discount rate for saving via concessionary interest rate
DR_d = discount rate for saving via intersubsidiary transfers
DR_f = discount rate for illegally repatriated project flows
r_g = market borrowing rate at home

We can describe each of the terms in the APV equation and show how these terms take care of the difficulties in evaluating foreign investment projects.

$- S_0 K_0$: The cost of the project is assumed to be denominated in foreign currency and incurred in year 0 only. It is converted into dollars at S_0.

$S_0 AF_0$: We reduce the project cost by the value, converted into dollars, of the blocked funds activated by the project. AF_0 is the face value of the blocked funds minus their value in the next best use.

$$\sum_{t=1}^{T} \frac{(S_t^* CF_t^* - LS_t^*)(1 - \tau)}{(1 + DR_e)^t}:$$ CF_t^* represents the expected legally remit-

table project cash flows on sales from the new project in year t, beginning after a year.[6] This is measured in foreign currency and converted into dollars at the expected exchange rate, S_t^*. From this is subtracted the lost income on sales from other facilities which are replaced by the new facility. If the lost income is measured in U.S. dollars, as it will be if sales are lost to the U.S. parent company, we do not multiply the lost income by S_t^*. If the lost income is measured in units of foreign currency, S_t^* applies to LS_t^*. Other funds remitted via intersubsidiary transfer pricing and other illegal means are included in a later term. The cash flows are adjusted for the effective tax rate, which is the higher of the domestic and foreign corporate rates. Any reduction from this level that results from moving funds from high-tax countries to low-tax countries can be added later. We assume here that the same tax rate applies to lost income on replaced sales as well as to new income. If the lost income would have faced a different tax rate, LS_t^* must be considered separately from CF_t^*. The discount rate is the all-equity cost of capital that reflects all systematic risk,

[6]As before in the book, asterisks stand for expected values. Quantities without asterisks are assumed to be known at the time of the investment decision.

including unavoidable country risk and exchange-rate risk.[7]

$$\sum_{t=1}^{T} \frac{DA_t \tau}{(1 + DR_a)^t}:$$ Depreciation is allowed against corporate taxes for projects located abroad as well as for those at home. The benefits of the depreciation allowances are the amounts of allowances times the corporate tax rates against which they are applied. We have given DA_t in dollar amounts and therefore have not included S_t^*. This will be appropriate if the higher tax rate is the rate in the United States; in this case allowances will be deducted against U.S. taxes. If the higher tax rate is the rate in the foreign country, DA_t will probably be in foreign-currency units, and we need to convert at S_t^*.

$$\sum_{t=1}^{T} \frac{r_g BC_0 \tau}{(1 + DR_b)^t}:$$ When debt is used to finance a project at home or abroad, the interest payments are tax-deductible. Whether or not the project in question fully utilizes its borrowing capacity and consequent tax savings, the tax savings on the amount that *could* be borrowed should be included as a benefit.[8] The annual benefit equals the interest payments that are saved from the tax reduction, the interest rate being the market borrowing rate at home. For example, if the project has a value of $1 million and the firm likes to maintain 50 percent of its value in debt, the project will raise borrowing capacity by $BC_0 = \$500,000$, and the interest payment on this amount, that is, $r_g BC_0$, should be included each year. This will be true even if the actual amount borrowed is larger or smaller than $500,000. For example, if $200,000 is borrowed on the $1 million project, an additional amount of $300,000 can be borrowed elsewhere in the corporation, with consequent tax offsets on the interest on $300,000. If $800,000 is borrowed, the project will reduce the capacity to borrow for other activities by $300,000, and the lower tax deductions elsewhere will offset the tax deductions on $300,000 worth of borrowing for the project. This leaves the interest on only $500,000 appropriate for inclusion as BC_0.

$$S_0 \left[CL_0 - \sum_{t=1}^{T} \frac{LR_t}{(1 + DR_c)^t} \right]:$$ The current value of the benefit of a concessionary loan is the difference between the face value of the loan and the present value of the repayment on the loan discounted at the rate of interest that would have been faced in the absence of the concessionary financing. This must be converted into dollars. For example, if a 10-year loan with a 10-percent interest rate and 10 equal principal repayments is made available when the market rate would have been 15 percent, the present value of the repayment on a £1 million loan is £833,959. This is shown in Table 15.1. The value of the subsidy is hence

---

[7] We are not yet ready to give a full account of country risk, which includes political risk. This will be covered in the next chapter.

[8] Borrowing capacity is not a limit imposed on the firm from outside. It results from the firm's decision on how much debt it wishes to carry.

TABLE 15.1
VALUE OF A £1-MILLION CONCESSIONARY LOAN

Year	Loan outstanding	Principal repayment	Interest payment	Total payment	Present value of payment
1	£1,000,000	£100,000	£100,000	£200,000	£173,913
2	900,000	100,000	90,000	190,000	143,667
3	800,000	100,000	80,000	180,000	118,353
4	700,000	100,000	70,000	170,000	97,198
5	600,000	100,000	60,000	160,000	79,548
6	500,000	100,000	50,000	150,000	68,849
7	400,000	100,000	40,000	140,000	52,631
8	300,000	100,000	30,000	130,000	42,497
9	200,000	100,000	20,000	120,000	31,111
10	100,000	100,000	10,000	110,000	27,190
					£833,959

£1,000,000 − £833,959 = £166,041. This amount has a current dollar value of $332,082 if, for example, $S_0 = 2.0$.

We should note that subsidized debt has potential effects on the tax shield from interest payments. We have considered corporate tax savings from debt in the previous term. This uses borrowing capacity and the market interest rate in the home country. This term will do whenever subsidized debt leaves total interest payments as without the subsidy. This might not, however, be so. For example, if total debt capacity is constrained by the total face value of debt being constant rather than by interest payments being constant, then the tax shield for the corporation will be smaller than shown.[9]

$$\sum_{t=1}^{T} \frac{TD_t^*}{(1 + DR_d)^t}:$$ By using the higher of the domestic and foreign tax rates

for τ we have taken a conservative approach. In practice, a multinational is likely to be able to move funds from high-tax locations to low-tax locations and defer the payment of taxes, thereby reducing the effective rate to a level below τ. Cash flows can be moved by adjusting transfer prices, head-office overhead, and so on, and the payment of taxes can be deferred by reinvesting in low-tax countries. The APV technique allows us to include these tax savings as a separate term. As we have mentioned, a two-step approach is possible. We can evaluate APV without a TD_t^* and see if it is positive. If it is, we need not do anything else. If it is not, we can see how much of a tax saving will be required

[9] The appropriate approach depends on whether, for example, the firm fixes the amount of debt it will bear or the annual interest payments. A general account of the valuation of subsidized financing can be found in Richard Brealey and Stewart Myers, *Principles of Corporate Finance*, 3rd ed., McGraw-Hill, New York, 1988.

to make APV positive and determine whether such a saving can reasonably be expected.

$\sum_{t=1}^{T} \dfrac{RF_t^*}{(1 + DR_f)^t}$: The cash flow we use for CF_t^* is, like the tax rate, a conservative estimate. CF_t^* includes only the flows which are remittable when transfer prices, royalties, and so on reflect their appropriate market values. However, a multinational might manipulate transfer prices or royalty payments to repatriate more income (as well as to reduce taxes). Any extra remittable income from international (and illegal) channels can be included after the APV from the legal cash flows has been computed, if the APV is negative. This two-step procedure can be applied simultaneously to both the extra remittable income and the extra tax savings that might be obtained through internal price and income tinkering.

We have described the numerators of the APV formula and shown how they take care of many of the difficulties in evaluating foreign investment projects which we cited earlier. We have not yet said much about the denominators in the APV formula.

SELECTING THE APPROPRIATE DISCOUNT RATES

So far we have said little about the discount rates other than that cash flows should be discounted at an all-equity rate that reflects risk. As we noted in Chapter 13, only the systematic component of total risk matters, and this risk requires a premium in the discount rate to reflect the shareholder's opportunity cost of capital. To some extent the additional risks of doing business abroad are mitigated by the extent to which cash flows from foreign projects are uncorrelated and therefore reduce the variance of corporate income. If there is risk reduction from having some independence of cash flows from different countries, but the pooling of flows from different countries is not directly available to shareholders, the diversification offered by the MNC should be reflected in discount rates as well as in the market value of the stock.[10] This is because the pooling of cash flow reduces the business risk.

The risks faced with foreign investments that are explicitly faced with domestic investments are foreign exchange risk and country risk.[11] These risks provide a reason, in addition to those previously cited, why the NPV technique is difficult to apply to foreign capital projects. Both country risk and exchange-rate risk can, for example, make the optimal capital structure change over time. This is difficult to incorporate within the weighted-average cost of capital used in the NPV technique. However, in the APV technique, where we use an

---

[10]As we mentioned in Chapter 13, the ability of the corporation to do what its shareholders cannot requires segmented capital markets that the corporation can circumvent.

[11]We recall from Chapter 9 that foreign exchange risk can exist for a completely domestic firm with local sales and production when competition from imports depends on exchange rates. This is why we say "explicitly."

all-equity cost of capital (DR_e) to discount cash flows, the capital structure matters only because of the effect on taxes, treated in a separate term.

Country risk and foreign exchange risk, like business risk, can be diversified by holding a portfolio of securities of different countries denominated in many different currencies. This means that the risk premium in the discount rate, which reflects only the systematic risk need not be very large.[12] It follows from our discussion of the CAPM in Chapter 13 that knowing the systematic risk requires that we have a covariance for the project with the market portfolio. It is extremely difficult to obtain such a project covariance, because there is no market value of the *project*, and no past data to use even if there were a market value. Moreover, the relevant risk premium for the APV approach must be for an all-equity investment. This adds even more difficulty when any existing risk premium reflects the company's debt. But these are only some of the problems in selecting appropriate discount rates. We have already mentioned the problem of the shareholder perspective, which is difficult when shareholders are from different countries and capital markets are segmented. Yet another problem is inflation and the connected question of the nature of the cash flows.

The primary question concerning how to treat inflation in the evaluation of foreign investments is whether we should discount at the "nominal" interest rate or the "real" interest rate—that is, the nominal rate minus the expected rate of inflation. This distinction between nominal interest and real interest is explicit in the Fisher equation presented in Chapter 7:

$$r = \rho + \dot{P}*$$

where ρ is the real rate, r is the nominal rate, and $\dot{P}*$ is the expected rate of inflation. The answer to which of the discount rates to use is that it does not matter provided we are consistent. That is, we shall reach the same conclusions if we discount nominal cash flows by the nominal rate or real cash flows by the real interest rate. We can also note that if capital markets are not segmented, that is, if there is a free flow of capital, the real interest rates in different countries will be similar.

It is frequently the case that we form an idea of the expected cash flow at today's prices. This is a "real" cash flow, and it is often adjusted upward at the expected rate of inflation to yield the expected "nominal" cash flow. If we use inflated values, we should discount at the nominal rate. Alternatively, we can

---

[12] In Appendix 15.2 we show that instead of including the country risk in the discount rate, we can incorporate it within the cash-flow term. This procedure, which can also be followed with other types of risk, involves putting cash flows into their "certainty equivalents." A method of dealing with risk that avoids the need to find certainty equivalents or risk premiums is to deduct from cash flows the cost of country risk insurance or a foreign exchange risk management program. This is the recommendation of Arthur I. Stonehill and Leonard Nathanson in "Capital Budgeting and the Multinational Corporation," *California Management Review*, summer 1968, pp. 39–54. The ability of shareholders to diversify foreign exchange risk has been examined by Jeffery A. Frankel ("The Diversifiability of Exchange Risk," *Journal of International Economics*, August 1979, pp. 379–393).

avoid inflating future cash flows (and then deflating them at the nominal discount rate) and instead leave cash flows in today's prices and discount at the real discount rate. The latter is in many ways a more straightforward procedure.

The advantage from using today's prices and the real rate extends to the use of today's exchange rates with foreign currency cash flows. This is so because if PPP can be expected to hold, exchange rates will mirror the inflation differential, and we shall obtain the same home currency cash flows from converting today's flows at today's exchange rates as by converting future (inflated) amounts at future (depreciated) exchange rates.

When foreign-currency cash flows are predetermined, or **contractual**, we do not have a choice between real and nominal discount rates and between current and future expected exchange rates. Examples of contractual cash flows are revenues from exports sold at fixed prices and depreciation allowances based on historical costs. The contractual amounts are fixed in nominal terms and should therefore be discounted at the nominal rate and converted into dollars at the expected future exchange rate. Contractual flows do not, therefore, lend themselves to simplification through the use of today's cash flows of foreign exchange at today's exchange rates. These conclusions can be derived by using the PPP condition and the Fisher equation.

Using Real Interest Rates and Today's (Real) Cash Flows and Exchange Rates

We will concentrate on the CF_t^* term of Equation (15.2), but our conclusions are valid for any other noncontractual terms in the computation. The cash-flow term is

$$\sum_{t=1}^{T} \frac{S_t^* CF_t^* (1 - \tau)}{(1 + DR_e)^t}$$

Since the numerator gives the expected U.S.-dollar cash flow, DR_e should be the nominal U.S. discount rate, reflecting the project's systematic risk and all-equity financing (with the effects of debt included later in APV). Using the Fisher equation and taking a U.S. perspective, we can write $(1 + DR_e)^t$ as

$$(1 + DR_e)^t = \left(1 + \rho_{US} + \dot{P}_{US}^*\right)^t \tag{15.3}$$

where ρ_{US} is the real rate of return. We can write definition (15.3) more precisely as

$$(1 + DR_e)^t = \left(1 + \rho_{US} + \dot{P}_{US}^* + \rho_{US}\dot{P}_{US}^*\right)^t = (1 + \rho_{US})^t \left(1 + \dot{P}_{US}^*\right)^t \tag{15.4}$$

This is similar to (15.3), since $\rho_{US}\dot{P}_{US}^*$ is the product of two small amounts—for example, $0.02 \times 0.10 = 0.002$—and is therefore unimportant.

If we think that exchange rates will be changing at a steady forecast rate $\dot{S}^*$, we can write

$$S_t^* \equiv S_0(1 + \dot{S}^*)^t \qquad t = 1, 2, \ldots, T$$

This condition is used in Chapter 13. If, in addition, we believe that cash flows in the foreign currency will grow at the foreign rate of inflation, we can write

$$CF_t^* = CF_1^*\left(1 + \dot{P}_{UK}^*\right)^{t-1} \qquad t = 1, 2, \ldots, T$$

where $\dot{P}_{UK}^*$ is the annual rate of inflation and CF_1^* is the initial cash flow, which we assume is unknown. Using this, our definition of S_t^*, and the Fisher equation, we have

$$\sum_{t=1}^{T} \frac{S_t^* CF_t^*(1 - \tau)}{(1 + DR_e)^t} = S_0 \frac{CF_1^*}{1 + \dot{P}_{UK}^*} \sum_{t=1}^{T} \frac{(1 + \dot{S}^*)^t(1 + \dot{P}_{UK}^*)^t(1 - \tau)}{(1 + \rho_{US})^t(1 + \dot{P}_{US}^*)^t} \qquad (15.5)$$

The magnitudes S_0 and $CF_1^*/(1 + \dot{P}_{UK}^*)$ have been placed in front of the summation because they do not depend on t.[13] We can reduce Equation (15.5) to a straightforward expression if we invoke the PPP condition.

We have been writing the precise form of purchasing power parity as

$$\dot{P}_{US} = \dot{P}_{UK} + \dot{S}(1 + \dot{P}_{UK})$$

If the best forecast we can make is that PPP will hold—even though we know that in retrospect we could well be wrong—we can write PPP in the expectations form:

$$\dot{P}_{US}^* = \dot{P}_{UK}^* + \dot{S}^*(1 + \dot{P}_{UK}^*)$$

By adding unity to both sides, we get

$$1 + \dot{P}_{US}^* = \left(1 + \dot{P}_{UK}^*\right) + \dot{S}^*\left(1 + \dot{P}_{UK}^*\right) = \left(1 + \dot{P}_{UK}^*\right)(1 + \dot{S}^*)$$

or

$$\frac{(1 + \dot{S}^*)\left(1 + \dot{P}^*_{UK}\right)}{1 + \dot{P}_{US}^*} = 1$$

By using this in Equation (15.5), we can write the APV cash-flow term in Equation (15.2) in the straightforward form

$$\sum_{t=1}^{T} \frac{S_t^* CF_t^*(1 - \tau)}{(1 + DR_e)^t} = S_0 \frac{CF_1^*}{1 + \dot{P}_{UK}^*} \sum_{t=1}^{T} \frac{1 - \tau}{(1 + \rho_{US})^t} \qquad (15.6)$$

All we need to know to evaluate this expression is the initial exchange rate, S_0; the initial cash flow at today's prices, $CF_1^*/(1 + \dot{P}_{UK}^*)$; the tax rate, τ; and

---

[13] We remove $CF_1^*/(1 + \dot{P}_{UK}^*)$ rather than just CF_1^* because we wish to have all expressions in the summation raised to the power t. The interpretation of $CF_1^*/(1 + \dot{P}_{UK}^*)$ is that it is the value of the initial foreign cash flow at today's prices.

the real discount rate that reflects the systematic risk, ρ_{US}. In reaching this conclusion, we assumed only that cash flows can be expected to grow at the overall rate of inflation, that PPP can be expected to hold, and that the Fisher equation does hold. Any noncontractual term can be handled in this straightforward way; we avoid forecasting inflation and exchange rates at which to convert the foreign-currency amounts. Our conclusion is based on the view that inflation and changes in exchange rates are offsetting—requiring PPP—and that local inflation and inflation premiums in interest rates are also offsetting—requiring the Fisher equation.

While it is reasonable to *expect* PPP and the Fisher equation to hold, when events are *realized*, it is very unlikely that they will have held. However, the departures from the conditions are as likely to be positive as negative. This is part of the risk of business. The risk is that realized changes in exchange rates might not reflect inflation differentials, and the interest rate might poorly reflect the level of inflation. This risk should be reflected in DR_e or ρ_{US}, which, as we have stated, should contain appropriate premiums.

When we are dealing with contractual values, we cannot use the real interest rate with uninflated cash flows. This is because the foreign-currency streams are nominal amounts that must be converted at the exchange rate at the time of payment/receipt and discounted at the nominal rate. What we have if the cash flows are contractual is

$$\sum_{t=1}^{T} \frac{S_t^* CF_t^* (1 - \tau)}{(1 + DR_e)^t} = \sum_{t=1}^{T} \frac{S_0 (1 + \dot{S}^*)^t CF_t^* (1 - \tau)}{(1 + DR_e)^t}$$

We cannot expand CF_t^* in order to cancel terms, since all values of CF_t^* are fixed contractually. We are left to discount at the nominal rate of interest, DR_e. We discount the nominal CF_t^* converted into the investor's currency at the forecast exchange rate.

When the profiles of cash flows or incremental effects such as tax shields vary in real terms and do not grow at the inflation rate (perhaps they initially increase in real terms and later decline), we cannot use PPP and the Fisher equation to reduce the complexity of the problem, even for noncontractual cash flows. We must instead use the APV formula—Equation (15.2)—with forecast nominal cash flows and the nominal discount rate.

Discount Rates for Different Items

Now that the method or methods for handling inflation with the discount rate have been explained, we are ready to describe the nature of the discount rates in the APV formula.

DR_e: This should be nominal for contractual cash flows resulting from sales made at fixed future prices. Since the cash flows are converted into dollars, the rate should be the nominal rate for the United States. DR_e should also be the all-equity rate, reflecting the project's systematic risk, including the risk from exchange rates. When the cash flows are noncontractual, as they will most generally be, we can use a real rate, today's actual exchange rate, and initial-period expected cash flows at today's prices, $CF_1^*/(1 + \dot{P}_{UK}^*)$. This makes the calculations more straightforward.

DR_a: Since in many countries depreciation is based on historical costs, DA_t will be contractual, and DR_a should therefore be the nominal rate. Since we have written DA_t directly in dollar terms, we should use the U.S. rate. The only risk premium should be for the chance that the depreciation allowances will go unused. If the investor feels very confident that the project will yield positive cash flows, this risk is small, and so DR_a should be the riskless nominal rate of the United States. This is true even if DA_t is measured in foreign currency units, provided we convert them into U.S. dollars.

DR_b: If the project's contribution to borrowing capacity is measured in nominal U.S. dollar terms—and it is very likely that it will be—we should discount at the U.S. nominal rate. The risk is that the tax shield cannot be used, and if this is considered small, we can use the riskless rate.

DR_c: The value of a concessionary loan depends on the interest rate that would otherwise be paid. If the loan repayments will be nominal foreign exchange amounts, we should use the nominal foreign interest rate that would have been paid.

DR_d and DR_f: Tax savings, additional repatriated income via transfer prices, and the deferment of tax payments via reinvestment in low-tax countries could be estimated at either today's prices or future prices. If the estimates of TD_t^* and RF_t^* are at today's prices and are therefore real, we must use a real rate, and if they are at future inflated prices, we must use a nominal rate. If the estimates are in U.S. dollars, as they probably will be, we must use a U.S. rate. Since the risk is that of not being able to find techniques for making these tax savings and additional remittances, the appropriate discount rate requires a risk premium. Donald Lessard advises the use of the same rate used for cash flows, DR_e.[14]

With the nature of the terms in the APV formula carefully defined and the factors influencing the discount rates also explained, we are ready to consider a realistic example of capital budgeting. We consider whether Aviva Corporation should build a jeans-manufacturing factory in Italy.

AN EXAMPLE

Suppose that as a result of the imminent entry of new firms into the Italian jeans market, Aviva is considering opening an Italian factory. Aviva hopes that by being on the spot it can be more responsive to local preferences for style and thereby avoid steadily losing sales to the new entrants. The construction costs of

---

[14]See Donald R. Lessard, *op. cit.* As we have already mentioned, this paper forms the basis of the APV technique explained here.

the plant have been estimated at Lit 2 billion, and it is believed that it will add $1 million to Aviva's borrowing capacity. Because of taxes on remitted earnings from Aviva's previously established sales subsidiary in Italy, the proposed factory can be partially financed with Lit 600 million, which, if it had been returned to the United States, would have faced taxes of Lit 400 million in Italy. Of this amount, credit for only Lit 280 million would have been received in the United States.[15] The funds would have been returned to the United States because nothing better could have been done with them.

Assume for simplicity that the current exchange rate between the lira and the U.S. dollar is Lit 1000/$, and so $S_0 = 0.00100$, and the spot rate is expected to move at a rate given by the relative inflation according to PPP. Italian inflation is expected to proceed at 25 percent, while U.S. inflation is expected to be 10 percent.

Jeans sales, which will begin when the plant is completed, after a year, are expected to average 50,000 pairs per year. At the beginning of the year of construction, the jeans have a unit price of Lit 20,000 per pair, and this is expected to rise at the general rate of inflation. The average production cost at material prices at the time of construction is Lit 15,000 per pair, and this cost is likely to keep in line with general Italian inflation.

The Italian market had previously been supplied by Aviva's main plant in California, and recent sales to the Italian market were 10,000 pairs per year. The most recent profit on U.S.-manufactured jeans was $5 per pair, and this can be expected to keep pace with general U.S. inflation. However, it was expected that in the absence of an Italian factory, Aviva would have lost 9.1 percent per annum of its Italian sales to the new entrants. This is why Aviva is considering opening an Italian plant of its own. It has learned that it must be in touch with local styles when local firms enter the market.

The factory is expected to require little in the way of renovation for 10 years. The market value of the plant in 10 years is extremely difficult to estimate, and Aviva is confident only in the belief that it will have some substantial value.

Aviva has by great art and ingenuity managed to arrive at an all-equity cost of capital that reflects the project's systematic risk (including country risk that is not covered by insurance, the deviation of exchange rates from predicted levels, and so on) of 20 percent. This allows for the fact that much of the risk can be diversified by the shareholders and/or avoided by insurance, forward cover, and so on.

In return for locating the factory in an area of heavy unemployment, Aviva will receive from the Italian government Lit 600 million of the Lit 1400 million it needs in addition to the previously blocked funds, at the subsidized rate of 10 percent. The principal is to be repaid in equal installments over 10 years. If Aviva had been required to borrow competitively in Italy, it could have expected

---

[15]The Italian government restricts remittances on "nonproductive" enterprises—hence the high cost of remitting earnings. We will assume that the factory is a productive enterprise and therefore subject only to appropriate corporate taxes.

a 35-percent borrowing cost, as opposed to its 15-percent borrowing cost in the United States. This is a little above the U.S. riskless rate of 12 percent. The remaining Lit 800 million that is needed for construction will be provided as equity by Aviva U.S.A. Income on the project is subject to a 25-percent tax in Italy and a 46-percent tax in the United States, and Italian taxes are fully deductible against U.S. taxes.

The U.S. Internal Revenue Service will allow Aviva to write off one-tenth of the dollar equivalent of the historical construction cost each year over 10 years. By using carefully arranged transfer prices and royalties, Aviva thinks it can reduce taxes by deferrals by $5000 in the initial year of operation, and it expects this to hold steady in real terms, but it does not expect to be able to remit more income than the amount declared.

We can show below that in terms of the notation used in defining APV in Equation (15.2), Aviva faces the following:

$$K_0 = \text{Lit } 2,000,000,000$$

$$BC_0 = \$1,000,000$$

$$AF_0 = \text{Lit } 600,000,000 - (\text{Lit } 600,000,000 - \text{Lit } 400,000,000)$$

$$= \text{Lit } 400,000,000$$

$$S_0 = 0.00100$$

$$S_t^* = 0.00100(1 - 0.12)^t$$

$$CF_t^* = \text{Lit } 50,000(20,000 - 15,000)(1 + 0.25)^t + (\text{scrap value when } t = 10)$$

$$LS_t^* = \$10,000(5)(1 + 0.1)^t(1 - 0.091)^t = \$50,000$$

$$CL_0 = \text{Lit } 600,000,000$$

$$LR_t = (\text{see Table 15.2})$$

$$DA_t = \$200,000$$

$$TD_t = \$5000(1 + 0.1)^{t-1} \quad \text{for} \quad t > 0.$$

$$RF_t = 0$$

$$\tau = 0.46$$

$$DR_e = DR_d = DR_f = 0.20$$

$$DR_a = DR_b = 0.12$$

$$DR_c = 0.35$$

$$r_g = 0.15$$

We will solve the problem by using all nominal values for cash flows and all nominal discount rates.

Many of the values attached to the terms of the APV formula are self-evident. For example, the construction cost is Lit 2,000,000,000, and the borrowing capacity is $1,000,000. The value of activated funds, AF_0, is their face value minus their value in their next best use. If the next best use is to bring them home and face taxes, the next best value is Lit 600,000,000 − Lit 400,000,000. We exclude the tax credit in the United States *on repatriated restricted funds* because it is smaller than the taxes paid in Italy; thus the effective tax rate is the Italian rate. (If the credit cannot be applied against other income, it has no value.) This means that if the blocked funds had been brought back, Lit 200,000,000 would have been received after taxes. We subtract this from the Lit 600,000,000 used in the project to get Lit 400,000,000 for AF_0.

The expected exchange rates are obtained from the definition $S_t^* \equiv S_0(1 + \dot{S}^*)^t$. We obtain $\dot{S}^*$ from the PPP condition; that is,

$$\dot{S}^* = \frac{\dot{P}_{US}^* - \dot{P}_{IT}^*}{(1 + \dot{P}_{IT}^*)} = \frac{0.10 - 0.25}{1.25} = -0.12$$

The cash flow, CF_t^*, is obtained by multiplying the expected sales of 50,000 pairs of jeans per annum by the expected profit per pair. The profit per pair during the construction year, when prices and costs are known, would be Lit 20,000 − Lit 15,000 if production could begin immediately, but by the initial year of operation the profit per pair is expected to rise to (Lit 20,000 − Lit 15,000)(1 + 0.25). The profit is expected to continue to rise at 25 percent per annum, with an expected cash flow by year t of

$$(Lit\ 20,000 - Lit\ 15,000)(1 + 0.25)^t$$

from each of the 50,000 pairs. The value of this is shown in Table 15.2. The present value of the cash flow at Aviva's chosen cost of capital of $DR_e = 0.20$ is also shown.

The scrap value of the project is uncertain. As a result, we can take a two-step approach to see whether the project is profitable without estimating a scrap value, since if it is, we can save time in our evaluation.

Replaced sales, LS_t^*, have most recently been producing a profit for Aviva U.S.A. of $5 \times 10,000 = $50,000$ per year. With the profit per unit expected to grow at the U.S. inflation rate of 10 percent and the number of units expected to decline by 9.1 percent, expected profits from replaced sales remain at their current level of $50,000 per year; the product of 1.10 and 1 − 0.091 equals unity.

The amount of the concessionary loan is $CL_0 = $ Lit 600,000,000. The repayments for the principal are at Lit 60,000,000 each year, with interest computed on the unpaid balance at 10 percent per annum. LR_t in Table 15.2 shows the annual loan repayments discounted at the market rate in Italy of $DR_c = 0.35$. The table also gives the values of the discounted net-of-tax depreciation allowances of $200,000 per year. This is 10 percent of the historical cost in dollars, $S_0 K_0$. We use the dollar cost because the depreciation is effectively

TABLE 15.2
ADJUSTED-PRESENT-VALUE MAGNITUDES FOR ITALIAN JEANS FACTORY

Year	S_t^* $/Lit	CF_t^* Lit	$S_t^* CF_t^*$ $	$S_t^* CF_t^* - LS_t^*$ $	$(1-\tau)\dfrac{S_t^* CF_t^* - LS_t^*}{(1+DR_e)^t}$ $
1	0.0008800	312,500,000	275,000	225,000	101,250
2	0.0007744	390,625,000	302,500	252,500	94,688
3	0.0006815	488,281,250	332,764	282,764	88,364
4	0.0005997	610,351,560	366,028	316,028	82,299
5	0.0005277	762,939,450	402,603	352,603	76,520
6	0.0004644	953,674,320	442,886	392,886	71,051
7	0.0004087	1,192,092,900	487,208	437,208	65,889
8	0.0003596	1,490,116,120	535,846	485,846	61,016
9	0.0003165	1,862,645,150	589,527	539,527	56,465
10	0.0002785	2,328,306,440	648,433	598,433	52,191
					749,733

TABLE 15.2
CONTINUED

Year	$\dfrac{DA_t\tau}{(1+DR_a)^t}$ $	$r_g BC_0\tau$ $	$\dfrac{r_g BC_0\tau}{(1+DR_b)^t}$ $	TD_i^* $	$\dfrac{TD_i^*}{(1+DR_d)^t}$ $	Outstanding loan Lit	Loan interest Lit	LR_t Lit	$\dfrac{LR_t}{(1+DR_c)^t}$ Lit
1	82,143	69,000	61,607	5,000	4,167	600,000,000	60,000,000	120,000,000	88,888,889
2	73,342	69,000	55,007	5,500	3,819	540,000,000	54,000,000	114,000,000	62,551,440
3	65,484	69,000	49,113	6,050	3,501	480,000,000	48,000,000	108,000,000	43,895,748
4	48,468	69,000	43,851	6,655	3,209	420,000,000	42,000,000	102,000,000	30,708,959
5	52,203	69,000	39,153	7,321	2,942	360,000,000	36,000,000	96,000,000	21,409,296
6	46,610	69,000	34,957	8,053	2,697	300,000,000	30,000,000	90,000,000	14,867,567
7	41,616	69,000	31,212	8,858	2,472	240,000,000	24,000,000	84,000,000	10,278,812
8	37,157	69,000	27,868	9,744	2,266	180,000,000	18,000,000	78,000,000	7,070,082
9	33,176	69,000	24,882	10,718	2,077	120,000,000	12,000,000	72,000,000	4,834,244
10	29,622	69,000	22,216	11,790	1,904	60,000,000	6,000,000	66,000,000	3,282,511
	519,821		389,866		29,054				287,787,548

against U.S. corporate taxes. These are at the rate $\tau = 0.46$. We have discounted depreciation allowances at the riskless dollar rate, $DR_a = 0.12$.

The debt or borrowing capacity of the project is such that Aviva can borrow $1,000,000 (which is half the dollar cost of construction) to obtain tax shields somewhere within its operations. The interest rate Aviva would pay if it took the tax shields by borrowing more at home is $r_g = 0.15$. This will save taxes on $0.15 \times \$1,000,000$ at the tax rate $\tau = 0.46$. We have discounted the saving from the tax shield at the riskless dollar rate, $DR_b = 0.12$.

The extra tax benefits, TD_t^*, of $5000 are assumed to keep pace with U.S. inflation. We have discounted $TD_t^* = \$5000$ at Aviva's cost of equity of 20 percent.

We can form an opinion concerning the feasibility of the jeans factory if we use the values of the terms as we have stated them, including the totals from Table 15.2, in the APV formula, Equation (15.2):

$$APV = -(0.001 \times 2,000,000,000) + (0.001 \times 400,000,000) + 749,733$$
$$+ 519,821 + 389,866 + 0.001 \times (600,000,000 - 287,787,548)$$
$$+ 29,054 + 0 = \$400,686$$

We discover that the APV is positive. This means that the project is worthwhile. Furthermore, the APV does not yet include any estimate for the market value of the factory and land at the end of 10 years. If Aviva feels that while it cannot estimate this value, it should exceed half the original cost in real terms, it can take an even more confident position. Half the original project cost is $1 million, and since this is a real value, it should be discounted at the real interest rate relevant for dollars. Using Aviva's risky rate, this is DR_e minus the U.S. expected inflation rate of 10 percent; that is, $DR_e = 0.20 - 0.10 = 0.10$. At this rate the present value of $1 million in 10 years is $385,543, which makes the APV clearly positive. The $385,543 would be subject to a capital-gain tax if it were to be realized because the entire project has been depreciated, but even after taxes the project would clearly seem to be worthwhile.

ACTUAL PRACTICE OF CAPITAL BUDGETING

The adjusted-present-value approach using the correct discount rate to reflect the contractual or noncontractual nature of cash flows and the systematic risk of the investment project requires management to take a very scientific view. We can expect that constraints on the knowledge of managers and the time available to make decisions will result in approaches that are more pragmatic than the approach we presented. According to a survey of multinational corporations this does appear to be the case. The survey was made of 10 U.S. multinationals by Business International to see how they analyze acquisitions.[16]

---

[16]See "BIMR Survey Reveals How U.S. Multinationals Analyze Foreign Acquisitions," *Money Report*, Business International, November 28, 1980. See also "Stress on Currency Fluctuations as MNCs Analyze Foreign Acquisitions," *Money Report*, Business International, November 5, 1980.

It showed that only 7 of the 10 corporations used any sort of discounting method at all.

Only one of the respondents in the Business International Survey said that it looked at synergy effects, that is, the effects the acquisition would have on other subsidiaries. Five of the ten firms used the same hurdle discount rate for all acquisitions, whatever the country. Projected exchange rates were used by five of the respondents, while two used the projected rate if they considered a currency to be unstable and the current rate if they considered it to be stable. The remainder used current rates to convert all currency flows, but it was not clear from the survey whether these flows were measured in current price terms. At least one company assumed that exchange-rate movements would be reflected in relative interest rates and therefore used the U.S. interest rate on cash flows converted into dollars at the current exchange rate.

A survey of the foreign-investment evaluation practices of 225 U.S. manufacturing MNCs conducted by Marie Wicks Kelly and George Philippatos produced results revealing practices somewhat more in line with theory than those found in the much smaller Business International survey.[17] For example, the majority of companies used cash-flow calculations and costs of capital which, while not exactly the kind explained in this chapter, are approximately in line with appropriate procedures.

SUMMARY

1 The net-present-value technique is difficult to use in the case of foreign investment projects. The adjusted-present-value technique is frequently recommended instead.

2 Cash flows from foreign investments can be seen in two different ways: from the investor's perspective and from the perspective of the project managers in the foreign countries. It is the investor's perspective which is relevant. Factors which can make a difference between cash flows from the different perspectives include blocked funds (which reduce project costs to investors), reduced sales from other corporate divisions, restrictions on remitting earnings, extra taxes on repatriated income, and concessionary loans. These factors can be included in the adjusted present value (APV).

3 The APV technique allows a two-step evaluation. The first step involves a conservative estimate that includes only estimated benefits of the project. The second step, including other benefits, is needed only if the first step gives a negative estimate.

4 The calculation of APV includes cash flows net of taxes and reduced earnings elsewhere, depreciation allowances, tax shields, the value of concessionary loans, and other potential benefits. Each item must be discounted at an appropriate discount rate.

5 Discount rates should reflect only the systematic risk of the item being discounted. Doing business abroad can help reduce overall corporate risk when incomes are more independent between countries than between operations within a particular country, and this can mean lower discount rates for foreign projects.

[17]Marie E. Wicks Kelly and George C. Philippatos, "Comparative Analysis of the Foreign Investment Evaluation Practices by U.S.-Based Manufacturing Multinational Companies," *Journal of International Business Studies*, winter 1982, pp. 19–42.

6 Discount rates can, however, be higher on foreign investment projects because of country risk and exchange-rate risk. These risks can be diversified by shareholders if they invest in a number of countries, and this reduces required risk premiums.

7 We must be consistent when we take care of inflation in foreign-project evaluation. We can use either real values of cash flows, and so on, and real interest rates, or nominal cash flows and nominal interest rates.

8 When we are dealing with noncontractual flows, we can choose the method of handling inflation that we prefer. However, with contractual flows, which are nominal amounts, we must use nominal discount rates. The choice of approach with noncontractual flows exists because of the PPP condition and the Fisher equation. These help ensure that inflation in cash flows will be offset by movements in exchange rates, and so on. However, the fact that PPP, and so on, are imprecise contributes risks. These should be incorporated in selected discount rates.

QUESTIONS

1 Will withholding taxes that are at rates below domestic corporate tax rates affect direct investment when full withholding tax credit is available? How will withholding tax rates affect the distribution of total tax revenues between countries?

2 A U.S. automobile manufacturer, National Motors, is considering building a new plant in Britain to produce is sports car, the Sting. The estimated construction cost of the plants is £50,000,000, and construction should be completed in a year. The plant will raise borrowing capacity by about $40,000,000. National Motors can reinvest £20,000,000 already held in Britain. If these funds were repatriated to the United States, they would face an effective tax rate of 46 percent. Inflation in Britain is expected to be at 15 percent; in the United states, at 10 percent. The current exchange rate is $S(\$/£) = 2.00$, and it is believed that PPP is likely to hold.

National Motors expects to sell the Sting with only minor modifications for 5 years, and after this period the plant will require remodeling. The value of the plant for future use is expected to be £40,000,000 in nominal terms after 5 years. The Sting will have an initial sticker price of about £8000, and it is expected that 10,000 will be sold each year. Production costs are estimated at £6000. These values are expected to move in line with the general price level in Britain.

National Motors also builds a two-seater car in Germany called the Racer and expects 4000 Racers to be replaced by the Sting. Since Racers are in short supply, 2000 of the 4000 Racers can be sold in Japan at the same profit as in Germany. The before-tax profit on the Racer during the initial year of producing the Sting is expected to be DM 5000 per car, with $S(DM/£) = 4.00$. This is expected to keep in line with German inflation, and PPP is expected to prevail between Britain and Germany.

Because National Motors will be building the Sting in Merseyside, an area of heavy unemployment, the British government has offered the company a loan of £20,000,000 at a 10-percent interest rate. The principal is to be repaid in five equal installments, with the first installment due at the beginning of the initial year of production. The competitive market rate in Britain is 20 percent, while in the United States, National Motors faces a borrowing rate of 12 percent and a riskless rate of 10 percent. The balance of the capital will be provided as equity. The tax rate in Britain is 50 percent, which is higher than the 46-percent rate in the United States. British tax law allows car plants to be depreciated over 5 years.

The British and U.S. tax authorities are careful that appropriate transfer prices are used so that no taxes can by saved by using intercompany pricing techniques. National Motors believes a 20-percent discount rate is appropriate for the project.

Should the Sting be built?

3 Which items in the previous question are contractual, and which are noncontractual? Could you discount the cash flows with a real rate of interest?

4 Compare the treatments of tax shields from debt in using the NPV and APV approaches to foreign investments.

BIBLIOGRAPHY

Adler, Michael: "The Cost of Capital and Valuation of a Two-Country Firm," *Journal of Finance*, March 1974, pp. 119–132.

Booth, Lawrence D.: "Capital Budgeting Frameworks for the Multinational Corporation," *Journal of International Business Studies*, fall 1982, pp. 113–123.

Eaker, Mark R.: "Investment/Financing Decisions for Multinational Corporations," in Dennis E. Logue (ed.), *Handbook of Modern Finance*, Warren, Gorham and Lamont, Boston, 1984. pp. 42-1–42-29.

Lessard, Donald R.: "Evaluating International Projects: An Adjusted Present Value Approach," in Donald Lessard (ed.), *International Financial Management: Theory and Application*, 2nd ed., Wiley, New York, 1985.

Shapiro, Alan C.: "Capital Budgeting for the Multinational Corporation," *Financial Management*, spring 1978, pp. 7–16.

Stonehill, Arthur I., and Leonard Nathanson.: "Capital Budgeting and the Multinational Corporation," *California Management Review*, summer 1968, pp. 39–54.

APPENDIX 15.1: A Survey of International Taxation

International taxation is a complex subject, and we can do little more than explain variations in the types of taxes encountered and the methods that can be used to help reduce them. We will view taxation questions in the most general terms.[18]

THE DIFFERENT FORMS OF TAXES

Corporate Taxes

Income taxes are the chief source of revenue for the U.S. government, and the corporate income tax is an important component of the total of income taxes. Income taxes are **direct taxes**, and the United States is dependent on direct taxes for a greater proportion of its total revenue than most other countries. Members of the European Economic

---

[18] For more detailed descriptions of international taxation in the United States, see Elizabeth A. Owens, *Bibliography on Taxation of Foreign Operations and Foreigners, 1968–75*, International Tax Program, Harvard Law School, Cambridge, Mass., 1976.

TABLE 15A.1
CORPORATE INCOME TAX RATES, 1989*
(Percentages)

Australia	49	Japan[†]	50
Canada	43	Netherlands	42
Denmark	50	New Zealand	48
Finland[†]	50	Singapore	33
France	42	Sweden	52
Hong Kong	17	United Kingdom	35
Ireland	36	United States	34
Italy	43	West Germany	50

*Actual rates in 1989 or schedules rates as of 1987.
[†]National plus local taxes.
Source: Vito Tanzi, "The Response of Other Industrial Countries to the U.S. Tax Reform Act," *National Tax Journal,* September 1987, p. 348, and Ernst and Whinney, *Corporate Taxation: A Worldwide Guide,* 1989 ed.

Community (Common Market) collect direct taxes, but these are augmented by a **value-added tax** or **VAT**, which is an **indirect tax**.[19] Many poorer countries have a tax on imports as their primary revenue source. Other taxes that are found are based on wealth, sales, turnover, employees, and so on. Despite variations in the proportion of total tax receipts derived from corporate and other income taxes, the corporate tax rates are remarkably similar in industrialized countries. Table 15A.1 shows, for example, that the rates are between 34 and 52 percent in a large number of nations. Outside the industrialized countries the rates that are charged vary considerably, with some tax havens charging no corporate tax at all. Countries with zero rates include the Bahamas and Bermuda. The absence of corporation taxes is designed to encourage multinationals to locate offices for sheltering income from abroad.

The United States considers that it has jurisdiction over all the income of its citizens and residents wherever it is earned. However, credit is given for taxes paid elsewhere as long as the credit does not cause taxes to fall below what would have been paid had the income been earned in the United States. While citizens and residents of the United States are taxed on their full income wherever it is earned, nonresidents are taxed only on their income in the United States. This is the practice in other countries. The resident versus nonresident status of a corporation is determined by where it is incorporated.

Some countries that appear to have low corporate tax rates have more normal rates when local corporate taxes are added. For example, while Switzerland has federal corporate rates below 10 percent, the local authorities, called **cantons**, have tax rates of between 5 and 40 percent. Different provincial rates in Canada can make rates vary up to 5 percent. Further variation and complication are introduced by the fact that some national tax authorities give full credit for local taxes, while others do not. In addition, there is considerable variation between countries according to what expenditures are deductible in determining taxable income and the amount of deductions.

---

[19]By definition, direct taxes cannot be shifted and are borne directly by those on whom they are levied. In contrast, indirect taxes can be shifted in part or in full to somebody who is not directly taxed. For example, corporate and personal income taxes are paid by those on whom they are levied. On the other hand, sales taxes and import duties charged to firms are at least in part paid by consumers. The consumer therefore pays indirectly.

Value-Added Tax (VAT)

A value-added tax is similar to a sales tax, but each seller can deduct the taxes paid at previous stages of production. If, for example, the VAT rate is 25 percent and a company cuts trees and sells $100 worth of wood to a furniture manufacturer, the tax is $25, since there are no previous stages of production. If the wood is made into furniture that is sold for $240, the furniture manufacturer must pay $60 minus the already collected VAT. Since the wood producer paid $25, the VAT of the manufacturer is $35. Since the eventual effect is the collection of 25 percent of the final selling price, the VAT is like a sales tax that is collected at each stage of production rather than only at the final retail stage.[20]

Because each payer receives credit for taxes paid at previous stages of production, there is an incentive to get complete records from suppliers. This reduces evasion but can give rise to complaints about burdensome, costly paperwork. The value-added tax has partially replaced income taxes on individuals in the European Economic Community. It has been promoted because it is a tax on spending and not on income. Taxes on income are a disincentive to work, while taxes on spending can be considered a disincentive to spend, that is, an incentive to save. Another advantage of VAT to countries promoting exports is that the rules of the General Agreement on Tariffs and Trade allow rebates of VAT to exporters, while a potential drawback is that VAT can distort patterns of output.

Import Duties

Before income tax and value-added tax became primary sources of revenue, import duties or tariffs (two terms for the same thing) were major sources of fiscal receipts.[21] Since goods entering a country are shipped to specific ports where policing can be intensive, import duties are a good source of revenue when income or sales records are poor. This partly explains why some underdeveloped countries depend on tariffs. Also, tariffs can explain why an automobile or refrigerator can cost 5 times more in some countries than in others. Because tariffs can be levied more heavily on luxuries than on necessities, they do not have to be regressive.[22]

Tariffs explain why some firms move production facilities abroad. For example, if automobiles made in the United States and sold in Britain face a tariff and this can be avoided if the vehicles are produced in Great Britain, a British plant may be opened. Tariffs are used to protect jobs that are believed to be threatened by cheap foreign imports. For example, if sales of imported footwear or automobiles increase while domestically produced goods face sluggish sales, there may be lobbying to impose tariffs or quantitative restrictions (quotas) on imports. Tariffs tend to distort the pattern of international trade because countries may produce goods and services for which they do not have a comparative advantage but on which they can make profits behind protective barriers. Duties have been imposed by the U.S. government in the form of **countervailing tariffs** when it was believed that foreign competitors were **dumping** (selling at lower prices abroad than at home) or receiving "unfair" export help from their governments.

---

[20]For more on VAT, see *Value Added Tax*, Price Waterhouse, New York, November 1979.

[21]Tariffs are also called **excise taxes**. They can be based on value (*ad valorem*) or on the weight of imports.

[22]With a regressive tax, the poor pay a larger *fraction* of their income or spending than do the rich. A tax can be regressive even if the rich pay a larger absolute *amount*.

Withholding Taxes

Withholding taxes are collected from foreign individuals or corporations on income they have received from sources within a country. For example, if a U.S. resident earns dividends in Canada, taxes will be withheld and paid to Revenue Canada. Credit is generally received on taxes withheld, and so the level of withholding primarily affects the amount of taxes received by the respective tax authorities. For example, if the U.S. resident has 15 percent withheld in Canada and is in a 25-percent tax bracket in the United States, the U.S. tax payable will be reduced to 10 percent of the income after credit for the 15 percent is given. Higher withholding rates therefore generally mean that more is collected by the foreign authorities and a smaller amount by the domestic government.

There are some circumstances in which the level of withholding does matter. Clearly, if the rate of withholding exceeds the effective tax rate at home, full credit may not be obtained. This can happen even if the tax *rate* at home is higher than the withholding rate if the definition of income or eligible deductions differs between the countries. For example, if little depreciation is deductible in the foreign country but generous allowances exist at home, the taxable income may differ, and more taxes may be paid abroad than are payable at home. There is an overall limitation on credit for taxes withheld that equals taxes payable in the United States, but when tax returns for a number of countries are combined, full credit may be obtained even when on an individual-country basis there would have been unused credit.[23]

Branch versus Subsidiary Taxes

An important element in corporate tax planning is deciding whether to operate abroad with a branch or with a subsidiary. A branch is a foreign operation that is incorporated at home, while a subsidiary is incorporated in the foreign country.

If a foreign activity is not expected to be profitable for a number of years, there may be an advantage to starting out with a branch so that negative earnings abroad can be used to offset profits at home in a consolidated tax return. U.S. tax laws and the tax laws of a number of other countries allow branch income to be consolidated. If a company expects positive foreign income and this income is not to be repatriated, there may be an advantage to a subsidiary. Foreign branches pay taxes on income as it is earned, while subsidiaries do not pay U.S. taxes until the income is repatriated. Whether this is sufficient reason to form an overseas subsidiary depends on relative tax rates and on whether the company wishes to repatriate earnings.

ORGANIZATIONAL STRUCTURES FOR REDUCING TAXES

The Foreign-Sales Corporation (FSC)

The **foreign-sales corporation** (FSC) is a device for encouraging U.S. export sales by giving a tax break on the generated profits. The possibility of establishing a foreign-sales corporation was part of the Tax Reform Act of 1984. Prior to this Act, the U.S. International Revenue Service offered tax breaks to exporters via the operation of

---

[23] When high levels of withholding are combined with low levels, the unused credit on the low levels of withholding is utilized by the high levels of withholding within the combined tax return. Even if the combined return does not provide full credit, unused credit can be carried back 2 years or forward 5 years.

domestic international-sales corporations (DISCs). While some DISCs still exist, the FSC has effectively replaced the DISC as the preferred tax-saving vehicle of exporters.

The main advantage offered by an FSC is that the goods or services "bought" by the FSC for subsequent sale do not have to be priced at **arm's length**, that is, at proper market value. Rather the FSC can use an artificial or **administered price** to increase its own profit and consequently reduce the profit—and tax—of the firm producing the U.S. goods or services for export. For example, if Aviva were to establish an FSC, Aviva itself could "sell" its jeans to its FSC for an artificially low price. Aviva's FSC could then sell the jeans abroad. Only a portion of Aviva's FSC's income is then subject to tax, and Aviva's own taxable income is reduced. That is, there is a shifting of income, by using the artificially low prices, from Aviva to its FSC. The tax paid by the FSC is less than the tax saving of Aviva.

There are, however, some limitations on the administrative prices and the portion of an FSC's income which escapes tax, as well as in the structure of an FSC. Some of the more important of the limitations and requirements are as follows:

1 An FSC must have its office in a possession of the U.S., or in a country with a tax information exchange program with the IRS.[24] This is to ensure the FSC is an "offshore" corporation.

2 Tax and accounting information must nevertheless be available at a location in the United States.

3 At least one director must not be a U.S. resident. This is also to ensure the FSC is "foreign."

4 An FSC may not coexist with a DISC that is controlled by the same corporation(s). An FSC may serve more than one corporation, but must have fewer than 25 shareholders.

5 Qualifying income is generated from the sale of U.S. "property," which essentially means goods or services produced or grown in the U.S., including leasing, rental property, and management services unrelated to the FSC.

6 The prices "paid" by the FSC to the producer can be set so that the FSC's income is the largest of the following three amounts:

a 1.83 percent of the FSC's revenue.

b 23 percent of the combined taxable income of the FSC and related suppliers associated with the export transactions.

c The FSC's income that would occur using arm's-length pricing.

The effect of this is that the worst that could happen is that the FSC's income would be as if the goods were priced at arm's length. However, in general the FSC can enjoy higher profits than this. These profits are taxed more favorably than if the profits had been made by the U.S. producer.

7 Only part of the FSC's income is taxed. If pricing is at arm's length, all the FSC's income is called **foreign-trade income**, and 30 percent of this is exempt from tax. If one of the two alternative administrative pricing rules is used, foreign-trade income involves adding the FSC's operating expenses to the taxable income—excluding the cost of goods sold—and $\frac{15}{23}$, or approximately 62.22 percent, of this is exempt. This can be very advantageous if expenses are low.

---

[24] The U.S. possessions are Guam, American Samoa, the U.S. Virgin Islands, and the Mariana Islands.

8 Domestic corporate shareholders of the FSC receive a 100-percent dividend-received deduction when disbursements occur, except for the taxable component of income under arm's-length pricing.[25]

80-20 Subsidiaries

If 80 percent or more of a corporation's income is earned abroad, dividends and interest paid by the corporation are considered foreign-source income by the U.S. Internal Revenue Service. An 80-20 subsidiary is formed to raise capital for the parent, since it is considered foreign by the IRS and therefore does not need to deduct withholding taxes. Payments made to 80-20 corporations may well be taxed by foreign governments, but when the income is consolidated, credit will be obtained. If an 80-20 corporation is incorporated in the Netherlands Antilles or in another country with a treaty with the United States permitting no withholding taxes, then when interest is paid by the U.S. parent to the 80-20 subsidiary, the parent can also avoid having taxes withheld. This means that a company can avoid withholding taxes completely by having an 80-20 corporation in a treaty country. However, as we mentioned in Chapter 14, since the passage of the Deficit Reduction Act of 1984, which removed the need for U.S. corporations to withhold tax on incomes paid to foreigners, the need for 80-20 subsidiaries has been reduced.

Internal Pricing

It is possible for a corporation to shift profits from high-tax countries to low-tax countries in order to reduce its overall taxes. However, the potential for U.S. corporations to do this is reduced by an important section of the U.S. Internal Revenue Code. Section 482 allows the Treasury to reallocate income and/or expenses to prevent evasion of taxes within commonly owned entities. The IRS requires internal prices to be as if they had been determined competitively. Of course, this does not apply to FSCs.

Tax Havens

Some countries charge extremely low corporate taxes to encourage corporations to locate within their jurisdiction, bring jobs, and so on. These countries include the Bahamas, Bermuda, and Cayman Islands, and Grenada, and they are all endowed with delightful climates. The ability of U.S. corporations to take full advantage of tax havens is limited by Section 882 of the U.S. Tax Code. This says that foreign corporations doing business in the United States are taxed at U.S. rates. There is therefore no obvious advantage to locating the corporate headquarters in the tax haven for doing business at home.

---

[25]By necessity, we have covered only the highlights. More details are contained in the IRS guides, and in materials available from U.S. accounting firms.

APPENDIX 15.2: Country Risk and Discount Rates

Let us define CF_t^* as the cash flow if confiscation does not occur, and let us assume that confiscation risk is the only country risk and that the probability that complete confiscation will occur in any year is a constant.[26] We shall write this probability as λ. With λ as the probability that confiscation will occur, $1 - \lambda$ is the probability that it will not occur. With $1 - \lambda$ as the probability that income will continue in each individual year, the probability that it will continue for 2 years is $(1 - \lambda)^2$, and for t years it is $(1 - \lambda)^t$. For example, if there is a 0.95 probability of nonconfiscation in any individual year, the probability of nonconfiscation for 2 years is $0.95 \times 0.95 = 0.90$. With CF_t^* as the cash flow if the investment has not been confiscated, the expected cash flow in year t adjusted for the probability that the investment will survive is

$$(1 - \lambda)^t CF_t^* \tag{15A.1}$$

We see from this expression that because CF_t^* is the cash flow if the investment is not lost, the expected cash flow that is adjusted for the probability of losing the investment is the smaller amount $(1 - \lambda)^t CF_t^*$. For example, if the expected cash flow is £100 if confiscation has not yet occurred and the probability of confiscation in each year is 0.02, then the probability-weighted expected cash flow in year 5 is $(0.98)^5 \times 100$, that is, £90, and in year 10 it is £82.

If we assume that the cash flow is a constant, $\overline{CF}$, the expression (15A.1) can be written as follows:

$$V = \sum_{t=1}^{T} \frac{(1 - \lambda)^t CF_t^*}{(1 + DR_e)^t} = \overline{CF} \sum_{t=1}^{T} \frac{(1 - \lambda)^t}{(1 + DR_e)^t} \tag{15A.2}$$

The summation $\sum_{t=1}^{T}(1 - \lambda)^t/(1 + DR_e)^t$ is a geometric series. By writing it in full as

$$G = \frac{1 - \lambda}{1 + DR_e} + \frac{(1 - \lambda)^2}{(1 + DR_e)^2} + \cdots + \frac{(1 - \lambda)^T}{(1 + DR_e)^T}$$

we have on multiplying both sides of the expression by $(1 - \lambda)/(1 + DR_e)$,

$$\frac{1 - \lambda}{1 + DR_e} G = \frac{(1 - \lambda)^2}{(1 + DR_e)^2} + \cdots + \frac{(1 - \lambda)^T}{(1 + DR_e)^T} + \frac{(1 - \lambda)^{T+1}}{(1 + DR_e)^{T+1}}$$

[26]An analysis that considers other events than confiscation has been provided by Alan Shapiro. See Alan C. Shapiro, "Capital Budgeting for the Multinational Corporation," *Financial Management*, spring 1978, pp. 7–16.

By subtracting, we get

$$G - \frac{1 - \lambda}{1 + DR_e}G = \frac{1 - \lambda}{1 + DR_e} - \frac{(1 - \lambda)^{T+1}}{(1 + DR_e)^{T+1}}$$

As T approaches infinity on a project with an infinite life, we find that

$$\frac{DR_e + \lambda}{1 + DR_e}G + \frac{1 - \lambda}{1 + DR_e}$$

That is,

$$G = \frac{1 - \lambda}{DR_e + \lambda}$$

We can therefore write Equation (15A.2) as follows:

$$V = \frac{\overline{CF}(1 - \lambda)}{DR_e + \lambda}$$

This can be compared with the value for the constant cash flow *without* country risk:

$$V' = \overline{CF} \sum_{t=1}^{T} \frac{1}{(1 + DR_e)^t}$$

By repeating the method for summing a geometric series, we get

$$V' = \frac{\overline{CF}}{DR_e}$$

as T approaches infinity. We find that we can allow for country risk by multiplying the cash flows by the probability that the firm will survive each year and dividing by the sum of the discount rate and the probability of confiscation.

THE GROWTH AND SPECIAL PROBLEMS OF MULTINATIONAL CORPORATIONS

The APV principle described in the previous chapter makes clear the importance of evaluating expected cash flows and risks when making foreign direct investments. But what makes expected cash flows and risks what they are? Furthermore, can anything be done to influence them? For example, can **transfer prices** of goods and services moving within a multinational corporation be used to reduce taxes or otherwise increase net cash flows, and can financial structure be used to reduce political risk? Indeed, can an MNC correctly measure the cash flows and political risks of foreign investments? These questions, which are central to the emergence and management of MNCs, are the focus of this chapter. In addition, we look at the problems and benefits that have been brought to the world by the often maligned MNC.

THE GROWTH OF MULTINATIONAL CORPORATIONS

It is foreign direct investments which have taken place in the past that have resulted in the growth of the multinational corporation. In the extensive example in the previous chapter Aviva's overseas direct investment was a result of the movement of indigenous firms into its market. This reason for overseas investment can be considered as strategic. It is especially important in dynamic and changing markets, such as publishing and fashion clothing, where subsidiaries must keep in line with local needs and where shipping time is vital. In addition to strategic reasons for direct investment, numerous other reasons have been put forward, and while these are not strictly financial, they deserve some mention in this book.

Reasons for the Growth of MNCs

Availability of Raw Materials   If there are mills producing denim cloth in other countries and the quality is good and the price is attractive, why should a firm like Aviva Corporation buy the material abroad, ship it to the United States, manufacture the jeans, and then ship the finished garments? Clearly, if the ability exists to manufacture the jeans in the foreign market, the firm can eliminate two-way shipping costs—for denim in one direction and jeans in the other—by directly investing in a manufacturing plant abroad.[1]

Many industrial firms, most particularly mining companies, have little choice but to locate at the site of their raw materials. If copper or iron ore is being smelted, it often does not make sense to ship the ore when a smelter can be built near the mine site. The product of the smelter—the copper or iron bars, which weigh much less than the original ore—can be shipped out to the market. But we still have to ask why it would be a foreign firm rather than an indigenous firm that would carry out the enterprise. With an indigenous firm there would be no foreign direct investment. One reason why foreign firms have an edge has to do with know-how and technical factors concerning integration of operations.

Integrating Operations   When there are advantages to vertical integration in terms of assured delivery between various stages of production and the different stages can be performed better in different locations (as with the smelting of ores), there is good reason to invest abroad. This reason for direct investment has been advanced by Charles Kindleberger, who along with Richard Caves did some of the earlier work on direct investment.[2]

Nontransferable Knowledge   It is often possible for firms to sell their knowledge in the form of patent rights and to license a foreign producer. This relieves a firm of the need to make direct investment abroad. However, sometimes a firm that has a production process or product patent can make a larger profit by doing the foreign production itself. This is because there are some kinds of knowledge which cannot be sold and which are the result of years of experience. Aviva, for example, might be able to sell patterns and designs, and it can license the use of its name, but it cannot sell a foreign firm its experience in producing and marketing the product. This points to another reason why a firm might wish to do its own foreign production.

---

[1]A model of overseas direct investment that considers transportation costs as well as issues involving stages of production and economies of scale has been developed by Jimmy Weinblatt and Robert E. Lipsey, "A Model of Firms' Decisions to Export or Produce Abroad," National Bureau of Economic Research, Working Paper 511, July 1980.

[2]We refer to Charles P. Kindleberger, *American Business Abroad*, Yale University Press, New Haven, Conn., 1969. See also Richard E. Caves, "International Corporations: The Industrial Economics of Foreign Investment," *Economica*, February 1971, pp. 1–27. A number of papers on direct investment are contained in John H. Dunning (ed.), *International Investment*, Penguin Books, Harmonsworth, U.K., 1972. For factors affecting the initial decision, the reader may consult J. David Richardson, "On Going Abroad: The Firm's Initial Foreign Investment Decision," *Quarterly Review of Economics and Business*, winter 1971, pp. 7–22.

Protecting Reputations Products develop good or bad names, and these are carried across international boundaries. Even people in the Soviet bloc, for example, know the names of certain brands of jeans. It would not serve the good name of Aviva Corporation to have a foreign licensee to do a shoddy job in producing jeans with the Aviva label. Similarly, it is important for multinational restaurant chains and fast food outlets to maintain homogeneous quality to protect their reputations. We find that there can be valid reasons for direct investment rather than licensing in terms of transferring expertise and ensuring the maintenance of a good name.

Exploiting Reputations Foreign direct investment may occur to exploit rather than protect a reputation. This motivation is probably of particular importance in foreign direct investment by banks, and takes the form of opening branches and establishing or buying subsidiaries. One of the reasons why banking has become an industry with mammoth multinationals is that an international reputation can attract deposits; many associate the size of a bank with its safety.[3] For example, a name like Barclays, Chase, or Citibank in a small, less-developed nation is likely to attract deposits away from local banks. Indeed, this is why many large industrial nations like the United States and Britain have pushed in negotiations of the General Agreement on Tariffs and Trade (GATT) for a liberalization of restrictions on services, including banking. It is also the reason why the majority of less developed nations have resisted this liberalization.

Protecting Secrecy Direct investment may be preferred to the granting of a license for a foreign company to produce a product if secrecy is important. This point has been raised by Erich Spitaler, who argues that a firm can be motivated to choose direct investment over licensing by a feeling that, while a licensee will take precautions to protect patent rights, it may be less conscientious than the original owner of the patent.[4]

The Product Life-Cycle Hypothesis It has been argued, most notably by Raymond Vernon, that opportunities for further gains at home eventually dry up.[5] To maintain the growth of profits, the corporation must venture abroad to where markets are less well penetrated and where there is perhaps less competition. This makes direct investment the natural consequence of being in business for a long enough time and doing well at home. There is an inevitability in this view that has concerned those who believe that American firms are

---

[3]Several other reasons for the multinationalization of banking were given in Chapter 11, including the value of information on financial markets and borrower quality, less onerous regulations, and so on.

[4]See Erich Spitaler, "A Survey of Recent Quantitative Studies of Long-Term Capital Movements," *IMF Staff Papers*, March 1971, pp. 189–217.

[5]Raymond Vernon, "International Investment and International Trade in the Product Life-Cycle," *Quarterly Journal of Economics*, May 1966, pp. 190–207.

further along in their life cycle development than the firms of other nations and are therefore dominant in foreign expansion.[6] However, even when U.S. firms do expand into foreign markets, their activities are often scrutinized by the host governments. Moreover, the spread of U.S. multinationals has been matched by the inroads of foreign firms into the United States, especially since the 1970s. Particularly noticeable have been auto and auto-parts producers such as Volkswagen, Toyota, Honda, Nissan, and Michelin Tires. Foreign firms have an even longer history as leaders in the U.S. food and drug industry (Nestlé, Hoffman-Loroche); in oil and gas (Shell, British Petroleum—as BP, and so on); in insurance, banking, and real-estate development; and in other areas.

Capital Availability and Organizational Factors   Robert Aliber has suggested that access to capital markets can be a reason why firms themselves move abroad.[7] The smaller one-country licensee does not have the same access to cheaper funds as the larger firm, and so larger firms are able to operate within foreign markets with a lower discount rate.

Richard Cyert and James March emphasize reasons given by organization theory, a theme that is extended to direct foreign investment by E. Eugene Carter.[8] The organization-theory view of direct investment emphasizes broad management objectives in terms of the way management attempts to shift risk by operating in many markets, achieve growth in sales, and so on, as opposed to concentrating on the traditional economic goal of profit maximization.

Avoiding Tariffs and Quotas   Another reason for producing abroad instead of producing at home and shipping the product concerns the import tariffs that might have to be paid.[9] If import duties are in place, a firm might produce inside the foreign market in order to avoid them. We must remember, however, that tariffs protect the firm engaged in production in the foreign market, whether it be a foreign firm or an indigenous firm. Tariffs cannot, therefore, explain why foreign firms move abroad, and yet the movement of firms is the essence of direct investment. Nor, along similar lines, can tax writeoffs, subsidized or even free land offerings, and so on, explain direct investment, since foreign firms usually are not helped more than domestic ones. We must rely on our other listed reasons for direct investment and the overriding desire to make

---

[6] Inevitable U.S. domination of key businesses in Europe and the world was a popular view in parts of Europe in the 1960s and 1970s. Particularly influential was J. J. Servan-Schreiber's *The American Challenge*, Hamish Hamilton, London, 1968.

[7] Robert Aliber, "A Theory of Direct Foreign Investment," in Charles P. Kindleberger (ed.), *The International Corporation: A Symposium*, M.I.T. Press, Cambridge, Mass., 1970.

[8] Richard M. Cyert and James G. March give an account of organization theory in *The Behavioral Theory of the Firm*, Prentice-Hall, Englewood Cliffs, N.J., 1963. E. Eugene Carter extends the theory to direct investment in "The Behavioral Theory of the Firm and Top Level Corporation Decisions," *Administrative Science Quarterly*, December 1971, pp. 413–428.

[9] A geometrical explanation of the effect of tariffs on direct investment has been developed by Richard E. Caves, *Multinational Enterprise and Economic Analysis*, Cambridge University Press, Cambridge, England, 1982, pp. 36–40.

a larger profit, even if that means moving abroad rather than into alternative domestic endeavors.

There have been cases where the threat of tariffs or quantitative restrictions on imports in the form of quotas have prompted direct investment overseas. For example, a number of foreign automobile and truck producers considered opening or opened plants in the United States to avoid restrictions on selling foreign-made cars. The restrictions were designed to protect jobs in the U.S. industry. Nissan Motors built a plant in Tennessee, and Honda built a plant in Ohio. For a period of time Volkswagen assembled automobiles and light trucks in the United States and Canada. Other companies making direct investments included Renault, Daimler-Benz, and Fiat.[10]

Avoiding Regulations   As we explained in Chapter 11 in our discussion of the multinationalization of banking, direct investment has been made by banks to avoid regulation. This has also been a motivation for foreign investment by manufacturing firms. For example, a case might be made that some firms have moved to escape standards set by the U.S. Environmental Protection Agency, the Occupational Safety and Health Administration, and other agencies. Some foreign countries with lower environmental and safety standards offer a haven to firms using dirty or dangerous processes. The items produced, such as chemicals and drugs, may even be offered for sale back in the United States.

Production Flexibility   A manifestation of departures from PPP is that there are periods when production costs in one country are particularly low because of a real depreciation of its currency. Multinational firms may be able to relocate production to exploit the opportunities that real depreciations offer. This requires, of course, that necessary technology can be transferred easily between countries and that trade unions or governments do not make the shifting of production too difficult. Small manufactured goods such as computer components and TVs lend themselves to such shuffling of production, whereas automobile production, with its international unions and expensive setup costs, does not.[11]

---

[10]Offsetting the incentive to produce within a country to avoid import tariffs is the preference that buyers of a product may have for imports. For example, it may be that a German car from Germany will be valued more than if the car were manufactured in the U.S.A. Sometimes the preference for imports can have strange effects on direct investment. For example, in 1988 the Japanese-based beer producer Kirin began producing in Canada for sale in the United States. In this way the beer remained an "import," with the associated shelf space and higher prestige, and yet transport costs and spoilage were reduced. At the same time as American beer drinkers were buying the Canadian-brewed product, Canadian consumers of Kirin could, until late 1989, purchase only beer brewed in Japan.

[11]The flexibility advantage of multinationals has been cited by a number of authors. See Victoria S. Farrell, Dean A. DeRosa, and T. Ashby McCown, "Effects of Exchange Rate Variability on International Trade and other Economic Variables: A Review of the Literature," *Staff Studies*, no. 130, Board of Governors of the Federal Reserve System, January 1984; Bruce Kogut, "Designing Global Strategies: Comparative and Competitive Value-Added Chains," *Sloan Management Review*, Summer 1985, pp. 15–28; and John H. Dunning, "Multinational Enterprises and Industrial Restructuring in the U.K.," *Lloyds Bank Review*, October 1985, pp. 1–19.

Symbiotic Relationships Some firms follow their clients when major clients make direct foreign investments. For example, large U.S. accounting firms which have knowledge of parent companies' special needs and practices have opened offices in countries where their clients have subsidiaries. These U.S. accounting firms have an advantage over local firms because of their knowledge of the parent, and because the client may prefer to engage only one firm in order to reduce the number of people with access to sensitive information. The same factor may apply to consulting, legal, and securities firms, which often follow their home-country clients' direct investments by opening offices in the same foreign locations.

Indirect Diversification We should not leave our discussion of factors contributing to the growth of MNCs without mentioning the potential for the MNC to indirectly provide portfolio diversification for shareholders.[12] This service will, of course, be valued only if shareholders are unable to diversify themselves. This means the existence of segmented capital markets that only the MNC can overcome. This argument was mentioned in Chapter 13 in the context of international asset pricing, where it was noted that the evidence is inconclusive.

Empirical Evidence on the Growth of MNCs

It should be apparent from glancing down the list of factors that can be responsible for the growth of MNCs that the relative importance of different factors will depend on the nature of the MNC's business. Partly as a result of this, the empirical evidence we have on MNCs tends to be limited to some stylized facts about the nature of the industries in which most direct investment occurs.

In an investigation of the characteristics of approximately 1000 U.S. publicly owned companies investing abroad, Irving Kravis and Robert Lipsey found a number of characteristics of investing firms vis-à-vis firms not investing abroad.[13] The characteristics were separated into those that could be attributed to the industry of the investor, and those distinguishing investing firms from other firms within their industry.

Investing firms spent relatively heavily on research and development; this was attributable both to the investors' industry and to the firms investing abroad within each industry. That is, the industries with heavy investments abroad spent more on R & D than other industries, and the firms that invested abroad spent more on R & D than the average spending of firms in their

---

[12] A formal theory of direct foreign direct investment based on indirect provision of portfolio diversification has been developed by Vihang R. Errunza and Lemma W. Senbet, "The Effects of International Operations on the Market Value of the Firm: Theory and Evidence," *Journal of Finance*, May 1981, pp. 401–417.

[13] Irving B. Kravis and Robert E. Lipsey, "The Location of Overseas Production and Production for Export of U.S. Multinational Firms," *Journal of International Economics*, May 1982, pp. 201–223.

industries. (This characteristic of foreign direct investment is consistent with the secrecy-protection explanation given earlier.) Investors were also more capital-intensive than noninvestors, this being mostly attributable to the industries investing overseas. (This is consistent with the capital-availability argument; capital-intensive investors presumably need to raise a relatively large amount of capital.) Other characteristics of investors were that they were large relative to both other industries and other firms within their industries, and that investing firms were more profitable.[14]

Kravis and Lipsey also noted that there appeared to be an order of countries when investing overseas. If an investor had made one foreign investment, it would most likely be in Canada. With two investments they would be in Canada and in Mexico or the United Kingdom. After this, investments were found in Germany, France, and possibly Australia.

Evaluation of direct-investment statistics also suggests that more investment occurs in those countries that have offered investors higher returns.[15] There also appears to be a connection between domestic economic activity and foreign investment, with good conditions at home discouraging investment abroad.

SPECIAL PROBLEMS FACING MULTINATIONAL CORPORATIONS: TRANSFER PRICING

While any firm with multiple divisions must price goods and services transferred between its divisions if it is to be able to judge its profit centers correctly, there are few if any political or tax implications of transfer pricing in the domestic context. The situation is very different for the multinational corporation.

The Measurement of Transfer Prices

If correct measures of prices of goods or services moving between corporate divisions are not available, management will have difficulty making APV calculations for new projects, and will even face difficulties judging past projects and performances of corporate divisions. But how are managers to calculate correct transfer prices?

The prices managers must determine are those of intermediate products moving through vertically integrated firms.[16] The most obvious source for these prices is the market. However, market prices do not always exist for intermediate products. Furthermore, even when there are market prices for the goods

---

[14]These conclusions are also supported by Irving B. Kravis, Robert E. Lipsey, and Linda O'Connor, "Characteristics of U.S. Manufacturing Companies Investing Abroad and Their Choice of Production Locations," Working Paper 1104, National Bureau of Economic Research, April 1983.

[15]See *International Letter*, Federal Reserve Bank of Chicago, no. 537, October 19, 1984.

[16]Indeed, *ceteris paribus*, the transfer-pricing problem increases with the degree of vertical integration in a company.

and services transferred between divisions within a firm, using these prices may result in incorrect decisions. Let us consider why.[17]

The theoretically correct transfer price is equal to the marginal cost.[18] This is because the price paid then correctly reflects the cost of producing another unit.[19] If a good or service transferred between corporate divisions is available in the marketplace, where it trades in a textbook-type "perfectly competitive" market, the market price will equal the marginal cost and this market price can then be used as the transfer price. However, goods and services moving between divisions are frequently available only in monopolistic or monopolistically competitive markets. In this case, market prices will typically exceed marginal costs. This means that by setting transfer prices equal to market prices a buying division will be paying above marginal cost for inputs. This will induce the use of too few inputs to achieve the profit-maximizing output from the firm's perspective. The firm's output of its final product will also be less than the profit-maximizing level. In addition, with transfer prices equal to market prices, and these being higher than the firm's marginal costs of the transferred goods and services, input combinations will be inappropriately intensive in products bought from outside the firm. That is, if, instead of setting transfer prices of intermediate products equal to market prices, the firm set them equal to its marginal costs, then buying divisions would correctly use more of the firm's own intermediate products.

While setting transfer prices equal to marginal costs will maximize the firm's overall profits, it will make it difficult to attribute the company's profit to the correct divisions; marginal costs are typically lower than market prices, so that divisions supplying intermediate products will show losses. This will make bonus allocations and expansion budgets difficult to determine properly. One way around this is to use marginal costs as the transfer prices that are paid, but to calculate divisional profitability at market prices. This requires, of course, that market prices of intermediate products be available, and that marginal costs be known. In reality, neither requirements is likely to be satisfied.

Strategic Considerations in Transfer Pricing

The repatriation of profits by a multinational firm from its overseas operations can be a politically sensitive problem. It is important that host governments do not consider the profit rate too high, or else the multinational is likely to face

---

[17]The background economic analysis behind the points made here was first provided by Jack Hirschleifer, "On the Economics of Transfer Pricing," *Journal of Business*, July 1956, pp. 172–184, and "Economics of the Divisionalized Firm," *Journal of Business*, April 1957, pp. 96–108.

[18]This assumes constant returns to scale. See Hirschleifer, *op. cit.*

[19]The rationale is the same as for selecting the quantity of any input that maximizes profits: profits are reduced by using less or by using more than the quantity of input at which the marginal revenue product of the input equals the input's marginal cost.

accusations of price gouging and lose favor with foreign governments. In order to give an appearance of repatriating a lower profit without reducing the actual profit brought home, the multinational can use transfer prices. It can set high transfer prices on what is supplied to a foreign division by the head office or by divisions in environments that are politically less sensitive. For example, it can extract high payments for parts supplied by other divisions or for general overheads. Alternatively, the multinational can lower the transfer prices of products which the foreign division sells to the head office or to other divisions. These methods of reducing foreign profits while repatriating income are particularly advantageous when foreign reinvestment opportunities are limited. Because host governments know these practices occur, it is a good idea to itemize all transfers so as to make it clear that not all flows are profits.

Transfer pricing to reduce overall corporate taxes can be advantageous. The multinational has an incentive to shuffle its income to keep profits low in high-tax countries and relatively high in low-tax countries. There are complications if within a country there are different tax rates on retained versus repatriated income. The gains from profit shuffling via transfer prices are limited by the legal powers of the Internal Revenue Service, and of taxing authorities in some other countries, to reallocate income if it is determined that transfer prices have distorted profits.[20]

A multinational firm is likely to be in a better position to avoid foreign exchange losses than a firm with only local operations. There have been times, especially under fixed exchange rates in the period before 1973, when the devaluation of certain currencies and the revaluation of others were imminent. Because of extensive involvement by central banks, the interest-rate differential between countries did not always reflect the anticipated changes in exchange rates, and so compensation was not offered for expected exchange movements. There were incentives for all corporations to reduce their holdings of the currencies which faced devaluation. However, an attempt to move from these currencies was viewed as unpatriotic when undertaken by domestic firms and as unfair profiteering when undertaken by multinationals. As a result considerable constraints were placed on moving funds in overt ways, but multinationals were in a better position than their domestic counterparts to move funds internally.

Transfer prices can be used to reduce import tariffs and to avoid quotas. When tariffs on imports are based on values of transactions, the value of goods moving between divisions can be artificially reduced by keeping down the transfer prices. This puts the multinational at an advantage over domestic firms.

---

[20] For a detailed account of the tax implications of transfer pricing see Donald R. Lessard, "Transfer Prices, Taxes, and Financial Markets: Implications of International Financial Transfers within the Multinational Corporation," *International Business and Finance*, 1979, pp. 101–135, and J. William Petty II and Ernest W. Walker, "Optimal Transfer Pricing for the Multinational Firm," *Financial Management*, winter 1972, pp. 74–87. We mghit note that if MNCs are in a position to reduce taxes in ways unavailable to local firms, this provides an additional reason for the growth of MNCs.

Similarly, when quotas are based on values of trade, the multinational can keep down prices to maintain the volume. Again, the multinational has an advantage over domestic counterparts, but import authorities frequently adopt their own "value for duty" on goods entering trade to help prevent revenues from being lost through the manipulation of transfer prices.

Large variations in profits may be a concern to shareholders. In order to keep local shareholders happy, fluctuations in local foreign profits can be reduced via transfer prices. By raising the prices of goods and services supplied to foreign operations or lowering prices on the sales of foreign operations, unusually high profits can be brought down so that subsequent falls in profits are reduced. Of course, shareholders are normally assumed to be concerned only with systematic risk and not with total risk, so that the premise that profit volatility is of concern to shareholders is open to criticism.

To the extent that transfer prices apply to financial transactions such as credits granted between corporate divisions, the scope for meeting the many strategic objectives we have described, such as reducing host-government criticism over profits and reducing taxes, are substantially enhanced. Indeed, when we add discretion over timing of repayment of credits, the MNC may be at a substantial advantage over nonmultinational competitors.[21]

Practical Considerations in Transfer Pricing

Transfer prices can be used to "window-dress" the profits of certain divisions of a multinational so as to reduce borrowing costs. The gains from having seemingly large profits by paying a subsidiary high transfer prices for its product must, of course, be balanced against the potential scorn of foreign host governments, higher taxes or tariffs that might result, and so on.

For the long-term survival of a multinational, it is important that interdivisional profitability be measured accurately. The record of profitability of different divisions is valuable in allocating overall spending on capital projects and in sharing other corporate resources. In order to discover the correct profitability, the firm should be sure that interdivisional transfer prices are the prices that would have been paid had the transactions been with independent companies—"arm's-length prices." This can be particularly difficult in the international allocation of such items as research and consulting services or headquarters overheads; there is rarely a market price for research or other services of corporate headquarters. Profit allocation will usually be according to the distribution of corporate sales, with the sales valued at the "correct" exchange rate. The advantages of preventing distortions in transfer prices must be balanced against the potential gains from using distorted transfer prices to

---

[21]See Lessard, *op. cit.* We recall that to some extent, timing discretion on credits is reduced by leading and lagging restrictions.

reduce tariffs, taxes, political risks, and exchange losses. This balance can be a difficult problem for multinational corporations.

SPECIAL PROBLEMS FACING MULTINATIONAL CORPORATIONS: COUNTRY RISK

As we mentioned in our account of capital budgeting in the previous chapter, when making overseas direct investments it is necessary to allow for risk due to the investment being in a foreign country. In this section we consider both the measurement and management of this so-called **country risk**, which, as with transfer pricing, takes on special importance in the multinational corporation.

The term "country risk" is often used interchangeably with the terms **political risk** and **sovereign risk**. However, country risk is really a broader concept than either of the other two, including them as special cases. Country risk involves the possibility of losses due to country-specific economic, political, and social events, and therefore all political risk is country risk, but not all country risk is political risk.[22] Sovereign risk involves the possibility of losses on claims to foreign governments or government agencies, whereas political risk involves the additional possibility of losses on private claims as well as on direct investments. Sovereign risk exists on bank loans and bonds and is therefore not of special concern to MNCs—unless they are banks. Since our concern here is with the risk faced on foreign direct investment, we are concerned with country risk and are not particularly interested in the subcomponent of country risk which consists of sovereign risk. Nevertheless, much of what we say about country-risk measurement applies to sovereign risk.

The Measurement of Country Risk

Among the country risks that are faced on an overseas direct investment are those related to the local economy, those due to the possibility of **confiscation** (which refers to a government takeover without any compensation), and those due to the possibility of **expropriation** (which refers to a government takeover with compensation, which at times can be generous[23]). As well as the political risks of confiscation and expropriation, there are political/social risks of wars, revolutions, and insurrections. While these are not the result of action by foreign governments specifically directed at the firm, they can damage or destroy an investment. In addition, there are risks of currency inconvertibility and restrictions on the repatriation of income beyond those already reflected in the CF_t^* term of the APV calculation in the previous chapter. The treatment of these risks requires that we make adjustments in the APV calculation and/or

---

[22] For example, see U.S. Comptroller of the Currency, news release, November 8, 1978.

[23] Clearly, when investors can count on timely and fair compensation at market value, there is no added risk due to expropriation.

allowances for late compensation payments for expropriated capital. The required adjustment can be made to the discount rate by adding a risk premium, or to expected cash flows by putting them into their certainty equivalent.[24]

We know that when we view the adjustment for risk in terms of the inclusion of a premium in the discount rate, only systematic risk needs to be considered. Since by investing in a large number of countries it is possible to diversify risk, the systematic component of economic and political/social risk can be very small. Risk diversification requires only a degree of economic and political/ social independence between countries. Diversification is made even more effective if the economic and political/social misfortunes from events in some countries provide benefits in other countries. For example, risk on diversified copper investments can be made arbitrarily small if war or revolution in African countries that produce copper raises incomes of South American producers of copper.

Before a company can consider how much of its country risk is systematic, it must be able to determine the risk in each country. Only later can it determine by how much its country risk is reduced by the individual country risks being imperfectly or even negatively correlated. But how can it determine each country's risk? The most obvious method is to obtain country-risk evaluations that have been prepared by specialists. But this merely begs the question how the specialists evaluate country risk. Let us consider a few of the risk evaluation techniques that have been employed.

One of the best known country-risk evaluations is that prepared by *Euromoney*, a monthly magazine that periodically produces a ranking of country risks. Euromoney's evaluation procedure is summarized in Figure 16.1.[25]

Euromoney consults a cross section of specialists. These specialists are asked to give their opinions on each country with regard to one or more of the factors used in their calculations. There are three broad categories of factors considered. These are analytical indicators (40 percent), credit indicators (20 percent), and market indicators (40 percent). Each of these broad categories is further subdivided into more specific components as shown in Figure 16.1.

The analytical indicators consist of economic indicators, an economic-risk evaluation, and a political-risk evaluation. The economic indicators are designed to reflect the ability to service debt, and are obtained from currently available data involving the ratio of external debt to GNP, the ratio of the balance of payments to GNP, and the ratio of debt-service payments to exports.[26] The economic-risk evaluation is provided by a panel of economists who are specifically asked to look forward in order to avoid being retrospective; the economic

---

[24]We have already mentioned that the two methods are conceptually equivalent. This is shown in Appendix 15.2.

[25]Figure 16.1 is based on the verbal description of the Euromoney method in "The Euromoney Country Risk Method," *Euromoney*, September 1988, p. 233.

[26]While the ratio of debt-service payments to export earnings provides an indication of the foreign exchange earnings that may be available for debt service, it does not reflect the diversity of goods and services earning foreign exchange. Presumably, a country with a single export is a poorer risk than a country with diversified export earnings, even if the two countries have the same ratio.

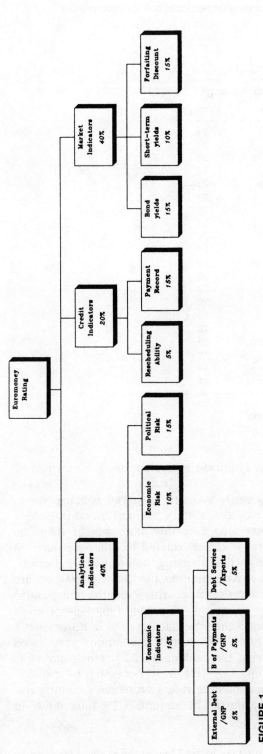

FIGURE 1
EUROMONEY'S COUNTRY-RISK RATING SCHEME.

TABLE 16.1
Euromoney's Country-Risk Ranking

Top twenty		Bottom twenty	
Country	Rating*	Country	Rating*
Japan	98	Guyana	24
West Germany	95	Malawi	24
United Kingdom	95	Honduras	23
Canada	94	Iran	23
Switzerland	94	Tanzania	23
United States	92	Iraq	21
Australia	91	Liberia	21
Austria	91	Bolivia	21
Sweden	91	Zaire	21
Belgium	90	Zambia	21
Netherlands	90	El Salvador	20
Finland	89	Ethiopia	20
France	88	Haiti	20
Spain	88	Peru	20
Italy	86	Angola	19
Taiwan	86	Cuba	19
Norway	85	Mozambique	19
USSR	85	Sudan	18
New Zealand	84	Uganda	14
China	83	Lebanon	11

*0 – 100.
Source: Euromoney, September 1988, p. 233.

indicators give the retrospective view. Political-risk evaluations are provided by political-risk specialists.

Credit indicators are based on how easily a country is viewed as being able to reschedule debt payments, and how well the country has performed in making payments in the past. The payments record carries more weight than the rescheduling ability, because the latter is closely related to other measures in the risk calculation, particularly those included among the economic indicators.

Market indicators are based on the risk premiums the financial markets are placing on the countries' bonds, their short-term securities, and the nonrecourse loans made to their exporters.[27] Large premiums are a sign of market-perceived risk. Of course, the market also considers the other factors used in Euromoney's ranking, and so there is double counting. However, if evaluations were based only on the market's perception of risk, the ranking would not help investors make their own investment decisions. For this it is necessary to evaluate whether the market is over- or underevaluating risk. Euromoney's country-risk rankings of the safest and riskiest 20 countries in September 1988 are shown in Table 16.1.

---

[27]Nonrecourse loans to exporters are discussed in Chapter 17 under the heading "forfaiting."

The Measurement of Political Risk

Particular attention has been devoted to the important subcategory of risk called political risk. It is worth briefly considering how this component of country risk has been measured.

Some idea of political risk can be obtained from an index such as the Political System Stability Index defined by Dan Haendel, Gerald West, and Robert Meadow.[28] This index uses data on socioeconomic characteristics, social conflicts, and government processes, and considers ethnic fractionalization, the rate of economic growth, the frequency of public demonstrations, riots, and coups d'état, and the power of the government to control civil disorder. Objective proxy measures are defined for all these factors. The index which is formed from combining these proxies ranks countries by their stability.

Harald Knudsen has computed political risk by comparing national aspirations with achievements on the grounds that when aspirations run ahead of achievements, there is national frustration.[29] Knudsen argues that when a high degree of foreign ownership is present, national frustration may trigger expropriation or destruction of foreign capital.

The studies of political risk described here all suffer from being unable to distinguish the different risks of different industries; they measure only the risk of the country.[30] Yet a number of studies show that some industries, especially those involving natural resources or utilities, involve a greater political risk.[31] Indeed, political risk may even differ between firms in the same industry. This potential for different political risks can to some extent be influenced by firms themselves, because there are a number of things firms can do to affect the odds of some political events. Let us consider some of the techniques that are available for reducing political risk.

Methods of Reducing Political Risk

Keeping Control of Crucial Elements of Corporate Operations   Some companies making direct foreign investments have tried to ensure that foreign operations cannot run well without the investor's cooperation. This can fre-

---

[28]The construction of the index is described in Dan Haendel, Gerald West, and Robert Meadow, *Overseas Investment and Political Risk*, Foreign Policy Research Institute, Philadelphia, 1974 (published in association with Lexington Books and D.C. Heath).

[29]Harald Knudsen describes his methodology in his article "Explaining the National Propensity to Expropriate: An Ecological Approach," *Journal of International Business Studies*, spring 1974, pp. 51–71.

[30]Most political-risk evaluations also are unable to allow for political instability in a country's region which might spill over and affect it, and for the danger or safety that might come from being a member of a political grouping. See John Calverly, *Country Risk Analysis*, Butterworths, London, 1985.

[31]It is apparent from the results of J. Frederick Truitt that there are different risks in different industries. See J. Frederick Truitt, "Expropriation of Foreign Investment: Summary of the Post World War II Experience of American and British Investors in Less Developed Countries," *Journal of International Business Studies*, fall 1970, pp. 21–34. See also Robert Hawkins, Norman Mintz, and Michael Provissiero, "Government Takeovers of U.S. Foreign Affiliates," *Journal of International Business Studies*, spring 1976, pp. 3–16.

quently be achieved if the investor maintains control of a crucial element of operations. For example, food and soft-drink manufacturers keep secret their special ingredients. Auto companies can produce vital parts, such as engines, in some other country and can refuse to supply these parts if their operations are seized.[32] The multinational oil companies have used refining capacity coupled with alternative sources of oil to reduce the probability that their oil wells will be expropriated. Similarly, many companies have kept key technical operations with their own technicians, who can be recalled in the event of expropriation or confiscation. This has not always been an effective deterrent, as more mercenary technicians can often be found if the salary is sufficient—or technicians can be provided by the communist bloc. Moreover, given sufficient time, local people can pick up the important skills.

Programmed Stages of Planned Divestment An alternative technique for reducing the probability of expropriation is for the owner of a foreign direct investment to promise to turn over ownership and control to local people in the future. This is sometimes required by the host government. For example, the Cartagena Agreement of 1969 requires the foreign owners of enterprises in the Andean countries of South America to lower their ownership, over time, to below 50 percent.

Joint Ventures Instead of promising shared ownership in the future, an alternative technique for reducing the risk of expropriation is to share ownership with foreign private or official partners from the very beginning. Such shared ownerships, known as **joint ventures**, have been tried by U.S., Canadian, European, and Japanese firms with partners in Africa, Central and South America, and Asia. Joint ventures as a means of reducing expropriation risks rely on the reluctance of local partners, if private, to accept the interference of their own government. When the partner is the government itself, the disincentive to expropriation is the concern over the loss of future investments. Joint ventures with multiple participants from different countries reduce the risk of expropriation, even if there is no local participation, if the government wishes to avoid being isolated simultaneously by numerous foreign powers.

Even if joint ventures with government-controlled enterprises work well while that government remains in power, they can backfire if the government is overthrown by the opposition in a polarized political climate. Extreme changes in governments have been witnessed so many times that the risks of siding with a government that falls are well known. In addition, even when the local partner is a private corporation, if expropriation means more ownership or control for the partner, there is likely to be muted local opposition at best. It is these reasons which may explain the observation that the risk of joint ventures has been greater than that of ventures with total U.S. ownership. A study of U.S.

---

[32]According to Roy E. Pedersen, who cited the case of IBM, the risk can be reduced by keeping all research and development at home. See Roy E. Pedersen, "Political Risk: Corporate Considerations," *Risk Management*, April 1979, pp. 23–32.

affiliates in the 1960–1976 period showed that joint ventures with host governments were expropriated 10 times more often than fully U.S.-owned ventures and that joint ventures with private firms were expropriated 8 times more often.[33]

Local Debt   The risk of expropriation as well as the losses from expropriation can be reduced by borrowing within the countries where investment occurs. If the borrowing is denominated in the local currency, there will often also be a reduction of foreign exchange risk. These obvious gains from engaging in local debt are limited by the opportunities. Those countries where expropriation is most likely tend to be the countries with the least-developed capital markets and host governments unwilling to make loans. The opportunities for reducing risk by having local people hold equity in the firm are also limited by the frequency shortage of middle-class shareholders in the high-risk countries and by the absence of a viable market in which to sell the primary issue.

Despite the techniques for reducing risk, some danger will remain. Fortunately, something can be done to reduce or eliminate the harmful consequences of political developments by purchasing investment insurance.

The Purchase of Investment Insurance

Many countries will insure their companies that invest overseas against losses from political events such as currency inconvertibility, expropriation, war, and revolution. In the United States this insurance is offered by the Overseas Private Investment Corporation (OPIC). This corporation has been in operation since the early 1970s, having replaced programs in effect since the Economic Co-operation Act of 1948. OPIC will insure U.S. private investments in the underdeveloped countries, where there tends to be more risk. Over 60 percent of non-oil-related investments in the underdeveloped countries are covered by OPIC.

In addition to investment insurance, OPIC offers project financing. This involves assistance in finding sources of funds, including OPIC's own sources, and assistance in finding worthwhile projects. Reimbursement for losses on loans is also offered. There is no coverage for losses due to changes in exchange rates, but there is also no need for such coverage because of the private means that are available, such as the forward and futures markets. OPIC charges a fee for complete coverage that is between 1 and 2 percent per annum of the amount covered on the insurance policy. Insurance must generally be approved by host governments and is available only on new projects. Since 1980, OPIC has joined with private insurance companies in the Overseas Investment Insurance Group. This has been done to move the insurance into the private sector of the economy.

[33]See David Bradley, "Managing Against Expropriation," *Harvard Business Review*, July–August 1977, pp. 75–83. For a survey of work on political risks, see Stephen Kobrin, "Political Risks: A Review and Reconsideration," *Journal of International Business Studies*, spring/summer 1979, pp. 67–80.

In Canada, foreign-investment insurance is provided by the Export Development Corporation (EDC). The Canadian EDC will insure against losses due to war, insurrection, confiscation, expropriation, and events which prevent the repatriating of capital or the transfer of earnings. This role of the EDC is similar to the role of OPIC. The EDC also offers insurance against nonpayment for Canadian exports, a function performed by the Export-Import Bank in the United States. The insurance coverage offered in the United Kingdom is very similar to the coverage offered by OPIC and the Canadian EDC, and similar programs exist in Australia, Denmark, France, Germany, Holland, Japan, Norway, Sweden, and Switzerland.

If the compensation provided by project insurers (1) is received immediately and (2) covers the full value of the project, the availability of insurance means that the only required adjustment for political risk is a deduction for insurance premiums from cash flows. We can deduct available premiums even if insurance is not actually purchased, since the firm will then be self-insuring and should deduct an appropriate cost for this.

Some of the political risk that MNCs face and that forces them to insure or take other steps is a result of their visibility. This is largely due to their immense size and the difficulty of regulating them. However, there are other factors that have made MNCs the target of criticism and concern. Let us end our discussion of the growth and special problems of MNCs by considering these criticisms and concerns, and why so much attention has been attracted by MNCs. We shall see that while some of the popular concerns over the power and practices of MNCs may be well founded, there are many benefits that have been brought through the transfer of technology and jobs that can be attributed to their direct investments.

Problems and Benefits from the Growth of MNCs

As we have mentioned, much of the concern about MNCs stems from their size, which can be formidable. Indeed, the profits of some of the larger corporations can exceed the operating budgets of the governments in smaller countries. It is the power that such scale can give that has led to the greatest concern. Can the MNCs push around their host government to the advantage of the shareholders and the disadvantage of the citizens of the country of operation? This has led several countries and even the United Nations to investigate the influence of MNCs. The issues considered include the following.

It can be difficult to manage economies in which multinationals have extensive investments, such as the economies of Canada and Australia. Since MNCs often have ready access to external sources of finance, they can blunt local monetary policy.[34] When the host government wishes to constrain economic

---

[34] While MNCs may reduce the effectiveness of monetary policy, they may also increase the effectiveness of changes in exchange rates on the balance of trade. In particular, they may speed up the increase in exports from countries experiencing depreciations by quickly moving their production to those countries to take advantage of the lower production costs.

activity, multinationals may nevertheless expand through foreign borrowing. Similarly, efforts at economic expansion may be frustrated if multinationals move funds abroad in search of yield advantages elsewhere. You do not have to be a multinational to frustrate plans for economic expansion—integrated financial markets will always produce this effect—but MNCs are likely to participate in any opportunities to gain profits. Furthermore, as we have seen, multinationals can also shift profits to reduce their total tax burden; they can show larger profits in countries with lower tax rates. This can make the MNC a slippery animal for the tax collector, even though it uses many local public goods provided from general tax revenues.

It has been argued that multinationals can make foreign exchange markets volatile. For example, it has been claimed that when the U.S. dollar is moving rapidly against the European currencies, the Canadian dollar swings even further. In particular, a declining value of the U.S. dollar against, for example, the German mark or sterling has been associated with an average larger decline of the Canadian dollar against the same European currency. Although the existence of this phenomenon has not been formally verified, MNCs have been blamed for such an effect. It has been claimed that when U.S. parent companies are expecting an increase in the value of the mark, sterling, and so on, they buy these foreign currencies and instruct their Canadian subsidiaries to do the same. With a thinner market in the Dominion currency, the effect of this activity could be greater movement in the value of the Canadian dollar than in the value of the U.S. dollar.

Concern has been expressed, especially within the United States, that U.S.-based multinationals can defy foreign policy objectives of the U.S. government through their foreign branches and subsidiaries. A firm might break a blockade and avoid sanctions by operating through overseas subsidiaries. This could cause even greater concern within some host countries. Why should companies operating within their boundaries have to follow orders of the U.S. government or any other foreign government? Multinational corporations present a potential for conflict between national governments. There is even potential for conflict within international/multinational trade unions. For example, in 1980 and 1981 Chrysler Corporation was given loan guarantees to help it continue in operation. The U.S. government insisted on wage and salary rollbacks as a condition. Chrysler workers in Canada did not appreciate the instruction from the U.S. Congress to accept a reduced wage.

Accusations have been made, most notably with regard to the oil industry, that multinationals can use monopoly power to withhold output to effect price increases for their products. Because the multinationals have such extensive operations, much of the data on which the governments must rely are often data collected and reported by the MNCs themselves. There is no guarantee that the data are accurate, and there is no easy way to enforcing controls and punishing culprits. This became one of the leading political issues of the 1980s.

Multinationals tend to concentrate and specialize their "good" and "bad" activities within certain locations. This can mean doing the research and development (R & D) within the home country. Highly trained university and technical-school graduates who find their employment and promotion opportunities diminished in their own country by the small scale of local operations would prefer locally owned and managed enterprises. This has been a controversial problem in countries that consider themselves "branch plant" economies. Canadian and Australian scientists and engineers have been particularly outspoken.[35]

At the same time as MNCs have improved prospects for some better-paid workers in their home countries, it has been argued that they have moved lower-wage jobs away from the home countries. For example, during 1966–1977, when the U.S. share of world exports fell from 16 to 14 percent, U.S.-based multinationals increased their share of world exports from 17 to 20 percent.[36] This suggests the U.S. multinationals had moved their production outside the United States. This is evident from looking at the location of production stamped on a large number of products with U.S. company names.

It is not uncommon to hear the view that because MNCs are so large they have reduced competition. However, the truth may be the opposite. In some industries such as automobiles, computers, steel, and shipbuilding, where a single country might support one or only a few firms in the industry, competition is increased by the presence of foreign MNCs. That is, the MNCs themselves compete in international markets, and without them monopoly powers in some sectors might be even greater.

Also on the positive side, MNCs have transferred technology and capital to less-developed nations (LDCs), and in this way helped accelerate their economic development.[37] U.S.- and Japanese-based MNCs have been particularly active building production facilities in LDCs.[38] For example, U.S. multinationals' share of manufactured exports of LDCs grew more than 58 percent during 1966–1983.[39] Their influence in Latin America has been particularly strong. The Japanese MNCs' share of LDC exports has also risen, particularly in Asian LDCs.[40]

There is little doubt that MNCs spread a common culture. Chain hamburger outlets become the same on Main Street in Iowa and on the Champs Elysées in Paris. Soft-drink bottles with a familiar shape can wash up on any beach, and

[35]The data support the claim that multinationals keep a disproportionate share of R & D activity at home. For example, according to the U.S. Department of Commerce, in 1977 only 10 percent of U.S.-based multinationals' R & D was spent by foreign affiliates, and these foreign affiliates employed only 13 percent of the MNCs' scientists and engineers. See U.S. Department of Commerce, Bureau of Economic Analysis, news release, June 2, 1981. See also Irving Kravis and Robert Lipsey, "The Effect of Multinational Firms' Foreign Operations on Their Domestic Employment," Working Paper 2760, National Bureau of Economic Research, March 1989.

[36]See "The World's In-House Traders," *Economist*, March 1, 1986.

[37]However, many have argued that the transferred technology is very often inappropriate.

[38]To the extent MNCs provide training, they may also add to the stock of human capital in LDCs.

[39]Magnus Blomstrom, Irving Kravis, and Robert Lipsey, "Multinational Firms and Manufactured Exports from Developing Countries," Working Paper 2493, National Bureau of Economic Research, June 1988.

[40]See Blomstrom, Kravis, and Lipsey, *op. cit.*

there is no obvious way of telling from which country they came. Hotel rooms are alike everywhere. The same corporate names and product names appear in every major Western language. Even architecture shows a common influence—the "international style." Many have decried this development, complaining that it is robbing the world of a good deal of its variety and local interest. Yet the local people demand the products of the MNCs. This is all part of the unending love-hate relationship between concerned people everywhere and the multinational corporation.

SUMMARY

1 MNCs have grown by making foreign direct investments. This requires that they find positive-APV projects.
2 Among the reasons MNCs have made direct investments are to gain access to raw materials, to integrate operations for increased efficiency, to avoid regulations, to protect industrial secrets and patents, to expand when domestic opportunities are exhausted, to avoid tariffs and quotas, to increase production flexibility and thereby profit from fluctuations in real exchange rates, to follow client MNCs, and to increase diversification.
3 MNCs are generally larger and more R & D-intensive than firms in general. These differences are characteristic both of the industries in which MNCs are found, and of the MNCs versus other firms within the same industries.
4 MNCs face two measurement problems to a greater degree than other firms, namely measuring transfer prices and country risks.
5 For maximum overall corporate profits and correct buy-versus-make decisions, transfer prices should be set equal to marginal costs. This means that the use of market prices as transfer prices is appropriate only if the market for intermediate products is competitive.
6 If intermediate-product markets are not competitive, prices will exceed marginal costs, and so, by using market prices of intermediate products, less than the optimal final output will be produced, and suboptimal use will be made of the MNC's own intermediate products.
7 Even if market prices equal marginal costs, so that transfer prices can be set equal to market prices, if one calculates divisional profits with these transfer prices, then supplying divisions may appear to be unprofitable even when they add to overall corporate profitability.
8 Transfer prices can be used to reduce political risk, taxes, foreign exchange losses, the impact of tariffs and quotas, and shareholder frustration resulting from fluctuating profits. Offsetting the gains from distorting transfer prices is the loss from losing information on divisional profitability.
9 Country risk is a broader concept than either political risk or sovereign risk. Country risk includes economic and social risk, as well as risk faced on private-sector investments.
10 There are a number of published rankings of country risks and political risks which can help in evaluations of direct investments.
11 Political risk can be reduced by keeping control of essential operations, by having a program of planned divestment, or by the use of local debt. Joint ventures can also reduce political risk, but they can backfire with changes in host governments.

12 Losses from political events can be reduced or eliminated by buying investment insurance. In the U.S., this is available from the Overseas Private Investment Corporation (OPIC).
13 MNCs have brought numerous problems. They can make it difficult to manage an economy; they may be able to defy the political directions of their own or foreign governments; they can concentrate skilled jobs at home and more menial jobs abroad. MNCs may also be able to manipulate prices and spread a common culture.

QUESTIONS

1 What examples can you list of foreign multinationals operating in the United States?
2 Which of the reasons for the growth of MNCs do you think are the primary reasons for the development of multinationals in the following industries?
  a Drugs and pharmaceutical manufacturing.
  b Automobile manufacturing.
  c Metal refining.
  d Hotel operation.
  e Commercial banking.
  f Energy development.
  g Fast food.
  h Fashion clothing.
3 Which explanation(s) of the growth of MNCs is/are supported by the evidence that MNCs are relatively capital-intensive?
4 What are the pros and cons of setting transfer prices equal to marginal costs?
5 Under what circumstances are market prices appropriate to use as transfer prices?
6 How can conflicts exist when a firm sets transfer prices for maximizing overall profits? Could these conflicts arise from differential tax rates, import tariffs, imminent changes in exchange rates, and political risks?
7 Why are risk premiums on bonds a useful way of ranking risks for direct investments, but not very useful for making bond purchasing decisions?
8 Why might country risk depend on the diversity of exports as well as on the value of exports versus debt-service payments?
9 In what ways might country risk be influenced by a country's political and economic associations and its geography?
10 Do you think the standard of living overseas has been raised by the direct investments of multinationals? Does this provide a reason for offering MNCs concessionary loans?

BIBLIOGRAPHY

Bird, Graham: "New Approaches to Country Risk," *Lloyds Bank Review*, October 1986, pp. 1–16.
Calvet, A. Louis: "A Synthesis of Foreign Direct Investment Theories and Theories of the Multinational Firm," *Journal of International Business Studies*, spring/summer 1981, pp. 43–59.
Calverley, John: *Country Risk Analysis*, Butterworths, London, 1985.

Casson, Mark: *The Firm and the Market: Studies on the Multinational Enterprise and the Scope of the Firm*, MIT Press, Cambridge, Mass., 1987.

Davidson, William H.: "Location of Foreign Direct Investment Activity: Country Characteristics and Experience Effects," *Journal of International Business Studies*, fall 1980, pp. 9–22.

Dunning, John H. (ed.): *International Investment*, Penguin, Harmondsworth, U.K., 1972.

____: *Economic Analysis and the Multinational Enterprise*, Praeger, New York, 1975.

Granick, David: "National Differences in the Use of Internal Transfer Prices," *California Management Review*, summer 1975, pp. 28–40.

Kobrin, Stephen J.: "The Environmental Determinants of Foreign Direct Investment: An Ex Post Empirical Analysis," *Journal of International Business Studies*, fall 1976, pp. 29–42.

Magee, Stephen P.: "Information and the Multinational Corporation: An Appropriability Theory of Direct Foreign Investment," in Jagdish N. Bhagwati (ed.), *The New International Economic Order*, M.I.T. Press, Cambridge, Mass., 1977.

Melvin, Michael, and Don Schlagenhauf: "A Country Risk Index: Econometric Formulation and an Application to Mexico," *Economic Inquiry*, October 1985, pp. 601–619.

Ragazzio, Giorgio: "Theories of the Determinants of Direct Foreign Investment," *IMF Staff Papers*, July 1973, pp. 471–498.

Rummel, R.J., and David A. Heenan: "How Multinationals Analyze Political Risk," *Harvard Business Review*, January/February 1978, pp. 67–76.

Vernon, Raymond: *Storm Over the Multinationals: The Real Issues*, Harvard University Press, Cambridge, Mass., 1977.

PART EIGHT

FINANCIAL
DIMENSIONS OF
INTERNATIONAL TRADE

The preceding four parts of the book, Part 4 to Part 7, have concentrated on international financial matters that are related to the flow of capital between nations. In this remaining part of the book we shift our attention to matters relating to the international flow of goods and services, that is, international trade.

Chapter 17 describes the financial instruments and other documents that are met with in international trade and in the financing of trade. The instruments and documents are introduced and explained in the context of an example involving an import into the United States. The example explains the roles of letters of credit, bills of exchange, bills of lading, credit insurance, and banker's acceptances in facilitating imports and exports. Distinctions are drawn between alternative ways of reducing credit risk via confirmed and unconfirmed letters of credit, and by credit insurance. Conditions under which different types of payment procedures are used are also described.

Several forms of export financing are explained in Chapter 17. These include short-term credits involving delayed payment dates on bills of exchange, and medium-term credits involving forfaiting. Forfaiting is particularly common in east-west transactions, where a form of trade called countertrade is frequently practiced. Chapter 17 describes various forms of countertrade and why they are used.

Chapter 17 ends with a description of some of the institutions that monitor and regulate international trade, such as the General Agreement on Tariffs and Trade (GATT). Since a substantial portion of international trade is between partners of free-trade pacts such as that of the European Economic Community

(EEC) and Canada and the United States, a brief overview of free-trade arrangements is given.

The last chapter of the book, Chapter 18, is devoted to an account of the factors influencing the extent to which exchange rates affect the sales and operating profitability of firms. (We recall that this extent was called operating exposure in Chapter 9.) Use is made of the traditional theory of the firm, with its emphasis on marginal cost and marginal revenue. It is shown that such factors as the elasticity of demand for imports or exports, and production flexibility, influence the amount of operating exposure. The chapter ends with a consideration of situations where unexpected effects of exchange rates, akin to those of the J curve, occur as a result of a combination of transaction and operating exposure.

THE INSTRUMENTS, INSTITUTIONS, AND ORGANIZATION OF INTERNATIONAL TRADE

EXTRA DIMENSIONS OF INTERNATIONAL TRADE

In ordinary domestic commercial transactions, there are reasonably simple, well-prescribed means of recourse in the event of nonpayment or other causes of disagreement between parties. For example, the courts can be used to reclaim goods when buyers refuse to pay or are unable to pay. The situation is substantially more complex with international commercial transactions, which by necessity involve more than one legal jurisdiction. In addition, a seller might not receive payment, not because the buyer does not want to pay, but because, for example, the buyer's country has an insurrection, revolution, war, or civil unrest, and decides to make its currency inconvertible into foreign exchange. In order to handle these and other difficulties faced in international transactions, a number of practices and institutional arrangements have been developed, and these are explained in this chapter.

In addition to different practices and institutions for ensuring payment and delivery in international versus domestic trade, national and international institutions have been established to finance and monitor international trade. This chapter will describe the roles of these institutions as well as explain practices such as forfaiting and countertrade that are unique to the international arena.

INTERNATIONAL TRADE INVOLVING LETTERS OF CREDIT: AN OVERVIEW OF A TYPICAL TRANSACTION

In order to give a general introductory overview of the documentation and procedures of international trade, let us suppose that after considering costs of alternative suppliers of cloth, Aviva has decided to buy cloth from the British denim manufacturer British Cotton Mills Ltd. An order is placed for 1 million yards at £4 per yard, with Aviva to receive the shipment in 10 months, and pay 2 months after delivery.

Assume that after having made the agreement with British Cotton Mills, Aviva goes to its bank, Citibank, N.A., in New York and buys forward (12 months ahead) the £4 million. Assume that at the same time Aviva requests a **letter of credit**, which is frequently referred to as an **L/C**, or simply as a **credit**.[1] An example of a letter of credit issued by Citibank, N.A., in New York is shown in Figure 17.1.[2] The letter of credit is a guarantee by Aviva's bank that if all the relevant documents are presented in exact conformity with the terms of the letter of credit, the British exporter will be paid. The most important part of the letter of credit is shown in the bottom left-hand corner of Figure 17.1. This is the promise by Citibank to make payment, and it makes the letter an "irrevocable negotiation," as noted at the top of the letter. Aviva Corporation will have to pay Citibank, N.A., a fee for the irrevocable letter of credit. Citibank will issue the letter only if it is satisfied with the creditworthiness of Aviva Corporation. If it is unsure, it will require some collateral.

A copy of the letter of credit will be sent to Citibank, N.A., in London. That bank will inform the British exporter's bank, Britbank, which will in turn inform British Cotton Mills of the credit advice. In our example, Citibank is both the "opening bank," as shown in the letterhead, and the "paying bank," as shown by the "drawn on" entry in the letter, while Britbank is the "advising bank." On receiving the credit advice, British Cotton Mills Ltd. can begin producing the denim cloth, confident that even if Aviva Corporation is unable to pay, payment will nevertheless be forthcoming from Citibank, N.A. The actual payment will be made by means of a **draft** (also called a **bill of exchange**), and this will be drawn up by the exporter or the exporter's bank after the receipt of the credit advice. The draft will stipulate that payment is to be made to the exporter at the exporter's bank, and therefore it is different from conventional checks, which are drawn up by those making the payment rather than by those who are to receive payment.

The draft corresponding to the letter of credit in Figure 17.1 is shown in part *a* of Figure 17.2. It was drawn up by the exporter, British Cotton Mills Ltd., and specifies that £4,000,000 is to be paid at the exporter's bank, Britbank. This is a **time** or **usance draft**, because the exporter, British Cotton Mills, is allowing a 60-day credit period.[3] The draft will be sent directly or via Britbank

---

[1] If Aviva frequently does business with British Cotton Mills, or if Aviva has had problems paying in the past, some other procedure is likely to be used. Such procedures are described later in the chapter.

[2] The format of the letter of credit shown in Figure 17.1 follows the standard recommended by the International Chamber of Commerce in 1971. The letter in Figure 17.1 was kindly provided by Citibank, N.A. Examples of letters of credit and other documents can be found in Leonard Back, *Introduction to Commercial Letters of Credit*, International Trade Services, Citibank, New York. The letter of credit we have presented is for a straightforward situation.

[3] The maturity of a time or usance draft is also sometimes referred to as its **tenor**.

Citibank, N.A.
NBG LETTER OF CREDIT, DIVISION ✶
111 WALL STREET, NEW YORK, N.Y. 10015

IRREVOCABLE NEGOTIATION DOCUMENTARY CREDIT	CREDIT NUMBER
	OF FNCB: 900000 OF ADVISING BANK

───── ADVISING BANK ─────

MAIL TO
Britbank Ltd,.
1 Floor Street,
London,
England

FURTHER TO OUR CABLE OF TODAY

MAIL TO / APPLICANT
Aviva   (Denim Clothing) Corp.
New York, New York

───── BY ORDER OF ─────

───── BENEFICIARY ─────

British Cotton Mills Ltd.
London, England

AMOUNT
£4,000,000   (Four Million British pounds sterling)

───── EXPIRY ─────

DATE IN   June 30, (next year)   FOR NEGOTIATION

WE HEREBY ISSUE IN YOUR FAVOR THIS DOCUMENTARY CREDIT WHICH IS AVAILABLE BY NEGOTIATION OF YOUR DRAFT(S) MARKED DRAWN UNDER OUR DOCUMENTARY CREDIT NO. INDICATED ABOVE.

DRAWN AT ⎯ SIGHT X 60 DAYS SIGHT ⎯ ⎯⎯⎯ DAYS DATE (DRAFTS TO BE DATED SAME DATE AS BILL OF LADING) ⎯ ⎯⎯⎯⎯⎯ OTHER

DRAWN ON ⎯ Citibank, N.A., New York, N.Y. . FOR ⎯⎯⎯ % INVOICE COST

DRAWN ON X Citibank, N.A. London, England (OVERSEAS BANK IF "CREDIT" IN FOREIGN CURRENCY) ⎯⎯⎯ FOR ⎯⎯⎯ % INVOICE COST

FOR DRAFTS ON TERM BASIS, DISCOUNT CHARGES FOR ⎯ SHIPPERS ⎯ BUYERS ACCOUNT

ACCOMPANIED BY THE FOLLOWING DOCUMENTS WHICH ARE INDICATED BY "X".

X COMMERCIAL INVOICE – ORIGINAL AND 2 COPIES

X CUSTOMS INVOICE – ORIGINAL AND 0 COPIES

⎯ INSURANCE POLICY AND/OR CERTIFICATE (TO BE EFFECTED BY SHIPPER, UNLESS OTHERWISE INDICATED BELOW)

⎯ INSURANCE TO INCLUDE WAR RISK

⎯ AIR WAYBILL CONSIGNED TO ⎯⎯⎯⎯⎯⎯⎯⎯⎯⎯⎯⎯⎯⎯⎯⎯⎯⎯⎯⎯⎯⎯⎯⎯⎯⎯⎯⎯⎯⎯⎯⎯ DATED LATEST: ⎯⎯⎯⎯⎯⎯⎯ 19 ⎯⎯⎯⎯

X ON BOARD ORIGINAL OCEAN BILL OF LADING OR CONTAINER BILL OF LADING OR BILL OF LADING BEARING CONTAINER ENDORSEMENT (IF MORE THAN ONE ORIGINAL HAS BEEN ISSUED, ALL ORIGINALS ARE REQUIRED)

ISSUED TO ORDER OF Citibank, N.A.

MARKED NOTIFY Aviva Corporation. New York, New York

MARKED: FREIGHT ⎯ COLLECT X PAID   DATED LATEST: June 20, (current year) 19 ⎯⎯⎯⎯

⎯ OTHER DOCUMENTS ⎯⎯⎯

COVERING: MERCHANDISE DESCRIBED IN THE INVOICE(S) AS: 1,000,000 yards of denim cloth

TERMS: ⎯ FAS LOCATION ⎯ FOB LOCATION X C & F LOCATION ⎯ CIF LOCATION ⎯ C & I LOCATION

SHIPMENT FROM: London, England
TO: New York, New York

PARTIAL SHIPMENTS X PERMITTED ⎯ PROHIBITED
TRANSSHIPMENTS X PERMITTED ⎯ PROHIBITED

X DRAFTS AND DOCUMENTS MUST BE PRESENTED TO NEGOTIATING OR PAYING BANK WITHIN 15 DAYS AFTER THE DATE OF ISSUANCE OF THE BILLS OF LADING OR OTHER SHIPPING DOCUMENTS BUT WITHIN EXPIRY.

X INSURANCE EFFECTED BY APPLICANT.

NEGOTIATING BANK TO FORWARD ALL DRAFTS AND DOCUMENTS LISTED HEREIN BY AIRMAIL IN A SINGLE MAILING TO CITIBANK, N.A., NBG LETTER OF CREDIT DIVISION 3, P.O. BOX 4566, GRAND CENTRAL STATION, NEW YORK, N.Y. 10017

We hereby engage with drawers and/or bona fide holders that drafts drawn, negotiated and presented in conformity with the terms of this credit will be duly honored on presentation, and that drafts accepted within the terms of this credit will be duly honored at maturity.
The amount of each draft must be endorsed on the reverse of this credit by the negotiating bank.

CITIBANK

AUTHORIZED SIGNATURE

PLACE, DATE, NAME AND SIGNATURE OF ADVISING BANK

FIGURE 17.1
IRREVOCABLE LETTER OF CREDIT (From Citibank, N.A.)

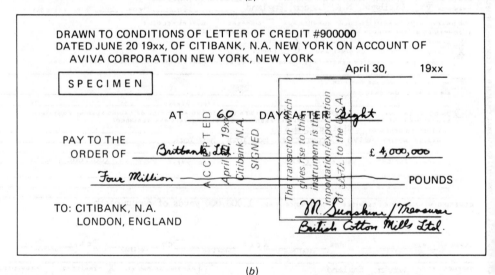

(a)

(b)

FIGURE 17.2
THE DRAFT AND BANKER'S ACCEPTANCE.

Ltd. to Citibank, N.A., in London, and that bank will **accept** the draft if it and other relevant documents that are presented to the bank are in exact conformity with the letter of credit. If the draft is stamped and signed by an officer of Citibank, it will become a **banker's acceptance.**[4] A banker's acceptance looks

---

[4]Citibank in London is the accepting bank because the draft is in pounds. If the draft were denominated in dollars, it would be accepted by Citibank in New York.

like the specimen in part *b* of Figure 17.2. British Cotton Mills Ltd. can sell the accepted draft at a discount to reflect the interest cost of the money advanced, but not to reflect any risk, since the draft has been guaranteed by a reputable bank. Alternatively, British Cotton Mills Ltd. can wait until payment is made to Britbank Ltd. and its account with the bank is credited. This will occur on June 30—2 months after the date on which the draft was accepted (April 30) and a year after the date of the sales contract.[5]

Citibank in London will forward the documents to New York. Citibank in New York will require payment from Aviva Corporation on June 30 of the dollar amount in the forward contract agreed to in the previous year for the purchase of £4 million. At the same time that Aviva's account is debited by Citibank in New York, Citibank will give the documents to Aviva. The New York and London offices of Citibank will then settle their accounts with each other. British Cotton Mills will have been paid via Britbank; Aviva will have paid Citibank in New York; Citibank in New York will have paid Citibank in London; and Citibank in London will have paid Britbank. Aviva will have the papers to receive the cloth. The transaction is complete. The steps are summarized in Figure 17.3.

Because the letter of credit in Figure 17.1 requires that certain documents be presented, it is a **documentary credit**. This is shown in the first line below the boxes at the top of the letter. The accompanying draft (Figure 17.2*a*) is referred to as a **documentary draft**. A **clean draft** does not require a letter of credit or other supporting documents and is used only when there is complete trust—for example, when goods are shipped between different divisions of the same multinational. If the documents are delivered upon the *acceptance* of a draft, the draft is an **acceptance draft**, and if the documents are delivered upon the *payment* of a draft, the draft is a **payment draft**.

The most important document that is required before a bank will accept a draft is the **bill of lading**. The bill of lading, or **B/L**, is issued by the carrier and shows that the carrier has originated the shipment of merchandise. The B/L can serve as the title to the goods, which are owned by the exporter until payment is made. Then, via the participating banks, the bill of lading is sent to the importer to be used for claiming the merchandise. An **order bill of lading** is a bill which gives title to a stated party. It can be used by that party as collateral for loans.

When goods are sent by air, the equivalent of the bill of lading is called an **air waybill**. This serves the same purpose as a bill of lading, being required for release of the goods and transferring ownership from seller to shipper to final buyer. A logistical difficulty with air waybills is ensuring they reach buyers before the goods which are to be claimed. The waybill may accompany the goods, but for reasons of safety—to ensure the right party receives the goods—waybills are better sent separately. There are proposals to use facsimile

---

[5]When payment is made upon the presentation of a draft, the draft is a **sight draft**. When payment is made after sight, the draft is a time draft (as in part *a* of Figure 17.2).

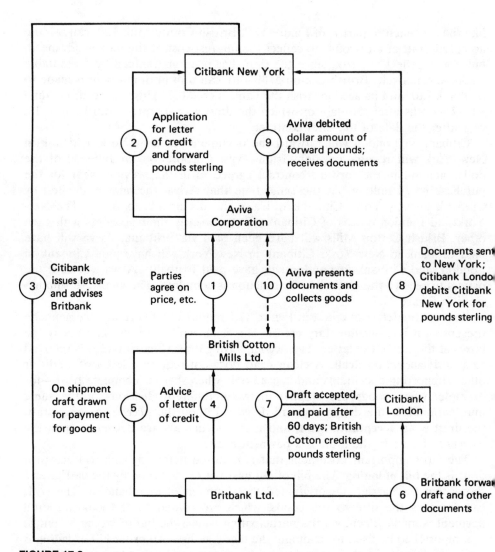

FIGURE 17.3
THE STEPS IN INTERNATIONAL TRADE. (Adapted from Leonard A. Back, Introduction to Commercial Letters of Credit, Citicorp, New York, undated.)

or Telex procedures, but these are hampered by the need to have the original document to claim goods.

ALTERNATIVE PAYMENT AND GUARANTEEING PROCEDURES

Open-Account and Consignment Sales

If Aviva and British Cotton Mills have been doing business with each other for many years and Aviva has established a reputation for prompt payment, Aviva may well try to avoid the expense of a letter of credit, for which banks charge a fee according to the credit rating of the importer and the value of the credit. Instead, Aviva might ask British Cotton Mills if it can order cloth on an **open account** basis, whereby the value of cloth shipped is added to the account Aviva keeps at British Cotton Mills. An invoice might be sent at the end of each month or after each shipment, allowing Aviva to pay by buying a clean draft, or simply by writing a check on an account denominated in the invoice currency. This saves collection fees as well as the cost of the letter of credit.

In situations of trust, goods are sometimes supplied on a **consignment** basis. In this case, payment is not made until after the buyer has sold the goods, and in the meantime the goods remain the property of the supplier.

Cash in Advance and Confirmed Credits

When there is no trust, as after a firm has developed a bad reputation for settling its accounts, perhaps having been late settling previous transactions with the supplier, payment may be required in advance. In this situation, cash is sent to the supplier's bank before the goods are shipped.

When an exporter's lack of trust concerns the importer's bank or the importer's government—perhaps the importer's bank is poorly capitalized, or the importer's government might freeze foreign exchange payments—and when the importer cannot pay cash in advance, the exporter can ensure payment by having a letter of credit guaranteed by a domestic bank. What happens in this situation is that the exporter asks the importer for a letter of credit, even though this will be issued by a bank of the importer's country. The exporter takes this letter to a bank at home and pays the domestic bank to guarantee, or **confirm**, the letter of credit. The result will be a foreign letter of credit with a domestic confirmation. The exporter will then be paid regardless of what happens to the importer's bank or in the importer's country. Nonpayment due to the failure of the importer's bank or action taken by the importer's government is the problem of the confirming bank and not the exporter, provided that the exporter has delivered the goods.

Export Insurance

Letters of credit must be purchased by the importer, and while the cost is not high—a mere fraction of a percent if the importer's credit is good—obtaining the letter may be inconvenient, and will reduce the importer's available credit for other purposes. For these reasons, an exporter may find that a sale is contingent upon not asking for a letter of credit. Indeed, pressure from other exporters who are not requiring letters of credit frequently means exporters can assume that any talk of letters of credit will mean no sale. In such a case exporters can buy export credit insurance. This insurance is arranged and paid for by the exporter and can cover a variety of risks.

It is possible to buy credit insurance against commercial risk only, or against both commercial and political risk. Insurance against both commercial and political risk will serve rather like a confirmed letter of credit in that the exporter will be paid whether the importer pays or not, and whether the importer's country allows payment or not. Insurance against commercial risk alone serves rather like an unconfirmed letter of credit in that the exporter will not be paid if the importer's government prevents payment. However, there are some important differences between letters of credit and export credit insurance. One of these differences is the presence of a deductible portion on insurance, whereas letters of credit typically cover 100 percent of credit.[6] The deductible means the exporter loses something if the importer does not pay. The uninsured portion of a credit is a contingent liability of the exporter. Clearly, the presence of a deductible makes credit insurance less desirable to exporters than confirmed letters of credit. However, a letter of credit may be unacceptable to importers and may be more costly.[7]

Typically there are two forms of export credit insurance. One form provides automatic coverage up to a stated limit on exporters' receivables from buyers whose credit the insurers have approved. This type of insurance is well suited to exporters who must quote commodity prices over the telephone, and accept orders if the buyers agree to these prices. For example, exporters selling lumber or wheat can buy credit insurance which covers all sales to approved buyers. This type of credit insurance is variously called **continuous**, **whole-turnover**, or **rollover** insurance.

A second form of credit insurance covers only specific contracts and specific risks. For this, an exporter must apply for coverage of the specific export credit. For example, if a firm receives an order for six large passenger planes, the exporter will have to apply to the credit insurer and state the specifics of the sale. This type of insurance is usually called **specific export credit insurance**.

The Rationale for Government-Provided Credit Insurance: An Aside

Even though export credit insurance can be purchased from private-sector insurance companies such as the large British-based insurance company Trade Indemnity, most governments sell export credit insurance themselves, usually through an especially established agency. For example, in the United States export credit insurance can be purchased from the Export-Import Bank (Ex-Im Bank), in Britain from the Export Credits Guarantee Department, and in Canada from the Export Development Corporation. Since governments do not typically provide fire, life, disability, automobile, and accident insurance, it is

---

[6]The deductible may be 10 percent or more of the amount insured. There are also other differences between letters of credit and credit insurance when an exporter is unable to deliver goods, when goods are damaged or lost in transit, and so on: credit insurance typically provides broader coverage than a letter of credit.

[7]For a more detailed treatment of the pros and cons of letters of credit and credit insurance see Dick Briggs and Burt Edwards, *Credit Insurance: How to Reduce the Risks of Trade Credit*, Woodhead-Faulkner, Cambridge, England, 1988.

worth asking why in the case of insurance of export credits it has become the norm for governments to arrange coverage. That is, why do governments step in to insure export credits rather than leave private insurance companies to provide the insurance at a competitively determined premium? Even apart from trying to subsidize exports because of the jobs and incomes they generate, there are "market failures" which might warrant government involvement, and arguments that the government may be able to provide the insurance more cheaply. Let us consider these arguments.

Credit insurance requires the insurer to keep current on the situation in different companies in a number of countries. A government can do this through its trade representatives stationed at its embassies and consular offices abroad. For private insurance companies to assess risks they all need to maintain overseas office.[8] Indeed, it might be that the market in each country could support only one credit insurer. Then the government might have to regulate the industry if it did not provide the credit insurance itself. That is, there may be elements of a **natural monopoly** in export credit insurance.

Another reason why governments might argue that they are better suited to provide export credit insurance than private insurance companies is that a government insurer can use other branches of government to provide muscle and thereby reduce country risk. For example, if a country decided it would no longer allow payment to foreign creditors, a government export credit agency might ask its government to threaten withdrawal of aid to the delinquent country.

A factor which supports official against private credit insurance, and which applies to export financing as well as to export insurance, is that there may be benefits to other firms in the exporting country if one of that country's companies makes an export sale. For example, if a U.S. engineering company wins a contract to supply machinery to China, there may be improved prospects for other U.S. companies to sell to China. That is, there may be positive externalities or spillovers that derive from an export contract. These positive externalities will not be considered by private export credit insurers in a competitive market, but a government agency can take them into account when deciding whether to provide export insurance or financing. That is, export insurance and financing have elements of a **public good**, and as is generally the case for public goods, they will be underprovided by profit-maximizing firms.

THE FINANCING OF INTERNATIONAL TRADE

Short-Term Financing: Banker's Acceptances

When an exporter gives credit to a foreign buyer by issuing a draft for some date in the future, the draft itself can be used by the exporter for short-term

---

[8]Alternatively, the insurance companies might buy information from a country-risk-evaluating company. However, the risk-evaluating company would need to maintain offices abroad if it were to be current on the situations in different countries.

financing. The procedure depends on whether the draft is issued in conjunction with a letter of credit.

If the exporter's draft is drawn in conjunction with a letter of credit, the draft will be sent to the bank that issued the letter of credit.[9] When this draft is stamped "accepted" by the bank and signed by an officer of the bank, it becomes a **banker's acceptance**. The exporter can sell the banker's acceptance in the money market at a discount that is related to the riskiness of the accepting bank. We note that it is the importer who determines which bank will accept the draft. The exporter can have the draft reaccepted or confirmed if the fee for confirmation improves the price received for the accepted draft by more than the cost of the reacceptance.[10]

If the exporter's draft is drawn without an importer's letter of credit, the draft is a **trade draft**. This can be sold in the money market, but because it is only a commercial rather than a bank obligation, the draft will face a higher discount than would a banker's acceptance. However, the exporter can pay a bank to accept the draft, and then sell this at a lower discount. The acceptance charge can be compared to the extra value received on the discounted draft. All documents including shipping documents will normally be provided to the bank accepting the draft.

When an exporter draws up a time draft, the exporter is granting the importer credit which the exporter may finance by selling the signed draft. When an exporter draws up a sight rather than a time draft, the exporter is not granting credit to the importer; there is no delay in payment. Nevertheless, a banker's acceptance may be created in this situation. This will happen if the importer draws up a time draft in favor of a bank, signs the draft, and has it accepted by the bank. The banker will immediately pay the importer the discounted value of the draft. The bank will then either sell the draft or hold it for collection. An importer might take this step to finance goods purchased from abroad before they are sold.

The time after sight on a banker's acceptance, whether created by the exporter or by the importer, is typically 30, 90, or 180 days. Consequently, banker's acceptances are only a mechanism for short-term trade financing.

Forfaiting: A Form of Medium-Term Finance

Forfaiting Explained   **Forfaiting** is a fast-growing form of medium-term financing of international trade.[11] It involves the purchase by a bank, the

---

[9]This is the situation in our earlier example.

[10]As we noted earlier, the reacceptance reduces the country risk for the exporter, who collects from his local bank provided the goods are delivered. It is the exporter's bank that loses if the accepting bank in the importer's country cannot honor its credit.

[11]In French it is called *a forfait*, and in German, *Forfaitierung*.

forfaiter, of a series of promissory notes, usually due at 6-month intervals for 3 to 5 years, signed by an importer in favor of an exporter.[12] These notes are frequently **avalled**, or guaranteed, by the importer's bank. The promissory notes are sold by the exporter to the forfaiting bank at a discount. The bank pays the exporter immediately, allowing the exporter to finance the production of the goods for export, and for the importer to pay later. The notes are held by the forfaiter for collection as they come due, without recourse to the exporter in whose favor the notes were originally drawn before being assigned. This absence of recourse distinguishes the forfaiting of promissory notes from the discounting of trade drafts, for which the exporter is open to recourse in the case of nonpayment.[13] This can all be summarized in the short definition:

Forfaiting is medium-term nonrecourse exporter-arranged financing of importers' credits.

The nature of forfaiting is also summarized in Figure 17.4 The figure shows what happens when a U.S. jeans-machine manufacturer sells its machines to a Russian jeans manufacturer. The unshaded arrows show the exchanges occurring at the time the export deal is made, while the shaded arrows show subsequent settlements.

Many forfaiting banks hold the promissory notes themselves and collect payments as they come due. Others buy notes for investors who have expressed interest in taking up the high-yielding paper, and still others arrange forfaiting and then trade the notes in the secondary market.[14]

The discount rates that apply to forfaiting depend on the terms of the notes, the currencies in which they are denominated, the credit ratings of the importers or of the banks avalling the notes, and the country risks of the importing entities. The spreads between forfaiting rates and Eurocurrency deposit rates, with which forfaiting rates move, are typically about one and a half times the spreads between straight Eurocurrency loans and deposits.[15] The higher spreads reflect the lack of recourse and interest-rate risk; the typical 5-year term of forfaiting deals means forfaiters have difficulty matching credit maturities with the typically much shorter-maturity Eurocurrency deposits and futures contracts. Although there have been some floating-rate agreements which have reduced interest-rate risk, fixed-interest-rate deals still predominate.

---

[12]Of course, the language of these promissory notes must be in accordance with legal requirements. These requirements are spelled out in the Geneva Convention of 1930, which has been signed by numerous countries, and the Bill of Exchange Act of 1882, which governs practice in Britain.

[13]The lack of recourse explains the origin of the term "forfaiting"; the buyer of the promissory notes forefeits the right of recourse.

[14]Forfaiting yields are relatively high because there is no recourse in the event the goods are not delivered, the importer does not pay, and so on.

[15]See Donald Curtin, "The Unchartered $4 Billion World of Forfaiting," *Euromoney*, August 1980, pp. 62–70.

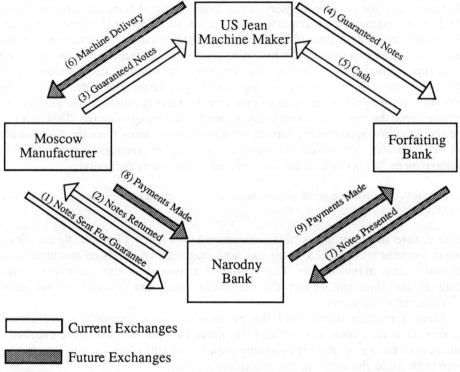

FIGURE 17.4
THE STEPS INVOLVED IN FORFAITING. Forfaiting is a means of providing medium-term import credits. The importer prepares promissory notes that are guaranteed by a bank. These are sent to the exporter, who then sells them for cash to a forfaiting bank. The bank may then sell the notes. The holder of the notes has no recourse to the exporter. The credit risk is entirely borne by the noteholder.

Forfaiting banks have shown considerable flexibility and often quote rates over the telephone once they know the name of the importer or the avalling bank.[16] This allows exporters to quote their selling prices after working out what they will net from their sales after forfaiting costs. Another advantage to the exporter is that because there is no recourse, the promissory notes are not carried on the exporter's books as a contingent liability. Yet another is that there is no need to arrange credit insurance. Of course, the advantage of forfaiting to importers is that they receive credit when it might not otherwise be offered or not be offered on the same terms.

The History of Forfaiting   As with the introduction of Eurodollars, the development of forfaiting probably owes its origins, but not its subsequent popularity, to the difficulties faced in east-west trade. (We recall that it has been

---

[16] The forfaiter may charge a **commitment fee** for this service.

argued that the Eurodollar market started because the Soviet Union wanted to hold U.S. dollars, but not to hold them in the United States.) The practice of forfaiting dates back to the early 1960s and the placing of orders by the eastern-bloc Comecon countries for capital equipment and grain. Many of these orders were placed with West German firms which were not in a position to supply credit themselves, or to arrange financing with banks or official lending agencies. That is, the exporters were unable to offer **supplier credits**, and they were unable to arrange **buyer credits** through lending institutions. Instead, they found banks which were willing to purchase the importers' promissory notes at a discount. One of the first banks to recognize the opportunity was Credit Suisse through its subsidary Finance A.G. Zurich.[17] The original deals involved the sale of U.S. grain to West Germany, which resold the grain to eastern European countries. Forfaiting allowed the U.S. exporters to be paid immediately and the eastern European buyers to receive medium-term credit.[18]

While originally viewed as "lending of last resort," forfaiting has grown in popularity, spreading from Switzerland and Germany, where it began, to London, later to Scandinavia and the rest of Europe, and eventually to the United States. Forfaiting is still not as important as payment by traditional time or usance bills of exchange or credit from official export financing agencies, but it has nevertheless become an important source of financing, especially for the medium-term maturities.[19]

Financing by Government Export Agencies

Because of the jobs and income that derive from a healthy export sector, it has become standard practice for governments around the world to help their exporters win contracts by offering export financing. This financing can be of short-, medium-, or long-term maturity, and takes a number of different forms.

A large part of official export financing takes the form of payments to exporters, with the foreign importers then paying the government agency. For example, the U.S. Export-Import Bank, which was established in 1934 and rechartered in 1945, pays U.S. exporters directly and then collects from the buyers of the U.S. exports, including interest on the credit advanced. This is a form of buyer credit. Buyer credits are offered in many countries. For example, the Export Credits Guarantee Department offers buyer credits to purchasers of British exports, and the Export Development Corporation provides buyer credits to buyers of Canadian exports.

Official export financing also takes the form of loans to domestic or foreign financial institutions, which in turn make loans to the importers. Sometimes only a portion of the funds required by the importers is made available to the

---

[17]See Werner R. Rentzman and Thomas Teichman, "Forfaiting: An Alternative Technique for Export Financing," *Euromoney*, December 1975, pp. 58–63.

[18]See Donald Curtin, *op. cit.*

[19]As we have seen, time drafts typically provide only short-term financing. Clearly, time drafts are a form of supplier credit.

financial institutions, the balance being provided by other lenders. In some countries, the export finance agency provides its component of the shared financing on a "first in, last out" basis. This means that the export agency commits its money before the private financial institution makes its contribution, and that the export agency gives the private financial institution the first claim on repayments. This and other financing practices have given rise to claims of hidden subsidies to exporters and to a number of disputes. Accusations that financing constitutes a subsidy have been especially common over interest rates charged on buyer credits. Some countries have tried to hide their subsidies by offering **mixed credits**, which are a combination of export credits at market interest rates and what the export agencies call "foreign aid." That is, some export agencies say that they are able to offer very low interest rates on export credits as a result of contributions by their countries' development aid agencies.[20]

It is not uncommon for official export agencies to offer guarantees to banks in the exporter's country if the banks offer buyer credits. This substantially reduces the risk to the banks, thereby reducing the interest rates they charge. In the United States, the Ex-Im Bank guarantees export credits that are offered by the Private Export Funding Corporation (PEFCO). PEFCO is a private lending organization that was started in 1970 by a group of commercial banks and large export manufacturers. PEFCO raises its funds through the sale of the foreign repayment obligations which it has arranged and which have been guaranteed by the Ex-Im Bank. PEFCO also sells secured notes on the securities market.

The need for special trade documents, such as letters of credit and trade drafts, the need for export financing, and the need for export insurance, are all greatly reduced or eliminated when international trade takes the form of countertrade. There are different variants to countertrade, and it is well worthwhile considering what these variants are and why countertrade occurs.

COUNTERTRADE

The Various Forms of Countertrade

Countertrade involves a reciprocal agreement for the exchange of goods or services. The parties involved may be firms or governments, and the reciprocal agreements can take a number of forms.

Barter   The simplest form of countertrade involves the direct exchange of goods or services from one country for the goods or services of another. No

---

[20]The bickering over interest rates on export credits was reduced in 1983 when the OECD countries agreed to link interest rates to a weighted average of government-bond yields and to all charge the same rate. See *International Letter*, no. 515, Federal Reserve Bank of Chicago, December 16, 1983.

money changes hands, so that there is no need for letters of credit or drafts, and since the goods or services are exchanged at the same time, there is no need for trade financing or credit insurance.

Often one of the parties in a barter deal does not want the goods that are received, and so a third party which specializes in brokering arranges to sell them. An example of a barter deal was the trading in 1978 of the Polish soccer star Kazimierz Deyna for photocopiers and French lingerie.[21]

Counterpurchase   Barter requires a *double coincidence of wants* in that the two parties in the transaction must each want what the other party has to provide, and want it at the same time. Because such a coincidence is unlikely, a different form of countertrade, called **counterpurchase**, is substantially more common than barter. With counterpurchase the seller agrees with the buyer either to

1 make purchases from a company nominated by the buyer (the buyer then settles up with the company it has nominated), or
2 take products from the buyer in the future (that is, the seller accepts credits in terms of products).

Counterpurchase can also involve a combination of these two possibilities. That is, the seller agrees to receive products at a future date from a company nominated by the buyer.

Counterpurchase frequently involves only partial compensation with products, and the balance in cash. These types of countertrade deals are called **compensation agreements**.

Industrial Offset   A large portion of countertrade involves reciprocal agreements to buy materials or components from the buying company or country. For example, an aircraft manufacturer might agree to buy engines or fuselage materials from a buyer of its aircraft. The materials or components may not be only for the aircraft sold to the company or country. For example, a military aircraft manufacturer might agree to buy engines for all its planes from a foreign producer if the engine manufacturer's country agrees to buy a large number of aircraft.

Buyback   This form of countertrade is common with capital equipment used in mining and manufacturing. In a buyback agreement the seller of the capital equipment agrees to buy the products made with the equipment it supplies. For example, the maker of mining equipment might agree to buy the output of the

---

[21]See *Euromoney*, September 1988, p. 54.

mine for a given period, perhaps 10 or 15 years. This is a guarantee to the equipment buyer that it can pay for the capital equipment whatever happens to the price of what it produces, provided, of course, it can ensure continued production. When the equipment buyer pays partly in terms of its product and partly in cash, then, as in the case of other counterpurchase agreements of this kind, the arrangement is called a compensation agreement.

Switch Trading   Switch trading occurs when the importer has received credit for selling something to another country at a previous time, and where this credit cannot be converted into financial payment, but has to be used for purchases in the country where the credit is held. The owner of the credit switches title to its credit to the company or country from which it is making a purchase. For example, a British firm might have a credit in Poland for manufacturing equipment it has delivered. If a firm finds a product in France that it wishes to purchase, the British firm might pay the French firm with its Polish credit. The French firm might agree to this if it wishes to buy something from Poland. Because it is difficult for the various parties to locate each other for a switch deal, most of them are arranged by brokers. With so much countertrade involving east-west transactions, many of these brokers are based in Austria, which is a bridge between east and west.

The relative importance of the different forms of countertrade that we have described is shown in Figure 17.5. The figure shows clearly that counterpurchase is the dominant form, and that barter is relatively unimportant.

Before leaving a description of the forms of countertrade we might mention that in the 1980s, in response to the deepening third-world debt crisis, some countries began to substitute commodities for debt payments. For example, in 1985 Peru began repaying the Soviet Union and other communist nations with

FIGURE 17.5
THE DIFFERENT FORMS OF COUNTERTRADE.
Source: Christopher Korth (ed.), *International Countertrade*,
Quorum, New York, 1985, p. 18.

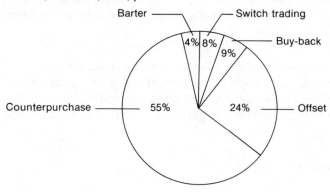

broiler chickens, shoes, and a variety of other products. Mexico also tried to arrange an oil-for-debt swap. These arrangements are a form of countertrade in that they circumvent the use of convertible currencies.

Reasons Why Countertrade Occurs

Given that countertrade is estimated to make up about 35 percent of east-west trade and about 10–20 percent of world trade, we might ask why trading agreements that are so difficult to arrange have assumed such importance.[22] That is, why do do many firms and countries decide against selling their products for a convertible currency and using this convertible currency to pay for what they buy?

A common reason for circumventing the use of a convertible currency and instead practicing countertrade is that a buyer in the countertrade does not have access to convertible currency. It is no accident that countertrade occurs where at least one party cannot obtain convertible currency to make payments. If one party cannot pay with convertible currency, then it must pay with goods, which is barter; with other companies' goods, which is counterpurchase; with credits, which could be a switch trade or a counterpurchase; and so on. Many communist countries and LDCs restrict access to convertible currency, and therefore many of the countertrades that occur involve a communist nation or an LDC.

Countertrade is also encouraged when prices are kept artificially high or low. For example, if the official OPEC oil price is above the market price, an oil seller might arrange a countertrade in which the oil is implicitly valued at the market price. The alternative of selling the oil at market price and using the proceeds for purchases is more likely to cause anger among other members of the OPEC cartel. More generally, countertrade allows goods to be exchanged internationally in specific transactions at relative prices which reflect genuine market values, while allowing nonmarket prices to be charged domestically. That is, countertrade is a way of circumventing problems caused by mispriced goods or currencies.[23]

THE INSTITUTIONS REGULATING INTERNATIONAL TRADE

A glance along the shelves at the vast range of goods we purchase from abroad, and a moment's reflection on the number of jobs which depend on export sales, should amply convince us that international trade is vital to our well-being, and that protectionism could do more to harm that well-being than almost any other development. Recognition of the potential damage that protectionism can bring

---

[22]See the surveys of countertrade summarized in Christopher Korth (ed.), *International Countertrade*, Quorum, New York, 1985.

[23]A denial of access to convertible currency can be considered a mispricing, in this case of the exchange rate; implicitly, the price of convertible currency is infinite if it cannot be purchased at any exchange rate.

has resulted in a number of post-World War II institutional arrangements designed to reduce protectionism and allow us to more fully exploit the benefits of trade. We shall quickly review the more important of these institutional arrangements in concluding our discussion of the organization of international trade. The two most important arrangements involve the regulation of the conduct of trade under the **General Agreement on Tariffs and Trade (GATT)** and the organization of trade in **free-trade areas**, which are sometimes called **customs unions** or **common markets**.

The General Agreement on Tariffs and Trade (GATT)

Established in 1947 closely on the heels of the IMF, GATT was intended to limit harmful trade practices, as the IMF was to limit harmful financial practices such as competitive devaluations. In its role as trade regulator, GATT has had limited success in reducing the level of damaging trade practices, but it is probably fair to say that without GATT, protectionism would likely be much worse.

Two of the central principles of GATT are:

1 Trade relations must be nondiscriminatory.
2 Export subsidies are not permitted.

The nondiscriminatory principle is effected via the **most favored nation** clause, which disallows offering better trade treatment to any country than is given to other GATT signatories. This means that all GATT members are treated in the same way as the most favored nation is treated. An exception has been made to allow free-trade areas or customs unions to exist, whereby members of the union can *all* be treated more favorably than nonmembers. The prohibition on export subsidies means that no advantage can be offered to domestic producers which would give them an advantage in foreign markets. Again, an exception has been made, this time for agricultural products. Where subsidies are shown to exist outside agriculture, countries are permitted to apply discriminatory tariffs to counteract the trade subsidies; these are usually referred to as **countervailing tariffs**.

GATT has managed to broker some general reductions in tariffs under the so-called **Kennedy** and **Tokyo rounds**, and has served a role in ruling on what trade practices are unfair. Since 1985, GATT has been stymied in its efforts to make progress in increasing free trade in services, although it has reached agreement, pressured largely by the U.S. and the European Economic Community, to include a discussion of services in the **Uruguay round** of meetings, which took place through the latter part of the 1980s.

The bureaucracy of GATT, which is centered in Geneva, Switzerland, has faced considerable difficulty dealing with **nontariff barriers**, many of which are insidiously hidden. Sometimes the hidden trade barriers are veiled in rules apparently aimed at protecting health, safety, and product quality, but having the distinct effect of favoring domestic producers.

Free-Trade Areas

When we include the European Economic Community and the world's largest bilateral free-trade agreement, that between Canada and the United States, along with the other customs unions that have been established, we find that a very substantial portion of international trade occurs within the regulations of trading agreements. Such agreements are therefore a reality that every business person involved in international trade must understand.

The European Economic Community (EEC), usually known these days simply as the Economic Community, has swollen in size since its establishment in the 1950s, to include Belgium, Britain, Denmark, France, Greece, Italy, Ireland, Luxembourg, The Netherlands, Portugal, Spain, and West Germany. Trade being an important component of economic activity within and between these nations, the EEC is the largest trading arrangement that exists. While the EEC has since its very beginning been an important factor in trade for countries such as the United States, its importance is reaching an entirely new level with the imminence of the complete removal of all tariffs and restrictions within the EEC in 1992. Companies operating outside the EEC under this new and final stage of trade deregulation have to face competition from firms inside the EEC that have favorable terms within the Community. For example, U.S. car makers selling in Britain have to face EEC tariffs, whereas German, Italian, and French car makers do not.

The U.S., which has traditionally been a staunch supporter of freer trade even if its rhetoric has often been sharper than its actions, made its own entry into trading agreements when, in January 1989, it signed the Free Trade Agreement (FTA) with Canada. Although it is not always noticed, the fact is that U.S. trade with Canada is substantially larger than U.S. trade with Japan, West Germany, or any other nation, and indeed, U.S.-Canadian trade is the largest bilateral trade on Earth. The comprehensive and detailed arrangement of the U.S.-Canadian FTA therefore means that each country has gained improved access to its largest foreign market. Tariffs are to be removed on a large range of products over a 10-year period from the original signing of the FTA in 1989. In addition, each country has greater freedom to invest in the other. For the U.S., one of the most important features of the FTA is Canada's agreement to give U.S. energy producers and consumers the same treatment given to Canadians. The FTA operates within the rules of GATT. Procedures have been put in place to resolve disputes, with the U.S. retaining its right to levy countervailing tariffs when it believes U.S. industry is being damaged by unfair trading practices.

With trading agreements existing between Australia and New Zealand, among the Caribbean nations, and in West Africa, Latin America, and Central America, some people have come to fear the consequences of a world that is divided into trading blocks. The pattern of localized freer-trading arrangements with unchanged or even increased protectionism levied against outsiders does not correspond to the principles envisioned by those who established GATT, and even if it brings some gains, is most distinctly a suboptimal development.

SUMMARY

1 Special procedures have evolved for dealing with the extra risks of international trade, and national and international institutions have been established to finance and regulate international trade.

2 Before shipping goods to foreign buyers, many exporters require buyers to provide a letter of credit from a reputable bank. This is a guarantee that the exporter will be paid if the goods are supplied in good order.

3 Payment is made by a bill of exchange, or draft, which is sent by the exporter to the importer or to the importer's bank. The importer or the importer's bank signs the draft. If the draft is payable on presentation, it is a sight draft. If it is payable at a future date, it is a time draft.

4 The shipper gives the exporter a bill of lading, the original copy of which is required for collection of the goods. The bill of lading is forwarded to the importer for the goods to be released.

5 When an exporter is confident an importer will pay, goods may be sold on an open account, and a bill presented after shipment. When an exporter suspects that an importer may not pay, cash may be demanded before shipment occurs.

6 When an exporter lacks trust in the importer's bank or country, the exporter can have the importer's letter of credit confirmed. A confirmed letter of credit is one way of avoiding country risk.

7 Export credit insurance is an alternative to letters of credit for avoiding commercial and/or country risks. Export insurance, however, typically involves a deductible portion of coverage and differs from letters of credit in other ways that are sometimes important.

8 Credit insurance may be a natural monopoly and be more effectively offered by an official rather than a private institution because a government may have more success avoiding nonpayment, and because a government may consider positive spillovers of trade deals.

9 Official export financing agencies often provide direct buyers' credits, as well as guarantees on credits to buyers granted by domestic or foreign financial institutions.

10 When an importer's bank which has issued a letter of credit accepts the associated time draft, or when an exporter has a time draft which was not issued against a letter of credit accepted by a bank, the resulting accepted draft is called a banker's acceptance. An importer can also create a banker's acceptance by drawing up a time draft signed by the importer in favor of a bank, paying the bank to accept it, and having the banker's acceptance discounted by the bank or in the money market.

11 Banker's acceptances are a means of short-term trade financing, typically up to 6 months. Forfaiting is a means of medium-term trade financing, with a typical term of 5 years.

12 Forfaiting involves the sale by an exporter of promissory notes issued by an importer and usually avalled by the importer's bank. The forfaiter has no recourse to the exporter in the event that, for whatever reason, the forfaiter is not paid.

13 Forfaiting is a particularly useful means of financing the sale of capital goods. The exporter is paid immediately, while the importer can make payments out of revenue generated by the products of the capital goods.

14 A substantial portion of east-west trade is countertrade. This may involve barter, an agreement to purchase products at a later date or from a designated supplier, an agreement to provide parts or to buy goods produced with capital equipment that has been supplied, or an agreement to switch credits.

15 Countertrade is motivated by foreign exchange controls and mispricing of products, and therefore often involves communist countries or LDCs.

16 The conduct of international trade is to a limited extent governed by GATT. Signatories to GATT agree to have nondiscriminatory tariffs by accepting the most-favored-nation principle, and they agree to not subsidize exports.

17 GATT has been forced to grant exceptions to its tariff policy. These exceptions are to permit the establishment of customs unions and to exempt agriculture from the prohibition on export subsidies. For these and other reasons, especially an emergence of nontariff barriers to trade, GATT has had limited success in encouraging freer trade. It might be, however, that without GATT, more restrictive practices would be present.

18 The majority of trade occurs between countries which are members of customs unions or free-trade agreements. The trend appears to be towards the establishment of trading blocs rather than towards globally free trade.

QUESTIONS

1 Why are letters of credit not used in domestic trade?

2 Why does the exporter provide the importer with the check for payment that the importer signs, rather than just allow the importer to send a check?

3 Why are banks willing to accept time drafts, making them bills of exchange, and why do importers and exporters arrange for banks to accept drafts?

4 Are cash terms likely when an importer can arrange a letter of credit?

5 Why is export credit insurance typically offered by government agencies?

6 Why do you think promissory notes used in forfaiting deals are normally avalled by the importer's bank?

7 What is the similarity between an aval and an acceptance?

8 Is forfaiting a form of factoring?

9 What form of trade financing is an exporter likely to seek first, and how would the choice depend on the export deal?

10 Why is counterpurchase so much more common than barter in countertrade?

11 How can a customs union or common market such as the EEC hurt a U.S. exporter?

12 Under what conditions might the emergence of a limited number of free-trade blocs lower standards of living?

BIBLIOGRAPHY

Back, Leonard A.: *Introduction to Commercial Letters of Credit*, Citibank, New York, undated.

Citibank: *Bankers' Acceptances*, Citibank, New York, undated.

Harrington, J.A.: *Specifics on Commercial Letters of Credit and Bankers' Acceptances*, Scott Printing Corp., Jersey City, N.J., 1974.

Korth, Christopher (ed.): *International Countertrade*, Quorum, New York, 1985.

Krugman, Paul R., and Maurice Obstfeld, *International Economics*: *Theory and Policy*, Scott-Foresman, Glenview, Illinois, 1988, Chapter 9.

Rentzmann, Werner F., and Thomas Teichman: "Forfaiting: An Alternative Technique of Export Financing," *Euromoney*, December 1975, pp. 58–63.

Södersten, Bo: *International Economics*, 2nd ed., Macmillan, London, 1980, Chapter 17.

Watson, Alasdair: *Finance of International Trade*, Institute of Bankers, London, 1976.

APPENDIX 17.1: International Commercial and Financial Abbreviations

COMMERCIAL ABBREVIATIONS

a.a.r.:	Against all risks (marine)
A/R:	All risks or against all risks (marine)
A.T.:	American terms
A/V:	Ad valorem
B.E.:	Bill of exchange
B/L:	Bill of lading
B.M.:	Board measure
Carr. pd.:	Carriage paid
c.& f.:	Cost and freight
c.i.f.:	Cost, insurance, freight
c.i.f.& c.:	Cost, insurance, freight, and commission
c.i.f.c.& i.:	Cost, insurance, freight, commission, and interest
c.i.f.i.& e.:	Cost, insurance, freight, interest, and exchange
C/R:	Company's risk
D/O:	Delivery order
E.& O.E:	Errors and omissions excepted
Ex.:	Out of
f.a.b.:	Free on board (French/German/Spanish)
F.A.S.:	Free alongside
f.c.s.:	Free of capture and seizure
f.o.b.:	Free on board
f.o.d.:	Free of damage
f.o.r.:	Free on rails at point of destination
f.p.a.:	Free of particular average
F.P.A.A.C.:	Free of particular average (American conditions)
F.P.A.E.C.:	Free of particular average (English conditions)
G/A:	General average
Grs.T.:	Gross ton
H.M.C.:	Her Majesty's Customs
Kd:	Knocked down
l.t.:	Long ton
M.I.P.:	Marine insurance policy
N/B:	Mark well (nota bene)
n.o.p.:	Not otherwise provided for

O/R:	Owner's risk
o.r.b.:	Owner's risk of breakage
S/D:	Sight draft
S.D.B.L.:	Sight draft, bill of lading attached
S/N:	Shipping note
S.P.A.:	Subject to particular average
s.t.:	short ton

FINANCIAL ABBREVIATIONS

A/S:	After sight
A/S:	At sight
A/T:	American terms
B/E:	Bill of exchange
B/P:	Bills payable
B/R:	Bills receivable
C.W.O.:	Cash with order
D/N:	Debit note
D/S:	Days (after) sight
L/A:	Letter of authority
L/C:	Letter of credit
P.L.C.:	Public limited company
R/A:	Refer to acceptor
R/D:	Refer to drawer
S/A:	Sociedad Anomina—corporation (Spanish, French, German)
S/D:	Sight draft
S.D.B.L.:	Sight draft, bill of lading attached
S/D D/P:	Sight draft documents against payment
W.B.:	Waybill
W/R:	Warehouse receipt

CHAPTER 18

OPERATING EXPOSURE

This chapter shows what changes in exchange rates imply for the cash flows of exporting and importing firms and is hence concerned with their operating exposure. For example, it describes the effects of exchange rates on an exporter's product price and sales (which affect cash inflows) as well as on production costs (which affect cash outflows). It explains how the elasticity of demand and the nature of production influence the extent to which profits are affected by changes in exchange rates. We shall discover how the effects of exchange rates depend on such things as the time span considered and the degree of competition from other firms. We shall consider a number of situations.

We reach the important conclusion in this chapter that even if a company has hedged its foreign exchange receivables and payables and has no foreign assets or liabilities, there is still an important element of foreign exchange exposure. This is the operating exposure which occurs because future profits from operating as an exporter or importer depend on exchange rates. The techniques of forwards, futures, options, and swaps used for hedging assets and liabilities are not designed to help eliminate operating exposure. Indeed, because operating exposure is so difficult to eliminate, it has been called **residual foreign exchange exposure**. We shall discover that the extent of operating or residual exposure depends on such factors as the elasticity of demand for the product, production-cost conditions, the currency relevant for income measurement, and whether inputs are produced domestically.

Before beginning, we should point out that some firms face operating or residual foreign exchange exposure without even dealing in foreign exchange. For example, restaurants in U.S. resorts that are visited by foreign tourists gain or lose customers according to the exchange rate. This happens despite the fact that they are generally paid in U.S. dollars and they pay for food, labor, rent, and interest in U.S. dollars. Similarly, industries which compete with imported goods face operating exposure. For example, U.S. firms that supply beef to U.S. supermarkets and that never see foreign exchange can find competition from foreign beef suppliers—in Canada and Latin America—more fierce when the U.S. dollar gains against other currencies, lowering prices of the non-U.S. product.

Since the links in the economic chain of interdependence are many, industries that provide supplies to U.S. resort hotels, U.S. beef producers, or other industries more directly involved in international trade will find themselves affected by changes in exchange rates. It should therefore be apparent that operating exposure makes the required perspective of management extremely broad. It should also be apparent that operating exposure is difficult to avoid with the exposure-reducing techniques we have met so far. But let us begin by examining what influences the extent of operating exposure. We consider separately the exporter and the importer.

THE EXPORTER

Competitive Markets in the Short Run

The most straightforward situation of operating exposure involves a perfectly competitive market, which by definition is a market where any one firm can sell all it wishes without affecting the market price. To put this in context, let us suppose that before a devaluation of the U.S. dollar, Aviva Corporation was able to sell in Britain all the jeans that it wished to produce at a dollar-equivalent price of $p_1^\$$ a pair. The dollar sign denotes that the price is in terms of Aviva's home currency. After a devaluation, Aviva Corporation will be able to sell all the jeans it wishes to produce at a higher price, $p_2^\$$. This is because with the U.S. dollar cheaper to foreigners, Aviva can charge a higher U.S. dollar price and yet leave the foreign exchange price unchanged or lower.

We can go further and say precisely how much higher the new price, $p_2^\$$, will be after a devaluation. To determine this, we define $p_1^\pounds$ as the price of Aviva's jeans in Britain before the devaluation and $S(\$/\pounds)$ as the predevaluation exchange rate. We can write the number of pounds that Aviva gets for each pair of jeans sold in Britain as $p_1^\pounds$ and say that

$$p_1^\pounds = \frac{1}{S(\$/\pounds)} \cdot p_1^\$ \tag{18.1}$$

This equation merely defines the relationship between the price charged in Britain in pounds and the price in dollars. If Aviva is operating in a competitive market, there are many other firms—at home, in Britain, and around the world —that are prepared to supply similar jeans. There is no reason for the foreign suppliers to change their pound prices just because the United States has experienced a depreciation/devaluation.

After a devaluation/depreciation to an exchange rate of $S'(\$/\pounds)$, the pound and dollar prices are related as follows:

$$p_2^{\pounds} = \frac{1}{S'(\$/\pounds)} \cdot p_2^{\$}$$

If the price of jeans in Britain is changing in line with the British inflation rate, $\dot{P}_{UK}$, and we can write $p_2^{\pounds} = p_1^{\pounds}(1 + \dot{P}_{UK})$, then

$$p_1^{\pounds}(1 + \dot{P}_{UK}) = \frac{1}{S'(\$/\pounds)} \cdot p_2^{\$} \tag{18.2}$$

That is, after the exchange value of the dollar falls to $S'(\$/\pounds)$, the price that Aviva should charge in Britain will move in line with the prices of other jeans suppliers. Prices of these other suppliers are assumed to change at the rate of British inflation. Equation (18.2) follows because Aviva can sell all it wishes at the price charged by other suppliers, and there is therefore no advantage to lowering its price after a devaluation.

Taking the ratios of Equation (18.1) and Equation (18.2), we get

$$1 + \dot{P}_{UK} = \frac{S(\$/\pounds)}{S'(\$/\pounds)} \cdot \frac{p_2^{\$}}{p_1^{\$}}$$

or

$$\frac{p_2^{\$}}{p_1^{\$}} = \frac{S'(\$/\pounds)}{S(\$/\pounds)}(1 + \dot{P}_{UK})$$

This tells us that after a devaluation of the dollar or an increase in the price of foreign exchange to $S'(\$/\pounds)$, the U.S. dollar price of jeans in Britain will rise by the combined rate of devaluation and British inflation. This is true no matter what the rate of inflation is in the United States. For example, if the dollar falls in value by 5 percent and Britain has 10-percent inflation affecting jeans (and other) prices, the dollar price that Aviva charges will go up 15 percent. Of course, the rate of inflation in the United States will determine production-cost increases and the extent to which the 15-percent gain in the dollar price of the product represents an increase in profitability.

The predevaluation and postdevaluation prices, $p_1^{\$}$ and $p_2^{\$} = [S'(\$/\pounds)/S(\$/\pounds)](1 + \dot{P}_{UK})p_1^{\$}$, are shown in Figure 18.1, where the price axes are drawn in home currency (\$) units. To keep the diagrams straightforward, we take the U.S. inflation to be zero so that the marginal cost curve, MC, does not shift. Since the firm is a perfectly competitive firm, the demand curve is a

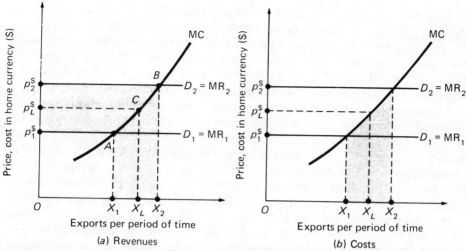

FIGURE 18.1
EXPORTER AND DEVALUATION IN A COMPETITIVE MARKET. A depreciation or devaluation raises the price an exporter can charge in terms of his or her own currency. In the perfectly competitive situation the price rises by the percentage of devaluation/depreciation plus the percentage of inflation in the United Kingdom. This raises profit-maximizing output, sales revenues, and the total cost of production. In the long run, new firms and the expansion of older firms reduce selling prices, output, and profits to original levels. If the country's exporters are a small part of the overall market, some benefits will remain.

horizontal line at the relevant price. Further, since additional units can be sold at a constant price, the horizontal demand curve is also the marginal revenue (MR) curve.[1] The marginal cost, MC, is assumed to increase as output increases.

In Figure 18.1, before the devaluation, our firm, Aviva Corporation, would have produced and sold X_1 units per period by seeking its optimum output where marginal revenue MR_1 equals marginal cost MC. This is the point of maximum profit. If output is less than X_1, MR > MC, and profit is increased by producing more and adding more revenue than costs. At an output greater than X_1, we have MC > MR, and profit is increased by producing less and thereby reducing costs by more than revenue.

If we are dealing with a situation without U.S. inflation, where all inputs such as the denim cloth are produced domestically, we can expect—at least in the short run—that MC will remain as before the devaluation. Foreign inputs will probably become more expensive after the devaluation, raising production costs and hence MC, but when inputs are all domestic there is no immediate reason

[1] In the long run newly entering firms will shift the demand or MR curve. We shall deal with this situation shortly.

for domestically produced inputs to cost more.[2] With the price and hence marginal revenue of jeans in dollar terms rising to $p_2^\$ = [S'(\$/£)/S(\$/£)](1 + \dot{P}_{UK})p_1^\$$ after the devaluation and the marginal cost remaining unchanged, Aviva will want to raise its production to X_2 per period. This is the new profit-maximizing output, where $MR_2 = MC$. We find that a higher price in dollars and a higher level of sales have resulted from the devaluation.

Part a of Figure 18.1 shows how revenues in units of domestic currency have increased because the price is higher and the sales are greater. Revenues will increase by the shaded area in part a. There is an unambiguous increase in cash inflows in terms of home currency after a devaluation. A simple reversal of interpretations in the diagram to determine the effects of a revaluation/appreciation will similarly show that there is an unambiguous decrease in cash inflows for an exporter when they are measured in terms of the home currency.

In the short run, with no U.S. inflation and per-unit costs of production unaffected by the devaluation, the total production cost will rise by only the cost of producing the additional quantity that is sold. Since MC is the cost of producing each additional item, the area under MC between X_1 and X_2 will be the additional cost incurred in providing the extra goods sold, $X_2 - X_1$. Hence, the total manufacturing cost will rise by the shaded area in part b of Figure 18.1. We can see that with revenues rising by the shaded area in part a and costs rising by the shaded area in part b, profits, which rise by the difference between revenues and costs, will rise by the area $p_2^\$ BAp_1^\$$ in part a. After a devaluation, the increase in cash outflows for production costs will always be less than the increase in cash inflows from export revenues.

How do we determine the amount by which total profits will increase? We note that with $p_2^\$$ exceeding $p_1^\$$ by the U.K. inflation and the percentage of the devaluation, the increase in nominal profits— even if output remains at X_1—will be equal to the sum of the U.K. inflation rate and the percentage of the devaluation multiplied by the original revenues. For example, with a 10-percent devaluation and 5-percent U.K. inflation, $p_2^\$$ exceeds $p_1^\$$ by 15 percent, and so if initial revenues were \$1000, nominal profits will rise by at least \$150. With output increasing, profits will rise by an even bigger percentage. This is clear from part a of Figure 18.1 by comparing the size of the extra profit, area $p_2^\$ BAp_1^\$$, with the original revenues given by the unshaded rectangle, $Op_1^\$ AX_1$. We can notice, also, that the flatter MC is, the greater is the increase in profit; production flexibility increases the gain from a depreciation/devaluation.

Long-Run Effects; Imported Inputs

Since the accurate forecasting of cash flows is an important job for the financial manager, we should not limit our discussion to the immediate effects of

---

[2]Later we do allow for U.S. inflation and for imported inputs with consequent movement in the long run. It should be clear that if the U.S. inflation and U.K. inflation are related according to PPP, that is, if $\dot{P}_{US} = \dot{P}_{UK} + \dot{S}(1 + \dot{P}_{UK})$, then MC will move by $\dot{P}_{US}$, which is as much as the vertical movement in $D = MR$, that is, $\dot{P}_{UK} + \dot{S}(1 + \dot{P}_{UK})$. Therefore the devaluation is not real and has no lasting effect.

devaluation on flows of revenues and production costs. When we are dealing with a firm in perfect competition with others, as we are here, it is important to appreciate that any increase in profits that will accompany a devaluation or depreciation will probably be temporary. A perfectly competitive market, by definition, involves the free entry of new firms. The additional profit that might be available after a real devaluation/depreciation (that is, one that does not just make up for differences in inflation) will serve as an incentive for new firms to get involved and existing firms to expand. This can bring the rate of profit back to its predevaluation/predepreciation level. Therefore, it is possible that only in the interim will the higher-than-normal profits be made. Hence, if Aviva is operating in a perfectly competitive market, management might not be too excited after falls in the exchange value of the dollar, even if they are real. Let us show these conclusions graphically.

The immediate higher profits after depreciation will induce firms in purely domestic endeavors to move into the export sector until the "last" firm to enter can reap a profit equal to the best it could achieve in some alternative endeavor. Competition from new firms might tend to move the price that the original firms such as Aviva can gain for their product back toward $p_1^{\$}$.[3] As a result, we would move back toward the predevaluation situation of price $p_1^{\$}$ and output X_1 with original cash flows. Extra profits will last only as long as it takes new firms to get involved. This will depend largely on the nature of the product.

We might want to note that if the devaluing country produces only a small fraction of the world's output of a particular good, then the free entry of firms *within* the country will have little effect when cutting into the extra profit from devaluation. This will be true because many new firms might enter the industry within the devaluing country without significantly affecting the world price. Prices might move back very little from $p_2^{\$}$, perhaps only to $p_L^{\$}$ in Figure 18.1. Output would be X_L. Profits would remain abnormally high and be given by the shaded area $p_L^{\$}CAp_1^{\$}$. Fortunately for Aviva Corporation, other countries also manufacture jeans.

There is another route that is possible through rising costs that can also limit the period of obtaining extra profit after a real devaluation and hence limit the postdevaluation/postdepreciation celebrations of the exporter. This involves the eventual reduction in the *real* devaluation via the inflation that the *actual* devaluation itself sets up. This will work in all market settings, not only in competitive markets, and so we will consider the effect separately. The effect will come about even if none of the inputs used by the firm under consideration are imported; in this case, after the devaluation there will be no immediate increase in costs. Cost increases will nevertheless take place eventually.

General import prices tend to rise after a depreciation or devaluation. To the extent that imports figure in the cost-of-living index, a devaluation will increase the cost of living and thereby reduce the buying power of wages. If efforts to

---

[3]The price will move back below $p_1^{\$}(1 + \dot{P}_{UK})$ because with no U.S. inflation, this price is higher than the original price, and so abnormal profits will still remain. Of course, $p_1^{\$}$ is a dollar price, and so after the devaluation of the dollar, the same dollar price $p_1^{\$}$ means a *lower* pound price.

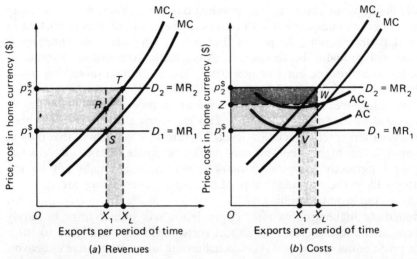

FIGURE 18.2
EXPORTER AND DEVALUATION IN A COMPETITIVE MARKET: EFFECT OF COST INCREASES. A devaluation will raise import costs and the costs of production. This means a reduction in the extent of real devaluation. Profit-maximizing output and profits will return to original levels. However, as long as some real devaluation remains, there will be extra sales and profits.

maintain real or price-adjusted wages result in wage increases to compensate for the higher cost of living, then production costs will rise. This is shown in Figure 18.2.

In part *a* of Figure 18.2, we show the marginal cost of production rising from MC to MC_L. Every unit is shown to cost more to produce as money wages rise. We can think of MC moving up by the U.S. inflation rate, and so we have

$$\frac{MC_L}{MC} = 1 + \dot{P}_{US}$$

at each output level. In order to retain an effective (or real) devaluation, we draw a smaller vertical shift in MC than in the demand curve, which, as we have already stated, shifts by

$$\frac{p_2^\$}{p_1^\$} = \frac{S'(\$/£)}{S(\$/£)}(1 + \dot{P}_{UK})$$

Indeed, the real extent of the devaluation/depreciation is the difference between the proportional shift in the price line, $D = MR$, and the proportional shift in the MC curve, since from the equations above this is

$$\frac{p_2^{\$}}{p_1^{\$}} - \frac{MC_L}{MC} = \frac{S'(\$/£)}{S(\$/£)}(1 + \dot{P}_{UK}) - (1 + \dot{P}_{US})$$

$$= \frac{S'(\$/£) - S(\$/£)}{S(\$/£)}(1 + \dot{P}_{UK}) - (\dot{P}_{US} - \dot{P}_{UK})$$

or the real devaluation/depreciation defined in Equation (9.18).

A word is in order as to why we might expect costs to rise less than the product price after a dollar devaluation. Only a fraction of the goods purchased by workers is produced abroad. Let us say, for example, that this fraction is 25 percent. If a 10-percent devaluation were to occur, this might at worst raise the price of imported goods by the same 10 percent. The price index of *all* goods and services purchased by workers would rise by about 2.5 percent as a result of a 10-percent increase in prices of only 25 percent of the goods.[4] If workers received wage increases to compensate completely for the price-level increase resulting from the devaluation, wages would rise by 2.5 percent, and this would be the extent of the upward shift in the cost curves (MC to MC_L and AC to AC_L). We see that the vertical shift in costs should be less than the amount of devaluation that determines the size of the shift in demand from D_1 to D_2. Because we can move MC and AC and the demand lines, $D = MR$, by any amounts relative to each other, Figure 18.2 can be used to show the effects of inflation *induced* by a devaluation/depreciation. It is also a valid representation when there is an *original* real devaluation with inflation in both countries.

If costs rise in the long run to MC_L and AC_L, output will end up only at X_L, where $MC_L = MR_2$, although the price will remain at the same level, $p_2^{\$}$, as before the increase in costs. Total revenues will rise from $Op_1^{\$}SX_1$ to $Op_2^{\$}TX_L$ as a result of the higher home-currency price and the larger quantity sold. The total cost is AC multiplied by the output, which before the devaluation was $Op_1^{\$}VX_1$. After the devaluation, at the output X_L, the total cost is area $OZWX_L$, which exceeds the predevaluation cost by the lightly shaded area in part *b* of Fig. 18.2. Since revenues rise by the shaded area in part *a*, or the entire shaded area in part *b*, and costs rise by the lightly shaded area in part *b*, profits rise by the difference, the darkly shaded area in part *b*.[5]

The dampening effect on profits from the competition-induced price reduction shown in part *a* of Figure 18.1 must be added to the profit reduction from

---

[4]Clearly, in a small "banana republic," where only masses of "bananas" are produced, perhaps as much as, say, 90 percent of the goods used could come from abroad, and these would be paid for with revenues from the sale of bananas. Then, the overall price index would rise by about as much as the devaluation, and the vertical shift of MC and AC would be the same as that of the demand curve.

[5]To simplify the argument, we have drawn area $Op_1^{\$}SX_1$ so that it is equal to area $Op_1^{\$}VX_1$. This means that before the devaluation, revenues equal costs, and profits are zero. Any profit after the devaluation is a result of the devaluation itself. We have also simplified the argument by ignoring the long-run envelope of AC curves.

higher costs. The effects will both contribute to a smaller profit increase from devaluation, but even firms that do not face extra competition from other producers will find profits shrinking because of rising costs brought about by the devaluation/depreciation that reduces the real change in exchange rates.

The effect of having imported inputs is, diagrammatically, precisely the same as the effect of general inflation through wage pressure that we have just discussed. Figure 18.2 will consequently also describe the effect of having imported inputs. If some of the inputs going into the production of our export good come from abroad—that is, they are **reexports**—a devaluation will probably make these inputs immediately more expensive to our exporting firm. As a result, MC and AC will both shift upward to the extent that imported inputs figure in production. We know that this vertical shift will be less than the shift in the selling price when at least some inputs are domestic. As before, the shift is given in Figure 18.2 by the MC_L an AC_L curves, and the output increase is smaller than it would be without imported inputs. Output increases to X_L, where MC_L cuts D_2. Profits rise by the darkly shaded area in part b of Figure 18.2.

The difference between the effect of imported inputs and our previous case of general devaluation-induced inflation is only in the immediateness of effect, with input prices probably rising much more quickly than with the link through wages. We should remember, however, that input and general inflation effects can work together in the long run. From this point on, we shall consider only the short run. We shall see that this can become complicated enough.

The Case of Imperfect Competition

There are a large number of imperfect-market settings, but in general we can say that in an imperfect market, a firm will still sell some of its product even if it raises the price. This will be the case when perfect substitutes are not available. It will occur frequently, since products of different firms generally have different characteristics.

Frequently, in imperfect markets, gains in profits can be maintained because new firms can be prevented from moving into a profitable firm's market. Devaluation gains, then, will be offset only to the extent that inputs are imported and through the general inflation route, not through the influx of new firms.[6] We shall not consider imported inputs or general inflation, and the gains in profit that we show will be permanent in the absence of these cost-increasing effects.

To examine a firm like Aviva in an imperfect-market setting, we allow for some inelasticity in demand; that is, we draw a conventional downward-sloping

---

[6]All that is necessary for the devaluation to have a lasting effect is that other firms *within our firm's own country or other devaluing countries* cannot easily enter our firm's market. This is why we claimed that Aviva was fortunate that jeans are produced in many different countries, which allows devaluation benefits to be long-lasting with *dollar* prices remaining higher.

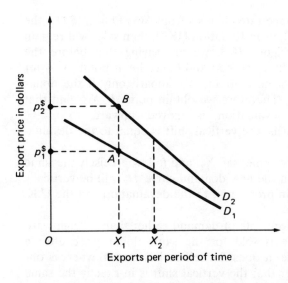

FIGURE 18.3
DEVALUATION AND THE DEMAND CURVE. For each sales level, the price that can be charged after the devaluation with sales unchanged rises by the percentage of the devaluation. This means that the demand curve shifts vertically by the percentage of the devaluation (plus any foreign inflation).

demand curve.[7] When, as before, we have the home currency on the vertical axis, what is the effect on this firm's demand curve then there is a devaluation/depreciation? We shall see that it will move vertically upward, just as in a competitive market. Indeed, the argument will differ little from the one we used in the discussion of competitive markets.

Let us consider any particular sales volume on demand curve D_1 in Figure 18.3, for example, X_1. Now when the demand curve is at the predevaluation level, D_1, a volume X_1 can be sold at the domestic-currency price $p_1^\$$. With the exchange rate $S(\$/\pounds)$, this means a foreign-currency price of $p_1^\pounds = [1/S(\$/\pounds)]p_1^\$$ *at this output* of X_1.

After the devaluation, the same quantity—that is, X_1—will be sold abroad if the foreign-currency price is raised in line with prices of other suppliers to $p_2^\pounds = p_1^\pounds(1 + \dot{P}_{UK})$. It is the foreign-currency price that always matters, and if Aviva keeps its pound prices in line with prices charged by other producers in the British market (which are assumed to rise at the U.K. inflation rate), it will remain competitive. This is because the British do not look at the price tag of a pair of U.S.-made jeans on sale in Britain in terms of the U.S. dollar. Rather, they consider the number of British pounds that must be paid for the jeans, just as a U.S. car buyer considers the dollar price of an imported car. It is the monetary unit of the country where the product is sold that influences the buyer's purchase decision. But at the devaluated/depreciated exchange rate of $S'(\$/\pounds)$, the new pound price of $p_2^\pounds = (1 + \dot{P}_{UK})p_1^\pounds$ means a dollar price of

$$p_2^\$ = S'(\$/\pounds)p_2^\pounds = S'(\$/\pounds)(1 + \dot{P}_{UK})p_1^\pounds \qquad (18.3)$$

[7]Of course, in a competitive market, the *industry* demand curve is also downward-sloping. Competitive-market *firms* were given horizontal demand because each is a small part of the market.

In other words, if, when the exchange rate changes from $S(\$/£)$ to $S'(\$/£)$, the dollar price changes from $p_1^\$$ to $p_2^\$$, as in Equation (18.3), then sales will remain unchanged at X_1. In terms of Figure 18.3, we are saying that before the devaluation at price $p_1^\$$, we will sell X_1 abroad and hence be at point A. After the devaluation, we will sell the same amount, X_1, aboard only if the dollar price is $p_2^\$ = S'(\$/£)(1 + \dot{P}_{UK})p_1^£$. Therefore we obtain point B. We find that the demand curve after the devaluation is moved upward to $p_2^\$ = [S'(\$/£)/S(\$/£)](1 + \dot{P}_{UK})p_1^\$$; that is, the vertical shift is equal to the devaluation plus the U.K. inflation.

We can now take another sales volume, say X_2, and follow precisely the same argument. Each and every point on the new demand curve D_2 will be vertically above the old demand curve, D_1, in proportion to the devaluation and the U.K. inflation.

We should think of vertical movements of demand rather than a "rightward shift" along the lines that "more is sold for the same dollar price after a devaluation." Although this is true, it does not tell us how much, whereas our argument in the text makes it clear that the vertical shift is in exactly the same proportion as the change in the exchange rate and U.K. inflation. Of course, we notice that since the vertical shift is always in the same *proportion* as the change in the exchange rate and the U.K. inflation, the *absolute* shift is less at lower prices on the demand curve. This is shown in Figure 18.3, with demand curve D_2 closer to D_1 at lower prices.

Part a of Figure 18.4 shows the vertical shift in the demand curve $(D_1$ to $D_2)$ from a U.S. dollar devaluation, along with the corresponding shift in the MR curve. We have assumed that the costs are constant in part b by drawing a flat MC.[8] It would complicate matters only a little to allow for increasing costs by also considering AC curves. Rising costs would tend to reduce the effects of devaluation on profits, but they would not eliminate these positive effects.

We see from Figure 18.4 that before the devaluation, the firm will produce X_1 per period, which is where MC = MR_1, and it will be able to sell this output at the price $p_1^\$$. After the devaluation, the firm will produce X_2 per period and sell this at the price $p_2^\$$. The increase in revenue from $Op_1^\$AX_1$ to $Op_2^\$A'X_2$ is represented by the total shaded area in part a of Figure 18.4. An important point to realize is that with a downward-sloping curve, the price increase from $p_1^\$$ to $p_2^\$$ is less than the vertical shift in the demand curve $(AC < AB)$. We discover that export prices when stated in the domestic currency rise *less than* the combined percentage of the devaluation and the U.K. inflation. This is different from the case of perfect competition, where we found the product price rising by an amount *equal* to the devaluation and the U.K. inflation.

With output rising from X_1 to X_2, costs will rise by this amount times the cost of manufacturing each of the units. Since each unit costs the manufacturer

---

[8]As in the case of perfect competition, for a given change in the exchange rate, U.S. inflation will change production costs but not the U.K.-based demand curve. To keep our diagrams straightforward, we assume that there is no U.S. inflation.

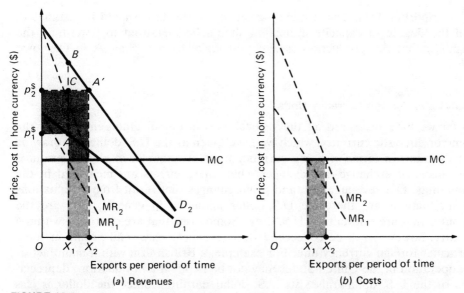

FIGURE 18.4
EXPORTER AND DEVALUATION IN AN IMPERFECTLY COMPETITIVE MARKET. In an imperfectly competitive market the home currency price of exports will increase by a smaller percentage than the devaluation. Sales will increase by a smaller fraction than in the case of perfect competition.

an amount given by the height of the MC curve, the total cost will rise by the lightly shaded area in part *b* of Figure 18.4 (shown also in part *a*). Profits will rise by the difference between the change in total revenue, given by the total shaded area in part *a*, and the change in total cost, given by the lightly shaded area. The change in profits is therefore represented by the darkly shaded area in part *a*, which is the difference between the total shaded area and the lightly shaded area.

The extent to which prices will rise, output increase, and profits be affected will depend on the slope (elasticity) of the demand curve and the slope of the MC curve, which we have made horizontal so that profits can be easily computed. The reader might note that if the firm is up against a rigid constraint in raising output, then MC can be vertical, and a devaluation will leave output and sales unchanged, with domestic-currency prices rising by the full percentage of devaluation and U.K. inflation—just as in the case of perfect competition. It has been observed, for example, that auto exporters have raised their home-currency prices in proportion to any depreciation/devaluation; that is, they have left foreign prices unchanged. This has been attributed to their inability to raise output in the short run. Why lower your foreign-currency selling price if you cannot satisfy any extra demand that this might create? The slopes of the demand and cost curves are thus vital parameters for effective financial planning in an exporting firm. The demand sensitivity of the firm should be estimated, and the degree of capacity utilization should be measured to determine the response that the production side should make to real changes in exchange rates.

Analysis in Foreign Currency Units

So far we have measured all the vertical axes in our diagrams in units of the home or domestic currency, which we have taken as the U.S. dollar. By drawing our diagrams in terms of home currency units, we have been able to examine the effects of exchange-rate changes when these effects are measured in the same units. Our revenue, cost, and profit changes that result from devaluations or revaluations are therefore U.S.-dollar amounts; in general, they are the amounts that are relevant for U.S. firms. Some firms that are operating within a country, however, will be concerned with revenues, costs, and profits in some particular foreign currency unit. For example, a British firm with a manufacturing operation in the United States may not be happy if a devaluation/depreciation of the U.S. dollar raises its U.S. dollar earnings. Since the dollar is less valuable, the higher U.S.-dollar earnings might bring fewer pounds than before the devaluation, or so it might seem. Similarly, a U.S. firm with a subsidiary in, for example, Canada, may not be thrilled if a depreciation of the Canadian dollar raises the Canadian-dollar earnings of its subsidiary. These higher earnings might, it might seem, be worth less in U.S. dollars. However, as we shall show, these possibilities need not concern parent firms.

Interest in the effects of a devaluation or revaluation, when measured in foreign currency units, should not be limited to firms with subsidiaries abroad. Any firm that denominates borrowing in some foreign currency—even if it enjoys only one location—will care about the effect of exchange-rate changes on its operating revenues, measured in units of the currency of its debt. For example, a U.S. firm that has borrowed in British pounds will care very much about its trading revenues as measured in pounds after an exchange-rate change. This is because the firm has payables in British pounds. Canadian firms that borrow in New York in U.S. dollars care about their U.S.-dollar revenues, since they are required to service U.S.-dollar debts. Any non-U.S. firms issuing Eurodollar bonds or borrowing in Eurodollar market will care about U.S.-dollar-denominated revenue, no matter where they are located. For all these reasons, we should consider the effects of exchange-rate changes on revenues, costs, and profits when measured in units of foreign currency. We will limit our discussion to an imperfect market; the competitive case, with a flat demand curve and an upward-sloping MC, is extremely similar and is left as an exercise for the reader.

As we said, the price that is relevant to a buyer is the price he or she has to pay in terms of his or her own currency. When there is no inflation and the price of Aviva jeans in Britain remains unchanged in terms of British pounds but changes in terms of U.S. dollars, there is no reason for sales in Britain to

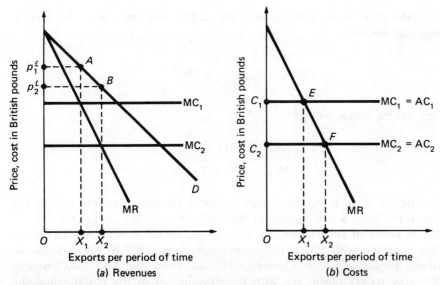

FIGURE 18.5
EXPORTER AND DEVALUATION IN AN IMPERFECTLY COMPETITIVE MARKET:
FOREIGN CURRENCY UNITS. The relevant price for demanders is the price
denominated in the buyers' currency. When we measure the vertical axis in the buyers'
currency, the demand and MR curves are unaffected by changes in exchange rates. If
production costs are unchanged in the producers' currency, a devaluation of that
currency will lower costs denominated in the buyers' currency. The export price will
decline in the buyers' currency after a devaluation.

change. It follows that when there is, for example, a devaluation of the U.S.
dollar, there is no reason for the demand curve for Aviva's jeans to shift if it is
drawn against the pound price. At the same pound price as before, the same
monthly volume of jeans will be sold. The demand curve in Figure 18.5, and
hence also the MR curve, is the same before and after the devaluation.[9]

The effect of changes in exchange rates on the cost curves is different from
the effect on the demand curve. When our diagrams are drawn in units of
foreign currency and there is an exchange-rate change, the cost curves will move
vertically in proportion to the exchange rate. Why is this so?

If it costs, say, MC_1 to produce an extra pair of Aviva's jeans and no inputs
are imported, then after a devaluation the production cost should still be MC_1
if the devaluation has not induced general inflation. However, before the
devaluation, with an exchange rate of $S(\$/\pounds)$, the cost in units of foreign
exchange was

$$MC_1^{\pounds} = \frac{1}{S(\$/\pounds)} \cdot MC_1^{\$}$$

[9]With inflation in Britain we could move the demand curve vertically upward by the U.K.
inflation rate. There is no need to do this to make our point.

After the devaluation to $S'(\$/£)$, with the dollar cost the same, the foreign exchange cost becomes

$$\text{MC}_2^£ = \frac{1}{S'(\$/£)} \cdot \text{MC}_1^\$$$

By simply taking ratios, we get

$$\frac{\text{MC}_2^£}{\text{MC}_1^£} = \frac{S(\$/£)}{S'(\$/£)}$$

That is, the MCs, in terms of British pounds, change in proportion to the exchange rate. Since a devaluation of the dollar means that $S'(\$/£) > S(\$/£)$, the MC, in terms of British pounds, falls as the dollar is devalued. In Figure 18.5, this is shown with MC moving downward from MC_1 to MC_2. Since we have drawn Figure 18.5 with a constant MC, we know that MC = AC, and so the AC curve moves downward with the devaluation of the dollar when the vertical axis is in British pounds.

With profit maximization requiring that MC = MR, we see from Figure 18.5 that a devaluation of the U.S. dollar should raise Aviva's jeans output from X_1 to X_2. With the demand curve remaining at D, the pound price will fall from $p_1^£$ to $p_2^£$. We see that even with the demand curve unshifted by a devaluation, the devaluation lowers the foreign exchange price of exports and raises the quantity sold.[10] With lower prices and higher sales, what has happened to revenues in terms of the British pound?

The answer clearly depends on whether sales have risen by a larger or smaller proportion than the reduction in price. If the increase in sales is greater than the price reduction, revenues will be higher. Such a situation requires that the elasticity of demand exceed unity, that is, it is elastic which we know to be the case by making a straightforward observation. Since MC is positive, and the firm produces where MR = MC, MR must also be positive. But with MR positive, an extra unit of sales, even though it requires a fall in price, must raise total revenue. We know, therefore, that pound revenues must rise, with area $Op_2^£BX_2$ necessarily greater than area $Op_1^£AX_1$.

Part b of Figure 18.5 gives the required curves for considering the effect of a devaluation on total costs. Since total costs are given by AC multiplied by the output, whether costs have increased depends on the slope of MR. Costs have changed from area OC_1EX_1 to area OC_2FX_2. Have costs increased, and if so, by how much? Well, continuing at this point without the help of mathematics is difficult. Mathematics helps us show that total costs, in terms of pounds, will increase after the dollar is devalued, but by a smaller amount than the increase

---

[10] By referring back to the equivalent home-currency diagram, Figure 18.4, the reader will see that while the pound price *falls*, devaluation *raises* the export price in terms of dollars (from $p_1^\$$ to $p_2^\$$). Figures 18.4 and 18.5 are, however, consistent.

in revenues. In terms of pounds, profits are therefore increased. This, along with the other results we have reached, is demonstrated in the appendix of this chapter.

THE IMPORTER

It would generally be presumed that importers will lose from a devaluation/depreciation and gain from revaluation/appreciation—the opposite of the effects for exporters. This presumption will normally be correct, with the exact magnitude of effect of exchange rates depending on such factors as the degree of competition and which currency we use for our analysis. The amount of change in cash flows is important information for the financial manager of an importing firm, whether the firm is importing finished goods for sale at home or some of the inputs used in producing its local output. If the goods are finished goods for sale, determining the effects of changes in real exchange rates requires that the financial manager know the elasticity of the market demand for the product. The financial manager must also decide on the relevant currency for measurement. We will begin by measuring in dollar amounts.

Analysis in Home Currency Units

Let us again consider Aviva Corporation and assume that it has decided to import finished jeans that are manufactured in Britain for sale in the United States. The most straightforward case is one in which Aviva can import whatever quantity of jeans it wishes at the same cost per pair. Being able to buy jeans at the constant cost $MC_1^\$$ means that we have the horizontal cost curve $MC_1 = AC_1$ shown in parts a and b of Figure 18.6. We can think of the constant cost per pair as being a constant cost that is faced whatever the exchange rate, $MC_1^\pounds$, translated at the predevaluation exchange rate.[11]

Assume that Aviva faces market demand conditions that are less than perfectly elastic in selling the imported British jeans in the U.S. market. This requires that there be not many other *sellers* of the same jeans. This could very easily be the case in practice if, for example, Aviva is licensed as the sole importer of these particular jeans in the United States.[12] This situation is very

---

[11] The cost curve for jeans will be flat if shipping and production costs in Britain are constant. The cost curve will also be flat if Aviva buys somebody else's jeans and it is one of the many buyers of these jeans. Every buyer, if sufficiently small, will be able to obtain whatever quantity it wants at the going price. This will mean that no buyer has any monopsony power. In fact, however, an assumption of constant costs is not necessary and only aids in computing total costs and profits.

[12] If the import were freely available to any importer or potential importer, any one firm would face a flat demand curve for the good at the going price. This perfect competition would put the demand curve at the level of the cost curve, and so no profit would be made above the normal return on the capital and enterprise involved.

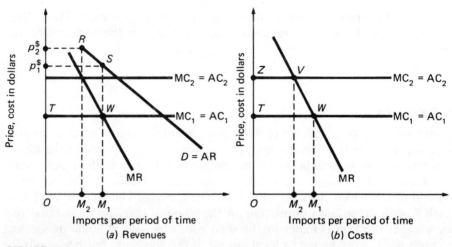

FIGURE 18.6
THE IMPORTER AND A DEVALUATION. If the importer's buying costs are unchanged from a devaluation in terms of the foreign supplier's currency, cost curves will move up by the percentage of devaluation when measured against the importer's currency. Demand curves will not be affected if they are drawn against the demander's currency. Only the amount demanded — a move along the curve — will be affected rather than the position of the curve. A devaluation will raise import prices and lower sales. The importer's profits will decline.

common. Many of the products produced in foreign countries are distributed and sold in each market by licensed firms.[13]

The demand curve is shown along with the associated MR and cost curves in Figure 18.6. Before the devaluation, Aviva Corporation will import and sell M_1 pairs of jeans per period, which is the profit-maximizing quantity where MR = MC_1. The jeans will be sold at the price $p_1^\$$ per pair, giving a total revenue in dollars of area $Op_1^\$SM_1$. The cost of the jeans, $MC_1 = AC_1$ per unit, gives a total cost of $OTWM_1$ dollars. The initial profit is the difference between total revenue and total cost, which is area $Tp_1^\$SW$ in Figure 18.6.

After a devaluation of the dollar to $S'(\$/£)$, there is no reason for the British-pound production cost to be affected. With the British-pound cost unchanged at $MC_1^£$ but the exchange rate now at $S'(\$/£)$, the new dollar cost must increase in proportion to the exchange value of the British pound against the dollar. The cost curves in parts a and b of Figure 18.6 shift vertically upward by the percentage of the dollar devaluation/depreciation.[14] The im-

[13] Our analysis is equally valid for a U.S.-based sales subsidiary of a foreign firm where we are specifically concerned with the profits of the subsidiary and not the foreign parent (for which the analysis of the exporter is applicable). Sales subsidiaries are common for automobiles, TVs, stereos, cameras, computers—and branded denim jeans.
[14] If we wish to allow for inflation in Britain, the vertical shift in MC can include this. We can keep the diagrams more straightforward by concentrating on the devaluation rather than inflation.

porter will reduce the amount imported and sold to M_2 per period, where $MR = MC_2$, and will sell this new amount, with the demand curve $D = AR$, at the price $p_2^\$$. We see that the effect of a dollar devaluation is to reduce imports and sales and raise prices.

The effect on revenues, costs, and profits of the importer is less obvious from Figure 18.6 than the effect on quantities and prices. Revenues have changed from $Op_1^\$SM_1$ dollars to $Op_2^\$RM_2$ dollars. However, we know from the straight-forward observation made for the exporter that as a result of a dollar devaluation, revenues have fallen for the importer. All profit-maximizing firms sell at a point where the demand curve for their product is elastic. This is because they choose to be where $MR = MC$, and since MC must be positive, MR is positive —that is, revenues are increased by additional sales, even though higher sales require lower prices. With the importer on an elastic part of his or her demand curve, the percentage reduction in the quantity sold must exceed the percentage increase in price—that is, revenues are reduced by a devaluation.

To determine the effect of a devaluation on profits, we must determine the effect on costs and compare this with the effect on revenues. This is not easily done with the diagrammatic analysis of Figure 18.6. However, as the mathematics in the appendix reveals, a devaluation also reduces the total costs of the imports; that is, area $OZVM_2$ is less than area $OTWM_1$. The appendix also reveals that provided we begin with positive profits, the reduction in costs is smaller than the reduction in revenues, and so the dollar profits of the importer fall from a devaluation/depreciation. The effects of a devaluation in terms of British pounds are more easily obtained from a digrammatic analysis than the effects in terms of dollars.

Analysis in Foreign Currency Units

The effects of a dollar devaluation in terms of British pounds are shown in Figure 18.7. With the cost of the jeans to Aviva Corporation at $MC^£$ and the demand curve at $D_1 = AR_1$, Aviva will import and sell M_1 pairs of jeans per period at the price $p_1^£$ per pair. The volume and the price were obtained by choosing the profit-maximizing position, where $MC^£ = MR_1$. We note, of course, that $p_1^£$ must equal $[1/S(\$/£)]p_1^\$$ and that $MC^£ = MC_1^\$/S(\$/£)$, where $p_1^\$$ and $MC_1^\$$ are the amounts in Figure 18.6.

Now, if the British-pound cost of the import does not change from a dollar devaluation, as previously argued, then $MC^£ = AC^£$ will remain in its original position. The quantity of items our importer can sell, however, will depend on the dollar price charged. At any level of sales—for example, M_1—the same quantity will be sold after the devaluation only if the dollar price remains unchanged. This must mean a lower British-pound price (lower by the percentage of the devaluation). In terms of British pounds, the demand curve of the American buyers of Aviva's imported jeans must shift vertically downward by the percentage of the dollar devaluation. This is shown as a move from

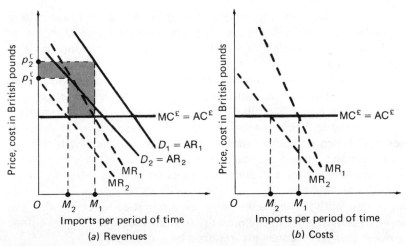

FIGURE 18.7
IMPORTER AND DEVALUATION IN FOREIGN CURRENCY UNITS. When inputs
are imported, a devaluation will raise production costs. Higher production costs
will lower the output of goods sold domestically and raise prices.

$D_1 = AR_1$ to $D_2 = AR_2$, with the associated MR curves moving from MR_1 to MR_2 in Figure 18.7.

Figure 18.7 tells us that a devaluation will reduce the profit-maximizing amount of imports from M_1 to M_2 (the same reduction as in Figure 18.6) and result in a lower British-pound price for the jeans (which, nevertheless, is a higher dollar price, as is seen in Figure 18.6). With both the quantity and price falling, the British-pound revenue must fall by the total shaded area in part a of Figure 18.7.

With the British-pound cost of the jeans unaffected by a devaluation/depreciation, but with a smaller amount imported, the total cost is reduced by the shaded area in part b of Figure 18.7. Profits will fall by the difference between the reduction in British-pound revenues and the reduction in British-pound costs. This fall in profits is shown by the heavily shaded area in part a of Figure 18.7. We conclude that an importer's pound profits are reduced from a devaluation/depreciation of the importer's currency. This should be no surprise because we saw previously that dollar profits are reduced, and with fewer pounds per dollar after the devaluation, pound profits must be reduced *a fortiori*.

Imported Inputs

Suppose that instead of importing finished jeans, Aviva is importing the denim cloth or perhaps cut denim that is ready for final manufacture in the United States. When a firm imports unfinished goods or other inputs for production, a

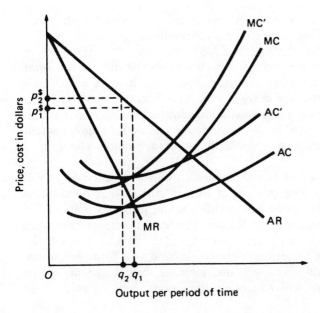

FIGURE 18.8
IMPORTER OF INPUTS AND DEVALUATION. When inputs are imported, a devaluation will raise production costs. Higher production costs will lower the output of goods sold domestically and raise prices.

devaluation of the domestic currency will raise production costs at each level of output.

When a firm is engaged in production, marginal costs and average costs will rise with output. The effect of a dollar devaluation will be to shift the rising cost curves upward, as shown in Figure 18.8. The amount by which costs increase depends on the importance of the inputs and on whether alternative sources of inputs are available and can be substituted. As Figure 18.8 shows, the effect of the dollar devaluation is to raise the product price and reduce the quantity manufactured and sold. In these circumstances the effect on profits becomes difficult to determine.

SUMMARY OF EFFECTS OF EXCHANGE RATES ON EXPORTERS AND IMPORTERS

Before we add the complications of forward hedging and the invoicing of exports or imports in different currencies, we shall find it useful to summarize what we have learned.

1 Even with no foreign assets or liabilities or foreign currency payables or receivables, changes in exchange rates will affect firms engaged in exporting or importing. This is called operating or residual risk and is very difficult to avoid.[15]

---

[15]It is difficult to hedge against residual or operating exposure because it depends on factors such as the elasticity of demand, the importance of imported inputs, and so on.

2 Devaluations raise export prices in home-currency terms and at the same time raise export sales. The reverse is true for revaluations.

3 Devaluations raise an exporter's profits. However, when the exporter is in a competitive environment, these increased profits may exist only in the short run. The gains are reduced by using imported inputs and may be in any case removed in the long run by the free entry of new firms into the industry. When the exporter is in an imperfectly competitive industry, the benefits of a devaluation can remain. However, even in the imperfectly competitive environment additional profits can be reduced by general inflation brought about by a devaluation.

4 Foreign-owned companies or companies with foreign-currency debts will care about receipts and payments in units of foreign currency. A devaluation will lower prices in foreign currency units (while raising prices in units of the devalued currency) and raise an exporter's sales. For firms in imperfect competition, revenues will increase because the percentage sales increase exceeds the price reduction. This follows because imperfectly competitive firms sell where demand is elastic. Production costs will also increase, but it can be shown mathematically that revenues will rise more than costs, and so profits will increase.

5 Import prices rise in units of the devalued currency and fall in units of foreign currency. The quantity of imports will fall from a devaluation. In an imperfectly competitive environment the importer's sales revenues will fall in terms of the devalued currency because price increases are smaller than quantity reductions. Costs will also fall, but not by as much as revenues. The profits of importers therefore decline from a devaluation. This is true whether we measure in terms of the local currency or in terms of foreign currency.

EFFECT OF CURRENCY OF INVOICING AND FORWARD HEDGING

In our discussion of operating exposure we have so far allowed the quantity sold and the price the exporter receives or the importer pays to vary immediately as the exchange rate changes. However, these variations in quantity and price do not always occur immediately. Often, quantities and prices are fixed for a period into the future in sales or purchase contracts. This temporarily postpones the effects of operating exposure, causes a translation/transaction exposure to be faced in addition to the operating exposure, and results in conclusions that are potentially different from those reached earlier. For example, exporters can lose from devaluations and importers can gain—the reverse of the normal effects.

The effect of changes in exchange rates depends on whether sales or inputs are covered by existing contracts and on which currency is used in the contracts. We will consider the following cases for exporters:

1 A fixed volume of exports has been promised for future delivery at prices fixed in dollars (or in pounds, which have been sold on the forward market), but inputs are subject to inflation or are at pound-contracted prices. This situation involves what is in effect a translation or transaction exposure on payables and the removal of this exposure on export revenues.

2 A fixed volume of exports has been promised for delivery at prices stated in pounds sterling, and the pounds have *not* been sold on the forward market. This situation involves a translation or transaction exposure on receivables.

We should note that what we shall be discussing involves the precontracting of prices and/or quantities. So far in this chapter we have taken price determination, production, and settlement as being contemporaneous. Clearly, there is then no transaction or translation exposure on receivables or payables, even though exchange rates do change profitability and therefore do leave some operating exposure. When we have the precontracting of prices and quantities, we have translation or transaction exposure and posponed operating exposure. Since this occurs frequently, we will sketch the potential consequences.

The Exporter with Exposed Inputs

Dollar Accounting   Assume that Aviva Corporation has fixed the dollar receipts from exports of a fixed number of pairs of jeans, either by selling the foreign exchange proceeds forward or by invoicing in dollars. With the dollar receipts per unit and the quantity supplied fixed, total revenues are fixed, and the gains/losses from operating exposure are temporarily eliminated.

While total dollar revenues will not change from a devaluation, costs could rise either via general inflation, induced by rising import prices, or because some inputs are imported at prices denominated in pounds which are not bought forward. Let us take input prices to be fixed in pounds, so that we have payables exposure on pounds and the situation shown in Figure 18.9.

The total revenue from sales is represented by area $Op_1^\$ SX_1$. However, costs could increase to $OHJX_1$. If Aviva's profits were minimal before the devaluation, the devaluation will result in losses equal to the area $p_1^\$ HJS$. We can see that a U.S. exporter might lose from a devaluation.[16] Of course, the loss is temporary and exists only while sales revenues are fixed and while more is paid for inputs.

If production costs as well as revenues from sales are fixed by buying forward foreign exchange for imported inputs and arranging a period of fixed dollar wages, then, of course, both costs and revenues will be unaffected by exchange rates while the various agreements are in effect. The exporting firm can therefore avoid temporary losses from a devaluation when foreign exchange is sold forward or invoicing is in dollars by trying also to fix dollar input costs, including wages, for the same period.

---

[16]Aviva would prefer to reduce output and sales to the level where MC_L cuts $p_1^\$$. Losses would be reduced a little if this were done, but with an agreement to deliver X_1, it might not be possible.

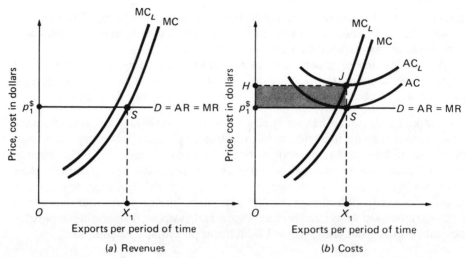

FIGURE 18.9
EXPORTER WITH PAYABLES EXPOSURE: DOLLAR ACCOUNTING. If a fixed number of goods are sold at a fixed dollar price, revenues will be unchanged after devaluations. We can think of economic exposure on revenues as being postponed. If a devaluation raises input costs, total costs will rise. This is because of transaction exposure if the prices of imported inputs are denominated in pounds. The higher input costs could reduce profits, and so exporters can lose from a devaluation.

We should note that the temporary decline in profits from a devaluation as a result of the precontracted importation of inputs is analogous to the temporary worsening of the balance of payments which in Chapter 5 was called the "J-curve effect." The balance of payments can temporarily worsen because the value of imports may increase in dollars, and this may offset extra revenues from exports. Our analysis in this chapter shows for an individual firm the J curve that is usually shown for the economy. The J curve for the firm or the economy is shown in Figure 18.10. The figure shows that if a devaluation takes place at time t_0, profits could temporarily fall or the balance of payments could temporarily worsen because of the payables denominated in foreign currency, but eventually the economic effects of the devaluation will begin to improve both profits and the balance of payments.

Pound Accounting   With the prices of jeans fixed in dollars from selling export proceeds forward or from dollar invoicing, these contracted dollars will represent fewer pounds. Production costs which are in dollars will also represent fewer pounds, but as long as some inputs are imported and become more expensive, revenues will fall more than costs. Thus profits will decline, or losses will increase. We find that exporters might lose not only in dollar terms but also in pound terms. This is no surprise, since lower profits in dollars are certainly

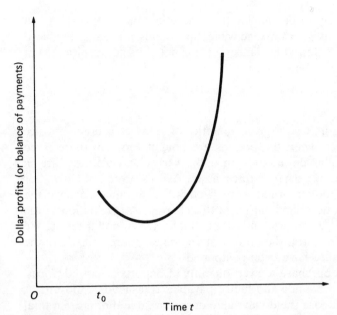

FIGURE 18.10
THE J CURVE. When the prices of imports are denominated in foreign currency, a devaluation can lower the profits of firms just as it can worsen the balance of payments of nations. The negative effects are temporary, and eventually the beneficial effects of a devaluation will begin to dominate.

lower profits in pounds after a dollar devaluation, because there are fewer pounds for each dollar.

The Exporter with Receivables Exposure

We have considered the case where the dollar receipts are fixed, either by selling foreign-currency-invoiced receivables forward or by invoicing in dollars. This eliminated operating exposure on revenues but left transaction exposure on payables. We can now consider what will happen when prices are precontracted in the foreign currency, but the foreign currency is not sold forward. This postpones the operating exposure and causes a transaction exposure on receivables.

It is relatively easy to compute the effect of Aviva's having precontracted to supply jeans to Britain at a fixed pound-per-pair price when the pounds have not been sold forward. A dollar devaluation would make these pounds more valuable by the percentage of devaluation—a gain on pound receivables—but postpone the effect of operating exposure. Production costs might also rise because of imported inputs or wage pressure from devaluation-induced inflation, but this effect is likely to be smaller than the effect on revenues, and so dollar profits will rise. This gain on receivables in pounds for jeans that have already been sold will be followed by gains on jeans not yet sold, resulting from the operating exposure described earlier.

The Importer

If Aviva has agreed to purchase a given quantity of jeans at a dollar invoice price, or at a pound price when the pounds are bought forward, there is no immediate effect of a dollar devaluation in dollar terms. Aviva's costs are in dollars and are unaffected by exchange rates, as are Aviva's revenues. Only after the period during which dollar prices were fixed will a devaluation have the operating-exposure effect described earlier in this chapter. A revaluation of the dollar will also leave costs, revenues, and profits unaffected in dollar terms. We have a case where there is no translation or transaction exposure and where the effects of operating exposure have been postponed.

If Aviva has agreed to purchase a given quantity of imports at pound prices, there is a fixed payable in pounds and hence payables transaction exposure. A dollar devaluation will increase the dollar value of this payable. For a given total revenue in dollars received on the contracted quantity, we have a reduction in dollar profits via losses on payables. The losses on payables will be followed by the importer's losses from operating exposure when prices are again raised.

A Reminder: Importance of Lags

If sales, delivery, and payment could all occur simultaneously, there would be no need to worry about the contract currency or the presence of forward agreements. There would be no receivables or payables in trade, and the only effects of changes in exchange rates would be those from the operating exposure described earlier in this chapter. The currency used for sales invoicing and forward market covering are important only when price agreements and payments are separated in time. This, however, frequently happens to be the case. We then have the combined effects of translation/transaction exposure and operating exposure.

An Example

Suppose that Aviva has contracted to sell 100 pairs of jeans per year to Britain at $24 per pair and to buy 200 yards of denim from Britain in this same period for £2 per yard. Suppose that 2 yards of denim is required per pair and that the labor cost for each pair is $8.

Suppose that at the time of contracting the exchange rate is $S(\$/£) = 1.5$ and that the dollar is then devalued to $S(\$/£) = 2.0$. Suppose also that the elasticity of demand for Aviva jeans in Britain is -2 and that after the contract expires Aviva raises the price of jeans to $25 per pair.

1 What are the gains/losses from the devaluation on the jeans sold and on the denim bought at the precontracted prices? (That is, what are the gains/losses from transaction exposure on payables and receivables?)

2 What are the gains/losses from the extra competitiveness of Aviva's jeans, that is, from operating exposure?

Assume that Aviva can buy all the denim it wishes at £2 per yard and that wages are not increased after the devaluation.

Effect of Transaction Exposure   Before the devaluation:

$$\text{Expected total revenue/year} = 100 \text{ pairs} \times \$24/\text{pair} = \$2400$$
$$\text{Expected total cost/year} = 100 \text{ pairs} \times 2 \text{ yd/pair} \times £2/\text{yd} \times \$1.5/£$$
$$+ \ 100 \text{ pairs} \times \$8/\text{pair}$$
$$= \$1400$$
$$\therefore \ \text{Expected profit} = \$2400 - \$1400 = \$1000/\text{year}$$

After the devaluation:

$$\text{Total revenue} = 100 \text{ pairs} \times \$24 \text{ pair} = \$2400$$
$$\text{Total cost} = 100 \text{ pairs} \times 2 \text{ yd/pair} \times £2/\text{yd} \times \$2/£$$
$$+ \ 100 \text{ pairs} \times \$8/\text{pair}$$
$$= \$1600$$
$$\therefore \ \text{Expected profit} = \$2400 - 1600 = \$800/\text{year}$$

We find that the exporter's profit on contracted quantities and prices of jeans supplied and denim purchased is *reduced* by $200 per year because of the transaction exposure.

Effect of Operating Exposure   Before the devaluation:

$$\text{Expected profit} = \$1000/\text{year} \quad \text{(as we just showed)}$$

After the contract expires: When the dollar price of jeans rises from $24 per pair to $25 per pair, the pound price falls from $24 ÷ $1.5/£ = £16 to $25 ÷ $2/£ = £12.5. This is a 21.875-percent price reduction. With a demand elasticity of −2, it will result in sales increasing by 43.75 percent to 143 pairs per year. It follows that after the contract expires

$$\text{Expected revenue} = 143 \text{ pairs} \times \$25/\text{pair} = \$3{,}575$$
$$\text{Expected cost} = 143 \text{ pairs} \times 2 \text{ yd/pair} \times £2/\text{yard} \times \$2.0/£$$
$$+ \ 143 \text{ pairs} \times \$8/\text{pair}$$
$$= \$2{,}288$$
$$\text{Expected profit} = \$3{,}575 - \$2{,}288 = \$1{,}287/\text{year}$$

We find that the exporter's profit is increased by $197 per year from the devaluation because of operating exposure.

In this specific example the firm is likely to feel happy about the devaluation because in the long run it will come out ahead. It should be clear, however, that temporary setbacks from transaction exposure on payables can be serious.

SUMMARY

1 An exporting firm in a competitive market will experience a temporary increase in sales revenues and production costs after a real devaluation/depreciation of its currency. Revenues will rise by more than the increase in costs, and so net profit flows will increase.

2 The higher temporary profit for a competitive firm will encourage new firms to get involved. This may limit the period of extra profit for any particular preexisting firm.

3 Higher input costs associated with a devaluation/depreciation can also limit profit improvements. Increases in input costs can result from the effect of a devaluation on wages via a general inflationary impact or from the need to import inputs.

4 The home-currency price of an exporter's product will rise by the percentage of the devaluation/depreciation and the foreign inflation rate when the product is sold in a competitive market.

5 An exporting firm in an imperfectly competitive market will experience an increase in revenues and costs after a devaluation/depreciation when amounts are measured in the firm's home currency. Revenues will rise by more than the increase in costs, and so profits will increase. The higher profits can persist if they are not offset by higher input costs. Revenues, costs, and profits that are measured in terms of foreign exchange will also increase from a devaluation.

6 The price of the goods sold by an exporter will, after a devaluation of the home currency, rise in terms of the home currency but fall in terms of the amount of foreign exchange. This happens because the home-currency price rises by a smaller percentage than the devaluation.

7 A devaluation raises the prices of imports in terms of the devalued currency and reduces the quantity that is imported and sold. Revenues and total costs in terms of dollars will fall, and so will the importer's profit. A revaluation lowers input prices and raises an importer's dollar revenues, total costs, and profits.

8 A devaluation lowers the prices of imports when these prices are measured in the foreign currency.

9 A dollar devaluation lowers an importer's revenue, costs, and profits in terms of the foreign currency. A revaluation will raise them.

10 When an arrangement exists to export to a foreign buyer a stated quantity at a price fixed in the home currency (or in foreign exchange that is sold forward), a devaluation can temporarily hurt the exporter through the route of fixed revenues with rising costs. This is true in both dollar and foreign currency units.

11 If prices in an export sales agreement are stated as foreign-currency amounts and these are not sold forward, a devaluation will raise the dollar revenues, costs, and profits of a U.S. exporter via both transaction and operating exposure.

12 An importer buying an agreed-upon quantity at an agreed-upon price in dollars (or with foreign exchange proceeds bought forward) will experience no change in dollar revenues, costs, or profits after a devaluation. An importer buying an agreed-upon

quantity at prices invoiced in foreign exchange will experience unchanged dollar revenues, increased dollar costs, and reduced profits.

QUESTIONS

1 Rank the following export industries according to the amount of increase in sales volume you would expect to result from a fall in the value of the U.S. dollar.
  a Wheat farming.
  b Automobile production.
  c Foreign travel to the United States.
  d Computer hardware.
  Use diagrams in your answers.
2 Rank the industries in question 1 according to the effects of a devaluation/depreciation on profits. You may assume that there are different amounts of imported inputs, different elasticities of demand, and so on.
3 Do you think that the United States is a sufficiently large importer of products in general so that the effect of a dollar depreciation would be eliminated by pressure on nominal wages from import price increases? How about Canada, Fiji, or Iceland?
4 Assume that the elasticity of demand for Aviva's jeans is -2.0. Assume that production costs are constant and that there is a 10-percent dollar depreciation.
  a By how much will the quantity sold increase?
  b By how much will dollar revenues increase?
  c By how much will foreign exchange revenues increase?
  d By how much will costs increase?
  e By how much will profits increase?
5 As in question 4, assume that Aviva's jeans face an elasticity of demand of -2.0 with constant costs, and assume also approximately half the total cost is accounted for by denim cloth, which is imported. To an approximation, what will this mean for your answers in question 4?
6 Redraw Figure 18.2 to show the *short-run effect* of a dollar *revaluation* on the profits of a U.S. exporter who sells in a competitive market.
7 Redraw Figure 18.2 to show the *long-run effects* of a dollar *revaluation* on the profits of a competitive U.S. exporter.
8 Redraw Figure 18.4 to show the effect of a *revaluation* of the dollar on a U.S. exporter in an imperfectly competitive market.
9 Redraw Figure 18.2 to show the effect of devaluation-induced cost increases when amounts are measured in foreign currency.
10 Why does a devaluation simultaneously raise export prices as measured in home currency and lower them as measured in foreign currency?
11 Redraw Figure 18.6 and Figure 18.7 to show the effect of a *revaluation* on revenues, costs, and profits.
12 Reconcile a rising domestic-currency price and a falling foreign-currency price for an imported good after a devaluation of the domestic currency. Why does this mean that the domestic-currency price rises by less than the percentage of devaluation/depreciation?
13 What would the availability of very close substitutes for an import mean for the elasticity of demand of the firm that exports our imports? Who will bear the burden of devaluation in this case?

14 Why does an exporter or importer face foreign exchange exposure and risk even if the firm has no foreign currency receivables or payables? Would it be difficult to hedge against this exposure and risk on the forward market?

15 Draw the revenue and cost diagrams for a British-owned firm which produces in and exports from the United States and cares about the British-pound amounts of sales, costs, and profits after a U.S.-dollar devaluation. Assume that the firm enters into a long-term sales agreement to provide X_1 per period at a fixed U.S. dollar price. [*Hint:* You need £ on the vertical axes and a horizontal AR line that will shift downward in terms of pounds after the devaluation. In the cost diagram, the MC and AC curves should be shifted downward.]

BIBLIOGRAPHY

Dufey, Gunter: "Corporate Finance and Exchange Rate Changes," *Financial Management*, summer 1977, pp. 23–33.

Flood, Eugene Jr.: "The Effect of Exchange Rate Changes on the Competitive Firm's Pricing and Output," unpublished, Massachusetts Institute of Technology, December 1981.

Hekman, Christine R.: "Measuring Foreign Exchange Exposure: A Practical Theory and its Applications," *Financial Analysts Journal*, September/October 1983, pp. 59–65.

Kalter, Elliot R.J.: "The Effect of Exchange Rate Changes upon International Price Discrimination," International Finance Discussion Paper 122, Board of Governors of the Federal Reserve, Washington, D.C.

Shapiro, Alan C.: "Exchange Rate Changes, Inflation and the Value of the Multinational Corporation," *Journal of Finance*, May 1975, pp. 485–502.

APPENDIX 18.1: Exchange Rates and the Exporter and Importer — A Mathematical Treatment

THE EXPORTER

Consider the situation of a U.S. firm that exports to the British market. We shall present the effects of a change in the value of the dollar, first in terms of dollar amounts and then in terms of British pounds.

Effects in Terms of Home Currency (Dollars)

The total dollar revenue, TR, of our U.S. firm from selling its entire output in Britain can be written as

$$TR = Sp^£q \tag{18A.1}$$

where S is the number of dollars per British pound, $p^£$ is the sales price in British pounds in Britain, and q is the number of units sold. The total cost of production for the quantity q, if each unit costs the same, can be written in U.S. dollars as

$$TC = cq \tag{18A.2}$$

where c is the cost per unit in home currency.

A profit-maximizing firm will always equate marginal revenue and marginal cost in determining the amount to sell or, equivalently, in determining what price to charge. That is, it sets

$$\frac{d\,TR}{dq} = \frac{d\,TC}{dq}$$

By taking Equation (18A.1) and Equation (18A.2) and differentiating, using the fact that $dS/dq = 0$, since changes in the production of our firm could have no effect on the exchange rate, we have

$$Sp^£ + Sq\frac{dp^£}{dq} = Sp^£\left(1 + \frac{q}{p^£}\frac{dp^£}{dq}\right) = c \tag{18A.3}$$

The definition of elasticity of demand is that it is the percentage change in quantity, dq/q, divided by the percentage change in the price the buyer pays, $dp^£/p^£$. Writing η for the absolute value of the elasticity (since the elasticity is otherwise negative) allows us to write Equation (18A.3) as

$$Sp^£\left(1 - \frac{1}{\eta}\right) = c \tag{18A.4}$$

so that

$$p^£ = \frac{c}{S(1 - 1/\eta)} \tag{18A.5}$$

Equation (18A.5) tells our U.S. firm how to set its price abroad in pounds according to the cost of production, the prevailing exchange rate, and the elasticity of demand. We recall that firms with some control over price will always sell at a point where $\eta > 1$, that is, where MR is positive. This follows because the firm produces and sells where MR = MC, and we know that extra units always have positive costs (that is, MC > 0), so MR must also be positive. The relationship (18A.5) consequently makes sense only when $\eta > 1$.

If we differentiate Equation (18A.5) with respect to S, since η and c are constants, we obtain

$$\frac{dp^£}{dS} = -\frac{c}{S^2(1 - 1/\eta)} = -\frac{p^£}{S} \tag{18A.6}$$

Since we know that $p^£$ and S are both positive, we know that $dp^£/dS < 0$. This negative derivative means that a devaluation of the dollar (an increase in S, the price of a British pound) will lower the profit-maximizing British pound price that a U.S. firm exporting to Britain should charge. This is seen in the text from Figure 18.5.

To determine what changes in the exchange rate do to U.S. dollar revenues, we can find $d\,\mathrm{TR}/dS$. We have

$$\frac{d\,\mathrm{TR}}{dS} = p^{\pounds}q + Sp^{\pounds}\frac{dq}{dp^{\pounds}}\frac{dp^{\pounds}}{dS} + Sq\frac{dp^{\pounds}}{dS} = p^{\pounds}q + Sq(1 - \eta)\frac{dp^{\pounds}}{dS} \qquad (18\mathrm{A}.7)$$

Now, Equation (18A.6) gives us $dp^{\pounds}/dS$, which when used in Equation (18A.7) gives

$$\frac{d\,\mathrm{TR}}{dS} = p^{\pounds}q - Sq(1 - \eta)\frac{p^{\pounds}}{S} = \eta p^{\pounds}q \qquad (18\mathrm{A}.8)$$

This expression tells us that $d\,\mathrm{TR}/dS > 0$, since every term is positive. This means that a devaluation of the dollar (an increase in S) will increase the U.S. dollar revenues of our firm from sales to Britain. In general, a devaluation/depreciation of a firm's own currency will raise the total revenue in domestic currency units from sales abroad. This is consistent with the finding in part *a* of Figure 18.1, part *a* in Figure 18.2, and part *a* of Figure 18.4 in the text.

To determine the effect of exchange rates on profits arising from trade, we must first examine the effect on costs, $d\mathrm{TC}/dS$. Since c is constant,

$$\frac{d\,\mathrm{TC}}{dS} = c\frac{dq}{cS} = c\frac{dq}{dp^{\pounds}}\frac{dp^{\pounds}}{dS} = -c\frac{dq}{dp^{\pounds}}\frac{p^{\pounds}}{S} \qquad (18\mathrm{A}.9)$$

In Equation (18A.9) we use $dp^{\pounds}/dS$ from Equation (18A.9). By introducing $\eta = -(dq/dp^{\pounds})p^{\pounds}/q$ we have

$$\frac{d\,\mathrm{TC}}{dS} = \frac{\eta cq}{S} \qquad (18\mathrm{A}.10)$$

Again, since the terms in Equation (18A.10) are all positive, $d\,\mathrm{TC}/dS > 0$, and we know that a devaluation of the dollar (an increase in S) will raise the dollar cost of production. This is consistent with the finding in part *b* of Figure 18.2 and part *b* of Figure 18.4 in the text.

We have learned that a devaluation/depreciation of the dollar will raise dollar revenues and dollar costs. The impact on profits will depend on which has risen more. Since dollar profits, ϕ, are given by

$$\phi = \mathrm{TR} - \mathrm{TC}$$

so that

$$\frac{d\phi}{dS} = \frac{d\,\mathrm{TR}}{dS} - \frac{d\,\mathrm{TC}}{dS}$$

we get

$$\frac{d\phi}{dS} = \eta p^{\pounds} q - \frac{cq\eta}{S} = \eta q\left(p^{\pounds} - \frac{c}{S}\right)$$

where the factor in parentheses is the "markup" per unit in pounds. Since this is positive if profits were originally made, a devaluation of the dollar unambiguously raises dollar profits.

Effects in Terms of Foreign Currency (British Pounds)

In terms of British pounds, we can write

$$\text{TR}^{\pounds} = p^{\pounds} q \quad \text{and} \quad \text{TC}^{\pounds} = cq/S$$

Equating MR and MC, that is, equating $d\,\text{TR}^{\pounds}/dq$ and $d\,\text{TC}^{\pounds}/dq$, again gives, as in Equation (18A.5),

$$p^{\pounds} = \frac{c}{S(1 - 1/\eta)}$$

and therefore, as in Equation (18A.6),

$$\frac{dp^{\pounds}}{dS} = -\frac{c}{S^2(1 - 1/\eta)} = -\frac{p^{\pounds}}{S}$$

Now,

$$\frac{d\,\text{TR}^{\pounds}}{dS} = p^{\pounds}\frac{dq}{dS} + q\frac{dp^{\pounds}}{dS} = q(1 - \eta)\frac{dp^{\pounds}}{dS}$$

and so using $dp^{\pounds}/dS$ from Equation (18A.6) allows us to write

$$\frac{d\,\text{TR}^{\pounds}}{dS} = \frac{cq\eta}{S^2} \tag{18A.11}$$

Since the terms in (18A.11) are positive, $d\,\text{TR}^{\pounds}/dS$ is unambiguously positive, so that a devaluation of the dollar will raise revenues in terms of British pounds. This is what we concluded in the text from Figure 18.5 and the added knowledge that demand must be elastic at chosen outputs of an imperfectly competitive firm. Also,

$$\frac{d\,\text{TC}^{\pounds}}{dS} = c\frac{d(q/S)}{dS} = \frac{c}{S}\frac{dq}{dS} - \frac{cq}{S^2}$$

But

$$\frac{dq}{dS} = \frac{dq}{dp^{\pounds}}\frac{dp^{\pounds}}{dS} = -\frac{dq}{dp^{\pounds}}\frac{p^{\pounds}}{S} = \frac{q\eta}{S}$$

Therefore,

$$\frac{d\,TC^£}{dS} = \frac{cq\eta}{S^2} - \frac{cq}{S^2} = \frac{c(\eta-1)q}{S^2} \qquad (18A.12)$$

Since (18A.12) is clearly positive, a devaluation of the dollar will raise production costs in terms of British pounds, even though this was not clear from part *b* of Figure 18.5 in the text. The effect on British-pound profits is given by

$$\frac{d\phi^£}{dS} = \frac{d\,TR^£}{dS} - \frac{d\,TC^£}{dS} = \frac{cq\eta}{S^2} - \frac{c(\eta-1)q}{S^2} = \frac{cq}{S^2} > 0$$

We discover that the British-pound value of profits for a U.S. firm selling in Britain will increase from a devaluation of the U.S. dollar.

THE IMPORTER

Effects in Terms of Home Currency (Dollars)

The total dollar revenue, TR, for a U.S. importer is

$$TR = p^\$ q \qquad (18A.13)$$

and the total cost, if each unit costs the same, is

$$TC = Sc^£ q \qquad (18A.14)$$

where $p^\$$ is the dollar sales price, q is the quantity imported and sold, $c^£$ is the fixed cost of the import in pounds, and S is the number of dollars per pound.

A profit-maximizing importer equates marginal revenue and marginal cost to determine the quantity to import and sell. By differentiating Equation (18A.13) and Equation (18A.14), we have

$$MR = \frac{d\,TR}{dq} = p^\$ + q\frac{dp^\$}{dq} = p^\$\left(1 - \frac{1}{\eta}\right)$$

where η is the absolute value of $(p^\$/q)\,dq/dp^\$$, and

$$MC = \frac{d\,TC}{dq} = Sc^£$$

Equating MR and MC gives

$$p^\$ = \frac{Sc^\$}{1 - 1/\eta} \qquad (18A.15)$$

and so, since $c^£$ is fixed,

$$\frac{dp^\$}{dS} = \frac{c^£}{1 - 1/\eta} = \frac{p^\$}{S} > 0 \qquad (18A.16)$$

That is, a dollar devaluation (an increase in S) will raise the dollar price of the good that is sold. We note that since firms always choose the elastic part of demand, our results make sense only when $\eta > 1$.

To determine the effect of exchange rates on U.S.-dollar revenues, we need $d\,\mathrm{TR}/dS$. We have

$$\frac{d\,\mathrm{TR}}{dS} = p^\$\frac{dq}{dS} + q\frac{dp^\$}{dS} = q(1 - \eta)\frac{dp^\$}{dS}$$

which, when we use Equation (18A.16), gives

$$\frac{d\,\mathrm{TR}}{dS} = \frac{p^£ q}{S}(1 - \eta) < 0 \qquad (18A.17)$$

since $\eta > 1$ for any profit-maximizing firm. We learn that a devaluation of the dollar (an increase in S) must reduce U.S.-dollar revenues, since the derivative is negative with $\eta > 1$. This is what we found in part a of Figure 18.6.

The effect of exchange rates on U.S.-dollar costs is given by $d\,\mathrm{TC}/dS$. Since $c^£$ is constant,

$$\frac{d\,\mathrm{TC}}{dS} = c^£ q + Sc^£\frac{dq}{dS} = c^£ q + Sc^£\frac{dq}{dp^\$}\frac{dp^\$}{dS}$$

which, when we use Equation (18A.16), gives

$$\frac{d\,\mathrm{TR}}{dS} = c^£ q - c^£ q\eta = c^£ q(1 - \eta) < 0 \qquad (18A.18)$$

since $\eta > 1$. We learn that a devaluation reduces dollar costs (expenditures on imports), which is what we claimed but were unable to demonstrate directly in part b of Figure 18.6.

With revenues and costs in dollar terms both falling for our importer from a devaluation, the effects on profits will depend upon which falls by a larger amount. We learn, from Equation (18A.17) and Equation (18A.18), that

$$\frac{d\phi}{dS} = \frac{d\,\mathrm{TR}}{dS} - \frac{d\,\mathrm{TC}}{dS} = q(1 - \eta)\left(\frac{p^\$}{S} - c^£\right)$$

If the imported good is sold at a profit, then $p^\$/S$, which is the selling price in the United States in pounds, must exceed $c^£$, the cost in pounds; that is, $(p^\$/S) - c^£ > 0$. Since $1 - \eta < 0$ (because $\eta > 1$ for a profit maximizer), we can conclude that $d\phi/dS < 0$, that is, that the dollar profits of an importer are reduced from a dollar devaluation or depreciation. This was claimed but not proved in the text. Similarly, dollar profits rise from a dollar revaluation or appreciation. Of course, it is important that there be an initial profit. If there are initial losses—that is, if $(p^\$/S) - c^£ < 0$—profits will increase from a depreciation and increase from an appreciation.

Effects in Terms of Foreign Currency (British Pounds)

In terms of British pounds, we can write $TR^£ = p^\$ q/S$, where as before $p^\$$ is the dollar price of the imported good, which is what is relevant to the buyer. We can also write $TC^£ = c^£ q$, where $c^£$ is the constant pound cost of the import. Equating MR and MC, that is, $d\,TR^£/dq$ and $d\,TC^£/dq$, again gives

$$p^\$ = \frac{Sc^£}{1 - 1/\eta} \tag{18A.19}$$

and therefore

$$\frac{dp^\$}{dS} = \frac{c^£}{1 - 1/\eta} = \frac{p^\$}{S} \tag{18A.20}$$

We know that

$$\frac{d\,TR^£}{dS} = \frac{d(p^\$ q)/dS - p^\$ q}{S^2} = \frac{p^\$ q(1 - \eta)}{S^2} - \frac{p^\$ q}{S^2}$$

when we use the result of Equation (18A.17). This gives

$$\frac{d\,TR^£}{dS} = -\frac{p^\$ q\eta}{S^2} < 0 \tag{18A.21}$$

We can see that a devaluation/depreciation of the dollar will unambiguously reduce British-pound revenues. This is inevitable, since dollar revenues are known to fall, as we have shown, and since there are also fewer pounds to the dollar after a devaluation. The effect of exchange rates on British-pound costs is

$$\frac{d\,TC^£}{dS} = c^£ \frac{dq}{dp^\$} \frac{dp^\$}{dS} = -\frac{c^£ q\eta}{S} < 0 \tag{18A.22}$$

where we use $dp^\$/dS$ from Equation (18A.20). We see that like the British-pound value of revenues, the British-pound value of the total costs of the imports must fall after a devaluation/depreciation.

The effect of exchange rates on profits is as follows:

$$\frac{d\phi}{dS} = \frac{d\,TR}{dS} - \frac{d\,TC}{dS} = -\frac{p^\$ q\eta}{S^2} + \frac{c^£ q\eta}{S} = \frac{q\eta}{S}\left(c^£ - \frac{p^\$}{S}\right)$$

That is, if the imported item is sold at a profit, so that, just as before, $(p^\$/S) - c^£ > 0$, we know that $d\phi/dS < 0$. In other words, an importer loses from a devaluation/depreciation. Since we have already learned that dollar profits are reduced by a devaluation, and since we know that there are fewer pounds per dollar after a devaluation, the lower pound profit from a devaluation should come as no surprise. Nor should the gains from a revaluation or appreciation.

THE INTERNATIONAL ECONOMIC ENVIRONMENT: A BACKGROUNDER TO THE INTERNATIONAL FINANCIAL SYSTEM, PAST AND PRESENT

This Addendum provides an overview of the international financial and economic environment for students who have not previously taken a course in international economics. There are six principal sections, covering:

1 Systems of fixed exchange rates.
2 The case for fixed versus flexible exchange rates.
3 Hybrid systems of exchange rates.
4 The history and possible future of the international financial system.
5 New theories of exchange rates.
6 Theories of exchange-rate volatility.

The Addendum can be read at any point in the course, but most naturally follows the determination of flexible exchange rates in Chapter 5.[1] The sequence of sections introduces the different types of exchange-rate systems and their implications before covering the historical experience with these systems. This order is designed to provide the reader with the necessary background to appreciate why some systems have failed. However, all topics are covered at a sufficiently nontechnical level to allow one to select a different sequence and/or to omit certain topics.

[1]The section on new theories of exchange rates does make reference to purchasing-power parity and interest parity, which are not covered until Chapters 6 and 7. However, both topics are explained briefly in the Addendum to ensure that it is self-contained.

SYSTEMS OF FIXED EXCHANGE RATES

When exchange rates are flexible, they are freely determined by the forces of supply and demand. When exchange rates are fixed, they are determined by governments or government-controlled authorities such as central banks. During the last century, several methods have been employed for fixing exchange rates, and these are described below. All these systems of fixed exchange rates involve mechanisms which automatically help correct deficits and surpluses in the balance of payments, a function performed by exchange rates themselves when they are flexible. One mechanism which has received particularly close attention is that involving prices. We shall explain the so-called **automatic price adjustment mechanism** as we explain the different systems of fixed exchange rates. This is done because the differences in price adjustment mechanisms help highlight the differences in the exchange-rate systems.

The Classical Gold-Standard System

Under a gold standard each country stands ready to convert its paper or **fiat money** into gold at a fixed price.[2] This fixing of the price of gold fixes exchange rates between paper monies. For example, if the U.S. Federal Reserve (the "Fed") agrees to buy and sell gold at $40 per ounce, and the Bank of England agrees to £20 per ounce, the exchange rate between the pound and dollar in the form of paper currency or commercial bank deposits will be $2/£. If the exchange rate is not $2/£, the foreign exchange market will not balance because it will be used for converting one currency into the other, but not vice versa. For example, if the exchange rate in the foreign exchange market is $1.60/£, the market will be used for converting dollars into pounds, but not for converting pounds into dollars. This is because it is cheaper for people buying dollars with pounds to buy gold from the Bank of England, ship the gold to the U.S., and sell it to the Federal Reserve for dollars. This roundabout method involves a cost of only £0.50/$ (assuming no cost of shipping gold) versus £0.63/$ = 1 ÷ ($1.60/£) on the foreign exchange market.[3] However, people buying pounds with dollars pay $1.60/£ on the foreign exchange market versus $2.0/£ via buying, shipping, and selling gold.[4] Since people are buying pounds with dollars but not dollars with pounds at an exchange rate of $1.60/£, there is a demand for pounds, but no supply of pounds. This excess demand for pounds will increase the exchange rate to $2/£. Similarly, if we begin with an exchange rate of $2.40/£, the foreign exchange market will be used by people buying dollars with pounds, but not by people buying pounds with dollars; the latter group will instead buy gold with dollars, ship the gold to Britain, and sell the gold for

[2] Fiat money is money whose face or stated value is greater than its intrinsic value. Its value comes from the edict or fiat that it must be accepted in discharge of financial obligations.

[3] Each dollar requires selling $\frac{1}{40}$ oz. of gold to the Federal Reserve, and to buy $\frac{1}{40}$ oz. of gold from the Bank of England costs £20 × $\frac{1}{40}$ = £0.50.

[4] Each pound requires selling $\frac{1}{20}$ oz. of gold to the Bank of England, and to buy $\frac{1}{20}$ oz. of gold from the Federal Reserve costs $40 × $\frac{1}{20}$ = $2.00.

pounds. With people selling pounds, and not buying pounds, the dollar value of the pound will fall until it reaches $2/£. That is, if the price of gold is $40/oz. in the U.S. and £20/oz. in Britain, the equilibrium exchange rate is $2/£.[5]

Price Adjustment under the Gold Standard

The price-level adjustment mechanism under the gold standard is known as the **price-specie adjustment mechanism**, where "specie" is just another word for precious metal. This mechanism was explained as early as 1752.[6] In order to explain the mechanism, let us continue to assume that gold is $40/oz. in the U.S. and £20/oz. in Britain and that at the resulting exchange rate of $2/£, Britain is buying more from the U.S. than the U.S. is buying from Britain. That is, let us assume that Britain has a balance-of-payments deficit with the U.S. The price-specie adjustment mechanism explains how the British deficit and the U.S. surplus are corrected in the following manner.

With Britain buying more from the U.S. than the U.S. is buying from Britain, there is an excess supply of pounds. With flexible exchange rates this will reduce the value of the pound below $2/£, but with a gold standard this will not happen because nobody will sell pounds in the foreign exchange market for less than $2. Rather, as soon as the pound dips even slightly below $2, people will sell pounds to the Bank of England in return for gold, ship the gold to the U.S., and sell the gold to the Federal Reserve for dollars. This gives people $2 for each pound. Therefore, the result of the British balance-of-payments deficit is the movement of gold from the Bank of England to the U.S. Federal Reserve.

The movement of gold from Britain, the deficit country, to the U.S., the surplus country, has effects on both countries' money supplies. This is because in standing ready to exchange gold for paper money at a fixed price, central banks have to make sure they have sufficient gold on hand for those occasions when many people wish to return paper money for gold. Prudent banking requires that a minimum ratio of gold reserves to paper money be held, and indeed, this used to be mandated in many countries, including the U.S., which required that the dollar be backed by at least 25 percent in gold reserves. The maintenance of a minimum reserve ratio means that as the Bank of England loses gold it is forced to reduce the amount of its paper money in circulation. At the same time, the increase in the Federal Reserve gold reserves allows it to put more paper money into circulation.

---

[5] We have based our argument on one-way arbitrage, that is, considering people who plan to exchange currencies and are looking for the cheaper of two methods: exchange via the foreign exchange market, or exchange via buying, shipping, and selling gold. An alternative way of reaching the same conclusion is with round-trip arbitrage, which involves showing that if the exchange rate in our example is not $2/£, people can profit by buying gold, shipping it to the other country, selling the gold for the foreign currency, and then selling the foreign currency for domestic money. When there are no transaction costs, one-way and round-trip arbitrage produce the same result. However, when it is costly to exchange currencies as well as ship, buy, and sell gold, round-trip arbitrage implies too large a possible range in the exchange rate.

[6] David Hume, "Of the Balance of Trade," in "Of Money," *Political Discourses*, 1752, reprinted in Richard Cooper, *International Finance*, Penguin, Baltimore, 1969.

In the minds of the eighteenth-century classical economists who described the working of the gold standard, the fall in the money supply in the deficit country would cause a general fall in prices. At the same time, the increase in the money supply in the surplus country (in the world we are describing, one country's deficit in the other country's surplus) would cause a general increase in prices.[7] With prices falling in the deficit country, Britain, and increasing in the surplus country, the U.S., there is a decline in British prices versus U.S. prices. This makes British exports more competitive in the U.S., helping them increase. At the same time, U.S. goods in Britain become less competitive than Britain's own **import substitutes**, so that British imports decline.[8] With British exports increasing and imports decreasing, Britain's deficit declines. Indeed, until the deficit has been completely eliminated there will be an excess supply of pounds, the sale of pounds to the Bank of England, the shipment of gold to the U.S., a decrease in the British money supply, an increase in the U.S. money supply, increasing competitiveness of British products at home and abroad, and a continued reduction in the British deficit.

The price-specie adjustment mechanism works not only via changes in relative prices *between* countries, but also via changes in relative prices *within* each country. In the deficit country, for example, the prices of nontraded goods will decline, but the prices of goods which enter international trade will remain unchanged. This is because prices of traded goods are determined by world supply and demand, not by the local money supply. The fall in the relative prices of nontraded goods in the deficit country will encourage local consumers to switch from traded goods to nontraded goods. At the same time, local producers will find it relatively more profitable to produce traded goods. The switch in consumer spending will free more exports, and the producers will produce more export items. These effects will be reinforced by developments in the surplus countries. The prices of nontraded goods there will rise in relation to the prices of traded goods, switching consumers toward traded goods and producers away from them. Altogether, we shall find more exports from deficit countries, fewer imports, and an improved balance of payments.[9]

Unfortunately for the effectiveness of the price-specie adjustment mechanism of the gold standard, governments were often tempted to abandon the required reserve ratio between gold and paper money when the maintenance of that ratio ran counter to other objectives. If a deficit is not allowed to reduce the money supply because, for example, the government thinks the reduction will raise

---

[7]The link between the money supply and prices the classical economists had in mind was the quantity theory of money. This theory predicts that prices increase and decrease in proportion to increases and decreases in the money supply.

[8]We show in Chapter 5 that even if Britain buys fewer imports from the U.S. because U.S. goods become more expensive, there can be an increase in the total *value* of imports. This will occur if the British demand for imports is inelastic.

[9]For an account of this and other fixed-exchange-rate adjustment systems, see Rudiger Dornbusch, *Open Economy Macroeconomics*, Basic Books, New York, 1980, or Leland Yeager, *International Money Relations: Theory, History, and Policy*, 2d ed., Harper & Row, New York, 1976, Chapter 5.

interest rates or unemployment to intolerable levels, the adjustment mechanism is lost. If, at the same time, the surplus countries with rising gold reserves do not print more paper money because of, for example, a fear of inflation, then both causes of a relative price-level adjustment are lost; we lose the lower prices in the deficit country and the higher prices elsewhere. The policy of not allowing a change in reserves to change the supply of money is known as **sterilization** or **neutralization policy**. As goals of full employment became common in the twentieth century, many countries abandoned their effort to maintain the required reserve ratio and focused on their local economic ills.

As a result of sterilization, the gold standard was not allowed to work. This is perhaps the most powerful criticism of the system. But that does not explain whether it *could have* worked. Some economists, most notably Robert Triffin, have said that it could not work.[10] Central to this view is the notion that prices are rigid downward (a feature of Keynesian economics) and that therefore deficits from gold outflows cannot be self-correcting, because prices cannot fall. Critics of the gold standard support this with evidence on the parallel movement of prices in surplus and deficit countries, rather than the reverse movement implied by the gold standard. It is true that without a decline in *absolute* prices, improving the balance of deficit countries is more difficult. However, it is *relative* prices which are relevant (including those of nontraded versus traded goods *within* the country), and these could decline if surplus countries' prices rose to a greater extent than those of deficit countries. If, therefore, prices are flexible upward and surplus countries' prices rise faster than those of deficit countries, we still have an automatic adjustment mechanism, although it is weaker than the mechanism that might have existed if absolute prices could fall. The other common criticism of the gold standard—that gold flows were frequently sterilized—is a valid criticism, but it is as much a criticism of the government for not allowing the gold standard to operate as it is of the gold standard itself.

A number of twentieth-century economists and politicians have favored a return to the gold standard. What appeals to the proponents of this system is the discipline that the gold standard placed on the expansion of the money supply and the check that this therefore placed on that creeping evil, inflation. The economists who prefer a return to the gold standard include Jacques Rueff and Michael Heilperin.[11] The politicians include the late French President Charles de Gaulle and New York Congressman Jack Kemp. A return to the gold standard, or some standard based on gold, would make exchange-rate forecasting a relatively straightforward task. The exchange rate in normal times would vary within limits known as **gold points**, which are set by the buying or

---

[10] Robert Triffin, "The Myth and Realities of the So-called Gold Standard," in *The Evolution of the International Monetary System: Historical Reappraisal and Future Perspective*, Princeton University Press, Princeton, N.J., 1964; reprinted in Richard Cooper, *International Finance*, Penguin, Baltimore, 1969.

[11] See Jacques Rueff, "Gold Exchange Standard: A Danger to the West," *The Times* (London), June 27–29, 1961, reprinted in Herbert G. Grubel (ed.), *International Monetary Reform: Plans and Issues*, Stanford University Press, Palo Alto, Calif., 1963, and Michael Heilperin, "The Case for Going Back to Gold," *Fortune*, September 1962, also reprinted in Grubel.

selling prices of gold at the central banks and by the cost of shipping it from country to country. Larger changes in exchange rates would occur when countries changed the price of their currency in terms of gold, and this would be a reasonably predictable event. Countries that were running out of reserves would raise the price of gold, while countries which were gaining reserves might lower it.

The Gold-Exchange and Dollar Standards

With a gold standard, exchange rates, or at least their ranges of potential variation, are determined indirectly via the conversion price of each currency vis-à-vis gold. When the gold standard came to an end with the depression of 1929–1933, the exchange-rate system which eventually replaced it in 1944 (after war and general disarray) offered direct determination of exchange rates. The system adopted in 1944 is called the **gold-exchange standard**.[12] This direct method of determining exchange rates allowed movement in exchange rates between **support points**. Support points were the exchange rates at which foreign central banks purchased or sold their currency for U.S. dollars to ensure that the exchange rate did not move beyond these points. In return for foreign central banks fixing, or **pegging**, their currencies to the U.S. dollar, the United States fixed the price of the dollar to gold, and so the gold-exchange standard involved:

1 The United States offering to exchange U.S. dollars for gold at an official rate, which for a long time was $35 per ounce.

2 Other countries offering to exchange their currencies for dollars around an official, or **parity**, exchange rate.

We will deal later with the history of the international financial system, but we can note that the ability to convert foreign *privately* held gold to dollars by the United States lasted until 1968, and the ability to convert foreign *officially* held gold lasted until 1971. With only the second part of the gold-exchange standard remaining in effect—that part involving the exchange of foreign currencies for dollars—the fixed exchange system from 1968 until the end of the Bretton Woods system in 1973 is best described as a **dollar standard**.

Under the gold-exchange standard and the dollar standard, countries which pegged their exchange rates to the U.S. dollar were required to keep the actual rate within 1 percent of the selected parity value. In order to ensure that the exchange vis-à-vis the dollar remained within the required 1 percent of official parity, it was necessary for central banks to intervene whenever free-market forces would have created an exchange rate that was outside the range. This intervention took the form of buying and selling the local currency for U.S. dollars at the upper and lower support points around official parity. The support

---

[12]The exchange-rate system adopted in 1944 is also called the **Bretton Woods system** after the town in New Hampshire at which its outlines were worked out.

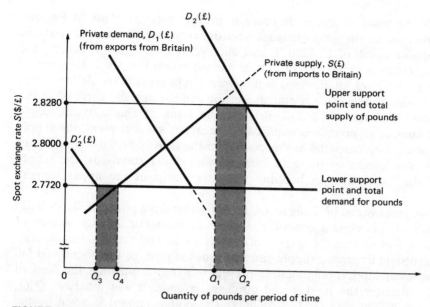

FIGURE A.1
THE WORKINGS OF THE GOLD-EXCHANGE AND DOLLAR STANDARDS. The
Bank of England stood ready to buy pounds at the lower support point and sell
pounds at the upper support point. This made the demand for pounds perfectly
elastic at the lower support point and the supply perfectly elastic at the upper
support point, ensuring exchange rates fell in the allowable range.

points meant adding to or reducing central-bank official reserves whenever the
uncontrolled exchange rate would have moved beyond the official limits. We can
illustrate the way these fixed exchange standards operated by using a diagram.

Suppose that the Bank of England has decided, as it did from 1949 to 1967,
that it wishes to peg the value of the pound sterling at a central value of \$2.80.
The upper and lower support points that the bank must maintain are \$2.8280/£
and \$2.7720/£. These are shown on the vertical axis of Figure A.1, which gives
the spot price of pounds in terms of dollars. The horizontal axis gives the
quantity of pounds, and so the diagram has the price and quantity axes familiar
from the theory of supply and demand. We have added to the diagram
conventionally sloping supply and demand curves for pounds drawn against the
price of pounds (measured in dollars). We have drawn the initial demand for
pounds, $D_1(£)$, intersecting the supply curve of pounds, $S(£)$, within the 1-per-
cent range allowed under the gold-exchange and dollar standards.

Suppose that for some exogenous reason there is an increase in demand for
British exports. This might, for example, be because of a general economic
expansion outside of Britain or a change in taste toward British goods. This will
shift the demand curve for pounds to the right, from $D_1(£)$ to $D_2(£)$, and the
demand for pounds will then intersect the private supply curve at an exchange

rate above the allowed ceiling. In order to prevent this, the Bank of England must, according to the gold-exchange and dollar standards, intervene at the upper support point of \$2.8280/£ and supply, in exchange for dollars, the pounds necessary to keep the rate from moving above this level. In terms of Figure A.1, the Bank of England will supply Q_1Q_2 pounds for dollars. This, with the private supply of OQ_1 pounds sterling and the demand curve of $D_2(£)$, would leave the rate at \$2.8280. Because the Bank of England will supply whatever number of pounds is required at the upper support point, the supply curve of pounds becomes flat at this point, like the heavily drawn line in Figure A.1. This is a feature of the gold-exchange and dollar standards; the supply curve of the local currency becomes perfectly elastic at the upper support point.[13]

Suppose that instead of rising to $D_2(£)$, the demand for pounds falls to $D_2'(£)$ as a result of, perhaps, a general slowdown in economic activity outside of Britain or a feeling that the quality of British goods and services has deteriorated. According to private supply and demand, the price of the pound will fall below the lower support point, and to prevent this from happening, the Bank of England will enter the market and purchase pounds. It will purchase Q_3Q_4 pounds with $2.7720 \times Q_3Q_4$ U.S. dollars. The dollar amount is given by the shaded area above Q_3Q_4; it represents the decline in dollar reserves of the Bank of England. It is hence the deficit in the balance of payments, measured in U.S. dollars. Because the Bank of England must demand whatever number of pounds is not wanted by private buyers, the demand for pounds that includes both private and official demand has a flat section at the lower support point. The total demand is the heavily drawn line in Figure A.1. This is another feature of the gold-exchange and dollar standards: the demand for local currencies becomes perfectly elastic at the lower support point.

Price Adjustment under the Gold-Exchange and Dollar Standards

In order to understand the price-level adjustment mechanism of the gold-exchange and dollar standards, we refer to Figure A.2. Suppose that after starting with $S_1(£)$ and $D_1(£)$ and a privately determined exchange rate within the allowed range, there is an increase in private demand for pounds to $D_2(£)$. As before, the Bank of England will be required to supply Q_1Q_2 pounds. These pounds will increase the money supply in Britain; they will enter the system as the Bank of England sells pounds for dollars. If we again assume that prices vary with the money supply, the increase in the number of pounds in circulation will raise British prices. At each exchange rate on our vertical axis, this will

---

[13] While in Figure A.1, the Bank of England supplies Q_1Q_2 pounds, it will be buying Q_1Q_2 times 2.8280 in dollars, which is the shaded area above Q_1Q_2 in the figure. The amount Q_1Q_2 is the gain in the Bank of England's foreign exchange reserves (its balance-of-payments surplus) valued in terms of pounds, and the area above Q_1Q_2 is the official British balance-of-payments surplus, valued in terms of dollars.

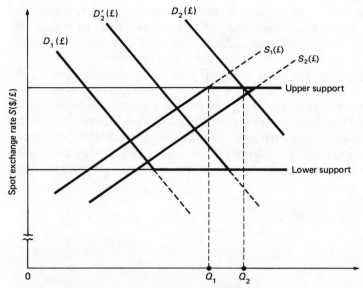

FIGURE A.2
THE PRICE-LEVEL ADJUSTMENT MECHANISM OF THE
GOLD-EXCHANGE AND DOLLAR STANDARDS. If the demand for
pounds moves to $D_2(£)$ and exceeds the supply at the upper support
point, the Bank of England must sell pounds in exchange for dollars.
Ceteris paribus, this increases the British money supply and prices.
Higher prices make British exports decline, shifting the demand for
pounds back toward $D_2'(£)$. Higher prices also increase imports into
Britain, and the currency supply curve shifts from $S_1(£)$ toward $S_2(£)$.
Shifts in currency demand and supply move exchange rates toward
their allowable limits.

lower the competitiveness of British goods. Exports will fall, and imports will
increase.

The decline in British exports will mean a lower demand for pounds, and the
demand curve will move back. We can assume that it will move to $D_2'(£)$. The
increase in British imports will mean a larger supply of pounds to the foreign
exchange market, and the private supply curve will move to the right. We can
move it to $S_2(£)$. With the demand and supply at $D_2'(£)$ and $S_2(£)$, the
free-market rate of exchange will return to the allowed range. We find that
intervention by a central bank affects the supply of money, local prices, and
exports and imports and thus restores free-market equilibrium. For example, a
balance-of-payments surplus raises the supply of money and hence prices; as a
result of this, exports are reduced, imports are increased, and the surplus is
thereby eliminated. Of course, if there is sterilization of the balance-of-payments surplus and the money supply is not allowed to increase, the price-level
adjustment mechanism will not work. Sterilization will eventually result in a
continued growth in foreign exchange reserves and a need to revise the parity

exchange rate. This makes exchange-rate forecasting a potentially highly rewarding activity for the financial executive, since the bank's need to change the parity value becomes clearly apparent in the foreign exchange reserve statistics. It is quite worthwhile to consider how forecasting can be done.

We have already noted that when exchange rates are determined on a gold standard, changes in exchange rates will follow large changes in gold reserves. For example, countries which are losing reserves will eventually be forced to raise the price of gold in terms of their own currency. This means a fall in the foreign exchange value of the currency. To take an example, if Britain were losing gold and raised its gold price from £20 per ounce to £25 per ounce while the U.S. price remained fixed at $40 per ounce, the exchange rate would change from

$$S(\$/£) = \frac{\$40/\text{ounce}}{£20/\text{ounce}} = \$2/£$$

to

$$S(\$/£) = \frac{\$40/\text{ounce}}{£25/\text{ounce}} = \$1.60/£$$

This is a devaluation of the pound. By keeping track of gold reserves, a financial executive could see that the central bank might be forced to raise the price of gold, that is, to devalue. The exact date would be difficult to predict, but actions based on such an assumption are unlikely to result in losses. A country that is losing reserves might manage not to devalue, but it certainly would not revalue, that is, raise the value of its currency by reducing the price of gold set by the central bank. This means that the financial manager would discover either that she or he was correct and a devaluation did occur or that the exchange rate remained as before. Thus there is an opportunity for a one-way bet, and the worst that is likely to happen is that no speculative gain will be made.

The "par" or middle exchange rate in a gold-exchange or dollar standard will respond to changes in reserve positions in a way that is similar to the response in a gold standard. The reserves held to defend the currency in a gold-exchange or dollar standard are made up of U.S. dollars, assets readily convertible to dollars, and gold. When these reserves are getting low, chances are that a devaluation, that is, a reduction in par value, will eventually take place. Indeed, speculation that a devaluation will occur is likely to make it occur. For example, prior to the 1980 devaluation of the Mexican peso, speculators had decided that a peso devaluation was imminent. They therefore sold pesos, and the Mexican authorities were required to purchase them at the lower support point. The pesos were purchased with U.S. dollars and hence the Mexican reserves were lowered. Eventually, reserves were so much reduced that the Mexicans were forced to devalue. The speculators' beliefs were vindicated. In a sense, their expectations were self-fulfilling.

The need to reduce the value of a currency in a country experiencing deficits and declining reserves depends on the ability of the central bank to borrow additional reserves. There are arrangements between central banks for exchanging currency reserves, and there are many lines for borrowing from international institutions such as the International Monetary Fund (which we will discuss later). The borrowing arrangements include **central-bank swaps**. Central-bank swaps involve, for example, the U.S. government making U.S. dollars available to the Bank of Canada when Canadian foreign exchange reserves are low. The Bank of Canada will temporarily swap these U.S. dollars for Canadian dollars. The swap will be reversed later, according to the original agreement. Often the swap will be reversed only after a number of years to allow the borrowing country to correct its balance of payments. Central banks also frequently borrow from private banks. The Bank of Canada, for example, borrowed heavily from both Canadian and U.S. commercial banks during the early and mid 1980s despite the fact that the exchange rate was supposed to be flexible. The ability of central banks to borrow from other central banks and from private banks and international institutions makes the forecasting of exchange rates more difficult. Revisions of par values can be delayed many years by countries with good credit ratings.

Another factor making exchange-rate forecasting under fixed rates difficult is the difference in the need to react to surpluses and deficits. Countries that are facing a deficit and losing reserves will eventually be forced into a devaluation because their reserves and ability to borrow will eventually be gone. On the other hand, the countries enjoying surpluses will be under no pressure to revalue their currencies and may instead allow reserves to keep growing. This represents one of the major problems with the gold-exchange and dollar standards, namely that the responsibility for adjustment, whether this be via a change in the exchange rate or via an automatic change in money supplies and prices, falls on deficit countries more heavily than on surplus countries. This problem of asymmetric need for adjustment between deficit and surplus countries under the gold-exchange and dollar standards is one of the major differences between these fixed-exchange-rate systems and the European Monetary System.

The European Monetary System (EMS)

At virtually the same time as the dollar standard collapsed, a new fixed-exchange rate system emerged among the European Economic Community (EEC) countries. This new system began in 1972 as the **snake**, which was designed to keep the EEC countries' exchange rates within a narrower band than had been adopted as part of a last-minute attempt to salvage the dollar standard.[14] The snake involved exchange rates being maintained within $1\frac{1}{8}$

---

[14]The wider band was part of the Smithsonian Agreement which was reached at the Smithsonian Institution in December 1971. We have more to say about the Smithsonian Agreement and wider bands later in this Addendum.

percent of selected par values, compared to $2\frac{1}{4}$-percent deviations allowed as part of the revision to the dollar standard in 1971. The snake was so called after the shape of the time path of EEC exchange rates moving within the wider band allowed for other exchange rates. The snake, with some refinements, because the **European Monetary system** (EMS) in 1979.

A central feature of the EMS is a **parity grid** that places an upper and lower limit on the possible exchange rates between each pair of member countries.[15] That is, there is a matrix showing for each pair of currencies the highest and lowest permitted exchange rate. These limits are $2\frac{1}{4}$ percent above and below the central or par rates.[16] If an exchange rate is at either limit, *both* countries are required to intervene. For example, if the Belgian franc is at its lower support point vis-à-vis the German mark, the Belgian authorities are required to buy Belgian francs *and* the German authorities are required to sell marks. The requirement that the Germans sell marks is unconditional, making the EMS fundamentally different from the gold-exchange and dollar standards. As we have seen, under the gold-exchange and dollar standards, if, for example, the pound was at its lower support point, Britain was required to buy pounds, but the U.S. was not required to cooperate by selling dollars. Under the EMS, Germany must sell marks if the mark is at its upper limit against the Belgian franc, whether or not Germany likes the implications of the increasing money supply the sale of marks brings about.

Partly because of the no-fault nature of the EMS, a **divergence indicator** was designed to identify if, for example, the Belgian franc was at its lower support point vis-à-vis the mark because of overly expansive Belgian monetary policy or overly restrictive German monetary policy. The divergence indicator is based on the value of the **European Currency Unit** (ECU).[17]

The ECU is an artificial unit defined as a weighted average of each of the EMS currencies plus the British pound and Greek drachma. Each EMS country is required to maintain its exchange rate within a specified range of the ECU, as well as within a specific range vis-à-vis the other individual EMS currencies. This serves to indicate which country is at fault when a currency approaches a limit vis-à-vis another currency, because the country at fault will also be close to its limit vis-à-vis the ECU. For example, if it is inflationary Belgian policy that is forcing the Belgian franc down vis-à-vis the German mark, the franc is also likely to be low against other currencies, and hence against the ECU. The country that is at fault is required to take corrective action or explain to other

---

[15]At the end of 1989, the member countries were Belgium, Denmark, France, Ireland, Italy, Luxembourg, the Netherlands, Spain, and West Germany. The remaining three EEC members are to join the EMS in 1990.

[16]That is, the matrix has eight currencies listed across the columns and down the rows, and has three exchange rates in each element: an upper limit, a par value, and a lower limit. Of course, the diagonal of the matrix is simply a line of 1's.

[17]The acronym of the European Currency Unit, *écu*, is the name of a silver coin that once circulated in France.

EMS members why it should not. Only as a last resort are par values realigned, although this has happened on several occasions.

The ECU serves additional role in denominating loans among the EMS countries. For example, if Belgium borrows from Holland to defend its exchange rate vis-à-vis the Dutch guilder or against the ECU, the loan can be denominated in ECUs. This reduces foreign exchange risk to the borrower and lender because the value of the ECU is likely to be more stable than the value of individual currencies.[18] The ECU is also used to denominate loans made by the **European Monetary Co-operation Fund**, or EMCF. The EMCF can make short-term and medium-term readjustment loans to EMS members out of a pool of funds it holds at the **Bank of International Settlements** located in Basle, Switzerland.

Price Adjustment under the EMS

Our explanation of the price-level adjustment mechanism of the gold-exchange and dollar standards applies also to the EMS, with the one major difference that with the EMS, both countries' money supplies are influenced by official intervention. For example, if the Belgian franc is at its lower support point versus the mark, the Belgian money supply declines and the German money supply increases. *Ceteris paribus*, this should reduce the Belgian price level and increase the German price level. This should improve Belgium's trade in comparison with Germany's because of the lowering of Belgian versus German prices. Because prices in both countries are contributing to the automatic adjustment, rather than one country as with the gold-exchange and dollar standards, the EMS mechanism is more effective. Furthermore, the requirement that both countries intervene helps overcome the problem of asymmetric needs for adjustment, a problem that detrimentally affected the functioning of the gold-exchange and dollar standards.

The EMS does allow for realignment of central values of the parity grid, and indeed there have been several realignments. Forecasting when this will occur is made difficult by the cooperation built into the EMS in terms of joint foreign exchange market intervention, intercountry short-term lending, and loans from the EMCF. Nevertheless, as with the gold-exchange and dollar standards, it does become evident when a currency needs to be realigned, not least because of the currency's value vis-à-vis the ECU. This means that speculators can sometimes guess which way the realignment will go. However, because it is fairly easy for a country to postpone realignment by borrowing from other members of the EMS, the timing of realignments is difficult to forecast. Adding to the difficulty of forecasting is the fact that other corrective measures are often taken, such as reversal of the policy that caused the movement of the exchange rate, meaning that expected realignments do not always take place.

[18]The ECU is like a portfolio of currencies. As such, it offers some diversification benefits.

Other Automatic Adjustment Mechanisms

National Income   The price-level adjustment mechanism requires flexibility of prices in order to operate. The macroeconomic revolution marked by the publication of *The General Theory of Employment, Interest and Money* by John Maynard Keynes, while focusing on a closed economy, spilled over into international finance and introduced an alternative adjustment mechanism that works if price flexibility does not exist.[19] This mechanism, popularized by the followers of Keynes, involves automatic adjustment via changes in national income. Like the price-level adjustment mechanism, the income adjustment system operates on the current account. The most straightforward way of describing Keynesian adjustment is to employ a Keynesian income-expenditure model and show how variations in national income work to correct balance-of-payments surpluses and deficits.

A straightforward model which will reveal the important features of income adjustment consists of the following equations:

$$Y \equiv C + I_0 + (\text{Ex}_0 - \text{Im}) \tag{A.1}$$

$$C = C_0 + cY \tag{A.2}$$

$$\text{Im} = \text{Im}_0 + mY \tag{A.3}$$

In these equations, Y is the national income or GNP, C is aggregate consumption of goods and services, I_0 is the given amount of aggregate investment or capital formation, Ex_0 is the given amount of exports, and Im is imports.

The national-income accounting identity is given by Equation (A.1), where, because it is not relevant for our purposes, we have omitted government spending. Y is the total value of *domestically produced* goods and services. Because it is difficult for government statisticians to separate consumption and investment of domestic goods from consumption and investment of imported goods, especially when domestic goods have imported components, C and I refer to the *total* consumption and investment of goods and services. In addition, exports, Ex_0, include re-exports, that is, items from abroad that are resold after reprocessing or used as inputs in exported products. Because Y refers to domestic production only, as the relevant output/income of a nation, and because C, I_0, and Ex_0 include imports, we must subtract imports, Im, to ensure the identity of (A.1). This is the most convenient approach from the viewpoint of a national-income statistician, because records of imports exist with customs agents, and records of consumption and investment reveal total amounts and do not show imported components separated from domestic components.

Equation (A.2) is the **consumption function**. The intercept, C_0, is the part that does not depend on income. The effect of national income on consumption

---

[19]John Maynard Keynes, *The General Theory of Employment, Interest and Money*, Macmillan, London, 1936.

is given by the **marginal propensity to consume**, c, which will be between zero and unity. Since C represents all consumption, it includes imports (Im), where the import equation itself is Equation (A.3). We assume that investment and exports are exogenous, or at least exogenous in relation to national income in the economy we are examining.

In order to discover how automatic adjustment via national income works, we can begin with an intuitive explanation. Suppose the balance of payments is initially in balance and that there is an exogenous increase in exports, Ex. This means an increase in national income via Equation (A.1), which itself indirectly further increases income via the extra induced consumption in Equation (A.2). The higher national income will increase imports via Equation (A.3). We find that the initial increase in exports that moved the balance of payments into surplus will induce an increase in imports, which will tend to offset the effect of exports. This is an automatic adjustment working via income. It is not apparent from our intuitive explanation that this adjustment, while tending to restore balance, will not be complete. In order to see this, we can employ our model.

If we substitute Equations (A.2) and (A.3) into the national-income accounting identity, Equation (A.1), we obtain

$$Y = C_0 + cY + I_0 + \text{Ex}_0 - \text{Im}_0 - mY \qquad \text{(A.4)}$$

By gathering terms, we can write Y as a function of exogenous terms:

$$Y = \frac{1}{1 - c + m}(C_0 + I_0 + \text{Ex}_0 - \text{Im}_0) \qquad \text{(A.5)}$$

The factor $1/(1 - c + m)$ is the **multiplier**. We can note that the larger the **marginal propensity to import**, m, the smaller will be the multiplier. The multiplier depends on the leakages from the circular flow of income, and by having imports, we add a leakage abroad, m, to the leakage into savings given by the marginal propensity to save, $1 - c$. The more leakages we have, the smaller the increase in income from any exogenous shock.

Let us allow exports to increase exogenously from Ex_0 to $\text{Ex}_0 + \Delta \text{Ex}$ and the corresponding increase in GNP to be from Y to $Y + \Delta Y$. We can therefore write

$$Y + \Delta Y = \frac{1}{1 - c + m}(C_0 + I_0 + \text{Ex}_0 + \Delta \text{Ex} - \text{Im}_0) \qquad \text{(A.6)}$$

Subtracting each side of Equation (A.5) from Equation (A.6), we have

$$\Delta Y = \frac{1}{1 - c + m} \Delta \text{Ex} \qquad \text{(A.7)}$$

The value of ΔY in Equation (A.7) gives the effect on national income of an exogenous change in exports. To find the induced effect on imports of this change in national income, we can use ΔY from Equation (A.7) in the import equation (A.3). Putting Equation (A.3) in terms of the new level of imports, $Im + \Delta Im$, after an increase in income to $Y + \Delta Y$, we have

$$Im + \Delta Im = Im_0 + m \cdot (Y + \Delta Y) \qquad (A.8)$$

Subtracting Equation (A.3) from Equation (A.8) on both sides gives

$$\Delta Im = m \, \Delta Y \qquad (A.9)$$

and substituting ΔY from Equation (A.7) in Equation (A.9) gives

$$\Delta Im = \frac{m}{1 - c + m} \, \Delta Ex \qquad (A.10)$$

Equation (A.10) tells us that the automatic adjustment working via national income will raise imports by $m/(1 - c + m)$ times the initial increase in exports. The value of $m/(1 - c + m)$ is, however, below unity. [Since the marginal propensity to consume is below unity, that is, $c < 1$, then $1 - c > 0$. We hence have m divided by itself *plus* the positive number $1 - c$. When a number is divided by a total larger than itself, the result is below unity. For example, if $c = 0.8$ and $m = 0.2$, imports will increase by only half of any exogenous increase in exports. If $c = 0.4$ and $m = 0.2$, the offset is only a quarter.] What we have is an adjustment process via national income that is not complete. While an exogenous change in exports will change imports in the same direction, imports will change by less than the initial change in exports, and so initial effects persist.

Income and income adjustment are relevant to the financial manager who is trying to forecast movements in exchange rates. If a country's national income is growing more rapidly than that of others *as a result of growth in exports*, then the country's foreign exchange reserves will increase, and eventually the currency will probably increase in value. Induced increases in imports resulting from export growth will only partially dampen the growth of reserves and the need to eventually revalue the currency. When a nation's income is growing from a growth in domestic investment, (I_0) or from growth in consumption (C_0), then foreign exchange reserves will shrink, and eventually the foreign exchange value of the currency will have to be reduced. The growth in income will raise imports but not exports, since exports are determined by the incomes of *other* nations.

There is an additional force, also working via changes in national income, that will help complete the automatic adjustment process. This force is induced changes in the money supply, which in turn affects interest rates, the rate of investment, national income, and imports. The process works as follows. If we start in balance and an exogenous increase in exports does not induce a sufficient rise in imports to offset the increase in exports, a surplus will remain. Under fixed exchange rates this will require the central bank to supply its currency to prevent its exchange rate from appreciating. This means an increase in the supply of money. A money-supply increase tends to lower the rate of interest. Lower interest rates stimulate investment, I, which will in turn both directly and indirectly work toward raising the national income, Y. Higher income will raise imports, Im, via Equation A.3, and help close the imbalance of payments.

The force that we have just described involves a lowering of interest rates working via capital investment, income, imports, and the current account. In addition, interest rates have an effect on capital flows and the capital account.

Interest Rates   The automatic interest-rate adjustment mechanism relies on the effect of the balance of payments on the money supply. We have seen that if the effects are not sterilized, a balance-of-payments deficit will reduce the supply of money, and a surplus will increase it. With a gold standard this occurs because a deficit means a gold outflow and a shrinking money supply, and a surplus means a gold inflow and an increasing money supply. In the gold-exchange and dollar standards, and in the EMS, the money supply also declines after deficits and increases after surpluses. In these cases the money supply declines because of intervention in the foreign exchange market. A deficit requires the local monetary authority to purchase its currency to keep the value up. Thus money is withdrawn from circulation. Similarly, a surplus requires the central bank to sell its currency and hence increase the supply of money. With this we can explain the interest-rate adjustment mechanism.

The interest-rate adjustment mechanism via the capital account involves the following. If a deficit occurs, it will reduce the money supply and raise the interest rate.[20] The deficit means surpluses elsewhere. Therefore the money supplies of other countries will be rising. This will reduce their interest rates. For both reasons there is a rise in interest differentials in favor of the deficit country. This will make investment (in securities, and so on) in that country appear relatively more attractive. The resultant inflows on the capital account should improve the balance of payments, thereby correcting the original deficit.

Because capital flows are highly responsive to interest-rate differentials when capital can flow without restriction, the interest-rate adjustment mechanism working via the capital account is likely to be the most effective mechanism in the short run. However, it is necessary that adjustment eventually occur via prices or national income and the current account. This is because capital inflows must be serviced. That is, there will be payments of interest which will appear as a debit in the invisible or service part of the current account. This means that in the future, the current-account deficit will increase.

---

[20]The interest rate will not increase as a result of a reduction in the money supply if there is a **liquidity trap**, which occurs if the demand for money is perfectly elastic. If they have ever existed, liquidity traps are probably limited to serious recessions, and will not hinder the interest-rate adjustment process in normal times.

Only if exchange rates are fixed need we rely on the automatic adjustment mechanisms we have described. If exchange rates are flexible, there is no need to invoke any of these mechanisms, because deficits and surpluses are avoided by immediate movements in exchange rates. This is a major advantage of flexible exchange rates, because the fixed-rate automatic adjustment mechanisms are likely to be more painful than a change in exchange rates. For example, for a deficit to be corrected via a lower price level, a lower national income, or higher interest rates, it is usually also necessary to suffer higher unemployment. Let us consider this argument for flexible versus fixed exchange rates along with some of the other arguments that have been advanced for and against fixed and flexible rates. These arguments remain of interest because central bankers have not given up intervening in foreign exchange markets, and because some countries still have fixed exchange rates—such as the members of the EMS and many less-developed countries.

THE CASE FOR FIXED VERSUS FLEXIBLE EXCHANGE RATES[21]

Arguments for Flexible Exchange Rates

Better Adjustment   As we have just said, one of the most important arguments for flexible exchange rates it that they provide a less painful adjustment mechanism than do fixed exchange rates. For example, an incipient deficit with flexible exchange rates will merely cause a decline in the foreign exchange value of the currency, rather than require a recession to reduce income or prices as fixed exchange rates would. We should note, however, that the decline in the value of a nation's currency still cures a balance-of-payments deficit by reducing real (price-level-adjusted) income and wages. We can make our products more competitive either by reducing prices in local currency or by reducing the foreign exchange value of that currency. For political and social reasons it may be impractical to reduce local-currency wages, so instead we can reduce the international value of the currency.

We can see how a currency devaluation or depreciation reduces real wages in two ways. First, it means more expensive imports, which raises the cost of living and thereby reduces the buying power of given local wages. Second, when the wages or incomes of the workers in different countries are ranked in terms of a common currency, the fall in the value of a currency will mean that wages and incomes in that country fall vis-à-vis those in other countries. It should hence be clear that a decline in the value of a currency via flexible exchange rates is an alternative to a decline in local-currency wages and prices to correct payments deficits. The preference for flexible exchange rates, on the grounds of better

---

[21]The classic case for flexible exchange rates has been made by Milton Friedman in "The Case for Flexible Exchange Rates," in *Essays in Positive Economics*, University of Chicago Press, Chicago, 1953, and by Egon Sohmen in *Flexible Exchange Rates: Theory and Controversy*, University of Chicago Press, Chicago, 1969.

adjustment, is based on the potential for averting adverse worker reaction by only indirectly reducing real wages.

Better Confidence It is claimed as a corollary to better adjustment that if flexible exchange rates prevent a country from having large persistent deficits, then there will be more confidence in the international financial system. More confidence means fewer attempts by individuals or central banks to readjust currency portfolios, and this gives rise to calmer foreign exchange markets.

Better Liquidity Flexible exchange rates do not require central banks to hold foreign exchange reserves, since there is no need to intervene in the foreign exchange market. This means that the problem of having insufficient liquidity (international foreign exchange reserves) does not exist with truly flexible rates, and competitive devaluations aimed at securing a larger share of an inadequate total stock of reserves will not take place.

Gains from Freer Trade When deficits occur with fixed exchange rates, tariffs and restrictions on the free flow of goods and capital invariably abound. If, by maintaining external balance, flexible rates avoid the need for these regulations, which are costly to enforce, then the gains from trade and international investment can be enjoyed.

Increased Independence of Policy Maintaining a fixed exchange rate can force a country to follow the same economic policy as its major trading partners. For example, suppose that the United States allows a rapid growth in the money supply, as it did during the Vietnam war. This will tend to push up U.S. prices and lower interest rates (in the short run), the former causing a deficit or deterioration in the current account and the latter causing a deficit or deterioration in the capital account. If, for example, the Canadian dollar is fixed to the U.S. dollar, the deficit in the United States will most likely mean a surplus in Canada. This will put upward pressure on the Canadian dollar, forcing the Bank of Canada to sell Canadian dollars and hence increase the Canadian money supply. In this case an increase in the U.S. money supply causes an increase in the Canadian money supply. It was for this reason that the United States was accused of "shipping" its inflation to the rest of the world. However, if exchange rates are flexible, all that will happen is that the value of the U.S. dollar will decrease against other currencies.[22]

The advantage of flexible rates in allowing independent policy action has been put in a different way in the so-called **optimum-currency-area argument**,

[22] For more on the theory and evidence of the linkage between the U.S. and other countries' money supplies under fixed and flexible exchange rates see Richard G. Sheehan, "Does U.S. Money Growth Determine Money Growth in Other Nations?," *Review*, Federal Reserve Bank of St. Louis, January 1987, pp. 5–14. For evidence that does not support the view that the U.S. shipped inflation abroad see Edgar L. Feige and James M. Johannes, "Was the United States Responsible for Worldwide Inflation under the Regime of Fixed Exchange Rates?," *Kyklos*, 1982, pp. 263–277.

developed primarily by Robert Mundell and Ronald McKinnon.[23] A currency area is an area within which exchange rates *are* fixed. An optimum currency area is an area within which exchange rates *should be* fixed. We can explain what constitutes an optimum currency area by asking what it would mean for the ECC to have a common currency, or alternatively, for the ECC currencies to be truly fixed to each other.[24] We can begin by asking what would happen if, for example, Britain suffered a fall in demand for its exports with resultant high unemployment, while the remainder of the ECC was booming.

Offsetting the fall in demand and easing the unemployment in Britain would require an expansion in the money supply. With a common currency throughout the ECC, this would involve the risk of inflation in the economies with full employment. We see that Britain cannot have an independent monetary policy. If, however, Britain has its own currency, then the money supply can be expanded to take care of Britain's problem. Moreover, even if the discretionary policy action is not taken, having a separate currency with a flexible exchange value means that this adjustment can be achieved automatically. The fall in demand for British exports would lower the external value of the pound, and the lower value would then stimulate export sales. In addition, a lower pound would encourage investors to built plants in Britain and take advantage of the cheap British wages vis-à-vis those in other countries.

The optimum-currency-area argument can be taken further. Why not have a separate currency with a flexible exchange rate for Wales, which is part of Britain? Then a fall in the demand for coal or steel, major products of Wales, would cause a fall in the value of this hypothetical Welsh currency, stimulating other industries to locate in Wales. A separate currency would also allow discretionary policies to solve the economic difficulties specific to the region. And if Wales, then why not Cardiff, a city in Wales, or even parts of Cardiff? Extending the argument to the United States, why shouldn't there be a separate northeastern dollar or a separate northwestern dollar? Then if, for example, there is a fall in the demand for the lumber of the northwest, the northwestern dollar will decline in value, and other industries will be encouraged to move to the northwest. But what limits this?

We can begin our answer by saying that there is no need to have a separate northwestern dollar if the people in the northwest are prepared to move to where opportunities are plentiful so that unemployment does not occur. We need a separate currency for areas from which factors of production cannot move or prefer not to move. This prompted Robert Mundell to argue that the optimum currency area is the **region**. A region is defined as an area within

[23]See Robert Mundell, "A Theory of Optimum Currency Areas," *American Economic Review*, September 1961, pp. 657–665, and Ronald McKinnon, "Optimum Currency Areas," *American Economic Review*, September 1963, pp. 717–725. See also Harry Johnson and Alexander Swoboda (eds.), *Madrid Conference on Optimum Currency Areas*, Harvard University Press, Cambridge, Mass., 1973.

[24]A commitment to reach a monetary union in stages beginning in 1990 was reached by all EEC members at a meeting of EEC leaders in Madrid in 1989.

which factors of production are mobile and from which they are immobile. Mundell argued that if currency areas are smaller than existing countries, then there is considerable inconvenience in converting currencies, and there is exchange-rate risk in local business activity.[25] In addition, thin currency markets can experience monopolistic private speculation. Mundell therefore limited the optimum currency area to something larger than a nation. This makes the problem one of asking which countries should have a common currency, or alternatively, truly fixed exchange rates.

The notion that the minimum feasible size of a currency area is limited by the greater risk and inconvenience of smaller areas is closely related to one of the leading arguments against flexible exchange rates: that they cause uncertainty and inhibit international trade. Let us begin with this in our discussion of the negative side of the flexible-exchange-rate argument.

The Case against Flexible Rates

Flexible Rates Cause Uncertainty and Inhibit International Trade and Investment It is claimed by proponents of fixed rates that if exporters and importers do not know the future exchange rate, they will stick to local markets. This means less enjoyment of the advantages of international trade and of making overseas investments, and it is a burden on everyone. To counter this argument, a believer in a flexible system can say the following:

1 Flexible rates do not necessarily fluctuate wildly, and fixed rates do change —often dramatically.[26] There have been numerous well-publicized occasions when so-called fixed exchange rates have been changed by as much as 25 percent. Many changes have taken place in the fixed value of British pounds, German marks, Israeli shekels, French francs, and Mexican pesos. In addition, there have been periods of relative stability of flexible exchange rates. For example, the Canadian dollar varied within a range of about 2 percent for a period of several years in the 1970s.

2 Even if flexible exchange rates are more volatile than fixed exchange rates, there are several inexpensive ways of avoiding or reducing uncertainty due to unexpected changes in them. For example, exporters can sell foreign-currency receivables forward, and importers can buy foreign-currency payables forward. Uncertainty can also be reduced with futures contracts, currency options, and

---

[25]This risk might be difficult to avoid with forward contracts and the other usual risk-reducing devices because the currency area is too small to support forward, futures and option markets. That is, the optimum currency area, like so many other things, is limited by the size of the market.

[26]Occasionally, proponents of fixed exchange rates refer to flexible rates as a "fluctuating exchange rate system." There is no such thing as a system of fluctuating rates, and those people who use this term are confusing "flexible"—which means able to move—with "fluctuation"—which means actual movement.

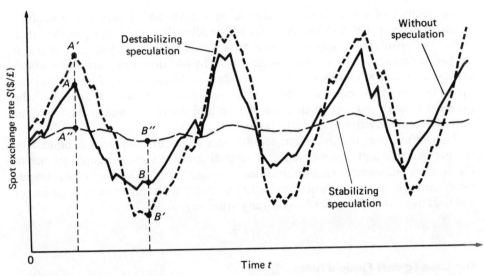

FIGURE A.3
STABILIZING AND DESTABILIZING CURRENCY SPECULATION. With destabilizing speculation
we expect variations in exchange rates to be larger than they would otherwise be. Profitable
speculation involving buying low and selling high should, however, reduce variability.

swaps. Furthermore, the cost of these uncertainty-reducing techniques is typically small.[27]

Flexible Rates Cause Destabilizing Speculation A highly controversial argument is that under flexible exchange rates, speculators will cause wide swings in the values of different currencies. These swings are the result of the movement of "hot money." (The expression is used because of the lightning speed at which the money moves in response to news items.) There are two counterarguments that can be made:

1 To be destabilizing, speculation will, in general, have to result in losses. The argument goes like this. To cause destabilization, a speculator must buy when the price is high to make it go higher and sell when it is low to make it go lower. In this way the variations in rates will be higher than they would otherwise be, as is illustrated in Figure A.3 If the rate without speculation follows the path shown, then to make the rate vary by more than this, pounds must be purchased when $S(\$/£)$ would have been at A [making $S(\$/£)$ rise to A'], sold when $S(\$/£)$ would have been at B [making $S(\$/£)$ fall to B'], and so on. But this means buying high and selling low, which is a sure recipe for a quick exit from any speculative game.

---

[27]This is shown in Chapter 9.

If speculators are to make a profit, they must sell pounds when $S(\$/£)$ would have been at A [forcing $S(\$/£)$ toward A''] and buy pounds when $S(\$/£)$ would have been at B [forcing $S(\$/£)$ toward B'']. In this way speculators will dampen variations in exchange rates and stabilize the market.[28]

2 Speculation with fixed exchange rates is destabilizing, and it can be profitable too. When a country is running out of foreign exchange reserves, its currency is likely to be under selling pressure, with the exchange rate at its lower support point. When speculators see this, they will sell the currency. Under fixed rates the central bank will purchase the currency sold by the speculators at the lower support price and use up foreign exchange reserves. This will make the shortage of reserves even worse, causing other holders of the troubled currency to sell. This will further lower foreign exchange reserves and eventually force the central bank to reset the rate at a lower level. This is highly destabilizing speculation. It is also profitable for the speculator.

With fixed exchange rates the speculators know in which direction the rate will move. For example, when the pound sterling was pegged at $2.8000/£ and experiencing downward pressure in the early and mid-1960s, a revaluation of the pound was exceedingly unlikely. By selling pounds the worst that could have happened was that the rate would not have changed. And if it had changed, there would have been a pound devaluation, and the speculator could have bought back the pounds later at a lower price. Similarly, when the German mark was fixed to the dollar and under heavy buying pressure in the early 1970s, everybody could have been confident that the mark would not be devalued. If anything, it would have been revalued, and a profit would have been made by buying German marks. The worst that could have happened was that the rate would not have changed. And so fixed-rate speculation is destabilizing, and because it provides one-way bets, may also be profitable.

Flexible Rates Will Not Work for Small Economies   This is a valid argument that has been made by a number of economists, including Robert Mundell. The argument begins by noting that a depreciation or devaluation of a currency will help the balance of payments if it reduces the relative prices of locally produced goods and services. However, a depreciation or devaluation will raise the prices of imports. This will increase the cost of living, which will put upward pressure on wages. If, for example, a 1-percent depreciation or devaluation raises import costs by a full 1 percent and most goods are imported (the country is a "banana republic" which produces a narrow range of outputs and imports most consumption goods), then if real wages are maintained, nominal wages must rise by

---

[28] It has been argued that if there is an imperfect signal that demand for a currency will be high in the next period, speculators may buy the currency even though they know the signal may not be correct. Then, if there is not another high-demand signal next period, speculators might sell their currency holdings, pushing the exchange rate lower than it would have gone. This can be destabilizing and, it is argued, may also be profitable. See Oliver D. Hart and David M. Kreps, "Price Destabilizing Speculation," *Journal of the Political Economy*, October 1986, pp. 927–952. For other special circumstances where destabilizing speculation can be profitable see Robert M. Stern, *The Balance of Payments*, Aldine, Chicago, 1973.

the amount of depreciation or devaluation. If wages rise 1 percent when the currency falls by 1 percent, the effects are offsetting, and changes in exchange rates, whether in flexible or pegged values, will be ineffective. In such a case the country may as well fix the value of its currency to the currency of the country which supplies the most imports.

Every country produces some of its consumer goods and services locally. Housing is always local (and often accounts for over 25 percent of consumption), and in many places most services, perishable foods, and so on, are too. This means that while the smallness of the economy is relevant, it does not mean that changes in exchange rates are completely ineffective. However, it is possible that even though some goods and services are produced locally, a depreciation will raise the prices of competing import items, allowing local producers to raise their prices. With this effect it is presumed that there is a lack of competition between local producers; but that may in fact occur in some small countries.

Flexible Rates Are Inflationary Rigid adherence to the gold standard involved a constraint on monetary authorities. They had to keep their money supplies and inflation under control. It is claimed by proponents of fixed rates that the dollar-exchange and dollar standards also involved discipline, since poor performance was readily apparent in statistics on declining foreign exchange reserves. This, it is said, gave the central bank public support for strong action. Flexible exchange rates, according to this argument, allow conditions to deteriorate without providing evidence to support strong corrective action. However, this argument fails to recognize that the exchange rate itself is daily evidence of poor economic performance. The need for corrective action is apparent to everyone. It is true that the problem can creep up rather than appear suddenly and dramatically. However, in order to believe that flexible rates are more inflationary than fixed rates, it is necessary to believe that central bankers are more concerned with evidence of declining reserves than with evidence of a declining currency value, or that central bankers are better able to act on evidence of declining reserves.

It has alternatively been argued that flexible exchange rates have an inherent inflationary bias because depreciations increase prices of traded goods, but appreciations do not cause parallel reductions in prices. This argument is based on a **ratchet effect** that is avoided with fixed rates; with fixed rates there are fewer changes in exchange rates to be subject to a ratchet. However, the empirical evidence does not support the existence of a ratchet.[29] Economists who believe that prices are related to the money supply are not surprised. This is because they believe that higher and higher price levels resulting from fluctuations in exchange rates would cause an excess demand for money that would reduce spending unless the higher prices were **accommodated** by the central bank expanding the money supply in line with higher prices.

[29] Morris Goldstein, "Downward Price Inflexibility, Ratchet Effect and the Inflationary Impact of Import Price Changes," *Staff Papers*, International Monetary Fund, November 1976, pp. 509–544.

Flexible Rates are Unstable Because of Small Trade Elasticities   If import demand or export supply elasticities are small, the foreign exchange market may be unstable in the sense that small disturbances to exchange rates can grow into extremely large disturbances.[30] Instability is possible because, for example, a depreciation can increase the value of imports by increasing import prices more than it decreases the quantity of imports. A depreciation can therefore increase the currency supply more than it increases the value of exports and currency demand. Consequently, a depreciation can cause an excess supply of currency, further depreciation, and so on. If this is the case, and other factors influencing currency supply and demand do not limit the movements in exchange rates once they begin, the government might wish to limit exchange-rate movements itself by fixing exchange rates. Of course, then the country must depend on the potentially painful price-level, income, and interest-rate adjustment mechanisms.

If, as is often argued, import and export demand are more elastic in the long run than in the short run, then exchange rates may be unstable in the short but stable in the long run. If this is so, it supports the practice of some governments of intervening to help ensure short-run order in the foreign exchange market, but of allowing longer-run trends in exchange rates to take their course. This type of foreign exchange intervention is a form of dirty float. Let us consider this along with some other intermediate types of exchange-rate systems that are not entirely fixed or flexible.

HYBRID SYSTEMS OF EXCHANGE RATES

Fixed and flexible exchange rates are only two alternatives defining the extremes of exchange-rate systems. In between these extremes are a number of other systems which have been practiced at various times.

Dirty Float

As we have just said, central banks sometimes intervene in the foreign exchange markets even when they have declared that exchange rates are flexible. We have suggested that a possible rationale for this practice is trade elasticities that are too small for exchange market stability.

Canada, which practiced floating exchange rates throughout the 1950s and has floated its currency since 1970, has the longest experience with flexible rates in this century of any major country. The Bank of Canada frequently intervenes to "maintain order" in the foreign exchange markets. Its policy is to try to prevent sharp changes in its exchange rate, but to allow market forces to operate over the long run. The purpose of this policy is to reduce short-run exchange-rate uncertainty, but to allow the exchange rate to reflect differential rates of inflation and other fundamental forces over the long run. The Bank of

---

[30]This is shown in Chapter 5.

Canada combines foreign exchange market intervention with interest-rate policy to stabilize its exchange rate. This model is a compromise between fixed and flexible exchange rates, and has been adopted by several other countries.

Wider Band

Another compromise between fixed and flexible exchange rates was tried for a very short while after December 1971, when the International Monetary Fund members decided at a meeting at the Smithsonian Institution in Washington, D.C., to allow the range of fluctuation of exchange rates to be $2\frac{1}{4}$ percent on either side of the official value. This gave a $4\frac{1}{2}$-percent total range of variation before the central bank would intervene, compared with the 2-percent range that existed from 1944 to 1971. The intention was to reduce the uncertainty about future exchange rates and at the same time allow more adjustment. The wider the band, the closer the system came to being a flexible-rate system.

The wider band was not tried by many of the major countries. Canada had opted for a completely floating rate before the Smithsonian meeting, and Britain and the other major European countries floated their currencies (some of which remained fixed to each other) shortly afterward.[31]

Crawling Peg

The **crawling peg** is an automatic system for revising the par or central value—the value around which the rate can fluctuate. This system can be combined with a wider band. The crawling peg requires the central bank to intervene whenever the exchange rate approaches a support point. However, the central value, around which the support points are set, is revised according to the average exchange rate over the previous weeks or months. If the rate tends to remain at or near, for example, the lower support point, the new central value will be revised downward. In this way the rate can drift up or down gradually, giving some degree of certainty without completely frustrating long-term fundamental trends.

Figure A.4 illustrates a crawling peg. Starting at time t_0, intervention points are defined which are above and below a middle or par exchange rate. The intervention points are shown by parallel lines. If the actual exchange rate hovers at the lower end of its allowed range, then at the next setting of the intervention points the middle value is set at the average actual value during the previous period. If the actual exchange rate moves to the lower end of the new allowable trading range, the intervention points are again lowered at the next setting of these points. In this way the exchange rate can drift according to fundamental forces such as inflation rates, but importers and exporters can be reasonably sure about exchange rates applying to short-term foreign-currency receivables and payables.

---

[31]For more on the wider band see John Williamson, "Surveys in Applied Economics: International Liquidity," *Economic Journal*, September 1973, pp. 685–746.

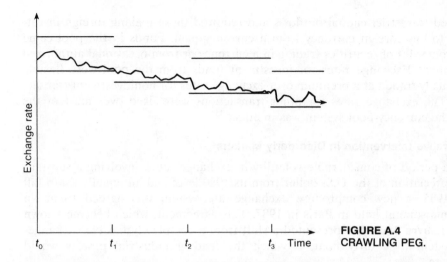

FIGURE A.4
CRAWLING PEG.

An alternative way of readjusting the band within which a currency can trade is according to recent rates of inflation.[32] This keeps exchange rates moving directly according to the purchasing power of currencies over long periods of time, but keeps them predictable in the short term. A crawling peg can also be based on balance-of-trade statistics or changes in external debt. Most examples of crawling pegs have involved countries experiencing very rapid inflation. Several South American countries have at some time tried a crawling peg.

Mixed Fixed and Flexible Rates

Another compromise between fixed and flexible exchange rates that has been tried is to have fixed exchange rates for some transactions such as those on the current account of the balance of payments, but to have flexible rates for other transactions such as those on the capital account.[33] This system is practiced by Belgium, which has a commercial exchange rate for imports and exports of goods and services, and a financial exchange rate for trading in financial assets. The commercial exchange rate is fixed, and the financial exchange rate is flexible. Only authorized banks are permitted to trade in the commercial market, while the financial market is open to all participants. The two tiers of the foreign exchange market are separated by a prohibition on buying foreign exchange in one market and selling it in the other.

Britain operated with two exchange rates for more than a quarter century while functioning under the Exchange Control Act of 1947. This act was

---

[32] In particular, the central value of the band vis-à-vis the U.S. dollar could be changed by the country's inflation minus U.S. inflation.

[33] This division of systems would be motivated by a desire not to exert influence over international trade, but to maintain control over capital flows.

designed to restrict capital outflows and required those making foreign investments to buy foreign currency from a **currency pool**. Funds in the pool came
only from sales of securities trading in a currency or from occasional authorized
additions.[34] Exchange rates for investment funds from the pool were flexible
and usually traded at a premium over exchange rates for noninvestment transactions. The exchange rates for other transactions were fixed over most of the
years the currency-pool system was in effect.[35]

Cooperative Intervention in Disorderly Markets

After a period of considerable volatility in exchange rates, involving a substantial appreciation of the U.S. dollar from its 1980 level and an equally sharp fall
after 1985, a new compromise exchange-rate system was agreed to at an
economic summit held in Paris in 1987. This agreement, which became known
as the **Louvre Accord**, represented a shift from a completely flexible exchange-
rate system to a dirty float in which the leading industrial powers would
cooperate.

The Louvre Accord followed the **Plaza Agreement** of 1985, in which the U.S.
accepted the need to intervene in the foreign exchange markets during unstable
times. The other leading industrial powers had recognized this need somewhat
earlier, but knew that intervention would not work without close cooperation,
given the very large size of private speculative capital flows. The Plaza Agreement was later confirmed at the 1986 Tokyo economic summit and reconfirmed
at other economic summits, most notably the 1987 meeting in Paris that resulted
in the Louvre Accord. These meetings took place against a background of
immense exchange-rate instability, and resulted in a new compromise between
completely flexible and completely fixed exchange rates.[36] The system that
emerged is not unlike Canada's approach of flexibility with intervention to
achieve orderly markets, but because it involves cooperation, it is a little
different from the Canadian dirty float.

The international financial system that emerged from the Louvre Accord can
be characterized as a floating exchange-rate system within rather wide bands
that are periodically revised, but where the intervention levels are not precisely
specified. The acceptable ranges of fluctuation have to be deduced from official
communiqués released after summit meetings, or from statements by senior

---

[34] As a result the size of the pool of each currency was determined by the value of investments
when the pool was established, subsequent realized gains on the value of investments, and special
authorized additions. The currencies covered by the Exchange Control Act varied during the time
the Act was in effect.

[35] Numerous other mixed exchange-rate systems have been tried, such as different exchange rates
for imports versus exports, different exchange rates for different imports, and so on, but these other
systems are combinations of different fixed rates, not mixtures of fixed and flexible rates. Those
interested in the other types of arrangements can consult the *Annual Report on Exchange Arrangements and Restrictions*, International Monetary Funds, Washington, D.C.

[36] The meetings up to and including the 1986 Tokyo summit involved the United States, Japan,
United Kingdom, West Germany and France, the so-called **Group of Five**, or **G-5**. Subsequent
meetings were expanded to include Canada—the U.S.'s largest trading partner—and Italy, and
became known as the **G-7 summits**.

officials of the nations involved. For example, it might be stated after a G-7 meeting that the leaders are satisfied with exchange rates in their recent trading range. Alternatively, after a substantial movement of exchange rates, the governor of a central bank or a treasury official might say they believe the dollar is too low or too high, and that if the markets do not adjust there could be intervention. Market participants react to these statements according to how credible they believe them to be, and, for example, buy currencies the authorities say are too cheap. This can help reduce the need for intervention and has been described as "talking" exchange rates in the officially desired direction.[37]

In this account of the many possible compromises between truly fixed and truly flexible exchange rates, we have given a rather patchy history of international finance. In order to provide a more systematic overview, we present below a brief chronology of international financial developments during the twentieth century. This chronology has been deferred so that we would be equipped with an understanding of the systems and events we describe. Our chronology should serve to give an historical perspective on the international financial system, and demonstrate that the international financial system is not static, but something that continues to evolve.

THE HISTORY AND POSSIBLE FUTURE OF THE INTERNATIONAL FINANCIAL SYSTEM

The Situation Before Bretton Woods, 1900–1944

Until 1914 the world was on a gold standard that was brought to an end by the First World War. As is usual in wartime, governments imposed currency controls and abandoned the commitment to convert their paper currencies into gold. Immediately after the First World War ended in 1918, there was a period of flexible exchange rates that lasted until 1926, during which time many countries suffered from hyperinflation. The gold standard was readopted in 1926 in an effort to bring inflation under control and to help cure a number of other economic ills such as sweeping protectionism, competitive devaluations, and so on.

For a gold standard to work, it is necessary that deficit countries allow the influence of deficits on their gold reserves to slow monetary growth. It is just as necessary that the surplus countries allow their increased gold reserves to liberalize their monetary policies. However, in practice, the burden of both types of adjustment was considered so great that frequently there was reluctance to behave in this way. Many countries began to manipulate exchange rates for their own domestic objectives. For example, the French devalued the franc in 1926 to stimulate their economy, and the undervalued currency contributed

---

[37] For a model of exchange rates in which there are imprecisely specified intervention points, and where these nevertheless add to foreign exchange market stability, see Paul R. Krugman, "The Bias in the Band: Exchange Rate Expectations under a Broad-Band Regime," National Bureau of Economic Research, Cambridge, Mass., 1987.

to the problems of the British pound. Then in 1928 the French decided to accept only gold and no more foreign exchange for reserves. When in 1931 the French decided that they would not accept any more pounds sterling and also that they would exchange their existing sterling holdings for gold, there was little the British could do other than make sterling inconvertible into gold. This they did in 1931. The ability to exchange currencies for gold is the central feature of the gold standard, and when other countries found their holdings of pounds no longer convertible, they followed Britain. By 1934 only the U.S. dollar could be exchanged for gold.

Since a full recovery from the depression of 1929–1933 did not take place until the onset of World War II, the conditions for any formal reorganizing of the international financial order were not present. The depression had provided an environment in which self-interested policies of "beggar thy neighbor"—competitive devaluations and increased tariff protection—followed the model established earlier by France. Since no long-lasting effective devaluations were possible and the great interruption of world trade eliminated the gains from international trade, such an environment hindered economic growth. When the war replaced the depression, no cooperation was possible, and it was not until July of 1944 that, with victory imminent in Europe, the representatives of the United States, Great Britain, and other allied powers met in the rural surroundings of Bretton Woods, New Hampshire to hammer out a new international financial order to replace the failed gold standard.

Bretton Woods and the IMF, 1944 – 1973

Of paramount importance to the representatives at the 1944 meeting at Bretton Woods was the prevention of another breakdown of the international financial order, such as the one which followed the peace after World War I. From 1918 until well into the 1920s the world had witnessed a rise in protectionism on a grand scale to protect jobs for those returning from the war, competitive devaluations designed for the same effect, and massive hyperinflation as the inability to raise conventional taxes led to use of the hidden tax of inflation. A system was required that would keep countries from changing exchange rates for competitive advantage. This meant that some sort of control on rate changes was needed, as well as a reserve base for deficit countries. The reserves were to be provided via an institution created for this purpose. The International Monetary Fund (IMF) was established to collect and allocate reserves in order to implement the Articles of Agreement signed at Bretton Woods.

The Articles of Agreement required member countries (of which there were 151 at the end of 1989) to:

1 promote international monetary cooperation,
2 facilitate the growth of trade,
3 promote exchange-rate stability,
4 establish a system of multilateral payments,
5 create a reserve base.

The reserves were contributed by the member countries according to a quota system (since then many times revised) based on the national income and importance of trade in different countries. Of the original contribution, 25 percent was in gold—the so-called **gold tranche** position—and the remaining 75 percent was in the country's own currency. A country was allowed to borrow up to its gold-tranche contribution without IMF approval and an additional 100 percent in four steps, each with additional stringent conditions established by the IMF. These conditions were to ensure that corrective macroeconomic policy actions would be taken.

The lending facilities have been expanded over the years. Standby arrangements were introduced in 1952, enabling a country to have funds appropriated ahead of the need so that currencies would be less open to attack during the IMF's deliberation of whether help would be made available. Other extensions of the IMF's lending ability took the form of:

1 The **Compensating Financing Facility**, introduced in 1963 to help countries with temporarily inadequate foreign exchange reserves as a result of events such as crop failures.

2 The **Extended Fund Facility** of 1974, providing loans for countries with structural difficulties that take longer to correct.

3 The **Trust Fund** from the 1976 **Kingston Agreement** to allow the sale of gold, which was no longer to have a formal role in the international financial system. The proceeds of gold sales are used for special development loans.

4 The **Supplementary Financing Facility**, also known as the **Witteveen Facility** after the then managing director of the IMF. It replaced the 1974–1976 **Oil Facility**, which was established to help countries with temporary difficulties resulting from oil price increases. This gives standby credits.

5 The **Buffer Stock Facility**, which grants loans to enable countries to purchase crucial inventories.

These facilities have been supplemented by the 1980 decision allowing the IMF to borrow in the private capital market when necessary.

As we have seen, the most important feature of the Bretton Woods Agreement was the decision to have the U.S. dollar freely convertible into gold and to have the values of other currencies fixed in U.S. dollars. The exchange rates were to be maintained within 1 percent on either side of the official party, with intervention required at the support points. This required the United States to maintain a reserve of gold, and other countries to maintain a reserve of U.S. dollars. Because the initially selected exchange rates could have been incorrect for balance-of-payments equilibrium, each country was allowed a revision of up to 10 percent within a year of the initial selection of the exchange rate. In this basic form the system survived until 1971.

The central place of the U.S. dollar was viewed by John Maynard Keynes, who was the British representative at Bretton Woods, as a potential weakness. Keynes preferred an international settlement system based on a new currency unit—the **Bancor**. However, the U.S. plan was accepted, and it was not until the 1960s that the inevitable collapse of the Bretton Woods arrangement was recognized by a Yale economist, Robert Triffin.[38] According to the **Triffin paradox**, in order for the stock of world reserves to grow along with world trade, the providers of reserves—primarily the United States but also Great Britain—must run balance-of-payments deficits. These deficits are the means by which other countries can accumulate dollar and pound reserves. Although the reserve-country deficits are needed, the more they occur, the more the holders of dollars (and pounds) will doubt the ability of the Federal Reserve (and Bank of England) to convert dollars (and pounds) into gold at the agreed price. This built-in paradox means that the system is doomed.

Among the more skeptical holders of dollars was France, which began in 1962 to exchange dollars for gold despite the objection of the United States. Not only were the French doubtful about the future value of the dollar, but they also objected to the prominent role of the United States in the Bretton Woods system. Part of this distaste for a powerful United States was political, and part was based on the seigniorage gains that France believed accrued to the United States by virtue of the U.S. role as the world's banker. **Seigniorage** is the profit from making money and depends on the ability to have people hold your currency or other assets at a noncompetitive yield. Every government which issues legal-tender currency can ensure that it is held by its own citizens, even if it offers no yield at all. For example, U.S. citizens will hold Federal Reserve notes and give up goods or services for them, even though the paper the notes are printed on costs very little to provide. The United States was in a special position because its role as the leading provider of foreign exchange reserves meant that it could ensure that foreign central banks as well as U.S. citizens would hold U.S. dollars. However, most reserves were and are kept in securities such as treasury bills, which yield interest. If the interest that is paid on the reserve assets is a competitive yield, then the seigniorage gains to the United States from foreigners holding U.S. assets is small. Indeed, with sufficient competition from (1) alternative reserves of different currencies and (2) alternative investments in the United States, the gains should be a normal and fair return on the assets.[39] Nevertheless, the French continued to convert their dollar holdings into gold. This led other countries to worry about whether sufficient gold would remain for them after the French had finished selling dollars.

By 1968, the run on gold was of such a scale that at a March meeting in Washington, D.C., a two-tier gold-pricing system was established. While the official U.S. price of gold was to remain at $35 per ounce, the private-market price of gold was to be allowed to find its own level.

After repeated financial crises, including a devaluation of the pound from $2.80/£ to $2.40/£ in 1967, some relief came in 1970 with the allocation of

---

[38] Robert Triffin, *Gold and the Dollar Crisis*, Yale University Press, New Haven, Conn., 1960.

[39] For an account and estimates of seigniorage gains, see the papers in Robert Mundell and Alexander Swoboda (eds.), *Monetary Problems of the International Economy*, University of Chicago Press, Chicago, 1969.

Special Drawing Rights (SDRs).[40] The SDRs are book entries that are credited to the accounts of IMF member countries according to their established quotas. They can be used to meet payments imbalances, and they provide a net addition to the stock of reserves without the need for any country to run deficits or mine gold. From 1970 to 1972, approximately $9.4 billion worth of the SDRs (or paper gold) was created, and there was no further allocation until January 1, 1979, when SDR4 billion was created. Similar amounts were created on January 1, 1980, and on January 1, 1981, bringing the total to over SDR 20 billion. No allocations of SDRs have occurred since 1981. A country can draw on its SDRs as long as it maintains an average of more than 30 percent of its cumulative allocation, and a country is required to accept up to 3 times its total allocation. Interest is paid to those who hold SDRs and by those who draw their SDRs, with the rate based on an average of money-market interest rates in the United States, the United Kingdom, Germany, Japan, and France.

The SDR was originally set equal in value to the gold content of a U.S. dollar in 1969, that is, 0.888571 gram or $\frac{1}{35}$ ounce. The value was later revised and based on 16 major currencies, and since January 1, 1986, the SDR has been valued in terms of five currencies as follows:

U.S. dollar	42%
German mark	19%
Japanese yen	15%
U.K. pound	12%
French franc	12%

The currency basket and the weights are revised every 5 years according to the importance of each country in international trade. The value of the SDR is quoted daily.

If the SDR had arrived earlier, it might have prevented or postponed the collapse of the Bretton Woods system, but by 1971, the fall was imminent. After only two major revisions of exchange rates in the 1950s and 1960s—the floating of the Canadian dollar during the 1950s and the devaluation of sterling in 1967 —events suddenly began to rapidly unfold. On August 15, 1971, the United States responded to a record $30-billion trade deficit by making the dollar inconvertible into gold. A 10-percent surcharge was placed on imports, and a program of wage and price controls was introduced. Many of the major currencies were allowed to float against the dollar, and by the end of 1971 most had appreciated, with the German mark and the Japanese yen both up 12 percent. The dollar had begun a decade of decline.

On August 15, 1971, the United States made it clear that it was no longer content to support a system based on the U.S. dollar. The costs of being a reserve-currency country were perceived as having begun to exceed any benefits

[40] See Fritz Machlup, *Remaking the International Monetary System: The Rio Agreement and Beyond*, Johns Hopkins Press, Baltimore, 1968, for the background to the creation of SDRs.

in terms of seigniorage. The ten largest countries were called together for a meeting at the Smithsonian Institution in Washington, D.C. As a result of the Smithsonian Agreement, the United States raised the price of gold to $38 per ounce (that is, devalued the dollar). Each of the other countries in return revalued its currency by an amount of up to 10 percent. The band around the new official parity values was increased from 1 percent to $2\frac{1}{4}$ percent on either side, but several EEC countries kept their own exchange rates within a narrower range of each other while jointly allowing the $4\frac{1}{2}$-percent band vis-à-vis the dollar. The snake, as the European fixed-exchange-rate system was called, became, with some minor revisions, the European Monetary System (EMS) in 1979.

The dollar devaluation was insufficient to restore stability to the system. By 1973 the dollar was under heavy selling pressure even at its devalued or depreciated rates, and in February 1973, the price of gold was raised 11 percent, from $38 to $42.22 per ounce. By the next month most major currencies were floating. This was the unsteady state of the international financial system as it approached the oil crisis of the fall of 1973.

The Flexible-Exchange-Rate Period, 1973 – 1985

The rapid increase in oil prices after the oil embargo worked to the advantage of the U.S. dollar. Since the United States was relatively self-sufficient in oil at that time, the U.S. dollar was able to weather the worst of the storm. The strength of the dollar allowed the United States to remove controls on capital outflows in January 1974. This opened the way for large-scale U.S. lending to companies and countries in need—and came just in time. The practice of paying for oil in U.S. dollars meant that the buyers needed dollars and that the sellers—principally the members of the Organization of Petroleum Exporting Countries (OPEC)—needed to invest their receipts. And so the United States began to recycle petrodollars, taking them in from OPEC on one side of the account and lending them to the oil buyers on the other.

It was not until 1976, at a meeting in Jamaica, that the system that had begun to emerge in 1971 was approved, with ratification coming later, in April 1978. Flexible exchange rates, already extensively used, were deemed to be acceptable to the IMF members, and central banks were permitted to intervene and manage their floats to prevent undue volatility. Gold was officially demonetized, and half of the IMF's gold holdings returned to the members. The other half was sold, and the proceeds were to be used to help poor nations. Individual countries were allowed to sell their gold holdings, and the United States, the IMF, and some other countries began sales. IMF sales were completed by May of 1980.

The Presidential election of 1980 and the subsequent adoption of **supply-side economics** by the Reagan Administration was followed by a period of growing U.S. fiscal and balance-of-trade deficits. Nevertheless, the U.S. dollar experienced a substantial appreciation, further adding to the U.S. trade deficit. This took place against the backdrop of the worsening third-world debt crisis which was aggravated by the high-flying dollar; since most of the debt was denominated in dollars, it was more expensive for the debtor nations such as Brazil and Mexico to acquire dollars to meet debt service payments. Adding to the difficulties of the debtor nations was a general disinflation which was particularly severe for the resource exports that were the source of much of the revenue of the debtor nations. Furthermore, because they had to meet debt payments, the debtors could not reduce production as they would normally do at low prices. Indeed, some debtor nations had to increase production to make up for lower prices, and this put even more downward pressure on their export prices.

With the third-world debt crisis deepening after 1980, the IMF and World Bank were thrust into the role of preventing default on large sovereign loans. In prescribing extremely tough fiscal remedies for the debtor nations, such as the elimination of food subsidies and other social programs, the IMF and to a lesser extent the World Bank became the object of anger among the debtor nations. Through all this uncertainty the U.S. dollar continued its upward movement, being fueled even further by uncertainty over the debt crisis it helped create. By 1985 the dollar was at such a high level that calls for protectionist measures to help U.S. exports finally helped reverse U.S. exchange-rate policy, which for over a decade had supported flexibility.

The Dirty-Float Era, 1985 –

Throughout the runup in the value of the dollar, the U.S. Adminstration repeatedly argued that the appreciating dollar was a sign of confidence in the U.S. economy, and that the free market would take care of exchange rates if they were seriously out of line. However, many economists argued otherwise, saying that the soaring U.S. dollar was the result of an exploding U.S. fiscal deficit that was too large to be financed by bond sales to Americans. Instead, the fiscal deficit required borrowing from foreign savers such as those of Japan and Germany. Bond purchases by Japanese, German, and other foreign investors meant a demand for U.S. dollars when paying for the bonds, and this pushed up the dollar's value. Furthermore, many economists argued that because a flexible exchange rate results in a balanced balance of payments, the capital inflow and resulting capital-account surplus required a matching current-account deficit, and this in turn was achieved by an overvalued U.S. dollar.

As the U.S. capital inflows and current-account deficits rose in tandem, the U.S. response was to leave fiscal policy in place, and instead push the dollar down by foreign exchange market intervention. The decision to take this tack was made at a meeting in the Plaza Hotel in New York in 1985. The Plaza Agreement marks a turning point in the fortunes of the U.S. dollar. During the following several years the U.S. dollar lost most of its earlier gains in value against the other leading currencies. Despite this spectacular depreciation, the U.S. trade balance worsened further.

With the plight of the dollar grabbing newspaper headlines, attention became focused on how to prevent the dollar falling further. Economic summits of the world's leaders were organized in which the volatility of exchange rates became a central issue. These summits culminated in the Louvre Accord reached in Paris in 1987, in which the G-7 industrial countries decided to cooperate on exchange-rate matters to achieve greater stability. This agreement marked a shift towards an orchestrated dirty, or managed, float. The reason for coordinating the management of the float was that the size of private capital flows had become so large that it had become difficult for the country whose currency was falling to muster sufficient exchange reserves to keep its exchange rate steady. However, since countries never run out of their own currencies, they can indefinitely prevent their exchange rates from increasing. Therefore, by agreeing to manage exchange rates cooperatively, it was felt that the authorities could keep them stable, even in the face of very heavy private speculation.

The agreement to intervene jointly in foreign exchange markets came in conjunction with an agreement for greater consultation and coordination of monetary and fiscal policy. This coordination was needed because, as we have seen, when countries work to maintain exchange rates, inflation starting in one country can be shipped to the others. For example, there was fear that if the U.S. maintained its very expansionary monetary and fiscal policy, the U.S. dollar would drop, forcing other countries to sell their currencies, and thereby increasing their money supplies. Japan, West Germany, and the other G-7 countries were afraid the U.S. fiscal deficit would eventually force the U.S. to expand its money supply, and therefore the agreement to cooperate with the U.S. was linked to U.S. efforts to reduce its deficit.

The system that emerged from the Louvre Accord, which has been reaffirmed in subsequent economic summits, is one that is based on flexible exchange rates, but where the authorities periodically let it be known what trading ranges of exchange rates they believe are appropriate. Intervention is used to try to maintain orderly markets. However, the threat of intervention helps provide stability, because the more the exchange rates change from their "approved" values, the more expectation speculators have of official intervention. For example, the more the dollar drops from summit-approved levels, the more speculators expect official dollar buying, and this leads the speculators to buy dollars themselves. This helps move the dollar toward approved levels.

THE FUTURE OF THE INTERNATIONAL FINANCIAL SYSTEM

If anything is clear from our brief description of the history of the international financial system, it is that it evolves in response to the environment it serves. For example, the shift from the gold standard to the standard adopted at Bretton Woods came in response to the beggar-thy-neighbor and protectionist exchange-rate policies of the depression and war. In reaction to these competitive devaluations, the system that was chosen was characterized by extreme rigidity of exchange rates. With the oil shock of the late 1960s and early 1970s, the rigidity of Bretton Woods could not provide the adjustment needed between oil-using and oil-producing nations, and so there followed after 1973 a period of exchange-rate flexibility. With the increasing financial and economic interdependence spawned by financial deregulation and the growth in trade, and with massive structural imbalances of trade and fiscal deficits, the unfettered flexibility of the 1970s and early 1980s was replaced by the more cooperative arrangements of the Plaza Agreement and Louvre Accord. The obvious question with important implications for the future conduct of international business is: where do we go from here?

The international financial system must cope with two challenging problems:

1 The third-world debt crisis.
2 The shift from U.S. economic hegemony to a shared U.S.-Japanese-European balance of economic power.

A review of these two problems suggests the possible direction of the international financial system.

The Third-World Debt Crisis

The Background The high interest rates on loans to countries such as Brazil, Mexico, and Argentina, and the rapid economic growth these countries had enjoyed in the 1970s, led even some of the most conservative banks from industrialized countries to make substantial fractions of their loans to developing nations. For example, for the largest 15 U.S. banks, developing-country loans at the outset of 1982 amounted to 7.9 percent of their assets and 150 percent of their capital. This means that default on all these loans would place the banks in technical insolvency. However, since many of the loans were made to governments or guaranteed by governments—so-called sovereign loans—few bankers seemed aware that defaults were possible. A commonly voiced opinion was that "countries don't go bankrupt, only companies go bankrupt." What was overlooked by the bankers in their complacency was that countries can go bankrupt *in terms of U.S. dollars*, and the vast majority of third-world debt was denominated in U.S. dollars.[41]

The debt crisis first became obvious when in August 1982, Mexico announced it could not meet scheduled repayments on its almost $100 billion of external debt. Within one year of that announcement, 47 debtor nations were negotiating with their creditors and international organizations such as the IMF and World Bank to reschedule payments.[42] The negotiations involved possible changes in magnitude, maturity, and currency composition of debt. Talk of a

---

[41]Clearly, if countries borrowed in their own currencies they could always repay debts; they have unlimited power to "print" their currencies. Of course, bankers would have been very wary of loans denominated in the borrowers' currencies, knowing that on repayment the currencies they received would probably have little value.

[42]It is worth noting that if the debtor nations had issued bonds rather than arranged bank loans, the inability to pay would have meant outright default, not rescheduling. For example, in a similar international debt crisis of the 1930s involving bonds, defaults occurred on the majority of foreign-issued U.S. dollar bonds. See Barry Eichengreen, "Resolving Debt Crises: An Historical Perspective," National Bureau of Economic Research, working paper 2555, April 1988.

"debtors' cartel" and default by debtors was matched against the threat of denial of future credits by the creditor banks and their governments. This was the background to the intense bargaining between debtors and creditors which stretched on throughout the 1980s. The creditors knew that debtors would repudiate if the value of repudiated debt exceeded the present value of the cost of repudiation in the form of denied access to future credit.[43]

The Causes Numerous factors combined to make the crisis as severe as it was. Taking developments in no particular order, we can cite the following:

1 In the two years 1979 and 1980 there was a 27-percent decline in commodity prices. In addition, at this time a recession swept developing and developed nations alike, so that quantities of commodities sold were declining along with commodity prices. This meant that export revenues of debtor nations which depended on commodity exports were plunging, and yet it was from these export revenues that they had to service debts. The loans had been granted and sought because of an expectation of increasing commodity prices and export revenues, and yet the very opposite occurred.

2 The debts were dominated in U.S. dollars, and in 1980 the U.S. dollar began a spectacular climb that by 1985 had almost doubled its value against the other major currencies. Bankers and borrowers had not anticipated this surge in the dollar.

3 Interest rates experienced an unprecedented increase after a switch to antiinflationary monetary policy in October 1979, with the U.S. prime rate topping 20 percent. This made the payment of interest difficult for many borrowers, and the repayment of principal just about impossible.

4 A substantial component of borrowed funds had not been devoted to investment which would have generated income to help service debts. Rather, much of the debt had been used to subsidize consumption. Furthermore, it was difficult to remove these subsidies, and so borrowing continued. Many debtor nations were on a knife edge, risking riots or revolution if they reduced subsidies, but risking isolation from creditor nations if they maintained them.[44]

The Fear The principal fear of officials was the consequence of bank failures brought about by outright defaults. This fear was based on the view that losses would exceed the capital of many banks, so that effects would not be limited to bank shareholders. Rather, losses would spill over to depositors.

---

[43]The problem of creditor-debtor bargaining clearly fits in the paradigm of noncooperative game theory, and indeed, the debt crisis spawned numerous papers in this vein. See, for example, Jonathan Eaton and Mark Gersovitz, "Debt with Potential Repudiation: Theoretical and Empirical Analysis," *Review of Economic Studies*, April 1981, pp. 289–309, and Ronald Giammarino and Ed Nosal, "Debt Overhang and the Efficiency of International Rescheduling," unpublished manuscript, University of British Columbia, December 1988.

[44]At the height of the debt crisis in the mid 1980s, visits by IMF officials to debtor nations to encourage reduced consumption-subsidization were frequently met with protests. In its efforts to force economic reorganization on debtors by making help contingent on a return to market forces, the IMF became a villain in the eyes of the poor in many developing nations.

There could be runs on banks if governments did not bail them out by purchasing bad debts. Bank bailouts were viewed by many as inflationary.[45] Many argued, therefore, that the consequences of the debt crisis would be financial panic and runaway inflation.

The Handling of the Crisis   The fact that the 1980s ended without widespread bank failures and financial chaos reflects the step-by-step rescheduling that has occurred, the long period of economic recovery that began in 1982 (the longest period of continuous economic growth during the century), and a number of steps taken by international organizations and banks. Some of the more notable of the actions taken are:

1 In 1982, the U.S. Treasury and Federal Reserve extended $1.7 billion of short-term credit to Mexico to help it maintain payments, and participated with other developed-country governments to grant loans to Brazil and Argentina. This was prompted by fear of collapse of highly exposed U.S. banks, which between them held approximately 35 percent of LDC debt.

2 Between 1982 and 1984, the IMF and the World Bank made $12 billion of standby credits available to the`six largest Latin American debtor nations on condition that they adopt austere economic policies. These policies included devaluations and elimination of subsidies, and were designed to bring about the required structural changes to deal with the problems over the long run.

3 In 1983 and 1984, private creditor banks agreed among themselves and with their debtors to reschedule payments, stretching the repayment interval. This required considerable cooperation because each creditor bank had to resist trying to take its money first.

4 In 1985, U.S. Secretary of Treasury, James Baker proposed $20 billion of additional private bank lending to the debtor nations, and offered to arrange $9 billion of new loans from the World Bank and the Inter-American Development Bank. The **Baker Initiative** showed recognition that the economic interdependence among nations required that debtors be able to continue buying crucial imports.

5 In 1988, led by Citibank of New York, the most exposed creditor banks began to write off bad debts to third-world countries. This reduced the debt carried on their books toward more realistic levels, and marked a recognition that the banks would accept the consequences of past mistakes.

6 In 1989 at the Paris G-7 meetings, Japan offered $65 billion over 5 years to needy nations. Some of the $65 billion was allocated to support the U.S. program to ease third-world debt.

7 Also in 1989, Mexico and a committee representing nearly 500 creditor banks agreed to the **Brady Plan**, named after U.S. Secretary of the Treasury

---

[45]This view is difficult to support if all that the governments did was prevent a collapse of their money supplies. In fact, failure of governments to prevent losses on deposits would almost certainly have been deflationary, as it was in the 1930s, and the maintenance of deposit levels, if done properly, should have been neutral.

Nicholas Brady. The plan allows each creditor to chose one of three options: they can forgive 35 percent of the principal of old loans, reduce interest rates to 6.25 percent, or provide new loans.

The experience with the third-world debt crisis shows how financially and economically interdependent we have become. Nations have come to recognize that failure of other countries' banks will spill over to their own banks, and economic setbacks among their customers will hurt their own firms that supply these customers. Through regular economic summits among national leaders, and through even more frequent contact among central bankers and other senior officials, countries have been cooperating. As with the physical environment, it has become recognized that the global good can no longer be achieved through independent, competitive action. The same conclusion emerges from considering the other major challenge that we listed, the changing balance of economic power.

Shifting Global Economic Power

At the end of the Second World War, the United States was the dominant power of the free world, and it is therefore little surprise that the international financial system adopted at Bretton Woods in July 1944 was the U.S. plan. As would be predicted by an application of game theory, in situations involving an overwhelmingly dominant player, solutions invariably unravel according to the dominant player's preferences.

The economic hegemony enjoyed by the United States at the end of the Second World War has been eroded by the phenomenal economic performance of Asian countries, most particularly Japan, and by the growing strength of an increasingly integrated Europe. This change in the balance of economic power is clear from Figure A.5. What the figure reveals is that today there is a much more even sharing of economic power between the U.S., Europe, and Japan. This means that we can no longer predict important economic changes, such as in the nature of the international financial system, simply by studying the preferences of any one country. In any situation involving three roughly equal players who can form coalitions, outcomes are notoriously difficult to predict. So what can we say about the likely evolution of the international financial and economic system in the face of this changed economic reality?

One clear consequence of the new balance of power is a need for each party to consult with the others. No single power can take the chance of triggering actions by the other two. This recognition of the need to cooperate has manifested itself in the G-7 summits, in the cooperative exchange-rate intervention policy of the Plaza and Louvre Accords, in the frequent meetings of leading central bankers under the aegis of the Bank for International Settlements in Basle, Switzerland, in the renewed attention paid to GATT during the Uruguay Round of tariff negotiations, and in numerous matters involving taxation, interest rates, and other policies. It seems likely that with increasing financial

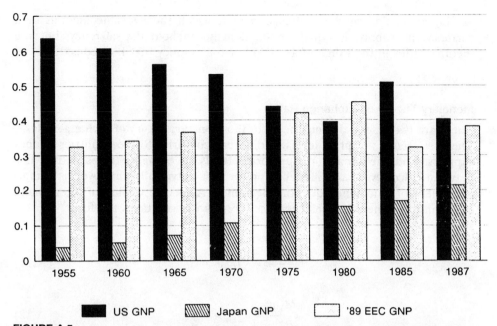

FIGURE A.5
THE CHANGES IN ECONOMIC POWER. The U.S. GNP as a fraction of the combined GNPs of the U.S., Europe, and Japan has diminished during the postwar period. The more even sharing of economic power makes it more difficult to predict changes in the international financial system. *Source:* International Monetary Fund, *International Financial Statistics*, Yearbook 1988.

and economic interdependence, the evolving international financial system will involve even closer cooperation.[46]

NEW THEORIES OF EXCHANGE RATES

There are two major classes of theories of exchange rates, those based on the *flow* supply versus the flow demand of a currency, and those based on the *stock* supply versus the stock demand.[47] In Chapter 5 we describe a flow theory of exchange rates where the demand for a currency is to pay for exports and the supply is to pay for imports. This is a flow theory because exports and imports are flows per calendar quarter or year that appear in the balance-of-payments account. In this Addendum, we describe several stock theories of exchange rates which were developed during the mid 1970s and early 1980s. All the theories

---

[46] Indeed, overtures by the Soviet Union to the Paris summit of 1989 indicate a recognition by the communist block that their future is closely tied to that of the West. In his letter to the summit leaders, Secretary Gorbachov offered to work closely with the West in economic matters.

[47] The flow demand or supply is the amount *per period of time*, such as the demand for a country's currency per month or per year. The **stock** demand or supply is the amount at *a given moment in time*, such as the amount of a country's currency being demanded at the end of a particular year.

are based on finding the exchange rate at which the available amount of a currency, its supply, is equal to the demand to hold the currency, but the theories differ in the range of assets other than money that they consider.

Monetary Theory of Exchange Rates

There are two essential components to the **monetary theory of exchange rates**.[48] The first relates the price levels in different countries to the countries' money supplies, and the second relates price levels to exchange rates.[49] The link between price levels and money supplies that is typically employed is a rearrangement of a demand equation for money. A specific version of the demand equation for money that has been used by John Bilson takes the form[50]

$$\frac{M_{US}}{P_{US}} = Q_{US}^{\alpha} e^{-\beta i_{us}} \tag{A.11}$$

$$\frac{M_{UK}}{P_{UK}} = Q_{UK}^{\alpha} e^{-\beta i_{uk}} \tag{A.12}$$

Here M_{US} and M_{UK} are respectively the U.S. and British money demands, P_{US} and P_{UK} are price levels, Q_{US} and Q_{UK} are real GNPs, i_{us} and i_{uk} are nominal interest rates, and α and β are parameters that are assumed to be positive and the same for both countries.

The left-hand sides of Equations (A.11) and (A.12) are the real money demands in the respective countries. (Division of any nominal variable by the price level converts it into a real variable. For example, dividing the nominal GNP, usually written as Y, by the price level gives the real GNP, usually written as $Q = Y/P$.) The real demand for money is how much money, in terms of the ability to buy real goods and services, the public wants to hold. Equations (A.11) and (A.12) assume that the real demand for money increases with the real GNP. This is because the real GNP equals the real amount of goods and services people produce and buy, and the more people buy, the more money they need

---

[48] The monetary theory of exchange rates is the flexible-exchange-rate form of the monetary approach to the balance of payments which pertains to fixed exchange rates. For a summary of the monetary approach to the balance of payments see Jacob A. Frenkel and Harry G. Johnson (eds.), *The Monetary Approach to the Balance of Payments*, Allen and Unwin, London, 1976, and Harry G. Johnson, "The Monetary Approach to the Balance of Payments: A Nontechnical Guide," *Journal of International Economics*, August 1977, pp. 251–268.

[49] The money supply is typically defined as currency held by the public plus all or some subset of deposits at commercial banks. The range of deposits included in the money supply depends on how broad a definition of money is being considered.

[50] John F. O. Bilson, "The Monetary Approach to Exchange Rates: Some Empirical Evidence," *Staff Papers*, International Monetary Fund, March 1978, pp. 48–75.

to hold for making purchases.[51] The extent that real money demand varies with real GNP depends on α.[52]

Equations (A.11) and (A.12) show that the demand for money in each country declines as that country's nominal interest rate increases. This is because the opportunity cost of holding money rather than buying bonds or some other interest-bearing asset is the nominal interest that would otherwise be earned.[53]

The assumption that the demand for money in each country depends on interest rates only in that country implicitly assumes that different countries' monies are not substitutable.[54] The alternative assumption, that different countries' monies are substitutable, would mean, for example, that the British view U.S. dollar holdings as satisfying their demand for money. In the extreme situation that different countries' monies are **perfectly substitutable**, changes in the money supply in any one country will not cause an excess supply of money because people in other countries will be prepared to hold the money. As we shall see, without an excess supply of money, there will be no depreciation in the exchange rate after an increase in the money supply as is predicted by the monetary approach.

The monetary approach to exchange rates assumes that people adjust their money holdings until the demand for money equals the supply of money. The way this occurs is as follows. If, for example, the supply of money exceeds the demand for money, the public attempts to spend the excess supply of money by buying goods and bonds. Of course, money does not disappear when it is spent, but rather ends up in somebody else's hands. However, the attempt to get rid of money does restore equilibrium between money supply and demand. This occurs because the buying of goods causes an increase in the price level, and the buying of bonds causes higher bond prices, which in turn mean lower interest rates. The higher prices and lower interest rates increase the nominal demand for money. The process continues until the demand for money has risen to match the supply. Similarly, an excess demand for money causes reductions in spending on goods and bonds, lower prices, higher interest rates, and a reduced demand for money. This continues until money demand has been reduced sufficiently to equal money supply.

If the money demand equals the money supply, we can interpret M_{US} and M_{UK} as money supplies as well as money demands. If we rearrange Equations

---

[51] Real GNP, which is the real amount produced, differs from real national expenditures, which is the amount people buy, by the change in inventories; production that is not sold is added to inventory. However, since inventory changes are typically small, real GNP differs little from real expenditures.

[52] The parameter α is the real income elasticity of real money demand.

[53] Interest rates appear as exponents of e for no other reason than that this produces a convenient form of the exchange-rate equation. This becomes apparent as we proceed.

[54] The monetary approach also implicitly assumes that bonds from different countries *are* substitutable. This assumption is implicit in the exclusion of bond demand and supply equations, thereby implying bond markets clear whatever happens to bond supplies. Later we drop the assumption that different countries' bonds are substitutable. This is done when we consider the portfolio-balance approach to exchange rates.

(A.11) and (A.12) to put the money supplies on the right-hand sides, we have

$$P_{US} = M_{US}Q_{US}^{-\alpha}e^{\beta i_{us}} \tag{A.13}$$

$$P_{UK} = M_{UK}Q_{UK}^{-\alpha}e^{\beta i_{uk}} \tag{A.14}$$

Equations (A.13) and (A.14) show that price levels in the two countries vary in proportion with the countries' money supplies. Price levels also vary inversely with real GNPs, and in the same direction as nominal interest rates.[55]

According to the monetary theory of exchange rates, the ratio of prices in two different countries is closely related to the exchange rate between the two countries' currencies. In particular, in the context of the U.S. and U.K., the monetary theory assumes that

$$S(\$/\pounds) = \frac{P_{US}}{P_{UK}} \tag{A.15}$$

where $S(\$/\pounds)$ is the exchange rate of dollars per pound. Equation (A.15) is known as the purchasing-power parity (PPP) principle and has the following rationale.[56]

Assume there are no taxes or shipping costs, and that a representative good costs \$10 in the U.S. and £6 in Britain. If the exchange were $S(\$/\pounds) = \$1.50/\pounds$ it would be possible to take \$9, purchase £6 on the foreign exchange market, buy one unit of the good in Britain, ship the good to the U.S., and sell it for \$10. There would be an arbitrage profit of \$1, and as many people tried to exploit the opportunity, which requires buying pounds with dollars, they would bid up the dollar price of the pound until the arbitrage was no longer profitable.[57] Alternatively, if the exchange rate were \$1.75/£, it would be possible to take £5.71, buy \$10 on the foreign exchange market, use the \$10 to buy one unit of the good in the U.S., ship the good to Britain, and sell it for £6. There would be an arbitrage profit of £0.29, which would encourage others to try and exploit the opportunity. This would involve buying dollars (selling pounds), which would push the dollar value of the pound below \$1.75/£. Only at \$1.67/£ does arbitrage become unprofitable. This is the exchange rate given by Equation (A.15), since with $P_{US} = \$10$ and $P_{UK} = £6$, we have

$$S(\$/\pounds) = \frac{P_{US}}{P_{UK}} = \frac{\$10}{£6} = \$1.67/\pounds$$

---

[55]The conclusion that prices vary in proportion to the money supply is a conclusion of the quantity theory of money, and indeed, the real-demand-for-money equations are rearrangements of the quantity equation. The quantity equation is usually written as $MV = PQ$, where M, P, and Q are defined above, and V is the velocity of circulation of money. We could rewrite the quantity theory as $M/P = QV^{-1}$ and them make $V = e^{\beta i_{us}}$. This is directly comparable to our money demand equations when $\alpha = 1$.

[56]The purchasing-power parity principle is discussed in Chapter 6.

[57]Alternatively, the arbitrage opportunity might be eliminated by changes in the pound and dollar prices of the good.

Substituting Equations (A.13) and (A.14) into Equation (A.15), we find[58]

$$S(\$/\pounds) = \frac{M_{\text{US}}}{M_{\text{UK}}} \left(\frac{Q_{\text{UK}}}{Q_{\text{US}}} \right)^{\alpha} e^{\beta(i_{\text{us}} - i_{\text{uk}})} \tag{A.16}$$

Equation (A.16) captures the essential features of the monetary approach to exchange rates.

An examination of Equation (A.16) shows that the first and most distinctive implication of the monetary approach is that the U.S. dollar value of the pound, $S(\$/\pounds)$, increases if the U.S. money supply increases more than the British money supply. The reason is that if M_{US} increases more than M_{UK}, U.S. prices increase more than British prices, so that according to the PPP principle, the dollar must fall vis-à-vis the pound.

The second prediction of the monetary approach characterized by Equation (A.16) is that the value of the pound increases if British real GNP increases faster than U.S. real GNP. This occurs because a higher real GNP means a higher demand for money, which, for a given supply of money, means an excess demand for money. This causes reduced spending—both on goods and on bonds—and a lower price level. According to the PPP principle, a lower price level means an appreciation of the exchange rate, in this case of the pound vis-à-vis the dollar. The prediction that faster growth of real GNP causes currency appreciation runs counter to what simple Keynesian models tend to predict. Keynesian models like that described earlier in this Addendum predict that faster growth of real GNP means faster growth of imports, a consequent faster growth of the supply of a currency, and a depreciating exchange rate. Monetarists argue that simple Keynesian models overlook the link between the goods and money markets, that is, the link between GNP and the demand for money. However, more sophisticated Keynesian models do contain such a link, and as a result are more eclectic in their predictions.

Another prediction of the monetary approach is that the higher are U.S. versus British interest rates, the higher is the U.S. dollar value of the pound. In terms of Equation (A.16), the higher i_{us} is, the higher is $S(\$/\pounds)$, because β is positive. A higher $S(\$/\pounds)$ means a higher value of the pound and lower value of the dollar. It follows that an unexpected jump in nominal interest rates will cause a currency to depreciate. The reason for this prediction of the monetary approach is that the higher nominal interest rates are, the lower is the real demand for money, and consequently, the lower is the equilibrium real money supply. The real money supply is reduced to its lower equilibrium level by an increase in the price level.[59] The PPP condition, Equation (A.15), requires that

---

[58] Because only freely traded commodities lend themselves to the type of arbitrage we have described, it can be argued that instead of using the overall price levels in Equation (A.15), we should use prices of traded goods. For the consequences of this see John F. O. Bilson, "Leading Indicators of Currency Devaluation," *Columbia Journal of World Business*, winter 1979, pp. 62–76.

[59] The price level increases because higher interest rates reduce money demand, thereby creating an excess supply of money. The excess supply of money causes extra spending, pushing up prices.

if the U.S. price level does increase because of higher U.S. interest rates, the U.S. dollar must lose value against the pound, that is, there must be more U.S. dollars per pound. Therefore, we reach the conclusion that the higher U.S. interest rates are relative to British interest rates, the lower is the value of the dollar. Flow theories of exchange rates such as that outlined in Chapter 5 tend to suggest otherwise, predicting that higher U.S. interest rates will increase the demand for U.S. interest-bearing securities, thereby increasing the demand for dollars and the value of the dollar.[60]

A prediction of the monetary approach with which a large number of economists will agree concerns the effect of expected inflation. It is generally accepted that *ceteris paribus*, higher expected inflation leads to higher nominal interest rates.[61] We have just seen that higher nominal interest rates cause a currency to depreciate. Therefore, the monetary approach predicts that higher expected inflation causes depreciation.[62] Because higher expected inflation suggests a future depreciation via the PPP condition (higher future prices mean a lower future currency value), what the monetary approach tells us is that the effect occurs immediately rather than later, after the expected inflation has occurred. The idea that expected future events are reflected immediately in spot exchange rates is an important ingredient of the **asset approach to exchange rates** considered next.

The Asset Approach to Exchange Rates

Exchange rates are relative prices of two assets: monies. The current value of an asset depends on what that asset is expected to be worth in the future. For example, the more valuable a stock is expected to become, the more it is worth now. Similarly, the more a currency is expected to be worth in the future the more it *is* worth now. It follows that today's exchange rate depends on the

---

[60] The evidence supports the prediction of the flow theory in that appreciations (depreciations) of the dollar are empirically associated with increases (decreases) in U.S. nominal interest rates. See Brad Cornell and Alan C. Shapiro, "Interest Rates and Exchange Rates: Some New Empirical Results," *Journal of International Money and Finance*, December 1985, pp. 431–442, and Gikas A. Hardouvelis, "Economic News, Exchange Rates and Interest Rates," *Journal of International Money and Finance*, March 1988, pp. 23–35.

[61] For the theory behind expected inflation and interest rates see Maurice D. Levi and John H. Makin, "Anticipated Inflation and Interest Rates: Further Interpretation of Findings on the Fisher Equation," *American Economic Review*, December 1978, pp. 801–812. For the evidence, see Maurice D. Levi and John H. Makin, "Fisher, Phillips, Friedman and the Measured Impact of Inflation on Interest," *The Journal of Finance*, March 1979, pp. 35–52.

[62] The flow theory's prediction of the effect of expected inflation depends on what is assumed to happen to *real* interest rates. For example, if real rates decline with increasing expected inflation, which will happen if the expected future depreciation of the inflating country's currency exceeds the increase in its nominal interest rate, then the flow theory predicts an immediate depreciation. It is worth noting that the monetary theory assumes there are no changes in relative real interest rates; all countries' real rates are assumed to be equal because all countries' bonds are assumed to be perfectly substitutable. The evidence cited in footnote 60 is inconsistent with the equal-real-rates assumption of the monetary theory. The fact that increases (decreases) in relative interest rates are associated with appreciations (depreciations) suggests that relative real interest rates change, and furthermore are positively correlated with nominal interest rates.

expected future exchange rate. In turn, the expected future exchange rate depends on what is expected to happen to all the factors reflected in future balance-of-payments accounts.

The asset approach to exchange rates, which has been articulated most clearly by Michael Mussa, looks at the current spot exchange rate as a reflection of the market's best evaluation of what is likely to happen to the exchange rate in the future.[63] All relevant available information about the future is incorporated into the current spot rate. Because new information is random, and could as easily be good as bad for one currency versus the other, the path of the exchange rate should contain a random component. This random component fluctuates around the expected change in the exchange rate. The expected change can reflect the implications of PPP—with more rapid inflation implying depreciation—or any other influence on exchange rates reflected in the balance-of-payments accounts.

The asset approach holds implications for the effect of fiscal policy as well as monetary policy. For example, it predicts that high fiscal deficits can result in an immediate depreciation. This would happen if the fiscal deficit caused people to expect future expansion of the money supply as the government printed money to make interest payments on its growing debt. The higher future money supply implies higher future prices, and via the PPP principle, this implies a future depreciation. The future depreciation translates into an immediate depreciation via the asset approach.

The asset approach offers an explanation for departures from PPP. Because expectations about the future are relevant to the current exchange rate, there is no necessity for the spot exchange rate to ensure PPP at every moment. For example, if a country is expected to experience rapid inflation, poor trade performance, or something else leading to a depreciation, the current exchange rate of that country's currency is likely to be below its PPP value. However, because the expected future exchange rate could be based on a tendency for PPP to be restored, the asset approach is not inconsistent with PPP as a long-run tendency. Nor, therefore, is the asset approach necessarily inconsistent with the long-run implications of the monetary approach.

The Portfolio-Balance Approach to Exchange Rates

The monetary approach to exchange rates assumes that people want to hold their own country's currency, but not the foreign country's currency. The **portfolio-balance approach** recognizes that people might want to hold both monies, although they might have a preference for one country's money, probably their own. The portfolio-balance approach makes the same argument for bonds. That is, it assumes people in both countries demand domestic and

[63] Michael Mussa, "A Model of Exchange Rate Dynamics," *Journal of Political Economy*, February 1982, pp. 74–104. This paper follows an earlier statement of the asset approach in Jacob A. Frenkel and Michael L. Mussa, "The Efficiency of Foreign Exchange Markets and Measures of Turbulence," *American Economic Review, Papers and Proceedings*, May 1980, pp. 374–381.

foreign bonds, or more generally, that people prefer diversified portfolios of securities. However, the portfolio-balance model does not just have demand equations for different monies and bonds in each country, showing how these demands are related to incomes, interest rates, and so on. Rather, it recognizes that supplies and demands for monies and bonds must balance, that is, markets must clear.[64] (The fact that the approach is based on diversification of portfolios and a requirement that markets balance explains its name.)

As we have explained, in the monetary approach each country's bond market is assumed to clear, whatever happens to the supply of or demand for any country's bonds. This assumption is implicit in the absence of equations for bond supplies and demands, and in the absence of any conditions for the bond markets to clear; without there being conditions showing when the bond markets clear, by implication they always clear. It is possible to rationalize this assumption of the monetary approach if it is argued that one country's bonds are perfectly substitutable for another country's bonds. This is because then, if the supply of a country's bonds is increased, the extra bonds will be held by residents or foreigners substituting these for foreign bonds they currently hold. Changes in the supply of one country's bonds are of such insignificance in the global context that the global demand for bonds equals the global supply without any noticeable effect on interest rates or exchange rates.

When we add bond demand equations and equilibrium conditions for bond demands to equal bond supplies for each country's bonds, as we do in the portfolio-balance approach, the implications of changing bond supplies and demands are different from those in the monetary approach. In particular, we find effects of bond supplies and demands on exchange rates and interest rates.

As an example of the implications of the portfolio-balance approach, let us consider the effect of an increase in a country's money supply brought about by the central bank buying the country's bonds in the open market.[65] The monetary approach predicts that eventually the exchange rate will depreciate by the percentage increase in the money supply. The portfolio-balance approach recognizes that, in addition to the direct effect of the money supply, there is also the effect of the excess demand for bonds caused by the central bank's purchase

---

[64]Therefore, the portfolio-balance model consists of demand and supply equations for money and bonds in all countries, as well as equations setting money and bond demands equal to supplies. We do not need to write down these equations in order to appreciate the essential features of the approach. Those who are interested can consult Pentti J. K. Kouri and Michael G. Porter, "International Capital Flows and Portfolio Equilibrium," *Journal of Political Economy*, May/June 1974, pp. 443–467, or Michael P. Dooley and Peter Isard, "The Portfolio-Balance Model of Exchange Rates," International Finance Discussion Papers, Board of Governors of the Federal Reserve, no. 141, May 1979. For a variant of a portfolio-balance model in which uncertainty in the price level is included to explicitly explain preferences for domestic over foreign money and securities see René M. Stultz, "Currency Preferences, Purchasing Power Risks, and the Determination of Exchange Rates in an Optimizing Model," *Journal of Money, Credit and Banking*, August 1984, pp. 302–316.

[65]Open-market purchase of bonds is one of the principal ways through which the money supply is increased in countries with well-developed money markets. By buying securities in the open market, central banks increase commercial bank reserves, and the extra reserves can in turn support increased bank deposits.

of bonds; when the central bank buys bonds, it reduces the supply of bonds available to the public, creating an excess demand. The excess demand for bonds pushes up bond prices and therefore lowers interest rates. This has further effects on the currency of the country that increases its money supply. Therefore, the portfolio-balance approach predicts a depreciation by a different amount when the money supply is increased by the central bank buying bonds than when it is increased in some other way.[66]

As another example of the predictions of the portfolio-balance approach, let us consider the effect of an increase in a country's real GNP. The monetary approach predicts an appreciation, as shown by Equation (A.16). The portfolio-balance approach suggests that the higher real GNP will also increase residents' savings, increasing their demand for domestic bonds more than their demand for foreign bonds. This will mean an excess demand for all bonds, but a relatively greater excess demand for the country's own bonds. An excess demand for bonds increases bond prices and lowers interest rates. Interest rates will fall relatively more in the country with the growing GNP, and this will depreciate its exchange rates. Because bonds are not perfect substitutes, the lower interest rates do not cause unlimited movements of capital, but rather are part of the short-run equilibrium. In that equilibrium the value of the currency of the country with increased GNP is different according to the portfolio-balance approach than according to the monetary approach.

Because it can explain changes in exchange rates via changes in bond supplies and demands, the portfolio-balance approach emphasizes the capital account of the balance of payments. Therefore, this approach is different from the flow approach to exchange rates explained in Chapter 5, which emphasizes the current account. However, despite the different emphasis of these approaches, they can both be adapted to explain a phenomenon we note in Chapter 1, that of volatile exchange rates. Let us consider how we can explain volatility in the form of "overshooting" of exchange rates. We begin with an overshooting theory which involves the PPP condition.

THEORIES OF EXCHANGE-RATE VOLATILITY

The Dornbusch Sticky-Price Theory[67]

In the monetary approach presented earlier, we assume that the PPP condition holds for the overall price level; P_{US} and P_{UK} in Equation (A.15) are the prices of baskets of *all* goods and services. If this assumption about PPP is relaxed, the monetary approach can generate exchange-rate overshooting, which occurs when exchange rates go beyond their new equilibrium before returning to it.

---

[66]For example, the money supply could be increased by reducing required reserve ratios of commercial banks.

[67]More complete accounts of the Dornbusch sticky-price theory can be found in Rudiger Dornbusch, "Expectations and Exchange Rate Dynamics," *Journal of Political Economy*, December 1976, pp. 1161–1176, and in Rudiger Dornbusch, *Open Economy Macroeconomics*, 2d ed., Basic Books, New York, 1988.

Let us suppose that PPP holds for internationally traded goods, but not for non-internationally-traded goods such as land and services. Let us also suppose that prices of nontraded goods are "sticky," that is, they move slowly toward their new equilibrium after a disturbance. In these circumstances, if the exchange rate falls in proportion to the percentage increase in a country's money supply, as suggested by the monetary approach, there remains an excess supply of money. [Traded-goods prices increase in proportion to the money supply because they move directly with the exchange rate, as shown by Equation (A.16), but nontraded-goods prices increase only slowly. Therefore, the overall price level increases less than the money supply, leaving the demand for money lower than the supply.] Eventually, the excess supply of money is eliminated via rising nontraded-goods prices, but in the interim the excess supply of money causes increased spending on goods and bonds.

The theory of overshooting exchange rates concentrates on the effect of the increased spending on bonds, arguing that this causes higher bond prices, and consequently lower interest rates. If a country has lower interest rates than other countries', capital leaves the country until the country's currency is expected to appreciate by the extent to which its interest rates are below other countries'.[68] In order for the currency to be expected to appreciate, the exchange rate must overshoot, going lower than its eventual equilibrium level. This means that prices of traded goods increase by even more than the increase in the money supply, thereby augmenting the increase in the price index. This increases the demand for money, as does the low interest rate, helping to maintain equality of supply and demand for money in the short run.

In the long run, the prices of nontraded goods increase in proportion to the increase in the money supply; they increase slowly, but do eventually catch up. This means that, in the long run, the exchange rate needs to depreciate only in the same proportion as the money supply, so that traded-goods prices increase by the same proportion as the increase in the money supply. Therefore, after overshooting beyond the new (lower) long-run equilibrium level, the exchange rate appreciates back to its new equilibrium. This appreciation reduces traded-goods prices, so that in the end, prices of traded and nontraded goods have increased in proportion to the money supply. Therefore, the overshooting is temporary, lasting only as long as nontraded-goods prices lag behind the increase in the money supply.

Varying Elasticities

If the demand for imports is inelastic in the short run, then depreciation can result in more being spent on imports; import prices increase by more than the quantity of imports declines, so that the value of imports increases. This means

---

[68]This is because the return from investing in a country consists of two components: the interest rate, and the change in value of the country's currency between the time of the investment, and the time of repatriation. Therefore, an expected appreciation of a country's currency compensates for lower interest rates in that country.

that the supply of a country's currency can increase with a depreciation. If the demand for the currency does not increase by as much as the supply because export demand is also very inelastic in the short run, a depreciation causes an excess supply of the currency. An excess supply means further depreciation. Therefore, while inelasticities persist there is depreciation, further excess supply, and so on. However, eventually, as elasticities of import demand and export supply increase, stability returns to exchange rates. Therefore, it is possible for exchange rates to overshoot.[69]

A particular variant of the varying-elasticities explanation of overshooting that has been advanced by Steven Magee is that previously agreed-upon export contracts make demand and supply elasticities effectively zero.[70] For example, if a stated quantity of wheat is purchased by Britain at a contracted U.S. dollar price, then a depreciation of the pound increases pound payments for wheat in proportion to the depreciation, causing an excess supply of pounds and further depreciation. What happens is that the British demand for imports has an elasticity of zero during the contract period. Only when the contract expires can the quantity purchased decline as a result of the higher pound price. In the interim, the exchange rate can overshoot.

Stock Adjustment and Flow Fluctuations

Overshooting of exchange rates can also be explained by arguments akin to those of the **accelerator model**.[71] Let us do this with the help of an example.

Suppose British investors save £10 billion each year and divide it evenly between British and U.S. investments. Suppose that they have accumulated £100 billion of investments in each country from their investments during previous years, but that suddenly, perhaps because of the election of a popular U.S. President or an unpopular British Prime Minister, British investors decide to increase their U.S. investments, to 60 percent of their portfolios.

After their portfolios have been adjusted the British will purchase £6 billion of U.S. investment and therefore £6 billion of U.S. dollars per year to pay for this investment. However, in order to readjust their accumulated portfolios the British must purchase another £20 billion of U.S. investments and U.S. dollars; with £100 billion in each country, having 60 percent of the portfolio in U.S. assets requires having £120 billion of U.S. assets. If the readjustment of the

---

[69]Speculators may stabilize exchange rates if the pattern is predictable. Therefore, we do not necessarily observe overshooting from varying elasticities. This is not the case for the Dornbusch model, where speculators do not prevent overshooting. This is because in that model, interest rates move to nullify the benefit of currency speculation; interest rates are low on the currency that is expected to appreciate.

[70]Steven Magee, "Contracting and Spurious Deviations from Purchasing Power Parity," in Jacob A. Frenkel and Harry G. Johnson (eds.), *The Economics of Exchange Rates: Selected Readings*, Addison-Wesley, Reading, Mass., 1978.

[71]The accelerator model offers an explanation of the business cycle—an overshooting of the GNP—based on assuming the stock of capital is proportional to national income. Many students will be familiar with the accelerator model because it is covered in introductory economics courses.

accumulated portfolios occurs during one year, the path of the British demand for dollars goes from £5 billion before the adjustment to £26 billion during the readjustment, and then back to £6 billion per year. Therefore, the demand for dollars is abnormally high during the period that accumulated portfolios are being readjusted, and this can cause the value of the U.S. dollar to overshoot. The basic reason is that accumulated portfolios are large relative to additions to portfolios, that is, stocks are large relative to flows.[72]

A reason why large shifts in desired portfolios might occur is that some forms of money do not pay interest. Normally, interest rates increase to make up for expected depreciations, so that investors do not switch assets because they anticipate a depreciation. Without interest being paid on money, this compensation is not possible. Consequently, large adjustments between different countries' monies can occur, causing large flow demands and exchange-rate overshooting.[73]

Other Theories of Overshooting

We have by no means exhausted the theories of overshooting. For example, Jeffery Frankel and Kenneth Froot have offered a theory of "speculative bubbles" in exchange rates, based on changes in the amount of attention portfolio managers pay to chartists, who extrapolate recent trends, and fundamentalists, who consider the fundamentals such as adherence of exchange rates to PPP.[74] Frankel and Froot argue that portfolio managers attach more weight to the predictions of the group that has been more accurate in the recent past. If chartists happen to be correct for a while, their predictions are followed, making their predictions correct, causing even greater attention to be paid to them, and so on. Because the chartists' predictions are self-reinforcing, it is only when exchange rates have become completely out of line with fundamentals that the chartists are likely to falter, making portfolio managers switch their attention to the advice of fundamentalists.[75]

[72] This explanation for exchange-rate overshooting has been advanced by Robert M. Dunn, Jr., *The Many Disappointments of Flexible Exchange Rates*, Essays in International Finance 154, Princeton University, December 1983.

[73] For variants of this explanation of volatility of exchange rates see Lance Girton and Donald Roper, "Theory and Implication of Currency Substitution," *Journal of Money, Credit, and Banking*, February 1981, pp. 12–30, and Ronald I. McKinnon, "Currency Substitution and Instability in the World Dollar Market," *American Economic Review*, June 1982, pp. 302–333.

[74] Jeffery A. Frankel and Kenneth Froot, "The Dollar as an Irrational Speculative Bubble: A Tale of Fundamentalists and Chartists," National Bureau of Economic Research, Cambridge, Mass., 1986. For an earlier model of overshooting based on different market players see Richard G. Harris and Douglas D. Purvis, "Diverse Information and Market Efficiency in a Monetary Model of Exchange Rates," *Economic Journal*, December 1981, pp. 829–847.

[75] We have given only a sampling of the many overshooting theories that have arisen in an attempt to explain exchange-rate volatility. Others that are worth mentioning include Peter Hooper and John Morton, "Fluctuations in the Dollar: A Model of Nominal and Real Exchange Rate Determination," *Journal of International Money and Finance*, April 1982, pp. 39–56, and Chau-Nan Chen, Ching-Chong Lai, and Tien-Wang Tsaur, "The Loanable Funds Theory and the Dynamics of Exchange Rates: The Mundell Model Revisited," *Journal of International Money and Finance*, June 1988, pp. 221–229.

SUMMARY

1 A gold standard involves the settlement of international transactions in gold and the open offer to exchange domestic paper money for gold at a fixed price. A deficit means an outflow of gold. The reduction in gold reserves reduces the local money supply and puts downward pressure on prices in the deficit country. The fall in prices stimulates exports and lowers imports. In the surplus (foreign) countries, the money supplies increase, raising prices in those countries. This causes a further reduction of relative prices in the deficit country. In addition, changes in relative prices within each country help eliminate a deficit or surplus.

2 The price-specie adjustment mechanism can be frustrated by a sterilization policy. This policy severs the link between gold flows and money supplies, so that the adjustment mechanism is lost.

3 Critics of the gold standard argue that prices in surplus and deficit countries showed parallel movement rather than the reverse movement implied by the gold standard. Downward price rigidity is responsible. However, an adjustment of relative prices will still occur if prices go up by more in surplus countries than in deficit countries. Another criticism of the gold standard is that governments did not allow it to work. This is as much a criticism of government as it is of the gold standard.

4 The gold-exchange standard required the U.S. to fix its exchange rate to gold, and other countries to fix to gold or to the U.S. dollar. This system operated from 1944 to 1968. From 1968 to 1973, the U.S. dollar was not fixed to gold, but most other currencies were still fixed to the dollar. This was called a dollar standard.

5 To maintain the fixed exchange rate in terms of the dollar, central banks must purchase or sell their local currency at the support points on either side of the parity value. If the free-market exchange rate would be above the upper support point, the central bank must sell its currency and purchase dollars. This raises official reserves and means a surplus in the balance of payments. It also raises the supply of money. At the lower support point, the central bank must purchase the local currency with dollars, which reduces official reserves and results in a deficit in the balance of payments. This lowers the money supply. Therefore, under fixed exchange rates, surpluses raise money supplies and deficits lower money supplies.

6 Because deficit countries which run out of foreign exchange reserves are eventually forced to devalue, it is possible to identify which currencies face devaluation. The need to revalue is less urgent than the need to devalue, making the timing of forecasts of revaluations more difficult.

7 The European Monetary System, EMS, is a fixed-exchange-rate system in which countries cooperate to maintain exchange rates. Exchange rates are fixed within limits set by a parity grid, which involves an upper and lower limit for each exchange rate. Exchange rates must also be maintained within limits vis-à-vis the European Currency Unit. This helps identify which country is at fault for any difficulties in maintaining exchange rates.

8 With both deficit and surplus countries intervening under the EMS, the burden of adjustment is shared.

9 Keynesian income adjustment involves a mechanism that restores equilibrium even if prices are inflexible. For example, if exports decline, causing a deficit, there will be a multiplier decline in national income, reducing consumption (including imports) and tending to restore equilibrium. The mechanism is, however, incomplete.

10 While income adjustment is incomplete, there is an additional mechanism working via income that is indirect and follows from changes in the money supply and interest rates. While a deficit persists, the supply of money will decline, raising the interest

rate, reducing investment, lowering income and imports, and hence helping to restore equilibrium.

11 Price and income adjustments, including indirect adjustment via the supply of money and investment, work on the current account. In countries with well-developed capital markets, adjustment via the capital account is the most effective mechanism. Deficits, which cause the money supply to decline and interest rates to rise, also raise capital inflows. This restores overall balance.

12 Arguments for flexible rates include better adjustment to payments imbalances, better confidence, more adequate foreign exchange reserves, and increased economic policy independence.

13 An optimum currency area is an area within which exchange rates ought to be fixed. The optimum-currency-area argument provides an alternative viewpoint with regard to the debate on fixed rates versus flexible rates. Having many small currency areas improves automatic adjustment and allows local monetary policy. However, it adds to uncertainty and introduces costs of exchanging currencies in local trade. The optimum currency area is the *region*, which is the area within which there is factor mobility. It is generally claimed that this area is at least as large as a country.

14 The case *against* flexible exchange rates includes the argument that they cause uncertainty and inhibit international trade. Counterarguments are that fixed rates, as they have worked in practice, have also been uncertain and that forward, futures and option contracts allow exporters and importers to avoid exchange risk at a low cost.

15 Another argument against flexible rates is that they allow destabilizing speculation. However, this requires that speculators incur losses, and in any case, speculation with fixed rates is destabilizing as well as profitable.

16 A valid argument against flexible rates is that they will not work for small economies because wages are likely to be forced up along with prices of imports, offsetting the effect of the depreciation. Other arguments are that flexible rates are inflationary, and that international trade elasticities are too small for foreign exchange market stability.

17 Alternatives to fixed-rate systems and flexible-rate systems include a fixed rate with a wide band, a crawling peg, fixed rates for some transactions and flexible rates for others, and a dirty float with intervention to maintain orderly markets. These combine attributes of both fixed-rate systems and flexible-rate systems.

18 The gold standard that was in effect at the start of the twentieth century came to an end with the depression of 1929–1933. From 1929 to 1944 many leading currencies were inconvertible, that is, there was no international financial system.

19 The IMF and the gold-exchange standard were established in the Bretton Woods Agreement of 1944. The IMF still functions after having gone through many changes, but the Bretton Woods system ended in 1973 when many major countries moved to flexible exchange rates. According to the Triffin paradox, the collapse of the gold-exchange standard was inevitable because growing reserves required continuing U.S. deficits, which reduce the acceptability of U.S. dollars as reserves. SDRs were an attempt to address the Triffin paradox.

20 Exchange rates were flexible from 1973 to 1985, with only infrequent interventions by central banks to maintain order. After September 1985 and the Plaza Agreement, action was taken to force down the dollar, and a dirty-float period began.

21 An agreement to coordinate foreign exchange market intervention and domestic economic policies was reached in the Louvre Accord of 1987. This marked a change to flexible exchange rates within a periodically revised but imprecisely specified band.

22 The third-world debt crisis reached a head in the early 1980s, when several Latin American borrowers were unable to meet scheduled payments. The causes of the crisis including falling prices of debtors' exports, a rapid appreciation of the U.S. dollar, high interest rates, and the use of debt for subsidizing consumption rather than for investment.

23 The much-feared bank failures due to the debt crisis did not occur because international institutions and private banks cooperated to provide credits. This cooperation was necessary to prevent panic in an interdependent financial and economic environment.

24 The global balance of economic power has shifted from U.S. dominance to a more even distribution of power between Europe, Japan, and the U.S. Stability requires cooperation among these economic powers.

25 The monetary approach to exchange rates is based on links between money supplies and price levels, and between price levels and exchange rates. The monetary approach predicts an exchange rate will depreciate by the excess of money growth in one country over another. It also predicts that faster growth of real GNP will cause appreciation, and that higher interest rates and expected inflation will cause depreciation.

26 The asset approach to exchange rates suggests that the current exchange rate depends on the expected future exchange rate. Since the expected future rate can depend on expected inflation or anything appearing in the balance-of-payments accounts, the asset approach is consistent with many other approaches.

27 The portfolio-balance approach assumes different countries' bonds are not perfect substitutes. As a result, changes in preferences for bonds of one country over another, or changes in bond supplies, can affect exchange rates.

28 If nontraded-goods prices are sticky, this can make foreign exchange rates overshoot their equilibrium. Other explanations of exchange-rate overshooting include varying elasticities of import demand and export supply, and portfolio readjustment causing jumps in currency supplies or demands during the readjustment.

QUESTIONS

1 How can government objectives such as the maintenance of full employment hinder the functioning of the gold standard? Would adjustment via income or via interest rates be inhibited in the same way?

2 Why might historical patterns of prices show parallel movements between deficit and surplus countries? Could gold discoveries and common movements in national incomes cause this?

3 Use Figure A.2 to show the effect of a fall in demand for British goods in terms of (*a*) the balance of payments measured in pound units and (*b*) the balance of payments measured in dollar units. Show also the movements of curves that the deficit and contraction in money supply will create in restoring equilibrium.

4 If the marginal propensity to consume *domestic* goods is 0.6 and the marginal propensity to consume all goods, including imports, is 0.8, what deficit will persist after Keynesian income adjustment if exports exogenously increase by $1 billion? Will changes in *foreign* national incomes improve adjustment?

5 Why can speculators make profits with less risk under fixed rates? From whom do they make their profits?

6 Assume that you are gong to poll the following groups:
  a Central bankers.
  b Academic economists.
  c Practicing business executives.
  d Consumer advocates.
  How do you think each group would weigh the arguments for and against flexible rates? What does each group have to gain or lose from more flexibility?
7 Why do we observe deficits or surpluses under "flexible" rates? Does this tell us something of the management of the rates?
8 Should Appalachia have its own currency? Should the members of the European Common Market (EEC) have separate currencies?
9 Will *re*valuations or appreciations work for small open economies? Why is there asymmetry in the effect of a revaluation and a devaluation?
10 Do you think that the collapse of the Bretton Woods system would have been less likely had surplus countries expanded their economies to ease the burden of adjustment on the countries with deficits?
11 How would you go about trying to estimate the seigniorage gains to the United States? [*Hint*: They depend on the quantity of U.S. dollars held abroad, the competitive rate of interest that would be paid on these, and the actual rate of interest.]
12 Why do you think some EEC countries adopted the snake? Does your answer have to do with optimum currency areas?
13 Australia and New Zealand do extensive trading with each other. Should they have fixed exchange rates?
14 Why have central bankers frequently intervened in the foreign exchange market under a system of flexible exchange rates? If they have managed to smooth out fluctuations, have they made profits for their citizens?
15 Which argument for fixed exchange rates do you think would be most compelling for Fiji? [*Hint*: Fiji's major "export" is tourism, and most manufactures and other consumer goods are imported.]
16 Do you think that problems might arise out of the difficulty of Americans in accepting a relative decline in economic power? What form might these problems take?
17 Why does the monetary approach imply that higher expected inflation causes a currency to depreciate?
18 What does the asset approach imply about the ability to make money by speculating in foreign exchange?
19 What are the differences and similarities between the monetary and portfolio-balance approaches to exchange rates?
20 What is the crucial assumption required for exchange-rate overshooting in the Dornbush model? Do you think this assumption is valid?

BIBLIOGRAPHY

Bilson, John F. O.: "The Monetary Approach to the Exchange Rate: Some Empirical Evidence," *Staff Papers*, International Monetary Fund, March 1978, pp. 48–75.

Dornbusch, Rudiger: *Open Economy Macroeconomics*, 2d ed., Basic Books, New York, 1988.

——: "Expectations and Exchange Rate Dynamics," *Journal of Political Economy*, December 1976, pp. 1161–1176.

Frenkel, Jacob A., and Harry G. Johnson (eds.): *The Monetary Approach to the Balance of Payments*, Allen and Unwin, London, 1976.

____ and ____ (eds.): *The Economics of Exchange Rates: Selected Readings*, Addison-Wesley, Reading, Mass. 1978.

Friedman, Milton: "The Case for Flexibility Exchange Rates," in *Essays in Positive Economics*, University of Chicago Press, Chicago, 1953.

Grubel, Herbert G.: *International Economics*, Richard D. Irwin, Homewood, Ill., 1977, Chapter 22.

Heller, H. Robert: *International Monetary Economics*, Prentice-Hall, Englewood Cliffs, N.J., 1974, Chapters 5 and 6.

Johnson, Harry G.: "The Monetary Approach to the Balance of Payments: A Nontechnical Guide," *Journal of International Economics*, August 1977, pp. 251–268.

____: "The Case for Flexible Exchange Rates, 1969," in George N. Halm (ed.), *Approaches to Greater Flexibility of Exchange Rates: The Burgenstock Papers*, Princeton University Press, Princeton, N.J., 1970; reprinted in Robert E. Baldwin and J. David Richardson, *International Trade and Finance: Readings*, Little—Brown, Boston, 1974.

Kouri, Pentti J. K., and Michael G. Porter: "International Capital Flows and Portfolio Equilibrium," *Journal of Political Economy*, May/June 1974, pp. 443–467.

Krugman, Paul R. and Maurice Obstfeld: *International Economics: Theory and Policy*, Scott Foresman, Glenview, Ill., 1988, Chapters 17–19.

McKinnon, Ronald I.: "Optimum Currency Areas," *American Economic Review*, September 1963, pp. 717–724.

Mundell, Robert A.: *International Economics*, Macmillan, New York, 1968, Chapter 12.

Sohmen, Egon: *Flexible Exchange Rates: Theory and Controversy*, rev. ed., University of Chicago Press, Chicago, 1969.

Willett, Thomas D., and Edward Tower: "The Concept of Optimum Currency Areas and the Choice between Fixed and Flexible Exchange Rates," in George N. Halm (ed.), *Approaches to Greater Flexibility of Exchange Rates: The Burgenstock Papers*, Princeton University Press, Princeton, N.J., 1970.

Yeager, Leland B.: *International Monetary Relations: Theory, History and Policy*, 2d ed., Harper & Row, New York, 1976.

NAME INDEX

SUBJECT INDEX